KT-221-401

Switzerland

Damien Simonis
Sarah Johnstone, Nicola Williams

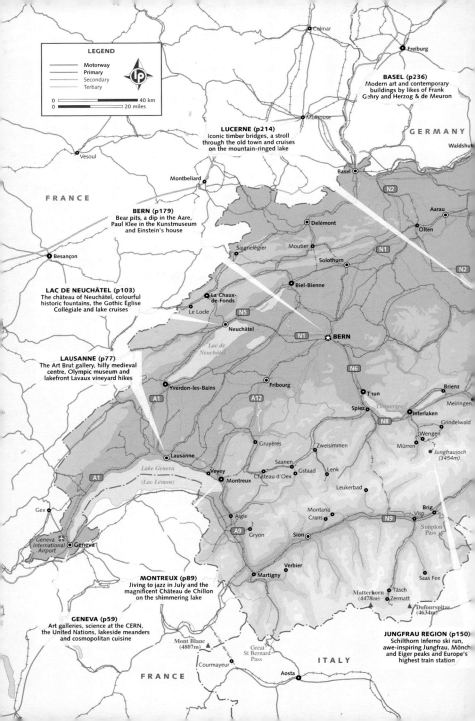

LEGEND

- Motorway
- Primary
- Secondary
- Tertiary

0 — 40 km
0 — 20 miles

BASEL (p236)
Modern art and contemporary buildings by likes of Frank Gehry and Herzog & de Meuron

LUCERNE (p214)
Iconic timber bridges, a stroll through the old town and cruises on the mountain-ringed lake

GERMANY

BERN (p179)
Bear pits, a dip in the Aare, Paul Klee in the Kunstmuseum and Einstein's house

FRANCE

LAC DE NEUCHÂTEL (p103)
The château of Neuchâtel, colourful historic fountains, the Gothic Église Collégiale and lake cruises

LAUSANNE (p77)
The Art Brut gallery, hilly medieval centre, Olympic museum and lakefront Lavaux vineyard hikes

MONTREUX (p89)
Jiving to jazz in July and the magnificent Château de Chillon on the shimmering lake

GENEVA (p59)
Art galleries, science at the CERN, the United Nations, lakeside meanders and cosmopolitan cuisine

JUNGFRAU REGION (p150)
Schilthorn Inferno ski run, awe-inspiring Jungfrau, Mönch and Eiger peaks and Europe's highest train station

ITALY

FRANCE

Colmar
Freiburg
Waldshut
Mulhouse
Vesoul
Montbéliard
Basel
Aarau
Olten
Besançon
Saignelégier
Moutier
Delémont
Solothurn
N1
N2
La Chaux-de-Fonds
Biel-Bienne
Le Locle
N5
Neuchâtel
N1
★ BERN
Lac de Neuchâtel
N6
Yverdon-les-Bains
Thun
Brienz
A1
Fribourg
A12
Spiez
Thunersee
Interlaken
Meiringen
N8
Grindelwald
Wengen
Gruyères
Zweisimmen
Mürren
Jungfraujoch (3454m)
Saanen
Lausanne
Château d'Oex
Gstaad
Lenk
Lake Geneva (Lac Léman)
Vevey
Montreux
Leukerbad
Gex
Aigle
Montana
Crans
Brig
Visp
Simplon Pass
A9
Gryon
Sion
N9
Geneva International Airport
Geneva
Verbier
Saas Fee
Martigny
Täsch
Zermatt
Matterhorn (4478m)
Dufourspitze (4634m)
Mont Blanc (4807m)
Great St Bernard Pass
Courmayeur
Aosta

RHEINFALL (p250)
Europe's largest waterfall, cruises on the Rhine and restaurants in Schloss Laufen

ZÜRICH (p194)
Dada at the Kunsthaus, shopping for chocolate, sunbathing by the lake and Switzerland's best clubbing

ST GALLEN (p251)
The extraordinary World Heritage-listed cathedral complex and abbey library, and the picturesque old centre

MÜSTAIR (p282)
Extraordinary Carolingian and Romanesque frescoes in the World Heritage-listed church of the Kloster St Johann

ST MORITZ (p282)
People-watching in this winter playground of the rich and famous, and the Hahnensee ski run

LAGO DI LUGANO (p296)
Views of Lugano and its lake from Monte San Salvatore or Monte Brè, the lakeside villages of Gandria and Morcote, and ancient fossils

VALLE MAGGIA (p302)
Huddles of grey stone villages, thundering waterfalls, babbling brooks and good food away from the glitz of Ticino's lakes

ELEVATION

4500m
4000m
3000m
2000m
1000m
0

GERMANY

AUSTRIA

LIECHTENSTEIN

ITALY

Leutkirch
Schaffhausen
Singen
Wangen
Konstanz
Friedrichshafen
Bodensee (Lake Constance)
Bregenz
Sonthofen
Frauenfeld
Winterthur
Baden
Zürich International Airport
N1
St Margrethen
Gossau
St Gallen
N1
Dornbirn
Herisau
Zürich
Wattwil
Appenzell
N13
Rapperswil
Zürichsee
Feldkirch
Zug
Buchs
N14
VADUZ
N3
Lucerne
Glarus
Sargans
N4
Schwyz
Schwanden
Stans
Lake Lucerne (Vierwaldstättersee)
Landquart
Sarnen
Altdorf
A13
Engelberg
Chur
Klosters
Mt Titlis (3239m)
A2
Davos
Oberalp Pass
N19
Arosa
Andermatt
Rhine
N28
St Gotthard Pass
N27
Swiss National Park
Müstair
N19
San Bernardino Pass
St Moritz
N13
N3
N27
A2
N29
Bormio
Bernina Pass
N3
Valle Maggia
A13
Bellinzona
Sondrio
Tirano
Locarno
Gravedona
Domodossola
Lago Maggiore
Lago di Como
Lugano
Verbania
Lovere
Como
A9

Destination Switzerland

If you could travel through only one European country, which might you choose? Italy? France? Germany? How about a taste of three in one? That can only mean Switzerland!

Known as a summer and winter sports paradise (just look at those glistening white 4000m-plus Alpine peaks and glittering lakes), Switzerland is where people first skied for fun. Illustrious names evoke all the romance and glamorous drama of the mountain high life: Zermatt, St Moritz, Davos, Gstaad, the Jungfrau, Verbier and more. One antidote to the exercise comes from the country's thermal baths, from Yverdon-les-Bains to Scuol.

Beyond the après-ski chic, edelweiss and Heidi lies a complex country of cohabiting cultures. It not only has four languages (Swiss German, French, Italian and Romansch), but the cultural variety to match. You could be chomping on sausages over beer in an oom-pah-pah *Stübli* one day and pasta over a glass of merlot in a granite *grotto* the next.

Cities like Geneva (the most cosmopolitan), Zürich (the most outrageous), Basel and Lausanne heave with heady artistic activity and sometimes incendiary nightlife.

The grandeur of the finest churches, such as the cathedrals in Lausanne and Bern, contrasts with sparkling but lesser-known treasures like the frescoes of Müstair or the abbey complex of St Gallen (both World Heritage sites).

The list of enchanting towns is endless: from Lucerne with its covered bridge to Neuchâtel and its fountains; from Gruyères, with its cheese, to Grimentz and its traditional timber houses; from the sgraffito-blazoned buildings of Engadine towns like Scuol and Zuoz.

Whether visiting the remotest Ticino villages or sampling the finest of Valais wines, you'll find Switzerland a chocolate box bursting with unexpected flavours.

KARL LEHMA

Outdoor Activities

MARTIN MOOS

Windsurfing (p49) on Switzerland's lakes is a popular activity

GLENN VAN DER KNIJFF

Skiing near Verbier at the heart of the Quatre Vallées (p124) offers 410km of runs

Hike towards the soaring peak of the Matterhorn (p134)

GARETH MCCORMACK

Landscapes

Looking out over Lake Geneva (p75) with the French Alps in the background

Listen to the cascading waters of the Rheinfall (p250)

Admire the flowering Alpine Eidelweiss (p41)

Take in a panoramic view of the Aletsch glacier from Jungfraujoch (p155)

Palaces & Parks

Wander around the impressive Schloss Schadau (p168), Thun

Visit the gardens of the Château de Gruyères (p106)

OTHER HIGHLIGHTS

- Sip and taste your way through the many quality vineyards around Lavaux (p88).
- Enjoy the stunning scenery and solitude at the amazing Swiss National Park (p280).

Take in the incredible vistas at the magnificent Schloss Vaduz (p308), Liechtenstein

Towns & Cities

Admire the painted houses on
St Augustinergasse, Zürich (p194)

Stroll the bustling Rathausplatz, Stein am Rhein
(p251)

Walking on the waterfront promenade at Quai du Mont-Blanc (p65) is a popular summer pastime in
Geneva

GLENN BEANLAND

Eat, drink and be merry al fresco style on Barenplatz, Bern (p186)

OTHER HIGHLIGHTS

- Mix it with the beautiful people in St Moritz's bars and clubs and ski to your heart's content (p282).
- Visit steamy Basel in summer for some of Switzerland's hottest weather and browse through some of the city's 35 museums (p236).

KARL LEHMANN

Admire the impressive interior of Spreuerbrücke, Lucerne (p214)

Go for a walk down the main street at Gruyères (p106)

CHRIS MELLOR

Festivals

Join in the fun at the Fasnacht (p317) festival

Be a part of Zürich's Street Parade (p200), Europe's largest street party

Let off some steam at the International Hot Air Balloon Week (p317) in Château d'Oex

Eating

GLENN BEANLAND

Fill your tummy at the Kornhauskeller (p186) underground bar and restaurant in Bern

Dip into some comfort food and find solace in a pot of steaming fondue (p52)

MARTIN MOOS

OTHER HIGHLIGHTS

- Hit the dance floor and quench your thirst at one of Zürich's many waterfront bars (p198).
- Smash marzipan-filled *marmites en chocolat* (chocolate cauldrons) and gorge on the sweet broken pieces at L'Escalade (p68).

GLENN BEANLAND

Satisfy your sweet tooth – mmmmm, chocolate (p52)

Traditional Architecture

Enjoy the lively atmosphere in Bern's medieval centre and gaze up at the zytglogge (p181) to check the time

GLENN BEANLAND

ROBERTO SONCIN GEROMETTA

Get out of the cities and admire the traditional mountain houses of Grindelwald (p151)

JOHN MCLEAN

Study the intricate window detail in Ardez (p279)

Open the door of the Grossmünster (p195) in Zürich and step inside

MARTIN MO

Contents

Regional Map Contents

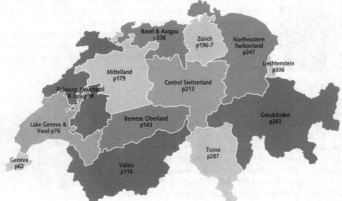

The Authors

DAMIEN SIMONIS

Coordinating Author; Lake Geneva & Vaud;
Valais; Graubünden; Ticino

The kaleidoscopic fare on offer in Switzerland would probably have passed Damien by had his other half not decided on moving to Lausanne on Lake Geneva. And yet it might have seemed an obvious place for him to be, speaking as he does French, German and Italian (not to mention the unofficial lingua franca, er, English!). The further he explores the place, from its tempting Italian eateries in Ticino to the top-of-the-world ski runs of Zermatt, the more he fails to understand how he didn't cotton on to the place earlier. Still, better late than never! Nowhere else in Europe has he found such a concentration of breath-taking natural beauty and cultural variety. Damien also updated the Destination: Switzerland; Getting Started; Itineraries; Snapshot; Food & Drink; Health; and Language chapters.

My Favourite Trip

An autumn favourite is to head east from home base Lausanne (p77), taking the high lanes through the Lavaux (p88) wine region, stopping off for a nibble and tipple at wine cellars along the way. From there, I like to put away some kilometres along the Rhône valley in Valais and making directly for Leukerbad (p132) and its thermal baths, where a first evening is well spent. From there, a detour leads up the Lötschental to Fafleralp (p133) for some healthy walking far from the regular tourist trails. Now it is time to swing south for some pre-season ski fun in Zermatt (p134), to try out the latest skis on the glacier on a weekend package that gets you dreaming of the white winter ahead!

Lausanne
Lavaux Wine Region
Fafleralp
Leukerbad
Zermatt

SARAH JOHNSTONE

Bernese Oberland; Mittelland; Zürich;
Central Switzerland; Basel & Aargau;
Northeastern Switzerland; Liechtenstein

Sarah covered the German-speaking parts of the country and came away (worryingly) with a Swiss accent and (surprisingly) with a rudimentary understanding of Schwyzertütsch. A freelance journalist based in London, she's previously worked for Reuters and several travel magazines. After nearly 10 Lonely Planet guidebooks (you think she'd learn) she still hates author bios. Sarah also updated the History; The Culture; Outdoor Activities; Directory; and Transport chapters.

My Favourite Trip

Visitors to the Bernese Oberland are forever looking out the train window and gasping words along the lines of 'Oh, my god, isn't it beautiful?' The journey between Grütschalp (above Lauterbrunnen, p156) and Mürren (p165) has this effect on me. If you arrive here as the sun is setting, the train really does seem to float along the horizontal ridge, while the peaks opposite shimmer purple and look tantalisingly within reach. In blazing sunshine, there's no such optical illusion. However, I'm happy to make this journey at any time, simply because it lands me in breathtaking Mürren.

Grütschalp & Mürren

NICOLA WILLIAMS   Geneva; Fribourg, Neuchâtel & Jura

Ever since Nicola moved to medieval Yvoire plump on the southern side of Lake Geneva, she has never quite been able to shake off that uncanny feeling that she is on holiday. A year on, a 1960s house in neighbouring Messery with a garden tumbling down the hillside towards that same glittering lake and Switzerland's mysterious Jura mountains beyond, is what she wakes up to each morning. Nicola has lived in France since 1997 and when not flitting into Geneva or delving into the Swiss countryside, she can be found at a desk writing. Nicola also updated the Environment chapter.

My Favourite Trip

There's always something to thrill to, living where I do: be it gorging on a truly authentic Asian feast (p71) in Geneva, viewing the latest MAMCO exhibition (p64), brunching in Carouge (p72) or indulging in a night out at the opera (I've just booked for *The Nutcracker*), Switzerland's oh-so-international city just doesn't tire. Elsewhere, riding the train up to Zermatt and skiing in the Matterhorn's shadow (p134); hanging out in the Engadine (p278) with friends during March's cross-country ski marathon (they do it, I don't); bombing down Davos' ab-fab luge track (p276) and or watching Jurassic cows (p114) being milked before farm breakfast (fresh-from-the-udder milk et al) are Swiss moments I'd repeat.

LONELY PLANET AUTHORS

Why is our travel information the best in the world? It's simple: our authors are independent, dedicated travellers. They don't research using just the Internet or phone, and they don't take freebies in exchange for positive coverage. They travel widely, to all the popular spots and off the beaten track. They personally visit thousands of hotels, restaurants, cafés, bars, galleries, palaces, museums and more – and they take pride in getting all the details right, and telling it how it is. For more, see the authors section on www.lonelyplanet.com.

Getting Started

With everything from soaring Alpine peaks in Zermatt to cavernous late-night dance clubs in Zürich, Switzerland offers a kaleidoscopic palette of options in a very small space. Whether you want to explore hidden jewels of medieval art in distant villages or the cutting edge of modern architecture in the humming cities, there is plenty of choice for the art buff. What other country offers at least three types of different national cuisine? You could set yourself a gastronomical route full of pleasant surprises. For the more energetic, the range of scenery and outdoor activities is almost unlimited. From cow-fighting to curling, hiking to hang-gliding, there is barely a sport or activity that isn't catered for here.

WHEN TO GO

When you visit Switzerland you will, at least in part, be dictated by where you want to go and what you intend to do, but there are good reasons for exploring at least parts of the country at any time of year.

See Climate Charts (p315) for more information.

Summer lasts roughly from June to September and offers the most pleasant climate for outdoor pursuits (apart from exclusively winter sports). In fact, many adventure sports, such as canyoning, are only offered during this time. The peak period is July and August, when prices are high, accommodation often fully booked and the sights packed. You'll find better deals, and fewer people, in the shoulder seasons either side of summer: in April, May and October. With the exception of the busy Easter break, spring is a beautiful time of year to explore the blooming countryside. In Ticino, flowers are in bloom as early as March. Hikers wanting to walk at high altitudes, however, should be equipped for snow and ice until well into June (and, in some tricky spots, all year).

The winter season in Alpine resorts kicks off in mid-December and moves into full swing around Christmas, closing down again when the snows begin to melt around mid-April. Between the summer and winter seasons, Alpine resorts all but close down (except where year-round glacier skiing is on offer). At the very best, they go into snooze mode and can even be a little depressing.

At any time, as you travel around the country you'll hit many different climatic conditions. The continental climate in the Alps tends to show the greatest extremes between summer and winter. Mid-August to late October generally has fairly settled weather, and is a good period for hiking trips.

DON'T LEAVE HOME WITHOUT...

- Valid travel insurance (p318)
- Your ID card or passport and visa if required (p322)
- Your driving licence (p329) and car documents if driving, along with appropriate car insurance (p326)
- Sunglasses in summer and winter (all that snow makes for sharp glare!)
- Hiking shoes for the mountains

COSTS & MONEY

Okay, let's get this over and done with quickly: Switzerland is an expensive place. Even people from the UK and Scandinavia will notice this, although the difference between Switzerland and its European neighbours has narrowed over the years, especially since the introduction of the euro in 2002 in Switzerland's neighbouring countries sent prices in those countries soaring. Indeed, UK estate agents specialising in holiday properties in ski resorts have started promoting Switzerland, as nearest rival France becomes 'too expensive'! The floods of Swiss swarming over the French and Italian borders for cheaper goods are largely a thing of the past. One very good piece of news is that petrol in Switzerland is cheaper than in its neighbouring countries (Austria, France, Germany and Italy).

Travellers from North America or Australia will find all of Europe more expensive, and the pain in Switzerland only marginally worse.

Your biggest expenses while in Switzerland are likely to be long-distance public transport, accommodation and eating out. In the most modest hotels, expect to pay at least Sfr70/100 per single/double. A full meal with 500ml of house wine for two can easily cost Sfr50 to Sfr60 and up per person.

But there are ways to keep costs down. Travel passes almost invariably provide big savings (see p327) on trains, boats and buses. It is essential to check these out and see which might suit you. Camping, sleeping in barns in summer (p313) and staying at youth hostels are cheap(ish) accommodation options. Preparing your own meals, not drinking alcohol and eating at the many supermarket and department-store restaurants will keep your food budget under control. Finally, a student card will entitle you to reduced admission fees for many attractions (see p316).

Your budget depends on how you live and travel. If you're moving around fast, going to lots of places, spending time in the big cities or major ski resorts, then your day-to-day living costs are going to be quite high; if you stay in one place and get to know your way around, they're likely to come down.

The minimum that budget travellers can expect to scrape by on is about Sfr80 to Sfr100 per day, and that's if they stick to camping/hostelling, self-service restaurants or self-catering, hitching (or have previously purchased a rail pass), hiking instead of taking cable cars, visiting only inexpensive sights and confining alcohol consumption to bottles purchased in supermarkets. Add at least Sfr30 a day if you want to stay in a budget pension instead, and a further Sfr30 for a wider choice of restaurants and sightseeing options. You still have to be careful with your money at this level; if you have a larger budget available, you will have no trouble spending it! Always allow extra cash for emergencies.

Admission prices on most museums and galleries range from Sfr5 to Sfr10, with a handful more expensive still. An expense that can blow any budget is trips on cable cars; these are rarely covered by travel passes (at best you can expect a 25% to 50% reduction). A short to medium ascent can cost Sfr10 to Sfr25. Return trips up and down Mt Titlis and Schilthorn exceed Sfr70.

HOW MUCH?

Local newspaper
Sfr2-2.50

City bus/tram ride
Sfr2-2.80

10-minute taxi ride
Sfr12-15

one-day ski-pass Sfr35-70

Bar of Toblerone
chocolate (100g) Sfr2.20

TRAVEL LITERATURE

Culture Shock – Switzerland (Shirley Eu-Wong) A curious and at times amusing look at how things are done in Switzerland, this book is part of a series and something of an etiquette guide.
Laughing Along with the Swiss (Paul Bilton) Published in Switzerland by Bergli, this is an often side-splitting outsider's handbook to the oddities of Swiss life. As Bilton points out, only the

TOP TENS

Our Favourite Festivals & Events

The Swiss have a calendar stuffed with festivals, ranging from curious local traditions to international music fests. We have chosen the following (in chronological order):

- Schlitteda (January), St Moritz, Pontresina and Silvaplana (p278)
- Vogel Gryff (mid- to late January), Basel (p240)
- Fasnacht (Carnival; February), Lucerne (p217)
- Sechseläuten (third Monday in April), Zürich (p200)
- Montreux Jazz (July), Montreux, Vaud (p90)
- Festival Internazionale di Film (August), Locarno (p300)
- Fête des Vendanges (Grape Harvest Festival; September), Neuchâtel (p110)
- Foire du Valais (October; cow fights feature), Martigny (p121)
- Zibelemärit (onion market; fourth Monday in November), Bern (p185)
- L'Escalade (11 December), Geneva (p68)

Our Favourite Ski Resorts

- Zermatt, Valais (p134)
- Davos-Klosters, Graubünden (p275)
- St Moritz, Graubünden (p282)
- Les Portes du Soleil, Champéry, Valais (p119)
- Verbier, Valais (p124)
- Saas Fee, Valais (p137)
- Wengen & Mürren, Bernese Oberland (p150)
- Crans-Montana, Valais (p130)
- Engelberg, central Switzerland (p229)
- St Luc & Chandolin, Valais (p131)

Top Museums & Galleries

Switzerland is not just for snowboarders and mountain-climbers. The country fairly bristles with important and intriguing museums and art galleries. Among the best are the following:

- Zentrum Paul Klee, Bern (p183)
- Fondation Beyeler, Basel (p237)
- Museum Jean Tinguely, Basel (p237)
- Kunsthaus, Zürich (p197)
- Fondation Pierre Gianadda, Martigny (p120)
- Musée de l'Art Brut, Lausanne (p81)
- Freilichtmuseum Ballenberg, outside Brienz (p171)
- Picasso Museum, Lucerne (p216)
- Musée International de la Croix Rouge et du Croissant Rouge, Geneva (p66)
- Musée Olympique, Lausanne (p82)

Swiss could 'make the Germans look untidy and the Texans poor'. Some overly-worn clichés aside, there are plenty of amusing truths (or near truths) in this light tome.

Little is the Light (Vitali Vitaliev) The Ukrainian-born journalist in this book takes an almost serious look at various European mini-states, including Liechtenstein.

Stamping Grounds: Liechtenstein's Quest for the World Cup (Charlie Connelly) Taking football as the centre pitch from which to launch a whimsical exploration of the little principality, Connelly has pulled off the remarkable trick of writing an engrossing account of this curious countryette.

Switzerland: A Village History (Paul Birmingham) Birmingham takes a different look at the balloon town of Château d'Oex, tracing its history as a rural village, through the impoverishment in the wake of the Napoleonic invasions and back to prosperity in the tourist age.

Take Me to Your Chalet (Eugene Epstein) The American-born writer has written several humorous accounts of life in Switzerland. A highly personal take on the country's idiosyncrasies, his books also include such titles as *Once Upon an Alp* and *Lend Me Your Alphorn*.

The White Spider (Heinrich Harrer) A classic of mountaineering literature, this is the account of a young climber and his ascent of the north face (the first ever) of the Eiger peak in 1938.

Ticking Along with the Swiss (Dianne Dicks) Dicks has collected 49 short stories on Switzerland by authors from as far afield as Australia, Canada, the USA and Ethiopia.

INTERNET RESOURCES

Lonely Planet (www.lonelyplanet.com) Can get you started with summaries on Switzerland, links to Switzerland-related sites and travellers trading information on the Thorn Tree.

My Swiss Alps (www.myswissalps.com) This site concentrates on mountain areas, hiking (with plenty of hiking route suggestions) and sports, particularly in the Bernese Oberland, Valais and Graubünden.

SBB/CFF/FFS (www.sbb.ch) The Swiss railway website allows you to check timetables and buy tickets online. It's in four languages, including English.

Swiss Info (www.swissinfo.org) A multilingual news and info site presented by the country's public broadcaster, Swiss Radio International. It also has a host of links, many of them tourism-related.

Switzerland Tourism (www.myswitzerland.com) The Swiss national tourist body's website has information on everything from local tourist office addresses to information on food and wine and links to Swiss mountain resorts.

Traveling.ch (www.traveling.ch) Another general site with loads of links and info ranging from embassy addresses to dinner recipes.

Itineraries

CLASSIC ROUTES

GENEVA TO ZÜRICH

Two Weeks / Geneva to Zürich

Forget your skis and hang up your hiking boots. This is a trip for the urbanites among us who want to mix up some metropolitan fire with some small-town charm. With the possibility now available to fly in to one hub and back home from another, this tour is eminently doable by either private car or public transport. And should you need to fly out from the same place, Geneva and Zürich are only separated by 2¾ hours by fast train. This trip can be done in either direction and plenty of variations suggest themselves en route.

Landing in **Geneva** (p59), immerse yourself in the most cosmopolitan of Switzerland's big cities. From Geneva, it's about 45 minutes by train northeast around the lake to bustling **Lausanne** (p77), the hilly lakeside city and seat of the International Olympic Committee. Follow the same glorious route through the Lavaux wine terraces to **Montreux** (p89), from where you head north to the medieval fortress town of **Gruyères** (p106) known especially for its fine cheese. Further north still, you arrive at **Fribourg** (p99), on the French-German language frontier, which you cross to make for the pretty national capital, **Bern** (p179), to the northeast. From here you drop down in the depths of Bern's cantons and the lakeside towns around **Interlaken** (p144). Nearby there is plenty of great skiing, hiking and other outdoor options. Our route swings north to another bewitching lady of the lake, the town of **Lucerne** (p214), before we change atmosphere completely by rolling onwards via **Zug** (p232) to Switzerland's most happening city, the once-stuffy banking town of **Zürich** (p194).

In order to give a little time to all the destinations on this route you will want at least two weeks, leaving two days apiece for places like Geneva, Lausanne, Bern, Lucerne and Zürich. The changes in scenery and culture on this 385km route are extraordinary.

THE GLACIER EXPRESS   7½ Hours / Zermatt to St Moritz

Although not quite as long as the Trans-Siberian, the classic rail journeys of Switzerland make up for the length in horizontal travel time with the spectacle of the vertical. Of the several scenic mountain rail trips on offer, perhaps the best is the Glacier Express, which runs from Zermatt, high in the southern Alps of Valais canton, northeast to St Moritz, via Chur, in Graubünden.

As Switzerland's Alpine resorts became increasingly popular with Europe's hoity-toity in the early 20th century, the idea for a train linking Zermatt and St Moritz grew. In 1930, the inaugural steam-train journey between the two Alpine towns took place. The excursion hasn't lost its appeal since. The 7½-hour trip can be done year-round and the literal high point of the trip is the crossing of the Oberalp Pass, at 2033m.

Starting in **Zermatt** (p134), the train winds slowly north down the valley to **Brig** (p138). From there it swings northeast along the pretty eastern stretch of the Rhône valley towards the Furka Pass (which it circumvents by tunnel) and descends on **Andermatt** (p233) before again climbing up to the Oberalp Pass. From there it meanders alongside the Vorderrhein river, passing through **Disentis/Mustér** (p272) before arriving in **Chur** (p264). The main train continues to **St Moritz** (p282), with a branch line heading northeast to **Davos** (p276).

The trip can be done in either direction. For practical details, see the Transport chapter (p331).

Of the many remarkable railway trips on offer in Switzerland, this is the most breathtaking. The 272km trip through Alpine country, surrounded by icy peaks, high mountain pastures and pretty towns, winds its way through 91 tunnels and over 291 bridges.

ROADS LESS TRAVELLED

LOST IN GRAUBÜNDEN & TICINO   Two to Three Weeks / Chur to Vals

Get well off the beaten trail on this circular road trip, taking in such gems as vivid Romanesque frescoes, quaint Engadine towns, remote Ticino villages, medieval castles, high mountain passes and two tempting thermal baths stops. Give yourself two to three weeks for this 685km trail.

With the exception of high wilderness mountaineering, this is one of the best routes for getting away from it all (with occasional options to jump back into the tourist fray). As a circular route, you can kick off anywhere, but we start in the Graubünden capital of **Chur** (p264), from where we head north for a quick detour to pretty **Maienfeld** (p274) and its vineyards. Make east for the skiing centres of **Klosters** (p275) and **Davos** (p276), where you leave the bustle behind to surge east into the lower Engadine valley, with pretty towns to admire like **Guarda** (p278) and **Scuol** (p279). In the latter, hang about for some great bath treatment. From there the road ribbons east to the Austrian border, which you cross to then head south through a slice of Austria and Italy, before veering back west into Switzerland to contemplate the frescoes at **Müstair** (p280). The road continues west and then southwest, passing through picture-postcard **Zuoz** (p281) before reaching chic **St Moritz** (p282). We then follow the Julier Pass mountain road that swings north and west, then dropping down the gorges of the **Via Mala** (p273) to the hamlet of **Zillis** (p273), another key art stop.

The road continues south and crosses into Ticino and the medieval castles of **Bellinzona** (p289). From there, steam on past lakeside **Locarno** (p299) and up the enchanting **Valle Maggia** (p302). Backtracking to Bellinzona, the main route takes you along the Valle Leventina, with a stop in **Giornico** (p291) and any high valley hamlets you fancy, before crossing the **Gotthard Pass** (p233) and **Andermatt** (p233) and then veering back east into Graubünden. Make a quick stop at the monastery of **Disentis/Mustér** (p272) before making one last highly recommended detour to the baths of **Vals** (p271), the last stop before Chur.

TAILORED TRIPS

WORLD HERITAGE SITES

In spite of all its natural wonders and considerably man-made beauty, Switzerland only boasts six Unesco World Heritage sites, all but one in the eastern half of the country. Starting in the north, **St Gallen** (p251) is the seat of a grand abbey and church complex that is home to one of the world's oldest libraries. On a similarly artistic note is the Kloster de St Johann (St John's Monastery) in **Müstair** (p280) in the far east of the country, graced with vivid Carolingian and Romanesque frescoes. Both sites were declared in 1983.

The canton of Ticino has two of the country's heritage sites. The first is the inspiring trio of defensive castles in **Bellinzona** (p288), added in 2000. The second site, **Monte San Giorgio** (p299), was added in 2003. A pyramid-shaped, wood-covered mountain (1096m) south of Lago di Lugano, it was selected by Unesco as the best fossil record of marine life from the Triassic period.

In the south of the country, the Jungfrau-Aletsch-Bietschhorn Alpine area (selected in 2001), was listed for its receding glaciers, especially the 24km-long **Aletsch Glacier** (p139). Finally, the old city centre of **Bern** (p179), which was listed in 1983, is the only Unesco site in the western half.

FAIRY-TALE CASTLES

It seems almost inevitable that Switzerland, being the home of chocolate confectionery and picture-postcard countryside, should also have its fair share of sugary-sweet, Disney-style castles. It doesn't disappoint. However enchanting (or enchanted) they may seem today, castles were often built for less romantic) reasons than one might daydream about today. Used as fortresses and prisons as well as sumptuous residences, they all have plenty of intriguing history.

The best known of them all, immortalised by Lord Byron and many others, is the **Château de Chillon** (p89), which juts out over Lake Geneva just outside Montreux. Not far to the north is the **Château de Gruyères** (p106), in the eponymous high-hill cheese-making town.

To the west, on or near the waters of Lac de Neuchâtel, are the witch's hat turrets of the **Château de Grandson** (p93), just outside Yverdon-les-Bains, and **Château de Vaumarcus** (p113), south of Neuchâtel. You can sleep over in the latter.

More lakeside castles stand proudly in Thun, notably **Schloss Thun** (p167) and **Schloss Schadau** (p168), and the altogether different, Italian-built, Escher-like **Castello Visconteo** (p299) at Locarno.

Away from the water, the most impressive castle scene is **Castelgrande** (p289), **Castello Montebello** (p290) and **Castello di Sasso Corbaro** (p290) at Bellinzona. In the Engadine valley is **Schloss Tarasp** (p279), just outside Scuol.

A curious cylindrical defensive castle in the north is the **Munot** (p249) in Schaffhausen.

Snapshot

'This couldn't be happening to us!' many an unsettled Swiss commuter cried when, on a warm June day in 2005, the Helvetic image of seamless efficiency took a dramatic hammering. In a country where trains delayed by a couple of minutes raise disapproving eyebrows, the entire national rail system ground to a halt at evening rush hour after a massive power surge. Service was only fully restored the following day.

Hundreds of thousands of Swiss were stranded in the chaos and reactions ranged from speechless disbelief through childlike amusement – clearly deep in the heart of some Swiss burns a longing for the occasional unexpected upheaval!

That rare humiliation for Swiss transport followed another sad episode for national pride – the sale of troubled national airline Swiss to Germany's Lufthansa at a bargain-basement price.

In summer it seemed even the gods had it in for the Alpine paradise. In July massive hailstorms pelted the Lavaux wine district, on Lake Geneva, into submission, destroying a good part of its vineyards. One month later, torrential flooding brought chaos to much of central and northern Switzerland. Four people died as waters cut off the capital, Bern, and dissected transport routes over the Alps into Italy. Some 700 people were evacuated from mountain resorts, as well as 300 from residential districts in Bern. Rhine river traffic was halted. The Engelberg mountain resort was cut off until well into September after the collapse of an access road. Damage was estimated at one billion francs. Ouch!

The Swiss are careful with money and conservative with their currency. Since the franc went into circulation in the 1850s, it has rarely been tampered with. The decision in early 2005 to drop the five-cent coin (by 2006–07), because it costs six cents to make, came as a minor earthquake in a country where any change tends to be viewed warily.

Money matters aside, the Swiss had some important decisions to make in 2005. In June they narrowly voted in favour of joining the European Union's Schengen system, which will mean dropping standard border controls with its EU neighbours and plugging into the Dublin Treaty shared police-data systems. In September, they took an even bolder step when voting in favour of extending free circulation of citizens (to be limited by quotas until 2011) from the older 15 member nations of the EU to the 10 new (mostly Eastern European) members that joined in 2004.

The debate was acrimonious, with Christoph Blocher's extreme right-wing UDC party raising the spectre of a flood of cheap labour from the East. Blocher lost on another count when, in June, Swiss gays won an important victory with the passing of a referendum to legally recognise same-sex couples (but not marriages) from January 2007.

So many referendums are enough to make you grab for a smoke, but those Swiss with a nicotine need did not get the chance to vote against a ban on smoking on all trains (and most other public transport), effective December 2005.

FAST FACTS

Population: 7.42 million

Non-Swiss nationals: 20% of population

Area: 41,285 sq km

GDP: €449 billion

GDP per person: Sfr54,000

GDP growth: 2.6%

Inflation: 1%

Unemployment rate: 3.7%

Average life expectancy: 78.6 (men), 83.7 (women)

Highest point: Dufourspitze at 4634m

History

As a historical reality, William Tell probably never existed. But as a national legend, the man who helped to drive out Switzerland's foreign rulers by shooting an apple off his son's head has perfectly embodied the country's rather singular approach to independence throughout the ages.

PRE-CONFEDERATION

Modern Swiss history is regarded as starting in 1291, but people had already been living in the region for thousands of years. The first inhabitants were Celtic tribes, including the Helvetii of the Jura and the Mittelland plain and the Rhaetians near Graubünden. Their homelands were invaded firstly by the Romans, who had gained a foothold by 58 BC under Julius Caesar and established Aventicum (now Avenches) as their capital. Then, Germanic Alemanni tribes arrived to drive out the Romans by AD 400.

The Alemanni groups settled in eastern Switzerland and were later joined by another Germanic tribe, the Burgundians, in the western part of the country. The latter adopted Christianity and the Latin language, laying the seeds for the division between French- and German-speaking Switzerland. The Franks conquered both tribes in the 6th century, but the two areas were torn apart again when Charlemagne's empire was partitioned in 870.

Initially, when it was reunited under the pan-European Holy Roman Empire in 1032, Switzerland was left to its own devices. Local nobles wielded the most influence, especially the Zähringen family – who founded Fribourg, Bern and Murten, and built a castle at Thun (see p167) – and the Savoy clan, who established a ring of castles around Lake Geneva, most notably Château de Chillon (see p89).

However, when the Habsburg ruler Rudolph I became Holy Roman Emperor in 1273, he sent in heavy-handed bailiffs to collect more taxes and tighten the administrative screws. Swiss resentment quickly grew.

SWISS CONFEDERATION

It was after Rudolph's death in 1291 that local leaders made their first grab for independence. It's taught in Swiss schools, although some historians see the tale as slightly distorted, that the forest communities of Uri, Schwyz and Nidwalden met on the Rütli Meadow (p224) in Schwyz canton on 1 August that year to sign an alliance vowing not to recognise any external judge or law. In any case, a pact does exist, preserved in the town of Schwyz (p226). It's seen as the founding act of the Swiss Confederation, whose Latin name, Confoederatio Helvetica, survives in the 'CH' abbreviation for Switzerland (used on car number plates and in Internet addresses, for example). The story of the patriotic William Tell, a central figure in the freedom struggle's mythology, also originates from this period (see the boxed text The William Tell Tale, p225).

In 1315, Duke Leopold dispatched a powerful Austrian army to douse this growing Swiss nationalism. Instead, however, the Swiss inflicted an

A comprehensive overview of the country's history, politics and society is provided by Jonathan Steinberg's *Why Switzerland?*

Learn about historical exhibitions being staged by the Swiss National Museum and its partners at www.musee-suisse .com. Many interesting themes from Swiss history are also discussed at length here, although mainly in German or French.

TIMELINE **1032**   **1273**

Swiss clans are united under the Holy Roman Empire, but left with much autonomy	Habsburg Emperor Rudolph I angers local 'William Tells' with heavy tax demands

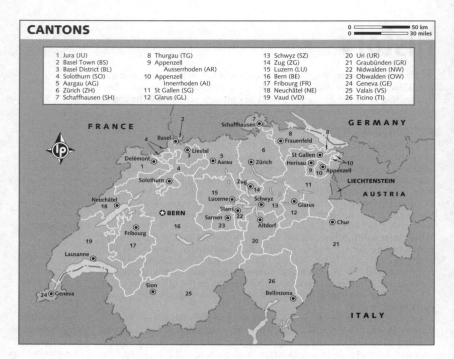

CANTONS

1 Jura (JU)	8 Thurgau (TG)	13 Schwyz (SZ)	20 Uri (UR)
2 Basel Town (BS)	9 Appenzell	14 Zug (ZG)	21 Graubünden (GR)
3 Basel District (BL)	Ausserrhoden (AR)	15 Luzern (LU)	22 Nidwalden (NW)
4 Solothurn (SO)	10 Appenzell	16 Bern (BE)	23 Obwalden (OW)
5 Aargau (AG)	Innerrhoden (AI)	17 Fribourg (FR)	24 Geneva (GE)
6 Zürich (ZH)	11 St Gallen (SG)	18 Neuchâtel (NE)	25 Valais (VS)
7 Schaffhausen (SH)	12 Glarus (GL)	19 Vaud (VD)	26 Ticino (TI)

Jura is the youngest of Switzerland's cantons, having only gained independence from Bern in 1979. Of 23 cantons, three (Appenzell, Basel and Walden) are divided in two to make the usual total of 26.

epic defeat on his troops at Morgarten and prompted other communities to join the Swiss union. The next 200 years of Swiss history was a time of successive military wins, land grabs and new memberships. The following cantons came on board: Lucerne (1332), Zürich (1351), Glarus and Zug (1352), Bern (1353), Fribourg and Solothurn (1481), Basel and Schaffhausen (1501) and Appenzell (1513). In the middle of all this, the Swiss Confederation gained independence from Holy Roman Emperor Maximilian I after a victory at Dornach in 1499.

Then, having made it as far as Milan, the rampaging Swiss suddenly lost to a combined French and Venetian force at Marignano in 1515. This stinging defeat prompted them to withdraw from the international scene and for the first time declare neutrality. For several centuries afterwards, the country's warrior spirit was channelled solely into mercenary activity – a tradition still echoed in the Swiss Guard that protects the pope.

REFORMATION

The country's neutrality and diversity combined to give Switzerland some protection when the religious Thirty Years' War broke out in 1618, although parts of it still suffered. The Protestant Reformation and the subsequent Catholic Counter Reformation had caused deep divisions and upheaval throughout Europe. In Switzerland, too, preacher Huldrych

1291   1515

Modern Switzerland 'begins' with independence pact signed at Rütli Meadow | Having finally dispatched the Habsburgs in 1499, the Swiss declare neutrality

Zwingli had started teaching the Protestant word in Zürich as early as 1519, as had Jean Calvin in Geneva. But Zentralschweiz (central Switzerland) remained Catholic.

So, unable to agree even among themselves, the Swiss couldn't decide which side to take in the Thirty Years' War and fortuitously stuck to their neutrality.

However, religious disputes dragged on inside Switzerland. At first, the Catholic cantons were sucked into a dangerous alliance with France, before eventually agreeing to religious freedom. At the same time, the country was experiencing an economic boom through textile industries in the northeast.

The French invaded Switzerland in 1798 and established the brief Helvetic Republic. But they were no more welcome than the Austrians before them, and internal fighting prompted Napoleon (now in power in France) to restore the former Confederation of cantons in 1803 (the Act of Mediation), with France retaining overall jurisdiction. Further cantons joined the Confederation at this time: Aargau, St Gallen, Graubünden, Ticino, Thurgau and Vaud.

After Napoleon's defeat by the British and Prussians at Waterloo in 1815, the Congress of Vienna peace treaty for the first time formally guaranteed Switzerland's independence and neutrality, as well as adding the cantons of Valais, Geneva and Neuchâtel.

Protestant Swiss first openly disobeyed the Catholic Church during 1522's 'affair of the sausages', when a printer and several priests in Zürich were caught gobbling Wurst on Ash Wednesday, instead of fasting as they should.

TOWARDS A MODERN CONSTITUTION

Civil war broke out in 1847, during which the Protestant army, led by General Dufour, quickly crushed the Sonderbund (or special league) of Catholic cantons, including Lucerne. In fact, the war lasted just 26 days, later leading German Chancellor Bismarck to dismissively declare it 'a hare shoot'. Victory by Dufour's forces was rapidly underlined with the creation of a new federal constitution in 1848 – largely still in place today – and the naming of Bern as the capital.

The constitution was a compromise between advocates of central control and conservative forces wanting to retain cantonal authority. The cantons eventually relinquished their right to print money, run postal services and levy customs duties, giving these to the federal government. However, they retained legislative and executive control over local matters. Furthermore, the new Federal Assembly was established in such a way as to give cantons a voice. The lower national chamber, or *Nationalrat*, has 200 members, allocated from the 26 cantons in proportion to population size. The upper states chamber, or *Ständerat*, comprises 46 members, two per canton.

The 780-page *Dunant's Dream: War, Switzerland and the History of the Red Cross*, by Caroline Moorhead, examines the triumphs, ethical dilemmas and occasional moral failures of the world's leading humanitarian organisation.

Lacking in mineral resources, Switzerland developed cottage industries and skilled labourers began to form guilds. Railways and roads were built, opening up Alpine regions and encouraging tourism. Between 1850 and 1860, six new commercial banks were established. The International Red Cross was founded in Geneva in 1863 by Henri Dunant.

Opposition to political corruption sparked a movement for greater democracy. In 1874, the constitution was revised so that many federal laws had to be approved by national referendum – a phenomenon for which Switzerland remains famous today. A petition with 50,000 signatures

1519	1847
Protestant Huldrych Zwingli starts preaching 'pray and work' in Zürich	'Hare shoot' civil war between Protestants and Catholics lasts just 26 days

can challenge a proposed law; 100,000 signatures can force a public vote on any new issue.

EARLY 20TH CENTURY

Despite some citizens' pro-German sympathies, Switzerland's only involvement in WWI lay in organising Red Cross units. After the war, Switzerland joined the League of Nations, but on a strictly financial and economic basis, without military involvement.

Although Swiss industry had profited during the war, the working classes had suffered as prices soared and wages fell. Consequently, a general strike was called in November 1918. With the country at a halt, the Federal Council eventually accepted some of the strikers' demands; a 48-hour week was introduced and the social security system was extended, laying the groundwork for today's progressive social state.

Switzerland was left largely unscathed by WWII. Apart from some accidental bombings (see Schaffhausen, p248), the most momentous event of the war for the country came when Henri Guisan, general of the civilian army, invited all top military personnel to the Rütli Meadow (site of the 1291 Oath of Allegiance) to show the world how determined the Swiss were to defend their own soil.

Although Switzerland proved a safe haven for escaping Allied prisoners, the country's banks have since been criticised for being a major conduit for Nazi plunder during WWII.

POST WWII

Switzerland's post-war history has been dominated by economic, social and political stability. The Swiss were horrified when these started to unravel slightly at the end of the 20th century, but recently have become reconciled to being a little more ordinary.

Geneva sociologist Jean Ziegler's The Swiss, the Gold and the Dead: How Swiss Bankers Financed the Nazi War Machine *offers a fascinating and controversial account of Switzerland's WWII history.*

THE SWISS WAY OF GOVERNMENT

- The make-up of Switzerland's Federal Council, or executive government, is determined not by who wins the most parliamentary seats, but by the 'magic formula', a cosy power-sharing agreement made between the four main parties in 1959.

- The Federal Council consists of seven ministers. All are part-time, even the president, and continue to hold down their everyday jobs.

- The president is drawn on a rotating basis from the seven federal ministers, so there's a new head of state each year.

- Until 2003, the 'magic formula' decreed the Free Democrats, Social Democrats and Christian Democrats had two council members each, with one going to the right-wing Swiss People's Party (SVP).

- In 2003, the anti-EU and anti-foreigner SVP, led by Christoph Blocher, won almost 28% of the vote and used this electoral success to wangle an extra place on the Federal Council. Controversially rewriting the 1959 compact, it took over the Christian Democrats' second seat.

- Many federal laws must first be approved by public referendum; there are several of these every year.

1863	1918
Pacifist Henri Dunant founds the International Red Cross in Geneva	Workers stage a general strike; the 48-hour week and social state follows

Immediately after the war, that certainly wasn't the case. While the rest of Europe was still recovering, Switzerland was able to forge ahead from an already powerful commercial, financial and industrial base. Zürich developed as an international banking and insurance centre, while the World Health Organization and many other international bodies set up headquarters in Geneva. Its much-vaunted neutrality led it to decline to actually join either the UN or the EU, but the country became one of the world's richest and most respected.

Then, in the late 1990s, a series of scandals forced Switzerland to begin reforming its famously secretive banking industry. In 1995, after pressure from Jewish groups, Swiss banks announced that they had discovered millions of dollars lying in dormant pre-1945 accounts, belonging to Holocaust victims and survivors. Three years later, amid allegations that they had been sitting on the money without seriously trying to trace its owners, the two largest banks, UBS and Credit Suisse, agreed to pay $1.25 billion in compensation to Holocaust survivors and their families.

Banking confidentiality dates back to the Middle Ages here, and was enshrined in law in 1934, when numbered, rather than named, bank accounts were introduced. However, in 2004, the country made another concession to that veil of secrecy, when it agreed to tax accounts held in Switzerland by EU citizens.

The year 2001 was truly Switzerland's *annus horribilus*. The financial collapse of the national airline Swissair, a canyoning accident in the Bernese Oberland that killed 21 tourists, an unprecedented gun massacre in the Zug parliament and a fatal fire in the Gotthard Tunnel, all within 12 months, prompted intense soul-searching.

However, when devastating floods washed through the country in 2005, causing several deaths and an estimated Sfr2 billion damage, there were fewer anguished cries about what was going wrong with Switzerland and more pragmatic debate on what should be done.

While swinging to the conservative right in its parliamentary government in 2003 (see the boxed text The Swiss Way of Government, opposite), the country also recognises that it's facing universal challenges, and has reached out more to the world. In 2002 it finally became the 190th member of the UN. In 2005 it joined Europe's 'Schengen' passport-free travel zone and, in theory, opened its borders to workers from the 10 new EU members.

It still isn't a member of the EU itself and, although the French-speaking regions would like it, doesn't look like becoming one any time soon. However, in many ways Switzerland no longer views isolation as quite so splendid.

Visit www.parliament .ch or www.admin.ch for more information on Switzerland's unusual political system, with its 'direct democracy', 'magic formula' and part-time politicians.

When Switzerland finally joined the UN in 2002, officials mistakenly ordered a rectangular Swiss flag to fly outside the organisation's New York headquarters. Swiss functionaries strenuously objected, insisting the UN run up the proper square flag pretty damn quick.

1940	2005
General Guisan's army turns out at Rütli to warn off potential WWII invaders	Summer floods sweep through Switzerland, causing an estimated Sfr2 billion damage

The Culture

THE NATIONAL PSYCHE

The Swiss consider themselves a bit different; a fundamental concept of their national identity has been 'Sonderfall Schweiz', or Switzerland as a special case. And despite moves towards more international cooperation recently, there's still much about the country that's idiosyncratic and unique. Not only does it bring four language groups – German, French, Italian and Romansch – under one national umbrella, it promotes 'direct democracy' with frequent referendums and practises 'armed neutrality', with a militia trained to do battle with an enemy that's not supposed to exist. While home to many global institutions, including the European headquarters of the UN, the country is yet to join the EU.

There are lots of stereotypes about Switzerland – chocolate, cheese, cuckoo clocks, precision watches and banking secrecy, Heidi, yodelling and the Alps – and just as many well-worn clichés surround the Swiss themselves. Thought of as dull, boring and overly cautious, ruthlessly efficient and hard-working, they inevitably display a touch of these attributes. In his rib-tickling *Xenophobe's Guide to the Swiss*, Paul Bilton even theorises that the national character is essentially a mountain farmer's: tough, independent, prepared for any emergency and, above all, insular, parochial and conservative.

However, Switzerland is such a diverse country that making any generalisations is foolhardy in the extreme. For a start, German-, French- and Italian-speaking Swiss all display similar attitudes to those of the Germans, French and Italians respectively. For every right-wing voter, there's always someone who's helped push through a wide range of progressive laws on subjects as different as gay marriage and voluntary suicide. There are marked differences between the older, more introspective generation and more outgoing younger people. Finally, for every well-meaning, if slightly dull, citizen, there are scores of happy, life-loving inhabitants.

Obtaining Swiss citizenship is notoriously difficult. Foreigners must approach the federal government, as well as their canton and commune, which have several ways of assessing an application, including panel interviews and public assemblies and votes.

ON GUARD

Machiavelli wrote that 'the Swiss are most armed and most free', but more than 400 years after their last major military excursion, even the Swiss are losing some of their enthusiasm for 'armed neutrality'.

While it's still the only Western nation to retain compulsory conscription, Switzerland's armed defences have been diminished. At the height of the Cold War, the country had more than 600,000 soldiers and 'universal militia' of reservists with a gun at home, comprising almost the entire male population. Today, every able-bodied Swiss man must still undergo military training and serve 260 days' military service between the ages of 20 and 36. However, community service is now an option, and the number of soldiers that can be mobilised within 48 hours has been scaled back to 220,000.

For many years, Switzerland maintained enough bunkers with food stockpiles to house just about the entire population underground in the event of attack. As army cost-cutting measures bite, however, some 13,000 military installations have recently been decommissioned.

But all is not lost. The enterprising army has, in part, turned to another trusty Swiss stand-by – tourism. The bunkers at Faulensee, for example, are now open to visitors (see the boxed text Bunker Mentality, p169).

In that respect, the Swiss – even though they consider themselves a bit different – are exactly like the rest of the world. You have to take everyone as you meet them.

LIFESTYLE

'They are,' wrote the UK's *Guardian* newspaper in 2004, 'probably the most fortunate people on the planet. Healthy, wealthy, and, thanks to an outstanding education system, wise. They enjoy a life most of us can only dream about. For ease of reference we commonly refer to them as the Swiss.' This deadpan doffing of the cap, from a nation that usually scorns 'dull' Switzerland, was prompted by yet another quality-of-life survey listing Geneva, Zürich and Bern among the planet's best cities. Those ratings haven't changed much since.

Urban Swiss don't enjoy a particularly different lifestyle from other Westerners; they just enjoy it more. They can rely on their little nation, one of the world's 10 richest in terms of GDP per capita, to deliver excellent health services, efficient public transport and all-round security. Spend a little time among them and you realise their sportiness, attention to diet and concern for the environment is symptomatic of another condition: they want to extract the most from life.

It's hardly surprising, then, that the Swiss have the greatest life expectancy in Europe; women here live to an average 83 years, men to 77. Switzerland isn't immune to modern worries, including AIDS and drugs, but the distribution of wealth in Switzerland is more even than in many contemporary societies. Most people can afford to rate friends and family – not work – as their top priority.

However, if you've not come to Switzerland to photosynthesise with envy, but are more interested in traditional culture, you'll find it in the rural regions, especially Appenzellerland or Valais. Here people still wear folk costumes during festivals and mark the seasons with time-honoured Alpine rituals. Every spring, shepherds decorate their cattle with flowers and bells before herding them, in a procession known as the *Alpauffahrt*, to mountain pastures where they both spend the summer. In autumn, the *Alpabfahrt* brings them down again.

POPULATION

Switzerland averages 172 inhabitants per square kilometre, with Alpine districts more sparsely populated and the urban areas more densely populated.

On a basic analysis, German speakers account for 64% of the population, French 19%, Italian 8% and Romansch under 1%. However, the situation is really more complex. 'German' speakers in Switzerland write standard or 'high' German, but they speak their own language, Schwyzertütsch, which has no official written form and is mostly unintelligible to outsiders. Linguists have identified at least two Romansch dialects and three variants of Italian, sometimes varying from valley to valley.

The various language communities have their differences of opinion; if it were left to the French-speaking regions, for example, Switzerland would have long been an EU member. However, spats only rarely go beyond words (see the boxed text Rocky Horror, p149).

SPORT

Ice hockey and football (soccer) are the two most popular spectator sports. Swiss football has been undergoing a recent renaissance, with the national squad winning a surprising, and infamously bad-tempered,

The Swiss have a strangely modest way of displaying wealth. For example, Hans J Bär, founder of private bank Julius Baer, admits in his autobiography to buying two identical limousines – to fool the neighbours into believing he owned only one.

Hoi – Your Swiss German Survival Guide, by Nicole Egger and Serge Liviano (www.bergli.ch), offers English speakers a frequently hilarious insight into Switzerland's most frequently spoken language.

play-off against Turkey to go into the 2006 World Cup. Although FC Basel and Zürich Grasshoppers still generally top the national league, FC Thun has also hit the international headlines with wins against Dynamo Kyiv and Sparta Prague in the European Champions League. Thun even gave London's mighty Arsenal a scare in 2005.

Of course, the biggest name in Swiss sport is tennis ace Roger Federer (at the time of writing still the unchallenged world number one). Additionally, former women's champion Martina Hingis hit the comeback trail late in 2005.

Tennis events include the Swiss Open in Gstaad (Allianz Suisse Swiss, p176) in July and an indoor tournament in Basel (p240) in October.

For traditional Swiss sports, see p49.

To check the latest cultural and sporting events in Switzerland, visit www.ticketcorner .com. Its booking line, ☎ 0900 800 800, costs Sfr1.19 per minute.

MULTICULTURALISM

Around 20% of people living in the country (more than 1.45 million) are immigrants who are residents but not Swiss citizens. This figure does *not* include the numerous seasonal workers, temporary residents, and international civil servants and administrators. Most of the permanent residents arrived after WWII, initially from Italy and Spain, and later from the former Yugoslavia.

The Swiss have reacted to this influx of immigrants as many other European countries. Parts of the populace appreciate the cultural wealth – and labour – these immigrants bring, while others have tended towards xenophobia. In 2002, a referendum trying to deny entry to asylum seekers arriving from other European countries was defeated by the narrowest of margins. A year later, however, the far-right SVP achieved enormous electoral success (see the boxed text The Swiss Way of Government, p30) and a proposed law to make naturalisation easier was voted down in a referendum.

MEDIA

Switzerland's media is mostly privately owned, although some broadcasters get state funding. It's independently minded, but can be worthy and conservative. The country's oldest and most distinguished organ is the *Neue Zürcher Zeitung*, founded in 1780 and now nicknamed the 'old aunt' for its fussy ways. (It's only begun putting photos on its front page in recent years.) The Geneva papers, especially *Le Temps*, provide an antidote, being progressive and pro-European.

The Swiss are bigger consumers of print media than TV, which is hardly surprising when you see how unexciting the broadcast fare is. Hundreds of small local newspapers dot the landscape to help feed this appetite for reading. For further details, see the boxed text Practicalities, p313.

THE NUMBERS GAME

Switzerland is virtually synonymous with numbered accounts and financial secrecy. It has seen the country become the fourth most important global financial centre, after New York, London and Tokyo, and the guardian of 27% of the world's offshore funds.

However, its policy of anonymity for account holders has also created damaging controversy. Since the 1990s scandal over dormant WWII accounts (see p30), banks have frozen accounts believed to belong to Al-Qaeda, agreed to tax accounts held by EU citizens and returned money looted from Nigeria by former dictator Sani Abacha.

Despite this, Swiss banks continue to have a reputation for opacity.

RELIGION

The country is split pretty evenly between Roman Catholicism (46%) and Protestantism (40%), mostly along cantonal lines that confusingly don't follow linguistic divisions. The main Protestant areas include Zürich, Geneva, Vaud, Thurgau, Neuchâtel and Glarus; strong Catholic areas include Valais, Ticino, Uri, Unterwalden and Schwyz, as well as Fribourg, Lucerne, Zug and Jura.

This split has been pivotal in the development of Swiss history and identity, but is less influential today. It still might have some residual bearing on, say, which school a Swiss person attends. However, in a recent nationwide poll, only 16% of the populace said religion was very important to them.

WOMEN IN SWITZERLAND

Gender equality has been a latecomer to the party in Switzerland. Women only won the right to vote in federal elections in 1971 and, as late as 1990, they still weren't permitted to participate in communal voting in parts of Appenzellerland.

Their countrymen's tardiness in acceding to their demands for suffrage and greater workplace recognition has meant a desperate game of catch-up for Swiss feminists. Switzerland was ahead of many when in 1999 it elected a woman president – the high-profile Ruth Dreifuss, who was also the first Jewish president. However, the World Economic Forum's 2005 Gender Gap Index placed Switzerland 34th out of 58 countries, well behind the Scandinavian nations, the UK and the US.

ARTS

Many foreign writers and artists, such as Voltaire, Byron, Shelley and Turner, have visited and settled in Switzerland. However, many home-grown creatives leave Switzerland to make a name for themselves abroad (see the boxed text I Didn't Realise They Were Swiss, p38).

Architecture

Switzerland's contribution to modern architecture has been pivotal, given that it's the birthplace of Le Corbusier (1887–1965), one of the most influential pioneers. Born Charles-Edouard Jeanneret-Gris in La Chaux-de-Fonds, Le Corbusier was famous for his economy of design, formalism and functionalism; without him, today's cities would look very different indeed. He spent most of his working life in France and his most famous constructions – Nôtre Dame du Haut chapel at Ronchamps in France and Chandigarh in India – are found outside Switzerland. However, the Villa Turque (Villa Schwob, see the boxed text The Concrete King, p112) can still be seen in his home town and the last building he ever designed is now a museum in Zürich (Le Corbusier Pavilion, p197).

Le Corbusier left a legacy of innovation and faith in modernism, which has helped contemporary Swiss architects push to the forefront. Basel-based partners Jacques Herzog and Pierre de Meuron are undoubtedly the best known, as creators of London's Tate Modern gallery, 2001 winners of the prestigious Pritzker Prize and the designers of the main stadium for the 2008 Beijing Olympics. However, Ticino architect Mario Botta also enjoys an international reputation, especially as the creator of San Francisco's Museum of Modern Art. Both of these practices have several noteworthy buildings in Basel and Botta's Church of San Giovanni Battista in Mogno (p303) is outstanding.

Assisted suicide is legal in Switzerland and much international debate, both for and against, has surrounded the role of Dignitas (www.dignitas .ch) in offering medical help to terminally or chronically ill foreign nationals who travel to the country.

Visit the Arts Council of Switzerland, Pro Helvetia (www.pro-helvetia.ch) for information on innovative projects promoting Swiss culture, both at home and abroad.

Other noteworthy modern Swiss buildings include Peter Zumthor's award-winning Therme Vals (see the boxed text Spas & Thermal Springs, p47), and the Kirchner Museum (p276) in Davos by architects Annette Gigon and Mike Guyer. For more details, ask Switzerland Tourism (p322) for its free, 128-page *Art & Architecture* book.

Rural Swiss houses vary according to the region. The Freilichtmuseum Ballenberg (see p171) outside Brienz showcases a wide variety.

Literature

In her coffee-table tome *Eigentlich Sind Wir Anders (We're Different Actually)*, photographer Christina Koerte visually subverts seven Swiss clichés, with ugly motorway service stations in Heidiland, an unheroic-looking William Tell and a cheeky look at Swiss food.

Thanks to a 1930s Shirley Temple film, Johanna Spyri's *Heidi* is the most famous Swiss novel. The story of a young orphan living with her grandfather in the Swiss Alps who is ripped away to the city is unashamedly sentimental and utterly atypical for Swiss literature. Otherwise, the genre is quite serious and gloomy.

Take the German-born, naturalised Swiss Hermann Hesse (1877–1962) for example. A Nobel Prize winner, he fused Eastern mysticism and Jungian psychology to advance the theory that Western civilisation is doomed unless humankind gets in touch with our own essential humanity – as in *Siddharta* (1922) and *Steppenwolf* (1927). Later novels, such as *Narzissus und Goldmund* (1930) and the cult *The Glass Bead Game* (1943), go on to explore the tension between individual freedom and social controls.

Similarly, the most recognised work by Zürich-born Max Frisch (1911–91), *Ich bin nicht Stiller* (1954; *I'm not Stiller/I'm not relaxed*) is a dark, Kafkaesque tale of mistaken identity. His *Homo Faber* (1957) examines how one engineer's cold-hearted affair with what turns out to be his daughter ultimately destroys them both. The book was adapted into the movie *Voyager*, with Sam Shepard and Julie Delpy, in 1991.

More accessible is Friedrich Dürrenmatt (1921–90), who created a rich seam of detective fiction. *Das Versprechen (The Pledge)*, a little masterpiece about how much sheer dumb luck – or lack of it – shapes our existence, was turned into a love-it-or-loathe-it film in 2001 by Sean Penn (starring Jack Nicholson). As a playwright, Dürrenmatt even penned comedies, such as *The Physicists*.

Green Henry (1854), by Gottfried Keller (1819–1900), is a massive tome revolving around a Zürich student's reminiscences and is considered one of the masterpieces of Germanic literature.

Music & Dance

Yodelling and alphorns are the two traditional forms of Swiss 'music'. Yodelling began in the Alps as a means of communication between

---

MY NAME IS…

The file on Swiss film is pretty thin, with few of the nation's movies having been released abroad. However, in 2005, locals were enjoying one home-grown hit that's not likely to be forgotten easily. Hilariously Swiss, *Mein Name ist Eugen* (My Name is Eugene) went on to win the national film prize that year.

Based on a popular children's book from 1955 from Klaus Schädelin, it follows 12-year-old Eugen and his rascally three friends as they journey from Bern to the mountains and down to Zürich in search of long-lost treasure.

In 2006, the same production team released another movie about events that at least created a blip on the international radar. *Grounding*, about the 2001 bankruptcy of national airline Swissair at least got overseas press coverage, if not – at the time of writing – a worldwide release.

> **ON HIS SOAPBOX**
>
> Switzerland is full of private galleries selling works to collectors, and a popular buy recently has been the work of Gianni Motti (1958–). This Italian artist has made Switzerland his home and, when not selling bars of soap made from Silvio Berlusconi's liposuctioned fat for US$18,000, he makes headlines pulling 'artistic' stunts.

peaks, but became separated into two disciplines. *Juchzin* consists in short yells with different meanings such as 'it's dinner time' or 'we're coming'. In *Naturjodel*, one or more voices sing a melody without lyrics.

Alphorns were used in the mountains to herd cattle. Long wind instruments 2m to 4m in length, they have a curved base and a cup-shaped mouthpiece. To learn more and see them made, visit Alphornbau Stocker (p221) outside Lucerne.

There's a symphony orchestra in every main city and music festivals throughout the year. Two of the most famous festivals, with worldwide reputations, are the Lucerne Festival (p217) and the Montreux Jazz Festival (p90).

One performance group definitely worth seeing is Öff Öff (www.oeffoeff.ch), which tours using a transportable 'Air Station' (rotating climbing frame) and has been described as a combination of dance and (how very Swiss!) mountaineering.

Yodelling has recently become trendy with Swiss city slickers, who find it an excellent way of releasing stress. Award-winning folk singer Nadja Räss has been at the revival's forefront, releasing two solo CDs.

Painting, Sculpture & Design

Aside from Dada (see the boxed text Completely Dada, p199), there haven't been many Swiss art movements. Homegrown painters and sculptors tend to be more individualistic. The painter who most concerned himself with Swiss themes was Ferdinand Hodler (1853–1918); he depicted folk heroes, like William Tell (see Kunstmuseum, p192), and events from history, such as the first grassroots Swiss vote (see Kunthaus, p197). Hodler also remained resident in Switzerland, unlike many fellow Swiss artists.

Abstract artist and colour specialist Paul Klee (1879–1940) spent most of his life in Germany, including with the Bauhaus school, although the largest showcase of his work is in Bern (see Paul Klee Centre, p183).

Likewise, the sculptor Alberto Giacometti (1901–66) spent most of his working life in Paris, but many of his trademark stick figures have made it back to Zürich (see the Kunsthaus, p197).

Many quirky sculptures by the Paris-based Jean Tinguely (1925–91) are clustered around Basel. In fact, there's a museum (p237) dedicated to the sculptor and one of his fountains (p239) is also here.

Swissworld (www.swissworld.org) offers a quick rundown on most aspects of Switzerland, from people and culture to science and economy.

One area where the Swiss tend to excel collectively is in graphic design. The 'new graphics' of Josef Muller-Brockmann (1914–96) and Max Bill (1908–94) are still extremely well regarded, as is the branding work by Karl Gerstner (1930–) for IBM, and the **Búro Destruct** (www.burodestruct.net) studio's typefaces (seen on many music album covers).

The country is also strong in product design and installation art. It gave the world Cow Parade – the different processions of life-sized, painted fibreglass cows that have decorated several different cities around the globe. The first herd, of more than 800 cows, had their outing in Zürich in 1998, and stray animals can still be found lurking around the country. Pipilotti Rist (1962–), whose City Lounge (Stadtlounge, p253) stands in St Gallen, also falls into this category.

I DIDN'T REALISE THEY WERE SWISS

Switzerland has always attracted celebrities – famous non-Swiss residents and former residents include Charlie Chaplin, Yehudi Menuhin, Audrey Hepburn, Richard Burton, Peter Ustinov, Roger Moore, Tina Turner, Phil Collins, the Aga Khan, Michael Schumacher and *Wallpaper* magazine founder Tyler Brûlé. Yet plenty of native Swiss have made their mark on the world stage too. Some people you may not immediately think of as Swiss include the following:

Ursula Andress (1936–) Actress, most famous for her bikini-clad appearance in the James Bond flick *Dr No*.

Sepp (Joseph) Blatter (1936–) Outspoken president of FIFA, world football's governing body.

Alain de Botton (1969–) Pop philosopher and globally best-selling author of the *Art of Travel* etc, who was born in Zürich.

Louis Chevrolet (1878–1941) Founder of the Chevrolet Manufacturing Company in 1911, producer of archetypal 'American' automobiles.

Le Corbusier (1887–1965) Architectural innovator, often believed to be French.

Carla del Ponte (1947–) Tough-gal public prosecutor at the International Criminal Court who's taken on former Yugoslav president Slobodan Milosevic.

Marc Forster (1969–) Oscar-winning director of *Monster's Ball* and *Finding Neverland*.

Albert Hofmann (1906–) The first person to synthesise and experiment with lysergic acid diethylamide (LSD).

Jean-Luc Godard (1930–) More-Swiss-than-French avant-garde film-maker.

Elisabeth Kübler Ross (1926–2004) Psychiatrist whose *On Death and Dying* articulated the famous five stages of grief: denial, anger, bargaining, depression and acceptance.

Erich von Däniken (1935–) Expounder of far-fetched early-history theories in the 1970s bestseller *Chariots of the Gods?*

SCIENCE

Science is important in Switzerland. The formula 'E=MC²' was coined by Albert Einstein when he was living in Bern (see Einstein Museum, p182) and the World Wide Web was born at the CERN (European Organisation for Nuclear Research) research institute (p66) outside Geneva. Furthermore, the Swiss themselves have more registered patents and more Nobel Prize winners (most in scientific disciplines) per head of population than any other nationality.

The country's pharmaceuticals industry is a major contributor to the economy, which makes it hardly surprising that Swiss voters take a very liberal approach when voting on issues like allowing stem-cell research. The two Swiss pharmaceutical giants are Novartis and Roche (the manufacturer of the much sought-after antiviral drug Tamiflu). Both are among the world's top 40 companies, according to the *Financial Times* newspaper.

Nestlé, founded in Switzerland more than 100 years ago, remains the world's biggest consumer food firm.

Helvetica: Homage to a Typeface, by Lars Müller, highlights Switzerland's pre-eminence on planet design, with a paean to an iconic font that appears everywhere from US tax forms to Windows and Mac iPhoto software.

Environment

THE LAND

Landlocked Switzerland – sandwiched between Germany, Austria, Liechtenstein, Italy and France – is essentially an Alpine country. The magnificent Alps and Pre-Alps in the centre and south make up 60% of the modest 41,285 sq km that Switzerland clocks on the European map. The mightily less-known, mysterious Jura Mountains in the west comprise another 10% and central Mittelland (otherwise known as the Plateau Central) makes up the rest. Farming of cultivated land is intensive, cows being moved to upper slopes to graze on lush summer grass as soon as the retreating snow line allows.

It is here that Europe's highest elevations smugly sit. The Dufourspitze (Dufour Peak; 4634m) of Monte Rosa in the Alps is Switzerland's highest point, but the Matterhorn (4478m) with its dramatic pyramidal cap is way better known; inhale incredulous views of it on the Zermatt–Gornergrat cogwheel train (p134) or while skiing in its shadow. Then of course there's Mont Blanc (4807m), a hulk of a mountain – Europe's highest to boot – shared with France and Italy. Enjoy the Swiss side of it with the Mont-Blanc Express (p122), Mont Blanc circuit (p124) or a simple stroll (on a clear day) along Geneva's Quai du Mont-Blanc (p65).

Southern Switzerland contains a series of high mountain passes that provide overland access into Italy. Glaciers account for a total area of 2000 sq km; most notable is the Aletsch Glacier, the largest valley glacier in Europe with an area of 169 sq km. Several glaciers proffer summer skiing, memorably the Glacier de Tsanfleuron (3000m) in Les Diablerets (p95).

Lakes are dotted everywhere except in the gentle Jura (p114) where the substrata rock is too brittle and porous. (These mountains peak at around 1700m and are less steep and less severely eroded than the Alps.) The most prolific source of lakes and rivers, including the mighty Rhine and Rhône, is central Switzerland's St Gotthard Massif (p233). The Rhône remains a torrent from its source to Martigny, from where it then flows west to create Europe's largest Alpine lake and Switzerland's best-known – Lake Geneva (Lac Léman in French).

From Lake Geneva in the southwest the Mittelland runs in a band to the Bodensee (Lake Constance) in the northeast. This region of hills is crisscrossed by rivers, ravines and winding valleys; it contains the most populous cities and is where much of the farming takes place. The sole canton entirely south of the Alps is Ticino, home to the northern part of Lago Maggiore. At 193m, this lake is the lowest point in the country.

WILDLIFE

With some of Europe's largest mountains and lakes and some of the strongest environmental legislation in its green fold, Switzerland's wildlife portfolio is rich, but not without risk. Experts reckon the last 150 years have blasted 200-odd plant and animal species in Switzerland into extinction, lark and otter included – and dozens more (such as the freshwater mussel, pretty purple monkey orchid and 81 bird species) hover on the brink.

Animals

The bearded vulture with its unsavoury bone-breaking habits and awe-inspiring 3m wing span only remains in the wild thanks to reintroduction

Meadow and pasture make up 45% of Swiss land, forest 24% and arable fields 6%.

Man meets Matterhorn in *Scrambles Amongst the Alps*, a mountaineering classic in which Edward Whymper describes his breathtaking ascent of Switzerland's most famous mountain in 1869 and the tragedy that befell his team coming down.

RULES OF THE WILD

- Leave the rural environment as you found it.
- Stick to the marked paths when hiking. Short cuts straight down a slope could be transformed into a watercourse during the next heavy rainfall and cause soil erosion.
- Don't pick Alpine wildflowers; they really do look lovelier on the mountainsides.
- Farm gates should be left as you found them.
- Approach wildlife with discretion; moving too close will unnerve wild animals.
- Don't light fires, except in established fireplaces.
- Take everything you bring into the mountains out again: rubbish, used packaging, cigarette butts and used tampons included.
- If you really can't avoid leaving some memento of your visit, such as faeces, bury it in the ground at least 100m away from any watercourse.

Follow young bearded vultures, Folio and Natura, as they flit around the Swiss National Park marked with satellite transmitters as part of the Bearded Vultures on the Move web project (www.wild .unizh.ch/bg). Get the background scoop at the Foundation Pro Bearded Vulture (www .bartgeier.ch).

programmes pursued by Alpine national parks, Swiss National Park (opposite) included. Extinct in the Alps by the 19th century, 21 captive-bred baby vultures in all were released into the park's Stabelchod Valley between 1991 and 2001, where they have since bred successfully and continue to prey. Since June 2005 the park has tracked two young bearded vultures live-time using satellite telemetry as part of a European project aimed at better understanding the vulture.

The European kestrel and golden eagle are other impressive birds to spot in protected Swiss Alpine skies. More plentiful than the vulture, the eagle nests with vigour in the Graubünden area and munches its way through marmots in summer, ungulate carcasses in winter. Markedly smaller is the Alpendohle, a relative of the crow; look for a flutter of jet-black feathers and yellow beak around mountain tops.

The most distinctive Alpine animal is the ibex, a mountain goat with huge curved and ridged horns. There are about 12,000 of them left in Switzerland and they migrate up to 3000m altitude. The chamois (a horned antelope) is more timid but equally at home on the peaks – it can leap 4m vertically. Marmots (chunky rodents related to the squirrel) are also famous residents, although they are hard to spot given they spend most of their lives darting in a maze of underground burrows or metres-long tunnels to escape from hungry predators. Come September, marmots hibernate, body temperatures bizarrely shooting every fortnight from between 3°C and 6°C to 38°C, where they remain for two days before plummeting back down to single digits. The reintroduced European lynx, mountain hare, ermine, weasel and fox are other Alpine residents, as is – experts say with bated breath – the European brown bear. Hunted into extinction in Switzerland by 1904, the lumbering mammal made a couple of controversial appearances when one crossed over the border from Italy in 2005 (see the boxed text A Little Animal Magic, p280).

The ibex was extinct in the Graubünden by 1650, prompting an enterprising soul a couple of centuries and a bit later to poach a couple from the Italian royal herd. In 1920 the first ibex bred from the pair was released into the Swiss National Park.

The rutting season in September and early October is easily the most impressive time to spot roe deer and larger red deer in forested regions and Alpine pastures. Fights can be fierce as stags defend their harem of hinds from other stoked-up males. With the rutting season done and dusted, the deer abandon Alpine pastures like the Swiss National Park for the sunnier slopes of warmer valleys like Engadine, Val Mustair and Vinschgau.

The noisy nutcracker with its distinctive sound and white-speckled brown plumage can be seen or heard practically everywhere you turn on pine forest hiking paths, be it on a Swiss National Park information panel (the nutcracker is the park's symbol) or high in a tree plucking out cone seeds with its long beak or stashing away nuts for the coming winter. Another ornithological treat – look out for it on rocky slopes and in Alpine meadows above 2000m – is the rock ptarmigan, a chicken-like species that has been around since the Ice Age, which moults three times a year to ensure a foolproof camouflage for every season (brown in summer, white in winter).

Plants

Climatic variation means that vegetation ranges from palm trees in Ticino to Nordic flora in the Alps. At higher altitudes, flowers bloom April to July, species depending. The famous Edelweiss, with star-shaped flowers, grows up to 3500m altitude. Alpine rhododendrons, known locally as Alpenroses, are numerous at 2500m. Spring gentians are small, violet-blue flowers. ·White crocuses are early bloomers (from March) at lower elevations.

Trees are a mixture of deciduous and conifers in the Mittelland. At an elevation of 800m conifers become more numerous. The red spruce is common at lower levels, while the arolla pine (*Arve* or *Zirbe* in German) and larch mostly take over higher up. At around 2000m, tall trees are replaced by bushes and scrub, which then finally give way to Alpine meadows.

Where to Watch Birds in Switzerland, by Marco Sacchi, Peter Ruegg and Jacques Laesser, is the definitive guide to birdwatching in Switzerland. It details 45 sights countrywide, including best times to spot them.

NATIONAL PARKS

Switzerland has just one national park, predictably called **Swiss National Park** (www.nationalpark.ch). Created in 1914, it gives hard-core protection to 172.4 sq km of coniferous forest (28%), alpine grassland (21%) and scree, rock or high mountains (51%) around Zernez (p280) in eastern Switzerland. Ibex, marmots and chamois are commonplace, 1800 to 2000 red deer roam around free as birds in summer, while the bearded vulture (reintroduced in 1991) is a rare treat for eagle-eyed visitors in the Stabelchod Valley. The main activity in the park is walking although it is limited, visitors being forbidden to stray off the 80km of designated footpaths. From November to May the entire national park is off-limits full stop.

Since 2000, Swiss conservation group ProNatura (see the boxed text Green Card, below) has been campaigning for the creation of another national park in Switzerland by 2010. State funding of Sfr10 million a year was approved in June 2005 on the back of the completion of feasibility studies aimed at locating the new national park: nature-rich hot contenders

Switzerland's Prix Ecosport awards sporting events (such as the Engadine Ski Marathon or Locarno Triathlon) that boost environmental awareness; read about past winners at www .prix-ecosport.ch, in German, French and Italian.

GREEN CARD

Environmental and wildlife organisations in Switzerland include:

Alpine Initiative (☎ 041 870 97 81, 027 924 22 26; www.alpeninitiative.ch; Kapuzinerweg 6, Altdorf) Mainly concerned with Alpine transport routes.

Birdlife Switzerland (☎ 044 457 70 20; www.birdlife.ch; Postfach Wiedingstr 78, Zürich) Swiss birdlife protection; visitor centres near Zürich and Berne.

Greenpeace Switzerland (www.greenpeace.ch in German & French) German speaking (☎ 044 447 41 41; Heinrichstrasse 147, 8031 Zürich); French speaking (☎ 022 731 02 09; Case Postale 1558, 1211 Geneva 1)

ProNatura French speaking (☎ 024 425 0372; www.pronatura.ch; Champ Pittet, 1400 Yverdon les Bains); German speaking (☎ 061 317 91 91; Postfach, 4018 Basel) Switzerland's largest conservation NGO dating to 1909 and responsible for national park and nature reserve management.

Wildlife Switzerland (☎ 044 635 61 31; www.wild.unizh.ch; Strickhofstrasse 39, Zürich)

WWF Switzerland (☎ 044 297 21 21; www.wwf.ch in German, French & Italian; Hohlstrasse 110, 8010 Zürich)

SUPPORT THE LOCAL ECONOMY – LEASE A COW!

Ramona, Ginette, Finette and a herd of other Alpine beauties with eyelashes to die for are there for the milking at **Wylerhof** (☎ 033 951 31 60; www.kuhleasing.ch in German & French; Stockmatte, Brienz), an Alpine dairy farm run by Helga and Paul Wyler in the Bernese Oberland. Lease the cow of your choice online for a month (Sfr2009) or the season (June to September Sfr380), invest half a day's manual labour on the farm and get 70kg to 100kg of cheese from your cow at a reduced rate.

---

include 600 sq km in Adula/Rheinwaldhorn near the San Bernardino Pass, a 349 sq km patch west of Locarno, 350 sq km snug against Matterhorn-proud Zermatt, and a pocket of the Muverans region.

A further 20% of Swiss land is protected to a substantially lesser degree by 600-odd nature parks, reserves and protected landscapes sprinkled around the country.

Two of the country's most precious sights deemed sufficiently incredible to star on Unesco's list of World Heritage Sights are green: pyramid-shaped Monte San Giorgio (1096m; p299), south of Lago di Lugano in Ticino, which safeguards the world's best fossil record of Triassic marine life from 245 to 230 million years ago; and southwestern Switzerland's spectacular Jungfrau-Aletsch-Bietschhorn mountain region (p139), where the Bernese Alps safeguard Europe's largest glacier and a rash of other equally stunning glacial creations.

Listen to the noise pollution of a jet plane; find out how much waste from households and small businesses is recycled annually; or hone in on an interactive air pollutant map at the Federal Office for the Environment (Bundesamt für Umwelt) at www .umwelt-schweiz.ch.

ENVIRONMENTAL ISSUES

Switzerland is extremely environmentally friendly, its citizens producing less than 400kg of waste each per year (half the figure for the USA). To say the Swiss are even more diligent recyclers than the Germans, with households religiously separating waste into different categories prior to collection, speaks volumes.

Hydroelectric power meets almost 60% of the country's energy demands and five Swiss nuclear power stations built between 1969 and 1984 provide the rest – and will continue to do so following the electorate's rejection in 2003 of an extension of a 10-year moratorium on the building of new plants that expired in 2000 and the *Strom ohne Atom* proposal calling for the closure of Switzerland's nuclear plants by 2014.

Gem up on Swiss ozone facts, figures and daily readings at www.ozone -info.ch (in German, French and Italian).

Mountain protection is of paramount importance in a country where the vast majority of land is Alpine, that shelters fragile ecosystems particularly vulnerable to pollution and environmental damage – and that receives 120 million-odd visitors a year. Global warming could have a serious impact on Switzerland because of the effect on Alpine glaciers. Since the 1950s the federal government has introduced various measures to protect forests, lakes and marshland from environmental damage and in 1991 it signed the Alpine Convention, which seeks to reduce damage caused by motor traffic and tourism.

Air pollution caused by vehicle emissions remains a major issue, with larger cities like Geneva tackling the problem head-on by introducing alternative circulation of vehicles with odd-/even-number plates in summer when ozone levels hit unacceptable highs. Reducing speed limits on motorways and encouraging motorists to leave their cars at home on chosen 'slow-up' days (www.slowup.ch in German and French) is another means of controlling air pollution. On a national level the country is gallantly trying to switch freight carriage from road to rail, which is less harmful to the environment; see the boxed text Road Tolls, p325 for details.

Outdoor Activities

Rafting, cycling, hiking, skiing, canyoning, snow golf, zorbing – Switzerland offers a world of adventure for the wild at heart. And those sports are only half of it. In a Victorian-era postcard sold at the Tourism Museum in Interlaken, a cartoonist imagines how, for example, *Die Jungfrau in der Zukunft* (the Jungfrau Region in the future) will appear. Dated 1896, the card envisages crowds of mountain-climbers trekking up glaciers as skiers slither downwards, and shows small planes zooming overhead while thrill-seekers paraglide off mountaintops. Apart from the Mary Poppins–style umbrellas used by the latter – and the big-bottomed women being carried by the gentlemen hikers – it's a surprisingly prophetic rendition of much of the Swiss landscape today.

Waffenlaufen is a uniquely Swiss race, where participants dress in military uniform and carry a rucksack and rifle over an 18km to 42km course.

ADVENTURE SPORTS

Rafting and canyoning are the two extreme sports most readily associated with Switzerland, and these and other adventure activities are mainly clustered around Interlaken (see p146), Lucerne (p217) and Engelberg (see p231). However, the best white-water rafting happens in Graubünden.

One of the largest operators with bases across the country is **Swissraft** (www.swissraft.ch). Otherwise look in individual chapters and destinations.

Activities include the following:

Bungee jumping/canyon jumping Tied by your ankle (bungee jumping) or your midriff (canyon jumping) to a long line, you leap off a cliff – before you look (from Sfr125).

Canyoning Described by some as 'white-water rafting without the boat', this controversial sport involves abseiling down waterfalls, rock-climbing and swimming through massive gorges. All in protective gear, of course (from Sfr110).

Hydrospeeding Kitted out in a helmet, wetsuit and scuba fins, participants lie on their stomachs, on top of specially designed, surfboard-like 'rafts' and ride the wild rivers, for example, in Graubünden (from Sfr120).

Zorbing This is an extreme sport even the faint of heart could comfortably choose (although perhaps not after a heavy night's drinking). You're strapped safely inside an inflated ball, inside another inflated ball, before being pushed head-over-heels down a hill. People who've zorbed in New Zealand say Swiss mountains are too steep to allow the leisurely roll-out that's the real thrill. But if Interlaken's closer than Rotorua, now's no time to compare (from Sfr95).

AERIAL SPORTS

There are more than 600 hot-air balloons in Switzerland, but **Château d'Oex** (www.chateau-doex.ch) is the best-known hub for this activity (from Sfr350). It's been the launch site for many round-the-world ballooning adventures, including the successful Breitling Orbiter journey in 1999 and some of Richard Branson's attempts. Every January the town hosts the **Semaine Internationale de Ballons à Air Chaud** (International Hot Air Balloon Week; www.festivaldeballons.ch), which is worth seeing just for the novelty-shape balloons. See also p96.

Paragliding and hang-gliding (from Sfr170) are possible just about anywhere there are mountains. Skydiving (from Sfr380) is also popular.

CYCLING

Thankfully, to enjoy cycling in Switzerland you don't have to be as good in the mountains as a Tour de France rider. Most bike paths, including the network of well-signposted national cycle routes, avoid too many

ACTIVITIES

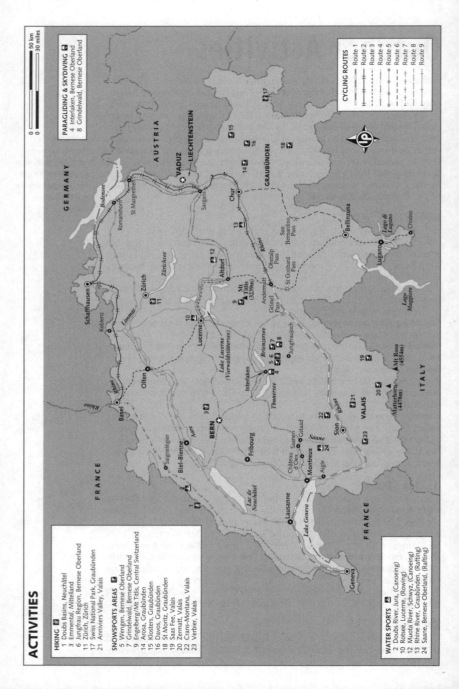

HIKING
1 Doubs Basins, Neuchâtel
3 Emmental, Mittelland
6 Jungfrau Region, Bernese Oberland
11 Zürich, Zürich
17 Swiss National Park, Graubünden
21 Anniviers Valley, Valais

SNOWSPORTS AREAS
5 Wengen, Bernese Oberland
7 Grindelwald, Bernese Oberland
9 Engelberg/Mt Titlis, Central Switzerland
14 Arosa, Graubünden
15 Klosters, Graubünden
16 Davos, Graubünden
18 St Moritz, Graubünden
19 Saas Fee, Valais
20 Zermatt, Valais
22 Crans-Montana, Valais
23 Verbier, Valais

PARAGLIDING & SKYDIVING
4 Interlaken, Bernese Oberland
8 Grindelwald, Bernese Oberland

WATER SPORTS
2 Doubs River, Jura, (Canoeing)
10 Rotsee, Lucerne, (Rowing)
12 Muota River, Schwyz, (Canoeing)
13 Rhine River, Graubünden, (Rafting)
24 Saane, Bernese Oberland, (Rafting)

CYCLING ROUTES
Route 1
Route 2
Route 3
Route 4
Route 5
Route 6
Route 7
Route 8
Route 9

GETTING IT COVERED

Whether you're simply going hiking, or you plan to canyon down a white-water river, it's important to have the right insurance. Mountain rescue can be very expensive, as can health care in Switzerland generally. Normal policies don't cover many of the activities in this section. You will need to pay a premium for winter-sports cover. Further premiums are necessary for adventure sports like bungee jumping and canyoning.

The vast majority of adventures pass off without injury. However, there's always a risk. There have been two tragic adventure-sports accidents in Switzerland in recent years (see p146), so back up your insurance by asking about the safety standards of the company you choose.

---

hills, following the courses of lakes or rivers instead. In a country that often seems to live by the motto 'two wheels good, four wheels bad', you'll find drivers are pretty courteous if you cycle on roads, there are lots of rental outlets (including numerous train stations) and you will have few problems transporting your bike by train (see p328).

Just about everything you could ever need while planning a cycling tour in Switzerland is available via **Veloland Schweiz** (www.veloland.ch, www.cycling-in-switzerland.ch), which includes details of lesser, regional trails as well as the following nine national routes:

Aare Route From the Grimsel Pass to Koblenz via Interlaken, Bern and Olten.

Alpine Panorama Route From St Margrethen on the Austrian border to Aigle near Lake Geneva, via Altdorf, Lake Lucerne and Fribourg.

Graubünden Route From Bellinzona to Chur.

Jura Route From Basel to Geneva running close to the northwestern border of the country.

Lakes Route From Lac Leman at Montreux to the southeastern end of the Bodensee near St Margrethen, via Gstaad, Lucerne and Sargans.

Mittelland Route From Lausanne on Lac Leman to Romanshorn on the Bodensee, via Biel, Olten and close to Zürich airport.

North–South Route From Basel to Chiasso via Lucerne, Andermatt and Lugano.

Rhine Route From Basel to Andermatt via Schaffhausen, the Bodensee (Lake Constance) and Chur.

Rhône Route From Geneva to Andermatt via Lausanne, Montreux and Sion.

All routes are well signposted in red with a bicycle icon. Hard-copy maps, should you want one, are also available from most Swiss bookshops or Switzerland Tourism (Sfr19.90).

There are 3300km of major national cycling routes in Switzerland. Between 1998 and 2004, when the Swiss postal service issued a special stamp, it was estimated that cyclists clocked up between 130 and 150 million kilometres on these paths.

HIKING

With 50,000km of designated paths (German: *Wanderweg*, French: *sentier*) at their disposal, it's no wonder the Swiss are mad-keen hikers and it's pretty easy for holidaymakers to join them. Bright-yellow direction signs along the trail make it difficult to get lost, and each usually gives an average walking time to the next destination. Of course, you should always wear proper hiking boots and take rain gear and a water bottle.

Trails are colour-coded according to difficulty. When yellow markers are painted on trees alongside a path, it's considered suitable for everybody. At higher altitudes, signs and markers for mountain paths (German: *Bergweg*, French: *sentier de montagne*) are painted white-red-white. These paths are deemed to be more suitable for experienced mountain walkers, though anybody with reasonable fitness and sturdy, nonslip footwear should be OK. High Alpine routes are white-blue-white.

To learn a little bit about the history of Nordic walking, as well as the best techniques, head to www.nordicwalking online.com. The German-language www.nordic -walking-online.de is more comprehensive and less commercial.

Some of the best hiking is in the Jungfrau Region, where you will find trails of varying difficulty and length. There's a fantastic all-day trail stretching from Grindelwald-First to Schynige Platte (or vice versa), and a much shorter, easy walk from Männlichen to Kleine Scheidegg. In the Swiss National Park (see p280) you can combine hiking with some wildlife-spotting.

One local passion is Nordic walking. If you see people rhythmically swinging themselves between two walking poles, don't be taken aback; they're simply working their upper bodies more and giving themselves a better cardio work-out. You might want to try it yourself. Snowshoe hiking is another recent trend in winter. For more details, see www .myswitzerland.com.

For walking suggestions and detailed route descriptions, see Lonely Planet's *Walking in Switzerland* by Clem Lindenmayer. Walks are detailed and accompanied by lots of maps.

The **Schweizer Wanderwegen SAW** (Swiss Hiking Federation; ☎ 061 606 93 40; www .swisshiking.ch in German; Im Hirshalm 49, CH-4125 Riehen) organises guided walking tours and produces good hiking maps. The **Schweizer Alpenclub** (Swiss Alpine Club; ☎ 031 370 18 18; www.sac-cas.ch in German & French; Monbijoustrasse 61, CH-3001 Bern) maintains huts for overnight stays at altitude; see p313.

MOUNTAINEERING

There are well-established mountaineering schools in Pontresina and Meiringen, and in many other locations. Zermatt is perhaps the most famous destination for experienced mountaineers, although the Eiger mountain in the Jungfrau Region is also popular. Ski mountaineering is also popular along the Haute Route in Valais. Verbier (p124), Zermatt (p135) and Saas Fee (p137) all offer good mountaineering.

The best organisation to contact is the **Verband Bergsportschulen Schweiz/ Association Suisse des Ecoles D'Alpinisme** (Swiss Mountain Sports School Association; ☎ 027 922 08 03; www.bergsportschulen.ch; Haus der Wirtschaft, Kerhstrasse 12, CH-3904, Naters), which has details of the 32 leading schools. Otherwise, try the **Swiss Mountain Guides' Association** (www.4000plus.ch), with its list of individual qualified guides. The **Schweizer Alpenclub** (☎ 031 370 18 18; www.sac-cas.ch in German & French; Monbijoustrasse 61, CH-3001 Bern) has details of mountain huts.

Mountaineering is not for the uninitiated and you should never climb on your own, or without being properly equipped/attired.

NOVELTY SPORTS

Switzerland is such a sports-loving nation that people have invented activities, or borrowed traditional activities from other countries, in their restless quest to test their limits.

Look out for the following throughout individual regions, although a high percentage of them seem to be offered in St Moritz.

Ski-joring Racers are pulled along on skis behind horses in this Scandinavian sport that came to Switzerland in the early 20th century. Several tournaments are still held around St Moritz (www .whiteturf.ch, www.stmoritz-concours.ch in German).

Dog-sledding Take the reins on a team of huskies, helped by an experienced driver (from Sfr6 for short runs, including on Jungfraujoch).

Cricket-on-ice (www.cricket-on-ice.com) Exactly as the name suggests, this is a tournament of the newly trendy gentleman's game on ice, which has been held by an eccentric mix of English, Swiss and Asian cricket lovers in St Moritz every February since 1989.

Trotti-biking Essentially the country cousin of the mini-scooter so popular with urban hipsters in the late 1990s, the Trotti-bike is used for whizzing down rural hills. Expect to pay Sfr15-20.

Using poles to swing your upper body in the Nordic walking technique burns 400 calories an hour on average, compared to the 280 for normal walking, and causes your heart to speed up by an extra five to 17 beats per minute.

Many books have been published on Switzerland's notoriously difficult Eiger mountain – from Heinrich Harrer's seminal *The White Spider* to Joe Simpson's *The Beckoning Silence*. Those planning to ascend the mountain themselves might appreciate Daniel Anker's photographic and historical record *Eiger: The Vertical Arena*.

A comprehensive source on spas and thermal baths in Switzerland is www.heilbad.org, although its information is reproduced in only German and French.

SPAS & THERMAL SPRINGS

If just the thought of all the adrenaline-pumping on these pages has you crying out for a nice cup of (herbal) tea and a good lie down, there are dozens of Swiss spas, clinics and health resorts where you can rest your feet, and submit yourself to world-class pampering. The following is just a small selection of leading spas and treatment centres; for more details contact **Switzerland Tourism** (www.myswitzerland.com), which produces a *Wellbeing* booklet.

Fashionable Spas

Clinique la Prairie (☎ 021 989 33 11; www.laprairie.ch in French; Clarens-Montreux; beautymed/revitalisation programmes per week from Sfr11,000/17,200) Switzerland's most famous spa, Clinique la Prairie is where the famous and *seriously* wealthy come for a complete anti-ageing overhaul. Specialising in 'scientific rejuvenation', or 'beautymed' treatments, it offers heavy-duty procedures like muscle-toning via electrical pulsing, microdermabrasion, botox, rejuvenating injections and even plastic surgery, as well as more usual spa treatments like whirlpool baths and (water-based) thalassotherapy.

Le Mirador (☎ 021 925 11 11; www.kempinski-mirador.com; Mont Pélerin, Montreux/Vevey; 2-night spa packages per person from Sfr700, spa day packages from Sfr310) One of Switzerland's finest grand-luxe resorts, Le Mirador has fabulous views of Lake Geneva, even from its glass-domed indoor/outdoor pool. Its relaxing Givenchy Spa offers facials, body wraps and stone therapy, plus anti-ageing and weight-loss programmes.

Park Hotel Weggis (☎ 081 926 80 80; www.phw.ch; Weggis; spa cottages per 2hr from Sfr260, s/d from Sfr340/515) The stand-out feature of this designer hotel's award-winning 'wellness' centre is its six private 'spa cottages' surrounded by a Japanese meditation garden. The cottages (open 10am to 9pm daily) contain a range of saunas, baths and whirlpools; one even has a TV and stereo. Massages and other treatments are offered here, and you can order milk baths or champagne for romantic breaks.

Hotel Crans Ambassador (☎ 027 485 48 48; www.crans-ambassador.ch; Crans-Montana; 2-night spa packages per person from Sfr790) The renowned Mességué-Phytotherm Centre here concentrates on detoxification through the use of medicinal plants, offering facials, Jacuzzi, hammam, herbal teas, cabbage compresses, massages and colonic irrigation.

Thermal Springs

These are among the more outstanding of the thermal bath options in Switzerland.

Therme Vals (☎ 081 926 80 80; www.therme-vals.ch; Vals) is one for the architectural buff. Peter Zumthor's award-winning building has been fashioned from concrete and quartzite to make it appear as if it's been hewn from rock. Inside, there's a Turkish bath, a deck pool with brilliant views and treatments including lymphatic drainage, thalassotherapy, reflexology, body peels and massages (foot, shiatsu, pregnancy or Hawaiian Lomi-Lomi, to name just a few). See p271.

Leukerbad (www.leukerbad.ch; Valais), at 1411m, is Europe's highest spa and pours out 3.9 million litres of water daily into 22 baths, six of them public. The best choice is either the huge **Burgerbad** (☎ 027 472 20 20; www.burgerbad.ch) with 10 thermal pools, a steam bath and Kneipp treatments, or **Lindner Alpentherme** (☎ 027 472 10 10; www.alpentherme.ch, www.lindner.de), combining centuries-old Roman-Irish baths with Chinese and Ayurveda treatments. See p132.

Wonderfully located between Lac de Neuchâtel and the Jura mountains, Yverdon-les-Bains, in Vaud, is known for its 14,000-year-old mineral springs. The waters are particularly good for arthritis/rheumatism or breathing difficulties, and are found in abundance at the modern **Centre Thermal** (☎ 024 423 02 32; www.cty.ch in French). This complex has three pools (both indoor and outdoor), whirlpool baths and treatment rooms. See p92.

More Roman-Irish baths are found at the **Engadin Bad Scuol** (☎ 081 861 20 00; www.scuol.ch; Scuol, Graubünden), with superb views of the Lower Engadine. See p279.

For something a bit different, try **Natur-Moorbad, Gontenbad, Appenzellerland** (☎ 071 795 31 23; www.naturbad.ch; Gontenbad, Appenzellerland) where you can dip in water from the moors (Sfr16) to help with stress or skin conditions, or luxuriate in a pampering rose bath (Sfr60 for two).

AVALANCHE WARNING

On average, 200 people a year are killed in the Alps by avalanches, and in Switzerland alone there are about 10,000 avalanches annually. Despite modern measures to help prevent them – ie crisscross metal barriers above resorts to prevent snow slips, controlled explosions to prevent dangerous build-up of snow and resorts' warning systems involving flags or flashing lights – skiers and boarders should never be complacent. Avalanche warnings should be heeded, and local advice sought before detouring from prepared runs.

Research suggests that most fatal avalanches are caused by the victims. So if you're going off-piste, or hiking in snowy areas, never go alone, take an avalanche shovel to dig out injured companions and be careful around narrow valleys below or close to ridges.

People's chances of being found and rescued are improved if they carry – and most importantly know how to use – a special avalanche radio transceiver. Such equipment is expensive, but it's foolhardy to forget it. Many boarders and off-piste skiers also now take a self-inflating avalanche balloon, which, if the worst happens, is designed to keep its owner above or close to the surface of the snow.

SKIING

Although budget travellers have turned their attention to the slopes in Eastern Europe, Switzerland still offers some of the best downhill skiing on the continent. Its big-name resorts, including Crans-Montana, Saas-Fee, Verbier and Zermatt, aren't cheap, but they are incredibly well equipped. The season generally lasts from mid-December to late March, although higher temperatures in recent years have curtailed the season. Nevertheless, at higher altitudes, some skiing is still possible into summer. Christmas through to February tends to be the best (and the busiest and most expensive) time.

Prices are generally quoted in this book for one day, or, if those are not available, two-day passes (and sometimes one week for an idea of the relative cost); but you can usually specify an exact number of days, or even buy parts of a day. You might pay anything from Sfr25 to Sfr65 per day, depending on the area. Free use of ski buses is usually included.

Equipment can always be hired at resorts; expect to pay about Sfr50 for snowboarding, downhill and cross-country skiing to get up for one day (daily rates decline over longer rental periods).

Cross-country skiing (German: *Langlauf,* French: *ski de fond*) is nearly as popular as downhill skiing, and Switzerland's trails compare to the best in Scandinavia. One particularly good area for cross-country is the Jura Mountains around Saignelégier (p115).

All major ski resorts listed have at least one ski school and you can join a group class (fees around Sfr40 to Sfr50 for half a day) or pay for individual tuition on a per-lesson basis. It shouldn't be necessary to arrange these in advance, but if you want to, **Swiss Snowsports** (☎ 031 810 41 11; www.snowsports.ch in German & French) has a list/clickable map of ski schools around the country.

Weekly package deals will give you a good run for your money if you're happy to stick to one resort. So, too, will limiting your skiing to specific areas in the resort. Young adults and senior citizens usually get discounts on ski pass prices.

Skiing in Switzerland is possible in the Bernese Oberland, central Switzerland, Graubünden, Lake Geneva, northeastern Switzerland and Valais regions; to check out a list of the top 10 ski resorts in Switzerland, see p20.

Check the latest snow and weather conditions for Swiss and other resorts at www.snow -forecast.com, which also includes skiing reviews.

SNOWBOARDING

Snowboarders love Switzerland. That's despite the expense of its resorts, which they usually gripe about. In the final analysis, any such complaints seem minor in the face of the country's magnificent terrain and facilities. There are lots of in-bounds cliffs, cornices and chutes for powder turns, great half-pipes and parks, as well as year-round boarding on the glaciers mentioned in the preceding section.

The biggest boarding meccas include Davos, the Laax-Flims area and the Engadine Valley (www.boarders-valley.com). That valley, which encompasses St Moritz, has been nicknamed 'the Hawaii of snowboarding' for the incredible runs created by its mix of north- and south-facing slopes.

Resorts such as Crans-Montana (p130), Grindelwald (p151), Saas Fee (p137), Verbier (p124), Zermatt (p134) plus Mt Titlis (p230), above Engelberg, are also popular snowboarding haunts.

SWISS SPORTS

Switzerland has three national sports. Apart from the following two, there's also *Steinstossen* (stone-throwing), most famously practised at the once-in-a-decade Unspunnenfest (see the boxed text Rocky Horror, p149).

Hornussen Taking its origins from medieval war games, this strange sport is played by two teams, one of which launches a 78g ball, or *Hornuss*, over a field. The other team tries to stop it hitting the ground with a *Schindel*, a 4kg implement resembling a road sign. To add to the game's bizarre quality, the *Hornuss* is launched by whipping it around a steel ramp with a flexible rod, in a motion that's a cross between shot-putting and fly-fishing, while the *Schindel* can be used as a bat to stop the 85m-per-second ball or simply tossed into the air at it. Some 16 to 18 players form each team.

Schwingen This is the Swiss version of Sumo wrestling, where two brawny young farm lads or, since 1992, gals, face off across a circle of sawdust 12m in diameter. Each leans in towards the other and grabs their opponent by the back of the very short hessian shorts that all contestants wear as overalls. Through a complicated combination of proscribed grips (including crotch grips), jerks, feints and other manoeuvres, each tries to wrestle their opponent onto his or her back. At the end of the contest, the winner dusts the sawdust off the loser.

WATER SPORTS

Switzerland shocked the world in early 2003 when its boat, *Alinghi*, won the world's most prestigious ocean-going yacht race, the America's Cup. However, the result wasn't that unpredictable, really. Although landlocked, the country is full of lakes where you can sail, windsurf, water-ski and even wakeboard – the waterborne equivalent of snowboarding. The lakes in the Bernese Oberland are all particularly well suited to these sports.

The Rotsee, near Lucerne, is a favourite place for rowing regattas. Rafting is possible on many Alpine rivers including the Rhine at Flims (p270) and Scuol (p279) and the Saane. Canoeing is mainly centred on

Follow the exploits of the Swiss-financed *Alinghi* team and its competitors in the 2007 America's Cup yachting competition at www.americascup.com.

FIFA, world football's governing body, is headquartered in Zürich. Its new, environmentally friendly offices were to open near the city's zoo in 2006.

EURO 2008

Switzerland and Austria will be the joint hosts of football's **European Championship Cup** (www .uefa.com, www.euro2008.com) in 2008. The 23-day tournament is due to kick off on 7 June 2008 at Basel's St Jakob Park (p243), designed by renowned architects Herzog & de Meuron. Bern's swanky new Stade de Suisse (p188) will be another venue in this, the largest sporting event ever to take place in Switzerland. Qualifying competitions begin in 2006.

the Muota River in Schwyz canton and on the Doubs River in the Jura. Paddleboats, or pedalos, are usually waiting for hire in lakeside resorts.

There are more than 350 beaches in the country, most of which are private and require an entrance fee (around Sfr5 per day).

Ironically, if you're interested in seeing Switzerland defend its America's Cup title in 2007, you'll have to go to Spain. The rules of the tournament dictate that the event be held in open seas and **Team Alinghi** (www .alinghi.com) has already built itself a base in Valencia.

Food & Drink

The land of Heidi is also the land of hearty. The eating can be excellent, not so much due to a rich indigenous menu, but because the country draws on three powerful neighbouring cuisines. Cooks in the French cantons take many of their cues from France, while the kitchens of Ticino lean towards Italy. To some the thought that the biggest chunk of the country looks to Germany and Austria for culinary clues may not seem like good news, but then they might not have thought about dessert!

The Swiss have some national munching icons. German Switzerland's potato-based rösti and the French melted cheese feasts of fondue and raclette, barely known beyond their respective cantons until the 1950s, are nationwide standards. And immigrants to Switzerland have enriched Swiss palates with imported cuisines, from Greek to Vietnamese.

All sorts of beers flow freely in the German cantons, but Switzerland is even more pleasing to wine-lovers. The bulk of its production comes from the French-speaking cantons and relatively little is exported. So your only chance to taste many of local drops is to come here – a rare and pleasing example of the limits of globalisation!

STAPLES & SPECIALITIES

Rösti (crispy, fried, shredded potatoes) is German Switzerland's star dish and by now a national favourite. Since the German and French parts of the country simply have to be different, the Swiss French cook it in oil and the Germans in butter or lard. Now as common (and cheap) as chips, you can buy it in vacuum-sealed packs in your local supermarket!

If you want to follow the raclette row or just find out the latest on what Swiss products have been awarded AOC denomination, see the official site www.aoc-igp.ch (in French and German).

Say Cheese!

The cheese (German: *Käse*, French: *fromage*, Italian: *formaggio*) with holes in it is a popular Swiss image. Contrary to popular belief, however, this cheese is not Gruyère (which comes from the similarly named town, see p106), but Emmental (from the Emme valley, see p191). There are plenty of other fine cheeses, including Etivaz (see the boxed text Looking Behind the Label, below), Tête de Moine from the Jura, the Tomme Vaudoise, Reblochon and Vacherin.

LOOKING BEHIND THE LABEL

A system of quality-control labelling of wines, much like those in neighbouring France and Italy, has long been in place in Switzerland. The AOC *(appellation d'origine contrôlée)* label denotes that a wine has been produced in its traditional area, by approved traditional methods and using approved ingredients. Anyone producing wine with the same name elsewhere is liable to prosecution.

Since the 1990s, the usage of AOCs has spread to other products. Etivaz, a raw milk cheese made in the Pays d'Enhaut in Vaud and ripened over eight months, was the first nonwine product to receive the AOC label in Switzerland. Nowadays, a big cheese debate rages over Raclette. Valais farmers claim the tangy round slabs of cheese used in the traditional dish (see p52) of the same name were first made in Valais – five centuries ago. The Ministry of Agriculture agreed in 2005, and so theoretically any cheese sold as Raclette must now come from that canton. Opponents in Switzerland and France protest that the word raclette refers to a dish, not a cheese, coming from the verb *racler* (to scrape – strips of the cheese are scraped on to plates as it melts under heat) and thus cannot be restricted to any one region. Stay tuned!

Indeed, the main French Swiss contribution to the dinner table is pots of gooey melted cheese. Raclette is the name of a meal and the cheese at its heart. Half-crescent slabs are screwed into a specially made 'oven' that melts the top flat side. As it melts, it is scraped off on to a diner's plate for immediate consumption with boiled potatoes and/or pickled onions and gherkins. Diners keep doing the rounds until they can stand no more.

Fondue (from *fondre*, to melt), which some claim originated in France, involves a different approach. A pot (the size can depend on the number of diners and the amount of space) is filled with cheese that is heated to melt, and kept on a slow burn throughout the evening (the trick is not to over- or under-do the heating). Diners dip morsels of food on slender forks into the cheese and munch. They say that if you lose your chunk in the cheese, you have to buy the next round of drinks. On the subject of drink, do not drink water while eating fondue. It cools and coagulates the cheese and makes for an unpleasant gut ache. As with raclette, the best accompaniment is a good local white wine (typically a Fendant from Valais). If you're getting stuffed but want more, the common trick is to swallow a *trou Normand* (Norman hole), a shot of high-octane liquor to burn some space in your tum. This might also occur before dessert, which ideally should be fluffy Gruyères meringues, topped with calorie-loaded double cream!

The classic fondue mix is of Emmental, Gruyère, white wine and flour, with potatoes and cubes of bread to accompany it. *Fondue moitié moitié* (half and half) mixes Gruyère with Vacherin Fribourgeois, *Savoyarde* (a French version) throws Comte cheese into the pot and there are plenty of other regional recipes. Common variants involve adding ingredients such as herbs, mushrooms or tomato.

> The Swiss have their own Marmite (Vegemite to Australians)! Cenovis is a dark spread made of beer yeast and vegetable extracts. Invented in 1931, it is high in Vitamin B1.

> *Müsli* (muesli) was invented in Switzerland at the end of the 19th century. The most common form of this very healthy breakfast is *Birchermüsli*, sometimes served with less-than-slimming dollops of cream.

Meeting Your Match

Fresh fish is the speciality in many lakeside towns. Perch and whitefish fillets are common. Lake Geneva is home to dwindling schools of *omble chevalier* (char), a meatier freshwater fish.

A wide variety of *Würste* (sausages) goes nicely with rösti and green salad. Veal is highly rated. In Zürich, it is thinly sliced, served in a cream sauce and called *Geschnetzeltes Kalbsfleisch*. A good dish from Schaffhausen is *Schaffhüser Bölletünne*, a savoury onion pie. *Rippli*, a pot of pork rib meat, is served in and around Bern with bacon, potatoes and beans. *Bündnerfleisch* is air-dried beef, smoked and thinly sliced, from Graubünden.

CRAZY FOR CHOCOLATE

In the early centuries after Christ's death, as the Roman Empire headed towards slow collapse on a diet of rough wine and olives, the Mayas in Central America were pounding cocoa beans, consuming the result and even using the beans as a system of payment.

A millennium later, the Spanish conquistador Hernando Cortez brought the first load of cocoa to Europe in 1528 but probably didn't think cocoa would catch on. Little did he know. Sweetened, it produced a beverage for which the Spaniards, and soon other Europeans, developed an insatiable thirst. The solid stuff came later.

Swiss chocolate built its reputation in the 19th century, thanks to pioneering spirits such as François-Louis Cailler (1796–1852), Philippe Suchard (1797–1884), Henri Nestlé (1814–90), Jean Tobler (1830–1905), Daniel Peter (1836–1919) and Rodolphe Lindt (1855–1909). Cailler established the first Swiss chocolate factory in 1819, near Vevey. Daniel Peter added milk in 1875 and Lindt invented *conching,* a rotary aeration process that gives chocolate its melt-in-the-mouth quality.

TRAVEL YOUR TASTEBUDS

Brisolée An autumn Valais dish of chestnuts cooked to be crunchy on the outside and soft on the inside, served with Alpine cheeses.

Cuchaule A saffron-scented bread served with la Moutarde de Benichon, a thick condiment made of cooked wine must, spices, sugar and flour. It is the first course in a traditional meal known as La Benichon, usually prepared in October.

Papet Vaudois A stew with potato and leek as its basis, but much more interesting if it includes cabbage sausage, itself a Vaudois speciality.

Taillée aux Greblons A Vaudois pastry, crispy on the outside and soft on the inside, with little dices of pork lard throughout.

Speaking of Graubünden, this canton has two particularly tasty local dishes. *Capuns* is a rich mix of *spätzli* dough, *Bünderfleisch,* ham and herbs, mixed together, cooked, then cut into tiny morsels that are wrapped in more *spätzli* with spinach. *Bizochel* (or *pizokel*) are little globs of *spätzli* boiled with herbs and then presented with a cheese *gratiné*. An Engadine speciality is *pian di pigna*, a dense potato, sausage and onion bake.

Autumn is hunting (and mushroom!) season. This is the time to sample fresh game, especially the various varieties of deer meat. Restaurants up and down the country will advertise the *Wildspezialitäten/specialités de gibier* (or *chasse)/cacciagione*.

Chocolate-loving Swiss gobble down more of the sticky stuff than anyone else in the world – a staggering 11.3kg per person per year.

Fruity Afters & Ladies' Thighs

Thurgau and Aargau are centres of fruit production (especially apples and pears, hence their use in drinks and food).

Fruit finds its way into typical sweets such *raisinée* (Vaud) or *vin cuit* (Fribourg). These are basically apple juice cooked over 24 hours into a dense, semi-hard mass used in tarts.

Cuisses de dame (ladies' thighs) is a sugary pastry deep-fried and in the vague shape of a thigh, and is found across the French cantons. Apart from the ubiquitous *Apfelstrudel* (apple pie), best served with vanilla sauce, the German cantons propose *Vermicelles*, a chestnut cream creation made to look like spaghetti and served with cream or ice cream.

For those who fear no calories, a must is meringue from Gruyères, topped with dollops of Gruyères double cream!

For Italian cuisine, see the boxed text What's Cooking in Ticino?, p298.

For a short history and explanation of everything you ever wanted to know about chocolate, especially in Switzerland, browse www.chocolat.ch.

DRINKS
Nonalcoholic Drinks

Tap water is fine but there is plenty of locally produced mineral water. In the French cantons you will come across Henniez and, in Valais, Aproz. Various mineral waters are produced in Graubünden (like Rhäzünser, Passugger and Valser).

Try the German Swiss soft drink Rivella, made in Rothrist. Uniquely, it's made with lactose. The blue-label (reduced-fat) version is probably the best introduction, but it also comes with red (original) and green (mixed with green tea) labels.

Suessmost is a nonalcoholic cider made in the German part of the country.

Coffee is more popular than tea – the latter will come without milk unless you ask for it. Hot chocolate is also popular, although disappointingly it often comes as powder in sachets to be added to a cup of hot milk.

Alcoholic Drinks

BEER & CIDER

In bars, lager beer comes in 300ml or 500ml bottles, or on draught *(Bier vom Fass, bière à la pression, birra alla pressione)* with measures ranging from 200ml to 500ml. The German part of the country is where most of the beer-guzzling is done. Feldschlösschen is a well-known brand that you will encounter around the country. Founded in 1876, it has been producing pils (lager) and dark beers for more than a century. Many smaller breweries are more closely identified with their area, such as St Gallen's Schützengarten, the country's oldest brewery (founded 1779).

Sauermost is the alcoholic-cider version of *Suessmost* and generally only found in the German cantons.

> The rate of liver cirrhosis is much higher in the French and Italian parts of Switzerland than in the German part.

WINE

The bulk of wine production takes place in the French-speaking part of the country, particularly in Valais and by Lake Geneva and Lac de Neuchâtel. Quality reds, whites and rosés are produced.

Much of the land north of the Rhône river in western Valais, which gets good sunlight from above the southern Alps, is given over to the grape. Some of the country's best wines come from here.

Two-thirds of Valais production is the dryish white Fendant, the most common accompaniment for fondue and raclette. Johannisberg is another excellent white, and comes from the Sylvaner grape. Look out for the sweeter Petite Arvine and Amigne whites.

The area's principal red is Dôle, made of Pinot Noir and Gamay grapes. Full bodied as an opera singer, it also has a firm fruit flavour. If you're looking for the Cadillacs of Valais reds, seek out drops made with the Humagne Rouge, Syrah, Cornalin and Pinot Noir grape varieties.

Some Valais dessert wines, like the Malvoisie (Pinot Gris) and Muscat, are also excellent.

> To learn more about Swiss wines and see when the upcoming wine fairs are being staged, check out www.swiss wine.ch.

The bulk of wine production in Vaud is done on either side of Lausanne. The Lavaux region (see the boxed text Vintners of Lavaux, p88) between Lausanne and Montreux produces some riveting whites, most born of the Chasselas grape and occasionally combinations of this with other types. The two *grands crus* from the area are Calamin and Dézaley.

The generic Vaud equivalent of the Dôle is the Salvagnin, divided into several labels and generally combining the Pinot Noir and Gamay. A home-grown offshoot is the Gamaret (created in the 1970s), which produces a throaty red.

Straddling Vaud and Valais is the Chablais wine-making area. Look for drops such as Yvorne whites from the Vaud side.

Lac de Neuchâtel is known above all for its fruity rosé, Oeil-de-Perdrix. And against an industry tendency to filter out impurities in whites, some producers from this canton are making unfiltered whites with considerable success. These need to be shaken up a little before serving and have a robust flavour.

In the Ticino, the favourite liquid for lunch is Merlot (around 88% of the canton's production). Some white Merlots are also made, and a handful of other grape varieties. The main wine-making areas are between Bellinzona and Ascona, around Biasca and between Lugano and Mendrisio.

German Swiss wines are less well known and produced in smaller quantities, but they count some good drops. About 75% are reds, especially Pinot Noir (Blauburgunder). The main white is Müller-Thurgau (a mix of Riesling and Sylvaner). Gewürztraminer is another dry white variety.

A TOUCH OF THE *BLEUES*

After a century on the index of banned beverages, absinthe (known as *la fée verte*, or green fairy) was legalised in Switzerland on 1 March 2005. This was good news for the Val-de-Travers (a valley in Neuchâtel canton), where villagers had long been forced to produce the liquor in clandestine fashion, if at all. About 10 types of the aniseed-based rocket fuel are produced here. The *bleue* (blue), as it is also affectionately known, typically has an alcohol reading approaching the Richter-scale proportions of 56% or more. For more on this fairy tale see the boxed text The Green Fairy, p113. Soon after the ban was lifted, one distillery in Val-de-Travers launched absINt 56, aimed at a hip, clubbing crowd and with a smidgin of mint to take the aniseed edge off. Its makers hope to conquer the clubs of the world. Smirnoff, move over.

Graubünden also produces some good Pinot Gris white varieties, as well as Blauburgunder in the Bündner Herrschaft region north of Chur.

One orders wine in multiples of the *déci* (100ml), a uniquely Swiss approach.

The annual Guide des Vins Suisses, published by Wend Verlag, is probably the most comprehensive guide to the country's wines. It carries extensive notes on wineries and the latest developments in wine-making across the country.

SPIRITS & SCHNAPPS

There is a choice of locally produced fruit brandies, often served with or in coffee. Kirsch is made from the juice of compressed cherry pits. Appenzeller Alpenbitter (Alpine Bitters) is a liquor made from the essences of 67 different flowers and roots. Damassine, which you are more likely to find in the French cantons, is made of small prunes and makes a good post-prandial digestive. A pear-based drop is the popular Williamine and Pflümli is a typical plum-based schnapps in the German cantons.

CELEBRATIONS

Fondue and raclette lend themselves to get-togethers. The intrinsically social nature of sharing a pot of bubbling cheese (fondue) or the ingredients for raclette makes an easy dinner-party option, whether in restaurants or at home.

One of the most impressive traditional feasts, if only for the sheer volume consumed, is La Saint-Martin, celebrated in the Jura around the Fête de la Saint Martin (Feast of St Martin; p116) on the second Sunday after All Saints' Day in November. At this time of year, in Switzerland and elsewhere in Europe, pigs were (and often still are) traditionally slaughtered. Fattened over the summer, they are ready for the butcher and for centuries on farms and in villages the slaughter would be followed by the salting of meat and the making of sausages. The work done, folk would then pass over to feasting to celebrate the day's toil. The main dishes for the feast: pork.

In the Jura nowadays you are unlikely to witness any sausage-making, but the tradition of feasting lives on, with particular energy in and around Porrentruy (p116). If anything, it has become increasingly popular through the years and some bars and restaurants in the region organise feasts for several weekends on the trot in October and November.

A typical pork binge consists of eating as many as seven courses, which few humans can complete. You might start with *gelée de ménage*, a pork gelatine dish. This will be followed by *boudin, purée de pommes et racines rouges* (black pudding, apple compote and red vegetables), piles of sausages accompanied by rösti and *atriaux* (a dish based on pork fat, sausage and liver, all roasted in sizzling fat). Then comes, if you will, the main (!) course, with *rôti, côtines et doucette* (roast pork, ribs and a green salad). Courses are copious, so don't wolf it all down from the beginning – you'll never make it to the roast! A liquor-soaked sorbet might follow to aid digestion, followed by a serving of *choucroute* (boiled cabbage enlivened by, hmm, bacon bits). Finally, a traditional dessert is *striflate en sauce de vanille,* strings of deep-fried pastries in vanilla sauce.

WHERE TO EAT & DRINK

For some enticing recipes that bring out the northern Italianate flair of Ticino cooking, take a look at *La Cucina Ticinese,* a trilingual book (but no English) published by FONA.

For sit-down meals you will generally wind up in a restaurant (the same word in French and German, *ristorante* in Italian). Many hotels, especially in the ski resorts, have their own. In the French cantons, many *brasseries* (beer bars) and cafés double as eateries. In Ticino, less-fancy eateries include the generally family-run *trattoria* and *osteria* (there is little to distinguish these nowadays). The *locanda* is similar and often offers a handful of rooms too. For authentic eating in rural Ticino, find a *grotto* (usually housed in a simple stone structure, once often used as simple houses or storage rooms, and generally partly built in the rocky walls of hill- or mountainsides on the edge of Ticino towns). Some wine bars *(Weinstübli)* and beer taverns *(Bierstübli)* in the German cantons also serve meals.

À la Mode de Chez Nous – Plaisirs de la Table Romande, by M Vidoudez and J Graniger, is a delightful introduction, in French, to the 'pleasures of Swiss French dining'.

Main meals in Switzerland are usually eaten from about noon, and a little later in the French and Italian parts of the country. At lunch you could opt for a cheapish, fixed-menu dish of the day *(Tagesteller, plat du jour* or *piatto del giorno).* Hours can vary quite substantially. Many restaurants will serve lunch from noon to 1.30pm, and as late as 2pm in the French and Italian cantons. Dinnertime can be as early as 6.30pm and in many places, especially in the German cantons and mountain resorts, you will have trouble being served after 9.30pm. On the other hand, in the cities you will find dining hours more generous, until as late as 11pm. Many places in the German cantons open right through the day from 11am to 11pm, although often they serve only cold dishes between the main meal times. All stay open for an hour or so beyond the kitchen closing time to allow diners time for dessert, coffee and an after-dinner tipple.

Most places have a day off *(Ruhetag, jour de fermeture, giorno di riposo).*

OUR TOP FIVE

This a quick selection (in strictly alphabetical order) of some of our favourite places to move mandibles, chosen for palate pleasure over price considerations. Turn to the appropriate page to initiate salivation.

Hotel Engiadina (☎ 081 864 14 21; www.engiadina-scuol.ch; tasting menu Sfr78; ☾ Tue-Sat) Gourmet Engadine cooking in the heart of Scuol. See p279.

Hôtel Terminus (☎ 027 455 13 51; www.hotel-terminus.ch; Rue du Bourg 1, Sierre; mains Sfr70-75, tasting menus Sfr120-185; ☾ Tue-Sat) One of Switzerland's leading chefs tickles your tastebuds. See p130.

Osteria Chiara (☎ 091 743 32 96; Vicolo della Chiara 1, Locarno; pasta & mains Sfr15-30; ☾ Tue-Sat) All the atmosphere of a traditional Ticino *grotto* and lovingly prepared Italian comfort food. See p301.

Pittaria (Theatergasse 12, Solothurn; snacks Sfr7.50-13.50; ☾ 10am-11pm Tue-Sat) The finest takeaway in the land – it's official! See p193.

Wirtshaus Taube (☎ 041 210 07 47; Burgerstrasse 3, Lucerne; mains Sfr18-40; ☾ 11am-midnight Mon-Sat) For good old Germanic munching. See p220.

Quick Eats

Budget travellers could seek out self-service restaurants in the larger Migros and Coop outlets, and in department stores such as Manor. These are usually open from around 11am to 6.30pm on weekdays and until 4pm or 5pm on Saturday. Manor serves the tastiest meals of the lot. A filling meal with drinks need not cost more than Sfr15 to Sfr20 per person.

Kiosks often sell cheap snacks that, like sausage and bread in St Gallen, are as much a regional speciality as are the fancy dishes. Takeaway kebab places are increasingly common in Swiss towns.

The Swiss like their biscuits – eating an average 6kg a year according to the local biscuit industry body, Biscosuisse.

VEGETARIANS & VEGANS

Dedicated vegetarian restaurants are more common in the cities, but you will usually find a pasta or rösti dish on most menus. *Fitnessteller* (fitness dish) for the health-conscious, are increasingly offered, especially in the ski resorts.

Even vegetarians will be able to sample *Alpermagaroninen,* basically a fancy version of macaroni cheese, which regularly arrives with cooked apple and onion. Soups are popular and sometimes contain small dumplings *(Knöpfli).*

EATING WITH KIDS

Children are generally welcome in most restaurants. Some even offer smaller, kid-sized menus and servings. Toddlers are usually fed straight from their parents' plates and if high-chairs aren't available, staff will improvise.

EAT YOUR WORDS

If you wish not only to be grateful for what you are about to receive, but also to have some idea of what it is, you will want to learn something of the names of dishes you may come across. To get an idea of how to pronounce them, turn to the Language chapter (p338).

Useful Phrases

The following phrases are in German (G), French (F) and Italian (I).

A table for..., please.
Einen Tisch für . . ., bitte. (G) *Une table pour. . ., s'il vous plaît.* (F) *Un tavolo per . . ., per favore.* (I)

May I see the menu, please?
Darf ich die Speisekarte sehen, bitte? (G) *Est-ce que je pourrais voir la carte, s'il vous plaît?* (F) *Posso vedere il menù, per piacere?* (I)

May I see the wine list, please?
Darf ich die Weinkarte sehen, bitte? (G) *Est-ce que je pourrais voir la carte aux vins, s'il vous plaît?* (F) *Posso vedere la carta dei vini, per piacere?* (I)

Bon appetit!
Guten Appetit! (G) *Bon appétit!* (F) *Buon appetito!* (I)

Good health/Cheers!
Prost! (G) *Santé!* (F) *Salute!* (I)

The bill, please.
Zahlen, bitte. (G) *L'addition, s'il vous plaît.* (F) *Il conto, per favore.* (I)

Is service included in the bill?
Ist die Bedienung inbegriffen? (G) *Est-ce que le service est compris?* (F) *È compreso il servizio?* (I)

I'm vegetarian.
Ich bin Vegetarier(in). (G) *Je suis végétarien(ne).* (F) *Sono vegetariano(a).* (I)

Food Glossary

These are some food terms that you may come across in German (G), French (F) and Italian (I):

boiled potatoes
Salzkartoffeln (G)	*pommes nature* (F)	*patate lesse* (I)

butter-fried trout
Forelle Müllerinart (G)	*truite à la meunière* (F)	*trotta frittata al burro* (I)

fillet of beef
Rindsfilet (G)	*filet de boeuf* (F)	*filetto di manzo* (I)

flat pasta/noodles
Nudeln (G)	*nouilles* (F)	*tagliatelle* (I)

fruit salad
Fruchtsalat (G)	*macédoine de fruits* (F)	*macedonia di frutta* (I)

grilled salmon
Grillierter Lachs (G)	*saumon grillé* (F)	*trotta salmonata alla griglia* (I)

ice cream
Eis (G)	*glace* (F)	*gelato* (I)

pasta
Teigwaren (G)	*pâtes* (F)	*pasta* (I)

pork
Schwein (G)	*porc* (F)	*maiale* (I)

rice
Reis (G)	*riz* (F)	*riso* (I)

sirloin steak
Zwischenrippenstück (G)	*entrecôte* (F)	*costata di manzo* (I)

soup
Suppe (G)	*potage* or *consommé* (F)	*zuppa* (I)

veal
Kalb (G)	*veau* (F)	*vitello* (I)

vegetables
Gemüse (G)	*légumes* (F)	*vedura* (I)

whitefish fillets (with almonds)
Felchenfilets *(mit Mandeln)* (G)	*filets de féra* *(aux amandes)* (F)	*filetti di coregone* *(alle mandorle)* (I)

Geneva

Super sleek, slick and cosmopolitan, Geneva is a rare breed of city. It's one of Europe's priciest. Its people chatter in every language under the sun and it's constantly thought of as the Swiss capital – which it isn't. This gem of a city superbly strung around the sparkling shores of Europe's largest Alpine lake is, in fact, only Switzerland's third-largest city.

Yet the whole world is here: the UN, International Red Cross, International Labour Organization, World Health Organization. You name it, they're in Geneva; 200-odd top-dog governmental and nongovernmental international organisations meting out world affairs with astonishing precision and authority. They fill the city's bounty of plush four- and five-star hotels with big-name guests. They feast on an incredulous choice of international cuisine, cooked up by restaurants to meet 'local' demand. And they help prop up the overload of banks, luxury jewellers and chocolate shops for which the city is known. Strolling through manicured city parks, sailing on the lake and skiing in the Alps next door are hot weekend pursuits.

But, ask critics, where's the urban grit? Not in the lakeside with its tourist boats, silky-smooth promenades and record-breaking high fountain. Not in its picture-postcard Old Town. No. If it's the rough-cut side of the diamond you're after, you need to dig into the Pâquis quarter, walk west along the Rhône's industrial shores or south into trendy Carouge where rejuvenated factories, alternative clubs and humble neighbourhood bars hum with attitude. This is, after all, the Geneva of the Genevois…or as close as you get, at any rate.

HIGHLIGHTS

- Watching a movie beneath the stars against a backdrop of legendary Lake Geneva at **Ciné Lac** (p73)
- Inhaling bohemia in Italianate **Carouge's** (p68) lounge-lazy café life
- Taking a **gastronomic tour** (p70) of the world, especially in rough-cut Pâquis
- Dashing like mad beneath the world's tallest fountain, the **Jet d'Eau** (p61) – or get wet!
- Getting your head around **CERN** (p66) or the monumental **Palais des Nations** (p65)

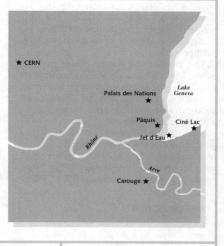

- POPULATION: 185,000
- AREA: 282 SQ KM
- LANGUAGE: FRENCH

GENEVA

HISTORY

Occupied by the Romans and later a 5th-century bishopric, rich old Geneva has long been the envy of all. Its medieval fairs drew interest far and wide, and in the 16th century John Calvin and his zealous Reformation efforts turned the city into 'Protestant Rome'. Savoy duke Charles Emmanuel took a swipe at it in 1602 but was repulsed by the Genevans, who still celebrate their victory (p68).

French troops made Geneva capital of the French Léman department in 1798, but in June 1814 they were chucked out and Geneva joined the Swiss Confederation. Watch-making, banking and commerce prospered. A local businessman founded the Red Cross in 1864 and as other international organisations adopted the strategically located city and birthplace of humanitarian law as their HQ, Geneva's future as an international melting pot was secured. After WWI the League of Nations strived for world peace from Geneva and after WWII the UN arrived. By the end of the 20th century, Geneva ranked among the world's 10 most-expensive cities, relying heavily on international workers and world markets (world demand generates 50% of cantonal GDP) for its wealth.

ORIENTATION

Geneva sits on the southwest lip of Lake Geneva (Lac Léman in French). The lakeside city is split by the westward progress of the Rhône, which meets the Arve River further west.

The main train station, Gare de Cornavin, is a few blocks north on the Rhône's north or right bank *(rive droite)*. Northeast is seedy, sexy Pâquis and the international Palais des Nations quarter, where many world organisations are.

South of the Rhône on the left bank *(rive gauche)* is Geneva's famous landmark, the Jet d'Eau fountain; the Rue du Rhône shopping district; the pedestrian Old Town *(vielle ville)*; and museum-studded Plain-

palais. Cross the Arve River to reach hip Carouge.

Maps

The tourist office distributes a free city map and there are some excellent searchable maps available on the City of Geneva website (www.ville-ge.ch).

INFORMATION
Bookshops

Book Worm (Map p65; ☎ 022 731 87 65; Rue Sismondi 5; ⏱ 10am-7pm Mon-Fri, 10am-5pm Sat) Second-hand English books in a café.

Off the Shelf (Map p62; ☎ 022 311 10 90; www.off theshelf.ch; Blvd Georges Favon 15; ⏱ 9am-6.30pm Tue-Fri, 10am-5pm Sat) English-language bookshop.

Emergency

See the inside front cover for emergency telephone numbers.

Police station (Map p65; ☎ 117; Rue de Berne 6)

Internet Access

For a list of free-access public wi-fi terminals in Geneva, see www.espritdegeneve.ch.

Charly's Checkpoint (Map p65; ☎ 022 901 13 13; www.charlys.com; Rue de Fribourg 7; per 15/65 min Sfr1/5; ⏱ 9am-midnight Mon-Sat, 2-10pm Sun) Has 40 machines.

Internet Café de la Gare (Map p65; ☎ 022 731 51 87; per 10/30/60 min Sfr2/4/6; ⏱ 8.30am-10pm Mon-Thu, 9.30am-11pm Fri & Sat, 9.30am-10pm Sun) In the train station, on the Place de Montbrillant side.

Internet Resources

City of Geneva (www.ville-ge.ch)

International Geneva Welcome Centre (www.cagi.ch)

Laundry

Wash your smocks for Sfr5 per kilogram at these places:

Lavseul (Map p65; Rue de Monthoux 29; ⏱ 7am-midnight)

Salon Lavoir (Map p62; Rue du 31 Decembre 12; ⏱ 6am-midnight)

Left Luggage

Aéroport International de Genève (☎ 0512 25 23 80; per day Sfr7; ⏱ 7am-7.30pm)

Gare de Cornavin (Map p65; Place de Cornavin; per 24hr small/large locker Sfr4/7; ⏱ 4.30-12.45am)

Media

World Radio Geneva (WRG; www.wrgfm.com; 88.4 FM) English-language radio station.

DID YOU KNOW?

Foreigners – 184 different nationalities no less – make up 45% of Geneva's population (2005).

GENEVA IN...

Two Days
Explore the left-bank **parks and gardens** (p63) and **Jet d'Eau** (below), then hit the **Old Town** (p70) for lunch and a stroll. Tummy full, **sail a seagull** (p74) to the **Parc de la Perle du Lac** (p65). Finish off with a dip in the water and aperitif at the **Bains des Pâquis** (p66). Indulge in a lazy **breakfast or brunch** (p72) on day two, preceded, or followed, by a museum visit. Fill up the afternoon with a **CERN** (p66) or **Palais des Nations** (p65) tour – or a good old spot of **shopping** (p73).

Four Days
Follow the two-day itinerary. Take your pick of the various **boat trips** (p69) on offer on the third day, perhaps venturing as far as **Hermance** (p69) or **Yvoire** (p69) in France for lunch. Hiring a **bicycle** (p66) for a lakeside spin or embarking on one of the city's **wacky walking tours** (p66) around Geneva's more obscure corners makes a fun fourth day.

Medical Services
Hôpital Cantonal (Map p62; ☎ 022 372 33 11, emergency 022 372 81 20; www.hug-ge.ch in French; Rue Micheli du Crest 24; � 24hr)
SOS Médecins à Domicile (☎ 022 748 49 50) Home/hotel doctor calls.

Money
Exchange offices, banks and ATMs are well distributed across the city.
American Express (☎ 022 717 86 98; www.american express.ch in German & French; Aéroport International de Genève; � 7am-9pm)

Post
Mont Blanc Post Office (Map p65; Rue du Mont-Blanc 18; � 7.30am-6pm Mon-Fri, 9am-4pm Sat)

Tourist Information
Information de la Ville de Genève (Map p62; ☎ 022 311 99 70; www.ville-ge.ch; Pont de la Machine; � noon-6pm Mon, 9am-6pm Tue-Fri, 10am-5pm Sat) City information point; ticketing desk for cultural events.
Genève Tourisme (Map p65; ☎ 022 909 70 00; www.geneve-tourisme.ch; Rue du Mont-Blanc 18; � 10am-6pm Mon, 9am-6pm Tue-Sat) Tourist office.

SIGHTS
Geneva's major sights are split by the Rhône that flows through the city to create its greatest attraction: the lake.

South of the Rhône
Get snapped in front of the **flower clock** in the Jardin Anglais, make a mad dash for it beneath the city's legendary fountain, then head south to the **Old Town** or stroll north-

east along the lake for the beach buzz of **Genève Plage** (p66).

JET D'EAU
This fabulous fountain, visible from the sky (ie from the aeroplane when you land) and other points of the lake on clear days, is easily Geneva's most impressive sight. The world's tallest **fountain** (Quai Gustave-Ador; � 9.30am-11.15pm Mar-Oct) shoots up water with incredible force – 200km/h, 1360 horsepower – to create a 140m sky-high plume. At any one time seven tonnes of water is in the air – much of which sprays spectators on the pier.

ESPACE ST-PIERRE
The hybrid mix of **Cathédrale de St-Pierre** (St-Peter's Cathedral; Map p64; Cour St-Pierre; admission free; � 9.30am-6.30pm Mon-Sat, noon-6.30pm Sun Jun-Sep, 10am-5.50pm Mon-Sat, noon-5.30pm Sun Oct-May) is

---

CENT SAVERS

To save a bob, visit Geneva's museums on the first Sunday of the month when admission to most is free. On other days, the Swiss Museum Pass kicks in.

Keypass (www.keytours.ch) is a Geneva city pass, valid for 24 hours (adult/child aged four to 12 Sfr49/25) or 48 hours (Sfr98/49), that includes admission to most museums, public transport and a clutch of city tours (including by bus, electric train and tram, or on foot). More details are available at the tourist office.

Route de Florissant
Route de Malagnou

questionable. Started in the 11th century, the style is Gothic with an 18th-century neoclassical façade tacked on.

Protestant John Calvin preached here between 1536 and 1564: see his seat in the north aisle and trace his life in the **Musée International de la Réforme** (International Museum of the Reformation; Map p64; ☎ 022 310 24 31; www.musee-reforme.ch; Rue du Cloître 4; adult/under 16/16-25yr Sfr10/free/7; 🕓 10am-5pm Tue-Sun). From here a passage leads to a **Site Archéologique** (Archaelogical Site; Map p64; ☎ 022 311 75 74; Cour St-Pierre 6; adult/under 7/7-16yr Sfr8/free/4; 🕓 10am-5pm Tue-Sun) with fine 4th-century mosaics. Atop the cathedral's 157-step **northern tower** (adult/under 16yr Sfr4/free; 🕓 9.30am-6.30pm Mon-Sat, noon-6.30pm Sun Jun-Sep, 10am-5.50pm Mon-Sat, noon-5.30pm Sun Oct-May) a city panorama fans out.

MAISON TAVEL

Little is left to remind you of the age of Geneva's oldest house, 14th-century **Maison Tavel** (Map p64; ☎ 022 418 37 00; Rue du Puits St-Pierre 6; admission free; 🕓 10am-5pm). Inside, enjoy an intriguing account of 14th- to 19th-century Genevan life.

ESPACE ROUSSEAU

The **Espace Rousseau** (Map p64; ☎ 022 310 10 28; www.espace-rousseau.ch; Grand-Rue 40; adult/under 7/7-18yr Sfr5/free/3; 🕓 11am-5.30pm Tue-Sun) is home to little bar an audiovisual display tracing the troubled life of the great thinker born here in 1712. En route you pass the 15th-century **Hôtel de Ville** (Map p64; Rue de l'Hôtel-de-Ville).

MUSÉE BARBIER-MUELLER

The **Barbier-Mueller Museum** (Map p64; ☎ 022 312 02 70; www.barbier-mueller.ch; Rue Jean Calvin 10; adult/under 12/student Sfr5/free/3; 🕓 11am-5pm) proves its dedication to world culture with an impressive collection of objects from so-called primitive societies: South American pre-Columbian art treasures, Pacific Island statues, and shields and weapons from Africa.

PARC DES BASTIONS & PLACE NEUVE

Giant 4.5m-tall figures of Bèze, Calvin, Farel and Knox – in their nightgowns ready for bed – loom large in **Parc des Bastions** (Map p62). The park's northern entrance hugs **Place Neuve** (Map p62), pierced by a statue of Red Cross co-founder Henri Dufour, who drew the first map of Switzerland in

INFORMATION
Canadian Consulate 1 A1
Hôpital Cantonal 2 C6
Information de la Ville de Genève 3 B5
Library in English 4 C4
New Zealand Consulate 5 A1
Off The Shelf 6 A5
Salon Lavoir 7 D5
UK Consulate 8 A2

SIGHTS & ACTIVITIES
Baby's Lounge 9 B5
Bains des Pâquis 10 C4
Genève Roule 11 C4
Horloge Fleurie 12 C5
Île Rousseau 13 B4
Jardin Botanique 14 B1
Jet d'Eau 15 D4
Les Corsaires 16 D4
Musée d'Art et d'Histoire 17 C6
Musée d'Arte Moderne et Contemporain (MAMCO) 18 A6
Musée d'Histoire Naturelle 19 D6
Musée International de la Croix Rouge et du Croissant-Rouge 20 A1
Musée Rath 21 B5
Palais des Nations 22 B1
Pâquis Express (see 73)
Parc de la Perle du Lac 23 C2
Parc de l'Ariana 24 A1
Parc des Bastions 25 B6
Patek Philippe Museum 26 A6
Petit Train Solaire 27 D4
Ski Nautique Club de Genève 28 C2
Tour d'Île 29 B5
Tramway Tour 30 B5

SLEEPING
Auberge de Jeunesse 31 C3
City Hostel 32 B3
Hôtel At Home 33 B4
Hôtel Beau-Rivage 34 C4
Hôtel de la Cloche 35 C4
Hôtel President Wilson 36 C3

EATING
Bistrot du Boucher 37 D5
Buvette des Bains (see 10)
Café des Bains 38 A6
Chez Kei 39 D6
Gelateria Arlecchino 40 D5
La Truffe Noire 41 A5
Le Pain Quotidien 42 C5
Le Pain Quotidien 43 A5
Les 5 Portes 44 C4
Les Saveurs de la Ferme 45 C5
ù bobba 46 B5
u jardinù bobba (see 46)

DRINKING
Arthur's 47 B5
Boulevard du Vin 48 B5
Nathan 49 A4
Olé Olé 50 B4
Omnibus 51 A5
Paillote 52 C3

ENTERTAINMENT
Bâtiment des Forces Motrices 53 A5
Bistr'Ok 54 C6
crem 55 C6
Dialogai 56 C3
Grand Théâtre de Genève 57 B5
Jet Set 58 A5
Le Zoo (see 60)
Les Scala 59 D5
L'Usine 60 A5
Maison des Arts du Grütli 61 B5
SIP 62 A6
Soda Bar 63 C6
Théâtre du Grütli (see 61)
Victoria Hall 64 B5

SHOPPING
Flea Market 65 B6

TRANSPORT
Avis 66 B3
Compagnie Générale de Navigation Ticket Booth & Boat Departures 67 C5
Europcar 68 B3
Hertz 69 C3
Parking du Mont Blanc 70 C5
Parking Plaine de Plainpalais 71 A6
Sixt 72 C4
Swissboat Departures 73 C4

1865. Geneva's lead theatre (p73) and the **Musée Rath** (Map p62; ☎ 022 418 33 40; Place Neuve; adult/under 18/student 18-25yr Sfr9/free/5; ☯ 10am-5pm Thu-Sun & Tue, noon-9pm Wed) are also here. Off the square, the **Maison des Arts du Grütli** (p73) is the place for contemporary photography, theatre and art happenings.

MUSÉE D'ART MODERNE ET CONTEMPORAIN

MAMCO (Museum of Modern & Contemporary Art; Map p62; ☎ 022 320 61 22; www.mamco.ch in French; Rue des Vieux-Grenadiers 10; adult/under 18/student Sfr8/free/6; ☯ noon-6pm Tue-Fri, 11am-6pm Sat & Sun), set in an industrial 1950s factory, plays host

to young, international and cross-media exhibitions.

PATEK PHILIPPE MUSEUM

A treasure trove of precision art, this **museum** (Map p62; ☎ 022 807 09 10; www.patekmuseum.com; Rue des Vieux Grenadiers 7; adult/child Sfr10/free; ☯ 2-5pm Tue-Fri, 10am-5pm Sat) displays exquisite timepieces from the 16th century to present.

OTHER LEFT-BANK MUSEUMS

Paintings, sculpture, room interiors and weapons fill the **Musée d'Art et d'Histoire** (Art & History Museum; Map p62; ☎ 022 418 26 00; Rue Charles Galland 2; admission free; ☯ 10am-5pm Tue-Sun). Kon-

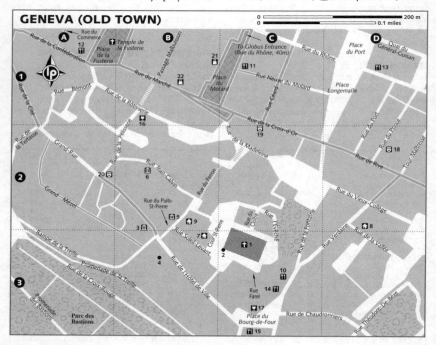

GENEVA (OLD TOWN)

rad Witz's *La pêche miraculeuse* (c 1440–44), portraying Christ walking on water on Lake Geneva, is a highlight.

Kids adore the stuffed bears, tigers and giraffes and Swiss fauna in the **Musée d'Histoire Naturelle** (Natural History Museum; Map p62; ☎ 022 418 63 00; Route de Malagnou 1; admission free; ⏱ 9.30am-5pm Tue-Sun).

North of the Rhône

Cross the water by **Pont du Mont-Blanc** (Map p62; Geneva's only road-traffic bridge, notorious for backlogs) or a footbridge, or sail a seagull (p74).

Flower gardens, statues and great views of Mont Blanc (clear days only) abound on this northern lakeshore promenade, Quai du Mont-Blanc, which leads past the fun-filled **Bains des Pâquis** (p66) to **Parc de la Perle du Lac** (Map p62), where Romans built ornate thermal baths. The peacock-studded lawns of **Parc de l'Ariana** (Map p62) further north ensnare the UN, a couple of museums and the **Jardin Botanique** (Botanical Garden; Map p62; admission free; ⏱ 8am-7.30pm Apr-Oct, 9.30am-5pm Nov-Mar).

PALAIS DES NATIONS

The **Palais des Nations** (Map p62; ☎ 022 917 48 60; Ave de la Paix 14; adult/under 6/6-18 yr/student Sfr8.50/free/4/6.50, passport obligatory; ⏱ 10am-noon & 2-4pm Apr-Oct, 10am-5pm Jul & Aug, 10am-noon & 2-4pm Mon-Fri Nov-Mar), home to the UN since 1966, was built between 1929 and 1936 to house the now-defunct League of Nations. Admission

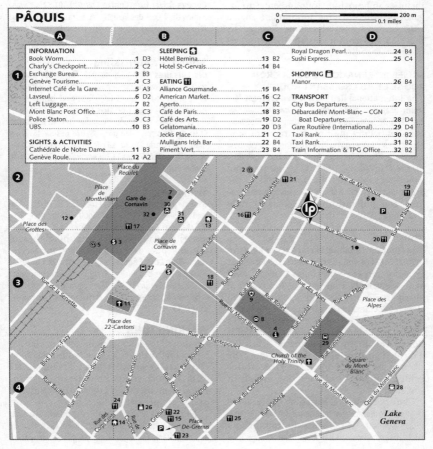

PÂQUIS

0 ——— 200 m
0 ——— 0.1 miles

A · **B** · **C** · **D**

INFORMATION		
Book Worm.....................1 D3	
Charly's Checkpoint............2 C2	
Exchange Bureau...............3 B3	
Genève Tourisme...............4 C3	
Internet Café de la Gare......5 A3	
Lavseul..........................6 D2	
Left Luggage....................7 B2	
Mont Blanc Post Office........8 C3	
Police Staton...................9 C3	
UBS.............................10 B3	

SIGHTS & ACTIVITIES	
Cathédrale de Notre Dame....11 B3	
Genève Roule..................12 A2	

SLEEPING	
Hôtel Bernina..................13 B2	
Hotel St-Gervais...............14 B4	

EATING	
Alliance Gourmande...........15 B4	
American Market...............16 C2	
Aperto.........................17 B2	
Café de Paris..................18 B3	
Café des Arts..................19 D2	
Gelatomania...................20 D3	
Jecks Place....................21 C2	
Mulligans Irish Bar............22 B4	
Piment Vert...................23 B4	

Royal Dragon Pearl............24 B4	
Sushi Express.................25 C4	

SHOPPING	
Manor........................26 B4	

TRANSPORT	
City Bus Departures............27 B3	
Débarcadère Mont-Blanc – CGN	
Boat Departures.............28 D4	
Gare Routière (International)...29 D4	
Taxi Rank.....................30 B2	
Taxi Rank.....................31 B2	
Train Information & TPG Office...32 B2	

THESE STREETS ARE MADE FOR WALKING

So say city planners, who have come up with nine thematic, colour-coded walks to steer pedestrians off the tourist track. Cedar trees, the comic Smurf-inspired Schtroumpfs architectural ensemble, Geneva's first reinforced-concrete housing estate and the romantic Bout de Monde (End of the World) are unexpected sights. Walks last two to four hours and are mapped out in French/English editions of *Genève à pied/ Geneva on Foot*. Get them at the tourist office or www.ville-ge.ch/plan-pietons.

---

includes an hour-long tour and entry to the gardens, where a grey monument coated with heat-resistant titanium, donated by the USSR to commemorate the conquest of space, sprouts.

MUSÉE INTERNATIONAL DE LA CROIX ROUGE ET DU CROISSANT-ROUGE

The **International Red Cross & Red Crescent Museum** (Map p62; ☎ 022 748 95 25; www.micr.org; Ave de la Paix 17; admission free; ۞ 10am-5pm Wed-Mon) is a compelling multimedia trawl through atrocities perpetuated by humanity. Against the long litany of war and nastiness, documented in films, photos, sculptures and soundtracks, are set the noble aims of the organisation created by Geneva businessmen and philanthropists, Henri Dunant and Henri Dufour, in 1864.

CERN

The **European Organisation for Nuclear Research** (☎ 022 767 84 84; visits-service@cern.ch; admission free; ۞ guided tours 9am & 2pm Mon-Sat), 8km west near Meyrin, is a laboratory for research into particle physics and was founded in 1954. It accelerates electrons and positrons down a 27km circular tube (the world's biggest machine) and the resulting collisions create new forms of matter – in 1996 it created antimatter for the first time. The lab can be visited by a free three-hour guided tour; book at least one month in advance.

Equally riveting is **Microcosm** (☎ 022 767 84 84; http://microcosm.web.cern.ch; admission free; ۞ 9am-5.30pm Mon-Sat), CERN's on-site multimedia and interactive visitors centre that runs physics workshops for children aged 12 and older.

Take bus No 9 marked 'CERN' from the train station (Sfr3, 40 minutes).

ACTIVITIES
Cycling & Blading

Rent a bike from **Genève Roule** (Map p62; ☎ 022 740 13 43; www.geneveroule.ch in French; Place de Montbrillant 17; ۞ 7.30am-9.30pm Apr-Oct, 8am-6pm Mon-Sat Nov-May) or its seasonal Jetée des Pâquis pickup point for Sfr10/60 per day/week (Sfr50 deposit). From May to October, borrow a bike carrying publicity for free.

Rafting

From April to October, raft white water with **Geneva Adventure Centre** (☎ 079 301 41 40; www.rafting.ch; 8 Quai des Vernets). An easy 7km-long Rhône canoe descent from the city takes four hours (with/without a guide Sfr70/60).

Sailing & Water-skiing

Les Corsaires (Map p62; ☎ 022 735 43 00; www.les corsaires.ch in French; Quai Gustave-Ador 33) rents yachts (per hour Sfr45 to Sfr70), speed boats (per hour Sfr60) and pedalos (per hour Sfr18).

Water-ski or wakeboard with **Ski Nautique Club de Genève** (Map p62; ☎ 078 663 35 13; www.sncg.ch in French; Parc de la Perle du Lac; per min Sfr3) or **Wake Up** (☎ 079 202 41 61; www.wake-up.ch in French; Genève Plage; per hr Sfr170).

Swimming

Swim at **Genève Plage** (☎ 022 736 24 82; www.geneve-plage.ch; Port Noir; adult before/after 5pm Sfr7/4.50, 6-16yr Sfr3.50; ۞ 10am-8pm mid-May-mid-Sep), a 1930s complex with shingle beach, outdoor pool and waterslide; or the legendary **Bains des Pâquis** (Map p62; ☎ 022 732 29 74; www.bains-des-paquis.ch in French; Quai du Mont-Blanc 30; adult/6-15yr Sfr2/1; ۞ 9am-8pm mid-Apr-mid-Sep) where Genevans have frolicked in the sun since 1872.

WALKING TOUR

Cosmopolitan buzz it might lack, but Geneva lays claim to a bunch of record breakers.

Start at the world's tallest fountain, the **Jet d'Eau (1)** which shoots up water at 200km/h. If you stand on the pier to view the fountain, prepare to get wet.

Next, walk west along Promenade du Lac to see the **horloge fleurie** (2; Flower Clock; Quai du Général-Guisan), Geneva's most photographed clock, crafted from 6500 flowers, which has ticked since 1955 and has the world's longest second hand (2.5m). If it happens to be on the hour, nip into the **Passage Malbuisson** (**3**; Rue du Rhône 40) to see 13 chariots and 42 bronze figurines dance to the chime of 16 bells on a fanciful 1960s clock. Then veer west for a coffee on **Île Rousseau** (**4**), one of five islands to pierce Europe's largest alpine lake.

Further west along the Rhône is 13th-century **Tour d'Île** (**5**), once part of the medieval city fortifications. Head south down cobblestone Rue de la Cité to Grand Rue and **Rousseau's birthplace** (**6**; p63). Cut onto parallel Rue Jean Calvin to visit the **Musée Barbier-Mueller** (**7**; p63) and the **Cathédrale de St-Pierre** (**8**; p61) before lunch on **Place du Bourg-de-Four** (**9**), Geneva's oldest square. From here, chestnut tree–lined **Promenade de la Treille** (**10**) leads to the world's longest

bench (126m) and cultured **Place Neuve** (**11**; p63). Finish with a slug of Swiss wine at **Boulevard du Vin** (**12**; p72).

GENEVA FOR CHILDREN

On and around the lake the kids will love the ducks and swans, boats (opposite), swimming (opposite), electric train tours (p68) and Tarzan-inspired tree park with tyres to swing from at **Baby Plage** (Quai Gustave-Ador), Geneva's baby beach. Parc de la Perle du Lac (p65) and **Bois de la Bâtie** (Bâtie Woods), where peacocks, goats and deer roam, have well-equipped playgrounds for toddlers.

The exhibits and Wednesday-afternoon workshops at the Musée d'Histoire Naturelle (p65) mesmerise children, as do many interactive exhibitions at MAMCO (p64).

Baby's Lounge (Map p62; ☎ 022 310 93 20; www .babyslounge.ch in French; Rue de la Cité 24) is ideal for hungry parents with under-fours.

TOURS

Pick up an English-language audioguide at the tourist office (Sfr10) for a 2½-hour walk around 26 of the left-bank sights. Or, you

---

WALK FACTS

Distance 2.5km
Duration 2 hours

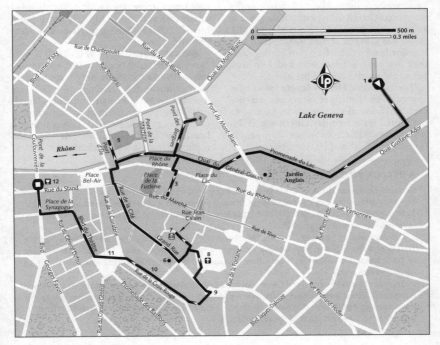

GENEVA

could enjoy an organised two-hour Old Town walking tour (Sfr15).

Tired feet can take a 45-minute **Tramway Tour** (Map p62; ☎ 022 781 04 04; Blvd St-Georges 36; adult/child Sfr8.90/5.90; ☻ 9am-7pm May-Oct) departing 12 times daily from Place du Rhône or Cour St-Pierre; a lakeside **Pâquis Express** (Map p62; ☎ 022 781 04 04; Blvd St-Georges 36; adult/child Sfr7.90/4.90; ☻ every 45 min 10am-dusk Mar-Oct) train tour along the right bank from Quai du Mont-Blanc; or a left-bank tour aboard **Petit Train Solaire** (☎ 022 735 43 00; 33 Quai Gustave-Ador; adult/child Sfr7/4; ☻ hourly 10.15am-10.15pm Jun-Oct) from the Jardin Anglais.

Between April and October, **Swissboat** (☎ 22 732 29 44; www.swissboat.com; 4-8 Quai du Mont Blanc) runs 40-minute to 2¾-hour thematic cruises on the lake.

FESTIVALS & EVENTS

Smashing marzipan-filled *marmites en chocolat* (chocolate cauldrons) and gorging on the sweet broken pieces is part and parcel of **L'Escalade** (www.escalade.ch in French), Geneva's biggest festival, which fills the city with frolics on 11 December. Torch-lit processions enliven the Old Town and a huge bonfire is lit in the cathedral square to celebrate the defeat of Savoy troops in 1602. A tall tale says the assault was repelled by a housewife who tipped a pot of boiling soup over a trooper's head, whacked him with her cauldron then raised the alarm.

The two-week **Fêtes de Genève** (www.fetes-de -geneve.ch in French) brings parades, open-air concerts and fireworks to the city in August. As party-mad is the one-day **Lake Parade** (☻ July or August), when DJs from around Europe spin tunes from 20 lakeside love-mobiles.

SLEEPING

Plug into a comprehensive list at www.ge neva-hotel.ch.

Budget

Pick up the annual *Info-Jeunes Genève* guide at the tourist office for a comprehensive list of hostels.

City Hostel (Map p62; ☎ 022 901 15 00; www.cityhos tel.ch; Rue de Ferrier 2; 3- or 4-bed dm per person Sfr28, sheets Sfr3.50, 2-bed dm incl sheets Sfr35, s/d Sfr58/85; ☻ reception 7.45am-noon & 1-11pm; ✗ P ▯) Spanking clean is the trademark of this organised hostel, where two-bed dorms give travellers a chance to double up on the cheap. Facilities include kitchen, free lockers, garage parking (Sfr10), laundry, TV room and Internet station (open 7.30am to 2am, per hour Sfr8).

Auberge de Jeunesse (Map p62; ☎ 022 732 62 60; www.yh-geneva.ch; Rue Rothschild 28-30; dm Sfr26, d with toilet Sfr75, d with shower & toilet Sfr85; reception ☻ 6.30-10am & 2pm-1am Jun-Sep, 6.30-10am & 4pm-midnight Oct-May; ▯) Pâquis' 350-bed apartment-block hostel serves its purpose handsomely: dorms max out at six beds, bathrooms tout hairdryers, there are facilities for disabled guests and a multi-machined laundry. Rates include breakfast and non HI-card holders pay Sfr6 more.

Hôme St-Pierre (Map p64; ☎ 022 310 37 07; www .homestpierre.ch; Cour St-Pierre 4; dm Sfr27, s/d with washbasin Sfr40/60; ▯) St-Pierre only takes women. In a centuries-old building, the place was founded by the German Lutheran Church in 1874 to put up German women coming to Geneva to learn French. Staying here is a home away from home and the view from the rooftop terrace is fab. Breakfast costs Sfr7.

A DETOUR INTO BOHEMIA

Geneva's bohemian streak strikes in fashionable Carouge, where the distinct lack of any real sights – bar 18th-century houses overlooking courtyard gardens and a **Musée de Carouge** (☎ 022 342 33 84; muse@carouge.ch; Place de la Sardaigne 2; admission free; ☻ 2-6pm Tue-Sun) displaying 19th-century ceramics – is part of the charm.

Carouge was refashioned by Vittorio Amedeo III, King of Sardinia and Duke of Savoy, in the 18th century in a bid to rival Geneva as a centre of commerce – until 1816 when the Treaty of Turin handed it to Geneva. Funky bars, restaurants, boutiques and artist's workshops fill its narrow streets today.

Tram No 12 or 13 links central Geneva with Carouge's plane tree–studded central square, Place du Marché, abuzz with market stalls Wednesday and Saturday morning. Horses trot along the streets during April's Fête du Cheval, while horse-drawn carriages line up on Place de l'Octroi in December to take Christmas shoppers for a ride.

DAY TRIPPER

Day trips from Geneva boil down to a boat trip to another lakeside hot spot, a mountain foray into the Jura or a meander into neighbouring France.

Oh-so-pretty French Yvoire, 27km northeast of Geneva on the lake's southern shore, is *the* spot where diplomats to dustmen while away weekend afternoons. The medieval walled village with a fishing port and fairytale castle (closed to visitors) has a few cobbled pedestrian streets to stroll, extraordinary flowers to admire, a restored medieval vegetable garden **Jardin des Cinq Sens** (Garden of the Five Senses; ☎ 72 82 04 50 80; www.jardin5sens.net; adult/4-16yr Sfr9/5.50; ☽ mid-Apr–mid-Oct) and an overkill of souvenir shops and touristy lunchtime spots. The CGN boat ride from Geneva's Jardin Anglais (day return Sfr35.20; 1¾ hours, May to September) is part of the day out.

Quaint Swiss Hermance, 16km northeast of Geneva on the French–Swiss border, lures a more discerning crowd with its narrow streets lined with medieval houses, the odd pricey art gallery and the legendary **Auberge d'Hermance** (☎ 022 751 13 68; www.hotel-hermance.ch in French; Rue du Midi 12; plat du jour Sfr19, menus Sfr68-125), one of the region's most prestigious culinary addresses, where chickens are baked whole and served in a magical salt crust. TPG bus E (Sfr4.60, 30 minutes, at least hourly) links Hermance with Rue de Pierre Fatio on Geneva's left bank.

Midrange

Hotel St-Gervais (Map p65; ☎ 022 732 45 72; www.stgervais-geneva.ch; Rue des Corps-Saints 20; s/d with wash-basin Sfr70/85, d with bathroom Sfr115) This quaint choice near the train station is a delight. Just like an old-fashioned auberge, rooms tout tartan carpets, wood furnishings and crisp white linen. Travellers with jumbo-sized suitcases beware: scaling the seven floors in the pocket-handkerchief lift is a squash and a squeeze.

Hôtel Bel'Esperance (Map p64; ☎ 022 818 37 37; www.hotel-bel-esperance.ch; Rue de la Vallée 1; s/d Sfr160/180; ✗) This small two-star hotel is a two-second roll home from the Old Town. Rooms are quiet and those on the 1st floor share a kitchen. Ride the lift to the 5th floor to discover a flower-filled rooftop terrace with table and chairs to lounge on.

Auberge de Carouge (☎ 022 342 22 88; Rue Ancienne 39; s/d/tr/q Sfr130/180/210/250; P) With its tree-shaded garden and the artsy scene of Théâtre de Carouge around the corner, this old Carouge hotel oozes appeal. Its room count is just a couple over a dozen so get in quick.

Hôtel At Home (Map p62; ☎ 022 906 19 00; www.hotel-at-home.ch; Rue de Fribourg 16; s/d/tr from Sfr100/140/160) At home is what At Home makes you feel. It rents kitchen-equipped apartments too, and surrounding eateries take you around the world.

Hôtel Bernina (Map p65; ☎ 022 908 49 50; www.bernina-geneve.ch; Place de Cornavin 22; s/d/tr/q from Sfr140/170/190/230; ✗) Spacious, if plain, rooms with TV, telephone and balcony ensure a decent – if unmemorable – night's sleep for punters keen to roll out of bed and into the train station. We assume the 'Attention! Pickpockets!' sign at reception means out on the streets, not in the hotel.

GAY & LESBIAN GENEVA

The key port of call is **Dialogai** (Map p62; ☎ 022 906 40 40; www.dialogai.org; Rue de la Navigation 11-13), which publishes a gay guide to the Geneva region and hosts candlelit dinners, Sunday brunch, film evenings, French-English discussion groups, club nights etc in its retro café; see its website for details.

The mainly male, expat **Gay International Group** (GIG; gig@360.ch) brings together 80-odd nationalities for monthly drinks and dinners.

Key entertainment spots include **Nathan** (Map p62; ☎ 022 733 78 76; Rue Baudit 6; ☽ 5pm-2am), a gay bar heaving with Geneva's most hip, especially at weekends; and gay night-club **Le Prétexte** (Map p64; ☎ 022 310 14 28; www.lepretexte.ch in French; Rue du Prince 9; admission Sfr10-20; ☽ 11pm-5am Thu-Sun).

Top End

Geneva is studded with four- and five-star hotels.

Hôtel Les Armures (Map p64; ☎ 022 310 91 72; Rue du Puits-St-Pierre 1; www.hotel-les-armures.ch; s/d from Sfr360/520, extra bed Sfr90; P ✗ ✗ ☐) This slumbering 17th-century beauty just oozes with history from every last beam. Beautifully placed in the heart of the Old

GENEVA

AUTHOR'S CHOICE

Hôtel de la Cloche (Map p62; ☎ 022 732 94 81; hotelcloche@freesurf.ch; Rue de la Cloche 6; s with/without bathroom Sfr110/80, d Sfr140/115, s with shower & toilet Sfr90-110, d Sfr110-140, extra bed Sfr15; ✕) Hôtel de la Cloche, an old-fashioned hotel in a bourgeois home, is part of a dying breed. And more is the pity. Monsieur Chabbey runs this small, one-star hotel with grace and panache, opening the door as a butler welcoming you home. Likewise, it is Monsieur Chabbey who delivers breakfast to each room from 8am every morning (each of the eight rooms have a table and chairs), sorts out the bill and so on. Elegant fireplaces, period furnishings, wooden floors and the odd chandelier add a touch of grandeur. Some rooms come with wrought-iron balconies that face the Jet d'Eau.

Town, it provides an intimate and refined atmosphere.

Hôtel Beau-Rivage (Map p64; ☎ 022 716 66 66; www.beau-rivage.ch; Quai du Mont Blanc 13; d/ste from Sfr495/1180; Ⓟ ✕ ❀ 💻 🍴) Run by the Mayer family for four generations, Beau-Rivage is a 19th-century jewel dripping in opulence. Sotheby's (actually based in the hotel) auctioned off the late Duchess of Windsor's jewellery here for millions in 1987, and celebrity names fill its guest book. A continental/buffet breakfast costs Sfr29/39.

Hôtel President Wilson (Map p62; ☎ 022 906 66 66; www.hotelpwilson.com; Quai Wilson 47; s/d from Sfr580; Ⓟ ✕ ❀ 💻 🍴) This shimmering five-star glass palace with spice-driven restaurant stars in the *Guinness Book of Records* as host to the world's most-expensive hotel room: its four-bedroom bullet-proof penthouse Imperial Suite – with lake view, private lift, table for 26 and library to entertain 40 – costs US$33,000 per night in 2003, so the book says. 'Rate on request' says the hotel. Meals here cost Sfr75 to Sfr128.

EATING

As the Swiss gastronomic capital, Geneva flaunts a fantastic choice of ethnic food, although quality occasionally plays underdog to interior design. For the culinary curious without a fortune to blow, Pâquis cooks up cheapish eateries from every corner of the globe.

Restaurants – South of the Rhône

Le Relais de L'Entrecôte (Map p64; ☎ 022 310 60 04; Rue du Rhône 49; starters/mains Sfr10/25) If *entrecôte* and fries (some say the best steak and chips in Geneva) are your cup of tea then this busy bistro wedged between designer shops is for you. Get here dot on to snag the table with a lake view.

ù bobba (Map p62; ☎ 022 310 53 40; Rue de la Corraterie 21; starters/mains Sfr15/30; 🕙 8am-3pm Mon, 8-12.30am Tue, Wed & Thu, 8-1am Fri, 10-1am Sat) A cultured crowd gathers at this dining spot, decked in red and gold and oozing attitude. Particularly hot is its u jardinù bobba, one of Geneva's best roof terraces. Inventive mains range from veal medallions with pistachio nuts (Sfr42) to Gorgonzola-dunked gnocchi (Sfr25).

Soupçon (Map p64; ☎ 022 318 37 37; www.soupcon.ch in French; Place du Bourg-de-Four 8; lunch/dinner mains Sfr25/40) Stark cream tablecloths, white china and a moneyed crowd add an urban edge to slick Soupçon, with a wooden decking terrace on busy Place du Bourg-de-Four. The cuisine is creative: think scallops strung on a lemongrass skewer.

Café du Centre (Map p64; ☎ 022 311 85 86; www.cafeducentre.ch; Place du Molard 5; plat du jour Sfr15-20, seafood platters Sfr39-350) It looks like a bog-standard century-old bistro from the outside, but peek at the lavish shellfish displayed in its window and you'll be raring to get in. A dandy terrace on Place du Molard tops off its culinary prowess.

La Truffe Noire (Map p62; ☎ 022 800 03 82; Blvd Georges Favon 4; starters/mains Sfr20/30; 🕙 Tue-Sat)

AUTHOR'S CHOICE

Café des Bains (Map p62; ☎ 022 321 57 98; www.cafédesbains.com; Rue des Bains 26; starters/mains Sfr15/40; 🕙 11am-3pm & 6pm-1am Mon-Fri, 6pm-1am Sat) No brand labels, beautiful objects and an eye for design are trademarks of this fusion restaurant where Genevan beauties flock. The king prawns, pan-fried with green pepper, sweet Thai basil and mango and served with a mint and apricot mousse, certainly won our hearts. Green almond and parmesan risotto woos vegetarians.

ASIAN CORNER

Geneva's most legendary (hence pricey) pan-Asian haunts are **Chez Kei** (☎ 022 346 47 89; Route de Malagnou 6; mains from Sfr30), the city's second-oldest ode to Chinese cuisine; and hip **Jecks Place** (Map p65; ☎ 022 731 33 03; Rue de Neuchâtel 14; mains from Sfr25), a moveable feast of Singaporean, Chinese, Malaysian and Thai.

Truffle junkies will be left breathless by this elegant boutique restaurant specialising in black truffles and cuisine from southwestern France. *Rapée de truffe* (grated truffle; Sfr48) followed by *cuisse de canard* (duck thigh) is a typical feast.

Au Pied de Cochon (Map p64; ☎ 022 310 47 97; Place du Bourg-de-Four 4; mains from Sfr30) Piggy feet are the house speciality at Au Pied de Cochon, where fat little trotters come stuffed, braised or pan-fried. A zinc bar and noisy wine-quaffing clientele complete the classic bistro picture.

Bistrot du Boucher (Map p62; ☎ 022 736 56 36; Ave Pictet de Rochemont 15; mains Sfr30-40) Beef cuts are the mainstay of this feisty meat number, a Parisian-style bistro with lace curtains, stained glass and Art Nouveau wood. *Entrecôte* (sirloin steak), *côte* (side), carpaccio or tartare are served with a choice of sauces, fries or risotto and salad. Baby-cow lovers will love or hate the sweet *tartare de veau*.

Auberge du Lion d'Or (☎ 022 736 44 32; Place Gautier 5, Cologny; mains Sfr100-150) Formal and packed with suits, the Lion d'Or is in the heart of Geneva's most expensive 'burb. Mouth-watering fish and seafood creations honour a fine wine list. Service and setting are immaculate and designed to impress.

Restaurants – North of the Rhône
Alliance Gourmande (Map p65; ☎ 022 901 10 03; www .alliancegourmande.com; Place De-Grenus 10; menus Sfr25; ☺ closed Sun) A clever mix of old and new – beamed ceiling, leg of ham–strung bar and designer chairs – invites gourmands to feast on all things tempting and tasty (the ricotta-stuffed king prawns in a whisky sauce are irresistible). Inventive tasting sessions tickle the tastebuds and cooking workshops (Sfr10, noon to 2pm Saturday) reveal some chef secrets.

Café de Paris (Map p65; ☎ 022 732 84 50; Rue du Mont-Blanc 26; steak & chips Sfr37) An impressionable dining experience: everyone here eats the same – green salad followed by *entrecôte* with a herb and butter sauce of legendary standing and as many supermodel-skinny fries as you can handle. Advance reservations are essential.

Les 5 Portes (Map p62; ☎ 022 731 84 38; Rue de Zürich 5; breakfast Sfr8.50-12.50, starters/mains Sfr10/20) The Five Doors is a favourite Pâquis port of call. Named after the five entrance doors it sports, the relaxed and fashionable eating joint embraces the whole gambit of moods and moments – romance, breakfast, solitary lunch, social brunch etc.

Buvette des Bains (Map p62; ☎ 022 738 16 16; www .bains-des-paquis.ch in French; Quai du Mont-Blanc 30; mains Sfr16; ☺ 8am-9.30pm) Meet Genevans at this earthy beach bar – rough and hip around the edges – at Bains des Pâquis (p66). Grab breakfast (Sfr10), a salad or *plat du jour* (Sfr10 to Sfr12), or dip into a *fondue au crémant* (champagne fondue). Dining is on trays and alfresco in summer.

Cafés
CALM (☎ 022 301 22 20; Rue Ancienne 36; brunch Sfr30, salads Sfr7) Divine quiches (Sfr12), Swiss bircher muesli and other house-baked goodies lure a discerning crowd to this kitchen-styled café just *comme à la maison* (like home) with a fabulous Italianate terraced garden out back.

Café des Arts (Map p65; ☎ 022 321 58 85; Rue des Pâquis 15; ☺ 11-2am Mon-Fri, 8-2am Sat & Sun) As much a place to drink as a daytime café, this trendy Pâquis hangout lures a local crowd with its Parisian-style terrace and artsy interior. Food-wise, think meal-sized salads, designer sandwiches and other titillating lunch dishes.

Les Recyclables (☎ 022 328 60 44; www.recyclables .ch; Rue de Carouge 53; ☺ 9am-11pm Mon-Sat; ☒) Sip coffee while glued to a book at this literary café with a difference. Committed to 'cultural recycling', Les Recyclables sells books and exchanges second-hand books for reading or edible matter.

Le Pain Quotidien (Map p62; ☎ 022 736 36 90; Blvd Helvétique; breakfast/brunch from Sfr15/32; ☺ 7am-6pm Mon-Fri, 8am-6pm Sat & Sun; ☒) Choose from a whole heap of breakfasts (continental, English etc) and brunches (classic, countryside etc) at this twin-set of rustic daytime spots.

B&B

A culinary kick-start to the day is what Geneva trendies do: CALM (p71), Buvette des Bains (p71), Soupçon (p70), Les 5 Portes (p71), Le Pain Quotidien (p71), Arthur's (right) and Alhambar (right) are breakfast and/or brunch favourites.

There's also a branch situated on Blvd Georges-Favon.

Quick Eats

Rue de Fribourg, Rue de Neuchâtel, Rue de Berne and the northern end of Rue des Alpes (all Map p65) are loaded with kebab, falafel and quick-eat joints. Eat in or take out at the following:

Piment Vert (Map p65; ☎ 022 731 93 03; www .pimentvert.ch in French; Place De-Grenus 4; menu Sfr24, starters/mains Sfr10/15; ☯ 11.30am-2.45pm & 5.30-10pm Mon-Fri, noon-4pm Sat) Fast, fresh, trendy is what this Sri Lankan bar aims for.

Globus (Map p64; ☎ 022 319 50 50; Rue du Rhône 50; ☯ 9am-10pm Mon-Sat) Snack-attack on sushi, sashimi, panini, tapas, antipasti, noodles and curry in the central department store.

Sushi Express (Map p64 & Map p65; ☎ 022 310 80 10; www.ekai.ch; Place du Bourg-de-Four 19; sushi platters from Sfr10; ☯ 11.30am-2.45pm & 5-9.30pm Mon-Fri, 11.30am-3.30pm & 4-8pm Sat) Consume raw fish from a clean-cut sushi bar. There's also a branch at Rue du Cendrier 18.

Self-Catering

Shop for Asian at **Royal Dragon Pearl** (Map p65; ☎ 022 731 16 41; Rue de Cornavin 1), for American at the **American Market** (Map p65; ☎ 022 732 32 00; Rue

LICK IT

Enviable choices for ice on the move:
Gelateria Arlecchino (Map p62; ☎ 022 736 70 60; Rue du 31 Decembre 1; per scoop Sfr3.50) Left-bank choice: chocolate and ginger, honey, peanut cream and mango are among the 40 flavours at this lip-licking parlour.
Gelatomania (Map p65; Rue des Pâquis 25; per scoop Sfr3) Right-bank choice: a constant queue loiters outside this shop where ice-cream maniacs wrap their tongues around exotic flavours like carrot, orange and lemon, cucumber and mint, lime and basil or pineapple and basil.

de Neuchâtel 3), and for stuff fresh from the farm at **Les Saveurs de la Ferme** (Map p62; ☎ 022 786 20 40; Cours de Rive 20). **Delicatessa Globus** (Map p64; Rue du Rhône 50) is the Harrods food hall of Geneva.

Central supermarkets in Geneva include the following:
Coop City (Map p64; Rue de la Confédération)
Aperto (Map p65; Gare de Cormavin; ☯ 6am-10pm)

DRINKING

In summer, the **paillote** (Map p62; Quai du Mont-Blanc 30; ☯ to midnight), with wooden tables inches from the water, is rammed. By 11pm the grassy lawns, quay and walls within a 20m radius of the kiosk overflow with merry punters.

Arthur's (Map p62; ☎ 022 810 32 60; www.arthurs .ch; Rue du Rhône 7-9; ☯ 7-2am Mon-Fri, 11-2am Sat) If Arthur was real he'd be called 007 and drink vodka martinis shaken not stirred at this drop-dead gorgeous lakeside terrace where aperitif lovers linger.

Omnibus (Map p62; ☎ 022 321 44 45; Rue de la Coulouvrenière 23) Angels trumpet at the bar and an old three-wheeler hangs outside at this retro hangout.

La Plage (☎ 022 342 20 98; Rue Vautier 19; ☯ 11-1am Mon-Thu, 10-2am Fri & Sat, 5pm-1am Sun) With bare wood tables, checked lino floor, green-wood shutters and tables outside, the beach in Carouge is a timeless drinking hole.

Qu'Importe (☎ 022 342 15 25; www.quimporte.ch in French; Rue Ancienne 1) Never Mind makes no bones about its mission in life: '*qu'importe le facon pourvu qu'on ait livresse*' ('Never mind the bottle as long as it gets you drunk…'), so said French Romantic poet and bar muse Alfred de Musset.

Olé Olé (Map p62; ☎ 022 731 38 71; baroleole@yahoo .com; Rue de Fribourg 11; tapas Sfr10-20) An industrial tapas bar with giant street-facing windows and a bar lit by naked bulbs ensures a stop with a difference near the train station.

Boulevard du Vin (Map p62; ☎ 022 310 91 90; www .boulevard-du-vin.ch in French; Blvd Georges-Favon 3; ☯ 11.30am-1.30pm & 5-11pm Mon-Thu, 5pm-2am Fri, 6pm-2am Sat) Wine sluggers will enjoy this excellent wine shop which doubles as wine bar with its weekly dégustation sessions. Food platters (Sfr10) add a gastronomic dimension.

Alhambar (Map p64; ☎ 022 312 13 13; www.al hambar.com in French; Rue de la Rôtisserie 10; ☯ noon-2pm Mon, noon-2pm & 5pm-1am or 2am Tue-Fri, 5pm-2am Sat, 11am-midnight Sun) Hidden behind a cinema, Alhambar cooks up a heady cocktail of drinks, DJs and food in a relaxed, convivial setting. Sunday brunch is worth rolling out of bed for.

La Clémence (Map p64; ☎ 022 312 24 98; www.la clemence.ch; Place du Bourg-de-Four 20) Indulge in a glass of red at this more than veritable Genevois institution fronting the city's loveliest square.

ENTERTAINMENT

Keep in the loop online with **nuit.ch** (www .nuit.ch in French).

Edgy mixed-bag entertainment venues include the following:

L'Usine (Map p62; ☎ 022 781 34 90; www.usine.ch in French; Place des Volontaires 4) A converted gold-roughing factory, entertainment ranges from dance nights, art happenings, cabaret and theatre to urban clubbing for night animals at Le Zoo (☎ 022 321 47 93, www .lezoo.ch, admission before 11pm/2am/5am Sfr5/10/15, open Friday and Saturday or Sunday). The entrance is on Quai des Forces Motrices.

Bâtiment des Forces Motrices (Map p62; ☎ 022 322 12 20; www.bfm.ch in French; Place des Volontaires 4) Geneva's one-time riverside pumping station (1886) is now a striking space for rock concerts, opera, ballet and other cultural events.

Bistr'Ok (Map p62; ☎ 022 329 33 95; www.bistrok .ch in French; Blvd des Philosophes 24) This ground-floor squat fronts Geneva's alternative cultural scene with its hybrid café-bar, cinema evenings, jam sessions and live bands.

Le Chat Noir (☎ 022 343 49 98; www.chatnoir.ch in French; Rue Vautier 13; concerts Sfr16-20) Nightly jazz, rock, funk and salsa gigs.

Nightclubs

SIP (Map p62; www.lasip.ch in French; Rue des Vieux Grenadiers 10) Soul Influence Product is 'not a nightclub', says the propaganda of this design-led space, an 1860s factory.

Soda Bar (Map p62; ☎ 022 312 00 98; www.sodabar .ch; Rue Étienne Dumont 3) Soul, salsa, funk and r'n'b; downhill from Place du Bourg Neuf.

crem (Map p62; ☎ 022 347 22 20; www.lacrem.ch in French; Blvd Helvétique 10) Gastronomic restaurant, lounge club, dance floor and bar so trendy its name doesn't carry an upper case.

There are also some mainstream nightclubs here:

Jet Set (Map p62; ☎ 022 732 13 13; Quai du Seujet 20; admission Sfr20)

X-S (Map p64; ☎ 022 311 70 09; Grand-Rue 21, entrance at Rue de la Pelisserie 19; admission Sfr10; ☉ 11pm-4am Thu, 11.30pm-5am Fri & Sat)

Cinemas

Watch films in English at **Rex** (Map p64; ☎ 0900 900 156; Confédération Centre 8, Rue de la Croix d'Or 11) or **Les Scala** (Map p62; ☎ 022 736 04 22; www.les-scala.ch in French; Rue des Eaux-Vives 23). Programmes are online at http://geneve.cinemas.ch (in French).

Ciné Lac (www.cinelac.ch in French; ☉ Jul & Aug) is a glorious summertime open-air cinema with a giant screen set up literally on the lakeside, which oozes romance. Watch a box-office hit against a twinkling backdrop of stars, boat lights and rippling water.

Theatre & Classical Music

Grand Théâtre de Genève (Map p62; ☎ 022 418 31 30; www.geneveopera.ch in French; Blvd du Théâtre 11) Geneva's opera, ballet, dance and theatre stage.

Victoria Hall (Map p62; ☎ 022 418 35 00; Rue du Général Dufour 14) Home to the Orchestre de la Suisse Romande.

Théâtre du Grütli (Map p62; ☎ 022 328 98 68; www .grutli.ch; Rue du Général Dufour 16) Experimental theatre and comedy.

SHOPPING

Designer shopping is wedged between Rue du Rhône and Rue de Rive. **Globus** (Map p64; Rue du Rhône 50) and **Manor** (Map p65; Rue de Cornavin) are the main department stores.

Grand-Rue in the Old Town and Carouge (p68) boast artsy boutiques. Something different can also be found at Geneva's twice-weekly **flea market** (Map p62; Plaine de Plainpalais; ☉ Wed & Sat).

GETTING THERE & AWAY
Air

Aéroport International de Genève (flight information ☎ 0900 57 15 00; www.gva.ch) has frequent connections to major European cities and many others worldwide. See p323.

Boat

The **Compagnie Générale de Navigation** (CGN; Map p62; ☎ 0848 811 848; www.cgn.ch) operates a steamer service from a jetty near Jardin Anglais to other villages on Lake Geneva. Many only sail from May to September, including those to Lausanne-Ouchy (adult 1st-/2nd-class single Sfr47.40/34.80, return Sfr73.60/54, 3½ hours). Passengers aged six to 16 pay 50% less and under sixes sail for nothing.

Those planning to stop off at other places en route should buy a Carte Journalière CGN (one-day CGN pass) costing Sfr74/55 in 1st/2nd class. Otherwise, the Swiss Boat Pass (Sfr35), available at any boat pier with a ticket office, yields a 50% discount on lake-steamer tickets for one year. Eurail and Swiss rail passes (see the boxed text Swiss Travel Passes, p327) are also valid.

Bus

International buses depart from the **Gare Routière** (Bus Station; Map p65; within Switzerland ☎ 0900 320 320, 022 732 02 30; www.coach-station.com; Place Dorcière). Buses run to a plethora of ski resorts, including Swiss Flaine and Verbier (both December to April), and to Chamonix (five daily, 1¾ hours, adult/child four to 12 Sfr49.50/25) in France.

Car & Motorcycle

RENTAL

Avis Airport (☎ 022 929 03 30); City (Map p62; ☎ 022 731 90 00; Rue de Lausanne 44)

Budget (☎ 022 717 86 75; Airport)

Easycar (www.easycar.com) Online, no-frills car rental operating out of Geneva airport.

Europcar Airport (☎ 022 717 82 37); City (Map p62; ☎ 022 732 52 52; Rue de Lausanne 37)

Hertz Airport (☎ 022 798 22 02); City (Map p62; ☎ 022 731 12 00; Rue de Berne 60)

Sixt Airport (☎ 022 717 84 10); City (Map p62; ☎ 022 732 90 90; Place de la Navigation 1)

Train

More-or-less-hourly connections operate between Geneva's main train station, **Gare de Cornavin** (Map p65; Place de Cornavin), and most Swiss towns, including Lausanne (Sfr20, 40 minutes), Bern (Sfr45, 1¾ hours) and Zürich (Sfr77, 2¾ hours). Pick up timetables at the **information office** (☎ 0900 300 300; ⏱ 8.30am-6.30pm Mon-Fri, 9am-4.45pm Sat).

Trains running southeast to/from Annecy, Chamonix and other destinations in France use Geneva's French Railways (SNCF) train station, **Gare des Eaux-Vives** (Ave de la Gare des Eaux-Vives).

For international connections see p326.

GETTING AROUND

Swiss rail pass holders (p327) travel for free on Geneva's trams and buses.

To/From the Airport

The quickest way to/from Geneva airport is by train: some 200 trains per day link the airport train station with Gare de Cornavin (Sfr2.80, eight minutes). Slower bus No 10 (Sfr2.80) also runs between the airport and Gare de Cornavin; get off at the '22 Cantons' stop. A metered taxi costs around Sfr30.

Boat

Yellow shuttle boats, Les Mouettes (the seagulls), crisscross the lake every 10 minutes between 7.30am and 6pm. Public transport tickets dispensed by machines at boat bays are valid.

Car & Motorcycle

Much of the Old Town is off-limits to cars. Street parking (1½-hour maximum stay) costs Sfr1.50 or Sfr2 per hour, and public car parks (www.geneve.ch/parkings in French) are well signposted: those parking in **Parking du Mont Blanc** (Map p62; Quai du Général-Guisan; per 25 min Sfr1) or **Parking Plaine de Plainpalais** (Map p62; Ave du Mail; per 40 min Sfr1) get one hour of free travel for two people on buses, trams and boats; validate your ticket in an orange TPG machine before leaving the car park.

Public Transport

Tickets for buses, trolley buses and trams run by **Transports Public Genevois** (TPG; ☎ 0900 022 021; www.tpg.ch in French) are sold at dispensers at stops and at the **TPG office** (⏱ 7am-7pm Mon-Sat), at the central train station: a one-hour ticket for multiple rides in the city costs Sfr2.80; a ticket valid for three stops in 30 minutes is Sfr2.20; and a city/canton day pass valid 9am to midnight is Sfr7/12. Schedules for **Noctambus night buses** (☎ 0900 022 021; www.noctambus.ch in French) are online.

Taxi

Pick one up from in front of the train station or call ☎ 022 331 41 33. Count on paying Sfr6.30 flag fall plus Sfr2.90 per kilometre.

Lake Geneva & Vaud

East of Geneva, Western Europe's biggest lake stretches like a giant liquid mirror between French-speaking Canton de Vaud (pronounced Voh; Waadt in German) on its northern shore and France to the south.

Known to most as Lake Geneva, to Francophones (except some in Geneva!) it is Lac Léman. Lined by the elegant city of Lausanne and a phalanx of pretty smaller towns, the Swiss side of the lake presents the marvellous emerald spectacle of tightly ranked vineyards spreading in terraces up the steep hillsides of the Lavaux area. These grapes and those grown to the west of Lausanne produce some fine tipples and it is possible to visit some *caveaux* (cellars). Modest beaches, often backed by peaceful woodland, dot the lake, and around Montreux the climate is mild enough for palm trees to thrive.

Jutting out over the waters of the lake near Montreux is the fairytale Château de Chillon, the first of many that await exploration a short way inland.

Lake-lovers can head north to Yverdon-les-Bains, which sits on the southern tip of Lac de Neuchâtel and offers the chance to relax in tempting thermal baths.

At its southeast corner the canton rises into the magnificent mountain country of the Alpes Vaudoises (Vaud Alps), a hikers' paradise in spring and summer, and skiers' haven in winter. Those addicted to the white stuff can even indulge in moderate summer skiing across the impressive Les Diablerets glacier.

In July, music rocks the lake with Montreux's international jazz get-together and Nyon's multifaceted Paléo music fest.

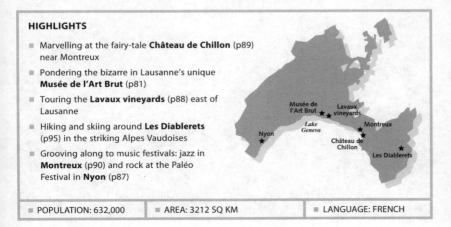

HIGHLIGHTS

- Marvelling at the fairy-tale **Château de Chillon** (p89) near Montreux
- Pondering the bizarre in Lausanne's unique **Musée de l'Art Brut** (p81)
- Touring the **Lavaux vineyards** (p88) east of Lausanne
- Hiking and skiing around **Les Diablerets** (p95) in the striking Alpes Vaudoises
- Grooving along to music festivals: jazz in **Montreux** (p90) and rock at the Paléo Festival in **Nyon** (p87)

■ POPULATION: 632,000	■ AREA: 3212 SQ KM	■ LANGUAGE: FRENCH

History

As early as 58 BC, Caesar's troops had penetrated what is now southwest Switzerland. In the succeeding centuries a mix of Celtic tribes and Romans rubbed along in peace and prosperity. Aventicum (today Avenches) became the capital, with as many as 20,000 inhabitants, and numerous other towns (such as Lausanne) flourished.

By the 4th century AD, the Romans had largely pulled out of Switzerland and Germanic tribes stepped into the vacuum. Christianised Burgundians arrived in the southwest in the 5th century and picked up the Vulgar Latin tongue that was the precursor to French. Absorbed by the Franks,

in 1032 Vaud became part of the Holy Roman Empire.

In the 12th and 13th centuries the Dukes of Savoy slowly assumed control of Vaud and embarked on the construction of impressive lakeside castles.

The Canton of Bern appreciatively took over those castles when, in 1536, it declared war on Savoy and seized Vaud. Despite the tendency of Bern's bailiffs to siphon off local wealth, by the 18th century Lausanne (the area's capital) was a thriving centre.

The French Revolution in 1789 had heavy consequences for its neighbours. On the urging of Fréderic César de la Harpe, leader of the Liberal Party, the Directorate in Paris placed Vaud under its protection

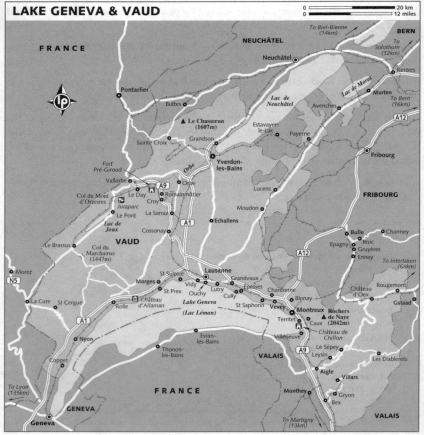

LAKE GENEVA & VAUD

in December 1797. The following month, Vaud was declared independent. In 1803 Napoleon imposed the Act of Mediation that created the Swiss Confederation in which Vaud, with Lausanne as its capital, became one of six separate cantons.

Orientation & Information

Vaud straddles the three main geographical regions of Switzerland: the Jura mountains in the west, the relatively flat plain of the Plateau Central (Mittelland), and a smidgen of the Alps in the southeast.

Along its northern flank it is bordered by the Neuchâtel and Fribourg cantons. To the south lies France (briefly interrupted by the frontier with Geneva canton) and to the southeast the Valais, while to the east the German part of the country starts with the canton of Bern.

The **Canton de Vaud tourist office** (Map p78; ☎ 021 613 26 26; www.lake-geneva-region.ch; Ave d'Ouchy 60, 1006, Ouchy, Lausanne; ⊙ 8am-5.30pm Mon-Fri) provides regional information, including hiking- and cycling-route brochures.

For information on Avenches and Payerne, which are part of Vaud, see p106.

In addition to the normal Swiss national holidays, the people of Vaud also take off St Basil's Day (2 January) and the Federal Day of Fasting (Lundi du Jeûne) on the third Monday in September.

Getting Around

The **Regional Pass** (7-day pass 1st/2nd class Sfr155/107) provides free bus and train travel throughout the canton three days in seven, and half-price travel on the other four days. It also gives 50% off CGN boat services as well as 25% off some cable cars (eg up to Les Diablerets glacier). There is a five-day version with two days of free travel (1st/2nd class Sfr129/89). Holders of one of the various Swiss rail passes (see p333) receive a 20% discount off the Regional Pass.

LAUSANNE

pop 116,330 / elevation 495m
This hilly city (loh-*san*), Switzerland's fifth largest (and third most visited after Geneva and Zürich), enjoys a blessed location. The medieval centre is dominated by one of the country's grandest Gothic cathedrals and,

among the museums, the unusual l'Art Brut collection stands out. Sports fans will love the Musée Olympique. Throughout the year Lausanne's citizens are treated to a busy arts calendar.

History

The Romans first set up camp on the lake at Vidy, a key halt on the route from Italy to Gaul that came to be known as Lousonna. In the face of an invasion by the Alemanni in the 4th century AD, Lousonna's inhabitants fled to the hilly inland site that became the heart of medieval Lausanne.

In 1529 Guillaume Farel, one of Calvin's followers, arrived in town preaching the Reformation but it wasn't until Bern occupied the city (not a shot was fired) seven years later that the Catholics were obliged to take notice.

From the 18th century, Lausanne exerted a fascination over writers and free-thinkers, attracting such characters as Voltaire, Dickens, Byron and TS Eliot (who wrote *The Waste Land* here).

Lausanne, with only 10,000 inhabitants, became capital of the Vaud canton in 1803. The city began to take on its present appearance with rapid development occurring from the latter half of the 19th century.

Today, Lausanne is a busy, vibrant city. Home to the Federal Tribunal, the highest court in the country, the International Olympic Committee (IOC), Tetra Pak and the multinational tobacco conglomerate Philip Morris, it also boasts a fairly boisterous wining and dining scene.

Orientation

The *Vieille Ville* (Old Town), with its winding, hilly streets topped by the cathedral, is north of the train station. Busy Rue Centrale runs along the valley that separates the *Vieille Ville* from another hill topped by Pl St François and its church. This square is the main hub for local transport, and off it to the east runs the shopping boulevard of Rue de Bourg. One of the country's top addresses in the 19th century (and on the Swiss version of Monopoly), it lost some of its class with the arrival of fast-food joints and poor renovation. Just west and downhill from Pl St François is Flon, an area of formerly derelict late 19th-century warehouses now partly taken over by a cinema

LAKE GENEVA & VAUD

LAUSANNE

0 — 300 m
0 — 0.2 miles

INFORMATION

Canton de Vaud Tourist Office	**1** B6
Lausanne Tourisme Tourist Office	**2** B6
STA Travel	**3** C4

SIGHTS & ACTIVITIES

Boat & Pedalo Hire	**4** B6
Fondation de l'Hermitage	**5** D1
Musée de l'Art Brut	**6** B1
Musée de l'Elysée	**7** C5
Musée Olympique	**8** C6
Sailing School	**9** B6

SLEEPING

Hôtel Beau-Rivage Palace	**10** C6
Hôtel du Port	**11** B6
Lausanne GuestHouse	**12** B4
Le Château d'Ouchy	**13** B6

EATING

Café de Grancy	**14** B4
Café du Vieil Ouchy	**15** B6

ENTERTAINMENT

Cinémathèque Suisse	**16** B3
Le V.O. et L'Ar'Lov Jazz Café	**17** C1
Palais de Beaulieu	**18** B1

TRANSPORT

CGN	**19** B6
Hertz	**20** C1

See Central Lausanne Map (p80)

LAKE GENEVA & VAUD

complex, art galleries, trendy shops, restaurants and bars. The city long ago enveloped the picturesque lakeside village of Ouchy.

Information

BOOKSHOP
With a broad selection of material on Switzerland and books in English, **Librairie Payot** (Map p80; ☎ 021 341 33 31; Pl Pépinet 4) is one of the best bookshop chains in French-speaking Switzerland.

INTERNET ACCESS
The city provides Wi-Fi hotspots (at Sfr0.30 a minute!) around town: Flon, Pl de la Palud, Pl St François, Pl de la Riponne, Pl du Port, Pl de la Navigation and Parc Mon Repos. You pay when you log on. **Fragbox** (Map p80; ☎ 021 311 89 69; www.fragbox.com; Rue de la Tour 3; per hr Sfr5; 🕙 9am-11.30pm Mon-Fri, 1.30-11.30pm Sat, 1.30-10pm Sun) is aimed at gamers but they have high-speed Internet connections.

LAUNDRY
You can wash those dirty socks and jeans at **Quick Wash** (Map p80; Blvd de Grancy 44; 🕙 8.30am-8.30pm Mon-Fri, 9am-8.30pm Sat & Sun). It costs about Sfr10 to wash and dry a load.

MEDICAL SERVICES
Lausanne's main hospital is the **Centre Hospitalier Universitaire Vaudois** (CHUV; Map p80; ☎ 021 314 11 11; Rue du Bugnon 46).

MONEY
Your first financial port of call is the **exchange office** (🕙 8am-7pm) in the train station. Otherwise, the city centre is full of banks. The **Banque Cantonale Vaudoise** (Map p80; Pl St François 10) has branches with ATMs all over town.

POST
The central **post office** (Map p80; Pl St François 15; 🕙 7.30am-6.30pm Mon-Fri, 8am-noon Sat) is handy. The house in which Edward Gibbon wrote much of *The History of the Decline and Fall of the Roman Empire* once stood on this site. The **main post office** (Map p78; Ave de la Gare 43) has extended hours at emergency counters.

TOURIST INFORMATION
There are two branches of the **Lausanne Tourisme tourist office** (☎ 021 613 73 73; www.lausanne-tourisme.ch). The **office** (Map p80; Pl de la Gare 9;

🕙 9am-7pm) in the train station is handiest for new arrivals. The other **office** (Map p78; Pl de la Navigation 4; 🕙 9am-6pm, 9am-8pm Apr-Sep) is next door to the Ouchy metro station. Ask about the Lausanne Card (Sfr15, valid for two days), which includes free public transport, 20% to 30% discounts on museums and discounts in some shops and restaurants.

City hall runs **InfoCité** (Map p80; ☎ 021 315 25 55; www.lausanne.ch/infocite; Pl de la Palud 2; 🕙 7.45am-noon & 1.15-5pm Mon-Fri). It has material on upcoming events in the city.

TRAVEL AGENCIES
The budget travel agency **STA Travel** (Map p78; ☎ 058 450 48 50; Blvd de Grancy 20) has several branches in the city.

Sights & Activities

CATHEDRAL & AROUND
The Gothic **Cathédrale de Notre Dame** (Map p80; 🕙 7am-7pm Mon-Fri Apr-Sep, 7am-5pm Oct-Mar), arguably the finest in Switzerland, stands proudly at heart of the *Vieille Ville*. Raised in the 12th and 13th centuries on the site of earlier, humbler churches, it lacks the lightness of French Gothic buildings but is remarkable nonetheless. Pope Gregory X, in the presence of Rudolph of Habsburg (the Holy Roman Emperor) and an impressive following of European cardinals and bishops, consecrated the church in 1275.

Although touched up in parts in succeeding centuries (notably the main façade, which was added to the original to protect the interior against ferocious winds), the building is largely as it was. The tiers of statues (mostly copies of the originals) around the entrance peer down at you with a chiding severity.

Inside, the most striking decoration is the 13th-century **rose window** in the south transept. The unusual geometric patterns comprise images relating to the seasons, signs of the Zodiac and the elements.

Just opposite the south flank of the cathedral are two minor museums. The **Musée Historique de Lausanne** (Map p80; ☎ 021 315 41 01; www.lausanne.ch/mhl; Pl de la Cathédrale 4; adult/student Sfr8/free; 🕙 11am-6pm Tue-Thu, 11am-5pm Fri-Sun Sep-Jun, 11am-6pm Mon-Thu, 11am-5pm Fri-Sun Jul & Aug) traces the city's history, and the **Musée de Design et d'Arts Appliqués Contemporains** (Map p80; ☎ 021 315 25 30; www.mudac.ch; Pl de la Cathédrale 6; adult/child/student Sfr8/free/5; 🕙 11am-6pm Tue-Sun Sep-Jun, 11am-6pm daily Jul & Aug) is a centre of modern design

LAKE GENEVA & VAUD

that frequently holds intriguing temporary exhibitions.

VIEILLE VILLE (OLD TOWN)

About 200m north of the Cathédrale stands the haughty, turreted **Château St Maire** (Map p80). This 15th-century castle was once the residence of the bishops of Lausanne and now houses government offices. In the streets between the cathedral and castle are several tempting eateries.

In front of the main entrance to the cathedral, a covered timber stairway leads down to Rue Pierre Viret, from where two more stairways lead further downhill, one to the modern Pl de la Riponne and the other to

CENTRAL LAUSANNE

INFORMATION		Palais de Rumine...........................16 B2	XIIIeme Siècle..............................31 C2
Banque Cantonale Vaudoise..............1 C3		Tour de l'Ale................................17 A1	
Centre Hospitalier Universitaire			**ENTERTAINMENT**
Vaudois.......................................2 D1		**SLEEPING**	Chorus..32 D3
Fragbox..3 B1		Hôtel des Voyageurs....................18 B2	D-Club...33 B2
InfoCité...4 C2		Hôtel Elite...................................19 B3	L'Atelier Volant............................34 A2
Lausanne Tourisme Tourist Office.....5 A4			Lecaféthéâtre...............................35 A2
Librairie Payot...............................6 B2		**EATING**	Loft Electroclub............................36 A2
Main Post Office............................7 B4		Brasserie Lausanne-Moudon...........20 C1	MAD – Moulin à Danse..................37 A2
Post Office....................................8 B3		Café de l'Hôtel de Ville.................21 B2	Opéra de Lausanne.......................38 C3
Quick Wash...................................9 A4		Café Romand...............................22 B3	Trixx Club.............................(see 37)
		Café-Restaurant du Vieux Lausanne.23 C2	
SIGHTS & ACTIVITIES		Le Vaudois..................................24 B2	**SHOPPING**
Cathédrale de Notre Dame.............10 C2			Globus..39 C2
Château St Maire..........................11 C1		**DRINKING**	La Ferme Vaudoise.......................40 B2
Église de St François.....................12 B3		Bar Tabac....................................25 C3	
Hôtel de Ville...............................13 B2		Café Luna....................................26 B2	**TRANSPORT**
Musée Cantonal des Beaux Arts.....(see 16)		Giraf Bar.....................................27 C2	Avis..41 B3
Musée de Design et d'Arts		Louis...28 A2	Enzo Location..............................42 A1
Appliqués Contemporains...........14 C2		Paparazzi.....................................29 C1	Europcar......................................43 A3
Musée Historique de Lausanne.......15 C2		Pinte Besson................................30 B2	Lausanne Roule............................44 A2

TEN O'CLOCK & ALL IS WELL!

Some habits die hard. From the height of the Cathédrale's bell tower, a *guet* (night watchman) still calls the hours into the night, from 10pm to 2am. Four times after the striking of the hour he calls out: *C'est le guet! Il a sonné dix, il a sonné dix!* (Here's the night watchman! It's 10 o'clock, it's 10 o'clock!). In earlier times this was a more serious business, as the *guet* kept a look out for fires around the town and other dangers. He was also charged with making sure the townsfolk were well behaved and the streets quiet during the solemn moments of church services.

medieval **Pl de la Palud** (Map p80). The latter's name suggests that this 9th-century market square was originally bogland. For five centuries it has been home to the city government, now housed in the 17th-century **Hôtel de Ville** (town hall; Map p80). The column with the allegorical figure of Justice that presides over the fountain dates from 1585, or rather it pretends to – the original is actually in the Musée Historique de Lausanne.

Rue du Pont descends from the eastern end of Pl de la Palud to Rue Centrale, which you cross to climb Rue St François up to the square of the same name. The name comes from the church, **Église de St François** (Map p80), which today is a bit of a hybrid but in the beginning formed part of a 13th-century Franciscan monastery. You can admire some restored frescoes inside. It is hard to imagine that the church and monastery once stood amid peaceful green fields! Rue de Bourg, off to the east, was for centuries home to the privileged bourgeoisie.

About 200m west of Pl de la Riponne stands the only surviving vestige of medieval Lausanne's defensive walls. The cylindrical **Tour de l'Ale** (Map p80), tucked away at the end of Rue de la Tour, was built in 1340 at the extreme western point of the medieval suburb of Ale. That we can admire the tower at all is due to those townspeople who opposed demolition plans in 1903.

MUSÉE DE L'ART BRUT

This extraordinary **collection** (Map p78; ☎ 021 315 25 70; www.artbrut.ch; Ave des Bergières 11-13; adult/child/student & senior Sfr8/free/5; ☺ 11am-6pm Tue-Sun Sep-Jun,

11am-6pm Jul & Aug), put together by French artist Jean Dubuffet, opened in 1976 in what was a late 18th-century country mansion.

Brut means crude or rough, and that's what you get. None of the artists had training but all had something to express. A few were quite mad, many (justly or otherwise) spent time in mental asylums or were plain eccentric. Their works offer a striking variety, and at times surprising technical capacity and an often inspirational view of the world.

There are sculptures made out of broken plates and discarded rags, faces made out of shells, sculptures in wood, paintings, sketches and much more. A wooden wall shown upstairs was taken from an asylum cell where Clément Fraisse carved designs with a broken spoon and, after that was confiscated, the handle of his chamber pot. Edmund Monseil, who spent most of WWII hiding in an attic, produced claustrophobic drawings on bits of paper, filled with glaring eyes surrounding the central figure or figures. The parade of works is as extensive as it is varied. To get there, take bus Nos 2 or 3 to Jomini stop.

PALAIS DE RUMINE

This neo-Renaissance pile was built to lord it over Pl de la Riponne in 1904 and, aside from the parliament of the Vaud canton, is home to several museums. This is where the Treaty of Lausanne was signed in 1923, finalising the break-up of the Ottoman Empire after WWI.

The main museum is the **Musée Cantonal des Beaux-Arts** (Fine Arts Museum; Map p80; ☎ 021 316 34 45; www.beaux-arts.vd.ch; Pl de la Riponne 6; adult/child/senior & student Sfr10/free/8, 1st Sun of the month free; ☺ 11am-5pm Fri-Sun, 11am-6pm Tue-Wed, 11am-8pm Thu), with many works by Swiss and foreign artists. The core of the collection is made up of works by landscape painter, Louis Ducros (1748–1810), and three other locals. The permanent collection is closed during the frequent temporary exhibitions.

The other **museum collections** (admission to each adult/child/senior & student Sfr4/free/2, 1st Sun of the month free; ☺ 11am-6pm Tue-Thu, 11am-5pm Fri-Sun) in the building cover natural history, zoology (with the longest – almost 6m – stuffed great white shark on show in the world), geology, coins, archaeology and history. The latter gives an overview of the history of the Vaud canton from the Old Stone Age to modern times.

MUSÉE OLYMPIQUE & AROUND

This **museum** (Map p78; ☎ 021 621 65 11; www
.museum.olympic.org; Quai d'Ouchy 1; adult/child/student
& senior Sfr14/7/9; ☯ 9am-6pm daily May-Sep, 9am-6pm
Tue-Sun Oct-Apr) is surprisingly interesting given
that its subject does not elicit universal interest. Housed in a lavish building in the
Parc Olympique, atop a tiered landscaped
garden, it tells the Olympic story from its
inception under Pierre de Coubertin to the
most recent competition using videos, ar-
chival film (usually including footage of the
most recent games), touch-screen computers and memorabilia from the games.

The **Musée de l'Elysée** (Map p78; ☎ 021 316 99
11; adult/child/student/senior Sfr8/free/4/6, 1st Sat of month
free; ☯ 11am-6pm) is worth keeping an eye on
if you like photography. It stages temporary
expositions that are often excellent.

THE LAKE

Lake Geneva (Lac Léman) provides plenty
of sporting opportunities. Contact the **sailing
school** (école de voile; ☎ 021 635 58 87; www.ecole-de
-voile.ch) at Ouchy for courses on windsurfing, water-skiing and sailing, and equipment rental for these activities. You can
also rent pedalos (Sfr20 an hour) and mo-
torboats (Sfr60 an hour) at stands in front
of the Château d'Ouchy. These stands also
offer water-skiing at Sfr35 for 15 minutes.

CGN (see p85) offers a range of boat
cruises.

In summer, head for the beach! The one
at **Vidy** is one of the nicer beaches, backed
by thick woods and parklands. Locals can
be seen cycling, rollerblading (in-line skat-
ing) or just strolling along the waterfront on
sunny weekends. Check out the remains of
Roman Lousonna and the adjacent **Musée Romain Lausanne-Vidy** (☎ 021 315 41 85; www.lausanne
.ch/mrv; Chemin du Bois de Vaux 24; adult/child/student
Sfr8/free/5; ☯ 11am-6pm Tue-Wed, 11am-8pm Thu, 11am-
6pm Fri-Sun), housed on the site of a Roman
villa and containing a modest collection of
ancient artefacts. It often stages temporary
expositions.

BOIS DE SAUVABELIN

Lausanne is remarkably blessed with green
spaces. Much of the lakeside is lined with
thick woodland and spacious picnic areas.
To the north stretches the bucolic expanse
of the **Bois de Sauvabelin** (Map p78). This
peaceful park is also home to the **Fondation**

THE REAL CAPTAIN NEMO

To the Swiss, he is the real Captain Nemo.
In 1960, Jacques Piccard (born 1922) and
a US Navy co-submariner took the deep-
sea submarine *Trieste*, originally designed
by his father, Auguste, down 10,916m to
the Marianas Trench in the South Pacific.
No-one has ever tried to repeat the feat,
and Piccard (father of the round-the-world
ballooner Bertrand) has dedicated most of
his life since to the defence of the sea and
lakes. In 2005 a lack of finance forced him
to reluctantly pull his 11-tonne *FA Forel*
mini-submarine out of the water for good.
In it he and his team had run scientific and
tourist excursions, principally on his home
turf in Lake Geneva.

---

de l'Hermitage (Map p78; ☎ 021 312 50 13; www
.fondation-hermitage.ch; Route du Signal 2; adult/child/
student/senior Sfr15/free/7/12; ☯ 10am-6pm Tue-Wed,
10am-6pm Fri-Sun & holidays, 10am-8pm Thu). This
charming 19th-century residence constantly
hosts high-calibre temporary art expositions. Take bus No 16 from Pl St François.

Tours

A guided **walking tour** (☎ 021 321 77 66; adult/
student & child/senior Sfr10/free/5; ☯ 10am & 3pm Mon-
Sat May-Sep) of the *Vieille Ville*, lasting one
to two hours, leaves from the front of the
Hôtel de Ville twice a day in spring and
summer. The tours are usually in French.
From July to mid-September there are free
guided visits of Cathédrale Notre Dame
four times a day, Monday to Friday.

Festivals & Events

In the first week of July the city hums with
performances all over town in the week-
long **Festival de la Cité** (www.festivalcite.ch).

For Switzerland's **national day** on 1 August, hire a pedalo (see left) in the early
evening and be ready on the lake for fireworks around 10pm.

The **Lausanne Marathon** (www.lausanne-mara
thon.com) is usually run towards the end of
October.

Sleeping

BUDGET

Lausanne GuestHouse (Map p78; ☎ 021 601 80 00;
www.lausanne-guesthouse.ch; Chemin des Épinettes 4;

dm Sfr30-35, s/d Sfr 89/100, without bathroom Sfr81/88; ℙ ☒ 🖳) An attractive mansion converted into quality backpacking accommodation near the train station. Many rooms have lake views. Hang out in the garden or terrace. Parking is Sfr10.

Camping de Vidy (☎ 021 622 50 00; www.camping lausannevidy.ch; Chemin du Camping 3; campsites per adult Sfr7.80, per tent Sfr9-19.20 depending on size of tent, per car Sfr3.50; ⊙ year-round) This campground is just to the west of the Vidy sports complex, on the lake. Take bus No 2 from Pl St François and get off at Bois de Vaux then walk underneath the motorway towards the lake.

MIDRANGE

Le Château d'Ouchy (Map p78; ☎ 021 616 74 51; www .chateaudouchy.com; Pl du Port 2; s/d up to Sfr175/280; ℙ ☒ 🖳) This is a whimsical castle (mostly built in the 19th century around the original medieval tower, complete with dungeon) enjoying a luxurious setting. Rooms are furnished in Louis XIII style but are showing signs of age.

Hôtel du Port (Map p78; ☎ 021 612 04 44; www .hotel-du-port.ch; Pl du Port 5; s/d Sfr182/234) A perfect location in Ouchy, just back from the lake, makes this a good choice. The better doubles look out across the lake and are spacious (about 20 sq m). Up on the 3rd floor are some lovely junior suites.

Hôtel Elite (Map p80; ☎ 021 320 23 61; www.elite -lausanne.ch; Ave Sainte Luce 1; s/d Sfr170/195; ℙ ☒ 🖳) A central family-run hotel set in quiet grounds with good-sized, comfortable rooms, decorated in subtle colours and equipped with cable TV. Some have a shower, others a full bath. Those with balcony enjoy pleasant views across the city.

Hôtel des Voyageurs (Map p80; ☎ 021 319 91 11; www.voyageurs.ch; Rue Grand St Jean 19; s/d Sfr200/250; ℙ 🖳) A handily located lodging for the historic centre of Lausanne, this hotel has comfortable if plain rooms. A nice touch is the free wi-fi throughout the premises.

TOP END

Hôtel Beau-Rivage Palace (Map p78; ☎ 021 613 33 33; www.beau-rivage-palace.ch; Pl du Port 17-19; s/d Sfr410/470; ℙ ☒ 🖳 🕮) Easily the most stunningly located hotel in town and one of only two five-star options, this place has it all. A beautifully maintained, early 19th-century mansion set in immaculate grounds, the hotel offers rooms with magnificent lake

and Alp views, a wellness centre and three restaurants.

Eating

Café de l'Hôtel de Ville (Map p80; ☎ 021 312 10 12; Pl de la Palud 10; ⊙ 9am-6pm Sun & Tue, 9am-11.30pm Wed-Sat) Grab one of the tiny, wobbly tables in summer or squeeze inside on a cold winters' day in this most congenial café in central Lausanne. It is ideal for a hot chocolate and languid read of the paper, surrounded by the buzz of animated conversation.

Café-Restaurant du Vieux Lausanne (Map p80; ☎ 021 323 53 90; Rue Pierre Viret 6; meals Sfr50-60; ⊙ Tue-Sat) An old stalwart, where good French and Swiss cooking comes in generous portions. Meat is the central theme, with dishes like *tartare de boeuf* (Sfr32) starring. In summer you can sit beneath the narrow pergola out the back.

Café Romand (Map p80; ☎ 021 312 63 75; Pl St François 2; mains Sfr17-25; ⊙ 11am-11pm Mon-Sat) A tatty sign leads you into an equally unpromising looking arcade. A few steps in and a push of the door takes you out of the 21st century and back to another era. The broad, somewhat sombre dining area littered with timber tables of all sizes attracts everyone from bankers to punks for hot traditional food, ranging from fine fondue to *cervelle au beurre noir* (brains in black butter). The kitchen operates all day, rare for this town.

Café de Grancy (Map p78; ☎ 021 616 86 66; www .cafédegrancy.ch; Ave du Rond Point 1; meals Sfr40-50; ⊙ 8am-midnight Mon & Wed-Thu, 8-1am Fri, 10-1am Sat, 10am-midnight Sun) An old-time bar resurrected with flair by young entrepreneurs, this spot has established itself as a hip hang-out with floppy lounges in the front, Wi-Fi, and a tempting restaurant out back. Wednesday is fondue night and brunch is offered on Saturday and Sunday.

Brasserie Lausanne-Moudon (Map p80; ☎ 021 329 04 71; Pl du Tunnel 20; mains Sfr25-40; ⊙ Mon-Sat) Set on two floors overlooking the square, this restaurant offers such enticing dishes as *medaillons de filet d'autruche au poivre vert* (ostrich filet medallions with green pepper). They do a good *tarte tatin* (apple tart) too.

Café du Vieil Ouchy (Map p80; ☎ 021 616 21 94; Pl du Port 3, Ouchy; mains Sfr18-37; ⊙ Thu-Mon) A simple but charming location for fondue, rösti and other classics. Follow up with a meringue smothered in *crème double de la Gruyère* (double thick Gruyère cream). Opt

LAKE GENEVA & VAUD

for the timber-lined upstairs dining in winter and the sunny terrace in summer.

Le Vaudois (Map p80; ☎ 021 331 22 22; Pl de la Riponne 1; mains Sfr25-35) Classic local Swiss cuisine, concentrating on fondues and meat dishes like the nationwide fave, Zürich's *émincé de veau à la zurichoise* (thin slices of veal prepared in a creamy mushroom sauce).

Drinking

Louis (Map p80; ☎ 021 213 03 00; Pl de l'Europe 9, Flon; ☺ noon-2.30pm & 7-10.30pm) Wine-lovers flock to this place to quaff fine tipples from around Europe. Attached is a Mediterranean-style bistro for light meals and a swanky restaurant upstairs. Outside is an extensive deck terrace on Voie du Chariot.

XIIIeme Siècle (Map p80; ☎ 021 312 40 64; Rue Cité-Devant 10; ☺ 10pm-4am Tue-Sat) In a grand medieval setting with stone vaults and huge timber beams, this is a great place for a beer or six.

Giraf Bar (Map p80; ☎ 021 323 53 90; Escaliers du Marché; ☺ 9.30pm-1am Tue-Thu, 9.30pm-2am Fri & Sat) This tiny smoke-filled bar fills up on a Friday and Saturday night. The giraffe-skin motif is repeated inside on lampshades and the music can reach back to the 1980s.

Pinte Besson (Map p80; ☎ 021 312 59 69; Rue de l'Ale 4; ☺ 11.30am-2.30pm & 6-11pm Mon-Sat) The city's oldest tavern has been serving up local wines to Lausannois punters since 1780. The place oozes the atmosphere of another age and makes no concessions to modern modishness. Squeeze in for a round of fondue and wine or just drop by for a couple of evening ales.

Bar Tabac (Map p80; ☎ 021 312 33 16; Rue Beau Séjour 7; ☺ 7am-9pm Mon-Wed, 7-1am Thu & Fri, 9-2am Sat, 9am-3pm Sun) Like a spruced corner tavern of old, this is the kind of thing Hemingway probably had in mind when he spoke of a 'clean, well lighted place'. Squeaky timber floors lend warmth and punters engage in animated chat at tables around the L-shaped bar.

Paparazzi (Map p80; ☎ 078 853 17 66; Rue de la Barre 1; ☺ 6pm-4am Mon-Fri, 6pm-midnight Sun) A dimly lit, classy lounge bar where, to start the evening, you can taste a variety of Italian wines or, if you arrive later, take a stronger drink and throw yourself into a comfy couch till late.

Café Luna (Map p80; ☎ 021 329 08 46; Pl de l'Europe 7; ☺ 4pm-1am Tue-Thu, 4pm-2am Fri, 2pm-2am Sat) It's a spacious, modern bar, with all angular dark furniture, huge, saucer-like suffused lights hanging from the ceiling and DJs

spinning all sorts of sounds from Thursday to Saturday.

Entertainment

Lausanne is one of the busier night-time cities in Switzerland, attracting young punters from as far off as Ticino and all over the western half of the country. In some bars you will find a handy free listings booklet, *What's Up* (www.whatsupmag.ch). Tickets for many shows can be bought in advance from **Ticketcorner** (☎ 084 880 08 00; www.ticketcorner .ch) or **Resaplus** (☎ 090 055 23 33; www.resaplus.ch).

LIVE MUSIC

Chorus (Map p80; ☎ 021 323 22 33; www.chorus.ch; Ave Mon Repos 3; admission free-Sfr35; ☺ 9pm-2am Thu-Sat) The appropriately dark and sometimes smoky ambience is perfect for local and international stars at Chorus, one of Lausanne's top jazz venues. It has food too.

Le V.O. et L'Ar'Lov Jazz Café (Map p78; ☎ 021 311 17 16; Pl du Tunnel 11; ☺ 5pm-4am) This venue, with red and pink low lighting, pulls in punters from all over town for tipples and occasional live music. It makes a good late night alternative to clubbing.

The Flon area is home to a number of fun venues.

Lecaféthéâtre (Map p80; ☎ 021 323 37 73; Rue de Genève 10; ☺ Tue-Sat) A hip yellow-hued cavern where a mixed crowd gathers for all sorts of live gigs (from jazz to turbo-folk), often free and starting around 10pm.

L'Atelier Volant (Map p80; ☎ 021 624 84 28; www .ateliervolant.ch; Rue des Côtes-de-Montbenon 12; ☺ 10pm-4am Thu-Sat) Like most of the buildings around this area, this venue is gaily painted and hard to miss. Salsa is a big theme on the 1st floor, but there are more mainstream hits on the ground floor and reggae on the 2nd floor.

CLUBS

MAD – Moulin à Danse (Map p80; ☎ 021 340 69 69; www.mad.ch; Rue de Genève 23; admission up to Sfr25; ☺ 11pm-4am Tue-Sun) With five floors of entertainment, MAD really is a crazy sort of place. Music themes can range from anything to trance to tranquil. Sunday is gay night (see opposite).

Amnésia (Map p78; ☎ 021 619 06 50; www.amnesia club.ch; Ave E Dalcroze 9; admission Sfr20; ☺ 11pm-5am) This place packs them in down on the lake. Apart from the club proper (with four dance floors) you can get limbered up in one of three attached bars beforehand and, in summer, get a snack in the restaurant on the beach (both open to 2am, May to October). Amnésia also organises occasional gay party nights.

D-Club (Map p80; ☎ 021 321 38 47; www.dclub.ch; Rue du Grand Pont 4; admission Sfr20-35; ☒ 10pm-5am Wed-Sat) D-Club is a heaving club where the DJs spin funk to house, especially the latter in all its latest sub-forms. Theme nights change regularly. To get here take the stairs down from Rue du Grand Pont and turn right before descending all the way into Pl Centrale.

Loft Electroclub (Map p80; ☎ 021 311 63 64; www .loftclub.ch; Pl Bel-Air 1; admission up to Sfr20; ☒ 11pm-4am Wed-Sat) Loft, a predominantly red bar and dance space just one level down the stairs of the Tour Bel-Air building, is another popular late-night option.

GAY VENUES

Trixx Club (admission free; ☒ 10pm-4am Sun) MAD hosts Trixx Club on Sunday night, *the* big club night for gays and lesbians throughout western Switzerland. Over the five floors is one dedicated to gals and another to guys.

CINEMA

Some of the cinemas around town show original language movies (watch for those marked 'vo' in the listings section of *24 Heures*).

Cinémathèque Suisse (Map p78; ☎ 021 331 01 00; www.cinematheque.ch; Allée E Ansermet 3, Casino de Montbenon) For classics and film cycles, head for this place, the seat of the Swiss film archives and the location of a fine café and restaurant.

THEATRE, OPERA & CLASSICAL MUSIC

Lausanne has a rich theatre scene for most of the year. Listings appear in the local paper *24 Heures*. Otherwise, pick up information on upcoming events at the InfoCité (see p79).

Palais de Beaulieu (Map p78; ☎ 021 643 21 11; Ave des Bergières 10) This venue stages concerts, operas and ballets. Lausanne has its own chamber orchestra and the renowned Rudra Béjart Ballet company.

Opéra de Lausanne (Map p80; ☎ 021 310 16 00; www.opera-lausanne.ch; Ave du Théâtre 12) Runs a season rich in events from September to May. Classics of opera alternate with classical music concerts and one-off presentations

of world music. Tickets can cost from Sfr15 to Sfr130 depending on the performance and seats.

Shopping

Rue de Bourg is lined with boutiques and jewellery stores. Otherwise head for Pl de la Palud and the surrounding pedestrian streets, where you will find department stores, fashion boutiques, wine and food speciality stores.

La Ferme Vaudoise (Map p80; ☎ 021 351 35 55; Pl de la Palud 5) This store sells an interesting array of cheeses, sweets, liqueurs and local farm produce.

Globus (Map p80; ☎ 021 342 90 90; Rue du Pont 5) The deli on the ground floor of Globus is full of costly Swiss and foreign goodies.

For grunge clothing and bargains away from the snooty central stores, hunt around the Flon, where you might also want to pop into the art galleries.

On Wednesday and Saturday mornings (6am to 2.30pm), produce markets set up on Rue de Bourg, Pl de la Palud and a couple of the other pedestrian streets around the square.

Getting There & Away

TRAIN

Three to four trains an hour run to/from Geneva (Sfr20, 35 to 50 minutes) and its airport (Sfr24, 45 to 60 minutes). One or two an hour travel to/from Bern (Sfr30, 60 to 70 minutes). Up to four trains an hour run to Yverdon-les-Bains (Sfr14.20, 20 to 45 minutes).

The station has a **left luggage service** (small/ big items per day Sfr4/7; ☒ 7am-8.30pm Mon-Sat, 9am-12.30pm & 1.30-7.30pm Sun). The **train information office** (☒ 8.30am-6.45pm Mon-Fri, 9am-5pm Sat) is close by.

BOAT

The company **CGN** (Map p78; ☎ 084 881 18 48; www.cgn.ch; Ave de Rhodanie 17) runs boats from Ouchy to destinations around Lake Geneva. From late May to late September there are frequent departures to all resorts, including the French side. There are no car ferries.

Up to 14 boats daily shuttle to and from Evian-les-Bains (France) in July and August (Sfr16/27.20 one way/return in 2nd class, 40 minutes), dropping to seven to nine boats the rest of the year. You can take less-frequent boats to places like Montreux

LAKE GENEVA & VAUD

(Sfr20.60, 1½ hours) and Geneva (Sfr34.80, about 3½ hours). A day pass to go anywhere on the lake costs Sfr55 (Sfr74 in 1st class).

CAR & MOTORCYCLE

Several motorways link Lausanne to Geneva and Yverdon-les-Bains (A1), Martigny (A9) and Bern (A9 then A12). Car-rental companies include **Avis** (Map p80; ☎ 021 340 72 00; Ave de la Gare 50), **Hertz** (Map p80; ☎ 021 312 53 11; Pl du Tunnel 17) and **Europcar** (Map p80; ☎ 021 319 90 40; Ave Louis Ruchonnet 2). **Enzo Location** (Map p80; ☎ 021 647 47 47; Ave de Beaulieu 8) offers a deal for Sfr20 a day plus 20c per kilometre.

Getting Around

Buses and trolley buses service most destinations (Sfr1.80 up to three stops, Sfr2.80 unlimited stops in central Lausanne for one hour, Sfr8 for 24-hour pass in central Lausanne). The Métro connects Ouchy with Gare (train station) and Flon (same prices as the buses). A second line is being built from Ouchy to Épalinges, in the northern suburbs.

Parking in central Lausanne is a headache. In blue zones you can park for free (one-hour limit) with a time disk (see p330). Most white zones are meter parking. Costs vary but can rise to Sfr2 an hour with a two-hour limit. The lower end of Ave des Bains is one of the few streets with some free parking spots.

If you need a taxi, call ☎ 080 080 58 05 or ☎ 084 481 08 10. A short ride from the train station to a central hotel will cost Sfr15 to Sfr20.

You can 'hire' bicycles (which carry advertising) for free from **Lausanne Roule** (Map p80; ☎ 021 312 31 09; www.lausanneroule.ch; Côtes de Montbenon 16) at Voie du Chariot in the Flon area. The bikes are available from 7.30am to 9.30pm, April to October. You leave a Sfr20 refundable deposit and ID. If you bring it back late, there's a Sfr10 fine and Sfr20 for each successive day.

AROUND LAUSANNE
La Côte

The coast between Lausanne and Geneva (known simply as The Coast) is sprinkled with fantasy castles, imposing palaces and immaculately maintained medieval towns. More than half of the Canton de Vaud's wine, mostly white, is produced along here. The towns along La Côte are on the train route between Lausanne and Geneva and some can be reached by CGN steamers (fares from Lausanne to Morges are Sfr12.60, Rolle Sfr19.40 and Nyon Sfr26.40).

LAUSANNE TO ROLLE

A pleasant walk west of Lausanne (about 6km from Ouchy) brings you to **St Sulpice**, a semi-suburban settlement whose jewel is the Romanesque church of the same name by the lake. A handful of restaurants are well placed to alleviate hunger. Take bus No 2 from Pl St François and change to bus No 30 at Bourdonette.

Some 12km west of Lausanne, the first town of importance is the wine-growing centre of **Morges**. Towering over its port is the 13th-century **Château** (☎ 021 316 09 90; Pl du Port; adult/child/student/senior Sfr7/free/5/6; ◷ 10am-5pm Tue-Sun Jul & Aug, 10am-noon & 1.30-5pm Mon-Fri, 1.30-5pm Sat & Sun Sep-Jun), built by the Savoy Duke Louis in 1286. Today it houses a trio of museums, among them the **Musée Militaire Vaudois** (stuffed with weapons and uniforms) and the **Musée de la Figurine Historique**, where 8000 toy soldiers are on parade! The town, which likes to sell itself as the 'flower of the lake', hosts a tulip festival from April to May.

Along the 26km stretch to the next major town, Nyon, are: the old village of **St Prex**, its centuries-old mansions bursting with the colour of creeping ivy and flower boxes; the stout **Château d'Allaman** (☎ 021 807 38 05; ◷ 2-6pm Wed-Sun), which houses the country's grandest treasure chest of antiques (ranging from carpets and furniture to ceramics and puppets, and covering styles from Gothic to Louis-Philippe and Biedermeier) that you can admire and (purse permitting) purchase; and **Rolle**, which also boasts a lakeside 13th-century Savoy castle (closed).

NYON TO COPPET

Nyon, of Roman origin but with a partly Celtic name (the 'on' comes from *dunon*, meaning fortified enclosure), is a busy lake town (population 16,330) at whose heart is a glistening-white, five-towered **château**. The castle was started in the 12th century and modified 400 years later. It houses the town's **historical museum** (due to reopen during mid-2006). Nearby, in what was a 1st-century basilica, the multimedia display of the **Musée Romain** (☎ 022 361 75 91; Rue Maupertuis; ◷ 10am-noon & 2-6pm Tue-Sun Apr-Oct, 2-

6pm Tue-Sun Nov-Mar) gives some insight into Nyon's Roman beginnings as the Colonia Iulia Equestris. Nyon also offers a wealth of lakeside dining, from fondue to Thai.

The town's **Paléo Festival** (☎ 022 365 10 10; www .paleo.ch) is an outdoor international music extravaganza (the biggest in Switzerland) lasting six days in late July. The event attracts more than 200,000 people for a feast of sounds ranging from rock through jazz to world music; tickets cost about Sfr50 per day at the venue (cheaper in advance).

Coppet, halfway between Nyon and Geneva, is a tightly packed medieval village with a handful of cosy hotels and restaurants. A short walk up the hill brings you to the 18th-century **château** (☎ 022 776 10 28; adult/student & senior Sfr8/6; ☯ 10am-noon & 2-6pm Jul & Aug, 2-6pm daily Easter-Jun & Sep), a rose-coloured stately home that belonged to the wily Jacques Necker, Louis XVI's banker and finance minister. The pile, sumptuously furnished in Louis XVI style, became home to Necker's daughter, Madame de Staël, after she was exiled from Paris by Napoleon. In her literary salons here she entertained the likes of Edward Gibbon and Lord Byron.

Lutry & Cully

About 4km east of central Lausanne, Lutry (population 8450) is a captivating village. Founded in the 11th century by French monks, it is perfect for an afternoon wander. The central **Église de St Martin et St Clément** was built in the early 13th century. A short way north is the modest **château**. Stroll along the slightly twee main street, lined with art galleries and antique stores. On the last weekend of September the town celebrates the annual wine harvest with parades and tastings.

The **Caveau du Singe Vert** (Green Monkey Cellar; ☎ 021 866 16 26; Grand Rue 38) hosts a couple of live gigs a month. Another good place for concerts, especially *chanson française* (French classics) is **Esprit Frappeur** (☎ 021 793 12 01; www.espritfrapeur.ch; Villa Mégroz, Ave du Grand Pont 20; admission up to Sfr50; ☯ 7.30pm-2am Tue-Sat, 5pm-midnight Sun). Bus No 9 runs to Lutry from Pl St François in Lausanne.

Five kilometres east of Lutry, the wine town of Cully (population 1800) is home to one of the country's finest hotels. The **Auberge du Raisin** (☎ 021 799 21 31; www.relaischateaux.ch/raisin; Pl de l'Hôtel de Ville 1; d Sfr350, apt Sfr490-580) started taking in weary travellers in the 15th century.

You have a choice of exquisite rooms and the restaurant (meals Sfr100 to Sfr200) is a gourmand's object of pilgrimage.

SWISS RIVIERA

Stretching east to Villeneuve, the Swiss Riviera rivals its French counterpart as a magnet for the rich and famous. The mild climate encourages palm trees and other subtropical flora to flourish barely an hour's drive from Alpine ski spots.

Lovers of panoramic train rides, steam trains and the like should inquire in either Vevey or Montreux about the many excursion options available in this area and to the Bernese Oberland.

VEVEY

pop 15,780 / elevation 385m

Vevey exudes a swanky ambience and has welcomed numerous celebrities, from Jean-Jacques Rousseau to Charlie Chaplin. Chaplin hung about for 25 years until his death in 1977. His former mansion in Corsier, the Manoir de Ban is destined to become a Chaplin museum in late 2007.

Orientation & Information

The hub of the town is Grande Pl, 250m to the left of the train station. The **tourist office** (☎ 084 886 84 84; www.montreux-vevey.com; ☯ 9am-6pm Mon-Fri, 9am-3pm Sat mid-May–mid-Sep, 8.30am-noon & 1-5.30pm Mon-Fri, 9am-noon Sat rest of year) is on the square in the La Grenette building.

Sights

The old streets east of Grande Pl and the lakeside promenades are worth exploring. Apart from that, the main entertainment comes from several museums.

The **Musée Suisse du Jeu** (Swiss Games Museum; ☎ 021 977 23 00; www.museedujeu.com; Rue du Château 11; adult/under 6/6-16yr/student & senior Sfr6/free/2/3; ☯ 11am-5.30pm Tue-Sun Mar-Oct, 2-5pm Tue-Sun Nov-Apr) is certainly the most amusing. The games are arranged according to themes – educational, strategic, simulation, skill and chance, and you can play several (explanations are in French). The museum is in the Château de la Tour de Peilz. To get there, take trolley bus No 1 to Pl du Temple.

Nestlé, with its headquarters located in Vevey since 1814, runs the **Alimentarium** –

VINTNERS OF LAVAUX

The serried ranks of lush, green, vine terraces that carpet the steep slopes above Lake Geneva between Lausanne and Montreux belong to the Lavaux wine region, which produces 20% of the Canton de Vaud's wine.

The villages of Lutry, Villette, Cully, Calamin, Epesses (which, by the way, hosts one of the lake's few nudist beaches), Dézaley, St Saphorin, Chardonne and Riex are among the wine centres. The two main wine types are Calamin and Dézaley and most of the whites (about three-quarters of all production) are made with the Chasselas grape.

It is possible to walk through much of the Lavaux wine country. Starting in Lutry, you can follow trails that lead you through hamlets like Grandvaux and down to lakeside Cully. In each it is often possible to visit *caveaux*. They tend to open between 5pm to 9pm Friday through Sunday. You could even walk all the way to Chardonne, about four hours' walk depending on what sort of detours you make along the way. From there head to a lakeside town to pick up a train back to Lausanne.

From Lutry you have the option of catching the **Lavaux Express** (www.lavaux.com in French and German; adult/child Sfr10/5; ☉ May-Sep) one of those tractor-driven tourist trains that does several circuits along wine trails between Lutry and Cully. For more information consult the website.

Musée de l'Alimentation (Food Museum; ☎ 021 924 41 11; www.alimentarium.ch; Quai Perdonnet; adult/child/student & senior Sfr10/free/8; ☉ 10am-6pm Tue-Sun). Completely refurbished in 2002, the lakeside museum takes an entertaining look at food and nutrition, past and present.

Musée Jenisch (☎ 021 921 29 50; www.museejenisch.com; Ave de la Gare 2; adult/child up to 12/student/senior Sfr15/free/7.50/13; ☉ 11am-5.30pm Tue-Sun) exhibits Swiss art from the 19th and 20th centuries and has a special section on Oskar Kokoschka, the Viennese expressionist. Another section is dedicated to prints and engravings by artists ranging from Dürer and Rembrandt to Canaletto and Corot.

Musée Suisse de l'Appareil Photographique (☎ 021 925 21 40; www.cameramuseum.ch; Grand Pl; adult/child/student & senior Sfr8/free/6; ☉ 11am-5.30pm Tue-Sun) concentrates on the instruments rather than the images they produce. Other museums in Vevey cover such topics as wine-growing and the history of the town.

Vevey is the capital of the Lavaux wine-growing region and once every 20 to 25 years the wine-growers descend on the town to celebrate a huge **summer festival**. The last time was in 1999, so we'll be waiting a while for the next one!

Sleeping

Riviera Lodge (☎ 021 923 80 40; www.rivieralodge.ch; Pl du Marché 5; dm from Sfr31, d Sfr80; Ⓟ) This place is a fun, central location housed in a converted 19th-century mansion. The rooftop terrace offers great views and you can use the kitchen to keep eating costs down. Dorm rooms sleep from four to eight. A buffet breakfast is extra at Sfr8.

Hôtel De Famille (☎ 021 923 39 30; www.hotelfamille.ch; Rue des Communaux 20; s/d Sfr150/240, without bathroom Sfr85/150; Ⓟ 🅇 🅛 🅡) Modern rooms in this centrally located hotel offer the standard comforts, but you will also have access to a sauna and roof terrace for a little sunbathing in summer.

Hôtel des Trois Couronnes (☎ 021 923 32 00; www.hoteldestroiscouronnes.ch; Rue d'Italie 49; s/d from Sfr295/380; 🅡 🅛 🅇 Ⓟ) This is Vevey's leading hotel, an elegant pleasure dome that's been in business since the mid-19th century. The hotel's three floors open onto interior galleries, and the décor – full of marble, period furniture and antiques – is all class. It has long been the choice of royalty and names from Thomas Mann to Saint-Saëns.

Eating & Drinking

Le National (☎ 021 923 76 25; Rue du Torrent 9; meals Sfr30-40; ☉ 11am-midnight Sun-Tue, 11-1am Wed-Thu, 11-2am Fri & Sat) Run by a young and enthusiastic team, this is a great place to eat and drink. On one side is a hip bar with oddly leaning glass-topped tables and stools or, for the more lounge-inclined, spots by the window. On the other side is the restaurant, where you can enjoy a mix of international dishes.

Le Mazot (☎ 021 921 78 22; Rue du Conseil 7; mains Sfr23-38) In the heart of the old town, this is an institute of classic local cooking, dominated by steaks and horse meat filets in the special Mazot sauce (they're not letting out the secret recipe). You can dine on the ground floor or the 1st floor in a timeless setting.

Restaurant du Port (☎ 021 921 20 33; Rue d'Italie 23; mains Sfr20-40; ☒ Tue-Sun) Just west of the old centre, this spot is a three in one. The most characteristic is the cosy *pinte* (not a glass measure but a traditional Vaudois eatery and tavern), but you can opt for the more anonymous main dining area or sit out on terrace with lake views. Food ranges from lake fish to fondue.

Getting There & Away

Vevey is 15 to 25 minutes from Lausanne by train (Sfr6.60) and five minutes from Montreux (Sfr3). Trolley bus Nos 1 and 3 run from Vevey to Montreux (Sfr3.20) and on to Villeneuve (Sfr4.60).

AROUND VEVEY

A steam train chugs along the 3km track from Blonay to Chamby, where a train museum houses steam engines and machinery. Entry and the return trip cost Sfr16/8 per adult/child, but it only operates on Saturday afternoons and Sundays from early May to late October. On four or five Sunday afternoons in summer the steam train departs from Vevey (adult/child Sfr37/23.50).

Spots near Vevey with good views and walks are Les Pléiades (1360m), accessible by train, Chexbres, a stop on the summer 'wine train' that runs to Puidoux, and Mont Pélerin (1080m) which is accessible by funicular and has a panoramic tower, Plein Ciel. En route to Les Pléiades is Lally, where **Les Sapins** (☎ 021 943 13 95; www.les-sapins.ch; s/d Sfr80/140, d with bathroom Sfr160; Ⓟ 🖳 🔁) is a good choice for accommodation and food. The views south to the Alps are fabulous. It organises snowshoe hikes in winter, among other things.

MONTREUX & AROUND

pop 22,570 / elevation 385m

In the 19th century, writers, artists and musicians (Lord Byron and the Shelleys among them) flocked from all over Europe to this pleasing lakeside resort. It has remained a magnet ever since, its main drawcards being peaceful waterfront walks and the Château de Chillon.

Montreux is best known to music lovers for its annual summer jazz festival (going since 1967). In 1971, Montreux casino was

the stage for a rather different kind of gig. Frank Zappa was doing his thing when the casino caught fire, casting a pall of smoke over Lake Geneva and inspiring the members of Deep Purple to pen their classic rock number, *Smoke on the Water*.

Orientation & Information

The lakeshore is fronted by a mix of 19th-century hotels, restaurants and shops, while the *Vieux Quartier* is a small cluster of quiet streets around Rue du Pont, high uphill. From the train station, on Ave des Alpes, take the lift or stairs from opposite the post office down to the shore. Here you'll find the **tourist office** (☎ 084 886 84 84; www.montreux-vevey.com; ☒ 9am-6pm Mon-Fri, 10am-5pm Sat mid-May–mid-Sep, 9am-noon & 1-5.30pm Mon-Fri, 10am-2pm Sat mid-Sep–mid-May), whose staff will help book hotels – a must in festival time.

Sights & Activities

CHÂTEAU DE CHILLON

This extraordinary, oval-shaped **castle** (Map p76; ☎ 021 966 89 10; www.chillon.ch; adul/childt/student & senior Sfr10/5/8; ☒ 9am-6pm Apr-Sep, 9.30am-5pm Mar & Oct, 10am-4pm Nov-Feb) was brought to the attention of the world by Lord Byron, and the world has been filing past ever since – they say the castle receives more visitors than any other historical building in Switzerland.

Occupying a stunning position on Lake Geneva, the 13th-century fortress is a myriad of courtyards, towers and halls filled with arms, period furniture and artwork. The landward side is heavily fortified but lakeside it presents a gentler face as a princely residence. Chillon was largely built by the House of Savoy and then taken over by Bern's governors after Vaud fell to that canton. In the **Chapelle St Georges** are medieval frescoes. And don't miss the spooky Gothic dungeons.

Byron made the place famous with *The Prisoner of Chillon*, his 1816 poem about François Bonivard, thrown into the dungeon for his seditious ideas and freed by Bernese forces in 1536. Byron carved his name into the pillar to which Bonivard was supposedly chained. Painters William Turner and Gustave Courbet captured the castle's silhouette on canvas, while Jean-Jacques Rousseau, Alexandre Dumas and Mary Shelley were all moved to write about it.

The castle is a 45-minute walk along the lakefront from Montreux. Otherwise take

LAKE GENEVA & VAUD

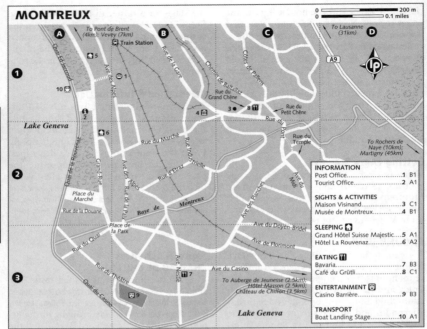

trolley bus No 1 (Sfr2.30), which passes by every 10 minutes.

MUSÉE DE MONTREUX

The **museum** (☎ 021 963 13 53; www.museemontreux .ch; Rue de la Gare 40; adult/child/student & senior Sfr6/ free/4; ☺ 10am-noon & 2-5pm Apr–early Nov) recounts the history of the town and locality. Displays range from a handful of Roman finds and coins through to period furniture, bathtubs and street signs. The streets inland and further uphill are the core of the original Old Town of Montreux and merit a wander far from the lake scene. The charming **Maison Visinand** (☎ 021 963 07 26; www.centreculturelmontreux.ch; Rue du Pont 32; ☺ 3-6pm Wed-Sun) is a cultural centre and theatre with regular exhibitions.

ROCHERS DE NAYE

A scenic railway from Montreux leads to this natural platform (2042m), from where you have remarkable views of Lake Geneva and the Alps. MOB trains cost Sfr49 return (Sfr55 in July and August, Sfr3 extra for steam trains).

SPAS

Montreux is a good place for a relaxing bath and beauty session. For a couple of suggestions on where to get the full works, turn to p47.

Festivals & Events

Montreux's best-known festival is **Montreux Jazz** (☎ 021 963 82 82; www.montreuxjazz.com) lasting two weeks in early July. Many free concerts take place every day, but count on spending around Sfr40 to Sfr100 for one of the big gigs. The music is not only jazz; past performers have included BB King, Paul Simon, Jamiroquai and Marianne Faithful.

The **Montreux–Vevey Music Festival** (☎ 090 080 08 00; www.septmus.ch; admission Sfr20-115) is a classical music fest (also known as Septembre Musical) held from late August to the end of September.

Sleeping

Auberge de Jeunesse (☎ 021 963 49 34; Passage de l'Auberge 8, Territet; dm from Sfr31; ☺ mid-Feb–mid-Nov; ▢) This modern, chirpy hostel is a 30-minute walk along the lake clockwise from

AUTHOR'S CHOICE

Hôtel Masson (☎ 021 966 00 44; www.hotel masson.ch; Rue Bonivard 5; s/d Sfr150/230 **P**) In 1829, this vintner's mansion was converted into a hotel. The old charm has remained intact and the hotel, set in magnificent grounds, is on the Swiss Heritage list of most beautiful hotels in the country. Just east of Montreux proper and back in the hills, it is best reached by taxi from Montreux centre, although you can walk it in about 30 minutes. It also has a small sauna and Jacuzzi for guests.

the tourist office (or take the local train to Territet or bus No 1). Dorms have two to eight beds.

Hôtel La Rouvenaz (☎ 021 963 27 36; www.montreux .ch/rouvenaz-hotel; Rue du Marché 1; s/d Sfr120/180; 🖵) A simple, family-run spot with its own Italian restaurant downstairs, you cannot get any closer to the lake or the heart of the action. The rooms are simple but pleasant and bright, and most have some sort of lake view.

Grand Hôtel Suisse Majestic (☎ 021 966 33 33; www.suisse-majestic.com; s/d Sfr200/280, with lake views Sfr250/330; **P**) With its two-tiered frontage and ranks of bright yellow awnings sheltering the balconies of those rooms looking out over the lake, this historic hotel (built in 1870) remains one of the most atmospheric on the waterfront. You can eat up the views on their terrace restaurant. Parking costs Sfr25.

Eating

Café du Grütli (☎ 021 963 42 65; Rue du Grand Chêne 8; mains up to Sfr28; 🕑 Tue-Sat) This eatery is hidden away in the old part of town and provides good home cooking, ranging from rösti with ham to hearty meat dishes and the inevitable fondue.

Bavaria (☎ 021 963 25 45; Ave du Casino 27; mains Sfr22-40; 🕑 Sun-Fri) The décor is a little 1970s, with horseshoe-shaped leather lounges gathered around some of the tables, but this is one of the rare spots in Montreux that you can get hearty, traditional cooking. Among the house specialities are a kaleidoscope of varieties of rösti, *fondue moitié-moitié* (literally 'half and half' cheese fondue, Sfr22), and entrecôte of…bison (Sfr38)! Wash them down with a range of Bavarian beers.

Pont de Brent (☎ 021 964 52 30; Route de Blonay; tasting menu Sfr180-240, mains Sfr40-80; 🕑 Tue-Sat) Set in a pretty country house, this is one of Switzerland's top restaurants and has three Michelin stars (one of only two in the country). A changing and imaginative menu is complemented by a fine wine list. It's northwest of Montreux in the hamlet of Brent, and is accessible by train.

Entertainment

Casino Barrière (☎ 021 962 83 83; www.casinodemon treux.ch; Rue du Théâtre 9; 🕑 11-3am Sun-Thu, 11-4am Fri & Sat) Resurrected in 2002, this casino has everything from slot machines to a pool (to cool off after burning off your millions).

Getting There & Away

From Lausanne, three trains an hour (Sfr9.80) take 20 to 35 minutes to reach Montreux. Scenic trains head up into the Bernese Oberland and Alps from Montreux (see p331). For boat services, see p73 and p85.

NORTHWESTERN VAUD

This part of the canton of Vaud is dominated by the Jura mountain chain and Lac de Neuchâtel.

YVERDON-LES-BAINS
pop 23,480 / elevation 437m

The Romans were the first to discover the healthy qualities of Yverdon's hot spa waters and since then the town has made its living from them. It's an enjoyable lakeside resort and Canton de Vaud's second-largest town.

Information

The **tourist office** (☎ 024 423 61 01; www.yverdon-les -bains.ch/tourisme; Ave de la Gare 1; 🕑 9am-6pm Mon-Fri, 9.30am-3.30pm Sat Jul & Aug, 9am-noon & 1.30-6pm Mon-Fri, 9.30am-3.30pm Sat May, Jun & Sep, 9am-noon & 1.30-6pm Mon-Fri Oct-Apr) has information on the town and surrounding area.

Sights & Activities

The Old Town core is clustered around the 13th-century **Château**, built by Peter II of Savoy. Inside, the **Musée du Château** (Musée d'Yverdon-les-Bains et Région; ☎ 024 425 93 10; adult/child/ student & senior Sfr8/4/7; 🕑 11am-5pm Jun-Sep, 2-5pm Oct-May) contains local prehistoric artefacts, arms, clothing and a Ptolemaic Egyptian mummy.

LAKE GENEVA & VAUD

Opposite the castle, the **Maison d'Ailleurs** (House of Elsewhere; ☎ 024 425 64 38; Pl Pestalozzi 14; www.ailleurs.ch; adult/child/student & senior Sfr7/4/5; 🕑 2-6pm Wed-Fri, noon-6pm Sat & Sun) is a science-fiction museum that features a mock-up of a spaceship, a room dedicated to HR Giger (of *Alien* fame) and masses of material dealing with the science fantasy worlds of figures ranging from Homer to Jules Verne and the present. The museum only opens when a temporary exhibition is on.

The lake offers the opportunity for various boat rides and other water activities, including windsurfing, water-skiing and sailing. Beaches stretch along 5km of the lakeside. One company that rents out boats, windsurfing kits and the like is **Les Vikings** (www.lesvikings.ch; Ave des Pins 34) at Yvonand, east of Yverdon along the lake.

SPAS

The water from the 14,000-year-old mineral springs starts 500m below ground. By the time it hits the surface it has picked up all sorts of salubrious properties from the layers of rock, and is particularly good for sufferers of rheumatism and respiratory ailments.

The **Centre Thermal** (☎ 024 423 02 32; www.cty .ch; 🕑 8am-10pm Mon-Fri, 9am-8pm Sat, Sun & holidays), the health complex off Ave des Bains, offers a wide range of treatments. Even if you feel fine you can enjoy bathing in indoor and outdoor pools (temperature 28° to 34°C) for Sfr16 for adults and Sfr10 for children. For Sfr25 you get access to the pools, saunas, hammams, a tropical shower, Japanese baths and a giant Jacuzzi.

Sleeping

Hôtel L'Ecusson Vaudois (☎ 024 425 40 15; www.ecu ssonvaudois.ch; Rue de la Plaine 29; s/d Sfr90/130; 🟢 💻) This hotel, with a ground-floor café, is the only central place. It has a handful of fresh, modernised rooms, some of which do not have their own bathroom and are a little cheaper.

Grand Hôtel des Bains (☎ 024 424 64 64; www .grandhotelyverdon.ch; Ave des Bains 22; s/d up to Sfr250 /444; 🅿 🟢 💻 🎦) The big daddy of them all, with all imaginable comforts and free entry to the thermal pools.

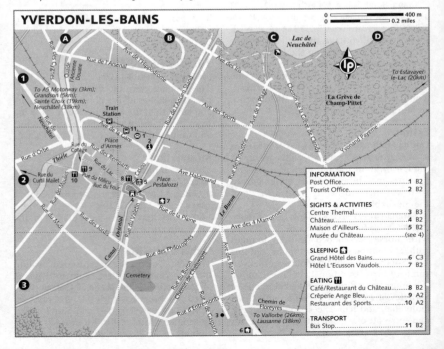

YVERDON-LES-BAINS

INFORMATION	
Post Office	1 B2
Tourist Office	2 B2

SIGHTS & ACTIVITIES	
Centre Thermal	3 B3
Château	4 B2
Maison d'Ailleurs	5 B2
Musée du Château	(see 4)

SLEEPING 🛏	
Grand Hôtel des Bains	6 C3
Hôtel L'Ecusson Vaudois	7 B2

EATING 🍴	
Café/Restaurant du Château	8 B2
Crêperie Ange Bleu	9 A2
Restaurant des Sports	10 A2

TRANSPORT	
Bus Stop	11 B2

Eating

Café/Restaurant du Château (☎ 024 425 49 62; Pl Pestalozzi 13; mains Sfr24-30) With its heavy dark timber beams and fine traditional meat and fish dishes, this classic mixes in a more modern tone with discreet furniture and lounge music. It also offers a limited pizza and pasta menu.

Restaurant des Sports (☎ 024 425 27 63; Rue du Milieu 47; mains Sfr25-35; ◯ lunch & dinner Tue-Sat, lunch Sun) Head upstairs for intimate dining at this straightforward but reliable place. The standard menu is limited to a few meat dishes, perch filets and the like. But it throws in a seasonal menu, which in autumn means game and snails.

Crêperie Ange Bleu (☎ 024 426 09 96; Rue du Collège 11; crepes Sfr7-10, salads Sfr10-13; ◯ Tue-Sun) If all the above sounds too heavy, pop by this cheerfully yellow diner. It's small and busy, with people packing in for the myriad versions of sweet and savoury crepes.

Getting There & Away

Regular trains run from Lausanne (Sfr14.20, 20 to 45 minutes). One or two an hour run to Neuchâtel (Sfr13.40, 20 minutes). An hourly train heads for Estavayer-le-Lac (Sfr6.60, 17 minutes).

AROUND YVERDON-LES-BAINS
Grandson

Grandson's stout, grey, 13th-century **Château** (☎ 024 445 29 26; adult/child/student & senior Sfr12/5/9; ◯ 8.30am-6pm) fell briefly to Charles the Bold in early 1476, but Swiss Confederate troops soon turned the tables and strung some of his routed Burgundian troops from the apple trees in the castle orchard.

The castle's **Musée d'Histoire** recounts the story of 1476 and other battles with dioramas, while the prize exhibit at its **Musée de l'Automobile** is Greta Garbo's white Rolls Royce.

Regular buses connect Yverdon with Grandson (Sfr2.60, 10 minutes). Or you could walk the 5km around the lake.

Sainte Croix
pop 4180 / elevation 1066m
This town high in the Jura Mountains has been hailed for its music boxes since the mid-19th century. The art of making these expensive items is documented in the **Centre International de la Méchanique d'Art** (☎ 024 454 77; Rue de l'Industrie 2; guided tour in French adult/child/student & senior Sfr12/7/10; ◯ 10.30am, 2pm, 3.30pm & 5pm Tue-Sun Jun-Aug, 2pm, 3.30pm & 5pm Tue-Sun Feb-May & Sep-Oct, 3pm Tue-Fri, 2pm, 3.30pm & 5pm Sat & Sun Nov-Jan). Music boxes contain a rotating spiked cylinder that bends and releases metal prongs, causing them to vibrate and hum melodiously. Some of the more elaborate boxes also incorporate miniature drums, bells and accordions. The best exhibits are the musical automata, such as the acrobats, a tiny Mozart and Pierrot the writer.

The town is otherwise none too scintillating, but makes a handy base for local winter sports. The highest point in the area is **Le Chasseron** (1607m), the focus for the area's downhill skiing and a two-hour walk from Sainte Croix. It provides a marvellous 360° panorama of the Alps, Lac de Neuchâtel and the Jura.

A local train runs from Yverdon (Sfr9.80, 36 minutes).

TO LAC DE JOUX

This little-visited corner of the canton to the north of Lac de Joux and its valley hides several gems. By car you could easily tour the area from Lausanne or Geneva in a day.

La Sarraz to Romainmôtier

From Lausanne take the N9 highway (not the motorway) towards La Sarraz. Its **castle** (☎ 021 866 64 23; tour of castle & museum adult/child/student & senior Sfr12/7/10; ◯ 1-5pm Tue-Sun Jun-Aug, 1-5pm Sat & Sun & holidays Easter-May & Sep-Oct), some of it dating from the 11th century, contains a museum devoted to the horse and carriage. From there follow a side road north to **Orbe** (where Nescafé was invented in 1938), which is interesting for the 13th-century **Tour Bernard** defensive tower and the **Musée de Mosaïques Romaines** (☎ 024 441 52 66; adult/child/student & senior Sfr4/2/3; ◯ 9am-noon & 1.30-5pm Mon-Fri, 1.30-5.30pm Sat & Sun Easter-Oct). The museum is a series of pavilions containing mosaics on the site of a 3rd-century Gallo-Roman villa, 1.5km north of town. In the first pavilion is the beautiful polychrome *mosaïque aux divinités*, which depicts the seven planetary gods (Jupiter, Saturn and co). The second one contains the *mosaïque du cortège rustique*, with several rural scenes including a man driving an ox-drawn cart.

From there it's 8km southwest to the hamlet of **Romainmôtier**, cupped in a lush green

LAKE GENEVA & VAUD

bowl of vegetation and wholly dominated by the Cluny order's **Abbatiale** (☎ 024 453 14 65; admission free; � 7am-8pm), a remarkable sandstone church whose origins reach to the 6th century. Upon and around its 11th-century Romanesque core were added new layers in higgledy-piggledy fashion over the ensuing centuries. Through the mixed Romanesque–Gothic entrance you step into the proud interior of the church, with its powerful pillars and faded frescoes. Of the couple of hotels and restaurants here, the pick is the lovely 17th-century **Hôtel au Lieutenant Baillival** (☎ 024 453 14 58; www.romainmotier.ch/publiinfo/baillival.html; s/d from Sfr100/160; ⓟ 🖳), full of antique furniture and rustic charm – call ahead to reserve one of the six rooms. It has its own restaurant.

Vallorbe to Lac de Joux

About 12km west along the N9 is the industrial town of **Vallorbe**. Its pleasant old centre astride the Orbe River is home to the **Musée du Fer et du Chemin de Fer** (Iron & Railway Museum; ☎ 021 843 25 83; adult/child/student Sfr10/6/9; ⓧ 9.30am-noon & 1.30-6pm Tue-Sun, 1.30-6pm Mon Apr-Oct, 9.30am-noon & 1.30-6pm Mon-Fri Nov-Mar), where you can see a blacksmith working at a traditional forge. Power for the furnace is derived from four large paddlewheels turning outside in the river. The railway section includes models and memorabilia. An hourly regional train from Lausanne to Vallorbe (Sfr16.20, 45 minutes) travels via La Sarraz. It makes a stop at Croy, from where it is just a short postal bus ride on to Romainmôtier (total trip Sfr15.20, 35 to 45 minutes).

A few kilometres outside Vallorbe is the underground **Fort Pré-Giroud** (Map p76; ☎ 021 843 25 83; adult/child/student & senior Sfr11/6/10; ⓧ noon-5.30pm Sat & Sun & holidays May-Oct), built in 1937 to ward off a possible attack from France. The seemingly unremarkable mountain chalet commands views across the Orbe Valley into France and below ground could accommodate 130 men. In its dormitories, canteens, kitchen, telephone exchange and infirmary now stand around 40 military mannequins. At the approaches are ranged artillery pieces and, down the hillside, five pillboxes. Bring warm clothing as the underground temperature is 8°C. The fort is a 40-minute walk from Vallorbe (follow the Fort 39-45 signs) or a nice drive through forests on a minor back road leading over the mountain ridge to Vaulion.

About 2km south of Vallorbe on the road to Lac de Joux at Mont d'Orzeires is **Juraparc** (☎ 021 843 17 35; www.juraparc.ch; adult/child Sfr4.50/3; ⓧ 9am-dusk Wed-Sun, 9am-6pm Mon-Tue), where North American bison roam about in the company of bears and wolves.

Shortly afterwards you reach the Col du Mont d'Orzeires pass and descend to Le Pont, a sleepy village at the northern end of the **Lac de Joux**. This is a quiet spot for water sports and the source of your dinnertime perch.

The main road south of the lake follows the Orbe river through Le Brassus and skirts the border on the French side (bring your passport). You could turn east at Le Brassus to climb to the Col du Marchairuz pass (1447m) and descend through pretty villages towards Lake Geneva.

ALPES VAUDOISES

The southeast corner of Vaud extends into a captivating Alpine nook. A five-day regional ski pass for the Alpes Vaudoises (Vaud Alps), including Les Diablerets glacier and Gstaad (see p175), costs Sfr225. Glacier skiing is an option in June and July and the hiking in summer is a dream. Contact the local tourist offices for chalets, apartments and B&B accommodation in advance.

AIGLE

pop 7670 / elevation 405m

A many-turreted castle surrounded by vineyards is the highlight of Aigle, the capital of the Chablais wine-producing region in southeast Vaud. The Chablais, which extends into neighbouring Valais, produces some of the country's best whites using the Chasselas grape.

The castle, on a gentle rise, is itself enough to induce you to stop by. Anyone with even a vague interest in wine will want to visit its **Musée de la Vigne et du Vin** (☎ 024 466 21 30; adult/child/student & senior Sfr9/5/6; ⓧ 10am-12.30pm & 2-6pm Tue-Sun Apr-Jun & Sep-Oct, 10am-6pm daily Jul & Aug). Two thousand years of wine-making are explained across 17 rooms. From July to September you can round off a visit with a free glass of local wine. Opposite the castle gates, the Maison de la Dîme houses the **Musée de l'Etiquette**, in which around 800 wine-bottle labels from around the world are displayed and explained. The naughty labels misappropriating names like 'champagne' are at times quite a laugh. You enter with the ticket from the Musée de la Vigne et du Vin.

There are several hotels should you wish to stay. Regular trains operate from Lausanne (Sfr14.20, 30 minutes) to Aigle via Montreux.

LEYSIN

pop 2780 / elevation 1350m

Leysin started life as a tuberculosis centre but is now a sprawling ski resort with 60km of runs. Many other sports are on offer, including a *via ferrata* – a vertical 'footpath' negotiated via cables and rungs. The **tourist office** (☎ 024 494 22 44; www.leysin.ch; Pl Large) is based in the New Sporting Centre. Take in the Alpine scenery from the revolving restaurant atop **Mt Berneuse** (2048m). The cable car costs Sfr20 return in summer, or Sfr37 for the lift and a day's skiing in winter.

Hiking Sheep (☎ 024 494 35 35; www.hikingsheep .com; dm/d Sfr30/80; P ☒ ☐) gets floods of accolades from happy backpackers. It's two minutes' walk from Grand Hotel station. It has a kitchen and good communal facilities. **Les Orchidées** (☎ 024 494 14 21; www.leysin.ch /orchidees; s/d Sfr80/140; P), a family hotel by Vermont station, has Alpine views and a decent restaurant.

To get to Leysin take the hourly cogwheel train that goes from Aigle (Sfr8.60, 30 minutes).

LES DIABLERETS

elevation 1150m

Overshadowed by the mountain of the same name (3209m), Les Diablerets is one of the key ski resorts in the Alpes Vaudoises. A number of fairly easy ski runs are open during June and July at **Glacier de Tsanfleuron** (3000m), which gives the Diablerets resort its recent official name, Glacier 3000. Whether you plan to ski or not, the views are fabulous.

Two cable cars run up to the glacier from the valley floor, both are linked to the village by bus: starting from Reusch or Col du Pillon you get to Cabane des Diablerets, where a further cable car whisks you almost to the summit at Scex Rouge. To ski from here all the way back down to Reusch is an exhilarating 2000m descent over 14km.

A one-day ski pass that takes in Les Diablerets, Villars and Gryon costs Sfr42. Including the glacier you pay Sfr55.

The town's **tourist office** (☎ 024 492 33 58; www .diablerets.ch), to the right of the train station, has more information.

Auberge de la Poste (☎ 024 492 31 24; www.auber gedelaposte.ch; Rue de la Gare; d Sfr200, s/d without bathroom Sfr70/140; P ☒ ☐) is a grand, inviting, timber hotel oozing mountain charm.

From Aigle take the hourly train via Le Sépey (Sfr12.40, 50 minutes).

VILLARS & GRYON

Villars (1350m) and nearby Gryon share the same local ski pass with Les Diablerets and in winter are linked by a free train for holders of the ski pass. For information on the area check out each village's websites: www.villars .ch and www.gryon.ch. If you want to buy ski passes in advance at reduced rates, check out www.easyski.ch.

The skiing is geared towards intermediate skiers. In summer the country is perfect for hiking. One great walk starts at the Col de Bretaye pass (reached by BVB train from Villars), takes you past the pretty Lac de Chavonnes and on through verdant mountain country to Les Diablerets. The walk takes about four hours, and from Les Diablerets you could catch a train to Aigle. The views from around the Col de Bretaye are magnificent, taking in the Dents du Midi and Mont Blanc.

In Villars, **Hôtel Suisse** (☎ 024 495 24 25; www.el gringo.ch/hotelsuisse; Rte des Hôtels; r per person Sfr50) offers the cheapest central accommodation, with compact, cheerful timber-walled rooms (doubles with their own shower). It can get a little rowdy with punters returning after a night in the club next door. For impressive Italian cooking, **La Toscana** (☎ 024 495 79 21; Rte des Hôtels; meals Sfr50-60; ☼ 6-11pm Wed-Mon) is the best bet and is located in the same complex as the hotel and aforementioned club, **El Gringo** (☼ 11pm-4am Fri & Sat in low season, nightly in ski season).

From Aigle you can reach Villars by an hourly bus (Sfr7.80, 40 minutes). Otherwise, you can continue with mainline trains to **Bex** (known for its nearby salt mines) and connect with local trains to Gryon (Sfr6, 25 to 30 minutes) and Villars (Sfr7.80, 40 minutes). The train running from Gryon to Villars is free with the ski pass. Occasional postal buses connect Villars with Les Diablerets via the Col de la Croix pass (closed in winter).

PAYS D'ENHAUT

This northeast corner of Canton de Vaud, the 'High Country', lies about midway between Aigle and Gruyères. In winter it could be considered the western, Francophone extension of the swank Gstaad ski scene, just over the cantonal frontier.

Château d'Oex is an attractive family resort with a nice selection of moderate ski runs, but the place is best known for all its hot air. Bertrand Piccard and Brian Jones launched their record-breaking, round-the-world, 20-day hot-air balloon ride from here in March 1999 (they landed in Egypt). For one week in the second half of January the place bursts into a frenzy of floating colour as the town hosts the annual **Semaine Internationale de Ballons à Air Chaud** involving around 100 hot-air balloons ranging from the standard floater to odd creatures such as a massive Scottish bagpipe player! Entry just to see and feel all the hot air up close is Sfr7 on the weekend (free on the weekdays). If you want to fly up, up and away, steady your nerves for fiscal turbulence. It costs up to Sfr350 per adult (half for children) for

about one hour. Cheese and sweets lovers should make a beeline for **Le Chalet** (☎ 026 926 66 77; www.lechalet-fromagerie.ch; meals Sfr30-40; ☺ 9am-7pm Tue-Thu & Sun, 9am-11pm Fri & Sat). This grand old cheesemaker is the place to gorge yourself on creamy fondue or raclette and dreamy meringues with double cream. And they make the cheese in front of you too (from 1.30pm to 3.30pm)! It is just behind the Coop supermarket opposite the MOB train station.

Less than 10km east is **Rougemont**, the other main centre. Both villages offer a variety of accommodation throughout the year. Summer activities include rafting and hiking.

The Château d'Oex **tourist office** (☎ 026 924 25 35; www.chateau-doex.ch; La Pl) is in the centre, below the hilltop clock tower. There are about 20 places to stay, ranging from chalets to a handful of rather overbearing big hotels.

The resort is on the scenic Montreux–Spiez train route serviced by MOB trains. From Montreux it takes one hour and costs Sfr17.60 (plus Sfr6 reservation fee on Panoramic Express trains only).

Fribourg, Neuchâtel & Jura

A far cry from the staggering Alpine scenes more readily associated with Switzerland, this gentle less-visited corner in the west of the country remains something of a 'secret'. From the evocative medieval cantonal capitals of Fribourg and Neuchâtel to the mysterious green hills and deep dark forests of the Jura, from the land of three lakes to charming villages like Gruyères and St Ursanne, it proffers a wealth of sights and scapes well off the beaten tourist track. Be it listening to frogs singing in lakeside bogs, marvelling at palatial ice creations between pine trees or following the call of the devilish green fairy into the wayward Val de Tavers, travelling here promises a brilliant sensory experience…and that includes for the taste buds. On the food front, there are monks' heads (strong, nutty-flavoured cheese) to be munched, one of Switzerland's best known AOC cheeses to be sampled and sweet feather-light meringues smothered in rich, thick double cream to blow the calorie count on. When it all gets too much, thousands upon thousands of kilometres of waistline-saving walking, cycling and cross-country skiing trails – not to mention sailing, skiing and wakeboarding on lake water – kick in.

This chapter covers (from south to north) the cantons of Fribourg, Neuchâtel and Jura, as well as the northwestern tip of the canton of Bern. The trio of lakes wedged between the Fribourg and Neuchâtel cantons – Lac de Neuchâtel, Lac de Morat and Bieler See – and the Fribourg canton fall mostly within the Plateau Central (Mittelland) plain. French rules everywhere bar the eastward edge of the latter canton where German predominates.

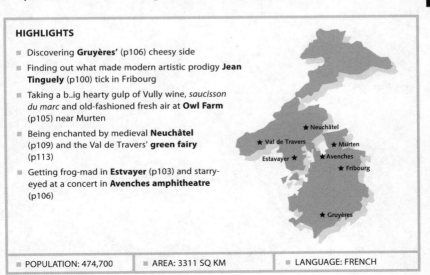

HIGHLIGHTS

- Discovering **Gruyères'** (p106) cheesy side
- Finding out what made modern artistic prodigy **Jean Tinguely** (p100) tick in Fribourg
- Taking a b..ig hearty gulp of Vully wine, *saucisson du marc* and old-fashioned fresh air at **Owl Farm** (p105) near Murten
- Being enchanted by medieval **Neuchâtel** (p109) and the Val de Travers' **green fairy** (p113)
- Getting frog-mad in **Estvayer** (p103) and starry-eyed at a concert in **Avenches amphitheatre** (p106)

★ Neuchâtel
★ Val de Travers
★ Murten
Estavayer ★
★ Avenches
★ Fribourg
★ Gruyères

■ POPULATION: 474,700	■ AREA: 3311 SQ KM	■ LANGUAGE: FRENCH

FRIBOURG, NEUCHÂTEL & JURA

History

The area's earliest inhabitants settled along Lac de Neuchâtel around 3000 BC and the second Iron Age in Europe is referred to as 'La Tène Period', after the settlement on the lake's eastern end where a store of weapons and utensils was discovered.

Influential Zähringen nobleman Berchtold IV (father of the fearless bear hunter who founded Bern) came up with Fribourg in 1157. It subsequently became a fortified eastern frontier post of the Burgundy realm and remained so until the Swiss thrashed Burgundy duke Charles the Bold once and for all at the infamous Battle of Murten (p104) in 1476, after which Fribourg was forced to join the Swiss Confederation.

Snooty old Neuchâtel, under the distant thumb of Frederick the Great of Prussia from 1707, remained aloof from the Confederation until 1815 when the Congress of Vienna obliged it – along with its northerly neighbour, the Jura – to turn Swiss.

Getting There & Around

Most of the region is well-covered by train tracks. Rail connections to and from the main cities – Fribourg and Neuchâtel – make light work of getting around. By road, the A12 motorway linking Bern with Lausanne and Geneva roars down the Canton de Fribourg's central spine. Navigating the more remote corners of the Jura is practically impossible without

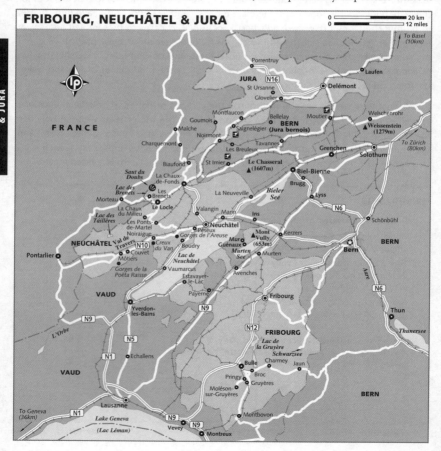

FRIBOURG, NEUCHÂTEL & JURA

your own two wheels or a sturdy set of hiking boots.

CANTON DE FRIBOURG

The southernmost of the three cantons, Canton de Fribourg (population 239,100) tots up 1671 sq km on the drawing board. Pre-Alpine foothills rise grandly around its cold craggy feet, cheesy Gruyères with its sprinkling of small mountain resorts pierces its central heart and the capital of Fribourg heads the canton up north. In the northwest, pretty lakeside villages and a wealth of vineyards and fruit orchards bask in a milder climate. The River Sarine traces the canton's central spine.

Variety of scape aside, what makes this canton fascinating is its linguistic divide: roughly, west speaks French (65% of the population), east speaks German (30%).

FRIBOURG

pop 33,000 / elevation 630m

Nowhere is Switzerland's *Röstigraben* (language divide) more keenly felt than in Fribourg (Freiburg) or 'Free Town', a medieval riverside city where inhabitants on the west bank speak French, on the east bank German. Throw Catholicism and a notable student population into the cultural cocktail and you get a fascinating town with a feisty nightlife and a refreshing waft of originality.

Its greatest moment in history – marked by the Murten–Fribourg dash (p105) and a linden tree (right) – saw a messenger sprint from Murten to Fribourg in 1476 to relay the glad tidings that the Swiss had defeated Charles the Bold…only to drop dead with exhaustion on arrival. Onlookers, saddened by this tragic twist, took the linden twig from the messenger's hat and planted it.

Orientation

Much of the Old Town is on the river's west bank, gathered around Cathédrale de St Nicholas and flowing into the low-lying spit of land called Auge cradled in the river's elbow.

From the train station, Ave de la Gare runs northeast, becomes Rue de Romont, and opens into the hub of town, Square des Places and Places Georges Python. From this square, the pedestrian-only shopping street Rue de Lausanne leads into the Old Town.

Information

BOOKSHOPS

Librairie Albert le Grand (☎ 026 347 35 35; www.al bert-le-grand.ch in French; Rue du Temple 1; ☉ 1-6.30pm Mon, 8.30am-6.30pm Tue, Wed & Fri, 8.30am-8pm Thu, 8am-4pm Sat) English books, maps and LP travel guides.

INTERNET ACCESS

Cyberworld (☎ 026 321 22 40; Rue de Lausanne 2; per hr Sfr10; ☉ 1pm-midnight)

INTERNET RESOURCES

Pays de Fribourg (www.pays-de-fribourg.ch) Lowdown on Fribourg land.

POST

Central post office (Ave de Tivoli 3; ☉ 7.30am-6.30pm Mon-Fri, 8am-4pm Sat)

TOURIST INFORMATION

Tourist office (☎ 026 321 31 75; www.fribourgtourism .ch; Ave de la Gare 1; ☉ 9am-6pm Mon-Fri, 9am-3pm Sat May-Sep, 9am-6pm Mon-Fri, 9am-noon Sat Oct-Apr)

Sights

The 12th-century **Old Town** was laid out in simple fashion, with Grand-Rue as the main traffic street and parallel Rue des Chanoines/Rue des Bouchers devoted to markets, church and civic buildings. The settlement later spread down the hill into Auge. The bridges here – quaint stone **Pont du Milieu** and cobbled, roof-covered **Pont du Berne** – proffer great views. Pont de Zaehringen, Route des Alpes and Chemin de Lorette are other prime vantage points.

Fribourg's famous **Tilleul de Morat** (Morat Linden Tree) stands in front of the Renaissance **town hall** (Grand-Rue).

CATHÉDRALE DE ST NICHOLAS

Before entering this brooding 13th-century Gothic **cathedral** (Rue des Chanoines), contemplate the main portal with its 15th-century sculptured portrayal of the Last Judgment. On your right as you enter is **Chapelle du Saint Sépulcre** with a sculptural group (1433) depicting Christ's burial with exceptional lifelikeness and movement.

A hike up 368 steps to the top of the cathedral's 74m-tall **tower** (adult/child Sfr3.50/1;

10am-noon & 2-5pm Mon-Wed, Fri & Sat, 10am-noon Thu, 2-5pm Sun Apr-Oct), the city's most recognisable landmark completed in 1490, is a Fribourg highlight.

ESPACE JEAN TINGUELY – NIKI DE SAINT PHALLE

Jump on the red button to watch *L'Retable de l'Abondance Occidentale et du Mercantilisme Totalitaire* (1989–90) – the centrepiece of this fantastic museum – make its larger-than-life, allegorical comment on Western opulence. Created in memory of Fribourg's modern artistic prodigy, Jean Tinguely (1925–91) in a tramway depot dating to 1900, the **Espace Jean Tinguely – Niki de Saint Phalle** (☎ 026 305 51 40; Rue de Morat 2; adult/under 16

Sfr6/free; 11am-6pm Wed & Fri-Sun, 11am-8pm Thu) showcases his machines and some of the wacky creations of French-American artist Niki de Saint Phalle (1930–2002) who worked/lived with Tinguely from the late 1950s until Tinguely's death.

ÉGLISE DES CORDELIERS

Inside 13th-century **Église des Cordeliers** (Rue de Morat 6; 7.30am-7pm Apr-Sep, 7.30am-6pm Oct-Mar) the large triptych (1480) above the high altar depicts the Crucifixion. Its mighty neighbour, the **Basilique de Notre-Dame de Fribourg** (Rue de Morat 1), shelters a beautifully restored 18th-century **Neapolitan crib** featuring 75 figurines re-enacting the nativity, annunciation and scenes from daily life.

FRIBOURG (FREIBURG)

0 -------- 300 m
0 -------- 0.2 miles

INFORMATION		
Central Post Office	1	A2
Cyberworld	2	C2
Librairie Albert le Grand	3	A2
Tourist Office	4	A2

SIGHTS & ACTIVITIES		
Basilique de Notre-Dame de Fribourg	5	C1
Cathédrale de St Nicholas	6	C1
Commanderie de St Jean	7	C2
Église des Cordeliers	8	C1
Espace Jean Tinguely – Niki de Saint Phalle	9	C1
Kuriosium Sonnenberg	10	B3
Musée d'Art et d'Histoire	11	C1
Musée Suisse de la Marionnette	12	D2
Town Hall	13	C2

SLEEPING		
Auberge de Jeunesse Fribourg	14	A2
Auberge de Zaehringen	15	D2
Hôtel du Sauvage	16	C2
Hôtel Elite	17	A2
Kuriosium Sonnenberg	18	C3
NH Fribourg	19	B2

EATING		
Auberge de la Cicogne	20	D2
Café de la Belvédère	21	D2
Café du Gothard	22	C1
Café du Midi	23	B2
La Petite Brasserie	24	B2
Les Halles	25	C1
Manora Restaurant	26	A2

DRINKING		
Brasserie Artisanale de Fribourg	27	D2
L'Apart	(see 19)	
Paddy Reilly's	28	B2
Plaza Lounge Bar	29	B2
TW	30	B2
Winebar	31	B1

ENTERTAINMENT		
La Spirale	32	D2
Morrison Room	(see 28)	
Service Culturel Regional	(see 4)	

TRANSPORT		
Bus Station	33	A2
Pertuis Funicular Station	34	B2
Upper Funicular Station	35	B2

FRIBOURG, NEUCHÂTEL & JURA

MUSÉE D'ART ET D'HISTOIRE

Fribourg's **Art & History Museum** (MAHF; ☎ 026 305 51 40; Rue de Morat 12; adult/under 16/student Sfr8/free/5; ☒ 11am-6pm Tue, Wed & Fri-Sun, 11am-8pm Thu), with an excellent collection of late-Gothic sculpture and painting, is housed in the Renaissance Hôtel Ratzé, with annexes in the former slaughterhouse and armoury. Gothic meets Goth in the underground chamber where religious statues are juxtaposed with some of Tinguely's sculptural creations combining animal skulls with metal machine components. The bench-clad museum garden, overlooking the river and pierced by a Niki de Saint Phalle sculpture, is one of the city's few green picnic spots.

MUSÉE SUISSE DE LA MARIONNETTE

Puppets rub shoulders in the **Swiss Puppetry Museum** ☎ 026 322 85 13; www.marionnette.ch in French; Derrière-les-Jardins 2; adult/child Sfr5/3; ☒ 10am-5pm Mon-Fri, 2-6pm Sat & Sun).

PLANCHE SUPÉRIEURE

Cross Pont du Milieu and head west towards the broad sloping square known as Planche Supérieure. The former **Commanderie de St Jean**, erected by the Knights of the Order of St John in the 13th century, dominates its eastern side and Chemin de Sonnenberg climbs from the square's western end to the **Kuriosium Sonnenberg** (☎ 026 322 03 50; www .corpaato.ch in French & German; Chemin du Sonnenberg 4; adult/12-16yr Sfr10/6; ☒ 10am-5pm Tue-Sun). Curious indeed, the gallery features surrealist and absurd works by *Le Boucher Corpaato* (the butcher Corpaato), alias jolly old butcher-painter Jean-Pierre Corpataux (b 1950) who apparently paints exclusively with a knife.

Sleeping

The tourist office has details of B&Bs in surrounding farms.

Auberge de Jeunesse Fribourg (☎ 026 323 19 16; Rue de l'Hôpital 2; dm Sfr30.65, s/d Sfr51.50/85; ☒ 7.30-10am & 5-10pm Mar–early Nov; P ☒) The rules are clear at this city hostel in one wing of the 17th-century Hôpital des Bourgeois, opposite Fribourg University. No smoking, no cooking or eating in rooms, and night owls must ring to enter after 10pm.

Kuriosium Sonnenberg (☎ 079 331 42 48; www.cor paato.ch; Chemin du Sonnenberg 4; s/d Sfr70/120; P) In a 19th-century house aplomb Mont Sonnenberg, this peaceful house opposite Fribourg's wackiest art gallery (left) has several simple rooms, breakfast included and bathrooms shared. Take bus No 4 from the train station to Planche Supérieure and hike up the hill.

NH Fribourg (☎ 026 351 91 91; www.nh-hotels.com; Grand-Places 14; s/d from Sfr150/220; P ☒ ☒ ☐) Notably modern in a lumbering apartment block, upmarket NH lures suits with its business facilities, modern décor, classy restaurant and Jacuzzi-clad suites.

Hôtel Elite (☎ 026 322 22 60; elitefribourg@bluewin .ch; Rue du Criblet 7; s/d/tr/q Sfr90/140/160/215) Nothing to look at from the outside, Hôtel Elite offers well-maintained rooms and competitive half-board rates should you wish to dine in its neighbouring restaurant.

Auberge de Zaehringen (☎ 026 322 42 36; www .auberge-de-zaehringen.ch in French; Rue de Zaehringen 13; ste for 1/2 people Sfr190/260; menus Sfr49-116; P ☒ ☒ ☐) This medieval mansion named after the Dukes of Zaehringen who founded Fribourg in 1157 dates to the 13th century – read: loads of lovely timber beams, grandiose halls and labyrinthine passages.

FRIBOURG, NEUCHÂTEL & JURA

AUTHOR'S CHOICE

Auberge aux 4 Vents (☎ 026 347 36 00; www.aux4vents.ch; Res Balzli Grandfrey 124; s/d Sfr120/170, s/d/tr/q without bathroom Sfr50/100/140/160; P ☒) 'Stylish' scarcely does justice to this imaginative and luxurious country inn where design of a wacky rustic nature prevails. Its eight rooms are individually designed ('by a bunch of adorable lunatics' says the hotel): the four-bedded 'dortoir' is Switzerland's most luxurious dorm; single red roses in vases plaster the walls of 'cathédrale'; while dreamy 'bleue' sports blue flowery period furnishings and a tub on rails that rolls out through the window for a bath beneath stars. Style or *what*? In the ambling gardens a cable car doubles as playhouse and smooching spot. There are swings, a pool, barbecue and tables that spill from the highly recommended conservatory-style restaurant to overlook a stunning medieval Fribourg panorama.

To get to the '4 Winds', 2km north in Grandfrey, drive north along Rue de Morat through 15th-century Porte de Morat and turn right immediately before the train bridge.

FRIBOURG, NEUCHÂTEL & JURA

Hôtel du Sauvage (☎ 026 347 30 60; www.hotel-sauvage.ch in French; Planche Supérieure 12; s/d from Sfr190/240; menus Sfr30 & Sfr40) Another medieval veteran, this one boasts 17 charming rooms in a twin set of 16th-century houses footsteps from the Sarine.

Eating

Café du Gothard (Rue du Pont Muré 16) Watch out for Tinguely's favourite eating haunt to reopen in 2006 after months of renovation. A kitsch mix of original 19th-century furnishings, Niki de Saint Phalle drawings and art nostalgia, the traditional bistro is legendary.

Les Halles (Pl des Ormeaux 1; meals Sfr15-17; ☒ 11am-6pm Mon-Sat) Market-driven creations with an inventive twist are the mainstay of this bright and bold eating hall above the market place.

La Petite Brasserie (☎ 026 321 36 46; Rue de Lausanne 25; starters/mains Sfr10/15; lunch menu Sf16; ☒ 9am-11.30pm Tue-Thu, 9-2am Fri & Sat) Giant windows overlooking people-busy Rue de Lausanne makes this free Wi-Fi zone a hot lunchtime spot. Cooking is modern European.

Café du Midi (☎ 026 322 31 33; www.lemidi.ch; Rue de Romont 25; salads Sfr6.50-21.50, menu fondue Sfr36) Fribourg's old boy pulls the punters on its busy pavement terrace with seven types of fondue and a menu fondue featuring air-dried beef, fondue and meringues with cream.

Manora Restaurant (Grand Places; meals Sfr15; ☒ 8am-7pm Mon-Wed & Fri, 8am-9.30pm Thu, 8am-6pm Sat) This glass shoebox heaves. Grab a tray, pick a cheap fill…and finish with a gander at the Tinguely fountain (created by the Fribourg artist for his mate, Swiss racing driver Jo Siffert, months before his deadly car accident in 1971) spouting out water in the park.

Café de la Belvédère (☎ 026 323 44 07; Grand-Rue 36; menu Sfr20; ☒ Tue-Sat) Sushi, sashimi, Thai and Chinese menus make a welcome change from the traditional norm. But the main reason to visit this bistro is for its staggering rooftop terrace.

Auberge de la Cicogne (☎ 026 322 68 34; www.la-cigogne.ch in French; Rue d'Or 24; starters Sfr20, mains Sfr25-78, menus Sfr80 & Sfr105; ☒ Tue-Sat) Eastern aromas waft over a couple of mains and desserts are divine at this highly revered establishment, constructed in 1771 in riverside Auge.

For a line-up of quick-eat kebab joints, hit Rue de l'Hôpital.

Drinking

TW (☎ 026 321 53 82; www.tmcafe.ch; Rue de Romont 29-31; ☒ 7am-11.30pm Mon-Wed, 7am-midnight Thu, 7-2am Fri, 9-2am Sat, 2-11.30pm Sun) Scale the tatty staircase next to the shoe shop to woo TW (Talk Wine) – a chic lounge bar where trendies drink and dance. Shots are hot and DJs spin everything from bastardelectro and breakbeat to house, bop and jazz.

Paddy Reilly's (Grand-Places 12; ☒ 4.30pm-2am Mon, 11-2am Tue-Thu, 4.30pm-3am Fri & Sat) If it's pints of the hard stuff you're after Irish Paddy's your man. Student night (read: cheap beer) is Monday.

L'Apart (Grand-Places 14; ☒ 2pm-3am Mon-Sat) A slick wooden-deck terrace fronts designled 'Apartment', tucked in the shadow of Paddy's.

Plaza Lounge Bar (Rue de Lausanne 91; ☒ to 4am) It serves food too (a good-value *menu du jour* kicks in at Sfr15.50), but the spacious bar is best suited for an aperitif on its vast pavement terrace.

BREWERIES BIG & SMALL

If it's big-name beer you crave, head for Fribourg's **Brasserie du Cardinal** (☎ 084 812 50 00; www.cardinal.ch in French & Dutch; Passage du Cardinal) where one of Switzerland's best-known lagers has been brewed since 1788. **Brewery tours** (☎ 058 123 22 16; admission Sfr10; ☒ 8.30-10am & 1.30-3pm Mon-Thu) demonstrate how water, malt and hops are turned into nine different types of Cardinal beer and take in the **Musée de la Bière Cardinal** (☎ 084 812 50 00; www.cardinal.ch; Passage du Cardinal; adult/under 12 with drink Sfr10/5; ☒ 2-6pm Tue & Thu), in the brewery cellar.

At the other end of the scale is small-time microbrewery **Brasserie Artisanale de Fribourg** (☎ 026 322 80 88; Rue de la Samaritaine 19; ☒ 8am-5pm Sat). Run by a couple of mates who began the enterprise as an amusing pastime (and now run it as a Saturday hobby!), the one-room brewery brews just 50 hectolitres a year. Pay Sfr4 for a bottle of its golden German-style Barbeblanche or Barberousse with subtle caramel and honey aromas, and Sfr4.50 for a bottle of black, Irish-style Old Cat stout.

THE FRIBOURG FUNICULAR

Nowhere else in Europe bar Fribourg does a funicular lurch up the mountainside with the aid of good old stinky sewage water. Constructed in 1899, the **Funiculaire de Fribourg** (ticket Sfr1.60; ⊙ 7-8.15am & 9.30am-7pm Mon-Sat, 9.30am-7pm Sun) links the lower part of the town with the upper every six minutes. The ride in one of two counterbalancing water-powered carriages from the lower Pertuis station (121m; Pl du Pertuis) to the upper station (618m; Route des Alpes) takes two minutes and includes bags of Old Town views.

Winebar (☎ 026 322 48 69; www.wine-bar.ch in French; Rue de l'Hôpital 39; ⊙ 7am-11pm Mon-Thu, 7-3am Fri, 2pm-3am Sat, 10am-11pm Sun) Young, fun and funky is the spirit of this student-driven, free WiFi venue. Special events (beach parties, Asetrix and Obelix soirées etc) fill weekends and munchies can be put to rest in its Le Bout du Monde restaurant.

Entertainment

Service Culturel Regional (☎ 026 350 11 00; Ave de la Gare 1; ⊙ 9am-6pm Mon-Fri, 9am-3pm Sat) Buy tickets for cultural events in the Service Culturel Regional adjoining the tourist office.

La Spirale (☎ 026 322 66 39; www.laspirale.ch in French; Pl du Petit St-Jean 39; admission Sfr10-35; ⊙ Wed-Sun) Jazz, blues, folk and flamenco musicians create a potent musical cocktail in this cellar club by the river. Wednesdays are dedicated to home-grown sounds.

Morrison Room (☎ 026 321 18 28; Grand-Places 12; ⊙ 9.30pm-2am Mon, 9pm-2am Wed, 10pm-2am Thu, 10pm-3am Fri, 10pm-1am Sat) Pub club above Paddy's.

To See (☎ 026 424 46 53; www.toseeclub.com in French; Passage Cardinal 2c; admission Sfr10-20, before 11pm often free; ⊙ 10pm-4am Wed, Fri & Sat, 10pm-3am Thu) Two dance floors, a select gallery and frenetic clubbing crowd. DJs spin all styles.

Fri-son (☎ 026 424 36 25; www.fri-son.ch; Route de la Fonderie 13; admission up to Sfr15, concerts up to Sfr40) Fri-son spins rap, reggae, soul, techno and house – and is one of western Switzerland's biggest stages for live concerts.

Getting There & Away

Trains travel hourly to/from Neuchâtel (Sfr19, 55 minutes), and more frequently to Geneva (Sfr37, 1½ hours) and Bern (Sfr12.40,

20 minutes). Regular trains run to Yverdon-les-Bains (Sfr16.80, 55 to 80 minutes) and Lausanne (Sfr22, 45 to 55 minutes).

Buses depart from behind the train station for Avenches (Sfr8.60, 25 minutes) and Bulle (Sfr14.20, 55 minutes) and Schwarzsee (Sfr14.20, one hour).

Fribourg is on the N12 between Lake Geneva and Bern.

ESTAVAYER-LE-LAC
pop 4330 / elevation 455m

A charming manicured lakeside enclave that has largely preserved its medieval core, Estavayer-le-Lac is a lovely little hideout. Pretty face aside, it is known for frogs – dead or alive.

Orientation & Information

From the train station walk 400m to town and the **Tourist Office** (☎ 026 663 12 37; www.est avayer-le-lac.ch in French; Rue de la Gare 14; ⊙ 8.30am-noon & 1.30-5.45pm Mon-Fri, 10am-noon & 2-4pm Sat, 10am-noon Sun Jul & Aug, 8.30am-noon & 1.30-5.45pm Mon-Fri, 10am-noon & 2-4pm Sat Apr-Jun & Sep, 10am-noon & 1.30-5.30pm Tue-Fri Oct-Mar).

Sights & Activities

The stars of the eclectic show at the **Musée Communal** (Regional Museum; ☎ 026 663 24 48; Rue du Musée 13; adult/child Sfr4/2; ⊙ 10am-noon & 2-5pm Tue-Sun Mar-Jun, Sep & Oct, 10am-noon & 2-5pm daily Jul & Aug, 2-5pm Sat & Sun Nov-Feb) are 108 stuffed frogs. François Perrier, a retired Swiss military fellow, spent the 1860s catching, stuffing and 'modelling' frogs.

Fairytale **Château de Chenaux** (1285–90), home to the Préfecture de Fribourg and *gendarmerie* (police station), cannot be visited but its ramparts can be strolled. The **Circuit des Remparts** takes you along much of the original 40m-long and 35m-wide rectangle interspersed with 16 gates and turrets galore. The largest tower, 32m-tall **Grand Tour**, could only be accessed via a door that stood 9m above ground level and was reached by a drawer bridge in medieval times.

Lac de Neuchâtel reins in a buoyant crowd with Alphasurf's **Téléski** (☎ 079 258 21 47; www.alphasurf.ch; 1/5/20 circuits Sfr5/20/50; ⊙ May-Sep) that tows water-skiers and wake-boarders around a cableway circuit from the end of a jetty at **Nouvelle Plage**. You can swim, sail and surf on the gravely beach here…or listen to a frogs' chorus in the **Grande Cariçaie**

(www.grande-caricaei.ch). The chain of marshy reed-fringed lakes strung along the southern edge of Lac de Neuchâtel is a stronghold for common green frogs, pool frogs, tree frogs and common toads. Watchtowers provide a bird's eye view of the unique frog land.

Sleeping & Eating

My Lady's Manor (☎ 026 663 23 16; www.myladysmanor .org; Route de la Gare; 1/2 or more nights per person with breakfast Sfr50/60; ☷ Mar-Oct; **P**) Grilling dinner in the flowery gardens, painting, or sleeping like a babe is all part of the charm at this stately B&B in a manor house near the station.

Abri-Côtier (☎ 026 663 50 52; www.abri-cotier.ch in French; Grande Gouille 1; dm Sfr20) The accommodation arm of Alphasurf, this shoebox gets packed with outdoor enthusiasts. Guests share a kitchen.

Hôtel Restaurant du Port (☎ 026 664 82 82; www .hotelduport.ch in French; Route du Port; s/d/tr/q Sfr80/ 130/150/160, menu du jour Sfr16, mains around Sfr30; **P**) Hôtel du Port sits plump between lake and Old Town – making it an easy stroll home wherever you are. Fish lovers make up the jovial crowd that dines here and lunch in the garden is a family choice.

Hostellerie du Château (☎ 026 663 10 49; www.au chateau.info in French & German; Rue des Granges 2; mains around Sfr20) Dine on the informal tree-shaded terrace or up top in the formal restaurant at this ode to regional cuisine where you can eat as many *cuisses de grenouilles* (frogs' thighs) as you like for Sfr32.

Les Lacustres (☎ 026 663 11 96; www.leslacustres .ch in French; Rue des Lacustres; ☷ Mar-Oct) For beach buzz hit this trendy waterfront café-restaurant where boarders eat, drink, play *pétanque* (French bowls) and lounge. Brunch is dished up Sunday and beach sushi is a Friday speciality.

Getting There & Away

Estavayer-le-Lac is on the road and train route between Fribourg (Sfr11.40, 40 minutes) and Yverdon (Sfr6.60, 17 minutes), or it's a short detour off the northbound N1 from Lausanne. Boats call in too (see p112).

MURTEN

pop 5650 / elevation 450m
This fortified German-speaking medieval village on the eastern shore of Murten See

(Lac de Morat) isn't called Murten (Morat) – derived from the Celtic word *moriduno* meaning 'fortress on the lake' – for nothing. In May 1476 the Burgundy duke Charles the Bold set off from Lausanne to besiege Murten – only to have 8000 of his men butchered or drowned in Murten Lake during the Battle of Murten. The fortifications that thwarted the duke (who escaped) create a quaint little lakeside town well worth an afternoon stroll today.

Canals link Murten See with Lac de Neuchâtel (west) and Bieler See (north) to form the Pays des Trois Lacs – a lake district crisscrossed with 250km-odd of marked roller-skating, cycling and walking paths.

Information

Tourist Office (☎ 026 670 51 12; www.murten.ch, in German; Französische Kirchgasse 6; ☷ 10am-noon & 2-5pm Mon-Fri Oct-Mar, 9am-noon & 2-6pm Mon-Fri, 10am-2pm Sat Apr-Sep)

Sights & Activities

Murten is a cobbled three-street town crammed with arcaded houses. A string of hotel-restaurants culminating in a 13th-century **castle** (closed to visitors) line Rathausgasse; shops and eateries stud parallel Hauptgasse, capped by the medieval **Berntor** city gate at its eastern end; while parallel Deutsche Kirchgasse and its western continuation, Schulgasse, hug the city ramparts. Scale the wooden **Aufstieg auf die Ringmauer** (rampart stairs) behind the **Deutsche Kirche** (German Church; Deutsche Kirchgasse) to reach the covered walkway traversing part of the sturdy medieval walls.

In a mill beyond the castle, the **Museum Murten** (☎ 026 670 31 00; www.museummurten.ch in French & German; Ryf 4; adult/child Sfr4/1; ☷ 2-5pm Tue-Sat, 10am-5pm Sun Apr-Oct, 2-5pm Tue-Sun Nov-Apr) displays artefacts discovered during the dredging of the Broye Canal in 1829 and cannons used in the Battle of Murten.

From May to September, shuttle boats operated by the **Société de Navigation sur les Lacs de Neuchâtel et Morat** (see p112) crisscross the lake and **Schifffahrtsgesellschaft drei Seen** (☎ 026 673 08 00; www.dreiseenschiffahrt.ch) organises Sunday brunch (adult/child six to 16 Sfr39/19.50), floating fondue evenings and other interesting food-orientated boat cruises.

Festivals & Events
Murten's three-day **carnival** is in early March and its 8000-runner **marathon**, the Murten–Fribourg race on the first Sunday of October, commemorates the dash by the messenger who relayed news of the Battle of Murten.

Sleeping & Eating
Many Murten restaurants are inside hotels; find cheaper eats on Hauptgasse.

Hotel Murtenhof & Krone (☎ 026 672 90 30; www .murtenhof.ch; Rathausgasse; s/d from Sfr80/100, menu Sfr29.50; P ⊠) The Murtenhof, in a 16th-century patrician's house, mixes old and new to create a very spacious sleeping and eating space. Eco rooms have basic furnishings but 'superior' ones ooze style – fancy a round bed! The terrace restaurant has 1st-class lake views and tasty perch filets in sherry and lime sauce or pan-fried in mango chilli.

Hotel Weisses Kreuz (☎ 026 670 26 41; www .weisses-kreuz.ch; Rathausgasse 31; s Sfr110-170, d Sfr160-280) A striking design-led interior contrasts to that of the historic exterior of the 'White Cross', a 15th-century tavern. Fish drives its restaurant.

Restaurant des Bains (☎ 026 670 23 38; www .restaurant-des-bains.ch in German; Ryf 35; mains Sfr30; ☯ 9am-midnight Tue-Sun Jun-Sep, Wed-Sun Oct-May) For lakeside dining, this is prime. A green lawn slopes down from its tabled terrace to the water where swans gag for crumbs. *Filets de perche* (perch filets) come in imaginative guises – including in local Vully wine.

Le Vieux Manoir au Lac (☎ 026 678 61 61; www .vieuxmanoir.ch; Rue de Lausanne 18, Meyriez; s/d from Sfr290/390, ste Sfr410-630, starters/mains from Sfr30/50; ☯ mid-Feb–mid-Dec; P ☐ ☙) This unabashedly luxurious timber Normandy house,

built as a whim on the lakeside in the early 1900s, is *the* ultimate splurge. For wooers wanting their loved one to say yes, there's one table for two at the end of a long jetty where you can dine in style (at sunset) for Sfr250 per person. Find it 1km south of Murten in Meyriez.

Drinking
Bar und Blumen (☎ 026 670 01 90; Rathausgasse 9; ☯ 10-12.30am Mon-Thu, 10-3am Fri & Sat, 11am-midnight Sun) 'Bar and Flowers' is just that – a minimalist café-bar that serves sushi after work and sells vases and flowers.

Irish Tavern (☎ 026 672 19 20; www.irish-tavern.ch; Hauptgasse 45; ☯ 10am-11.30pm Mon-Thu, 10-3am Fri & Sat) Irish watering hole with beamed interior. For wine, don't miss its L'Oenothèque du Muratum next door.

Getting There & Around
From the **train station** (Bahnhofstrasse), 300m south of the city walls, hourly trains operate to/from Fribourg (Sfr10.40, 30 minutes), Bern (Sfr12.40, 35 minutes) via Kerzers (Sfr3.50, nine minutes), and Neuchâtel (Sfr11.40, 25 minutes). Hourly trains to/from Payerne (Sfr7.20, 20 minutes) stop at Avenches (Sfr3.20, seven minutes). Murten train station rents **bicycles** (☎ 051 221 15 52; per day Sfr31).

Seasonal boats sail from Murten to/from Neuchâtel (p112). By car, Murten is on the N1 linking Lausanne with Bern.

AROUND MURTEN
Agricultural with the odd village or farm thrown in for an overnight roll in the hay (see p313), Murten's surrounding green

---

AUTHOR'S CHOICE

Eulenhof (Ferme du Hibou; ☎ 026 673 18 85; www.fermeduhibou.ch; Rue du Château 24, Mur; camping on straw adult/child Sfr26/16, dm adult/child Sfr25/35, d Sfr90-120, dinner mid-May–mid-Sep Sfr27, Sun lunch mid-May–mid-Sep Sfr27-40; ☯ Jan-Oct; P ⊠) Nowhere do guests get a warmer welcome and more authentic regional cuisine than at Owl Farm, run by farmer Willy and wife Nadja. Well placed on the Sentier du Vins de Vully (Vully wine trail), many guests arrive on foot or by bicycle. Terraced gardens sport tables, a pond, swing and spectacular lake views. There are various animals to see and tennis-ball chasing Spake and his mate Sasha for canine entertainment. Rooms are spotless; pine bunk beds fill a spacious dorm in a converted barn; and blankets to thwart off straw prickles are laid on for campers kipping in the hay barn (bring your own sleeping bag). Advance reservations for accommodation, dinner and Sunday lunch are essential. To get here from Murten 13km away, drive north around the lake, following the lake road as far as Guénaux, then head inland for 1km to Mur village.

fields offer a gulp of fine old-fashioned fresh air. Farmers trustingly pile up carrots on the roadside for motorists to buy (Sfr10 for a 10kg sack) and open their lettuce fields and apple orchards to the agriculturally curious as part of the **Inforama Seeland** (www.inforama.ch in German) green tourism project. On the western side of the lake, Vully wine is produced from grapes grown on the slopes of Mont Vully (653m).

Avenches

Roman Aventicum, 8km southwest of Murten, grew on the site of the ancient capital of the Celtic Helvetii tribe and was a major centre in the 2nd century AD, with a population 10 times that of the modern village. But its 5.6km of defensive ramparts failed to withstand attacks by the Alemani tribe in the late 3rd century and by the 5th century the town was insignificant.

Its Roman glory days are evoked in the **amphitheatre**, host to the **Musée Romain** (Roman Museum; ☎ 026 675 17 27; Ave Jomini; adult/under 16 Sfr4/free; ✆ 10am-noon & 1-5pm Tue-Sun Apr-Sep, 2-5pm Tue-Sun Oct-Mar) and an audience of 12,000 during its summer opera season. For tickets (Sfr70 to Sfr160), contact the **tourist office** (☎ 026 676 99 22; www.avenches.ch in French; Pl de l'Église 3).

Payerne

Payerne, 10km southwest, is dominated by the 11th-century five-apse Romanesque **Église Abbatiale** (☎ 026 662 67 04; Pl du Marché). The magnificent sandstone complex boasts fine sculptural decoration and frescoes, hosts art exhibitions (admission up to Sfr12), classical concerts (tickets Sfr20 to Sfr30) and free organ concerts at 6.15pm on the first Saturday of each month. Payerne **tourist office** (☎ 026 660 61 61; www.payerne.ch in French; Pl du Marché 10; ✆ 8am-noon & 1.30-6pm Mon-Fri), beside the church, has details.

Kerzers

Head 11km northeast from Murten to Kerzers where tropical butterflies flutter alongside hummingbirds and other exotic birds at **Papiliorama** (☎ 031 756 04 60; www.papiliorama.ch in French & Dutch; adult/4-15yr/parking Sfr13/7/3; ✆ 9am-6pm Apr-Oct, 10am-5pm Nov-Mar). Indigenous butterflies flit about in the **Swiss Butterfly Garden**, night creatures from Latin America hide in **Nocturama** (✆ 10am-

6pm Apr-Oct, 10am-5pm Nov-Mar), and in **Jungle Trek** (to open 2006) intrepid explorers can do just that.

The Swiss tropical gardens are a 20-minute walk from Kerzers train station, linked to Murten by train. Shuttle buses (adult/child Sfr2/1) run between Kerzers and the gardens.

GRUYÈRES & AROUND

pop 1490 / elevation 830m

Cheese is what this quaint pre-Alps village – with a fairytale castle so dreamy Sleeping Beauty would never wake up – is all about. Featherweight meringues drowned in thick double cream and a chocolate factory just down the road create a deadly gastronomic cocktail for food junkies.

Tummy matters aside, medieval Gruyères is a riot of 15th- to 17th-century houses tumbling down a hillock. It's cobbled heart will look even prettier by 2008 when a five-year, Sfr5 million project to repave its streets will be complete; buy a virtual cobble at www.pave-gruyeres.ch (in French).

Gruyères gets its name from the emblematic *gru* (crane) brandished by the Counts of Gruyères between the 11th and 16th centuries. Note the hard AOC Gruyère cheese made here for centuries carries no 's'.

Information

Tourist Office Gruyères (☎ 026 921 10 30; www.gruyeres.ch in French; Rue du Bourg 1; ✆ 10.30am-noon & 1.30-4.30pm Mon-Fri year-round, 9am-5pm Sat & Sun Jul–mid-Sep); Moléson (☎ 026 921 85 00; www.moleson.ch)

Sights

CHÂTEAU DE GRUYÈRES

This bewitching turreted **castle** (☎ 026 921 21 02; adult/6-16yr Sfr6.50/2; ✆ 9am-6pm Apr-Oct, 10am-4.30pm Nov-Feb), home to 19 different Counts of Gruyères who controlled the Sarine Valley from the 11th to 16th centuries, was rebuilt after a fire in 1493. Inside, you can visit its dungeon, view period furniture, tapestries and modern 'fantasy art'.

MUSEUM HR GIGER

Biomechanical art fills the **HR Giger Museum** (☎ 026 921 22 00; www.hrgigermuseum.com; adult/6-16yr Sfr12/5; ✆ 10am-6pm May-Oct, 11am-5pm Nov-Apr), dedicated to the man behind the sci-fi uniforms in the *Alien* movies – Chur-born Zürich-based Giger (b 1940). Opposite the

FRIBOURG, NEUCHÂTEL & JURA

Museum Bar HR Giger (◷ 10am-8.30pm Tue-Sun) is kitted out in the same weird and wacky surrealist style.

A combined museum and château ticket costs Sfr14.

CHEESE DAIRIES

The secret behind Gruyère cheese is revealed at the **Maison du Gruyère** (☎ 026 921 84 00; www.la maisondugruyere.ch; adult/child/student Sfr5/2/4; ◷ 9am-7pm Apr-Sep, 9am-6pm Oct-Mar) in Pringy, 1.5km from Gruyères. Cheese-making takes place four times daily between 9am and 3pm and can be watched through glass windows. The tourist train from Gruyères (p108) stops here.

At the **Fromagerie d'Alpage de Moléson** (☎ 026 921 10 44; adult/child Sfr5/3; ◷ 9.30am-10pm mid-May–mid-Oct), a 17th-century Alpine chalet 5km southwest of Gruyères in Moléson-sur-Gruyères, cheese is made using old-fashioned methods at 9.45am and 2.45pm.

Both dairies sell cheese (Sfr1.98 to Sfr2.40 per 100g) and serve fondue, *soupe du chalet* (a thick 'n hearty vegetable and potato soup topped with Gruyère double cream and cheese), *soupe à l'oignon au Gruyères* (Gruyère-topped onion soup) and other typical mountain dishes in their dairy restaurants.

Cheese is still produced in a couple of traditional mountain chalets along the **Sentier des Fromageries**, a trail that takes walkers through green Gruyères pastures. Ask at the Maison du Gruyère for the brochure outlining the two-hour walk (7km to 8km).

Activities

Moléson-sur-Gruyères (elevation 1100m), 5km southwest of Gruyères, is popular in summer for via ferrata, go-karting, hiking and mountain biking, with plenty of well-marked trails, including a gentle 1½-hour **Sentier Botanique** (botanical trail) from Moléson village. In winter there is easy downhill skiing from the Moléson peak (2002m) and a 4km-long **sledge track** linking mid-station Plan-Francey (1520m) and the village.

Sleeping & Eating

Le Pâquier (☎ 026 912 20 25; www.lepatchi.ch; Rue de la Gare 10, Le Pâquier; s/d/tr Sfr60/90/120; P ▣) Three years of hard graft has paid off for Hedwige and André who run this *maison d'hôtes* in a restored 19th-century manor. Nightly rates are for a bathroom-clad room with breakfast *or* kitchenette, making it handy for families and self-caterers. Find Le Pâquier 3.5km northwest of Gruyères.

Hostellerie Saint-Georges (☎ 026 921 83 00; www .st-georges-gruyeres.ch in French; s/d from Sfr130/180, menus Sfr45 & Sfr79) 'Sweet dreams' is the house motto at this stylish 14-room inn where hefty beams, fireplaces, embroidered bedspreads and the odd chandelier add a noble touch. The former Michelin-starred chef cooks up strictly poetic creations.

Chalet de Gruyères (☎ 026 921 21 54; www.chalet -gruyeres.ch in French; Rue du Château 53; fondues & raclettes Sfr28; ◷ lunch & dinner Mon-Sun) Feast on Alpine fodder (fondue, raclette, grilled meats) in this cosy chalet strung with cow bells or on its shaded Terrasse du Chalet opposite. Its *croûte en fromage* is super-loaded

FRIBOURG, NEUCHÂTEL & JURA

GRUYÈRE: FAST FACTS

▪ A cow consumes 100kg of grass and 85L of water a day to produce 25L of milk.

▪ Cheese-makers need 400L of milk to make one 35kg wheel of Gruyère.

▪ There are allegedly 75 different Alpine scents in Gruyère cheese. Vanilla, orchid, violet, chestnut, mint, wood shavings, hazelnuts, fresh grass…you name it, it's there.

▪ Approximately 330 million litres of milk are processed into 27,500 tons of cheese in 200-odd dairies in the Fribourg, Neuchâtel, Jura and Vaud cantons; Gruyères cows yield 5.7 million litres a year.

▪ A mild (*doux*) Gruyère is left to mature for five to six months, a semi-salted (*mi-salé*) for seven to eight months, a salted (*salé*) for nine to 10 months, a reserve (*réserve au surchoix*) for at least 10 months, and a deliciously strong-tasting mature (*vieux*) for at least 15 months.

▪ Two-thirds of Gruyère production is consumed in Switzerland; the EU and North America eat the rest.

with cheese, meringues come with the thickest Gruyère double cream ever, while coffee comes with a whole pot of the creamy stuff.

Auberge de la Halle (☎ 026 921 21 78; Rue du Château; menus Sfr33, Sfr41.50 & Sfr43; ☺ Wed-Mon) Less touristy than some, Auberge de la Halle is known for its meal-sized *soupe du chalet* (soup of mushrooms, pasta, cheese etc, Sfr15) and *sérac* (*fromage frais* made from the whey of Gruyère). Its special menu (Sfr12) for *'vos gastronomes en culottes courtes'* (little gourmands in short trousers) are popular.

Getting There & Around

From Fribourg, Gruyères can be reached by hourly bus or train (Sfr16.80, 40 minutes to one hour) to Bulle then hourly bus or train (Sfr3.30, 15 to 20 minutes) from there. Gruyères is a 10-minute walk uphill from its train station. One or two buses a day connect Gruyères train station with Gruyères village and Moléson.

The N12 motorway from Vevey to Fribourg passes by Bulle. From there take the N11 road south to Gruyères. Otherwise, take the N11 north from Lake Geneva via Aigle.

Cars must be left in the free parking area at the village entrance. An electric **tourist train** (☎ 079 542 28 30; www.petit-train.info; adult/6-12yr Sfr6.50/4; ☺ 9am or 10am-7pm Mar-Oct) tootles between the car park, château and Maison du Gruyère.

BROC & BULLE

Experience Willy Wonka's chocolate thrills and spills at the **Nestlé-Caillers chocolate factory** (☎ 026 921 51 51; adult/under 16 Sfr4/free; ☺ 1.30pm & 4pm Mon, 9am, 11am, 1.30pm & 4pm Tue-Fri), 2km north of Gruyères in Broc. But don't expect to get anywhere near the production line; visits comprise a video of how chocolate is made – and free samples.

Five kilometres northwest of Gruyères, **Bulle** (elevation 771m), the main transport hub for the area, is worth a brief look for its 13th-century **château** (now administrative offices) and **Musée Gruérien** (☎ 026 912 72 60; www.musee-gruerien.ch in French; Rue de la Condémine 25; adult/under/student 16 Sfr6/free/5; ☺ 10am-noon & 2-5pm Tue-Sat, 2-5pm Sun).

CHARMEY & THE SCHWARZSEE

From Broc it is a pretty climb into the pre-Alps of Canton de Fribourg. **Charmey** (elevation 876m) is the centre of local skiing with 30km of downhill slopes (1630m) accessible via the Rapido Sky cable car. In summer, it's a haven for walkers and mountain bikers. The **tourist office** (☎ 026 927 55 80; www.charmey.ch; ☺ 2-6pm Tue-Sun), across the car park from the cable car, has trail details, including some around Vanil Noir, the region's highest point.

Head east for another 11km and you hit German-speaking territory (the 'Wilkommen' sign is a dead giveaway) and the hamlet of **Jaun** with its twin-set of churches. The older one with a wood shingle roof shelters **Cantorama** (☎ 026 929 85 72; admission Sfr4, concerts Sfr20; ☺ 2-5pm Sat & Sun May-Oct, 2-5pm Tue & Thu Jul & Aug), a sacred music centre with displays on traditional Fribourgeois chants and host to choral concerts. The newer church (1910) has an unusual cemetery where wooden crosses dating from the 1980s to present feature carvings of the deceased's job in life. From Jaun the road climbs up to the **Jaunpass**, just inside Bern canton.

SOUNDS OF SILENCE

Silence is sweet for the 26 Carthusian monks who live in almost complete silence in Switzerland's only such still-functioning monastery, the solitary 13th-century **Chartreuse de la Valsainte**, 6km north of Charmey as the crow flies. Behind high walls, well away from the outside world, the cream-robed fathers and brothers here lead a spartan life dedicated to prayer and manual work. They rise at 5.30am, those assigned the duty of chopping wood, for heating, in the surrounding forests are allowed a simple breakfast of cheese. The rest wait until midday to eat. Once a week, the community is allowed 'out', the monks dividing into two groups for a 3½-hour hike – and chat – in the green surrounds. Sunday recreation is the only other opportunity for shared debate.

The 62-cell monastery cannot be visited. Only men can attend Sunday mass at 7.45am in the chapel, but the **Chapelle de la Valsainte** (☎ 026 927 11 37), outside the compound, is open to all.

Northeast of Charmey is the mountain lake of **Schwarzsee** (Black Lake; www.schwarzsee.ch), elevation 1046m, a magical setting for winter skiing and summertime hiking. About 2km north of the village is Karl Neuhaus' **Eis Paläste** (Ice Palace; ☎ 026 419 11 80; adult/under 16 Sfr6/3; ☼ 2-9.30pm Wed-Sun Dec-Mar), a fantastical construction of turrets, bridges, domes, grottoes and crystal palaces between pine trees – built solely from ice. Illuminated at night, an evening stroll along the sand paths (not to mention a picnic in an igloo) is magical.

Another fascinating trip is to drive past La Valsainte to the end of the road, from where a three-hour marked trail leads to the lake.

CANTON DE NEUCHÂTEL

The focus of this heavily forested 800 sq km canton (population 166,500), northwest of its Fribourg counterpart, is Lac de Neuchâtel – the largest lake entirely within Switzerland. Canton capital Neuchâtel sits plump on its northern shore and the gentle Jura Mountains rise to the north and west. Watch-making has been a mainstay industry since the 18th century and the canton's two other large towns – La Chaux-de-Fonds and Le Locle – remain firmly on the so-called 'Watch Valley' tourist trail.

Together with Biel and Murten lakes, Neuchâtel falls into the Pays de Trois Lacs (Land of Three Lakes) trio. With France bang next door, French is *the* language of this rural land.

NEUCHÂTEL

pop 31,740 / elevation 430m

Its Old Town sandstone elegance, the airy Gallic nonchalance of its café-life and the gay lakeside air that breezes along the shoreline of its glittering lake makes Neuchâtel disarmingly charming. The small university town – complete with spirited *comune libre* (free commune) – is compact enough to discover on foot while the French spoken here is said be Switzerland's purest.

Information

BOOKSHOP

Payot Librairie (Rue du Seyon; ☼ 1.30-6.30pm Mon, 9am-6.30pm Tue-Fri, 8.30am-noon Sat) Maps, guidebooks and English-language fiction.

> **DID YOU KNOW**
>
> Neuchâtel's town observatory gives the official time-check for all of Switzerland.

LAUNDRY

Salon Lavoir Lavmatic (Rue des Moulins 27; ☼ 8am-8pm)

POST

Central Post Office (Place du Port; ☼ 7.30am-6.30pm Mon-Fri, 8.30am-noon Sat)

TOURIST INFORMATION

Tourist office (☎ 032 889 68 90; www.neuchateltourism .ch; Hôtel des Postes, Pl du Port; ☼ 9am-noon & 1.30-5.30pm Mon-Fri, 9am-noon Sat Sep-Jun, 9am-6.30pm Mon-Fri, 9-4pm Sat, 10am-2pm Sun Jul & Aug)

Sights

Eight *promenades touristiques* (tourist walks) are marked around town and an electric **train** (☎ 032 889 68 90; Pl du Port; adult/child Sfr6/3; ☼ tours Sat & Sun May, Jun & Sep, daily Jul & Aug) ferries tired/tiny feet around the main sights, which takes around 45 minutes.

OLD TOWN & CHÂTEAU

The streets are lined by fine, shuttered 18th-century mansions and studded with fanciful gold-leafed fountains topped by anything from a banner-wielding knight, **Fontaine du Banneret** (Rue Fleury), to a maiden representing Justice, **Fontaine de la Justice** (Rue de l'Hôpital) – see a copy on the street and the original in the Musée d'Art et d'Histoire.

Heading uphill along Rue du Château, walk through the medieval city gate to view the **Tour des Prisons** (☎ 032 717 71 02; Rue Jehanne de Hochberg 5; admission Sfr1; ☼ 8am-6pm Apr-Sep). Scale it for lake and Alpine views. Inside the largely Gothic **Église Collégiale** a mix of Romanesque elements (notably the triple apse) looms large. Facing the main entrance is a statue of Guillaume Farel, who brought the Reformation to town, following which the cathedral was obliged to swap sides.

Behind the church is the 15th-century **château** (☎ 032 889 60 00; admission free; ☼ guided tours hourly btwn 10am-noon & 2-4pm Mon-Sat, 2-4pm Sun Apr-Sep) with a pretty shady courtyard you can wander in. Summertime guided tours (45 minutes) allow you to poke your nose around the castle's innards.

FRIBOURG, NEUCHÂTEL
& JURA

MUSÉE D'ART ET D'HISTOIRE

The **Art & History Museum** (☎ 032 717 79 25; www
.mahn.ch in French; Esplanade Léopold Robert 2; adult/under
16 Sfr7/free, Wed free; ☼ 10am-6pm Tue-Sun) is notable
for three clockwork androids made between
1764 and 1774 by watchmaker Jaquet Droz.
The Writer can be programmed to dip his
pen in an inkpot and write up to 40 characters, while the Musician plays up to five tunes
on a real organ. The Draughtsman is the simplest, with a repertoire of six drawings. The
androids are activated on the first Sunday of
the month at 2pm, 3pm and 4pm.

Activities

The port buzzes with summer fun. Pl du
12 Septembre is one big playground, while

Marine Service Loisirs (☎ 032 724 61 82; Port de la Ville;
☼ May-Sep) rents out motor boats (Sfr55 per
hour), pedalos (Sfr20 per hour), aquabikes
(Sfr20 per hour) and two- or four-seated
pedal-powered buggies to cruise along the
silky-smooth quays. **Neuchâtel Roule** (☎ 032
717 77 75, 076 417 50 91; www.neuchatelroule.ch in French;
Faubourg du Lac 3), with a seasonal **portside kiosk**
(☼ 7.30am-9.30pm Jun-Oct), rents bicycles for
free (Sfr15 or €20 deposit) and the **Société
de Navigation sur les Lacs de Neuchâtel et Morat**
(see p112) organises lake cruises.

Festivals & Events

Parades, costumes and drunken revelry ensure fun at the **Fête des Vendanges** (Grape
Harvest Festival), the last weekend in Sep-

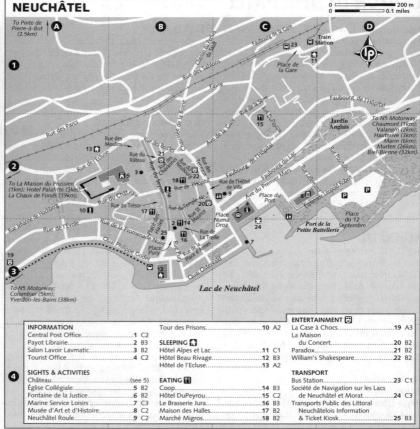

NEUCHÂTEL

INFORMATION	
Central Post Office	1 C2
Payot Librairie	2 B3
Salon Lavoir Lavmatic	3 B2
Tourist Office	4 C2

SIGHTS & ACTIVITIES	
Château	(see 5)
Église Collégiale	5 B2
Fontaine de la Justice	6 B2
Marine Service Loisirs	7 C3
Musée d'Art et d'Histoire	8 C2
Neuchâtel Roule	9 C2

Tour des Prisons	10 A2

SLEEPING	
Hôtel Alpes et Lac	11 C1
Hôtel Beau Rivage	12 B3
Hôtel de l'Ecluse	13 A2

EATING	
Coop	14 B3
Hôtel DuPeyrou	15 C2
Le Brasserie Jura	16 B3
Maison des Halles	17 B2
Marché Migros	18 B2

ENTERTAINMENT	
La Case à Chocs	19 A3
La Maison	
du Concert	20 B2
Paradox	21 B2
William's Shakespeare	22 B2

TRANSPORT	
Bus Station	23 C1
Société de Navigation sur les Lacs	
de Neuchâtel et Morat	24 C3
Transports Public des Littoral	
Neuchâtelois Information	
& Ticket Kiosk	25 B3

LIFE IN THE COMMUNE

Neuchâtel's so-called **Commune Libre du Neubourg et Alentours** (Free Commune of Neubourg and Surroundings; www.leneubourg.ch in French) – a good mate of Paris' Montmartre (a self-declared free commune since 1920) – boils down to a good excuse to party. Founded in 1979, it embraces a trio of Old Town streets – Rue de Neubourg, Rue des Fausses-Brayes and colourfully frescoed Rue des Chavannes, otherwise dubbed Rue des Peintres (Painters' St) with the free-thinking motto *'voir d'un œil sentir de l'autre'* (look with one eye, feel with the other) scribed as a footnote on the unofficial street sign pinned up next to the official one.

Various jazz festivals, February's Fête de la Chandeleur, June's Fête de l'Été et de al Musique, not to mention the annual Fête des Vendages in late September when the wine flows like there's no tomorrow, are but some of the spirited festivals celebrated with gusto by the bohemian souls behind the commune.

---

tember. Jazz, pop and rock set the lakeside jiving during June's open-air **FestiNeuch** (www.festineuch.com in French).

Sleeping

Hôtel de l'Ecluse (☎ 032 729 93 10; www.hoteldelecluse.ch; Rue de l'Ecluse 24; s/d from Sfr100/150; P 💻) Squished in between commercial buildings, yes, but this fine house boasts modernised rooms with brass beds, elegant décor and kitchenettes. Breakfast is served in the bar and there are a couple of terraces for guests to lounge in.

Hôtel Alpes et Lac (☎ 032 723 19 19; www.alpesetlac.ch in French; Pl de la Gare 2; s/d Sfr125/180, with lake view Sfr150/210; P 🍴 💻) Opposite the station, this stately 19th-century hotel dating from 1872 markets its 30 comfortable modernised rooms with Wi-Fi (Sfr5 per 30 minutes, Sfr11 for 24 hours) as *bon chic contemporain*. Weekend rates are competitive.

Hôtel Beau Rivage (☎ 032 723 15 15; www.beau-rivage-hotel.ch in French; Esplanade du Mont Blanc 1; s/d from Sfr210/255, mains/menu Sfr38/49; P 🍴 🍴 💻 🍷) Overlooking the lake and sculpture-studded gardens, this majestic ship of a hotel is ab fab – as are the culinary wonders of chef Jean-Baptiste Molinari. Breakfast costs Sfr24.

Hôtel Palafitte (☎ 032 723 02 03; www.palafitte.ch; Route des Gouttes-d'Or 2; pavilion on the lake/shore Sfr490/660; P 🍴 🍴) If cutting-edge technology and architecture are your thing then Neuchâtel's other five-star wonder – a work of art 3km west of Neuchâtel centre in Monruz – will thrill. Stylish self-contained pavilions tout plasma TV screens, Jacuzzi and remote-control everything. Lakeside units have a terrace, fully-equipped office and bathrooms spilling into the lake. Breakfast costs Sfr30.

Eating

Local specialities include tripe and *tomme neuchâteloise chaude* (baked goat cheese starter).

Le Brasserie Jura (☎ 032 725 14 10; Rue de la Treille 7; lunch menu Sfr16.50, mains Sfr15-35; 🕐 Mon-Sat) With a name like Jura Brasserie, this hot spot couldn't be more local. Food is cooked to fill. *Tripes à la Neuchâteloise* (Neuchâtel-style tripe) is the menu star and vegetarians are well catered for with vegetable rösti, veg-stuffed ravioli or six-cereal ravioli doused in goat cheese sauce.

Maison des Halles (☎ 032 724 31 41; www.maisondeshalles.com; Pl des Halles; mains from Sfr35; 🕐 Tue-Sat) Gourmands plump for tasty Maison des Halles inside a turreted 16th-century mansion. Cuisine is French.

La Maison du Prussien (☎ 032 730 54 54; www.hotel-prussien.ch; Au Gor du Vauseyon, Rue des Tunnels 11; mains from Sfr30; 🕐 Mon-Sat) This one-time brewery in a grand old house, enclosed by woods and cradled by the impetuous babbling of a nearby brook, is a treat – and it has great rooms too. Hop aboard Cormondrèche-bound bus No 1 from Pl Pury, get off at Beauregard and head down the stairs to your right following the signs.

Hôtel DuPeyrou (☎ 032 725 11 83; www.dupeyrou.ch in French; Ave DuPeyrou 1; starters/mains Sfr20/50, menus Sfr79-139; 🕐 Tue-Sat) DuPeyrou presides like a mini-Versailles over manicured gardens. Built between 1765 and 1770, it regales with gastronomic dining in an 18th-century ambience.

Pinte de Pierre-à-Bot (☎ 032 725 33 80; Rue Pierre-à-Bot 106; starters/mains Sfr10/25, fondue for 2 Sfr28-32) It is a short drive from the town centre but worth it. Built in 1928 as the town's golf clubhouse, the green was moved in the 1970s and the

FRIBOURG, NEUCHÂTEL & JURA

clubhouse turned into a restaurant – famed for its 20 fondues including ones with Guinness, champagne, curry and 1000 herbs. *Fondue Neuchâteloise* is a mix of local Gruyère, garlic and kirsch.

Central supermarkets:
Coop (Rue de la Treille 4)
Marché Migros (Rue de l'Hôpital 12)

Entertainment

Paradox (☎ 032 721 33 77; www.paradoxclub.com in French; Rue du Râteau; ☾ 10.30pm-4am Thu-Sat, à l'étage 5pm-1am or 2am Tue-Sun) Funk, deep house, mental groove…anything goes at this trendy steel space with dance floor downstairs, bar *à l'étage* (1st-floor bar).

William's Shakepeare (☎ 032 725 85 88; Rue des Terreaux 7) Modest disco-pub in the commune.

La Case à Chocs (☎ 032 721 20 56; www.case-a-chocs .ch in French; concerts Sfr10-15; Quai Philippe Godet 16; ☾ Thu-Sun) Alternative venue in a converted brewery with live music, occasional cinema and art shows.

La Maison du Concert (☎ 032 724 21 22; www.maisonduconcert.ch in French; Rue de l'Hôtel de Ville 4) Revitalised old theatre with plans to open a bistro.

Getting There & Away
BOAT
From May or June to October, **Société de Navigation sur les Lacs de Neuchâtel et Morat** (☎ 032 729 96 00; www.navig.ch in French; Port de la Ville) runs boats to/from Estavayer-le-Lac (Sfr16.20, 1¾

hours), Yverdon-les-Bains (Sfr25, 2½ hours), Murten (Sfr18.20, 1¾ hours) and Biel (Bienne; Sfr26, 2½ hours).

TRAIN
From the **train station** (Ave de la Gare), a 10-minute walk northeast of the Old Town, hourly trains run to/from Geneva (Sfr37, 1¼ to 1½ hours), Bern via Kerzers (Sfr17.60, 35 minutes), Basel (Sfr34, 1½ hours), Biel (Sfr11.40, 20 minutes) and other destinations. Around two per hour run to/from Yverdon (Sfr13.40, 20 minutes).

Getting Around
Local buses hit transport hub Pl Pury where **Transports Public du Littoral Neuchâtelois information & ticket kiosk** (TN; ☎ 032 720 06 58; www.tnneuchatel.ch in French; Pl Pury; ☾ 7am-6pm Mon-Fri, 8.30-11.30am Sat) is located. Tickets cost Sfr1.70 to Sfr2.50 (Sfr0.40 more from the driver), depending on the length of the journey. Bus No 6 links the train station and Pl Pury.

AROUND NEUCHÂTEL
Day trips from Neuchâtel abound.

Inland
Chaumont (1160m) is a beautiful spot to soak up views across the three lakes to the Alps. From Neuchâtel ride bus No 7 to La Coudre, then take the 13-minute panoramic **funicular**

THE CONCRETE KING

Few know that Le Corbusier (1887–1965, see p35), invariably perceived as French rather than Swiss, was born in La Chaux-de-Fonds at Rue de la Serre 38. Charles Edouard Jeanneret (the groundbreaking architect's real name) spent his childhood in the clock-making town whose concrete, Soviet-style grid-plan clearly found its way somewhere into his young psyche.

After brief stints in the Orient and Berlin, Le Corbusier returned to La Chaux in 1912 to open an architectural office and build Villa Jeanneret-Perret, otherwise called La Maison Blanche ('the white house'), for his parents. The architect who, a few years later would become a serious pal of Germany's Walter Gropius and the Bauhaus movement, lived in the house until 1917 when he left Switzerland for Paris' bright lights. Two years later his parents, unable to afford the upkeep of the house, left.

La Maison Blanche (www.villa-blanche.ch; Chemin de Pouillerel) is one of 11 points on a Corbusier trail that La Chaux's **Tourist Office** (☎ 032 889 68 95; info.cdf@ne.ch; Espacité 1, Pl Le Corbusier), a five-minute walk north of the train station along Ave Léopold Robert, has information on. Derelict for years, Le Corbusier's family home was made a historic monument in 1979 and adopted in 2000 by the Association Maison Blanche which has restored the modern architecture treasure and opened it to visitors.

Mediterranean-inspired **Villa Turque** (☎ 032 912 31 31; www.ebel.ch in French; Rue du Doubs 167; admission free; ☾ 11am-4pm 1st & 3rd Sat of every month), the other La Chaux house Le Corbusier designed, was taken over by the self-dubbed 'architects of time', Ebel luxury watch-makers, in 1986.

THE GREEN FAIRY

It was in the deepest darkest depths of Couvet in the Val de Travers – otherwise dubbed the Pays des Fées (Fairyland) – that absinthe was first distilled in 1740 and produced commercially in 1797 (although it was a Frenchman called Pernod who made the bitter green liqueur known with the distillery he opened just a few kilometres across the French–Swiss border in Pontarlier).

From 1910, following Switzerland's prohibition of the wickedly alcoholic and ruthlessly bitter aniseed drink, distillers of the so-called 'devil in the bottle' in the Val de Travers moved underground. In 1990 the great-grandson of a pre-prohibition distiller in Môtiers came up with Switzerland's first legal aniseed liqueur since 1910 – albeit one which was only 45% proof alcohol (instead of 50% to 75%) and which scarcely contained thujone (the offensive chemical found in wormwood, said to be the root of absinthe's devilish nature). An *extrait d'absinthe* (absinthe extract) quickly followed and in March 2005, following Switzerland's lifting of its absinthe ban, the **Blackmint – Distillerie Kübler & Wyss** (☎ 032 861 14 69; www.blackmint.ch; Rue du Château 7, Môtiers) distilled its first true and authentic batch of the mythical *fée verte* (green fairy) from valley-grown wormwood. Mix one part crystal-clear liqueur with five parts water to make it green.

(☎ 032 720 06 00; one way/return Sfr4.60/9.20) up the mountain.

About 2km beyond Neuchâtel, **Valangin** presents a white turreted **château** (☎ 032 857 23 83; adult/child Sfr5/3; ⏱ 10am-noon & 2-5pm Tue-Thu, Sat & Sun Apr–mid-Dec). Inside you'll find period furniture, arms, artwork and Neuchâtel lacework which you can watch being made on the first Sunday of each month from 2pm to 5pm. Take Villars-bound TN bus line V from Pl Pury to Valangin (seven minutes).

Clocks and Le Corbusier are the only reasons to push northwest to **La Chaux-de-Fonds** (population 38,500), the canton's largest city (and Switzerland's highest). The drab grid-plan town was a household name in Europe as the centre of precision watch-making in the 18th and 19th centuries and stills manufactures timepieces today. Its **Musée International d'Horlogerie** (☎ 032 967 68 61; www.mih.ch in French; Rue des Musées 29; adult/12-18yr/family Sfr10/6/22; ⏱ 10am-5pm Tue-Sun) tells the tale. Hourly trains run from Neuchâtel to/from La Chaux-de-Fonds (Sfr10.40, 30 minutes).

Along the Lake

Family-scale vineyards have clothed the hills on the northwest shore of Lac de Neuchâtel since the 10th century. Neuchâtel tourist office has a list of cellars where wine can be sampled.

At Hauterive, 3km northeast of Neuchâtel, **Laténium** (☎ 032 889 69 17; www.latenium.ch in French; adult/7-16yr/family Sfr9/4/20; ⏱ 10am-5pm Tue-Sun) is an archaeological trip back in time from local prehistory to the Renaissance.

Take bus No 1 from Pl Pury to the Musée d'Archéologie stop.

Southbound, **Château de Vaumarcus** (☎ 032 836 36 10; www.chateauvaumarcus.ch in French; admission by guided tour adult/child/family Sfr8/5/20; ⏱ 2-5pm Wed-Sat, 11am-5pm Sun Apr-Aug) is a keep with witches-hat turrets and wooded vineyard surrounds rescued from ruin in the 1980s. It now houses the excellent restaurant, **Le Cour du Peintre** (starters/mains Sfr10/30, lunch menus Sfr19-48). Charles the Bold allegedly slept here in March 1476, and you can take his room, the only guest space in the house (doubles Sfr290), complete with Louis XIII furniture, modern bath and four-poster bed. Guided castle tours include admission to the castle-based Fondation Marc Jurt, an art foundation that hosts changing contemporary art, sculpture and installation exhibitions.

Val de Travers

Hikers march from Vaumarcus to the Val de Travers to marvel at the enormous abyss known as the **Creux du Van** (Rocky Hole – *van* is a word of Celtic origin meaning rock). This spectacular crescent moon wall, a product of glacial erosion, interrupts the habitually green rolling countryside hereabouts in startling fashion. This enormous gulf on the cantonal frontier with Vaud is 1km long and plunges 440m to the bottom (the first 200m is a sheer stony drop).

The Creux is most easily reached on foot from Noiraigue, 22km southeast of Neuchâtel along the N10 or by hourly train from Neuchâtel (Sfr6.60, 20 minutes). The round-trip hike can take up to five hours depending on the route you follow.

Continuing along the N10 or on the same train from Neuchâtel (Sfr10.40, 35 minutes), you reach **Môtiers** with its pretty castle, absinthe distillery and **Maison des Mascarons** (☎ 032 861 35 51; Grande-Rue 14; adult/child Sfr5/2; ☒ 2.30-5.30pm Tue, Thu, Sat & Sun May–mid-Oct), a local arts, crafts and history museum. Immediately south from here another great ring walk (around 4½ hours) takes you through the **Gorges de la Poëta Raisse** to high green plains, forest and, finally, a crest at 1448m.

MONTAGNES NEUCHÂTELOISES

The west of the canton is dominated by the low mountain chain of the Jura, which stretches from the canton of the same name (right) to the northeast and into Canton de Vaud in the southwest. Cross-country skiers, walkers and cyclists will find the hills here – the Montagnes Neuchâteloises – inspirational.

Le Locle

pop 10,315 / elevation 950m

Incredibly, the whole lucrative Swiss watch business began ticking in this straggly town when Daniel Jean-Richard (1665–1741) established a cottage industry in the manufacture of timepieces here. His name continues to be lent to luxury watches manufactured by Jean Richard (www.danieljeanrichard .ch) in nearby La Chaux-de-Fonds.

Grand 18th-century rooms filled with all manner of clocks make the **Musée de l'Horlogerie du Locle** (Watchmaking Museum; ☎ 032 931 16 80; www.mhl-monts.ch in French; Route des Monts 65; adult/10-18yr/family Sfr7/4/17; ☒ 10am-5pm Tue-Sun May-Oct, 2-5pm Tue-Sun Nov-Apr), inside Château des Monts, tick.

About 2km west, a series of underground mills carved out of the rock to exploit subterranean water flowing into the Doubs River makes for an unusual day out at the 17th-century **Moulins Souterrains du Le Col-des-Roches** (☎ 032 931 89 89; www.lesmoulins.ch in French; admission by guided tour adult/child/family Sfr12/7/28; ☒ 10am-5pm May-Oct, 2-5pm Tue-Sun Nov-Apr), 2km west of Le Locle. Take the Le Locle–La Brévine bus to get here.

Le Locle is 8km by train (Sfr3.20, six minutes, at least hourly) from La Chaux-de-Fonds.

Les Brenets & Saut du Doubs

A scenic excursion lies 6km from Le Locle. Le Doubs River, which springs forth inside France, widens out at the peaceful village of **Les Brenets**, just inside Swiss territory. For the next 45km on its serpentine northwestern course from here, the river forms the border between the two countries before making a loop inside Switzerland and then returning to French territory.

About a one-hour walk along **Lac des Brenets** (Lac de Chaillexon on the French side) the river will bring you to the **Saut du Doubs**, a splendid crashing waterfall where the river cascades 27m to a natural pool. Hikers might prefer a great 4½-hour loop. From Les Brenets, follow signs for Les Recrettes (most easily reached along a narrow asphalt road). From here you head across a clearing on the edge of the forest that stands on the steep slopes above the river to the **Belvédère** (1075m), a magnificent point high above a bend on the Doubs with views across to the gentle green countryside of France. Take the forest trail (impassable in winter) for about an hour to **Roches de Moron**, then head downhill through the woods to **Lac de Moron** and follow the trail along its southern shore. It gradually climbs away from the lake and river (about an hour) until you reach the Saut du Doubs waterfall. From here it's an easy hour's walk back to Les Brenets.

For non-walkers, **NLB** (☎ 032 932 14 14; www .nlb.ch) runs regular boats from Les Brenets to the waterfall up to 11 times a day from June to September (one way/return Sfr7/12), and three daily in April, May and October.

Trains from Le Locle to Les Brenets (Sfr3.20, seven minutes) are frequent.

CANTON DE JURA

The northernmost of the three cantons, clover-shaped Canton de Jura (840 sq km, population 69,100) is a more-rural-than-rural, mysterious peripheral region that has always come last. Its grandest towns – including its capital – are little more than enchanting villages, while deep forests and impossibly green clearings succeed one another across the low Jura mountains.

While the Jura mountain range proper extends south through Canton de Neuchâtel and Canton de Vaud into the Haut-

CENT SAVER

If you are intending to travel a lot by bus or train in a day, you should get a Carte Journalière Région CJ (Sfr16), allowing unlimited travel on Chemins de Fer du Jura (CJ) trains and buses for 24 hours. Canton aside, the Carte Journalière Arc Jurassien (Sfr25) also covers the Jura Bernois and as far south as Le Locle (opposite) and Les Brenets (opposite).

Jura in neighbouring France, it is here that its Jurassic heart lies. Saignelégier, 45km north of Neuchâtel in the south of the canton, is the main port of call for tourist information.

FRANCHES MONTAGNES

Settlers only began trickling into these untamed 'free mountains' in the 14th century. Heavily forested hill country marking the northern end of the Jura range, the area – undulating at roughly 1000m – is sprinkled with hamlets and is ideal for walking, mountain biking and cross-country skiing. The Doubes River kisses its northern tip.

At an elevation of 1000m and with a population of 2140, **Saignelégier** (www.saignelegier.ch), the main town, won't hold your interest for long unless you're in town for August's annual **Marché-Concours**, a horse show. The tourist office, **Jura Tourisme** (☎ 090 112 34 00; crs@jura .ch; Rue de la Gruère 1; 🕑 9am-noon & 2-6pm Mon-Fri, 10am-4pm Sat) covers the whole Jura and has ample information on accommodation options, including farm-based B&Bs.

For **cross-country skiing**, take your pick of a trio of hamlets: **Montfaucon**, 5km northeast; **Le Noirmont**, 6km southwest; or **Les Breuleux**, 7km south. **Goumois**, bang-slap on the Swiss–French border (officially in France) 8km west of Saignelégier, is a canoeing and rafting mecca. **Goumois Évasion** (☎ 03 81 44 21 30, 06 81 24 02 03; www.goumois.com in French; Chemin des Seignottes) organises canoeing, rafting and kayaking trips along the Doubs River to Soubey (€27, four to five hours) and St-Ursanne (€45, nine hours over two days) in the Swiss Jura. Straightfoward canoe/kayak rental costs €6 for 1½ hours.

Saignelégier is on the train line between La Chaux-de-Fonds (Sfr13.40, 35 minutes, almost hourly) and Basel (Sfr26, 1½ with a change at Glovelier).

For panoramic views across the Jura, the Bieler See and the Alps, head to **St Imier**, 18km south of Saignelégier in the Jura Bernois, then follow the minor road south towards Villiers. The first turn left (east) takes you along a winding (and in winter snowbound) road to **Le Chasseral** (1607m), a launch pad for hang-gliders.

NORTHERN JURA

Three towns within easy reach of one another are strung out across northern Jura, never far from the French frontier.

Delémont
pop 11,490 / elevation 413m

Canton de Jura's capital moored alongside the Scheulte River is modest. Its Old Town preserves a whiff of years gone by, with uneven houses topped by improbably tall tiled roofs peeping over 18th-century **Église de St Marcel** and the so-called **château** (really a grand stately manor). The **Musée Jurassien d'Art et d'Histoire** (☎ 032 422 80 77; Rue du 23 Juin 52; adult/child Sfr6/free; 🕑 2-5pm Tue-Sun) displays a hodgepodge of local paintings, religious art and objects from various Jura churches and traditional household furnishings. Motorists can follow the signs 3km north out of town to the **Chapelle de Vorbourg**, a dramatically located centre of pilgrimage.

St Ursanne
pop 870 / elevation 430m

A pretty 30-minute motor west of Delémont takes you through beautiful countryside to the most delightful village in the canton – medieval St Ursanne on the north bank of the Doubs River. As early as the 7th century a small centre of worship existed here on the site of the present grand, 12th-century **Église Collégiale**, a mostly Gothic church with a splendid Romanesque portal on its southern flank and an intriguing crypt. The Gothic cloister is a cool, soothing retreat. Around the church are clustered ancient houses, the 16th-century town gates and a lovely stone bridge over the Doubs River. For tourist information, accommodation and the lowdown on kayaking on the Doubs, hit **Jura Tourisme** (☎ 032 461 37 16; Rue du Quartier 18).

Trains link St Ursanne train station, 1km east of the town centre, with Delémont (Sfr6.60, 20 minutes) and Porrentruy (Sfr4.60, 12 minutes) and buses poodle

---

MONKS' HEADS

For eight centuries, villages around the Bellelay Abbey in the Jura Bernois (just across the border from Canton de Jura, 8km north of Tavannes on the N30 highway between Moutier and St Imier) have produced a strong, nutty flavoured cheese. Until the French Revolution it went by the name of Bellelay or monks' cheese. In 1792 revolutionary troops marched in, obliging the monks of Bellelay to take their leave. The troopers found a pile of these cylindrical cheeses in the cellars and dubbed them *têtes de moine* (monks' heads). Perhaps they had in mind the curious way in which one 'slices' them. A knife is used to scrape shavings off the top of the cheese in a circular motion, vaguely reminiscent of the monks' tonsure. Nowadays, the *tête de moine* is produced all over the Jura and a nifty device, the *girolle* has been invented to slice it.

---

along narrow country roads to and from nearby villages. Walking trails are a dime a dozen; to foot it to Porrentruy pick up the steep and picturesque uphill trail north to the Col de la Croix (789m).

Porrentruy
pop 6750 / elevation 425m

From Col de la Croix, the road dips down quickly through forest and into a plain to the last Jura town of importance before heading into France – pretty Porrentruy. Fine old buildings line the main street, Grand Rue, against a dramatic backdrop of the bulky **château** (really a set of buildings raised at different periods). Thirteenth-century **Tour de Refouss** stands aloof amid the various 18th-century structures now occupied by government offices.

The tastiest time to visit **Porrentruy** (www .porrentruy.ch in French) is during its **Fête de la Saint Martin**, a centuries' old feast on the second Sunday after All Saints' Day in November, marking the end of the rural working year. Now, as then, the festival is a fabulous excuse to gorge yourself on all sorts of sausages, cold meats and puddings. **Jura Tourisme** (☎ 032 466 59 59; www.juratourisme.ch in French & German; Grand Rue 5; ☽ 9am-noon & 1.30-6pm Mon-Fri, 10am-4pm Sat) have more information.

Accommodation is abundant and includes **Hôtel de la Poste** (☎ 032 466 18 27; Rue des Malvoisins 15; s/d from Sfr80/150), which has a bunch of reasonable rooms and a bar open until 3am; and the more upmarket Churchill Pub– and clubclad, three-star **Hôtel du Cheval Blanc** (☎ 032 466 15 15; Rue du 23 Juin 15; s/d from Sfr100/170). All over town, bakeries cook up sensational *gâteau de fromage* (cheesecake) on Friday morning.

Trains proceed fairly regularly southeast to St Ursanne and Delémont. Buses serve neighbouring villages in the Ajoie plains.

FRIBOURG, NEUCHÂTEL & JURA

Valais

With the 10 highest mountains in Switzerland – all over 4000m – this scenic canton offers pinnacles of pleasure for those who enjoy the high life.

A certain supply of snow plus challenging slopes makes the Valais region one of the most popular in the world for skiing. A series of mountain valleys cuts south into the Alps from the Rhône valley, which slices east to west through the canton, leading to ski resorts as varied in scenery and challenges as they are culturally mixed. Depending on your choice of ski resort, you can ski from Francophone Switzerland into France or German Switzerland into Italy and back in the same day!

The Alps are as stunning in summer, offering limitless hiking possibilities for all levels, including the classic Mont Blanc circuit through Switzerland, France and Italy.

Long a region of struggling farmers until the advent of Alpine tourism, the canton is dotted with delightful high mountain villages and, lower down in the Rhône valley, vineyards that provide some of the country's best wines – the whites are a perfect accompaniment to a local cheese speciality, raclette, about which you can learn more on p52.

The Valais is not just about yomping and chomping. Martigny hosts one of the country's key art centres and Sion is notable for its medieval core, dramatic castle and museums.

Valais is also good for soothing nerves and tired muscles in its thermal bathing centres, notably those of Leukerbad.

VALAIS

HIGHLIGHTS

- Skiing, snowboarding and hiking in the shadow of Switzerland's emblematic **Matterhorn** (p135), or, for those with the right stuff, scaling it
- Checking out the world-class art exhibitions at Martigny's **Fondation Pierre Gianadda** (p120)
- Cheering along your favourite bovine in the spring and autumn cow battles in the villages of the **Val d'Hérens** (p129)
- Exploring the medieval centre, castle and basilica of **Sion** (p126)
- Frolicking in the regenerative thermal baths of **Leukerbad** (p132) while admiring the massive mountain stone walls around the town

★ Leukerbad
★ Sion
★ Val d'Hérens
★ Fondation Pierre Gianadda
★ Matterhorn

| ■ POPULATION: 281,000 | ■ AREA: 5224.5 SQ KM | ■ LANGUAGE: FRENCH & GERMAN |

VALAIS

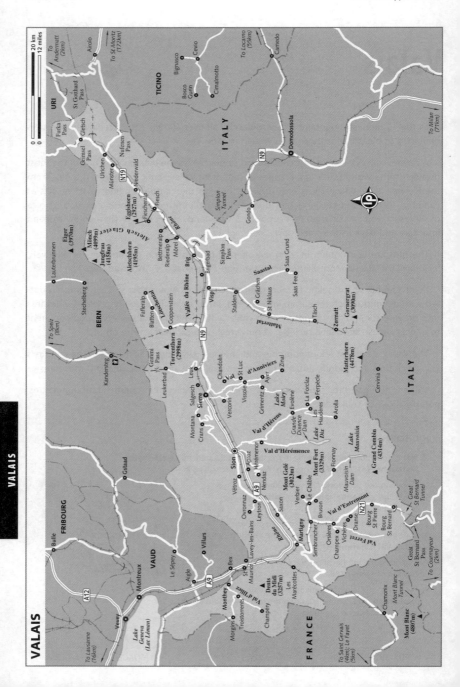

History

As in neighbouring Vaud, Julius Caesar was an early 'tourist' in these parts. Historians fail to record whether he packed his skis, but we do know the Roman leader brought an army to conquer the Celtic community living in the valley, penetrating as far as Sierre. Once under Roman domination, it appears the four Celtic tribes of the Valais were peaceably integrated into the Roman system. Artefacts and archaeological remains still attest to the passage of the rambling general and his boys from Rome.

Sion became a key centre in the valley when the Bishop of Valais blessed the town with his presence, making his home there from AD 580. By 1000, the bishop's power stretched from Martigny to the Furka Pass.

That power did not go uncontested. A succession of Dukes of Savoy managed to encroach on the bishops' territory and a Savoyard army besieged Sion in 1475. With the help of the Swiss Confederation, the city was freed at the battle of Planta. Internal opposition was just as weighty and the independently minded communes that made up the Valais region stripped the bishops of their secular power in the 1630s, shifting the levers of control into the hands of the Diet, a regional parliament.

The Valais was not invaded again until Napoleon Bonaparte called by in 1798. The little man with big plans was determined to dominate the routes into Italy. Valais joined the Swiss Confederation in 1815.

Orientation & Information

The Rhône carves a broad, sunny valley from east to west between the serried ranks of the Bernese Alps to the north and the Valaisan Alps that mark the southern frontier with France and Italy. French speakers dominate the lower valley, while German has been used in the upper (eastern) half of the canton since the 6th century.

Information is available at the regional tourist office, **Valais Tourisme** (☎ 027 327 35 70; www.matterhornstate.com, www.wallis.ch; Rue de Pré Fleuri 6, Sion; ⏰ 8am-noon & 1.30-5.30pm Mon-Fri).

Getting There & Around

The smoothest routes are from Italy to Martigny (via the Great St Bernard Pass and Tunnel) and Brig (via the Simplon Pass and Tunnel). The most direct route from Chamonix in France to the Valais is by road from Martigny. The N9 highway enters the canton in the east via the Furka Pass and passes through main junctions like Brig. In Sierre it becomes the dual carriageway A9 motorway, continuing to Sion, Martigny and then north to follow Lake Geneva to Geneva. The same route is served by a major rail line, with a branch route into Italy via the border town of Domodossola.

The Adventure Card Wallis is a general transport card for the Oberwallis (German-speaking Upper Valais) area and entitles holders to two, three or five days' (Sfr89/109/169) unlimited travel on trains and buses in the area within a one-month period. It gives you 50% off on most lifts and sporting activities on those days too.

Special bus passes for Sion + Region and Martigny + Region are available in summer. Together they cover the whole of Lower Valais. The Martigny Pass includes the *Mont Blanc Express/St Bernard Express* trains. The Sion version includes some cable-car discounts. Ask at the towns' tourist offices about the passes. Another pass is the Valais Central pass, which runs from Martigny to Leukerbad. It gives you three days' unlimited transport within a week (adult/child Sfr48/38).

LOWER VALAIS

The western, predominantly French, half of the Valais region is rich in history, art and snow-sport options, and the source of the some of Switzerland's best wines.

WESTERN VALAIS & VAL D'ILLIEZ
Champéry & Les Portes du Soleil

The hamlet of Champéry (population 1180) in the Val d'Illiez is at the heart of an extensive, international ski paradise known as **Les Portes du Soleil** (Gateway to the Sun; www.portesdu soleil.com). With a total of 208 lifts and 650km pistes of all classes (intermediates predominate) spread out on the Swiss and French sides of the frontier, there is plenty of ski fun for all. Cross-country skiing is abundant too – 243km of trails. There are also eight snowparks for snowboarders.

To get to the pistes you have several options. Passing through the largely uninteresting town of Monthey, you swing southwest. At Troistorrents, the road forks. You can

VALAIS

continue 8km to Champéry, or branch west to Morgins. Lifts operate from both villages. The main town on the French side is Avoriaz. Ski passes for a day for the whole area cost Sfr55/37/44/46 per adult/child to 16/senior/student or youth.

Croix de Culet (1963m) affords an eagle's view of the nearby Dents du Midi mountain peaks. The viewpoint is only a short wander from the top of the Planachaux cable car.

Champéry's ski lifts operate from June to August for hikers and mountain bikers. The Planachaux cable car operates as late as October in good weather.

The **Champéry tourist office** (☎ 024 479 20 20; www.champery.ch) will tell you more. Another source of info is www.chablais.info.

From Aigle (20 minutes along the track from Martigny to Lausanne), a train runs via Monthey every hour to Champéry (Sfr12.40, one hour).

St Maurice

You'd never know that this quiet village (population 3680), named after an early Christian martyr, was the site of an ancient and horrible massacre. Maurice and his Christian companions in a Roman army unit are said to have been cut to pieces in AD 302 for refusing to march against other Christians or worship the ancient gods of Rome. Their faith was commemorated by the construction of the 11th-century **Abbey Church**. The town castle also has a **military museum** (☎ 024 486 04 04; www.stmaurice.ch; Ave d'Agaune 15; adult/child Sfr6/3; ☒ visits 3pm Tue-Sun Nov-Apr, 10.30am, 2pm, 3.15pm & 4.30pm Tue-Sun Jul & Aug, 10.30am, 3pm & 4.30pm Tue-Sun May, Jun, Sep & Oct). Trains from Martigny run around three times an hour (Sfr6, 15 minutes).

Lavey-les-Bains

Although just inside the cantonal frontier of neighbouring Vaud, Lavey-les-Bains is south of St Maurice along the motorway. The **thermal baths** (☎ 024 486 15 55; www.lavey-les-bains.ch; admission for up to 3hr adult/4-16yr Sfr22/14; ☒ 9am-9pm Sun-Thu, 9am-10pm Fri & Sat) here comprise three pools (indoor and outdoor), Jacuzzis, steam baths and saunas. Children under four may not enter.

Local postal buses run from St Maurice, on the train line between Geneva and Brig, to Lavey (Sfr2.80, 10 minutes).

MARTIGNY

pop 14,050 / elevation 476m

It might be the oldest town in Valais, but Martigny has a modern and somewhat muddled feel. While not immediately compelling, it does offer a handful of considerable cultural attractions, including reminders of the city's ancient Roman masters, who controlled the area from 15 BC.

Orientation & Information

Tree-lined Place Centrale is where the action is. Sitting at one of the long line of pavement cafés and bars, the locals watch the world pass by. The **tourist office** (☎ 027 721 22 20; www.martignytourism.ch; Place Centrale; ☒ 9am-noon & 1.30-6pm Mon-Fri, 9am-noon & 2-6pm Sat in summer, also 10am-noon & 4-6pm Sun Jul & Aug, closed Sat afternoon & Sun rest of year) can help with inquiries.

Sights & Activities

The main attraction is the **Fondation Pierre Gianadda** (☎ 027 722 39 78; www.gianadda.ch; Rue du Forum; adult/student/senior Sfr15/8/13; ☒ 9am-7pm Jun-Nov, 10am-6pm Dec-May), a spacious art gallery rambling across an area of pretty parkland. The latter doubles as a showplace for contemporary sculpture, with contributions from the likes of Henry Moore and Alexander Calder. This delightful setting, established in 1978, attracts top-class art exhibitions from around the world and people from all over the western half of the country to admire them.

Included in the entry price is access to a couple of unrelated but curious permanent exhibitions. Above the main art gallery is the **Musée Archéologique Gallo-Romain**, housing coins, pots and sculptures from Roman and pre-Roman times found in the vicinity. The finest piece is the head of a bronze bull.

Mighty bulls are replaced by horsepower in the **Musée de l'Auto** (Automobile Museum), on the same premises. Some 50 polished-up automobiles dating from the late 19th century on look ready to take to the road at any moment.

The Roman Empire withstood barbarian pressure for a long time, and the restored **Roman Amphitheatre** (admission free) is again the scene of occasional summer concerts. The visitor is given free rein to wander round every aspect of the site.

The baroque **Église de Notre Dame des Champs** (Our Lady of the Fields; Rue de l'Eglise) hides remains of Romanesque and Gothic churches, and even a 4th-century baptistery. By the Dranse river, the **Chapelle de Notre Dame de la Compassion** (Our Lady of Compassion) is curious for its ex-voto paintings. Perched above the chapel is **Château de la Bâtiaz** (Bâtiaz Castle; www.batiaz.ch in French; ⏰ 4-6pm Thu, 11am-6pm Fri-Sun mid-May–mid-Oct). It is worth the climb up the hill for the views over surrounding vineyards alone. On display inside is a collection of remakes of medieval war engines and instruments of torture. Suitably sickened, you can stop off at the castle tavern for some refreshment.

Festivals & Events

Pigs don't fly, but cows certainly fight. At least they do in Martigny. The 10-day October **Foire du Valais** (Valais Regional Fair) ends with a bovine bash-about of epic proportions (see the boxed text Close Cow Encounters, p129). Tickets are around Sfr16 for seats and Sfr10 to stand.

If the idea of watching crunch-tackle cows doesn't thrill you, there's sizzling action at the **Foire du Lard** (Bacon Fair) in December. Local residents have been picking on the prize porkers since the Middle Ages.

Sleeping

Hôtel Beau Site (☎ 027 722 81 64; Chemin Dessus; www .chemin.ch; s/d Sfr70/130) Sometimes it's worth going the extra kilometre (actually 6km from central Martigny). This charming four-storey rural getaway was built in 1912. In summer or winter, its bucolic position with views of

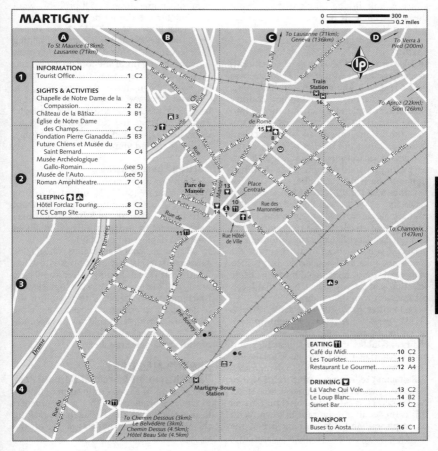

MARTIGNY

0 _____ 300 m
0 _____ 0.2 miles

To St Maurice (18km); Lausanne (71km)
To Lausanne (71km); Geneva (136km)
To Verra à Pied (200m)

To Aproz (22km); Sion (26km)

To Chamonix (147km)

INFORMATION
Tourist Office.............................1 C2

SIGHTS & ACTIVITIES
Chapelle de Notre Dame de la
Compassion............................2 B2
Château de la Bâtiaz...............3 B1
Église de Notre Dame
des Champs.............................4 C2
Fondation Pierre Gianadda.......5 B3
Future Chiens et Musée du
Saint Bernard.........................6 C4
Musée Archéologique
Gallo-Romain......................(see 5)
Musée de l'Auto.....................(see 5)
Roman Amphitheatre...............7 C4

SLEEPING 🏠 🏕
Hôtel Forclaz Touring...............8 C2
TCS Camp Site.........................9 D3

EATING 🍴
Café du Midi...........................10 C2
Les Touristes..........................11 B3
Restaurant Le Gourmet...........12 A4

DRINKING 🍷
La Vache Qui Vole...................13 C2
Le Loup Blanc........................14 B2
Sunset Bar..............................15 C2

TRANSPORT
Buses to Aosta.......................16 C1

To Chemin Dessous (3km);
Le Belvédère (3km);
Chemin Dessus (4.5km);
Hôtel Beau Site (4.5km)

Martigny-Bourg Station

VALAIS

the hills and down to the Rhône valley make it a peaceful spot. It has its own restaurant with a terrace. To get here follow the road from the roundabout of Rue des Champs-du-Bourg to Chemin sur Martigny. Local bus No 5 heads up here hourly (25 minutes).

Hôtel Forclaz Touring (☎ 027 722 29 42; www.hotel forclaztouring.ch; Rue du Léman 15; s/d Sfr100/150) Yes, it is an awful concrete block with purple door and window frames, but inside the rooms are comfortable and reasonably spacious, if utterly functional. The 6th-floor restaurant with mountain views is a winner.

TCS camping ground (☎ 027 722 45 44; Rue de Levant 68; person/tent/dm Sfr7.40/9.20/21) This camping venue has a swimming pool, sports facilities and good views of the countryside, and is a half–hiking boot's distance from the town centre. It has its own restaurant, bar and shops.

Eating

Le Belvédère (☎ 027 723 14 00; www.lebelvedere.ch in French; Chemin Dessous; mains Sfr26-42; ☻ lunch & dinner Thu-Sat, lunch Sun) About 3km south of Martigny up a narrow, high-climbing country road, this is a splendid mansion turned into a fine restaurant. You can enjoy views out over the Rhône valley and such succulent dishes as *tournedos de filet de boeuf et son foie gras poêlé* (a tournedos of Val d'Herens beef with pan-fried foie gras). See the directions for the Hôtel Beau Site.

Café du Midi (☎ 027 722 00 03; Rue des Marronniers 4; mains Sfr20-35; ☻ Wed-Mon) Tucked away in the pleasant old centre of Martigny by the church, this is an old-style café and restaurant. They don't make places like this any more, and it's perfect if you are after fondue or an *assiette valaisanne* (aka *Walliserteller*, a dish principally made up of mixed cold meats, a cheese selection and a few pickles). Note that locals eat this dish with their hands.

Les Touristes (☎ 027 722 95 98; Rue de l'Hôpital 1; meals Sfr45-55; ☻ Tue-Sun) A classic, straight-up-and-down locale, with white linen and wooden chairs and tables, makes for a pleasing ambience for an Italian meal over good local wine. On sunny days head upstairs to the terrace.

Restaurant Le Gourmet (☎ 027 722 18 41; www .le-gourmet.ch; Ave du Grand St Bernard 74; meals Sfr100-190; ☻ daily) Housed in the Hôtel du Forum, this is the leading restaurant in town. With its amphorae and salmon-pink décor, the dining area transmits reminders of the city's Roman past. The menu changes regularly. You may find such items as the *terrine de lapin au foie gras et pistaches* (rabbit terrine with foie gras and pistachios).

Drinking

La Vache Qui Vole (☎ 027 722 38 33; Place Centrale 2B; ☻ 10.30-1am) The 'Flying Cow' is an inviting, laid-back lounge bar, where good local wines are the order of the day. You can sit out on the terrace and it also offers snacks and a limited menu.

Verre àPied (☎ 027 720 16 16; Rue des Prés-Beudin 20; ☻ 10.30am-1pm & 5-9pm) Don't be put off by the enormous four-star hotel in which this fine little wine bar is located. This is one of the best-stocked places in town, but the ungenerous hours mean you'll probably want to come for pre-dinner drinks only.

Le Loup Blanc (☎ 027 723 52 52; Place Centrale; ☻ 10-1am) The 'White Wolf' offers something for everyone. It's a modern bar that is great for wine tasting (local and foreign wines) and if you want to stay to eat, the menu offers a variety of Italian and local dishes.

Sunset Bar (www.sunset-bar.com in French; Rue du Léman 15; ☻ 6pm-1am Tue-Sat) Set inside the Hôtel Forclaz building, the bar attracts the occasional local DJ or band Thursday to Saturday. Sets start around 9pm.

Getting There & Away

Martigny is on the main rail route running from Lausanne (Sfr22, 50 minutes) to Brig (Sfr24, 50 to 65 minutes). Buses go from Martigny via Orsières and the Great St Bernard Tunnel to Aosta in Italy (Sfr30.60, at least two departures per day).

The private **Mont-Blanc Express** (☎ 027 721 68 40; www.tmrsa.ch) usually goes hourly to Chamonix (Sfr31, 1½ hours) in France. There are up to 12 trips per day in the high season. Martigny is also the departure point for the *St Bernard Express*, which goes to Le Châble (Sfr9.80, 27 minutes); ski lift or bus connection for Verbier) and Orsières (Sfr9.80, 28 minutes) via Sembrancher.

AROUND MARTIGNY
Val d'Entremont & Great St Bernard Pass

The *St Bernard Express* train from Martigny to Orsières branches south at Sembrancher, heading south to the Italian border along the Val d'Entremont. **Orsières** is just off the main road to the Col du Great St-Bernard

---

A SHAGGY DOG TALE

Since the 11th century, monks have maintained a hospice at the Great St Bernard Pass to give spiritual succour to people in the mountains and on occasion rescue travellers lost in the snow. And so the legend of the St Bernard dogs was born, as it was they who frequently found the lost souls and did the rescuing. The dogs have long stopped doing the work and in 2004, the handful of ageing monks who had long raised them and maintained a museum at their mountain hospice shocked all and sundry by announcing they could no longer take care of the dogs ('who seem to have become more important than us,' remarked one). A multi-millionaire from Geneva stepped in and saved the day, putting up the money to create a museum in Martigny (next door to the Roman Amphitheatre, due for completion in 2006) as well as kennels to preserve the race. And to keep the tourists happy, a posse of the doggies will be taken up to stay at the hospice each summer, as usual. The **kennels and museum** (adult/child/senior Sfr7/5/6; 🕙 9am-7pm Jul & Aug, 9am-noon & 1-6pm Jun & Sep) operate in summer only.

---

and like-named tunnel, and marks the beginning of the little-visited **Val Ferret**. While in Orsières you may be tempted to stop by **L'Hôtel des Alpes** (☎ 027 783 11 02; lunch/dinner set menu Sfr65/115; 🕙 lunch & dinner Thu-Sun, lunch Mon). A former hostelry for lonely travellers en route to and from the Great St Bernard Pass, it is now an enticing village-square restaurant. It offers mouth-watering set-meal options (which start as low as Sfr30 at lunch and rise as high as Sfr180 in the evening) in a rustic setting. Those in the know insist the best time is autumn, when freshly hunted game meat takes pride of place. It also has a handful of modest rooms.

A branch road leads to **Champex**, which sits by a looking-glass lake. From Orsières it's a 1¾-hour walk. A cable car operates in winter and summer to La Breya (2374m), where the views include the Grand Combin (4314m) to the east.

Animal lovers with a vehicle could follow the N21 road further south towards Drance. Turn off for Drance and head for Vichères. Keep your eyes peeled for a signed walking track that leads off the road a couple of kilometres before reaching the hamlet. This trail leads down along the Combe de l'A hill range and eponymous stream. In September it is a good walk for deer-spotting.

The N21 continues south to the Italian border, which you can cross by tunnel or the winding mountain road, depending on your preferences (views or time?) and weather conditions.

Although the **hospice** (☎ 027 787 12 36; www.gs bernard.ch; dm Sfr17-45, d Sfr56-69) is snowed in for up to six months of the year, it remains open to people who wish to sleep overnight or just get a bite to eat. Five brothers of the St Bernard order and seven lay workers stay up here through the long winter. The only way up or down is on foot (snow shoe or skis) from the entrance to the road tunnel 7km downhill. It is essential to call ahead and find out if it is open and if there is space. In winter especially, you must call again just before you plan to arrive, as bad weather may make it inadvisable. If you decide not to go, let them know, because if they expect you and you don't turn up, they will wonder whether you have gotten lost or caught in an avalanche. This small courtesy becomes a necessity in the mountains.

To get to the hospice from Martigny in summer, take the *St Bernard Express* train to Orsières (see opposite) and change for the connecting bus (45 minutes). The total cost from Martigny is Sfr18.50. Otherwise the bus won't go past Bourg St Pierre.

MONT BLANC
elevation 4807m

From numerous points in southwest Switzerland you can see this mighty Alpine peak, and although it's not in Switzerland there are times you think it close enough to touch. In France the main ski resort is Chamonix, popular with folks in Geneva and easily accessible by road from there and a little less easily by train and bus from Martigny. The biggest ski attraction is **Vallée Blanche**, a 20km glacier dangling from the side of Mont Blanc that constitutes the world's longest ski run. On the Italian side, the main resort is Courmayeur. For information on skiing in Chamonix and Courmayeur, check out www .chamonix.com and www.courmayeur.com.

See p122 for travel details. There are also buses from Geneva. The lower reaches of the mighty mountain reach into Switzerland like lava flow and hikers might want to take on the 215km **Mont Blanc circuit** in summer, about a third of which passes through Switzerland. The walk reaches a maximum altitude of more than 2500m and typically takes 10 to 14 days. In Switzerland there are a number of good places to commence, including Champex (p123) and the Col de la Forclaz pass, reached by bus from Martigny.

VERBIER

pop 2500 / elevation 1500m

With its first ski lift only built in 1947, Verbier is but a young pup of a ski resort. It also attracts a youthful, trendy crowd of skiers and snowboarders, who often look cooler than the snow below their feet. In the high season, Verbier becomes a major party village, with as much ice clinking in whisky tumblers at local bars as you'll find on the slopes.

Orientation & Information

Verbier is scenically situated on a southwest-facing ledge above Le Châble, the local rail terminus. The resort proper is uphill from Verbier village. The hub of Verbier is Place Centrale, where you will find the **tourist office** (☎ 027 775 38 88; www.verbier.ch; ☒ 8am-noon & 2-6.30pm Mon-Fri, 9am-noon & 4-6.30pm Sat, 9am-noon Sun). Hours are longer in peak season. Just off the square is the post office and postal bus terminus. Verbier is mostly shut from late October to early December and during May. That includes the cable cars. The resort has a free bus service in the high season. Families, children and senior citizens get substantial discounts on lift prices for skiing and hiking.

Activities

Verbier is at the heart of the **Quatre Vallées** (Four Valleys) ski area, which offers 410km of runs and 94 ski lifts. A ski pass for the whole area costs Sfr62. Cheaper passes excluding Mont Fort are also available. The Four Valleys area stretches east to Nendaz and Thyon.

The skiing is exciting and varied, with opportunities for the experts to flaunt their off-piste skills, particularly at Attelas and Mont Fort (3329m; have fun on the moguls!). Mont Fort is high enough to allow summer skiing on its glacier.

Maison du Sport (☎ 027 775 33 63; www.maisondu sport.ch), behind the post office, offers ski-mountaineering, heli-skiing and other interesting (and expensive) options, including a five-day trek along the Haute Route to Zermatt. They can even arrange a tennis coach for you!

With the snow gone in summer, Verbier offers plenty of hiking. From Les Ruinettes, it takes two hours to ascend to the ridge at Creblet, and down into the crater to Lac des Vaux.

If being on the top of a mountain isn't high enough, then you can take to the air by hang-gliding or paragliding. Solo and tandem flights are available. **Centre de Parapente** (☎ 027 771 68 18; www.flyverbier.ch) and **Max** (☎ 027 771 55 55), based in the Hotel Rosa Blanche, both offer 30-minute tandem flights from Sfr170.

Festivals & Events

The resort faces the music in July when it hosts the **Verbier Festival & Academy** (☎ 027 711 82 82; www.verbierfestival.com), a prestigious classical music and spoken-word event. Sports events include **Xtreme Freeride Contest** (www2 .xtremeverbier.com). The name of the competition might be a little lax in the spelling department, but the event does spell a lot of fun, with snowboarders going through a range of exciting moves.

Sleeping

Private rooms and chalets are reasonable, but book in advance. Most places shut in spring and autumn and prices are considerably higher in winter than in summer.

Hôtel Garbo (☎ 027 771 61 62; http://hotelgarbo.com; Rue de Médran 5; d up to Sfr250) If you don't mind a bit of chaos at the end of the day when skiers gather in the various nooks and crannies for a bite and drink (until as late as 2am), this party hotel's rooms are as good as any, clean, comfy and all with own bath and cable TV. Some have balconies and mountain views. Downstairs it also has the Netsu sushi and fusion food bar. It's 100m off Place Centrale.

Hôtel De La Poste (☎ 027 771 66 81; www.hotelposte verbier.ch; Rue de Médran 12; per person half board up to Sfr200; ⓟ ⓡ) A mountain chalet-style place that is centrally located and has no-nonsense accommodation. Prices drop to less than half in summer. Timber dominates in the mostly bright rooms and the food is hearty.

Eating

With about 45 restaurants and eateries spread about the resort and its runs, you won't go hungry in Verbier. The range spreads from as cheap and imaginative as chips to a handful of serious gourmet options.

La Channe Valaisanne (☎ 027 771 15 75; Rue des Creux; fondue per person Sfr28-34; ☺ daily in season) For a choice of 14 types of fondue (including one with mustard and cognac), or simply a raclette with local cheese, this makes a cosy and very Swiss option when hamburgers, pizza and poor Mexican begin to lose their charm. It's about 50m off Place Centrale.

Au Vieux Valais (☎ 027 775 35 20; www.vieux-valais .ch; Rue de Médran; mains Sfr20-40; ☺ daily in season) Voted 'mountain restaurant of the year' by *The Good Skiing and Snowboarding Guide* in 2005, this place is handily placed by the main lift down to Le Chable and up to Les Ruinettes. It does all the local cheesy classics, along with a sizzling *fondue bourguignonne* (a beef fondue in which cubes of meat are dipped into boiling oil).

Drinking

Pub Mont Fort (☎ 027 771 48 98; Chemin de la Tinte 10; ☺ 3pm-1.30am daily Nov-Apr & mid-Jun–Aug) Phalanxes of after-drinking skiers gather over two storeys in this Verbier classic near the base of Attelas cable car. Happy hour (half-price tipples) is 4pm to 5pm daily (January to April only). Shots are the order of the night and closing time seems to be interpreted broadly. Downstairs it also serves up food.

Taratata (☎ 079 456 25 02; Place Centrale; ☺ 10pm-4am Dec-Apr, Jul & Aug) One of the handiest of the four or five clubs in Verbier. It shuts from late April to late June and from September to November.

Getting There & Away

Trains from Martigny run hourly year-round, take 30 minutes and terminate at Le Châble. From there you either get a bus or, when it's running, the cable car. The full trip costs Sfr15.20 and takes about 50 minutes.

VAL DE BAGNES

From Le Châble it's a 19km drive south and up to Lac de Mauvoisin (Lake Mauvoisin) and its impressive dam. Several hiking trails fan out from here, including one that crosses the mountain frontier with Italy over the Fenêtre du Durand pass (2797m) and down into the Valpelline valley in Italy's Val d'Aosta region. Three daily buses run on weekends and holidays from Le Châble. You may find the simple, lone hotel at the base of the dam open, but don't count on it.

OVRONNAZ

Few foreign visitors cotton on to this small but pleasing family ski resort with thermal baths. From Martigny, head east up the A9 as far as the Leytron turn-off. From Leytron, which is on the north side of the motorway, a winding mountain road leads 10km to Ovronnaz. The **tourist office** (☎ 027 306 42 93; www.ovronnaz.ch) is at the north end of the village near the Coop supermarket.

The skiing is limited and mostly for intermediates, but makes for a pleasant day on the slopes. The highest lift reaches 2500m. What makes it especially fun is combining the slopes with bath time. A combined lift pass and entry to the **Thermalp baths** (☎ 027 305 11 11; www.thermalp.ch in French; ☺ 9am-8.30pm) costs Sfr53 (a saving of Sfr8 on paying for them separately).

There is only a handful of hotels, but the tourist office can help with various B&Bs and apartments.

Buses run from Martigny (change at Leytron) hourly (Sfr13.40, about one hour). You have similar options from Sion.

SION

pop 27,700 / elevation 490m

Sion (Sitten in German) has a dramatic backdrop, sheltered by the twin battlement hills of Valére and Tourbillon.

The capital of Valais has retained much of its attractive medieval architecture. A helter-skelter of cobbled streets ramble from the Château de Tourbillon's perch down to the old town centre, passing a collection of museums, churches and historic houses along the way.

Orientation

The French-speaking town lies north of the Rhône. The train station is downhill and south of the old town centre, facing the modern, commercial heart of Sion. Most of the areas of interest are within walking distance of the station, along Ave de la Gare and Rue de Lausanne.

VALAIS

Information

Sion has a **post office** (Place de la Gare 11; 8am-6.30pm Mon-Fri, 9am-4pm Sat) and a **tourist office** (027 322 77 27; www.siontourism.ch; Place de la Planta; 8.30am-12.30pm & 2.30-5.30pm Mon-Fri, 9am-12.30pm Sat).

Sights & Activities

A one-off ticket to all museums (Passeport tous musées) is available for Sfr12. It is valid for two days over a 15-day period.

CHÂTEAU DE TOURBILLON

It's a rough trek uphill to this **castle** (027 606 47 45; Rue des Châteaux; admission free; 10am-6pm mid-Mar–mid-Nov), and all that's left are ruins of the exterior walls. However, the view of the town is well worth the climb.

BASILIQUE DE VALÈRE

On the hill opposite the Château de Tourbillon, this fortified height contains a **basilica** (Rue des Châteaux; adult/child/family Sfr3/2/6; hourly visits 10.15am-4.15pm Tue-Sun, plus 5.15pm Jun-Sep) dating in part to the 12th century. The world's oldest playable organ juts out from the inside wall opposite the apse like the timber stern of a medieval caravel. Built in the 15th century, it was restored in the early 2000s. Concerts are held here every now and then, especially for the Festival International de l'Organ Ancien et de la Musique Ancienne (International Ancient Organ and Music Festival), held here on Saturday afternoons (from 4pm) from mid-July to mid-August. In the front part of the church where the organ is are 15th-century frescoes, the best of the them depicting St Sebastian.

The interior of the church is divided by a wall. In medieval times such divisions were typical. On the main altar side would gather the clergy and nobles, while the plebs would be herded into the other side. In the 17th century the Pope ordered such divisions be removed, but here the clergy resisted. In the end, it was never taken down, but a doorway inserted instead. This is the part you pay to see. Just inside are the beautifully carved choir stalls. The apse is covered with bright frescoes. Downhill from the basilica, before exiting through the gate in the complex's medieval walls, is the **Musée Cantonal d'Histoire** (027 606 47 10; adult/child/family combined with basilica Sfr7/4.50/15; 11am-5pm Tue-Sun Oct-May, 11am-6pm daily Jun-Sep). It offers a blend of medieval ar-

tefacts and modern bric-a-brac. From the basilica you have a commanding panoramic view across the city.

MAISON SUPERSAXO

Built by Georges Supersaxo in 1505, this impressive **residence** (Passage de Supersaxo; admission free; 8am-noon & 2-6pm Mon-Fri) offers a keyhole peek into the lives of the rich and powerful in 16th-century Switzerland. Supersaxo built the house to provoke his friend-turned-enemy, the bishop of Sion. The provocation backfired when Supersaxo was exiled.

OTHER MUSEUMS

Local art, ancient and modern, is highlighted in the **Musée Cantonal des Beaux-Arts** (Museum of Fine Art; 027 606 46 90; Place de la Marjorie 15; adult/child/family Sfr5/2.50/10; 10am-noon & 2-6pm Tue-Sun). Workmanlike paintings and sculptures on display fail to give the museum the lustre of the Louvre, but it's an opportunity to view the region through local eyes. The collection is lodged in the impressive grey stone Château de la Marjorie et Vidonnat.

You can learn more about Sion's Roman invaders and the lives of medieval folk at the **Musée Cantonal d'Archéologie** (Archaeological Museum; 027 606 47 00; Rue des Châteaux 12; adult/child/family Sfr4/2/8; 1-5pm Tue-Sun). Among the displays are various models and dioramas.

Just up the road from these two museums is the **Ancien Pénitencier** (027 606 47 07; Rue des Châteaux 24; adult/child/family Sfr6/3/12; 11am-5pm Tue-Sun Oct-May, 11am-6pm daily Jun-Sep), until the 1990s the town prison. Since 2000 its cells, which have been given a lick of paint but still retain a vaguely sinister air, have been the site of regular expositions.

It's stuffed animals a-go-go at the **Musée Cantonal d'Histoire Naturelle** (Museum of Natural History; 027 606 47 30; Ave de la Gare 42; adult/child/family Sfr3/1.50/6; 1-5pm Tue-Sun).

CHURCHES & TOWERS

At the heart of the compact old town, two churches stand side by side. The **Cathédrale de Notre Dame du Glarier** dates largely to the 15th century, although some earlier elements remain. The smaller **Église de St Théodule** dates to the 16th century. Up Rue de la Tour from the churches is a stout reminder of Sion's medieval past, the **Tour des Sorciers** (Wizards' Tower), one of the watchtowers in the one-time city walls.

Sleeping

In addition to various (mostly modern) hotels, the tourist office can provide a list of chalets and B&B-style accommodation in the area around Sion.

Hôtel du Rhône (☎ 027 322 82 91; www.bestwestern.com; Rue de Scex; s/d Sfr132/190; ▢) Fronted by a pretty fountain, this modern block offers spacious if somewhat bland rooms. Parking costs Sfr10.

SYHA Hostel (☎ 027 323 74 70; www.youthhostel.ch; Rue de l'Industrie 2; dm/d Sfr29/72) Behind the train station, rooms in this clean, bright youth hostel are mostly equipped with four beds, although there are some doubles. You can sit outside the modern building in the yard in summer.

Eating

Rue du Grand-Pont is lined with eateries and bars.

Grand Pont (☎ 027 322 20 96; Rue du Grand-Pont 6; meals Sfr30-40; ☷ Mon-Sat) One of the best. Whether outside on the pavement terrace or inside the spacious dining area with its art-covered walls, you can try anything from guacamole to healthy servings of salad. There are some Asian options too, but skip the pasta.

L'Enclos de Valère (☎ 027 323 32 30; Rue des Châteaux; mains Sfr25-40; ☷ Tue-Sat) This French restaurant is magnificently set on the road leading up to Tourbillon and boasts a shady garden where you might chomp into a *filet de poulain aux poivres noir, vert et de Sichuan*

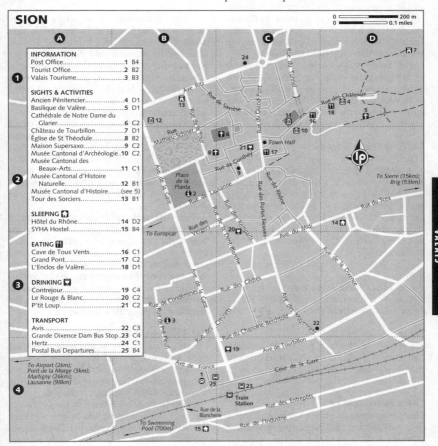

(foal fillet with black, green and Sichuan peppers). There's a kids' menus too.

Cave de Tous Vents (☎ 027 322 46 84; Rue des Châteaux 16; meals Sfr40-60; ☷ daily Jun-Nov, Mon-Sat Dec-May) Wander downstairs into this perfect cellar atmosphere for local dining, including such favourites as raclette and fondue, and an assortment of hearty meat dishes. It's great in winter.

Drinking

Contrejour (☎ 027 323 21 11; Ave de la Gare 6; ☷ 6pm-1am Mon-Thu, 6pm-2am Fri & Sat) Easily the hippest hangout in town, this is a slick lounge bar, with good wines and mood music, all done for the best-dressed scions of Sion.

Le Rouge & Blanc (☎ 027 323 80 82; Rue des Remparts 10; ☷ 3pm-midnight Mon-Thu, 3pm-1am Fri & Sat) A rowdy pub-style place that caters to all comers, from the pool players who hang out the back to the better-dressed punters lounging about near the street-side windows.

P'tit Loup (☎ 079 358 36 67; Rue de Conthey 6; ☷ 5pm-midnight Tue-Thu, 5pm-1am Fri & Sat) Hard rock is the rage here. A grunge of leather jackets jockey for position at the bar, vibrating like guitar strings to the heavy sounds reverberating from a powerful stereo system.

Getting There & Away

AIR

The **airport** (☎ 027 329 06 00; www.sionairport.ch; Route de l'Aéroport) is 2km west of the train station; bus No 1 goes there (Sfr3.40). There are year-round flights to Zürich (50 minutes), London and Corsica. During the ski season shuttle buses operate direct from the airport to resorts such as Crans Montana, Verbier and Zermatt.

BUS

Postal buses leave from outside the train station. For information, call ☎ 027 327 34 34 or ask at the train station.

TRAIN

All trains on the express route between Lausanne (Sfr28, 50 to 70 minutes) and Brig (Sfr17.60, 35 to 50 minutes) stop in at Sion.

CAR & MOTORCYCLE

The A9 motorway passes by Sion. There's free parking by the swimming pool, five minutes' walk west of the youth hostel.

Europcar (☎ 027 323 86 86; Rue de Lausanne 148) is at Garage Delta. **Hertz** (☎ 027 322 37 42; Ave Ritz 33) is at Garage du Nord, and there's also **Avis** (☎ 027 322 20 77; Ave de Tourbillon 23-25).

AROUND SION
Val d'Hérémence

Little explored, this valley is worth the trip to visit one of the great engineering feats of modern times. Stretching about 30km south of Sion, the valley is sectioned off at its southern end by the enormous Grande Dixence dam. At 284m, it is the highest dam in the world.

From Sion, follow the signs for this valley and the Val d'Hérens, which share the same road as far as Vex, where you branch right (southwest).

After **Hérémence**, distinguished by its strange-looking Cubist-style concrete church, come two small hamlets, Prolin and Mâche. The heavily wooded and deep valley narrows as you gain altitude, finally opening up into a small plain before the road narrows to track status. It then makes a final series of switchbacks up to the base of the dam, which seems to rise up into the sky.

Just before embarking on that road you'll see a huddle of houses called **Pralong**, home to a couple of bijou hotel-restaurants that make handy bases for walkers in the area. Try the **Val des Dix** (☎ 027 281 12 13; www.grande-dixence .com in French; r per person Sfr52), which has spotless, timber-lined rooms and a snug restaurant downstairs.

Take the **cable car** (adult/child return Sfr9/4.50; ☷ 9.30am-12.20pm & 1.15-6.20pm) from the dam base to the top. As you stare across the milky green water, remember that six million cubic metres of cement stand between this lake and the valley stretching out below.

Hikers can do a circuit of the lake or cross over into the next valley and make for Arolla, a six-hour trek for the fit.

Val d'Hérens & Val d'Arolla

Locals of this valley pride themselves on their authentic way of life, which includes dressing and working in traditional costume. The best day to see people dressed up this way in the valley's villages is Sunday.

Coming up from Sion, you pass through Vex and then **Euseigne**. Just before reaching the latter, the road passes under Gaudiesque-looking rock pinnacles commonly known

---

CLOSE COW ENCOUNTERS

It might sound like a load of bull, but cow fights are a serious business in Valais. Known as the *Combats de Reines* (*Kuhkämpfe* in German), cow fights are organised in villages, in particular on the Val d'Hérens, to decide which beast is most suited to lead the herd to summer pastures. These Moo-Hammad Ali wannabes charge, lock horns then try to force each other backwards.

The winner, acclaimed to be the herd's 'queen', can be worth Sfr20,000. Genetic selection and embryo freezing are used to get effective contenders to the field of combat. Once selected, they are fed oats concentrate (believed to act as a stimulant) and sometimes wine.

Contests take place on selected Sundays from late March to late May and from August to late September and are usually accompanied by much consumption of Valaisan wine. Combatants rarely get hurt so visitors shouldn't find the competition distressing. There is a grand final in Aproz (a 10-minute postal bus ride west of Sion) in May on Ascension Day, and the last meeting of the season is held at Martigny's Foire du Valais in early October.

---

as the **Pyramides d'Euseigne**. They have been eroded into their strange form over thousands of years. Some 8km further south is the valley's main town, **Evolène**. Here is where you will find most of the valley's accommodation and a huddle of restaurants. **Hôtel Arzinol** (☎ 021 283 16 65; www.hotel-arzinol.ch; s/d Sfr55/110) offers a range of cheerful rooms in a timber chalet. The best have a balcony and on cold winter nights you can sit by the fire in the house's lounge room.

Another 5km and you reach the hamlet of **Les Haudères**. Here the road forks. To the left, one leads 7km up to another pretty mountain settlement, **Ferpècle**, which represents the end of the road and the start of some mountain hiking in the shadow of the Dent Blanche (4357m).

The other road heads right, rising steeply onto a wooded mountain ridge before dropping down into another remote valley, the **Val d'Arolla**. After 11km you roll into a modest ski resort. To the east you can make out the Dent Blanche and to the southwest the Pigne d'Arolla (3796m), one of half a dozen peaks of 3600m or more that encircle the village of Arolla.

Set in gardens thick with larch trees, the deciduous conifer typical of the valleys here, the **Grand Hotel & Kurhaus** (☎ 027 283 70 00; www.kurhaus.arolla.com; r per person Sfr86) stands in splendid isolation a couple of kilometres beyond Arolla and has been in business since 1896. Cheaper rooms come without bathroom.

Four to seven daily buses from Sion run up the valley to Evolène (Sfr13.40, 45 minutes) and some roll on to Arolla (change at Les Haudères, Sfr20, 1¼ hours), which is 41km from Sion.

SIERRE & AROUND
pop 14,360 / elevation 540m

The French and German languages compete for prominence in Sierre (Siders in German), although French is favoured. Great weather also comes up victorious, as this is one of Switzerland's sunniest towns. The **tourist office** (☎ 027 455 85 35; www.sierre-salgesch.ch; ◷ 8am-7pm Mon-Fri, 8am-noon Sat, 8am-7pm daily high season) is in the train station.

Sights & Activities

History is reflected in the numerous **châteaux** and **grand houses** in and around the town. The tourist office's *Promenade des Châteaux* brochure has walking routes but most buildings are private and can only be viewed from outside.

Of these, the most inviting is the 16th-century **Château de Villa** (☎ 027 455 18 96; www.chateaudevilla.ch; Rue Ste-Catherine 4), set on high ground about a 20-minute walk from the train station along Ave du Marché. The walk itself is curious, as it takes you into the older part of the town, some of which is still littered with postage stamp–sized vineyards! The château is home to the **Musée du Vin** (◷ 2-5pm Apr-Nov), a modest display of old wine presses and other memorabilia showing how the grape nectar used to be made and stored. The château is worth visiting for other reasons though. First there is the **Oenothèque** (wine store; ◷ 10.30am-1pm & 4.30-8.30pm), with its extensive collection of wines, some of which you can taste before buying. Then there is the restaurant (see p130).

A 10-minute walk, partly past vineyards, from the Château de Villa is the **Château Mercier**, which is set with a series of other villas,

VALAIS

AUTHOR'S CHOICE

Hôtel Terminus (☎ 027 455 13 51; www.hotel
-terminus.ch; Rue du Bourg 1; s/d Sfr120/190;
☒ 🖳 🅿 Sfr8) Recently transformed into
one of the region's top addresses, this is a
gourmet pilgrimage site with snazzy digs.
Rooms are pleasingly laid out with modern
furniture (touches like plasma TV and wi-
fi). Ask about the big doubles in the loft.
The chef behind the restaurant, Didier de
Courten, was voted the 2006 Cook of the
Year by the prestigious *Gault-Millau* restaurant guide. The restaurant (mains Sfr70-75,
tasting menus Sfr120-185; 🕑 Tue-Sat), in
yellow and black (and with a lovely terrace),
is the high altar of avant-garde cooking.

orangery and former stables in a pretty park.
The whole lot is used for major receptions
and similar events, but you can wander the
grounds any time.

Just 3.5km away from Sierre and on
the other side of the language frontier is
the wine hamlet of **Salgesch** (Salquenen to
Francophones). You can follow a walking
route through Sierre and vineyards from
the Château de Villa. In Salgesch you will
find the **Weinmuseum** (🕑 2-5pm Apr-Nov), part
of the museum in the Château de Villa,
and loads of wineries such as the excellent
Gregor Kuonen & Söhne.

Sleeping & Eating

Bois de Finges (☎ 027 455 02 84; www.tiscover.ch
/camping-bois-de-finges; sites per person/tent only/car & tent
Sfr6.40/10.40/17; 🕑 late Apr–early Oct; 🅿 🏊) East of
the town centre, an area of protected woodland contains several camping grounds, including this one, which is prettily located on
the forest edge and near the Rhône.

Château de Villa (☎ 027 455 18 86; www.chateaude
villa.ch; Rue Ste-Catherine 4; raclette Sfr30; 🕑 daily) Giving the Terminus a run for its money, the
château proposes a marvellous raclette feast,
tasting six types of cheese (washed down
with excellent local wine).

Getting There & Away

Around two trains an hour stop at Sierre
on the Geneva–Brig route. The town is
the leaping-off point for Crans-Montana;
a red SMC shuttle bus (*navette*, free) from
outside the station runs to the nearby fu-

nicular station for Montana (Sfr11.40, 15
minutes).

CRANS-MONTANA
pop 7000 / elevation 1500m

Visitors to this trendy twin resort about
15km northwest of Sierre are as interested
in show as snow. Once favoured by the likes
of President Kennedy and film stars, it now
tends to attract new rich Russians. The skiing is mostly intermediate but excellent. As
host of the European Masters Golf Tournament every September, the local courses, one
of them designed by Spanish player Seve Bal-
lesteros, are among the best in the country.
The resort is a modern, sprawling affair, but
set along a string of shimmering lakes.

The **tourist office** (☎ 027 485 04 04; www.crans
-montana.ch; 🕑 8.30am-6.30pm Mon-Sat, 10am-noon
& 4-6pm Sun Dec-Apr & mid-Jun–Aug, 8.30am-noon &
2-6pm Mon-Fri, 8.30am-noon Sat rest of the year) has
branches in the Scandia building on Rue
Centrale in Crans and the post office building on Ave de la Gare in Montana.

The ski area comprises 160km of slopes,
41 lifts and 50km of cross-country tracks.
Crans-Montana area ski passes cost Sfr56/34/
48 per adult/child/youth and senior for one
day. For about 20% more you can include the
Plaine-Morte Glacier (3000m). Five ski schools
are scattered about the resort.

In summer, hiking and golf are the prime
activities. The golf courses include nine and
18 holes. Prices range from Sfr40 to Sfr80.
Contact the **golf club** (☎ 027 485 97 97; www.golf
crans.ch; 🕑 May-Oct). The tourist offices can tell
you about adventure sports, from canoeing
to mountain climbing.

Sleeping & Eating

You can book online through the resort
website (www.crans-montana.ch). It is often
cheaper and sometimes more homey to lodge
in private homes than in hotels (of which
there are about 50). This can also be arranged
through the tourist office.

Auberge du Petit Paradis (☎ 027 481 21 48; www
.petit-paradis.com; s/d Sfr75/130; 🅿) Situated just
below Crans in the hamlet of Bluche, this
is a cosy place at a price you'll find hard to
beat anywhere else in the resort. Rooms are
spotless with typical wood panelling.

Hôtel Mont-Blanc (☎ 027 481 31 43; www.hotel
-montblanc.ch in French; Plans Mayens; s/d Sfr165/280; 🅿)
Just outside Crans to the northwest, this

VALAIS

spot is known for its grand balcony terrace, perfect for eating up the Alpine views along with the food. The place has 10 rooms and three suites.

Hostellerie du Pas de l'Ours (☎ 027 485 93 33; www .relaischateaux.com/pasdelours; Rue du Pas de l'Ours; ste Sfr430-650; P ☒) For sheer splendour, this grand timber 'castle' is one of the best places to stay. Just nine suites, all done with impeccable taste, combine stone with timber to create a truly warm welcome. The Jacuzzis in the rooms help too. It's in central Crans.

Le Raphaele (☎ 027 480 31 50; Rue du Pas de l'Ours; pizzas Sfr18-20, meat mains Sfr30-46; ☒ daily) Apart from having the distinction of being one of the very few places here to open year-round, this spot does pretty good pizza and quite reasonable food in general. In autumn the game menu is enticing.

Le Pavillon (☎ 027 481 24 69; Route de Rawyl; mains Sfr35-46; ☒ Wed-Mon) Overlooking Lac Grenon, one of the pretty little lakes where much of the resort is strung, this small but warm dining option allows you lake views from inside and out. The menu includes fresh fish (depending on what the markets offer). Try the *filet de saumon grillé, poêlé de fenouil et tomates* (grilled salmon fillet with pan-fried fennel and tomatoes). It's about halfway between Crans and Montana (bus stop Pavillon).

Getting There & Away

See opposite for information on getting to Crans-Montana. Free shuttles move around the resort area.

VAL D'ANNIVIERS

Traditionally Sierre has had a close relationship with the people of the Val d'Anniviers, who would winter in their mountain homes and come to Sierre in summer to work in the vineyards. Some continue to do so. The valley is dotted by pretty towns and offers some fine skiing options.

From Sierre, the main road south winds up steeply on the east flank of the valley, arriving after 13km in the medieval village of **Vissoie**, with its 13th-century watchtower and 12th-century church. It is a valley crossroads for five ski stations (www.sierre-anniviers .ch). You can get a ski pass for the whole area (adult/child/student Sfr45/27/38), which totals 220km of ski runs. About 11km along a narrow road winding back north towards Sierre is **Vercorin** (☎ 027 455 58 55; www.vercorin.ch),

a pleasant family resort with limited (35km of pistes) but enjoyable skiing and a handful of places to stay and eat. It is also accessible direct from Sierre via Chippis. In summer you could take a one-hour walk (signposted) south to **Val de Réchy**, especially tempting in late September, when it is often possible to spot sizable groups of deer.

Closer and much more tempting are the combined stations of **St Luc** (☎ 027 475 14 12; www .saint-luc.ch) and **Chandolin** (☎ 027 475 18 38; www .chandolin.ch), with 75km of broad, sunny ski runs and fairytale panoramas. St Luc is 4km east of Vissoie, up a series of switchbacks, and Chandolin another 4km to the north. The latter is the prettier of the two, a huddle of timber houses hanging on for dear life to the steep slopes at around 2000m. While here, visit the **Espace Ella Maillart** (admission free; ☒ 10am-6pm Wed-Sun), dedicated to the remarkable Swiss adventurer who lived in Chandolin when she wasn't exploring the remote corners of Afghanistan and Tibet, or winning races as a champion sailor and skier. In summer, there are plenty of walking options, including the Chemin des Planètes (Planets Trail), an uphill amble from Tignousa (above St Luc) to the **Weisshorn Hotel** (☎ 027 475 11 06; www.chez.com /hotelweisshorn; r per person half board Sfr110), with models of planets in the solar system along the way (a variant sees you leaving the path at Uranus and following a trail past several mountain lakes to Lac de la Bella-Tola). The hotel, opened in 1884, is at 2337m and accessible on foot or by mountain bike only (or on skis in winter, when luggage is transported for you from St Luc).

The funicular from St Luc to Tignousa (Sfr13/8 per adult/child return) doesn't run between seasons. The walk from St Luc to Tignousa and on to Lac de la Bella-Tola is four hours. There are plenty of accommodation and eating options in Chandolin and St Luc.

Back down in Vissoies you could continue along the main road for **Zinal** (☎ 027 475 13 70; www.zinal.ch) via the hamlet of Ayer. At Zinal, too, there is good skiing, although the village is nothing special.

Another story is **Grimentz** (☎ 027 476 20 01; www.bendolla.ch), 7km up a winding road from Vissoies into a side valley. It is one of the prettiest mountain towns in Valais, its burned-timber houses huddled over narrow lanes and adorned with geranium-filled

VALAIS

flower boxes (some local citizens have the job of maintaining hanging pots of geraniums along several kilometres of the approach road to Grimentz!). The town makes a lovely base for local skiing. The 8km road south along La Gougra stream to the turquoise waters of **Lac de Moiry** (2249m) is open only in summer. Another 3km brings you to a second, smaller dam, where the road peters out. Before you, the Glacier de Moiry sticks out its dirty white tongue, a 1½-hour hike away.

In Grimentz, **Hotel de Moiry** (☎ 027 475 11 44; www.hoteldemoiry.ch; r per person half board Sfr105) is a modest, comfortable option with all the trappings of a warm mountain chalet. Eat heartily in the restaurant downstairs. How about a *tartiflette*, a potato and bacon pie coated in a layer of Reblochon cheese? There's a vegetable version too.

Up to eight postal buses a day run from Sierre to Vissoie, where you make connections for Chandolin (Sfr14.20) via St Luc, Zinal (Sfr15.20) and Grimentz (Sfr13.40). All these trips take about one hour from Sierre. In summer three buses run the 20 minutes from Grimentz to Lac de Moiry (Sfr9.80).

UPPER VALAIS

The German eastern half of the Valais is dominated by the country's most powerful image, the soaring Matterhorn peak. A cluster of 4000m peaks and pretty Swiss German towns act as a year-round magnet for sport and nature lovers.

LEUKERBAD

pop 1430 / elevation 1411m

Leukerbad (Loèche-les-Bains in French) is the largest mountain thermal centre in Europe. The Romans settled here and in the 19th century it was popular with travellers negotiating the Gemmi Pass to/from the Bernese Oberland. From the 1980s until the late 1990s, the municipality undertook massive renovation works with dodgy debts that finally resulted in a scandal, jail for various people involved and the placement of the entire area under financial surveillance.

The majestic mountain walls that encase the village like an amphitheatre grander than anything the Romans could have conceived makes for an awe-inspiring backdrop to your outdoor bathing meditations. The grey rock walls rise out of pretty green and wooded fields.

Orientation & Information

This attractive resort is 16km north of Leuk along a spectacular road. The **tourist office** (☎ 027 472 71 71; www.leukerbad.ch; ☼ 9am-noon & 1.15-6pm Mon-Fri, 9am-6pm Sat, 9am-noon Sun Jul-Nov & Dec-Apr, 9am-noon & 1.15-5.30pm Mon-Sat rest of year) is in the centre. In the same complex you'll find the town hall, post office, a parking garage and the bus station. Cars are not used in the centre at night.

Sights & Activities

There are six main thermal bath installations, but the biggest and best is **Burgerbad** (☎ 027 472 20 20; www.burgerbad.ch; Rathausstrasse; adult/child/student Sfr22/12/17; ☼ 8am-8pm Sun-Thu, 8am-9pm Fri & Sat). It has a number of different pools, inside and outside, including whirlpools and water massage jets. The complex also has a sauna and fitness studio, which cost extra. Another centre is **Lindner Alpentherme** (☎ 027 472 10 10; www.lindner.de; ☼ 8am-8pm Oct-Mar, 8am-7pm Apr-Sep), where a two-hour treatment in the Roman-Irish bath (reservation required) costs Sfr59, including an extra three hours in the thermal pools. They cost Sfr16/12 per adult/child for three hours without extras. Children under six are not admitted. The tourist office can give details of training and regeneration programmes and medical treatments.

A cable car ascends the sheer side of the northern mountain ridge to the **Gemmi Pass** (2350m). It's a good area for hiking. The cable car is Sfr18.50/26 one way/return, or it takes two hours to walk up.

The main **skiing** area is the Torrenthorn (2998m), yielding mostly runs of medium difficulty, but there are also a few easy ones and a demanding run that descends 1400m. One-day ski passes cost Sfr44/26/35 per adult/child six to 11 years/student and senior.

Sleeping & Eating

Weisses Rössli (☎ 027 470 33 77; weissesroessli@bluemail.ch; s/d with hall shower Sfr50/100) Just off the central Dorfplatz, this is a cheerful place, with flower boxes on the little balconies and a welcoming, homey feel. A good breakfast is included and the proprietor is helpful. It has a restaurant serving up typical Valais fare downstairs.

VALAIS

FEBRUARY'S FREAKY MONSTERS

The Lötschental is little known to outsiders, but many have heard vague telling of the Tschäggättä, masked and hairy monsters that flit about the valley's settlements around Fasnacht time from 2 February until Ash Wednesday. Wearing old clothes covered in thick sheep or goat pelts, tied around the waist with a thick belt from which hangs a fat cowbell, these fellows don scary, locally made wooden masks and gloves dipped in soot. Traditionally (until about the mid-20th century) they would stalk villagers from noon to 6pm, rubbing the soot into any victims they could lay their hands on. Nowadays a few women join in this long, traditionally male activity. They tend to prowl around in the evening and, thankfully, are a little more respectful of their soot-loathing victims.

How the tradition was born is a matter of conjecture. One theory suggests these 'monsters' aimed to ward off the vestiges of winter and evil spirits (similar figures appear in other parts of Europe, from Austria to Sardinia), but another one sees the origin in a band of masked thieves that operated in the valley in the 11th century.

If you're in the valley on 3 February, you can catch a parade of Tschäggättä from Blatten to Ferden.

Hôtel de la Croix Fédérale (☎ 027 472 79 79; www .croix-federale.ch; Kirchstrasse 43; s/d Sfr99/180) With its timber-lined rooms and friendly downstairs restaurant, this is a good central deal. Wood-panelled rooms, especially the doubles, are spacious and light and you're a short sprint from the Lindner Alpentherme baths. Downstairs, the Walliser Kanne (mains Sfr20 to Sfr35; ☻ Friday to Wednesday) restaurant offers a wide range of dishes, from tried and true local standards to a range of vegetable-laden rösti (crispy, fried, shredded potatoes) options, pasta and warm winter polenta (a thick mush made of cornmeal boiled in water or stock) dishes.

Lindner Alpentherme (☎ 027 472 10 00; www.lind ner.de; Dorfplatz; s/d Sfr200/400; 🖳 🅿 🕮) This is quite a complex, plonked down smack in the centre of town with its 135 rooms and tempting bath installations. Apart from the standard rooms, already elegantly appointed (and whose price halves in the low season), there is a whole range of bigger and better rooms and suites to choose from.

Getting There & Away

Leuk is on the main rail route from Lausanne to Brig. From Leuk an hourly blue postal bus goes to Leukerbad; last departure is 7.45pm (Sfr13.40, 30 to 35 minutes).

LÖTSCHENTAL

This westernmost valley of the series of valleys and glaciers that together make up the Aletsch region, mostly accessible from villages east of Brig (see p139), is an engaging and little-visited foretaste. Most people who venture into the area only make it as far as Goppenstein, 9km north of the N9 road, to load their cars onto the half-hourly Lötschbergtunnel train that whisks them to Kandersteg in the Bernese Oberland (Sfr20 to Sfr25 per car, 15 minutes). More trains are put on in summer.

Beyond Goppenstein, the road swings gradually northeast along a wild valley, a far cry from the ski jet set hue and cry of Crans-Montana, Verbier or Zermatt. Trundle through a series of villages to the end of the valley at **Fafleralp**, little more than a huddle of chalets and a wonderful mountain hotel, the Hotel Fafleralp.

The icy finger of the **Langgletscher** glacier stretches down towards the village and is the object of a fairly easy 1½-hour hike from the car park that marks the end of town. Other walks into the mountains, creased by the cascading waters of glacial waterfalls and largely bereft of any vegetation but a touch of Alpine grass, are also possible. To further whet your appetite, see www.loetschental.ch (in German).

Cross-country skiing is possible in the vicinity and there's even a little downhill action on the **Lauchneralp** at **Wiler**, 3km southwest of Blatten.

Up to 12 postal buses run from Goppenstein to Blatten, and on to Fafleralp (32 minutes) from June to October.

VISP

pop 6580 / elevation 650m

About the most visitors see of Visp is the train station as they change rides to get from the

VALAIS

AUTHOR'S CHOICE

Hotel Fafleralp (☎ 027 939 14 51; www.fafler alp.ch in German; per person up to Sfr84) Settled amid woods at the end of the Lötschental valley, this is a delight for those seeking a rustic getaway. Rooms are made of local wood and there's not a telephone or TV in sight. It's like being in a big family home, with cosy dining and lounge areas for those who don't want to get out in the snow. The hotel remains open in winter (often weekends only), although snow cuts the road off as far down as Blatten (4km southwest). An utterly fable-like atmosphere settles on the place then. If you reserve at the hotel they will pick up your luggage from Blatten and you will walk the 4km in snow shoes.

---

main line to the Geneva–Brig train line up to the Zermatt and Saas Fee ski resorts. The old centre is attractive enough with its cobbled streets and shuttered windows. Take the 2½-hour hike up the hill to the wine-growing village of **Visperterminen**; an occasional bus (Sfr6) does the same trip in 25 minutes.

Should you get stuck here, there is a cluster of hotels near the train station. Trains run every hour or so to Zermatt (Sfr32, 65 minutes). For Saas Fee you need to take the hourly postal bus (Sfr14.20, 45 minutes). If you take the Zermatt train, parking is free in Visp at the 'park and ride' car park between the station and the post office.

BRIGERBAD

Halfway between Visp and Brig but more easily accessible from the former are Brigerbad's open-air **thermal baths** (☎ 027 946 46 88; www.brigerbad.ch in German). The pools range from frivolous to curative. The five open-air **pools** (adult/child Sfr12/6; ☯ 9.30am-6pm late May-Sep) have a water temperature of 27°C to 37°C. Postal buses from Visp (Sfr2.80, 12 minutes) leave more or less hourly.

ZERMATT

pop 5420 / elevation 1605m
One word says it all: Matterhorn (4478m). The legendary peak towers over the town of Zermatt, acting like a magnet to ski fans, snowboarders and mountaineers. On 13 July 1865 Edward Whymper (who stayed at the grand Monte Rosa hotel) led the

first successful ascent of the mountain. The climb took 32 hours but the descent was marred by tragedy when four team members crashed to their deaths in a 1200m fall down the North Wall. Many mountaineers still come to conquer the peak, but a few unlucky individuals never leave. Their names are etched in stone in the town's cemeteries.

Skiers and snowboarders prefer going down to climbing up. The town doubled in size during the ski boom that raged in the 1960s and 1970s. For the rich and stylish, Zermatt is a place to see (as well as ski) and be seen (skiing or otherwise).

Information
INTERNET ACCESS
You can go online for free (or bring your laptop for a wi-fi moment) at **Papperla Pub** (☎ 027 967 40 40; www.papperlapub.ch).

TOURIST INFORMATION
The town has a **tourist office** (☎ 027 966 81 00; www.zermatt.ch; Bahnhofplatz 5; ☯ 8.30am-noon & 1.30-6pm Mon-Fri, 9.30am-noon & 4-6pm Sat & Sun late Sep–mid-Jun, 8.30am-6pm Mon-Sat, 8.30am-noon & 1.30-6pm Sun mid-Jun–Sep).

Alpin Center (☎ 027 966 24 60; www.zermatt.ch/alpin center in German; Bahnhofstrasse 58; ☯ 8am-noon & 2-6pm mid-Nov–Apr & Jul-Sep) contains the ski and snowboard school and the mountain guides office (Bergführerbüro). For climbing the Matterhorn they recommend previous experience, one week's preparation and the small matter of Sfr1130 per person. Also ask here about Haute Route ski-touring and heli-skiing. In the off-season you can reach them by phone only from 9am to 11am and from 2pm to 5pm Monday to Friday.

Sights
Views from the cable cars and gondolas are almost uniformly breathtaking. The cogwheel train to **Gornergrat** (3090m) is a highlight. The mountain railway (Sfr36 one way) takes 25 to 43 minutes and there are two to three departures per hour. For the best views of the Matterhorn sit on the right-hand side. Alternatively, it takes around five hours to walk up from Zermatt to Gornergrat.

Hinter Dorf, off Zermatt's main street, is the oldest part of the village. It's crammed with tumbledown wooden Valais homes, a world away from the flashy boutiques by the church. The stone discs on the stilts of the storage barns are intended to keep out the rodents.

A walk in the **cemetery** is a sobering experience for any would-be mountaineer, as numerous monuments tell of deaths on Monte Rosa and the Matterhorn. The **Alpine Museum** (adult/child/senior Sfr8/free/4; ☼ 10am-noon & 4-6pm daily Jul-Sep, 4-6pm Mon-Sat rest of year) has exhibits about mountain ascents, local fauna, the development of Zermatt and famous visitors. Around the back is the **English church**, where there are more mountaineering epitaphs. A pair from Cambridge University in England was lost in the mountains in August 1959. Their bodies were found 30 years later.

Activities

Zermatt has numerous demanding slopes to test the experienced and intermediate skier in three main skiing areas: **Rothorn, Stockhorn** and **Matterhorn Glacier Paradise** (formerly Klein Matterhorn). In all, there are 245km of ski runs, and free ski buses simplify transferring between areas. February to April is peak time but in early summer the snow is still good and the lifts are less busy. Beginners have fewer options on the slopes.

The Klein Matterhorn is topped by the highest cable-car station in Europe (3820m), providing access to the highest skiing on the continent. It's also the most extensive summer skiing in Switzerland (up to 21km of runs), and the starting point for skiing at the

ZERMATT

INFORMATION	
Alpin Center.................................1	A3
Tourist Office..............................2	A1

SIGHTS & ACTIVITIES	
Alpine Museum...........................3	A3
Cemetery....................................4	B3
English Church............................5	A2
Gornergrat Cogwheel Train	
Station...................................6	B1
Mountain Guides Office & Ski	
School.................................(see 1)	

SLEEPING	
Hotel Bahnhof............................7	B1
Hotel Couronne..........................8	B4
Parkhotel Beau Site....................9	C3

EATING	
Restaurant Ross-Stall...............10	B1
Restaurant Stockhorn..............11	C4
Restaurant Weisshorn..............12	A4

DRINKING	
Broken Bart Disco....................13	A3
Papperla Pub............................14	B4
Schneewittchen..................(see 14)	
S'alt Hirschi.............................15	B3

VALAIS

Italian resort of Cervinia. This opens up a potential total ski area of 313km of downhill runs. The No 7 run down from the border is an exhilarating, broad avenue, great for intermediates and above. Be aware that bad weather can close the lifts leading up to the Klein Matterhorn on either side. Runs can be icier on the Italian side too (the skiing in Cervinia is best in March), but there are plenty of options and it is fun to indulge in the Italian atmosphere for a day. Don't leave it too late to get the lifts back up, or you could find yourself staying overnight!

When you take the cable car to Klein Matterhorn, if the weather is good, take the lift up to the top of the mountain. From here (3883m) you are virtually on top of Europe, with 360° views of the Swiss Alps (from Mont Blanc to Aletschhorn) and deep into Italy.

From September to late November you can head to Zermatt for a weekend package that involves testing several pairs of the latest skis to hit the market on a limited set of runs around the Klein Matterhorn glacier. This can cost from Sfr304 per person in a one-star hotel (double room) to Sfr419 in a five-star. The price includes breakfast, ski pass and test-ski rental.

A day pass for all ski lifts in Zermatt (excluding Cervinia) costs Sfr67/34/57 per adult/child/senior and student and Sfr75/38/64 including Cervinia.

Festivals & Events

On 15 August, Zermatt comes alive to the sound of music with the Alpine **Folkloreumzug** (Folklore parade), involving 1400 participants. In September, look out for the **Zermatt Festival**, a series of chamber music concerts given by a skeleton crew of the Berlin Philarmonic in venues around the village.

Sleeping

Zermatt offers plenty of accommodation, from five-star luxury down to rooms in private houses and chalets. There are about 120 hotels, hostels and similar, along with more than 200 holiday apartments (which you can usually book only for one-week blocks).

Hotel Bahnhof (☎ 027 967 24 06; www.hotelbahnhof.com; Bahnhofstrasse; dm Sfr33, s/d with shower Sfr76/96; ☿ closed around mid-Oct–mid-Dec) This hotel is opposite the train station and a mountaineer's mecca. It has 12-bed dorms and a shower on every floor. There are also compact, wood-panelled rooms. Prices are without breakfast, but there's a kitchen.

Hotel Blauherd (☎ 027 967 22 91; www.hotels-suisse.ch/blauherd; Wiestistrasse; s/d Sfr95/190; ☒) Although a bit of a walk from the centre, this very friendly chalet-style hotel is a fine option. Rooms are clean and cosy, the buffet breakfast is generous and you can use the pool in the nearby Hotel Cristiania, about 50m down the road. They will pick you up at the train station.

Hotel Couronne (☎ 027 966 23 00; www.hotel-couronne.ch; Kirchstrasse 15; s/d/ste Sfr162/264/304) This is in an excellent location overlooking the river. The best rooms are the south-facing ones with balcony, all of which enjoy views of the Matterhorn. There's a sauna (free) and you can take breakfast in the Wintergarden, again with views towards the Matterhorn.

Parkhotel Beau Site (☎ 027 966 68 68; www.parkhotel-beausite.ch; Brunnmattgasse 9; s/d half board Sfr240/400; ☒) The standard rooms in this opulent option are already very nice, done in walnut. If you want to pay a little more, there are all sorts of options on bigger and better doubles and suites. On the premises you have access to various saunas and steam baths, a pool and whirlpool.

Eating

Restaurant Ross-Stall (☎ 027 967 30 40; Bahnhofplatz 50; meals Sfr50; ☿ daily mid-Jun–Apr) Housed in a typical-looking Valais house near the train station, this place specialises in fondue, which it does very well. Head downstairs for the main dining area and dig in to a meal consisting of *Walliserteller* starter, fondue washed down with Fendant white wine and sorbet with local alcohol (like Williamine) to finish.

Restaurant Stockhorn (☎ 027 967 17 47; Riedstrasse 11; fondue Sfr35, mains Sfr35-40; ☿ daily mid-Jun–Sep & mid-Nov–Apr) This place is what you have in mind when looking for a warm, cuddly, Alpine chalet. If it's fondue or raclette you want, stay downstairs. Here you will also see a very strange old machine with weights and cogs that turns chickens (order in advance) on a spit! For meat specialities cooked over wood fire, head upstairs.

Restaurant Weisshorn (☎ 027 967 57 52; Am Bach 6; fondue Sfr25-28, meals Sfr40-50; ☿ daily mid-Jun–Sep & mid-Nov–Apr) The garish mural of Chichenitza, the Mexican temple, contrasts with the orange glowing Matterhorn table lamps.

The food range is just as odd, from nachos and quesadilla to fondue. The more adventurous will be unable to resist the chilifondue with mango, pineapple and nachos! Wash down with Heida white wine.

Drinking

Papperla Pub (☎ 027 967 40 40; www.papperlapub .ch; Steinmattstrasse 34; ☷ 2.30pm-2am) This is *the* après-ski pub in Zermatt, especially if it's a slow time in the season (like January). Around the circular bar arranged on a couple of levels are high tables with stools or, if you prefer, low lounges. A DJ is usually in action and there's no shortage of ski-resort drinking hijinks. Next door, proceed downstairs to the Schneewittchen club (open to 4am), run by the same people.

S'alt Hirschi (☎ 027 967 42 62; Hinterdorfstrasse 44; ☷ 9pm-2am daily Dec-Apr, otherwise sometimes 9pm-2am Fri & Sat) In the old part of the village, this quiet little bar set up in a traditional timber dwelling is an atmospheric spot for a *Glühwein* (mulled wine) or other poison. It serves a limited range of food in winter but there is none available in summer.

Broken Bar Disco (☎ 027 967 19 31; Bahnhofstrasse 41; ☷ 10pm-4am) Down in a vaulted cellar of the Hotel Post, this is a popular dance dive where you can jive on a keg and expend any energy left over after the day on the slopes. The Hotel Post is home to various bars and eateries in the one complex.

Getting There & Away

CAR

Zermatt is car-free. Dinky little electric vehicles are used to transport goods, serve as taxis and so on around town. At the moment, drivers have to leave their vehicles in the huge open parking area in Täsch (Sfr7.50 per day), or in one of the several covered garages there and take the train (Sfr7.80, 12 minutes) into Zermatt. In 2005, the village voted to open the road as far as Zermatt and build parking stations at the village entrance, but it could be a while before this happens.

TRAIN

Hourly trains depart from Brig (Sfr34, 85 minutes), stopping at Visp en route. The scenic route is operated by a private railway. Zermatt is also the starting point of the *Glacier Express* to Graubünden, one of the most spectacular train rides in the world (see p23).

SAAS FEE

pop 1600 / elevation 1800m

Hemmed in by a menacing grey amphitheatre of 13 implacable peaks over 4000m, backed by the threatening ice tongues of nine glaciers, little Saas Fee (1792m) looks positively feeble in the revealing light of summer. It is perched on a ledge above Saas Grund (1560m), a slightly drabber partner town further from the piste action. Although bits of the old village, with its chalets and timber barns on stilts, survive, this is largely a modern creation, less charming than its westerly neighbour Zermatt but equally full of twinkling cheer in the winter ski season.

Orientation & Information

Saas Fee spreads out in a long line. The village centre and ski lifts are to the left (southwest) of the bus station.

The **tourist office** (☎ 027 958 18 58; www.saas-fee .ch; ☷ 8.30am-noon & 2-6.30pm Mon-Fri, 8am-7pm Sat, 9am-noon & 3-6pm Sun) is opposite the post office and bus station. Opening hours reduce slightly in the off-season. The local Guest Card earns various discounts.

Sights & Activities

Skiing is the primary activity. About 100km of ski runs are more suited to beginners and experts, though intermediates have sufficient choices. Snowboarding is also good, but off-piste skiing is hazardous, due to the many glaciers. A general lift pass costs Sfr61/37 per adult/child for one day and Sfr340/204 for one week. Ski-mountaineering is possible along the famous Haute Route all the way to Chamonix.

The tourist office has a map of 280km of summer **hiking** trails in the region. In winter, 20km of marked footpaths remain open.

The highest underground funicular (metro) in the world operates all year to **Mittelallalin** (3500m), ascending 500m in 2½ minutes. It gives access to the Feegletscher, a centre for summer skiing (July and August) with 20km of runs above 2700m. Under the top station is the **Ice Palace** (adult/child Sfr4/2), 10m below the surface of the ice. It expounds on glacier-related topics. From Saas Fee to Mittelallalin by cable car then funicular costs Sfr69 return (children are half-price).

VALAIS

Sleeping

Ask for the tourist office accommodation brochures. There are more than 360 chalet options scattered around Saas Fee and about 60 hotels.

Hotel Alpenblick (☎ 027 957 16 45; www.alpenblick -saas-fee.ch in German; r per person Sfr80) This largish chalet-style place left of the bus station and next to the swimming pool has rooms arranged as two doubles with shared living area. There are also apartments rented for weekly blocks. This place overlooks a fantastic garden.

Hotel Sonnenhof (☎ 027 958 13 13; www.hotel -sonnenhof.ch in German; s/d Sfr130/260) A centrally located mid-size hotel, this spot is family friendly and offers vegetarian food in its restaurant. Rooms are straightforward, with some wood panelling, carpet and TV. It is a quiet location with a spot of garden.

Romantik Hotel Beau-Site (☎ 027 958 15 60; www .beausite.org; s/d Sfr220/396) This classy hotel offers, aside from spacious, comfortable rooms, a tempting wellness centre and pools, which range from the Felsgrotte ('cliff grotto') to various steam baths, thalassotherapy and a Finnish sauna. You'll hardly have time for the ski runs!

Eating

Zur Mühle (☎ 027 957 26 76; mains Sfr15-20; ☯ daily) For some typical Valais grub, you could pop by here. Rösti is the mainstay and comes in various forms, such as Walliserteller (with ham, onions and cheese mixed in). It is located atop the town's river.

Carl-Zuckmayer-Stube (☎ 027 957 21 75; meals Sfr50; ☯ Tue-Sun) Sit outside on the terrace for a hearty dish of deer schnitzel with glazed apple, chestnuts, red cabbage and Brussels sprouts.

La Ferme (☎ 027 958 15 69; meals Sfr70-80; ☯ 11.30am-midnight) On the main street near the tourist office, this place with country chalet airs has a rustic feel, with farm implements hanging from the walls. It specialises in meat dishes (and a good *fondue chinoise* at Sfr48).

Fletschhorn (☎ 027 957 21 31; www.fletschhorn .ch; tasting menu Sfr140-190; ☯ 10am-midnight daily mid-Dec–Apr & mid-Jun–Oct) This is one of the top 20 restaurants in Switzerland, offering gourmet cuisine with a French leaning. It's in a quiet location beyond the northern part of the village (get staff to pick you up in the electric car).

Drinking

About a dozen bars are strung out along the long main street of Saas Fee. For cocktails, drop by **Metrobar** (☎ 027 957 14 10; ☯ 4pm-1am).

Getting There & Away

Hourly buses depart from Brig (Sfr16.80, one hour) and Visp (Sfr14.20, 45 minutes). From Brig it is marginally faster to get the train and change at Visp. You can transfer to/from Zermatt at Stalden Saas.

Saas Fee is car-free. Park at the entrance to the village, where the first 24 hours in winter costs Sfr15 (covered parking). It gets cheaper after the first day and if you use the local Guest Card.

BRIG

pop 11,880 / elevation 688m

With the number of road and rail routes bumping into each other here, it's likely you'll spend a night in this bustling burgh.

Orientation & Information

The centre is south of the Rhône and east of its tributary, the Saltina. On the 1st floor of the train station is the **tourist office** (☎ 027 921 60 30; www.brig.ch; ☯ 8.30am-6pm Mon-Fri, 9am-1pm Sat Oct-Jun, 8.30am-6pm Mon-Fri, 9am-6pm Sat, 9am-1pm Sun Jul-Sep). Postal buses leave from outside the train station. Directly ahead is Bahnhofstrasse, leading to the centre of town.

Sights

STOCKALPERSCHLOSS

Kaspar Jodok von Stockalper (1609–91), a man with an eye for business who dominated the Simplon Pass trade routes, did so well that he built this castle caprice in the middle of Brig. He even dubbed himself the 'Great Stockalper'. Locals didn't agree and obliged him to hightail it to Italy. However, the **castle** (☎ 027 921 60 30; Alte Simplonstrasse 28; adult/child/7-16yr Sfr7/free/3; ☯ hourly 50-min guided visit 9.30-11.30am & 1.30-4.30pm Tue-Sun May-Oct), with it's Eastern-style onion domes, is a suitably three-dimensional memorial to one man's self-worth. You can wander the gardens and main court at leisure (admission free, open 6am to 10pm April to October and 6am to 8pm November to March).

Sleeping & Eating

Restaurant Matza (☎ 027 923 15 95; Alte Simplonstrasse 18; s/d with hall showers Sfr40/80) This place provides simple food and a basic flop for the night. While there's nothing special about it, it is in the old centre and perfectly serviceable. It's closed Sunday unless you pre-book.

Hotel de Londres (☎ 027 922 93 93; www.hotel-de londres.ch; Bahnhofstrasse 17; s/d Sfr70/120) The décor is rather '70s, with gaudily coloured curtains, thick dull carpet and reddish wood panelling, but the place is comfortable and right on the old town's pedestrian-only central square, Stadtplatz (in spite of the official address), a five-minute walk from the train station.

Restaurant zum Eidgenossen (☎ 027 923 92 07; Geissplatzji; mains Sfr14-36; ☾ Wed-Mon) Head to the 1st floor for a Valais mountain chalet– style ambiance in which to enjoy local specialities and more interesting slabs of exotic meats including kangaroo (Australia), kudu (South Africa) and wapiti (Canada).

Hotel du Pont (☎ 027 923 15 02; Marktplatz 1; meals Sfr20; ☾ daily) There's something for everyone here, from fish to pasta. House specialities, however, revolve around meat, anything from a beef tournedos (Sfr45) to a *fondue chinoise* (about Sfr40 per person). It's closed for around three weeks at Christmas.

Getting There & Away

Brig is on the *Glacier Express* line from Zermatt to St Moritz and the main line between Italy (Milan via Domodossola) and Geneva (Sfr55, two to 2¾ hours). Trains from Brig also run to Locarno (Sfr49, 2½ hours) in Ticino, via Domodossola (take your passport).

THE GOMS & ALETSCH GLACIER

Exiting Brig, you enter another world. Approaching the source of the mighty Rhône river (here known as the Rotten), the broad and deep valley begins to narrow as you gain altitude. The drama of pine-clad mountainsides and poetry of terraced vineyards clinging to south-facing hills that so characterises the west of the canton gives way to a more rural, Germanic scene. Known as the Goms, a string of mostly pretty villages (one of the first of them invitingly named Bitsch) of timber chalets, geranium-filled flower boxes and onion-domed churches stretches northeast, waiting to be counted off like so many rosary beads. On either side of the ever-narrower turquoise torrent that is the Rhône stretch billiard table–green fields with scattered farmhouses.

PULVERISING COW PATS

The good folk of Riederalp, ever on the lookout for new distractions, came up with a new/old summer sport in 2005. In the old days, farmers leading cattle down from the high Alpine plains at the end of summer would smash up and spread as far as possible the animals' droppings to promote the growth of grass. Inspired by this now-forgotten tradition, locals held their first-ever Chüefladefäscht (cow pat festival) in September 2005. The aim of the game: to give as many cow pats as possible a good thumping with a golf club– style instrument. 'Four!' they might have shouted, as cow pats flew all over the shop at fields above the Aletsch Glacier. For those who like a flutter, the townsfolk had another idea. They demarked 49 squares on a field and let the cows out. Bet on the square in which you think one of the beasts will first drop a pat…

Aletsch Glacier

The bucolic valley idyll of the Goms, however, hides great Alpine drama. For to the north, out of view from the valley floor, lies the icy spectacle of the Aletsch Glacier (Aletschgletscher), at 24km the longest in the Alps. It stretches from the Jungfrau (4158m) in the Bernese Oberland to a plateau above the Rhône. Its southern expanse is fringed by the Aletschwald, one of the highest pine forests in Europe (2000m).

ORIENTATION & INFORMATION

There are three resorts on the southern rim of the glacier, separated from the forest by a ridge of hills. The westernmost is **Riederalp** (☎ 027 928 60 50; www.riederalp.ch in German), followed by **Bettmeralp** (☎ 027 928 60 60; www .bettmeralp.ch) and finally **Fiescheralp** (☎ 027 970 10 70; www.goms.ch in German), all at an altitude of just short of 2000m. Each has a tourist office, as do the towns in the valley floor from where cable cars depart to reach them. All these places are car-free.

ACTIVITIES

The best thing about the glacier is that it can be easily visited. If you do nothing else in the Goms, stop at Fiesch and take the two **cable cars** (☎ 027 971 27 00; www.eggishorn.ch in

VALAIS

German; adult/child return Sfr42.80/21.40; ☣ every 30 min 8am-6pm Jun-Oct) up to the **Eggishorn** (2927m). This is most exhilarating in summer. As you float up over the green fields, champing cows and then, above the tree line, the stark olive, brown and grey Alpine landscape, nothing can prepare you for the sight that awaits on exiting the gondola.

Streaming down in a broad curve around the Aletschhorn (4195m), the glacier looks like a frozen six-lane motorway. In the distance, to the north, you can check off some of the country's greatest peaks: the Jungfrau, Mönch (4109m), Eiger (3970m) and Finsteraarhorn (4274m). If you scamper up the loose and rocky rise, topped by an antenna, to the west of the cable car exit, you might espy Mont Blanc and the Matterhorn in the distance.

While gawping at this wonder of nature (the whole Aletsch area is a Unesco World Heritage site), consider the grim news. The main glacier (the Grosser Aletschgletscher) covered 163 square kilometres in 1856, 128 square kilometres in 1973 and just 87 square kilometres today . In another couple of generations it may well be gone. The Grosser Aletsch Glacier is one of a series in these mountains.

Chase away these depressing thoughts with some physical activity. In summer the Aletsch area offers some inspiring hiking routes (an easy option is to take the cable car up, walk to the glacier and then walk back down to Fiescheralp, the midway station). In winter, there is some fine skiing among the three Alpine ski villages. Of the three hamlets, the one in the middle (Bettmeralp) is perhaps the handiest and prettiest. Each offer limited accommodation as well as some eating options. They are far more interesting than the three cable car–access towns in the Rhône valley, respectively Mörel, Betten and Fiesch. Once up in the villages, your ski pass will allow you to move between all three during the day's skiing.

In the Aletsch region there are 99km of ski runs and 35 lifts. The skiing is mostly intermediate or easy. Ski passes cost Sfr45/23 per adult/child per day, or Sfr54/27 including the lifts up from the valley towns.

SLEEPING & EATING
Hotel Toni (☎ 027 927 16 56; www.hotel-toni.ch in German; Aletschpromenade 9; s/d Sfr80/160) In the middle

of Riederalp village and a stumble from the lifts, this is a cheerful medium-sized hotel.

Bettmerhof (☎ 027 928 62 10; www.bettmerhof.ch; s/d Sfr165/320) You can't get much closer to the lifts in Bettmeralp. The rooms in these chalet-style digs are pretty standard for this kind of mountain hotel, with lots of wood panelling, carpet and, in some cases, balconies. Families should ask about the family suites. They have their own restaurant and pizzeria.

Hotel Eggishorn (☎ 027 971 14 44; www.hotel-egg ishorn.ch; r per person Sfr100) This attractive hotel, with a variety of rooms, all of them offering marvellous views, is near the Eggishorn cable car, and so well placed for the skier or hiker anxious to get up to the glacier.

GETTING THERE & AWAY
The base stations for these resorts are on the train route between Brig and Andermatt. Cable-car departures are linked to the train arrivals. Mörel up to Riederalp costs Sfr8 each way, the same as from Betten up to Bettmeralp. Some versions of the ski pass include these cable cars. Various Swiss transport passes give you half-price on these cable cars.

From Fiesch to the Furka Pass
The trail out of the Valais continues northeast away from Fiesch, with still more postcard-cute villages along the way, including **Niederwald**, where Cäsar Ritz (1850–1918), founder of the hotel chain, was born and is now buried. Of them all, **Münster** is easily the most charming. Tightly packed chalets drop down the hill from a bright white church. A brook babbles contentedly through the heart of the village and weary travellers take delight in the **Hotel Croix d'Or et Poste** (☎ 027 974 15 15; www.hotel-postmuenster.ch; s/d Sfr118/236), the extraordinarily flower-laden hotel gathered around a little snippet of square on a bend in the main road through the village. Germany's literary giant Goethe slept in here in 1779. The 38 rooms are elegant, with different décor in each.

At **Ulrichen** you must make a decision. You can turn southeast down a narrow road that twists its way south out of the Valais and into the mountains that separate the canton from Ticino. Impressively barren country that at times reminds one of western Ireland, at others of the Spanish Pyrenees and still others of nothing you have ever seen, leads you to the **Nufenen Pass** (Passo di Novena) at

2478m, probably the most remote gateway into Switzerland's Italian canton. Dropping down the other side, the first major town you will encounter is **Airolo** (p291), 24km east of the pass along the quiet, almost gloomy Val Bedretto.

Should you decide to push on east of Ulrichen, you will head slowly upwards towards **Gletsch**. From here the mighty **Grimsel Pass**, with its spectacular views west over several lakes in Bern canton and the eastern Valais, lies a short, steep drive north, but it is often closed even in summer (see also p174).

Marking the cantonal frontier with Uri canton is the **Furka Pass** (2431m), the run up to which offers superlative views over the Rhône glacier to the north. Open in summer only, it is the gateway into southeast Switzerland, but you can get your car on to a car train in **Oberwald** to negotiate the trip underground when the pass is shut. The train surfaces at Realp (see p233).

VALAIS

Bernese Oberland

It's impossible to do the Bernese Oberland justice on paper. German poet Goethe and English romantic Lord Byron both eulogised its waterfalls and glaciers. Mark Twain wrote that no opiate compared to walking through it. Yet even these great talents failed to capture the majesty of a place that has to be seen to be believed.

No amount of hyperbole about sparkling vistas where snow-capped peaks line up like bowling pins – or talk of sheer valleys, verdant pastures and crystal-clear lakes (blah, blah, blah) – could ever communicate the sheer outrageous beauty of Switzerland's Alpine heartland. So don't take anyone else's word for it, just visit.

The 'big three' peaks of the Eiger, Mönch and Jungfrau lie at the region's heart and the most talked-about trip is the train ride to Europe's highest station at Jungfraujoch. However, everyone finds their favourite spot, whether in the breathtakingly serene Lauterbrunnen valley, on the ridges above Grindelwald or in some remote area around Kandersteg.

Cable cars thread up mountain slopes to incomparable outlooks and lake steamers glide past waterfront castles, so you're not required to exert much energy. But even confirmed city types usually find themselves inspired to hit the hiking trails that crisscross the landscape.

Thrill-seekers rush to jump off the mountains around Interlaken, while families head to Ballenberg to see gentle Swiss traditions re-enacted. All sorts, it seems – from Sherlock Holmes fans around Meiringen to jetsetters in Gstaad – get a kick out of this incomparable region.

And if words can't convey how good the Bernese Oberland looks, professional photographers seem at a loss too. Listen to the postcard carousels creak in souvenir shops, as customers push them round in circles in search of something that lives up to their memories.

HIGHLIGHTS

- Enjoy the heavenly **hike** (p149) between Schynige Platte and Grindelwald-First
- Float up to the scenic car-free resorts of **Mürren** (p165) and **Gimmelwald** (p166)
- Hit the heights of **Schilthorn** (p166) or **Jungfraujoch** (p155)
- Paraglide from the peaks above **Interlaken** (p146) or **Grindelwald** (p152)
- Get up close and personal with the magnificent **Trift Glacier** (p172)

Interlaken ★   Schynige Platte ★   Trift Glacier ★
★ Grindelwald
Schilthorn ★   Mürren ★   ★ Jungfraujoch
Gimmelwald

BERNESE OBERLAND

| POPULATION: 897,502 | AREA: 5907 SQ KM | LANGUAGE: GERMAN |

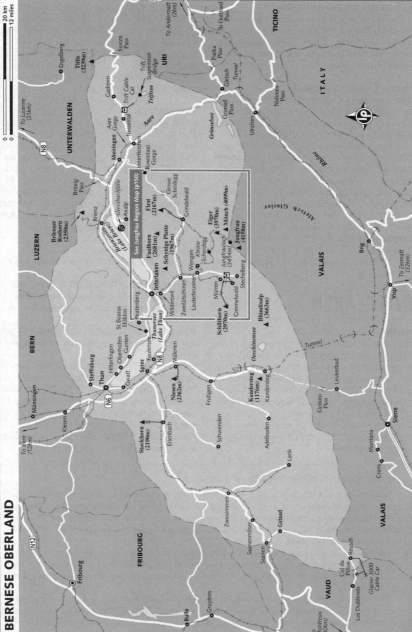

BERNESE OBERLAND

BERNESE OBERLAND

Orientation & Information

This region covers the southern part of the canton of Bern, stretching from Gstaad in the west to the Susten Pass (2224m) in the east. **Berner Oberland Tourismus** (www.berneroberland.ch) offers online information only.

Getting There & Around

The Bernese Oberland is easily accessible by road and train from most major Swiss airports, including Basel, Bern, Geneva and Zürich, as well as from Lucerne.

If you intend spending most of your holiday here, it's worth investigating the **Berner Oberland Regional Pass** (www.regiopass-berneroberland.ch; for 7/15 days Sfr220/265; ☉ May-Oct), offering free travel on three/five days on certain routes, plus discounts on others.

Alternatively, the Jungfrau Region, at the heart of the Bernese Oberland, has its own **Jungfraubahn Pass**. Note that a Swiss or Eurail Pass alone will only take you so far into the Jungfrau Region. See p151 for more information.

INTERLAKEN

pop 5094 / elevation 570m

Standing in Interlaken's large central park, gazing at the Jungfrau massif in the distance, it's possible to sense the romance of a place that first attracted early package tourists in the 19th century. But the view these days regularly interrupted by paragliders coming in to land – as this attractively mountain-ringed town has become one of the world's top adventure-sports destinations.

Interlaken makes a convenient base, because good transport links mean you can easily visit most of the Bernese Oberland from here on day trips. However, the town's touristy strip of souvenir shops and its restless, ski-resort vibe aren't quite as appealing as the calm and even better panoramas deeper inside the Jungfrau Region.

Orientation

Most of Interlaken is coupled between its two train stations: Interlaken West and Interlaken Ost. Each station has bike rental and money-changing facilities and behind each is a landing stage for boats on Lake Thun and Brienzersee (Lake Brienz). The main street, Höheweg, runs between the two stations. You can walk from one to the other in less than 30 minutes, passing the huge central park, Hohe-Mätte, as you do.

Information

Hospital (☎ 033 826 26 26; Weissenaustrasse 27) West of the centre.

Kikireon Internet (☎ 033 823 32 32; Postgasse 6; per min Sfr0.30; ☉ 11.30am-10.30pm) Computer shop with Internet connection, including for laptops. Asian keyboards available.

Main post office (Postplatz; ☉ 8am-noon & 1.45-6pm Mon-Fri, 8.30-11am Sat) Telephones and stamp machines outside.

Rocco's Latino Bar (☎ 033 827 87 83; Chalet Hotel-Oberland, Am Marktplatz; per min Sfr0.30; ☉ 8am-12.30pm)

Tourist office (☎ 0800 55 85 55, 033 826 53 00; www .interlakentourism.ch; Höheweg 37; ☉ 8am-7pm Mon-Fri, 8am-5pm Sat, 10am-noon & 5-7pm Sun Jul & Aug, 8am-noon & 1.30-6pm Mon-Fri, 9am-noon Sat rest of year) Halfway between the stations. There's also a hotel booking board outside its office and at both train stations.

SWITZERLAND: THE BIRTHPLACE OF TOURISM

If Switzerland's tourist infrastructure seems to run like a well-oiled machine, it's because the country has had more practice at welcoming foreign visitors than nearly any other. Thomas Cook, the man behind today's international travel group, only conducted a few tours of Scotland before the railway companies there refused to cooperate further. So in the early 1860s Cook began looking farther afield.

He announced in his regular newsletter that he planned to tour the Jungfrau Region and the response was huge. More than 62 people joined him entering Switzerland on his inaugural trip in 1863, when he had planned for just 25. Soon afterwards, mountain railways began opening up the territory.

The English upper class had already made the Alps its private playground, and the region was soon to be publicised by writers like Mark Twain, but Thomas Cook's regular jaunts became a huge success among less well-heeled visitors and laid the groundwork for today's mass tourism.

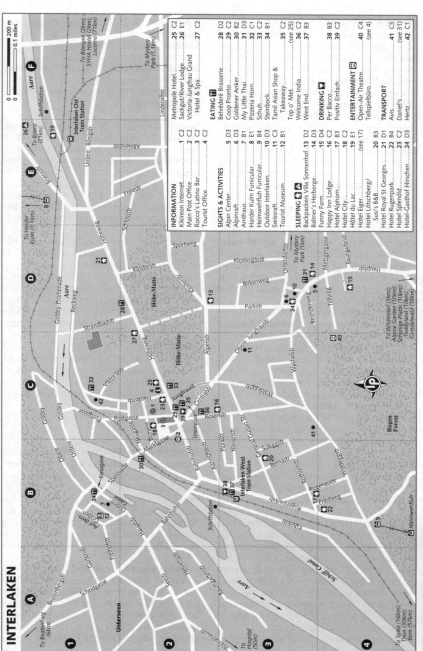

Sights & Activities

As a regional gateway, Interlaken itself possesses few attractions. However, its biggest and newest is **Mystery Park** (☎ 0848 50 60 70; www.mysterypark.ch; adult/child/student Sfr48/28/38, late entry after 3.30pm Sfr28; ⏲ 10am-6pm). This otherworldly theme park looms large on the outskirts, with expensive re-creations of a Mayan temple, Egyptian pyramid, Indian Vimana, Stonehenge and a highly visible 'Sphere'. It's the brainchild of Erich von Däniken, the Swiss author of the 1970s bestseller *Chariots of the Gods*, and its displays (including crop circles in summer) are meant to get you thinking about aliens. Sceptics need not apply. There's a free shuttle bus from Interlaken Ost once or twice an hour.

For an altogether more nostalgic atmosphere, head across the Aare River to Interlaken's charming old quarter of **Unterseen**. Near the 1471 Amthaus, there's a humble **Tourist Museum** (☎ 033 822 98 39; Obere Gasse 26; adult/child Sfr5/3; ⏲ 2-5pm Tue-Sun May-Oct), which details how the surrounding areas opened up in the 19th century.

Two funicular trips into the surrounding hills are worth making. A **nostalgic funicular** (adult/child return Sfr10/7) will take you up to family-friendly **Heimwehfluh** (☎ 033 822 34 53; www.heimwehfluh.ch; adult/child Sfr6/5, bobsled run Sfr5; ⏲ 9.30am-5pm Apr-Oct), where there's a wonderful view, a model-train display and a toboggan ride all the way back down the hill.

Alternatively, **Harder Kulm** (☎ 033 822 34 44; www.harderkulm.ch in German; single/return Sfr14.60/Sfr24; ⏲ Apr-Oct) has a panoramic restaurant and many hiking paths.

EXTREME SPORTS

Switzerland is the world's second-biggest adventure-sports destination, just behind New Zealand, and Interlaken is its busiest hub. Everything you can think of in this regard is offered from here (although the activities take place in the greater Jungfrau Region). There's river rafting on the Lütschine, Simme and Saane Rivers, canyoning in the Saxetet, Grimsel or Chli Schliere gorges, and canyon-jumping at the Gletscherschlucht near Grindelwald (see p152). In addition, you can paragliding off any number of mountains, bungee jumping, skydiving, ice-climbing, hydro-speeding and much more.

The major operators, each able to arrange most sports, include the following:

Alpin Center (☎ 033 823 55 23; www.alpincenter.ch; Hauptstrasse 16)
Alpinraft (☎ 033 823 41 00; www.alpinraft.ch; Hauptstrasse 7)
Outdoor Interlaken (☎ 033 826 77 19; www.outdoor-interlaken.ch; Hauptstrasse 15)
Swissraft (☎ 033 823 02 10; www.swissraft.ch; Obere Jungfraustrasse 72)

Bohag (☎ 033 822 90 00; www.bohag.ch in German; Gsteigwiller bei Interlaken) and **Scenic Air** (☎ 033 826 77 17; www.scenicair.ch, www.skydiveswitzerland.com) conducts scenic flights, skydiving and other activities.

Prices are from Sfr90 for rock climbing, Sfr95 for rafting, Sfr125 for bungee jumping, Sfr110 for canyoning, Sfr120 for hydro-speeding, Sfr140 for paragliding and Sfr380 for skydiving.

The vast majority of excursions are without incident, but there's always a small risk of injury. Two tragically fatal accidents – canyoning in the Saxetet Gorge and bungee jumping off the Stechelberg-Mürren cable car – about five years ago fortunately have not been repeated, but it's always a good idea to ask about safety records and procedures.

Sleeping

Ask your hotel for the useful Guest Card, which offers discounts on local sporting facilities and free bus transport across town, and call ahead during the low season, as some places close.

BUDGET
Hostels

Balmer's Herberge (☎ 033 822 19 61; www.balmers.ch; Hauptstrasse 23; dm Sfr24-27, d Sfr60-70; ⏲ year-round; 🖳) Switzerland's oldest private hostel is a legend, known for its fun, frat-house atmosphere. This *Animal House* buzzes with the adrenalin of those coming down from adventure sports and there's always something social happening. In summer, Balmer's also opens a huge tent along Gsteigstrasse, about 800m south.

Backpackers Villa Sonnenhof (☎ 033 826 71 71; www.villa.ch; Alpenstrasse 16; dm/d Sfr33/98; r with Jungfrau view per person extra Sfr5; ⏲ reception 7.30-11am & 4-9pm, to 10pm summer; 🖳) Widely regarded as the cleanest and most genteel of Interlaken's hostels, this place still has plenty going on. There's a small kitchen, a lounge and table tennis in the garden. The old steamer trunks and balconies with views of the Jungfrau are nice touches, too.

Funny Farm (☎ 079 652 61 27; www.funny-farm.ch; Hauptstrasse; dm without sheets Sfr25, dm with shower & toilet Sfr35; 🍸) Funny Farm is halfway between a squat and an island shipwreck. There's a ramshackle house surrounded by makeshift bars and a swimming pool, but guests don't care; they're here for the party and revel in such anarchism.

Also available are these places:

Happy Inn Lodge (☎ 033 822 32 25; www.happy-inn .com; Rosenstrasse 17; dm Sfr22, s/d/tr Sfr38/76/96, breakfast extra Sfr8) OK hostel, recently spruced up a little, with cheap prices, central location and noisy bar.

SYHA hostel (☎ 033 822 43 53; www.youthhostel.ch /boenigen; Aareweg 21, am See, Bönigen; dm/d Sfr30/86; 🕙 reception 7-10am & 4-10pm to 11.30pm summer, hostel closed mid-Nov–late-Jan, except Christmas/New Year) Quite a way from town with a scenic garden on the waterfront. Take bus No 1.

Hotels & Pensions

Hotel Lötschberg/Susi's B & B (☎ 033 822 25 45; www.lotschberg.ch; General Guisan Strasse 31; B&B s/d Sfr95/125, hotel s/d from Sfr115/155; ✖ P) The individually decorated rooms at this place are thoughtfully designed and charming, almost as if you're staying in a private home. They do tend to be quite small, though, particularly in the attached B&B.

Camping

Sackgut/River Lodge (☎ 033 822 44 34; Brienzstrasse; camp sites per adult/car Sfr9.50/4, tent Sfr7.50/17.50, tent

---

AUTHOR'S CHOICE

Hotel Rugenpark (☎ 033 822 36 61; www.ru genpark.ch; Rugenparkstrasse 19; s/d/tr/f Sfr85/130/ 165/200, without bathroom Sfr65/105/140/175; 🖵 ✖ P) Its newish owners, Chris and Ursula, have already done wonders in transforming this into an incredibly sweet B&B. Rooms remain humble, but the place is spotless and public areas have been enlivened with colourful cushions, beads and travel trinkets. There's a hammock and child's swing in the large garden, where Monty the dog likes to roam, while a large breakfast buffet is served and some rooms have Jungfrau views. Most of all, you feel at home and your knowledgeable hosts are always ready to help with local tips.

---

bungalow for 4 people Sfr98; 🕙 May–mid-Oct) Sackgut's the only camp site actually in the town, and now has a row of bungalows along the waterfront, which it offers under the River Lodge banner.

MIDRANGE

Hotel-Gasthof Hirschen (☎ 033 822 15 45; www.hirsch en-interlaken.ch in German; Hauptstrasse 11; s/d from Sfr90/180) Under new management and having undergone a Sfr400,000 renovation in 2004, this 16th-century heritage-listed Swiss chalet is enjoying a new lease of life. Rooms are now 'rustic modern', with parquet floors, bathroom pods and wireless LAN. The in-house Swiss restaurant (mains Sfr15 to Sfr40, open Wednesday to Monday) has also been refurbished.

Hotel Alphorn (☎ 033 822 30 51; www.hotel-al phorn.ch; Rugenaustrasse 8; s/d Sfr120/140) Tucked away in a quiet street, allowing it to offer ample parking. It also belongs to a very small group of hotels and hires out Smart cars to guests as part of its accommodation package. Renovated rooms in the adjoining Hotel Eiger are Sfr20 more per person.

Hotel Splendid (☎ 033 822 76 12; Höheweg 33; s/d Sfr90/120, s/d with shower & toilet Sfr135/210) This friendly hotel is on a central corner, but you hear surprisingly little noise from the rooms. These come in a range of decorative styles, from Swiss traditional to something approaching modern.

Hotel City (☎ 033 822 10 22; www.city-hotel.ch; Am Marktplatz; standard s/d Sfr110/150, superior s/d Sfr140/210) There's lots of classic Scandinavian décor here, from stylish padded armchairs, geometric lampshades, sauna-style wood panelling and a cylindrical fireplace. But if you don't get a kick out of that retro vibe, go for one of the renovated or more contemporary rooms.

Hôtel du Lac (☎ 033 822 29 22; www.dulac-inter laken.ch; Höheweg 225; s/d Sfr150/270) In a great spot overlooking the river near Interlaken Ost train station, this hotel has been in the same family for generations, and although it has a slight mish-mash of styles it retains more than enough of its former belle époque glory to remain immensely charming.

Metropole Hotel (☎ 033 828 66 66; www.metropole -interlaken.ch in German; Höheweg 37; s/d Sfr195/295, breakfast Sfr25) As the tallest concrete highrise on Interlaken's horizon, this is impossible to miss. However, with an exterior this ugly, staying here is a boon: while you enjoy lofty views of the town and Jungfrau, you're also saved from looking at the Metropole.

Hotel Royal St Georges (☎ 033 822 75 75; www .royal-stgeorges.ch; Höheweg 139; s/d Sfr175/280) Down the road is this lovingly restored Art Nouveau gem. It has a slightly stuffy air about it, but it's still quite delightful.

TOP END

Victoria-Jungfrau Grand Hotel & Spa (☎ 033 828 28 28; www.victoria-jungfrau.ch; Höheweg 41; s/d from Sfr560/680, d with Jungfrau views from Sfr780; ☐ ☒ ℙ ☒) The reverent hush and impeccable service here (as well as the prices) hark back to the era when only royalty and the seriously wealthy travelled. A perfect melding of well-preserved Victorian-era features and modern luxury help make this Interlaken's answer to Raffles – with plum views of the Jungfrau to boot.

Eating

Welcome India (☎ 033 822 52 04; Rosenstrasse 7; mains Sfr11-32, weekday lunch menus Sfr14.50-16.50; ☯ lunch & dinner Dec-Oct, dinner Nov) Decorated like a true curry house with carved wooden statues and a garish mixture of black, orange and yellow, this is the best of several local Indian restaurants. The menu includes Punjabi and northern Indian specialities.

Pizzeria Horn (☎ 033 822 92 92; Hardererstrasse 35; pizzas Sfr13-20, other mains Sfr20-35; ☯ dinner Thu-Mon) This quirky old-fashioned restaurant looks like it's been the same for decades, with pink tablecloths covering wooden tables, dried tobacco sheaths hanging from the ceiling and four romantic alcoves. But why should it change? The atmosphere is wonderfully warm and familiar, while the tasty pizzas emerging from the central wood-fired oven are the real deal.

West End (☎ 033 822 17 14; Rugenparkstrasse 2; mains Sfr15-36; ☯ dinner Mon-Sat) Amuse yourselves with the wine list and remember that good things come to those who wait, as you survey the incongruous Swiss interior of this buzzing, congenial Italian restaurant. Many of the pasta and other dishes are freshly homemade and can take a while to arrive at your table, but when they do, they're usually delicious.

Belvéderè Brasserie (☎ 033 828 91 00; Höheweg 95; mains Sfr18-36; ☯ lunch & dinner) Although attached to the boring-look Hapimag hotel village, this brasserie has upbeat contemporary décor, with excellent international cuisine such as

monkfish medallions in saffron sauce and veal in merlot sauce, alongside a handful of Swiss stalwarts. It's closed on Tuesdays from December to May and for all of November.

Goldener Anker (☎ 033 822 16 72; www.anker.ch in German; Marktgasse 57; mains Sfr18-38; ☯ 4-11.30pm daily, from 10am Sat & Sun) Its interior rebuilt after the 2005 floods, this well-respected establishment continues to serve interesting dishes, ranging from chicken fajitas and red snapper to ostrich steaks. It also has a roster of live bands and international artists.

Steinbock (☎ 033 822 18 43; Kreuzgasse 5; mains Sfr15-35; ☯ lunch & dinner Tue-Sat) While there are dozens of phoney and/or overpriced Swiss restaurants lining Höheweg, this humble tavern is one in which locals also eat. Another good option for Swiss food is the Hirschen (see p147).

For coffee and cake, or a cocktail, try **Top o' Met** (☎ 033 828 66 66; Höheweg 37) on the top floor of the Metropole Hotel, which has excellent views. **Schuh** (☎ 033 822 94 41; Höheweg 56; ☯ 8am-10.30pm, to 9pm in winter) also works as a Viennese-style coffee house. Skip dinner here, however, as the tinkling, Barry Manilow–style piano and overwhelmingly pink interior can feel like being trapped in a 1970s B-movie.

Good cheap eats include **Tamil Asian Shop & Takeaway** (☎ 033 822 23 30; Uniongasse 1; all menus Sfr10.90; ☯ 10.30am-10.30pm) and **My Little Thai** (☎ 033 822 01 75; Hauptstrasse 19; mains Sfr12.50-20.50; ☯ 10.30am-12.30am) next to Balmer's.

There's a supermarket opposite each train station and another, **Coop Pronto** (Höheweg 11; ☯ 10-10pm Mon-Sat), in between them.

Drinking

Positiv Einfach (Centralstrasse) This cosy little DJ bar place feels more local and dignified, with its slick, low-lit interior.

Per Bacco (☎ 033 822 97 92; Rugenparkstrasse 2; ☯ 9-1am Mon-Sat) This is a fairly chi-chi wine bar, attracting a slightly more sophisticated and well-dressed older crowd.

The bars at Balmer's, Funny Farm and Happy Inn Lodge are usually the most lively drinking holes for 20-something travellers, although you'll also find older locals in the Happy Inn.

Entertainment

There are twice-weekly performances of Schiller's *Wilhelm Tell* between late June

BERNESE OBERLAND

ROCKY HORROR

The rivalries between Switzerland's linguistic communities are usually low-key, but when they do erupt it's often over the most unlikely things. Take the German-speaking canton of Bern and French-speaking Jura separatists as an example. They've been tussling over a 65kg piece of rock for more than 20 years.

The 200-year-old Unspunnen Stone (*Unspunnenstein*) is a focal point of Switzerland's Alpine Games, which since 1805 have symbolically asserted national unity and are now held about once every 10 years. The stone was first kidnapped from an Interlaken museum in 1984 by the French-speaking 'Beliers', who lay claim to part of Bern's territory. They kept it hostage for 17 years, while also demanding Jura's devolution from Switzerland and entry into the European Union.

In 2001, the stone was suddenly given back in mysterious circumstances, and engraved with the EU flag. Just four years later there was another theft, again from Interlaken, where the travelling games were due to be held that year.

The **Alpine games** (Unspunnenfest; ☎ 033 826 53 53; www.unspunnenfest.ch) feature yodelling, Alphorn playing, *Schwingen* wrestling and stone-throwing, preferably of the historic Unspunnen Stone. With floods swiftly following the theft, the 2005 Interlaken games were postponed until September 2006. At the time of writing, the stone still hadn't reappeared.

and mid-September, staged in the open-air theatre in the Rugen Forest. The play is in German but an English synopsis is available. Tickets are available from **Tellspielbüro** (☎ 033 822 37 22; www.tellspiele.ch; Höheweg 37; tickets Sfr26-48) in the tourist office, and from some hotels.

GETTING THERE & AWAY

Trains to Lucerne (Sfr29) depart hourly from Interlaken Ost train station. Trains to Brig (via Spiez and Lötschberg) and to Montreux (via Bern or Zweisimmen) depart from Interlaken West or Ost.

Main roads head east to Lucerne and west to Bern, but the only way south for vehicles without a big detour round the mountains is to take the car-carrying train from Kandersteg, south of Spiez.

Should you wish to hire a car in Interlaken for trips further into Switzerland, big-name rental companies **Avis** (☎ 033 822 19 39; Waldeggstrasse 34a), near a 24-hour petrol station, and **Hertz** (☎ 033 822 61 72; Harderstrasse 25), are both reasonably central.

GETTING AROUND

You can easily get around Interlaken on foot, but taxis and buses are found at each train station. Alternatively, you can pick up scooters, motorbikes and small cars for zipping around town at **Daniel's** (☎ 033 822 01 75; www.daniels-rental.ch; Hauptstrasse 19), among others.

AROUND INTERLAKEN

SCHYNIGE PLATTE

One of the most memorable day trips from Interlaken is to this 1967m plateau. There's an **Alpine garden** (admission Sfr4) with 500 types of flora, including Edelweiss. There's also a collection of thousands of toy bears at **Teddyland** (admission free).

Despite all this, the main attraction is the hiking and the views. The **Panoramaweg** is an easy two-hour circuit, while the trail to **Grindelwald-First** is one of the best in the region. If you're here in July or August, don't miss the **moonlight hikes** here.

You reach the plateau on a **cog-wheel train** (www.schynigeplatte.ch, www.jungfraubahn.ch; one way/return Sr33/54; ☺ closed late Oct–late May) from Wilderswil, a short train ride from Interlaken Ost. If you don't have your own boots with you, there is, amazingly, free boot-testing on Schynige Platte (see the websites for details).

ST BEATUS HÖHLEN

A bus ride from Interlaken, a 1½-hour walk or a short Sfr7 boat ride, you'll find the attractive **St Beatus Caves** (☎ 033 841 16 43; adult/child/student Sfr17/9/15; ☺ 10.30am-5pm Apr–mid-Oct). They're supposed to have sheltered St Beatus in the 6th century, but it's their stalagmites, stalactites and underground lakes that make them interesting.

The accompanying museum can easily be missed.

JUNGFRAU REGION

If the Bernese Oberland is Switzerland's Alpine heartland, the Jungfrau Region within it is the holiest of the holy. Dominated by the famous Eiger, Mönch and Jungfrau (Ogre, Monk and Virgin) mountains, it boasts the country's highest density of dramatic scenery. In every direction you turn – whether on a hike from Grindelwald Männlichen, in a cable car to Schilthorn, or a hotel room in Mürren – you're faced with outstanding natural beauty. With hundreds of kilometres of walking trails in the region, you're able to observe the landscape from many angles, but it never looks less than astonishing.

The 'big three' peaks have an enduring place in mountaineering legend, particularly the 3970m Eiger, whose fearsome north wall claimed many lives and remained unconquered until 1938. Reaching great heights is easier today; it takes just hours to whiz up by train to Jungfraujoch (3454m), the highest station in Europe.

Orientation & Information

Two valleys branch southwards from Interlaken. The broad valley curving to the east is dominated by Grindelwald. The valley running more directly south leads to Lauterbrunnen, from where you can reach several car-free resorts on the hills above – Wengen on the eastern ridge, Mürren and Gimmelwald on the west. These latter two villages are reached either via mountainside Grütschalp or via Stechelberg farther along the Lauterbrunnen Valley floor.

Between the two valleys stands the holy grail of Jungfraujoch, Europe's highest train station. It's usual to travel in a loop, say, from Interlaken to Grindelwald, to Kleine Scheidegg at the bottom of the Eiger, to Jungfraujoch, back to Kleine Scheidegg and on to Wengen, Lauterbrunnen and Interlaken. However, the trip can also be taken in the opposite, anticlockwise direction, or you can retrace your steps.

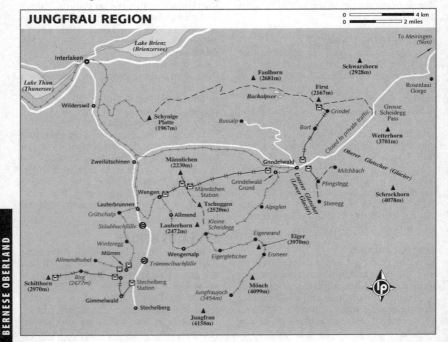

JUNGFRAU REGION

BERNESE OBERLAND

Schilthorn, the region's other main lookout point, is reached via Mürren.

Mountain-top journeys are only really worth making on clear days. Conditions are volatile in the mountains, and the outlook changes frequently, but it's always a good idea to check a webcam before you leave. A good selection is found at www.jungfrau bahn.ch, although tourist office websites and www.swisspanorama.com are also very helpful.

Staying in resorts entitles you to a Gästekarte (Guest Card), good for discounts throughout the entire region. Ask your hotel for the card if one isn't forthcoming.

Getting There & Around

Hourly trains depart for the region from Interlaken Ost station. Sit in the front half of the train for Lauterbrunnen or the back half for Grindelwald. The two sections of the train split up where the two valleys diverge at Zweilütschinen. The rail tracks loop around and meet up again at Kleine Scheidegg at the base of the Eiger, from where the route goes up and back to Jungfraujoch.

Swiss Passes are valid as far as Grindelwald in one direction and Wengen and Mürren in the other; beyond that, holders get a 25% discount. Eurail and Inter Rail Passes are not valid beyond Interlaken, although they are good for a 25% discount on Jungfrau journeys. The Swiss Half-Fare Card is valid within the entire region.

Jungfraubahnen (Jungfrau Railways; ☎ 033 828 72 33; www.jungfraubahn.ch) offers its own pass, providing five days of unlimited travel throughout the region for Sfr165 (Sfr120 with Swiss Pass, Swiss Card or Half-Fare Card), though you still have to pay half-price from Eigergletscher (just past Kleine Scheidegg) to Jungfraujoch.

Sample fares include the following: Interlaken Ost to Grindelwald Sfr9.80; Grindelwald to Kleine Scheidegg Sfr30; Kleine Scheidegg to Jungfraujoch Sfr104 (return); Kleine Scheidegg to Wengen Sfr23; Wengen to Lauterbrunnen Sfr6; and Lauterbrunnen to Interlaken Ost Sfr6.60. Check out the website for a complete and up-to-date list.

Many of the cable cars close for servicing at the end of April and at the end of November.

GRINDELWALD

pop 4166 / elevation 1090m

Below the imposing Eiger mountain, Grindelwald's lengthy main thoroughfare threads along the floor of a picturesque valley. Nicknamed the 'glacier village', for its proximity to two large seas of ice, Grindelwald is a bustling winter ski resort and year-round hiking mecca.

Orientation & Information

The centre is east of the train station. At either end of the village, Terrassenweg loops north off the main street and takes a scenic, elevated east–west course. Below and south of the main street is the Schwarze Lütschine river.

Postal buses and local buses depart from near the train station, and a post office is nearby. Local buses are free with the Guest Card in winter.

The **tourist office** (☎ 033 854 12 12; www.grindel wald.com; Dorfstrasse; ☼ 8am-noon & 1.30-6pm Mon-Fri, 8am-noon & 1.30-5pm Sat, 9am-noon & 1.30-5pm Sun summer & winter high season, 8am-noon & 1.30-5pm Mon-Fri, 9am-noon Sat low season) is in the Sportzentrum.

Sights & Activities

The **Oberer Gletscher** (Upper Glacier) is renowned for its blue hues. It's a 1½-hour hike east from the village, or catch a local bus (marked Terrassen Weg–Oberer Gletscher, Sfr6.80 one way) to the Hotel-Restaurant Wetterhorn. Fifteen minutes from the bus stop, then (pant!) up 890 log stairs, after you pay your entrance fee (adult/child Sfr6/3), you'll find a terrace offering wonderful views.

Gletscherschlucht (Glacier Gorge; admission Sfr6; ☼ 10am-5pm May-Oct, to 6pm Jul & Aug) is a 35-minute walk south of the village centre, past Gletscherdorf (see p153) camping ground. This is a popular spot for canyon-jumping expeditions. At the end of the 1000m gorge, you can also spy the tongue of the **Unterer Gletscher** (Lower Glacier).

HIKING

The best hiking in Grindelwald is above the village – around Männlichen, First and Pfingstegg – reached by taking the relevant cable car up from the village. Some of these areas can just as easily be approached from Wengen or Schynige Platte, so see p154 for details.

WINTER SPORTS

The region of First (see p154) offers many **ski** runs stretching from Oberjoch at 2486m right down to the village at 1050m. Most are intermediate or difficult. From Kleine Scheidegg or Männlichen there are long, easy runs back to Grindelwald. Grindelwald is also a good base for **cross-country skiing** (33km of trails).

Grindelwald Sports includes the skiing school.

OTHER ACTIVITIES

In the tourist office, **Grindelwald Sports** (☎ 033 854 12 90; www.grindelwaldsports.ch in German) organises mountain climbing, canyon-jumping and glacier bungee jumping. **Paragliding Grindelwald** (☎ 079 779 90 00; www.paragliding -grindelwald.ch) organises simple jumps from 1200m at First (from Sfr160) and hikes to and jumps from Schreckhornhütte (Sfr490), with many options in between.

Festivals & Events

The **World Snow Festival**, where competitive international teams create enormous ice sculptures, is in mid-January. In July there's **Schwingen** (Swiss, Sumo-style wrestling) at nearby Grosse Scheidegg, while the **Eiger Bike Challenge**, over a 90km course through the valley and surrounding mountains, races by in August.

Sleeping

If you're looking for a holiday chalet instead of a hotel, the tourist office has a full list.

HOSTELS

These first two hostels are reached by buses to Bussalp, Terrasenweg and Waldspitz. Services run at least hourly between 9am and 5pm, with a gap at lunchtime. The 30-minute uphill walk sets off from the road that follows the rail tracks on the northern side. Don't miss the small sign on the brown-and-white house indicating the steep footpath up to the right.

SYHA hostel (☎ 033 853 10 09; www.youthhostel.ch /grindelwald; Terrasenweg; 4-/6-person dm from Sfr31/35, d with/without bathroom Sfr76/102; ☻ reception & check-in from 3.30pm Mon-Sat, from 5pm Sun, hostel closed btwn seasons) Perched high on a ridge, with spec-

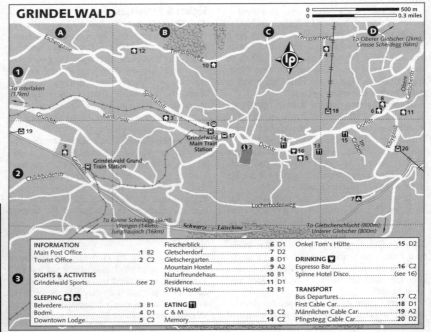

GRINDELWALD

INFORMATION		
Main Post Office...................................**1** B2	Fiescherblick......................................**6** D1	Onkel Tom's Hütte.........................**15** D2
Tourist Office.....................................**2** C2	Gletscherdorf...................................**7** D2	
	Gletschergarten..............................**8** D1	**DRINKING** 🍷
SIGHTS & ACTIVITIES	Mountain Hostel..............................**9** A2	Espresso Bar....................................**16** C2
Grindelwald Sports.......................(see 2)	Naturfreundehaus.........................**10** B1	Spinne Hotel Disco.....................(see 16)
	Residence..**11** D1	
SLEEPING 🏠🏔	SYHA Hostel...................................**12** B1	**TRANSPORT**
Belvedere...**3** B1		Bus Departures..............................**17** C2
Bodmi...**4** D1	**EATING** 🍴	First Cable Car...............................**18** D1
Downtown Lodge..............................**5** C2	C & M...**13** C2	Männlichen Cable Car.................**19** A2
	Memory...**14** C2	Pfingstegg Cable Car...................**20** D2

BERNESE OBERLAND

tacular views, this excellent hostel is spread across a cosy wooden chalet (with six-bed dorms) and a modern annexe (with four-bed dorms). Take the bus to Gaggi-Säge.

Naturfreundehaus (☎ 033 853 13 33; www.natur freundehaeuser.ch; Terrassenweg; dm Sfr34-39; ☺ closed low season) Decorated in a simple, traditional Swiss fashion, this also has a great back garden with a wonderful valley outlook. Take the bus to the Naturfreundehaus stop.

Downtown Lodge (☎ 033 853 08 25; www.down town-lodge.ch; dm without breakfast Sfr35-40; 🖳) Grindelwald's most conveniently located hostel is modern, clean and friendly. However, the surrounds are not as atmospheric as at the SYHA.

Mountain Hostel (☎ 033 853 39 00; www.mountain hostel.ch; dm/d with shared bathroom from Sfr34/88) Near the Männlichen cable-car station, this big, blue, modern complex is a good base for sports junkies.

CAMPING

Gletscherdorf (☎ 033 853 14 29; www.gletscherdorf.ch; adult Sfr9.20, plus camp site Sfr6-17; ☺ for tents May–late Oct, for caravans year-round) Near the Pfingstegg cable car, this is the most convenient and well equipped of several camping sites, with views of the Eiger. A supplement is payable for very short stays.

HOTELS & PENSIONS

Gletschergarten (☎ 033 853 17 21; www.hotel-gletscher garten.ch; s/d from Sfr120/220; ✖ ℗) Quaint and charming without being cloying, Gletschergarten's appealing rusticity is complemented by all mod cons, including a lift, hairdryers and in-room safes. Every room has a balcony.

Fiescherblick (☎ 033 854 53 53; www.fiescherblick .ch; s/d from Sfr105/170) Another excellent hotel in the same mode as the neighbouring Gletschergarten.

Residence (☎ 033 854 55 55; www.residence-grindel wald.ch in German; s/d from Sfr90/150; ✖ ℗) Seated in a quiet location on the eastern side of the village, this is friendly, cosy and modern. There's a terrace restaurant overlooking the Wetterhorn. It's closed in November.

Bodmi (☎ 033 854 18 18; www.bodmi.ch; s/d from Sfr185/265; 🖳 ✖ ℗) Also in a quiet location, further along from the youth hostel and under the First cable car, this elegant family-run hotel offers well-furnished, generously sized rooms with good views, and has a good

restaurant. Call ahead and they'll collect you from the train station. Terrassenweg buses stop outside, too.

Belvedere (☎ 033 854 57 57; www.belvedere-grindel wald.ch; s/d from Sfr255/350, ste from Sfr490; 🖳 ✖ ℗ 🐾) This nine-storey, four-star hotel enjoys some of the best views in the village and its rooms are special too. The suites, in particular, mix old and new, with wood-beamed ceilings, bed niches and all mod cons. Public rooms include a lounge in Louis Philippe style.

Eating

Onkel Tom's Hütte (☎ 033 853 52 39; Im Graben 4; pizzas from Sfr13-30; ☺ 4-10.30pm Tue, noon-2pm & 4pm-midnight Wed-Sun) Usually, the biggest problem in this sweet mini-chalet is getting a table. It serves good pizzas, in three sizes to suit any appetite.

Memory (☎ 033 854 31 31; mains Sfr15-25; Dorfstrasse; ☺ 11.30am-10.30pm) The most casual eatery in the Eiger Hotel is an unpretentious choice for steaks, sandwiches, jacket potatoes and burgers. It also does tasty rösti and fondue.

C & M (Café und Mehr; ☎ 033 853 07 10; mains Sfr7.50-38; ☺ 8.30am-11.30pm Wed-Mon) There's a stupendous view from this café's rear terrace, where you can enjoy an ice cream, coffee and cake or a beer. The place also does some fantastic modern international/seasonal cuisine, with the daily changing menu including things like perch on mashed pumpkin with risotto and entrecôte of venison.

Fiescherblick (☎ 033 854 53 53; mains Sfr25-45, menus Sfr28-75; ☺ 6pm-late; ☺ closed after Easter, mid-Oct–mid-Dec) This hotel has a small bistro, but its main attraction is its GaultMillau-rated gourmet restaurant, with a range of Swiss and international cuisine.

Drinking

The misleadingly named **Espresso Bar** (☎ 033 954 88 88), in the Spinne Hotel, is a popular watering hole. The hotel also has a **disco** (admission free; ☺ Mon-Sat winter, Thu-Sat summer) with a DJ and occasional live music.

Getting There & Away

See p151 for train fares. Grindelwald can also be reached by the main road from Interlaken. A smaller road continues from the village over the Grosse Scheidegg Pass (1960m). It's closed to private traffic, but from early July to early October postal buses (two hours) travel this scenic route to Meiringen (see p174).

BERNESE OBERLAND

SKIING THE JUNGFRAU REGION

Grindelwald, Männlichen, Mürren and Wengen are all popular skiing destinations, plus there's a demanding run down from the Schilthorn. In all, there are 205km of prepared runs and 45 ski lifts. A one-day ski pass for either Grindelwald-Wengen or Mürren-Schilthorn costs Sfr56 (Sfr28 for children, Sfr45 for 16 to 19 year olds, Sfr50 for those over 62). Ski passes for the whole Jungfrau ski region cost Sfr120/60/96/108 for a minimum two days, but switching between ski areas by train can be slow and crowded. In 2006, as part of new measures to heighten skiers' awareness of safety issues, a speed limit of 30km/h was introduced on certain runs above Grindelwald.

AROUND GRINDELWALD
Männlichen

On the ridge dividing the Grindelwald and Lauterbrunnen valleys, Männlichen (2230m) is one of the region's top lookout points. The world's longest **cable car** (☎ 033 854 80 80; www.maennlichenbahn.ch) route connects Grindelwald-Grund to Männlichen (Sfr30/Sfr50 one way/return, Sfr30 return 3pm to 5pm in summer). Another cable car comes up the other side of the ridge, from Wengen (Sfr23/Sfr38 one way/return).

From the top Männlichen station, walk 10 minutes up to the crown of the hill to enjoy the view. At the southern end of the ridge are Tschuggen (2520m) and Lauberhorn (2472m), with the 'big three' looming behind. From here, you notice the difference between the two valleys – the broad expanse of the Grindelwald Valley to the left, and the glacier-formed Lauterbrunnen Valley to the right with its steep sides. To the north you can see a stretch of Thunersee.

If you wish to stay overnight, there's the **Berggasthaus Männlichen** (☎ 033 853 10 68; berggasthaus@maennlichen.ch) or an **igloo camp** (www.maennlichen.ch) in winter.

A classic hike from Männlichen is the scenic **Panoramaweg** down to Kleine Scheidegg, which heads south to Honegg, and skirts around the Lauberhorn ridge to reach Rotstöckli and Kleine Scheidegg in 1½ hours.

First

A cable car goes to **First** (☎ 033 828 77 11; www.go first.ch; one way/return Sfr30/50), where there are 100km of paths, half of which stay open in winter. From here, you can hike up to **Faulhorn** (2681m; 2½ hours) via Bachalpsee (Lake Bachalp). As you proceed along the ridge to Bachalpsee, there are excellent unfolding panoramas of the Jungfrau massif; at Faulhorn, there's a restaurant and a 360° panorama. From here, you can choose to continue on to Schynige Platte (another three hours), and return by train. Or you can hike to Bussalp (1800m, 1½ hours) and return by bus to Grindelwald (Sfr19.80).

Other hikes go to Schwarzhorn (three hours), Grosse Scheidegg (1½ hours), Unterer Gletscher (1½ hours) or Grindelwald (2½ hours). By the First cable-car summit station, there's the **Berggasthaus First** (☎ 033 853 12 84).

Pfingstegg

Yet another cable car goes to **Pfingstegg** (☎ 033 853 26 26; www.pfingstegg.ch in German; single/return Sfr11.20/Sfr17; ☺ May-Oct). From here, you can take short hiking trails to Stieregg, near the Unterer Gletscher. Check to see whether the trail to **Hotel Wetterhorn** (☎ 033 853 12 18; www .hotel-wetterhorn.ch in German) at the base of the Oberer Gletscher (1½ hours) via the Restaurant Milchbach (one hour) is open. Along this, you pass the **Breitlouwina**, a geologically fascinating terrace of rock scarred with potholes and scratches caused by moving ice.

There's also a popular summer **bobsled** ride at Pfingstegg.

KLEINE SCHEIDEGG

This place is a mere huddle of buildings around the train station, yet it occupies an enviable position at the base of the Eiger. Most people only linger for a few minutes while changing trains for Jungfraujoch, but Kleine Scheidegg (2061m) is also a good base for hiking. There are short, undemanding trails, one hour apiece, to Eigergletscher, down to Wengernalp, and up the Lauberhorn behind the village. (These areas become intermediate ski runs from early December to April.) Alternatively, you can hike the Eiger Trail from Eigergletscher to Alpiglen (2¼ hours).

The train station has local information and money-changing facilities as well as a small post office.

BERNESE OBERLAND

THE HILLS ARE ALIVE WITH THE SOUND OF HINDI

Confused by the curry buffet at Jungfraujoch? The answer is simple really. India's huge movie industry just adores a mountain, a waterfall or a lake as the backdrop to its unashamedly escapist song-and-dance sequences. So when the traditional location of Kashmir became too risky for Bollywood film crews to venture into, Switzerland began acting as its stunt double, its stand-in.

As a result, more Bollywood movies are now shot in the Alpine confederation than in any other foreign country, and thousands of loyal fans are following in their movie idols' footsteps here. Since the huge hit *Dilwale Dulhania Le Jayenge* was filmed here in 1995, dozens of other Indian blockbusters have followed and the number of Indian tourists to Switzerland has more than doubled. Huge tour groups arrive in the pre-monsoon months of May and June to visit their favourite locations, including Gstaad (p175), Engelberg/Titlis (p229) and Geneva (p59).

Basic dormitory accommodation can be found in **Restaurant Bahnhof Röstizzeria** (☎ 033 828 78 28; dm/s/d Sfr46/78/156, half board extra Sfr17), also in the train station, and the more recently renovated **Restaurant Grindelwaldblick** (☎ 033 855 13 74; dm Sfr40, half board extra Sfr21; ☺ closed Nov & May), eight minutes' walk towards Grindelwald.

Hotel Bellevue Des Alpes (☎ 033 855 12 12; s/d from Sfr170/270) is a formerly grand Victorian hotel – rambling, creaky and atmospheric. It has a world-beating location and a rather macabre history of people using its telescopes to observe mountaineering accidents on the Eiger.

JUNGFRAUJOCH

Don't be deterred by the fact that everyone else wants to go to Jungfraujoch (3454m), nor by the fact that the trip is expensive (about Sfr175 from Interlaken). It's one of those once-in-a-lifetime trips that you have to experience first-hand to know what it's all about. And there is a reason why about two million people a year visit this, the highest train station in Europe; the views from the so-called 'top of Europe' are indisputably spectacular. Remember not to overdo things, though, because at this altitude there's one-third less oxygen in the air than at sea level.

The last stage of the train journey, from Kleine Scheidegg, passes through nearly 10km of rock before arriving at the sci-fi Sphinx metereological station. (Little wonder that the tunnel, which was opened in 1912, took 16 years to drill.) Along the way, you stop several times inside the Eiger and Mönch, at Eigerwand and Eismeer, where there are viewing platforms, panoramic windows and vertiginous views.

Good weather really is essential for this journey; check on www.jungfrau.ch or call ☎ 100 62 from within Switzerland. Don't forget to take warm clothing, sunglasses and sunscreen. There's snow and glare up there all year and there's really no point coming all this way to stay indoors at Jungfraujoch.

Within the Sphinx weather station, where the trains disgorge their passengers, there's an ice palace gallery of ice sculptures, restaurants, places to send emails, souvenir shops and indoor viewing terraces.

However, outside there are spectacular views of the **Aletsch Glacier** (see p139), as well as distant landmarks like the Jura mountains and the Black Forest in Germany.

It's possible to walk across the glacier behind the Mönch on a marked path, enjoy a bit of tame skiing or boarding, drive a team of husky dogs or enjoy a range of other activities. If you cross the glacier along the prepared path, in 50 minutes you reach the **Mönchsjochhütte** (☎ 033 971 34 72; ☺ closed btwn seasons) at 3650m. This mountain hut offers dorms, refreshments and a great view across the mountains fringing the glacier.

From Interlaken Ost, the journey time is 2½ hours each way and the return fare is Sfr172.80 (Swiss/Eurail Pass Sfr126.40/111). The last train back is at 6.10pm in summer and 4pm in winter. However, there's a cheaper 'good morning' ticket of Sfr148.60 (Swiss/Eurail Pass discounts available) if you take the first train (6.35am from Interlaken) and leave the summit by noon. From 1 November to 30 April the reduction is valid for both the 6.35am and 7.35am trains, and the noon restriction doesn't apply.

Getting these early trains is less effort if you start from deeper in the region. Stay overnight at Kleine Scheidegg and you can pick up the excursion-fare train at 8.02am in summer and at 8.02am or 9.02am in winter. From here, the 'good morning' return is Sfr65, instead of the full return of Sfr102 (Sfr52 with the Jungfrau Railways Pass). The farthest you can walk is up to Eigergletscher (2320m), which only saves you Sfr6.80/11.40 one way/return from Kleine Scheidegg.

Even the ordinary return ticket to Jungfraujoch is valid for one month, so you can use that ticket to form the backbone of your holiday travel, venturing as far as Grindelwald and stopping for a few days' hiking, before moving on to Kleine Scheidegg, Jungfraujoch, Wengen and Lauterbrunnen.

LAUTERBRUNNEN

pop 2683 / elevation 806m

Lauterbrunnen's wispy Staubbach Falls (Staubbachfälle) inspired both Goethe and Lord Byron to compose poems to their ethereal beauty. However, contemporary Lauterbrunnen tends to attract a less high-faluting crowd. Friendly and full of unpretentious lodgings, the town is simply a great base for nature-lovers wishing to hike through the surrounding region.

The **tourist office** (☎ 033 856 85 68; www.wengen -muerren.ch; ☼ 8am-noon & 2-6pm daily May-Sep, 8am-noon & 2-5pm Mon-Fri rest of year) is across from the train station, while the post office, bank, most hotels and sights are to the left of the station (as you face the tourist office).

Hotel Horner has Internet access for Sfr12 per hour and a dance bar (open until late).

If you're travelling to the car-free resorts above, there's a multistorey **car park** (☎ 033 828 71 11; www.jungfraubahn.ch; per day/week Sfr12/54) by the station, but you must book ahead. There is also an open-air car park by the Stechelberg cable-car station, charging Sfr8 for a day.

Sights & Activities

Especially in the early-morning light, it's easy to see how the famous **Staubbachfälle** captivated several writers with their threads of spray floating down the cliffside.

The **Trümmelbachfälle** (☎ 033 855 32 32; www .truemmelbach.ch; adult/child Sfr10/4; ☼ 9am-5pm Apr-Nov, 8am-6pm Jun-Sep), on the other hand, are more of a bang-crash spectacle. Inside the mountain, up to 20,000L of water per second corkscrews through a series of ravines and potholes shaped by the swirling waters. The

falls drain from 24 sq km of Alpine glaciers and snow deposits. You reach the starting point via stairs or a lift and walk to the various 10 stages. A bus (Sfr3) from the train station takes you to the falls, which are along the valley floor towards Stechelberg. Take a raincoat, as you get quite damp – making this an ideal excursion in poor weather.

The valley floor is also good for **cross-country skiing** during the winter.

Sleeping & Eating

Camping Jungfrau (☎ 033 856 20 10; camp sites per adult/tent from Sfr10.30/6, dm from Sfr26; ☼ year-round) This Rolls Royce of a camping ground offers supreme comfort and superb facilities. It even has wooden huts on site, although the whole setup might not appeal to those looking to get away from it all. It's a few minutes' walk south after the end of the main street, right near the Staubbach Falls.

Valley Hostel (☎ 033 855 20 08; www.valleyhostel .ch; dm/tw/d/f Sfr25/56/64/112; ☼ reception 10am-1pm & 2-10pm; ▯) Flying the Korean flag from the back garden facing the railway line, this clean, modern place has kitchen facilities, an attached laundromat and a cat.

Chalet im Rohr (☎ 033 855 21 82; r per person Sfr28) Its verandas bedecked with a blaze of multicoloured flowers and flags, this wooden chalet is pretty as a picture from outside, but much more humble on the interior. Still, the owners and many regular guests are friendly and have a good sense of humour.

Hotel Staubbach (☎ 033 855 54 54; www.staubbach .com; s/d/tr/f Sfr90/100/150/170, s/d without bathroom from Sfr60/80) Next door, this hotel is better quality but still fairly old-fashioned, with an informal, friendly atmosphere. The best rooms have balconies, but these come with a Sfr10 supplement in summer.

Hotel Oberland (☎ 033 855 12 41; mains Sfr16.50-35) Received wisdom has it that this is Lauterbrunnen's best eating option and received wisdom is right. It serves a superior sort of rösti, pasta, salad and Swiss speciality.

WENGEN

pop 1050 / elevation 1350m

Especially popular with British holidaymakers, Wengen rightfully boasts about its 'celestial views'. Perched on a mountain ledge, this car-free resort has a long view

(Continued on page 165)

MARK HONAN

Château de Chillon (p89), Montreux

Sailing (p49), Lake Geneva

MARK HONAN

WITOLD SKRYPCZAK

Cathédrale de St-Pierre (p61), Geneva

View over Montreux (p89)

GLENN VAN DER KNIJFF

CHRIS MELLOR

Gorner Glacier from Gornergrat (p134)

Bahnhofstrasse, Zermatt (p134)

GLENN VAN DER KNIJFF

GLENN VAN DER KNIJFF

Gornergrat (p134), above Zermatt

Val de Bagnes (p125), Valais

GRANT DIXON

DAVID TOMLINSON

Oberer Gletscher (p151), Grindelwald

Restaurant, Wengen (p156)

ROBERTO SONCIN GEROMETTA

Ski trekking, Jungfrau Region (p152)

MARK HONAN

KARL LEHMANN

Paraglidling (p43), Mt Rigi

HUGH WATTS

Old Town and Münster (p182), Bern

Rathaus (p239), Basel

ADINA TOVY AMSEL

Sechseläuten parade (p200), Zürich

Cathedral (p253), St Gallen

Grossmünster (p195), Zürich

MARTIN MOOS

Mountain hut, Swiss National Park (p280)

Scuol (p279), the Engadine

JOHN MCLEAN

Hiker crossing stream, Swiss National Park (p280)

MARTIN M

MARTIN MOOS

Cable car, Diavolezza (p283)

MARTIN MOOS

Switzerland–Liechtenstein border sign

Church, Triesenberg (p310), Liechtenstein

MARTIN MOOS

GLENN VAN DER KNIJFF

Gandria (p297), Ticino

GLENN VAN DER KNIJFF

Promenade, Ascona (p301)

Castello di Montebello (p290), Bellinzona

MARTIN MOOS

Market stalls, Lugano (p292)

MARTIN MOOS

(Continued from page 156)

down the Lauterbrunnen valley to peaks that remain snow-capped all year.

The **tourist office** (☎ 033 855 14 14; www.wengen -muerren.ch; ◷ 9am-6pm daily, closed Sat & Sun Nov & Mar-Apr) is minutes from the train station, taking a left at Hotel Silberhorn and continuing 100m farther on. Next door is the **post office**. Internet access is available a few steps along, at **Rock's Bar**.

The high point in Wengen's calendar is the international **Lauberhorn downhill ski race** in late January. The ski runs are reached by the cable car to Männlichen, or by train to Allmend, Wengernalp or Kleine Scheidegg. There's also a **ski school** (☎ 033 855 20 22). The same areas are excellent for hiking in the summer (see p154 for details on hiking from Männlichen). Some 20km of paths stay open in winter too. The hike down to Lauterbrunnen takes about an hour.

Sleeping

Old Lodge Backpackers (☎ 078 745 58 50; www.old -lodge.ch; dm Sfr25-40, r Sfr35-60) This place looks pretty much as the name suggests, making it easily recognisable as you approach it down the path below Wengen's train station. In fact, it's a huge, rambling old lodge, with basic facilities, but it boasts a lively atmosphere and fantastic views.

Hotel Bären (☎ 033 855 14 19; www.baeren-wengen .ch; s/d from Sfr70/120, in winter from Sfr90/160) Also reached by looping back under the rail track and down the hill, this sweet little chalet hotel has a peaceful atmosphere and decent, if compact, rooms. Note that the rates it normally quotes include half-board.

Hotel Belvedere (☎ 033 856 68 68; www.belvedere -wengen.ch; s/d from Sfr100/160, in winter Sfr145/250) Set in leafy grounds, the Belvedere is notable for its wonderfully preserved Art Nouveau sitting room and good views. There's a range of renovated and unrenovated rooms.

Eating

Hotel Bären (☎ 033 855 14 19; mains Sfr18-42; ◷ 11.30am-2pm & 6-11pm Tue-Sat, 6-11pm Sun & Mon) This family-run hotel puts a modern, international twist on Swiss food, and its restaurant is worth visiting, even if you're not staying.

Da Sina (☎ 033 855 31 72; pizzas Sfr12-27, other mains Sfr14-42; ◷ 11.30am-11.30pm high season, 11.30am-2pm

AUTHOR'S CHOICE

Hotel Caprice (☎ 033 856 06 06; www.ca price-wengen.ch; standard d with view Sfr160-300, in winter Sfr460) If you're looking for pure luxury in the Jungfrau mountains, it's hard to think of a better place. Whereas most other top-end establishments in the region are opulent, historic and slightly overblown, the interior of this boutique hotel is modern and chic. The colour scheme is understated, with black, muesli and white tones, and the lounge has a stylish Scandinavian-style fireplace. Most importantly, the Caprice doesn't try too hard; you get the feeling that the charming service and excellent French food all just come naturally. It's closed between seasons.

& 6-11.30pm rest of year) In good weather, you can enjoy the terrace of this popular pizzeria-cum-steakhouse, while there's an attached pub/disco for après-ski entertainment.

Chili's the Wengen Saloon (most mains Sfr12-25) This is a young hang-out near the tourist office with drinks, bar food and a downstairs disco bar (winter only).

Café Gruebi (☎ 033 855 58 55; mains Sfr7-16; ◷ 8.30am-6pm Mon-Sat, 1-8pm Sun) Above the main street and run by a husband-and-wife team, Gruebi offers cheap Swiss eats and home-made cakes (baked almost daily by the…husband).

MÜRREN

pop 320 / elevation 1650m

Arriving on a clear evening, as the train from Grütschalp seemingly floats along the horizontal ridge towards Mürren, the peaks across the valley feel so close that you could reach out and touch them. And that's when you'll think you've died and gone to Heidi heaven. Car-free Mürren is simply one of the most stunning spots in the region.

The **tourist office** (☎ 033 856 86 86; www.wengen -muerren.ch; ◷ 8.30am-7pm Mon-Sat, to 9pm Thu, 8.30am-6pm Sun high season, 8.30am-7pm Mon-Sat, 8.30am-5pm Sun shoulder seasons, 8.30am-5pm Mon-Sat low season) is in the sports centre.

The main pursuits in the village are hiking and skiing, plus staring slack-jawed at the scenery.

In summer, the **Allmendhubel funicular** (one way/return Sfr12/7.40) takes you above Mürren to a panoramic restaurant. From here, you can set out on many hikes, including the famous **Northface Trail** (2½ hours), via Schiltalp to the west, which offers outstanding views across the Lauterbrunnen valley. There's also an easier **Children's Adventure Trail** (one hour).

In winter, there are 50km of prepared ski runs nearby, mostly suited to intermediates, and a **ski school** (☎ 033 855 12 47). Mürren is known for the **Inferno Run** (Inferno-Rennen in German) down from Schilthorn in mid-January. Inaugurated in 1928, the difficult course now attracts nearly 2000 amateur skiers each year. It's also the reason for all the devilish soft-toy souvenirs.

Sleeping & Eating

Eiger Guesthouse (☎ 033 856 54 60; www.eigerguest house.com; d with/without bathroom from Sfr130/Sfr110, in winter Sfr140/120, dm Sfr40-70; 🖳) Run by a friendly and on-the-ball Swiss-Scottish couple, this humble abode offers pretty good value. Besides clean, freshened-up and comfortable rooms, you get a generous buffet breakfast.

Hotel Alpenruh (☎ 033 856 88 00; www.schilthorn .ch; s/d Sfr115/190, in winter Sfr140/260; 🖳 ✕) Lots of loving detail has gone into this much-lauded chalet hotel near the Schilthorn cable car. Funky wreaths decorate every door and knick-knacks brighten up the stairwell. Past guests praise the service, food and views.

Hotel Edelweiss (☎ 033 86 56 00; edelweiss@ muerren.ch; s/d Sfr95/190) While something of a concrete box from outside, this modern hotel does perch spectacularly on the edge of the cliff and offers vertiginous views through the large windows of its lounge and restaurant.

Eiger Hotel (☎ 033 855 54 54; www.hoteleiger.com; s/d from Sfr200/280; ✕ 🍴) This elegant four-star establishment is most noteworthy for the absolutely amazing view from its swimming pool: the picture-windows frame not just the mighty Eiger, but the Mönch and Jungfrau, too.

Tham's Snacks & Drinks (☎ 033 856 01 10; mains Sfr15-28; ⏱ noon-9pm daily Jul & Aug, on demand in low season) Tham's serves Thai, Singaporean, Malaysian and other Asian dishes cooked by a former five-star chef who's literally taken to the hills to escape the rat race.

Restaurant La Grotte (☎ 033 855 18 26; mains Sfr16.50-35; ⏱ 11am-2pm & 5-9pm) This is the Hotel Blumental's rustic restaurant, highly regarded for its fondues and flambées, although it's becoming slightly touristy in summer. Both it and Tham are along the lower main thoroughfare.

GIMMELWALD

pop 140 / elevation 1370m

Tiny Gimmelwald has long been a bolthole for hikers and other adventurers wanting to escape the worst tourist excesses of the region. The secret is out, though, and this mountainside village – where you can sleep in the hay of what is now one of Switzerland's most famous barns – is becoming more popular (although, really, the views are better in Mürren).

The surrounding hiking trails include one down from more scenic Mürren (30 to 40 minutes) and one up from Stechelberg (1¼ hours). Cable cars are also an option (Mürren Sfr7.40, Stechelberg Sfr7.80).

Sleeping & Eating

Esther's Guest House (☎ 033 855 54 88; www.esthers guesthouse.ch; r per person Sfr40-45) Esther's is a lovely B&B, serving its own jam and organic produce at breakfast. However, it's better known for its barn where, from June to October, you can enjoy the novelty – and surprising comfort – of sleeping in hay (Sfr22 including breakfast and shower).

Mountain Hostel (☎ 033 855 17 04; www.mountain hostel.com; dm Sfr20; ⏱ check-in 5.30-10.30pm; 🖳) A backpacking legend, this basic, low-ceilinged but incredibly friendly place now has a communal outdoor hot tub, where you can bathe while enjoying mountain views.

Pension Gimmelwald (☎ 033 855 17 30; www.pen siongimmelwald.ch; s/d Sfr87/135) Even the owners describe this as simple and rustic, but few want more in back-to-nature Gimmelwald. The restaurant, where most meals range from Sfr14 to Sfr26, is famous for its 'Gimmelwalder Horse Shit Balls' (an interestingly shaped sweet made from chocolate, almonds and sugar).

SCHILTHORN

There's a fantastic 360° panorama from the 2970m **Schilthorn** (www.schilthorn.ch), one that's possibly even better than from Jungfraujoch. On a good day, you can see from Titlis around to Mont Blanc, and across to the German Black Forest. Yet, some visitors seem more preoccupied with practising their delivery of the line, 'The name's Bond, James

Bond', than taking in the 200 or so mountains. That's because a few scenes from *On Her Majesty's Secret Service* were shot here in late 1968/early 1969 – as the fairly tacky **Touristorama** below the **Piz Gloria** revolving restaurant will remind you.

From Interlaken, take a Sfr115 excursion trip (Half-Fare Card and Swiss Pass 50% off, Eurail Pass 25% off) going to Lauterbrunnen, Grütschalp, Mürren, Schilthorn and returning through Stechelberg to Interlaken. A return from Lauterbrunnen (via Grütschalp) and Mürren costs about Sfr100, as does the journey up and back via the Stechelberg cable car. A return from Mürren is Sfr65. Ask about discounts for early-morning trips.

En route from Mürren, the cable car goes through the Birg station (2677m), where you can also stop to take in fantastic views.

THE LAKES

Anyone who travels to Interlaken for the first time from Bern will never forget the moment they clap eyes on Thunersee (Lake Thun). As the train loops past green pastures and tidy villages on the low southern shore, some people literally gasp at the sight of the mountains across the blue waters outdoing any picture-postcard image.

Brienzersee (Lake Brienz), flanking Interlaken to the east, doesn't have so many people lunging for their cameras. However, it's still very attractive and – before the 2005 floods at least – was said to be the cleanest lake in Switzerland.

Steamers run on both lakes from April to mid-October. There are no winter services on Brienzersee, whereas special cruises continue on Thunersee. For more information contact **BLS** (☎ 033 334 52 11; www.bls.ch). A day pass valid for both lakes costs Sfr50 (Sfr70 in 1st class, children half-price). Passes are also available for seven days or longer. Eurail Passes, the Regional Pass and the Swiss Pass are valid on all boats, and Inter Rail and the Swiss Half-Fare Card get 50% off.

The most famous ferry on Thunersee is the *Blümlisalp*, a paddlesteamer built in 1906.

THUN

pop 40,236 / elevation 563m

Thun (pronounced toon) is a historic town with a strong feeling of youth, where he-

donistic crowds sun themselves at waterfront pavement cafés and funky shops fill the unusual medieval arcades.

The turreted castle sitting on the hill above is still the town's most visible feature, but today all Swiss most readily associate Thun with its football team. Having unexpectedly felled several European footballing Goliaths in recent years, minnows FC Thun have won a place in the nation's heart.

Orientation

The town sits on the northern tip of its namesake lake, along the Aare River. The river separates the train station (which has bike rental and money-exchange counters) from the medieval centre around the castle. A sliver of land midstream, linked to both banks by footpaths and roads, has the pedestrianised street Bälliz running along it. The central area can easily be covered on foot.

Information

Main post office (☎ 033 224 88 30; Bahnhofplatz; ☽ 7.30am-7pm Mon-Fri, 8am-noon Sat) Opposite the train station.
Manor (☎ 033 227 36 99; Bahnhofstrasse 3; ☽ 9am-6.30pm Mon-Fri, 9am-9pm Thu, 8am-4pm Sat) Internet access is available on the 1st floor of this supermarket.
Tourist office (☎ 033 222 23 40; www.thunersee.ch; Bahnhofplatz; ☽ 9am-6pm Mon-Fri, 9am-noon & 1-4pm Sat Jul & Aug, 9am-noon & 1-6pm Mon-Fri, 9am-noon Sat rest of year)

Sights & Activities

It's just a joy to wander through Thun, taking in the street scenes of coffee drinkers by river weirs, of ad hoc street stalls, and of cake-shop windows lined with confectionery footballs and other FC Thun sweets.

One street that should definitely not be missed is the split-level **Obere Hauptgasse**. Here, a series of quirky shops line the cobbled pavement where cars drive – with a pedestrian footpath built along the top of these shops' roofs and another row of stores and bars in turn lining this footpath.

The 12th-century hilltop castle, **Schloss Thun**, once belonged to Duke Berchtold V of the powerful Zähringen family. Now it contains a **historical museum** (☎ 033 223 20 01; www.schlossthun.ch; adult/child Sfr7/2; ☽ 10am-5pm daily Apr-Oct, 1-4pm Sun Nov-Jan, 1-4pm daily Christmas, New Year, Feb & Mar), with local artefacts from prehistory to the 19th century.

BERNESE OBERLAND

There's another castle, **Schloss Schadau**, on the shore of the lake, but you can't go inside. Should you wish to cycle out here, free city bikes are available for loan from **Thun Rollt** (Aarefeldstrasse; passport & deposit of Sfr20; ☺ 7.30am-9.30pm May-Oct).

Sleeping & Eating

Hotel zu Metzgern (☎ 033 222 21 41; www.zumetzgern .ch in German; Untere Hauptgasse 2; s/d without bathroom 1st night Sfr60/120, thereafter Sfr55/110; ☺ reception Tue-Sun) You'll find spartan but comfortable rooms above the popular restaurant of this historic hotel (1361). Downstairs, the chef uses organic ingredients in Swiss classics and interesting-sounding international recipes like lamb with a pistachio-herb crust, red-wine risotto and dahl with coconut vegetables (mains Sfr19 to Sfr38).

Hotel Emmental (☎ 033 222 01 20; www.essenund trinken.ch in German; Bernstrasse 2; s/d Sfr80/160) Looking like a funky Swiss farmhouse in the middle of town, this is an eye-catching building. The ornately carved eaves have been sanded back to natural wood, while the slatted window shutters beneath them

have been painted a fashionable mint green. Inside, the rooms are stylish with vaguely 1970s bathrooms and not too much noise floats up from the popular bar below (well, not when we've stayed).

Hotel Freienhof (☎ 033 227 50 50; www.freienhof.ch in German; Freienhofgasse 3; s/d from Sfr165/215, with water views Sfr185/235; ☒ ℗) This leading hotel is in a lovely location facing the river, where you can feel the town's vibrant character. Rooms are sleek and modern, plus there's an excellent restaurant.

Essen und Trinken (☎ 033 222 48 70; Untere Hauptgasse 32; mains Sfr19-32; ☺ 5.30-11.30pm) Operated by the same concern as Hotel Emmental, this restaurant bills itself mainly as a trendy Tex-Mex venue, but also has fondue and rösti on the menu.

Altes Waisenhaus (☎ 033 223 31 33; Bälliz 61; mains Sfr26-35; ☺ 9am-midnight) This spacious waterfront restaurant at the start of the pedestrian zone gets lots of mealtime traffic for its excellent Italian cuisine. However, it's equally popular as a quick stop-off for homemade cake and ice cream, or an alcoholic drink.

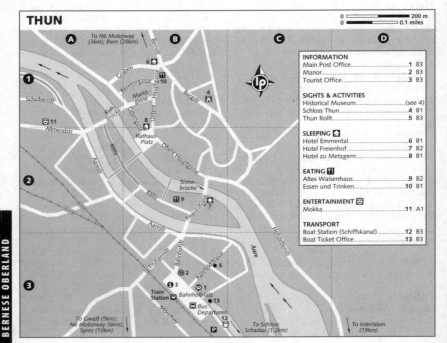

THUN

INFORMATION	
Main Post Office	1 B3
Manor	2 B3
Tourist Office	3 B3

SIGHTS & ACTIVITIES	
Historical Museum	(see 4)
Schloss Thun	4 B1
Thun Rollt	5 B3

SLEEPING 🅖	
Hotel Emmental	6 B1
Hotel Freienhof	7 B2
Hotel zu Metzgern	8 B1

EATING 🍴	
Altes Waisenhaus	9 B2
Essen und Trinken	10 B1

ENTERTAINMENT 🎭	
Mokka	11 A1

TRANSPORT	
Boat Station (Schiffskanal)	12 B3
Boat Ticket Office	13 B3

BERNESE OBERLAND

BUNKER MENTALITY

It used to be said that Switzerland didn't have an army, Switzerland was an army, and at the height of the Cold War this tiny country's attachment to compulsory national service meant that it had nearly one million soldiers on a 48-hour call-out. With recent army cuts, however (see the boxed text On Guard, p32), that's all changed, and the *Artilleriewerk* at Faulensee is among the first of 13,000 decommissioned facilities to fall back on that other Swiss standby – tourism.

The formerly **top-secret bunkers** (☎ 033 654 25 07; artfort@bluewin.ch) here were built to house troops defending Thun, Spiez and the Lötschberg railway. Now, during summer, they're open to the public on the first Saturday of every month (adult/child Sfr9/5, 2pm to 5pm April to October). Cleverly disguised as farmhouses, the entrances to the bunkers are guarded by cannons, and connected by underground tunnels in which you'll find offices, laboratories, kitchens and cramped sleeping quarters.

Visitors are organised into ad hoc groups, and guided through the facility on the hour and half hour. Tours last 1½ to two hours, and you'll need warm clothing and good shoes. To ask about English explanations, call or email ahead. (With a group of six, you can also arrange a visit to the Swiss Army Museum Collection in Thun.)

Faulensee can be reached by bus from Spiez train station and from Interlaken West by boat (Sfr18/31 single/return).

Entertainment

Each Thursday in July and August there are free folklore performances in Rathausplatz. Thun's most famous club is **Mokka** (www .mokka.ch in German; Allmendstrasse 14). However, the industrial area where most of the town's clubs are located could be up for redevelopment; check on the website for the latest details.

Getting There & Away

Thun is on the main north–south train route from Frankfurt to Milan and beyond. From Interlaken West, Thun is Sfr14.20 each way by train, Sfr28 by boat.

SPIEZ

pop 11,924 / elevation 628m

Hunched around a horseshoe-shaped bay, with a medieval castle rising out of its midst, the oft-overlooked town of Spiez is resplendent in summer with coloured blooms. Its lush vegetation includes a vineyard, for which its well known.

Orientation & Information

The **tourist office** (☎ 033 654 20 20; www.thunersee .ch; ☽ 8am-6pm Mon-Fri, 9am-noon & 2-6pm Sat summer, 8am-noon & 2-6pm Mon-Fri winter) is outside the train station. It is open shorter hours in the shoulder seasons and has an Internet terminal. Seestrasse, the main street, is down to the left, and ultimately leads to the castle (15 minutes).

Sights & Activities

The castle, **Schloss Spiez** (☎ 033 654 15 06; www .spiez.ch in German; adult/child/concession Sfr7/2/5; ☽ 2-5pm Mon, 10am-5pm Tue-Sun Easter–mid-Oct, 10am-6pm Jul–mid-Sep), displays portraits of its former masters, the influential von Bubenburg and von Erlach families and fine examples of medieval rooms. But the highlight is the view, whether from the banqueting hall or from the vertiginous tower (which also sports 13th-century graffiti).

Near the castle is the small **Heimat und Rebbaumuseum** (admission free; ☽ 2-5pm Wed, Sat & Sun May-Oct) with exhibits on wine culture and cultivation.

There there's a vintage wine festival, the **Läset-Fescht**, in September.

Sleeping & Eating

Hotel Des Alpes (☎ 033 654 33 54; Seestrasse 34; s/d from Sfr80/140) Little personal touches in the decoration and a friendly air help make this relatively humble abode one of Spiez's nicer places to stay.

Strandhotel Belvédère (☎ 033 655 66 66; www.bel vedere-spiez.ch; Schachenstrasse; s/d from Sfr130/270; ☽ Mar-Jan) This refined four-star hotel mixes traditional furnishings with modern spa facilities. Overlooking the lake from a quiet but central spot, it has a gourmet French restaurant (mains from Sfr36.50).

Hotel Bellevue (☎ 033 654 84 64; www.bellevue -spiez.ch; Seestrasse 36; s/d from Sfr75/125; **P**) This option is between the train station a lake. Its rooms are perfectly adequate, and little more, although some of them do enjoy good views.

You'll find many, rather ordinary, pizza and pasta places around the boat station.

Getting There & Away

From Interlaken West, Spiez is Sfr9.20 each way by train. By boat it's Sfr13.60 from Thun and Sfr18 from Interlaken West.

LAKE THUN
Castles & Museums

As well as the castles within Thun and Spiez themselves, there are a couple others dotted around Thunersee (Lake Thun). These are easily reachable by boat for a right royal day out.

Schloss Oberhofen (☎ 033 243 12 35; Oberhofen; adult/child Sfr5/1; ⏰ 2-5pm Mon, 10am-5pm Tue-Sun mid-May–mid-Oct) is probably the best of the bunch. Bernese troops wrested it from Habsburg control after the Battle of Sempach (1386) and it now documents Bernese life from the 16th to the 19th centuries. There's a medieval chapel, an ornate Napoleonic drawing room and, its biggest draw, a Turkish smoking room. In the landscaped **gardens** (admission free; ⏰ 10am-dusk, mid-Mar–mid-Nov) there's a children's chalet with toys.

Another advantage of choosing to visit this castle is that just east of it, on Wichterheer Estate, lies the stunning **Sammlung im Obersteg** (☎ 033 243 30 38; Wichterheer Estate, Oberhofen; adult/student Sfr8/6; ⏰ 10am-noon & 2-5pm Tue-Sat, 10am-5pm Sun mid-May–mid-Oct). This is a fine private collection of modern art, much better than anything you'd expect to find here, with works by Picasso and Chagall.

Oberhofen is 25 minutes by boat from Thun (services approximately hourly), or you can take a bus (14 minutes, every quarter of an hour).

Schloss Hünegg (☎ 033 243 19 82; www.schlosshuen egg.ch in German; Staatsstrasse 52, Hilterfingen; adult/child Sfr8/1.50; ⏰ 2-5pm daily, plus 10am-noon Sun mid-May–mid-Oct) is also more plush than the castles in Spiez and Thun. With heavy brocades, carpets and furniture in its fabulous 19th-century bathrooms and salons, and gleaming nickel-plated bathtub and taps in the bathroom, it provides a fascinating mix of neo-Renaissance and Art Nouveau styles.

Water Sports

All manner of water sports are practised on Thunersee, from swimming, sailing and messing around in small boats to windsurfing, water-skiing and wake-boarding. The Thun tourist office has a complete list of centres and schools in its *Thunersee* brochure, or see www.thunersee.ch.

Camping Gwatt (☎ 033 336 40 67; camping.gwatt@ tcs.ch; Gwattstrasse 103; adult & car Sfr10.90, tent Sfr8.40-10.40, Modulhotel per person Sfr30-90; ⏰ May-Oct) offers windsurfing, as well as family/group accommodation in its unusual 'Modulhotel' – five large plastic tubes laid on their side and fitted with bunk beds.

BRIENZ
pop 2921 / elevation 566m

Right on the edge of its aqua-coloured namesake lake, looking across the water to the mountains opposite, Brienz is a sleepy little village fitting for a day or two's escape from the world. As a convenient base for visiting the well-known Freilichtmuseum Ballenberg, it's also the centre of Switzerland's wood-carving industry and within easy reach of the popular Giessbach Falls. However, it suffered badly during the 2005 floods, becoming one big mudslide, and had a long, hard task returning to normality.

Orientation & Information

The train station, boat station, Rothorn Bahn and post office are all within a stone's throw of each other in the centre. The **tourist office** (☎ 033 952 80 80; www.alpenregion.ch; ⏰ 8am-6pm daily Apr-Oct, 8am-noon & 2-6pm Mon-Fri Nov-Mar) is in the train station.

Sights & Activities

The **Rothorn Bahn** (☎ 033 952 22 22; www.brienz-rot horn-bahn.ch; single/return Sfr46/72, 25% discount with Swiss Pass; ⏰ hourly from 7.30am-4.30pm daily May-Oct) is the only steam-powered cogwheel train still operating in Switzerland, climbing 2350m, from where you can embark on several hikes or just enjoy the views. A standard diesel train is used instead of a steam engine before 9.30am and again around lunchtime, so check with the office if you that's important for you. Sometimes there's a train decorated with pictures of Hopp the Steam Railway Ghost – to keep the children happy. Walking to the top from Brienz takes around five hours.

There are many touristy shops and boutiques along Hauptstrasse, selling locally carved statues, music boxes and cuckoo clocks. Several outlets also open their attached workshops, including **Jobin**, which has been in business since 1835. There's more to see in its **Living Museum** (☎ 033 952 13 00; Hauptstrasse 111; admission Sfr5, guided tour Sfr15; ☺ 8am-7pm daily Apr-Nov, 8am-6pm Mon-Sat Dec-Mar, individual entry not allowed 11.30am-2pm) than you'll find at **Walter Stähli** (☎ 033 951 06 06; Hauptstrasse 41; tours free; ☺ 8am-7pm).

Sleeping & Eating

Camping Aaregg (☎ 033 951 18 43; www.aaregg.ch; camp sites per adult/car & tent Sfr11/18; ☺ Apr-Oct) This lakeside camp site was devastated by the 2005 floods, but vowed to rebuild its facilities to the same excellent standard. It's a 10-minute walk east of the train station, in the opposite direction to the town centre.

SYHA hostel (☎ 033 951 11 52; www.youthhostel.ch /brienz; Strandweg 10; 10- & 14-bed dm Sfr25.40, d Sfr60.80; ☺ reception closed 10am-5pm) The nearby hostel is adequate, rather than appealing, with large dorms and quite basic facilities, although it has good lake views. The hostel is closed from mid-October to January.

Hotel Weisses Kreuz (☎ 033 952 20 20; www.weisses kreuz-brienz.ch in German; Hauptstrasse 143; s/d/tr Sfr110/ 160/175) Conveniently located close to the train station, this old-fashioned chalet building has all modern amenities, and an interesting list of past guests that ranges from Goethe and Byron to Richard Nixon. The restaurant also seems quite popular locally.

Hotel Lindenhof (☎ 033 952 20 30; www.hotel-lind enhof.ch; Lindenhofweg 15; s Sfr120-160, d Sfr160-230) Brienz's most interesting hotel is spread over five buildings higher up the hill than Schönegg. There's a range of individually decorated rustic rooms, encompassing everything from flowery murals and canopy beds to forest themes, bales of hay above the bed and a 'smuggler's retreat'. An 'eyrie' bedroom offers wonderful views.

Tea-Room Hotel Walz (☎ 033 951 14 59; Hauptstrasse 102; menus Sfr18-30; ☺ 8am-10.30pm daily, 8am-6.30pm Thu-Tue in winter) This place has healthy meals, biscuits and cakes. The latter includes the unfortunate-sounding but tasty speciality Brienzer Krapfen, pastries filled with dried pears.

Seerestaurant Löwen (☎ 033 951 12 41; Hauptstrasse 8; most mains Sfr20-42; ☺ mid-Mar–late Dec) Take a seat on the lakeside terrace and choose from a wide range of fish dishes, including perch in beer batter, catfish in wholegrain mustard, and monkfish in green curry sauce. Meatlovers and vegetarians are also catered for.

Getting There & Away

From Interlaken Ost, Brienz is accessible by train (Sfr7.20) or boat (Sfr19.80, April to mid-October). The scenic Brünig Pass (1008m) is the road route to Lucerne.

AROUND BRIENZ
Freilichtmuseum Ballenberg

The **Ballenberg Open-Air Museum** (☎ 033 952 10 30; www.ballenberg.ch; adult/child Sfr16/8; ☺ buildings 10am-5pm daily, grounds 9am-6pm mid-Apr–end Oct) is a kind of Disneyland-like rural Switzerland of yore. East of Brienz, this 80-hectare park contains some 100 authentic century-old buildings, in which traditional Swiss crafts and customs – from hat-making and bobbin-lace making to herding cows decked with ribbons and bells back to base – are displayed. The houses were brought here from all over the country and show a range of regional architectural styles. There are more than 250 farm animals, woodlands and a range of gardens, with vegetables and medicinal herbs on site.

Ballenberg is too big to absorb in one visit, so don't even try. Instead, pick up a plan at the entrance (Sfr2), check the times of special demonstrations on the board, and work out an itinerary.

There are two entrances, at the west and east of the site, and car parks at each. The nearest train station is Brienzwiler. A good option is to take the bus (Sfr3 each way) that leaves from outside Brienz train station. It's often packed, but at least you can get off at one entrance and leave by the other, without having to retrace your steps.

Giessbachfälle

It's their setting on a wooded hillside overlooking Brienzersee that makes the 500m-tall **Giessbach Falls** worth visiting. An old-fashioned funicular runs up from the boat station (one way/return Sfr4.50/6) but the walk doesn't take long. Various footpaths traverse the surrounding hillside. Giessbach is easily reached by boat (return from Brienz Sfr13.60, from Interlaken Ost Sfr27).

The room categories at the grand old 19th-century **Grand Hotel Giessbach** (☎ 033

952 25 25; www.giessbach.ch; s Sfr130-170, d Sfr150-330; May-Oct) overlooking the falls say it all: 'Nostalgic', 'Romantic' and 'Bellevue'. It's idyllically situated high on the mountain above the lake, surrounded by forest. Some just come on a day trip from Interlaken for lunch in the panoramic restaurant.

EAST BERNESE OBERLAND

The Hasli Valley (Haslital), east of the Jungfrau Region, is a popular hiking spot, and a good base for embarking on tours across the Grimsel and Susten passes.

MEIRINGEN

pop 4660 / elevation 595m

When the writer Arthur Conan Doyle left his fictional detective Sherlock Holmes for dead at the base of the Reichenbach Falls near Meiringen, he ensured there was a corner of Switzerland that would forever remain English-eccentric. Every 4 May, fans in deerstalker hats and tweed capes still congregate here for the anniversary of Holmes' 'death'.

Meiringen's other claim to fame is for being the sweet-toothed birthplace of meringue. For many visitors, though, it's simply a good base for taking hikes, especially through two nearby river gorges and across

Europe's highest and longest pedestrian suspension bridge.

Orientation

The town is north of the Aare River. As you exit the train station (bike rental available), you'll see the main post office and bus station opposite. Head straight ahead past the Hotel Meiringen, turn right onto the main thoroughfare, and in a few minutes you'll reach the tourist office.

Information

alpenregionCARD (6/13 days Sfr35/55; Apr-Oct) Offers a range of discounts, including for boats, some scenic bus routes, cable cars, the Freilichtmuseum Ballenberg, the Reichenbachfall funicular and the Rothorn Bahn.

Tourist office (☎ 033 972 50 50; www.alpenregion.ch; Bahnhofstrasse; 8am-12.30pm & 2-6pm Mon-Fri, 8-11am & 4.30-6pm Sat, 4.30-6pm Sun Jul & Aug, 8am-noon & 2-6pm Mon-Fri, 8am-noon & 3-5pm Sat rest of year)

Sights & Activities

Gazing over the mighty **Reichenbachfälle** (Reichenbach Falls), where the water cascades to the ground with a deafening roar, you can see how Arthur Conan Doyle thought them perfect for dispatching his increasingly burdensome hero, Sherlock Holmes. In 1891, in *The Final Problem*, Conan Doyle acted like one of his own villains and pushed both Holmes and Holmes' arch-enemy, Dr Moriarty, over the precipice here. From that moment on, fans have been flocking

---

BRIDGE OVER MELTING WATERS

Meiringen's latest attraction comprises a glacier underneath Europe's longest and highest pedestrian suspension bridge. Opened in 2005, the 102m-long **Triftbrücke** (Trift Bridge; www.trift.ch in German) is already a huge hit with hikers who come to balance above the majestic Trift glacier, as it becomes melt-water more swiftly than it once did. It's a simultaneously impressive and terrifying sight, as one wrestles with both vertigo and pessimism about the warmer global future.

The bridge was built in response to hikers' requests and can be reached because the local power company has opened its renovated cable car to public use. To get to the base station, catch any bus from Meiringen heading to Sustenpass or Gadmen and alight at 'Käppel bei Nessental, Trift' (Sfr8.60, Swiss Pass valid). Alternatively, catch the MIB train from Meiringen to Innertkirchen Post and pick up a bus there.

The **cable car** (☎ 033 982 20 11; www.grimselstrom.ch; one way/return Sfr10/18; 9am-4pm Jun-Oct) takes you up to 1022m, from where it's a 1½-hour walk to the bridge (1870m). The high Alpine scenery is so spectacular that you might want to spend a couple of days up here and, if so, you can overnight in one of two mountain huts: the **Windegghütte** (www.windegghuette.ch in German), 20 minutes from the bridge, or the **Trifthütte** (www.trifthuette.ch in German), three hours above it.

The hike from the cable-car base station to the bridge takes about 3½ hours. Tourist offices in Meiringen and Brienz can provide flyers with a basic map.

to the site. (This is despite the fact that, after Conan Doyle failed in his quest to become a 'serious' writer, he gave in to public pressure and resurrected Holmes in 1903's *The Hound of the Baskervilles*).

Reichenbach funicular (☎ 033 972 90 10; www .reichenbachfall.ch; adult one way/return Sfr6/8, child Sfr3/5; ☷ 9am-6pm Jul & Aug, 9-11.45am & 1.15-5.45pm daily May, Jun, Sep & Oct) carries you from Willigen, south of the Aare River, to the top. It takes nearly an hour to walk back down to Meiringen. Alternatively, you can take the steep paths up the side of the falls to the village of Zwirgi. At Gasthaus Zwirgi, you can rent Trotti-bikes (adult/child Sfr19/14) and ride back to Meiringen.

Zwirgi is at the start of the scenic **Reichenbach Valley**, which runs towards Grindelwald. A path leads to the village of Rosenlaui and the **Gletscherschlucht** (Glacier Gorge; ☎ 033 971 24 88; www.rosenlaui.biz; adult/child Sfr7/3.50 ☷ 9am-6pm Jun-Sep, 10am-5pm May & Oct). The walk back to Meiringen takes at least two hours, but hourly buses also ply the route from June to September.

If you're a real fan, you might care to visit the **Sherlock Holmes Museum** (☎ 033 971 42 21; www.sherlockholmes.ch; Bahnofstrasse 26; adult/child Sfr4/3, combined with Reichenbachfall funicular Sfr11/7; ☷ 1.30-6pm Tue-Sun May-Sep, 4.30-6pm Wed-Sun rest of year) in the basement of the English church back in Meiringen.

Otherwise, it's better to keep to exploring the region. Less than 2km from the town, towards the village of Innertkirchen, is the steep and narrow **Aareschlucht** (Aare Gorge; ☎ 033 971 40 48; www.aareschlucht.ch; adult/child Sfr7/3.5; ☷ 8am-6pm daily Jul & Aug, plus 9-11pm Wed & Fri, 9am-5pm Apr-Jun & Sep-Oct). The gorge has two entrances: the main western entrance near Meiringen and the lesser-used eastern one near Innertkirchen. The **MIB** (☎ 033 982 10 11; www.grimselstrom.ch; adult one way/return Sfr3/6, child Sfr2/3; ☷ 6am-7pm) is a train running half-hourly on weekdays, less often on weekends, from Meiringen and Innertkirchen to Aareschlucht West, near the western entrance.

There's skiing and snowboarding in the region (mainly intermediate and also some beginner runs; Sfr52 for a day pass). The tourist office can provide details on this, as well as on mountaineering and paragliding.

For a after season, a **cable car** (☎ 033 971 34 17; return summer/winter Sfr48/40) runs to the nearby 2250m-high revolving restaurant,

AUTHOR'S CHOICE

Hotel Victoria (☎ 033 972 10 40; www.victoria-meiringen.ch; Bahnhofplatz; s/d/tr from Sfr130/180/250; ☐ ☒) Stylish but relaxed, the Victoria is Meiringen's equivalent of a design hotel. Orchids, artfully arranged pieces of fruit, blue lounge chairs and dark hardwood floors give warmth to otherwise white rooms. A handful of board games is welcomingly scattered around the guest lounge.

the **Alpen Tower** (☎ 033 972 53 26; www.alpentower .ch in German; ☷ Jul & early Dec-Mar).

Sleeping

Hasli Lodge (☎ 033 971 59 00; www.haslilodge.ch; Kirchgasse 11; dm Sfr35-40, s Sfr60-65, d Sfr100-120; ☐) This has swiftly become the cool place to hang out in Meiringen for adventure-sports fans, hikers, backpackers, musicians and the like. A converted budget hotel (the 'Weisses Kreuz' emblem is still on the carpet), its rooms are quite old, but decent. There's a popular bar/restaurant with a brief menu.

Hotel Rebstock (☎ 033 971 07 55; www.hotel-rebstock.ch in German; Bahnhofstrasse; new s/d Sfr125/180, old s/d with bathroom Sfr90/150, old s/d without bathroom Sfr75/120; ☒ ℗) The Rebstock is a hotel of two halves. The 14 light-filled, minimalistic bedrooms in its new wing cater to upmarket tastes; the 14 in its older wing are growing slightly shabby, but still offer good value.

Park Hotel du Sauvage (☎ 033 971 41 41; www .sauvage.ch; Bahnhofstrasse; s/d from Sfr110/200) Sherlock Holmes' creator, Arthur Conan Doyle, once stayed in this opulent belle époque gem, and today it honours his memory by hosting many murder-mystery weekends.

Eating

Hotel Victoria (bistro menu Sfr11-30, restaurant menu Sfr24-44; ☷ 9am-midnight) With its new terrace and accompanying garden dotted with a few quirky sculptures, this is a good spot for a not-too-formal bite. The cuisine is mostly modern European, with a supplementary sushi menu on Fridays and Saturdays.

Hotel Alpbach (☎ 033 971 18 31; Kirchgasse 17; mains Sfr24-48; ☷ 8.30am-midnight) The traditional wooden interior is patently a modern re-creation, but the food is the genuine article. Dishes range from Chinese meat

BERNESE OBERLAND

ALPINE PASS TOURS

Between early July and early October, you can spend a full sunny day enjoying a wonderful four-Alpine-pass tour from Meiringen. From here, it's possible to make a circular bus trip crossing the Grimsel, Nufenen, Gotthard and Susten passes, enjoying stupendous views of snowy peaks, lakes and several glaciers along the way.

At the time of writing, the bus left Meiringen at 9.20am and returned at 5.30pm. However, the tours on offer change each year, so check with **Berner Oberland Postal Bus** (☎ 0900 304 304, 033 828 88 38; www.postalbus.ch/travel) for all the latest details. Alternatively, you'll find information at Meiringen's train station or at the **postal bus office** (☯ 8.15-11.15am) opposite. Reservations are advisable.

The fare is Sfr118 for adults or – and here's the major selling point – Sfr25 for holders of a Swiss Pass. Children travel free.

There is a range of other routes from Meiringen (including to Grosse Scheidegg and Grindelwald, see p153) or Andermatt (p234).

Of course, if you have a car, you can set your own itinerary. Do note, however, that the passes are closed to all traffic from late October to late June.

---

fondue or rösti with veal to noodles with Indian-style giant prawns.

Café Brunner (☎ 033 971 14 23; Bahnhofstrasse 8; menus Sfr14.50-18.50; ☯ 7am-8pm) One of the town's best purveyors of meringue, this café also does a range of salads, savoury pancakes and other simple meals.

Getting There & Away

Frequent trains go to Lucerne (Sfr18.80, 80 minutes; with a scenic ride over the Brünig Pass) and Interlaken Ost (Sfr10.40, 30 minutes, via Brienz). In summer, buses and cars can take the pass southeast (to Andermatt), but the road southwest over Grosse Scheidegg (to Grindelwald) is closed to private vehicles.

WEST BERNESE OBERLAND

At the western side of the Jungfrau are Simmental and Frutigland, dominated by two river valleys, the Simme and the Kander. Farther west is Saanenland, known mainly for the ski resort of Gstaad.

KANDERSTEG

pop 1165 / elevation 1176m

Turn up in Kandersteg wearing anything but sturdy boots and you'll attract a few odd looks. Hiking is this town's raison d'être, with 550km of surrounding trails, both summer and even winter. Skiing and climbing are other popular activities.

The **tourist office** (☎ 033 675 80 80; www.kandersteg.ch; ☯ 8am-noon & 1.30-6pm Mon-Fri, 8am-noon & 1.30-4.30pm Sat Jun-Sep, 8am-noon & 2-5pm Mon-Fr Apr-Jun & Oct-Nov, 8am-noon & 2-6pm Mon-Fri, 8am-noon & 2-4.30pm Sat Dec-Mar) can help with suggested hiking routes. The office is in the village centre, straight ahead from the train station then left on the main street.

To the east is the spectacular **Oeschinensee** (Lake Oeschinen; www.oeschinensee.ch), beautifully situated among the mountains. An old-fashioned chair lift, the **Rodelbahn** (☎ 033 675 11 18; one way/return Sfr14/19; 8.45am-4.45pm May-Oct, 7.30am-6.15pm Jun-Sep) takes you to within 20 minutes of the lake by foot. Once there, it takes an hour to walk back down to Kandersteg.

In winter there are 75km of cross-country ski trails, including the iced-over Oeschinensee, while 55km of hiking tracks stay open. The limited downhill skiing is suited to beginners and day passes cost Sfr34.

The **Blausee** (Blue Sea) and its namesake **nature park** (☎ 033 672 33 33; admission Sfr4.50) lie 5km to the north of Kandersteg (reachable by bus or on foot). This lake is famous for its fresh trout.

Sleeping

Kandersteg's popularity with hikers means there's lots of cheaper accommodation, but many places are closed between seasons.

Ruedihus (☎ 033 675 81 81; www.doldenhorn-ruedihus.ch; s/d from Sfr100/200) This gem of a cosy chalet dating from 1753 has been wonderfully renovated to combine quaintness with comfort. With low ceilings, small windows and antique furniture, it's in a field south of the Hotel-Pension National.

Doldenhorn (☎ 033 675 81 81; www.doldenhorn-rue dihus.ch; s/d from Sfr120/200) Less unique but also slightly grander than its sister Ruedihus, this chalet has a range of individually decorated rooms, from traditional to more modern, and a well-regarded restaurant.

Hotel Victoria Ritter (☎ 033 675 80 00; www.hotel -victoria.ch; s/d from Sfr125/210) This was once a coach tavern, now transformed into an elegant hotel. The Victoria side has traditional 19th-century décor, while rooms in the Ritter are more modern. Also an excellent choice for food.

Camping Rendez-vous (☎ 033 675 15 34; www.camp ing-kandersteg.ch; camp sites per adult/car Sfr7.50/3, tents Sfr6-12; ☼ year-round) A relaxed site by the chair lift to Oeschinensee, this has decent washing and toilet facilities, as well as a shop. Its restaurant has a range of hearty fare (from Sfr14) including hamburgers and schnitzels.

Basic accommodation is available at **Hotel-Pension National** (☎ 033 675 10 85; dm Sfr30-38, s/d/tr Sfr60/100/120), and the huge **Pfadfinderzentrum** (International Scout Centre; ☎ 033 675 11 39; www.kisc.ch; camp sites Sfr10.50; dm Sfr21-27). To reach the Hotel-Pension National, turn right on the main street from the train station and follow the road for 15 minutes. A further 15 minutes on, you'll come to the Pfadfinderzentrum.

Getting There & Away
Kandersteg is at the northern end of the Lötschberg Tunnel, through which the trains trundle to Goppenstein (30km from Brig) and onwards to Iselle in Italy. See www.bls.ch /autoverlad for more details. The traditional way to head south is to hike; it takes a little over five hours to get to the Gemmi Pass and a further 1¾ hours to reach Leukerbad.

GSTAAD
pop 2500 / elevation 1100m
Synonymous with the international jet set, and fittingly twinned with Cannes in France, the resort of Gstaad appears smaller than its reputation – too little for its fur-lined ski boots. Renowned as a haunt of Sean Connery, Roger Moore, minor European royalty, heiresses like Paris Hilton and various wannabes, it's a picturesque but tiny village crouched beneath the hilltop fairytale turrets of its leading hotel, the Gstaad Palace. Cartier, Gucci, Hèrmes, Louis Vuitton and Rolex are piled high in the chi-chi boutiques lining the pedestrianised Promenade, and it offers better après-ski window-shopping than actual skiing. While its principal competitive sports are seeing and being seen, ordinary mortals might enjoy the hiking opportunities.

Orientation & Information
The train station is in the centre, parallel to the main street, Hauptstrasse. Walk straight ahead past Hotel Bernerhof to Hauptstrasse, turn right and go 200m east along the pedestrian-only section to reach the centre and the tourist office.

Information
The three-day Easyaccess card (Sfr33) offers some free transport, guided tours and swimming and discounts on many activities.

There's a **tourist office** (☎ 033 748 81 81; www .gstaad.ch; Promenade; ☼ 8.30am-6.30pm Mon-Fri, 9am-noon & 1.30-5pm Sat & Sun Jul, Aug & Dec-Mar, 8.30am-noon & 1.30-6.30pm Mon-Fri, 10am-noon & 1.30-5pm Sat rest of year).

Activities
'Where does one actually ski in Gstaad?'; that's an oft-repeated complaint in this little resort. There is some **skiing**, but lifts around the village only go up to around 2200m, meaning snow is not guaranteed. Runs tend to be blue or easy red. For more varied skiing, head to neighbouring resorts like Saanen, Saanenmöser, St Stephan and Zweisimmen. These are only some of the places included in the Region Ski Gstaad, totalling 250km of runs. In all, 69 lifts are covered, some as far afield as Château d'Oex and Les Diablerets glacier (see p95). The regional pass is available for a minimum of two days (Sfr97); for single days, buy specific sectors (Sfr26 to Sfr52).

Snowboarding is better, especially above the Eggli cable car, where there are snow-making machines. From here, you can reach the Videmanette area by chairlift and this offers some more challenging pistes.

There is a plethora of other activities. **Hiking** is possible in four valleys radiating out from Gstaad. An undemanding excursion is to walk to Turbach, over the Reulisenpass, and down to St Stephan or to Lenk in the adjoining Simmen Valley (around 4½ hours total). From either resort, a train runs back to Gstaad (change at Zweisimmen).

BERNESE OBERLAND

There's **rafting** on the Saane and nearby rivers, from May to September, from about Sfr82 to Sfr108. One large operator is **Alpinzentrum Gstaad** (☎ 033 748 41 61; www .alpinzentrum.ch), which also offers climbing, glacier tours and jeep safaris. The tourist office has details of other operators, including several offering canyoning and paragliding.

Festivals & Events
During July, Gstaad hosts the annual **Allianz Suisse Open** (☎ 033 748 83 83; www.swiss opengstaad.com) tennis tournament. Quaint Saanen nearby hosts a **Yehudi Menuhin Festival** (☎ 033 748 83 33; www.menuhinfestivalgstaad.ch) of classical music every August. It's held in Saanen's 15th-century Mauritian church and in a marquee in Gstaad.

Sleeping
All hotel prices are high-season prices and drop at other times of the year.

SYHA hostel (☎ 033 744 13 43; www.youthhostel.ch /saanen; dm Sfr31; ☺ reception 8-10am & 5-9pm, 8-10am & 4-10pm winter, closed mid-Oct–mid-Dec & sometimes Apr & May) This very pleasant hostel is at Chalet Rüblihorn in nearby Saanen, just four minutes away by train.

Hotel Alphorn (☎ 033 748 45 45; www.gstaad-al phorn.ch; Gsteigstrasse; s/d Sfr130/240; **P**) Try this if you're not A list, but want to make believe (sort of). Ten minutes from the centre near the ski school, it's a rustic Swiss chalet with renovated rooms, a small bar and generous buffet breakfast.

Post Hotel Rössli (☎ 033 748 42 42; www.posthotel roessli.ch; Promenade; standard s/d Sfr140/260) Another simple chalet hotel with pleasantly renovated rooms, this time the oldest hotel in town. Only doubles are available in the high season.

Hotel Olden (☎ 033 744 34 44; www.hotelolden .com; s/d Sfr380/420) Part-owned by Formula One boss Bernie Ecclestone, this central chalet has exclusive rooms, decorated in a belle époque style with a tub or steam bath in each room.

Gstaad Palace (☎ 033 748 50 00; www.palace.ch; s/d from Sfr350/600; ❄ ✗ **P** ⛵) The ultimate in luxury, this turreted fairytale palace casts its haughty gaze over the village from its hilltop vantage point. It's another Bollywood favourite, while the resort's top disco, Green Go, is also found up here.

Eating & Drinking
Post Hotel Rössli (☎ 033 748 42 42; Promenade; mains Sfr17-27) This place has a reasonable, decently priced restaurant that serves Swiss staples.

Hotel Bernerhof (☎ 033 748 88 44; www.bern erhof-gstaad.ch; mains Sfr18-40, menus from Srf45) Another good restaurant within a hotel, with reasonable prices. It offers upmarket Chinese.

Spoon des Neiges (www.chlosterli.com; mains Sfr52-65, fixed 3-course menu Sfr105) Famed French chef Alain Ducasse has opened this restaurant in Le Chlösterli (www.chlosterli.com), an amazing restaurant/bar/club complex a 10-minute drive from town. An old Swiss inn that's been transformed with postmodern design, Chlösterli has a 6m-tall glass wall dividing the public spaces from the kitchens, a bunch of lit monitors, like a tree of fire, instead of a fireplace, and some stools that look like hay bales. There's also a cheaper restaurant, Alpen Bistro (mains Sfr35 to Sfr50).

Charly's (☎ 033 744 15 44; Promenade) Renowned for its apple tart, patisseries and chocolate, the most famous tea room in town has reopened in a new home with a huge aquarium and 'interesting' paintings on its façade.

Chesery (☎ 033 744 24 51; Lauenenstrasse; menus from Sfr140-160; ☺ noon-2pm & 6.30-9.30pm Tue-Sun Dec-Apr & Jun-Oct) Founded by the Aga Khan in the 1960s, this ritzy – and pricey – chalet

---

MOUNTAIN FEAST

If Gstaad's ritzy restaurants aren't for you, in season you can head for the area's good batch of mountain restaurants at the summit station of the cable cars up from the valley floor. The gourmet **Berghaus Eggli** (☎ 033 748 96 12) and the family-friendly **Berghaus Wispile** (☎ 033 748 96 32) even host fondue, raclette and wine evenings in winter, where guests head home on skis.

Further above Eggli is the gimmicky-but-fun **Videmanette Berghaus** (☎ 026 925 87 44), where staff dress in army uniforms and guests eat from a *Gamelle*, an army-issue food container. Above the nearby village of Schönried, **Horneggli Berghaus** (☎ 033 744 27 57) has a hunting theme. Most cheap mains are about Sfr25.

restaurant goes from strength to strength, with chef Robert Speth recently named GaultMillau chef of the year. Downstairs there's a bar.

Hush (☎ 033 748 15 00; Promenade) The sister bar of the Mayfair establishment in London and also owned by Roger Moore's son, Geoffrey (among others), this brasserie, lounge and club is a favourite haunt of the beautiful people.

Getting There & Away

Gstaad is on the Golden Pass route between Montreux (Sfr23, 1½ hours) and Spiez (Sfr24, one hour 20 minutes; change at Zweisimmen). You can get to Geneva airport (Sfr45, three hours) via Montreux. A postal bus goes to Les Diablerets (Sfr12.40, 50 minutes) about five times daily. Highway 11 is the principal road connecting Aigle and Spiez, and it passes close to Gstaad at Saanen.

Mittelland

The flat Swiss 'middle ground' embodies its nation's commitment to political compromise and linguistic plurality. Despite being home to the capital, it's not the most cosmopolitan or the most power-obsessed place in the country. Though it's largely German-speaking – with an infamously slow, lilting dialect – it retains pockets where French has equal footing.

This situation arises from history. Once an important city-state during the medieval era, Bern lost territory in the 1798 French invasion and was an unthreatening choice in establishing a capital in 1848. Geneva was too French, Zürich too German, Bern just right.

Yet, while Bern's political success has lain in being middling, its aesthetic qualities are anything but. This might be one of the most understated capitals on the planet, but it's one of the most appealing. Its 15th-century old town has an idyllic appearance, with terraced stone buildings, covered arcades, clock towers, church spires and cobbled streets. Add its compact space, laid-back pace and small-town friendliness, and its charm becomes irresistible.

Around Bern the countryside is just as benignly beautiful, with small villages and hundreds of farms dotted across rolling green hills. If the Mittelland can't claim to be the most energetic place in Switzerland, it can boast of being one of the most fertile. Fittingly, one of the products you can see being manufactured here is holey Emmental cheese, which on the international market does the trick as 'Swiss'.

Finally, along the eastern border of the region you approach Switzerland's so-called Röstigraben, or German–French linguistic divide. Here, the baroque town of Solothurn has the distinct atmosphere of a French village despite being formally German-speaking.

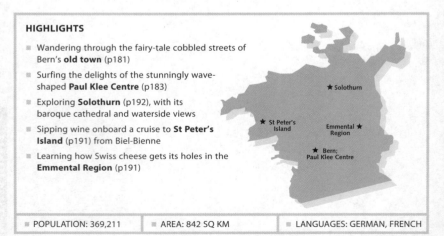

HIGHLIGHTS

- Wandering through the fairy-tale cobbled streets of Bern's **old town** (p181)
- Surfing the delights of the stunningly wave-shaped **Paul Klee Centre** (p183)
- Exploring **Solothurn** (p192), with its baroque cathedral and waterside views
- Sipping wine onboard a cruise to **St Peter's Island** (p191) from Biel-Bienne
- Learning how Swiss cheese gets its holes in the **Emmental Region** (p191)

★ Solothurn

★ St Peter's Island

Emmental ★ Region

★ Bern; Paul Klee Centre

▪ POPULATION: 369,211   ▪ AREA: 842 SQ KM   ▪ LANGUAGES: GERMAN, FRENCH

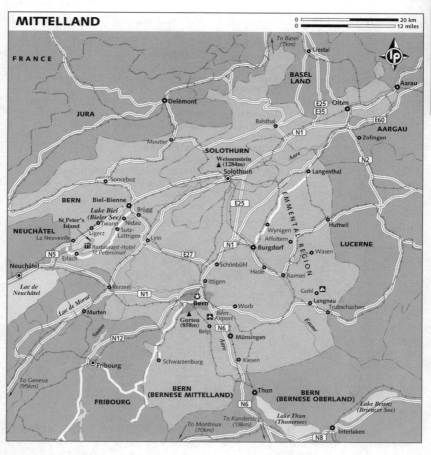

Orientation & Information

Switzerland's Mittelland (Schweizer Mittelland/Le Plateau Central) is a flat plain between the Alps and the Jura, comprising mainly the northern part of canton Bern (Berner Mittelland/Le Plateau Bernois) and the canton of Solothurn (Soleure).

The regional tourist office is **Schweizer Mittelland Tourismus** (☎ 0313 28 12 28; www.smit.ch in German), but the Bern **tourist office** (☎ 031 328 12 12) dispenses region-wide information to personal callers.

Getting There & Around

Bern has a small airport, while road and rail links into the region are excellent in every direction. Some train services within the region are operated by smaller, private companies.

BERN

pop 122,707 / elevation 540m

You won't spend long in Bern without hearing or reading the name Unesco. (Indeed, you just have.) Switzerland's capital is so proud of its medieval town centre it wants everybody to know that the UN Educational, Scientific and Cultural Organization has declared this a World Heritage Site.

No-one would argue with that 1983 protection order. On the city's long, curving and cobbled streets, lined with tall, 15th-century terraced buildings and arcades, you often feel as if you're in some kind of dizzying architectural canyon. From the surrounding hills, you're presented with an equally captivating picture of parallel rows of red roofs, all crammed on a spit of land within a bend of the Aare River.

Be warned, though: like Canberra in Australia and several other world capitals, Bern (Berne in French and sometimes in English) only got the gig by being the compromise candidate. It was simply the easiest choice for French and German speakers to agree on when the new Swiss Confederation came to life in 1848. So even today this remains an essentially provincial town –

with a parliament and bunch of bureaucrats attached.

Orientation

Because the compact town centre is contained within a sharp U-shaped river bend, access to some main streets is restricted to pedestrians and trams. The main train station is at the mouth of this 'U' and within easy reach of the main sights.

Information
BOOKSHOPS

Atlas (☎ 031 311 90 44; Schauplatzgasse 21; ⏰ 9am-6.30pm Mon-Fri, 9am-10pm Thu, 9am-4pm Sat) Travel books and backpacking accessories.

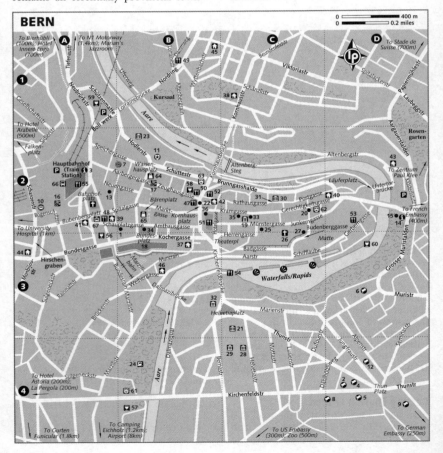

Stauffacher (☎ 031 311 24 11; Neuengasse 25;
🕑 8am-6.30pm Mon-Fri, 8am-9pm Thu, 8am-4pm Sat)
Fiction and nonfiction books in English and French.

BUSINESS HOURS
Some shops do not open Monday morning;
otherwise, business hours are standard for
Switzerland (see inside front cover).

DISCOUNT CARD
BernCard (per 24/48/72hr Sfr17/27/33) Admission to
the permanent collections of all museums, plus free public
transport and discounts on city tours.

EMERGENCY
Police station (☎ 031 321 21 21; Waisenhausplatz 32)

INTERNET ACCESS
Inside Internet Bar (www.iib.ch in German; Aarberger-
gasse 46; per hr Sfr7-9; 🕑 11-12.30am Mon-Sat, noon-
10pm Sun)

MEDICAL SERVICES
Emergency doctor, dentist, pharmacist (☎ 0900
57 67 47; 🕑 24hr)
University hospital (☎ 031 632 21 11;
Fribourgstrasse; 🕑 24hr) West of the centre, has a
casualty department.

MONEY
SBB Change office (Basement, Hauptbahnhof; 🕑 7am-
8pm Mon-Fri, 9am-5pm Sat & Sun)

POST
Main post office (Schanzenstrasse; 🕑 7.30am-9pm
Mon- Fri, 8am-4pm Sat, 4-9pm Sun)

TOURIST INFORMATION
Bern Tourismus (information ☎ 031 328 12 12, hotel
reservations ☎ 031 328 12 10; www.berninfo.com;
Ground Level, Hauptbahnhof; 🕑 9am-8.30pm daily
Jun-Sep, 9am-6.30pm Mon-Sat, 10am-5pm Sun Oct-May)
Excellent tours and free hotel bookings. The office also
distributes the informative *Bern Guide*.
Tourist office (🕑 9am-6pm daily Jun-Sep, 10am-4pm
daily Mar-May & Oct, 11am-4pm Fri-Sun Nov-Feb) Across
the river by the bear pits.

Dangers & Annoyances
Bern's hard drugs problem is less noticeable
than before, but some addicts still congregate around the train station at night.

Sights
ZYTGLOGGE & CITY FOUNTAINS
Bern's flag-bedecked medieval centre is
an attraction in its own right, with 6km of

covered arcades and cellar shops/bars descending from the streets. After a devastating fire in 1405, the city was rebuilt in today's sandstone, as opposed to the earlier wood.

An enduring focal point is Bern's clock tower or **Zytglogge** (*Zeitglockenturm* in High German), which was once part of the city's western gate (1191–1256). It's reminiscent of the Astronomical Clock in Prague's old town square in that crowds congregate to watch it chime – and then wonder why. The clock's revolving figures begin twirling at four minutes before the hour, after which the actual chimes begin. Tours enter the tower to see the clock mechanism between May and October (contact the tourist office).

It's said the clock tower helped Albert Einstein (see right) hone his theory of relativity, developed while working as a patent clerk in Bern. The great scientist surmised, while travelling on a tram away from the tower, that if the tram were going at the speed of light, the clock tower would remain on the same time, while his own watch would continue to tick – proving time was relative.

Another Bern landmark is its series of 11 decorative **fountains**. Built around 1545, they all depict characters from history and/or folklore and are concentrated along Marktgasse as it becomes Kramgasse and Gerechtigkeitsgasse. However, the most famous lies in Kornhausplatz; it's the **Kindlifresserbrunnen** (Ogre Fountain), which depicts a giant, snacking…on children.

MÜNSTER

Its lofty spire is in all senses the high point of the 15th-century Gothic **Münster** (Cathedral; tower admission payable halfway up Sfr4; ⏰ 10am-5pm Tue-Sat, 11.30am-5pm Sun Easter-Nov, 10am-noon & 2-4pm Tue-Fri, to 5pm Sat, 11.30am-2pm Sun rest of year, tower closes 30 min earlier). At 100m, it's Switzerland's tallest and those with enough energy to climb the 344 narrow winding stairs (you can stop at 254) are rewarded with stupendously vertiginous views – all the way to the Bernese Alps on a clear day.

Back on terra firma, look at the decorative **main portal** depicting the Last Judgment. The mayor of Bern is shown going to heaven, while his Zürich counterpart is being shown into hell.

Don't forget to also wander through the **Münster Plattform** behind the cathedral. This small patch of parkland drops away suddenly into a steep cliff, and you need the public **lift** (admission Sfr1.20) in the corner to travel down to Badgasse and the **Matte** (www.matte.ch in German) area on the river plain below. In good weather, a café on the platform serves coffee, cake and hot chocolate.

EINSTEIN HAUS

The world's most famous scientist developed his special theory of relativity in Bern in 1905, and the small **Einstein Museum** (☎ 031 312 00 91; www.einstein-bern.ch; Kramgasse 49; adult/student & senior Sfr6/4.50; ⏰ 10am-7pm Apr-Oct, 1-5pm Tue-Fri, noon-4pm Sat Feb, Mar & Nov–mid-Dec, closed mid-Dec–Jan) was given a facelift recently to celebrate the centenary of that discovery.

The humble apartment where Einstein lived with his young family while working as a low-paid clerk in the Bern patent office has been redecorated in the style of the time. However, numerous multimedia displays now flesh out the story of the subsequent general equation – $E=MC^2$, or energy equals mass times the speed of light squared – which fundamentally changed humankind's understanding of space, time and the universe.

Upstairs, there's a short biographical film; choose between the German, French and English soundtrack.

BUNDESHÄUSER

The 1902 **Houses of Parliament** (☎ 031 322 85 22; www.parliament.ch, www.bundeshaus.ch in German; Bundesplatz), the home of the Swiss Federal Assembly, are built in an impressive Florentine style, and contain statues of the nation's founding fathers, a stained-glass dome adorned with cantonal emblems and a huge, 214-bulb chandelier. When the Parliament is in recess, there are hourly free 45-minute **tours** (⏰ 9am-4pm Mon-Sat, plus 5pm, 6pm & 7pm Thu) in different languages. During parliamentary sessions, you can watch from the public gallery. A passport or other national ID is always needed to gain entry.

The car park in front of the parliament was reclaimed for public use during the recent refurbishment of Bundesplatz. At night, 26 illuminated **water jets**, representing every Swiss canton, now spout from the square's pavement. However, these are frequently turned off during the day for markets and other events.

BÄRENGRABEN & ROSENGARTEN

Bern sounds like it has something to do with bears, and indeed it does. Founded in 1191 by Berthold V, a powerful Duke of Zähringen, the city derived its name from his first hunting success in the area – a bear, or *Bärn* in the local dialect. Today, there are still **Bärengraben** (bear pits; ⊙ 9am-5.30pm Apr-Sep, 9am-4pm Oct-Mar) in the city, where five animals live. They're very cute and undoubtedly well cared for, but animal lovers might not approve. Even the authorities are considering a replacement 'bear park'.

Next door, in the tourist office (see p181 for opening times), you'll find the **Bern Show**. This is a 'multimedia' display explaining Bern's history using a huge model of the city and other props; kids love it even if their parents might find it a bit tacky. There's a rolling programme of 20-minute English, German and French versions.

Up the hill is the fragrant **Rosengarten** (rose garden), where the view over the town is stupendous.

ZENTRUM PAUL KLEE

The **Paul Klee Centre** (☎ 031 359 01 01; www.zpk .org; Monument in Fruchtland 3; adult/child/concession Sfr14/6/12, special exhibitions extra Sfr2; ⊙ 10am-5pm Tue-Sun, 10am-9pm Thu) is Bern's Guggenheim, an eye-catching building by an acclaimed contemporary architect filled with popular modern art.

Renzo Piano's remarkable building curves up and down like ocean waves, forming three 'hills' in the agricultural landscape on the outskirts of town. It's a pity about the main road whizzing by, but the architecture is a refreshing blast of modernity in olde worlde Bern.

The structure's middle hill houses the main exhibition space, showcasing 4000 rotating works from Paul Klee's prodigious and often playful career. Interactive computer displays built into the seating mean you can get the low-down on all the Swiss-born artist's major pieces.

The other two 'hills' are given over to conferences, concerts, administration and a hands-on **children's museum** (admission Sfr15).

The best way to get here is take bus No 12 from Bubenbergplatz to Zentrum Paul Klee, but if you take tram No 5 from Bahnhofplatz to Ostring, you will also be within walking distance. Both services run regularly.

HISTORICHES MUSEUM BERN

Blockbuster exhibitions have dominated the **Bern Historical Museum** (☎ 031 350 77 11; www.bhm .ch; Helvetiaplatz 5; special exhibitions adult/concession Sfr13/8; ⊙ 10am-5pm Tue-Sun, 10am-8pm Wed) in recent years. A superb, nearly two-year-long exhibition on Einstein and $E=MC^2$ winds down at the end of 2006, by which time work will be underway on a new building for special exhibitions. By 2008, the permanent collection, including a marvellous selection of tapestries, will be back in the main building.

KUNSTMUSEUM

The permanent collection at the **Museum of Fine Arts** (☎ 031 328 09 44; www.kunstmuseumbern.ch in German; Hodlerstrasse 8-12; adult/student Sfr7/5, special exhibitions Sfr8-18; ⊙ 10am-9pm Tue, 10am-5pm Wed-Sun) includes works by Italian artists such as Fra Angelico, Swiss artists like Ferninand Hodler, and others such as Picasso and Dali. However, it's the interesting temporary exhibits you want to watch out for.

OTHER MUSEUMS

The following are all near Helvetiaplatz, on the southern side of the Kirchenfeldbrücke.

The **Museum für Kommunikation** (Museum of Communication; ☎ 031 357 55 55; www.mfk.ch; Helvetiastrasse 16; for either permanent or special exhibitions adult/concession Sfr9/6, combined Sfr13/10; ⊙ 10am-5pm Tue-Sun) houses items from antique phones and stamps to electronic communication.

The **Schweizerisches Alpines Museum** (Swiss Alpine Museum; ☎ 031 351 04 40; www.alpinesmuseum.ch; Helvetiaplatz 4; adult/concession Sfr9/6; ⊙ 2-5pm Mon, 10am-5pm Tue-Sun) outlines the history of Alpine mountaineering and cartography, with the help of impressive relief maps.

Items at the **Naturhistorisches Museum** (Natural History Museum; ☎ 031 350 71 11; www.nmbe.unibe .ch in German; Bernastrasse 15; adult/student Sfr7/5; ⊙ 2-5pm Mon, 9am-5pm Tue-Fri, 9am-6pm Wed, 10am-5pm Sat & Sun) include the taxidermied, moth-eaten remains of Barry, the most famous St Bernard rescue dog.

GURTEN

A little over 3km south of the town centre is the Gurten hill, whose peak boasts two restaurants, a miniature railway and an adventure playground. You can also enjoy fine views as you hike down the mountain (about one hour), following the clearly marked paths. To get here, take tram No 9 heading to Wabern, alight at Gurtenbahn and change to the **funicular** (www.gurtenbahn.ch in German; adult one way/return Sfr5/9, child Sfr2.50/4.50; ☼ 7.10am-10pm) to the top. You can also do this whole trip on the Sfr12 version of the city pass.

Activities

In summer, the open-air **Marzili pools** (www.aare marzili.ch in German; admission free; ☼ May-Sep), beside the Aare River, are the perfect place to get a tan; there's even a topless bathing area. Only strong swimmers should take a dip in the river itself.

Red-signed bicycle routes run parallel to the river and the city provides free loans of bikes, via the scheme **Bern Rollt** (☎ 079 277 28 57; www.bernrollt.ch in German; huts at Bahnhofplatz & the western end of Zeughausgasse; ☼ 7.30am-9.30pm daily May-Oct). ID and a refundable Sfr20 are required as a deposit.

Walking Tour

Start at Bundesplatz, in front of the **Parliament** (**1**; p182). After enjoying the water jets (if they're turned on), head straight ahead past the right side of the building down a small flight of stairs and follow the terrace around to the left. From here, you have an excellent view across the River Aare. At Casinoplatz, turn left and right again until you come to the square facing the **Cathedral** (**2**; p182). The fountain over your left shoulder is the **Moses fountain** (**3**). Veer right into the small park behind the cathedral, the so-called **Münster Plattform** (**4**; p182). Now catch the **lift** (**5**; admission Sfr1.20) down to the area on the river plain known as **Matte** (**6**). The district of craftsmen, dockworkers and ar-

---

WALK FACTS

Distance 5km
Time 1½ hours

---

tisans during medieval times, it had its own distinctive dialect. More recently, during the floods of 1999 and 2005, Matte suffered extensive flood damage, and some evidence of that could still be visible.

Continue until you come to **Laüferplatz** (**7**), with its fountain depicting the cheeky city herald who once allegedly told off the French king for not understanding Bernese German. Cross **Untertorbrücke** (**8**). Here you could add to the walk by heading up and back to the **Rosengarten** (**9**; p183) for a brilliant view of the city's red rooftops. For a less taxing circuit, however, loop right until you come to the **bear pits** (**10**; p183).

Now it's time to plunge into the heart of the old district. Walk right up Gerechtigkeitsgasse into Kramgasse. These two historic streets were very recently repaved and the small stream between the city fountains restored. As you head away from the bear pits, you'll pass the **Gerechtigkeits fountain** (**11**), the **Samson fountain** (**12**) and **Zähringer fountain** (**13**). At Kreuzgasse, make a little detour to see the **Rathaus** (town hall; **14**), before heading for the tour's endpoint, the **Clock Tower** (**15**; p181).

Bern for Children

Young children find Bern particularly enchanting, with its romantic old town, **clock tower** (p181) and storybook **fountains** (p181). They don't worry too much about the morality of the **bear pits** (p183), and they love the **Bern Show** (p183) much more than their adult companions. To keep little ones fresh, jump on a tram for some of your sightseeing or, with older children, borrow free city bikes from **Bern Rollt** (left).

As part of the children's museum at the **Paul Klee Centre** (p183) there's an open studio where children four years and over are encouraged to create their own works of art, based on Klee's designs. The **Museum**

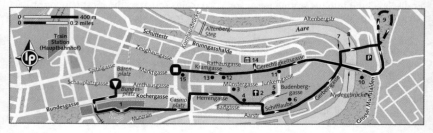

of **Communication** (p183) and **Natural History Museum** (p183) also have visual elements that will appeal.

Older boys might enjoy a tour of the **Stade de Suisse** (p188) football stadium, while an outing to **Gurten** (p183) seems tailor-made for young families.

Bern also has a **zoo** (☎ 031 357 15 15; www .tierpark-bern.ch; ⏰ 8am-6.30pm summer, 9am-5pm rest of year), take tram No 19 to Tierpark to get there, and **puppet theatre** (☎ 031 311 95 85; www .berner-puppentheater.ch; Gerechtigkeitsgasse 31).

Festivals & Events

Bern canton has a public holiday on 2 January (Berchtoldstag). On the fourth Monday in November, Bern hosts its famous **onion market** (*Zibelemärit*), where traders take over the town centre. Legend has it that the market dates back to the great fire of 1405, when farmers of Fribourg canton helped the Bernese to recover and were allowed to sell their produce in Bern as a reward. In reality, the market probably began as part of Martinmas, the medieval festival celebrating the start of winter. In any case, today the onion market is an excuse for pure, often bizarre, revelry, as people walk around throwing confetti and hitting each other on the head with plastic hammers, while many street performers add to the carnival atmosphere.

Bern has a **jazz festival** (www.jazzfestivalbern.ch) in early May and hosts the **Gurten Rock Festival** (www.gurtenfestival.ch in German) in mid-July. August's **Aare swimming race** (www.aareschwuemme.ch in German) is a lively spectacle.

Sleeping

BUDGET

Hostels

Hotel Glocke Backpackers Bern (☎ 031 311 37 71; www.bernbackpackers.com; Rathausgasse 75; dm 1st/ subsequent nights Sfr36/31, tw Sfr39/44, s/d without bathroom Sfr70/125, d with bathroom Sfr165; 🖥 ✖) Reasonably new bedrooms, clean bathrooms, a kitchen and sociable lounge make this many backpackers' first choice, but its central location also means plenty of street noise. Dorms are mixed occupancy.

SYHA hostel (☎ 031 311 63 16; www.youthhostel.ch /bern; Weihergasse 4; dm Sfr35; ⏰ reception 7-10am & 3-10pm, 5-10pm winter) Scenically located by the river, below the Parliament building and well away from traffic noise, this is a large,

friendly hostel, although the building is not particularly new. The paths down the hill are signposted, or take the Marzilibahn funicular (one way Sfr1.10).

Hotels

Hotel National (☎ 031 381 19 88; www.nationalbern.ch in German; Hirschengraben 24; s/d without bathroom from Sfr55/100, s/d/f with bathroom Sfr85/130/180; 🖥) A quaint, charming hotel, the National wouldn't be out of place in Paris, with its wrought-iron lift, sprigs of lavender and Persian rugs over newly surfaced (but still creaky) wooden floors. The friendly owners leave the doors of vacant rooms open, so you can look in and choose the one you fancy.

Marthahaus Garni (☎ 031 332 41 35; www.martha haus.ch; Wyttenbachstrasse 22a; dm Sfr39, s/d without bathroom Sfr65/95, s/d/tr with bathroom & TV Sfr110 /125/155; 🖥 ✖) Located in a residential location, this five-storey building feels like a friendly boarding house. Clean, simple rooms have lots of white and a smattering of modern art, plus there's a kitchen. Take tram No 9 to Viktoriaplatz.

Hotel Landhaus (☎ 031 331 41 66; www.landhaus bern.ch; Altenbergstrasse 4; dm Sfr30, d without bathroom from Sfr110, d/f with bathroom from Sfr140/180; 🖥 ✖ 🅿) This historic hotel has a stripped-back modern interior, with spiral wooden stairs and spacious individually renovated rooms. There's a very relaxed, friendly atmosphere and a guest kitchen. Only the claustrophobic, stall-like dorms prove a disappointment.

Camping

Camping Eichholz (☎ 031 961 26 02; www.camping eichholz.ch; Strandweg 49; camp sites per person/car Sfr7.50/3.50, tent Sfr7-9, bungalows per person Sfr17.50-25; ⏰ May-Sep; 🖥) The nicest place to camp near Bern is south of the city, near the river. Take tram No 9 to Wabern to get there.

MIDRANGE

With government workers accounting for a large proportion of their clientele, many midrange hotels sport a brisk, businesslike atmosphere.

Hotel Belle Epoque (☎ 031 311 43 36; www.belle -epoque.ch; Gerechtigkeitsgasse 18; s/d Sfr245/340; 🖥 ✖) A lovely and romantic old-town hotel with opulent Art Deco furnishings, the Belle Epoque's standards are so exacting it even cleverly tucks away modern aberrations –

MITTELLAND

like the TV – into steamer-trunk-style cupboards, so as not to spoil the look. It costs less on weekends.

Hotel Arabelle (☎ 031 301 03 05; www.arabelle .ch; Mittelstrasse 6; s Sfr120-135, d Sfr135-195; ☐ ☒) Small rooms feature bright colour schemes and parquet floors, adding character to what could have been a merely functional hotel. Nicer than its central sister, the Ador, it's only a short bus ride from the train station. Take bus No 12 to Mittelstrasse to get there.

Hotel Allegro (☎ 031 339 55 00; www.allegro-hotel .ch; Kornhausstrasse 3; s/d with views from Sfr250/290, without views Sfr215/255, ste from Sfr600; ☒ ☐ ☒) Cool and modern without being too pretentious, this curved sliver of a building just above the old town offers excellent views from its front rooms. Others look down into the unusual atrium. Decor ranges from sleek 'Asiatic' to brassy 'Broadway' and there's even a Paul Klee–themed suite. Suites cost Sfr400 on weekends.

Hotel Astoria (☎ 031 378 66 66; www.astoria-bern .ch; Zieglerstrasse 66/Eigerplatz; s/d from Sfr130/180; ☐ ☒ ℙ) Not too soulless inside for a business hotel, the Astoria creates a sense of cosiness with dark-wood panelling and fluffy white duvets. It's also five minutes from the centre.

Hotel Bären (☎ 031 311 33 67; www.baerenbern .ch; Schauplatzgasse 4 & 10; s Sfr150-220, d Sfr200-300; ☐ ☒) You're paying for the supremely convenient location and thoroughly professional service in this hotel and its sister. The rooms are clean, comfortable and modern, but relatively generic and small. Its sister hotel, Hotel Bristol (☎ 031 311 01 01; www.bristolbern .ch; Schauplatzgasse 10), offers the same services and rates.

Hotel Innere Enge (☎ 031 309 61 11; www.zghotels .ch; Engestrasse 54; s/d from Sfr220/260; ☐ ☒ ℙ) Not tonight, Josephine. But the French empress did stay (c 1810) in this historic mansion, set in parkland on the edge of town. After waking to Alpine views in your Art Nouveau room, saunter down to breakfast in the unforgettable park pavilion and spend your nights in the attached Marian's Jazzroom.

The following are also available:

Hotel City (☎ 031 311 53 77; www.hotelcity.ch; Bubenbergplatz 7; s/d Sfr130/180) Generously sized rooms that are slick and modern, although overwhelmingly pale green. Very central location.

La Pergola (☎ 031 381 91 46; www.hotel-lapergola .ch; Belpstrasse 43; s/d Sfr120/150) Another good-value

business hotel that's not too sterile. About 10 minutes from the centre.

TOP END
Bellevue Palace (☎ 031 320 45 45; www.bellevue-palace .ch; Kochergasse 3-5; s/d Sfr350/460; ☒ ☐ ☒ ℙ) Bern's power brokers, and international statesmen like Nelson Mandela, gravitate towards Bern's only five-star hotel. Near the parliament, and recently renovated, it's the address to choose if you need to impress. Rates are cheaper on weekends.

Eating
BUDGET
Markthalle (Bubenbergplatz 9) This buzzing central arcade is full of cheap eateries, serving everything from pizza slices and kebabs to noodles. Most places have stools perched at bars or stand up tables.

Sous le Pont (☎ 031 306 69 55; Schützenmatte; snacks & light meals from Sfr5-15; ⏱ 11.30am-2pm & 6pm-midnight Tue-Fri, 6pm-2am Sat) Organic meat and lots of vegetarian options are on the menu in the semichaotic surrounds of Reitschule (see p188). Every Wednesday evening, there's a speciality evening showcasing a different cuisine.

There's also an outlet of the vegetarian buffet restaurant **Tibits** (meals per 100g Sfr3.70) in the main train station.

MIDRANGE & TOP END
Kornhauskeller (☎ 031 327 72 72; Kornhausplatz 18; most mains around Sfr32-38; ⏱ 11.45am-2.30pm & 6pm-12.30am Mon-Sat, 6-11.30pm Sun, bar 5pm-1am Mon-Wed, 5pm-2am Thu-Sat, 5pm-12.30am Sun) Bern's surprisingly ornate former granary is now a stunning subterranean restaurant. Below tall vaulted arches covered in frescoes, well-dressed diners enjoy Mediterranean cuisine; on the mezzanine level above, beautiful people sip cocktails alongside historic stained-glass windows. With a neighbouring café as well, this is, in many ways, just as good as Schwellenmätteli (see opposite).

Santorini (☎ 031 312 18 12; Gerberngasse 34; mains Sfr20-40; ⏱ 11.30am-2pm & 5pm-midnight Tue-Fri, 5pm-midnight Sat) Probably Bern's sole GaultMilau-rated Greek/Mediterranean restaurant, Santorini is one of many good reasons to come to the Matte quarter, reopened after the 2005 floods.

Lorenzini (☎ 031 310 50 67; Hotelgasse 10; mains Sfr20-55; ⏱ 11.30am-2.30pm & 6-11.30pm Mon-Fri, to

AUTHOR'S CHOICE

Schwellenmätteli (☎ 031 350 50 01; Damazi-
quai 11; meals Sfr18-55; ☯ 9am-11pm) 'Bern's
Riveria' announces a sign near these two
very classy restaurants on the Aare, and the
experience certainly shouldn't be missed.
At night, the cool glass cube that is the
restaurant Terrasse overlooks an illuminated weir, while Casa behind it enjoys a
cosier atmosphere. Both concentrate on
Italian/Mediterranean–influenced cuisine,
although you can come for just a coffee
or drink on the open-air terrace.

midnight Sat) The Lorenzini complex of bars,
enotoca (lounge) and Italian restaurant is
popular with a young professional crowd
looking for merely a coffee and panini, or
a full meal of home-made pasta or other
Tuscan cuisine.

Altes Tramdepot (☎ 031 368 14 15; Am Bärengraben;
mains Sfr18-38, menus Sfr15-25; ☯ 11am-midnight)
Don't be deterred by its touristy location by
the bear pits; even locals recommend this
cavernous microbrewery. Swiss specialities
sit alongside international dishes with an occasional Australian bent. Plus, there's a separate children's menu.

Ringgenberg (☎ 031 311 25 40; Kornhausplatz 19;
mains Sfr20-42; ☯ 11.15am-2.15pm & 5.30-10pm Mon-Sat)
Despite the pristine white tablecloths, this is
a relaxed, brasserie-style eatery, with an emphasis on modern Mediterranean cuisine.

Du Nord (☎ 031 332 23 38; Lorrainestrasse 2; mains from
Sfr17-35; ☯ 8-12.30am Mon-Fri, 9-12.30am Sat, 4-11.30pm
Sun) This gay-friendly casual restaurant in the
Lorraine quarter serves well-priced modern
international cuisine to a trendy, alternative
crowd. It also has a bar and hosts occasional
gigs.

Anker (☎ 031 311 11 13; Kornhausplatz 16; mains
Sfr16-35; ☯ 7.30am-11.30pm Mon-Thu, 7.30am-midnight
Fri & Sat, 9.30am-6pm Sun) Unleash your inner
tourist in this smoky Swiss restaurant, where
the usual fondues, röstis etc are dished up on
kitschy red-and-white check tablecloths.

Della Casa (☎ 031 311 21 42; Schauplatzgasse 16;
mains Sfr28-40; ☯ 8am-11.30pm Mon-Fri, 8am-3pm Sat)
Offering a much more refined take on the
local cuisine, this historic old restaurant
specialises in different types of *Bernerplatte*,
selections of meat with sauerkraut, potatoes
and beans.

Drinking

Bern has a very healthy nightlife, with more
bars than any guidebook could list. See the
Bern Guide, available from the tourist office, for more details.

BARS & LOUNGES

Kornhauskeller (opposite) and Altes Tramdepot, (opposite) and several clubs, also
have bars.

Eclipse (☎ 318 47 00; Gurtengasse 6; ☯ 7-12.30am
Mon-Wed, 7-3.30am Thu-Sat) These neighbouring bars are popular with hip young 20-
somethings. During the day, people come
for snacks, lunch or merely to chill out on
the lounge chairs, but come evening they're
heaving with eager wannabes out for a good
time with cocktails and DJs.

Art Cafe (☎ 318 20 70; Gurtengasse 6; ☯ 7-12.30am
Mon-Wed, 7-3.30am Thu-Sat) Sister establishment
of Eclipse.

Pery Bar (☎ 311 59 08; Schmiedenplatz 3; ☯ from
5pm Mon-Sat) Another popular venue with a
young crowd, the Pery Bar boasts a good-
time atmosphere and pavement tables in
summer.

Café des Pyrenees (Kornhausplatz 17; ☯ Mon-Sat)
With its mixed crowd of wine-quaffing cli-
ents, this lovely Bohemian joint has the atmosphere of a traditional Parisian café/bar.

Du Theatre (☎ 031 311 17 71; Hotelgasse 10; ☯ from
6pm Mon-Sat) Part of the upmarket Lorenzini
complex, this chic lounge bar has a cool
30-something crowd parked on its plump
1970s leather sofas. But even slightly older
drinkers are also in evidence at DüDü, as it's
affectionately called.

NIGHTCLUBS

Bierhübli (☎ 031 301 92 92; Neubruckstrasse 43; ☯ lounge
from 7pm Mon-Sat, club according to programme) The
huge old hall here (with balcony) hosts
mainstream international bands and various
club nights, but the chic DJ lounge is open
six nights a week. In summer, there's a beer
garden. Take bus No 11 to Bierhübli to get
there.

Wasserwerk (☎ 031 312 12 31; www.wasserwerkclub
.ch; Wasserwerkgasse 5; ☯ Thu-Sat, some Wed) The
main techno venue in town, this has a bar,
club and sometimes live music. It boasts
that both Moby and the Prodigy played
here in their heyday. An alternative cinema, Cinematte, sits around the side of the
building.

Reitschule (☎ 031 306 69 52; www.reitschule.ch in German; Schützenmatte; ☺ daily) While determinedly cleaning up its act this infamous – and ramshackle – centre for alternative arts, music and theatre still attracts local slackers, students and curious tourists.

Gaskessel (☎ 031 372 49 00; www.gaskessel.ch; Sandrainstrasse 25) Inside this graffiti-covered domed building in Marzili is another counter-cultural centre, with lots of trance and rap and some popular gay evenings.

Entertainment

PERFORMING ARTS & CLASSICAL MUSIC

Dampfzentrale (☎ 031 311 63 37; www.dampfzentrale .ch in German; Marzilistrasse 47) This refined performing-arts centre combines jazz, funk and soul music gigs with avant-garde art exhibitions and dance. It's in a pleasant riverside spot and serves a brilliant Sunday brunch.

Stadttheater Bern (☎ 031 329 51 51; www.stad theaterbern.ch; Kornhausplatz 20) Opera, dance and classic music are performed here, as well as German-language plays.

SPORT

Bern's new 32,000-seat **Stade de Suisse** (www .stadedesuisse.ch in German & French; tours adult/child Sfr20/15) will be one of four Swiss venues when Austria and Switzerland co-host football's Euro 2008 championship. Built over the demolished Wankdorf Stadium (which hosted the 1954 World Cup final) the new stadium is home to the local Young Boys team and already hosts international matches.

Outside matches, tours of the ground are available. The complex, which is topped by the world's largest expanse of solar panelling ($8000m^2$), also contains shops and restaurants.

Shopping

The shops situated in the western half of Bern's old town are considered more affordable, while those to the east are more exclusive.

There are open-air **vegetable, fruit and flower markets** (Bärenplatz & Bundesplatz) each Tuesday and Saturday (daily in summer). Waisenhausplatz has a general market on Tuesday and Saturday. On the first Saturday of the month there's a craft market in front of the cathedral.

Getting There & Away

AIR

Bern-Belp airport (☎ 031 960 21 21; www.flughafen bern.ch) is a small airport with connections to London City and Lugano on **Darwin Airline** (www.darwinairline.ch) and to Munich on Lufthansa, among others. **Fly Be** (www.flybe.com) also flies here from Birmingham and Southampton in England.

BUS & TRAIN

Postal buses depart from the western side of the train station. By rail, there are services at least hourly to most destinations, including Geneva (Sfr45, 1¾ hours), Basel (Sfr36, 70 minutes), Interlaken Ost (Sfr25, 50 minutes) and Zürich (Sfr45, one hour).

CAR & MOTORCYCLE

There are three motorways intersecting in the city's north. The N1 (E25) is the route from Neuchâtel in the west and Basel and Zürich in the northeast. The N6 connects Bern with Thun and the Interlaken region in the southeast. The N12 (E27) is the route from Geneva and Lausanne in the southwest.

There are several underground parking spots in the city centre, including one at the train station (Sfr2.50 per hour). 'Park & Ride' parking is free at Guisanplatz, Wankdorf in the north, Neufeld in the northwest and Gangloff, Bümpliz in the southwest.

Getting Around

TO/FROM THE AIRPORT

There's a shuttle bus (Sfr15 one way, 20 minutes) between Bern-Belp airport and the train station, which is coordinated with flight arrivals and departures. A **taxi** (☎ 031 333 55 55) costs about Sfr40.

BUS & TRAM

Getting around on foot is easy in the centre, but buses and trams operate. Tickets, available from dispensers at stops, cost Sfr1.90 (maximum six stops) or Sfr3.20. A day pass for the city network is Sfr12 (Zones 10/11). If you're planning on clubbing, **Moonliner** (www.moonliner.ch in German) night buses depart Friday and Saturday nights from Bahnhofplatz at 12.45am, 2am and 3.15am; passes aren't valid and fares start at Sfr5.

BIEL-BIENNE

pop 49,157 / elevation 429m
Situated right on the *Röstigraben*, Switzerland's French–German divide, double-barrelled Biel-Bienne is the country's most bilingual town. Locals switch language fluently in mid-conversation, and sometimes it's difficult to know which one to choose.

In nobody's language is this Switzerland's most picturesque town. Despite a reasonably well-preserved historic centre and an interesting, slightly grungy alternative culture, it's the lake that laps Biel-Bienne's shores that's its biggest draw.

Orientation & Information

Biel-Bienne is at the northern end of Lake Biel (Bieler See, Lac de Bienne). The train station lies between the lake and the old town and has bicycle-rental and money-exchange counters. The old town is about a 10-minute walk north of the station (or take bus No 1).

Main post office (☎ 032 321 18 40; Bahnhofplatz 2; 🕐 7.30am-6.30pm Mon-Fri, 8am-4pm Sat)

Tourist office (☎ 032 329 84 84; www.biel-seeland.net; Bahnhofplatz 12; 🕐 8am-12.30pm & 1.30-6pm Mon-Fri, to 8pm Thu, 9am-3pm Sat)

Sights & Activities

At the heart of the old town lies the **Ring**, a plaza with a 16th-century fountain. The

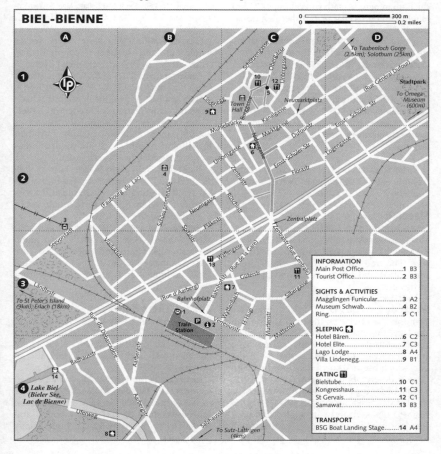

INFORMATION	
Main Post Office	1 B3
Tourist Office	2 B3

SIGHTS & ACTIVITIES	
Magglingen Funicular	3 A2
Museum Schwab	4 B2
Ring	5 C1

SLEEPING	
Hotel Bären	6 C2
Hotel Elite	7 C3
Lago Lodge	8 A4
Villa Lindenegg	9 B1

EATING	
Bielstube	10 C1
Kongresshaus	11 C3
St Gervais	12 C1
Samawat	13 B3

TRANSPORT	
BSG Boat Landing Stage	14 A4

name harks back to bygone days when justice was dispensed here. The community bigwigs would sit in an intimidating semicircle to pass judgment on the unfortunate miscreants brought before them. Leading from the Ring is Burggasse, where there's the step-gabled town hall and theatre, the Fountain of Justice (1744) and shuttered houses.

Outside town, the **Magglingen funicular** (Seilbahn Magglingen, Funiculaire Macolin; ☎ 032 322 45 11; www.funic.ch in German & French; Seevorstadt; one way/return Sfr2.60/4.20) takes you up the Magglingen hill, where there are hikes and views.

Roughly a 30-minute walk along the road to Solothurn (or take bus No 1) is the **Taubenloch Gorge** (Taubenlochschlucht, Les gorges du Taubenloch). A path runs along its 2.5km length (no entry charge, but there's a donation box).

There are a couple of museums in town, the best of which include these:

Museum Schwab (☎ 032 322 76 03; Seevorstadt 50; admission Sfr5; ☺ 10am-noon & 2-5pm Tue-Sat, 11am-5pm Sun) It contains prehistoric relics from around the lakes of Biel, Murten and Neuchâtel.

Omega-Museum (☎ 032 344 92 11; Stämpflistrasse 96; ☺ on request) It showcases notable watches, from that worn by Lawrence of Arabia, to one that's been to the moon.

Bieler Braderie, held on the last weekend in June, is one of the biggest markets in the country.

Sleeping

Sutz-Lattrigen (☎ 032 397 13 45; www.camping-sutz .ch in German; camp sites per person/car Sfr10/6, tent Sfr7-9; ☺ Apr-Oct) This is a well-equipped site by the lake. The train to Sutz runs every 30 minutes (Sfr3) and brings you to within 1km of the site.

Lago Lodge (☎ 032 331 37 32; www.lagolodge .ch; Uferweg 5; dm Sfr25-30, s/d Sfr57/74; ☺ reception 10am-10pm; ▯) Between the train station and the lake, this place resembles an American motel, with its simple rooms laid out in a row over two storeys. Reception is in the bar, which brews its own delicious beer and is accordingly popular. Breakfast costs Sfr8.

Villa Lindenegg (☎ 032 322 94 66; www.lindenegg .ch in German & French; Lindenegg 5; s Sfr95-175, d Sfr150-250; ℗) Tucked away in a pleasant park just minutes from the centre, this small 19th-century villa offers elegance and per-

sonal service at a very affordable price. The rooms are a mix of modern and historic, and a few have balconies.

Hotel Elite (☎ 032 328 77 77; www.hotelelite.ch; Bahnhofstrasse/Rue de la Gare 14; s/d Sfr190/280, Fri & Sat Sfr150/190; ▯ ✖ ℗) The renovated Art Deco rooms are light and airy in this most upmarket of Biel hotels, providing every luxury you need.

Hotel Bären (☎ 032 322 45 73; www.rel-rutschi.ch; Nidaugasse 22; s/d Sfr100/150) This central hotel provides a good back-up option, with pleasant enough rooms. Reception is in the restaurant below.

Eating

St Gervais (☎ 032 322 48 22; Untergasse/Rue Basse 21; menus Sfr14.50; ☺ 9.30-12.30am Mon & Wed-Sat, 9.30am-3pm Tue, 2pm-12.30am Sun) Underneath vaulted arches, or at its popular pavement tables, this alternative-style eatery serves wholesome and frequently organic dishes, from curries to Italian-influenced dishes.

Samawat (☎ 032 323 88 81; Waffengasse/Rue des Armes 1; mains Sfr14.50-27.50; ☺ 9am-11pm Tue-Sat, 11.30am-8pm Sun) A delightful, slightly kitsch Afghani café/restaurant reflecting Biel-Bienne's growing multi-ethnicity, this serves a wide range of dishes, including Afghan tortellini with lentil sauce and yogurt. Samawat is closed for two weeks in August.

Bielstube (☎ 032 322 65 88; Rosius 18; mains Sfr20-36; ☺ 11am-2.30pm & 6pm-midnight Mon-Fri, from 9am Sat) An intriguing mix of Creole and Swiss food is served by this historic restaurant in the middle of the old town.

Kongresshaus (☎ 032 329 19 60; Zentralstrasse 60; menus Sfr15.50-18.50; ☺ 11am-11pm) Cheap lunch menus, vegetarian and meat-based, are served in the restaurant of this most unusual 1950s building – an A-line shape made from concrete.

Getting There & Away

Biel-Bienne can easily be reached by train from Bern (Sfr14.20, 30 minutes), Solothurn (Sfr10.40, 20 minutes), Neuchâtel (Sfr11.40, 20 minutes) and Murten (Sfr12.40, 50 minutes).

However, a more enjoyable connection in summer is by **BSG boat** (☎ 032 329 88 11; www.bieler see.ch in German & French). Services go to Murten (one way/return Sfr37/72, four hours) and Neuchâtel (Sfr24.80/49.80, 2½ hours) daily in summer.

Solothurn can be reached along the Aare River. There are five departures per day (except on Monday) and it takes around 2½ hours (Sfr25/50). See also p193.

AROUND BIEL-BIENNE

Several wine-growing villages line the western shore of Lake Biel, while the nature reserve of **St Peter's Island** (St Peterinsel/Île de St Pierre) lies in the middle. Actually, falling water levels mean this is no longer an island proper, but a long, thin promontory jutting out into the lake from the southwest shore near Erlach. It is possible to take a 1¼-hour stroll along this causeway from Erlach, but because of the difficulties in reaching Erlach from Biel-Bienne (you need to catch a train to La Neuveville and an infrequent bus to Erlach) it's easiest to catch a boat from Biel-Bienne (Sfr13.40, 50 minutes).

Political theorist Jean-Jacques Rousseau spent, he said, the happiest time of his life on St Peterinsel and the 11th-century monastery where he resided is now the renowned **Restaurant-Hotel St Petersinsel** (☎ 032 338 11 14; www.st-petersinsel.ch in German & French; d Sfr220-270, s/d without bathroom Sfr95/155).

Visiting the island makes a relaxing day trip and if you buy a return ticket (Sfr26.80), you're entitled to get off and on as often as you like, including at the wine-growing villages of **Twann/Douanne** and **Ligerz/Gléresse**. The latter has a **funicular** (www.vinifuni.ch in German & French; adult one way Sfr5.20) to the hilltop settlement of Prêles, where there are views to the Bernese Alps on a clear day.

If you're more interested in swimming, there are spots at Erlach, on St Peter's Island and at La Neuville.

The neighbouring Lac de Neuchâtel and Lake Murten are connected to Bieler See by canal, and day-long tours of all three lakes are offered from 13 May to 20 October. Boats are run by two boat companies: **BSG** (☎ 032 329 88 11; www.bielersee.ch in German & French), based in Biel, and **LNM** (☎ 032 729 96 00), based in Neuchâtel. The three-lake tours depart around 9am to 10am, but ring ahead, as timetables change yearly; expect to pay about Sfr56 (with BSG) or Sfr52 (for a day-pass with LNM). Other regular lake services operate only in spring and summer, though there are special cruises (eg fondue evenings) in winter and autumn.

EMMENTAL REGION

Holey cheese, Batman! Sorry, that really *was* cheesy, but then, having given its name to one of Switzerland's most famous dairy products, the yellow stuff is what the Emmental Region is largely about. The valley (Tal in German) of the Emme River is a rural idyll east of Bern. Picturesque towns and villages, full of chalets with overhanging roofs, line the riverbanks.

Orientation & Information

Emmental tourist office (☎ 034 402 42 52; www .emmental.ch in German; Schlossstrasse 3, Langnau; ☻ 2-5pm Mon, 8am-noon & 2-5pm Tue-Fri)

Sights & Activities

The **Emmentaler Schaukäserei** (Emmental Show Dairy; ☎ 034 435 16 11; www.showdairy.ch; admission free; ☻ 8.30am-6.30pm) at Affoltern lets you see Emmental cheese being made into huge wheels (60kg to 130kg). Various production stages are instigated at 9.10am, 10.35am, 12.40pm, 2.05pm, 4.10pm and 5.35pm, although at any time you can listen to a succession of short videos explaining how milk becomes cheese. If you pay close attention, you will learn how Emmental derives its pockmarked, adolescent complexion. **Affoltern** is 6km east of Burgdorf; to reach it by public transport take the train from Burgdorf to Hasle Rüegsau, then postal bus No 195 (Sfr5.80). There's roughly one bus an hour, apart from a long wait around lunchtime. **Kiesen**, on the train route running southeast of Bern (Sfr7.80), also has the **Milchwirtschaftliches Museum** (Museum of Dairy Products; ☎ 031 45 33 31; admission free; ☻ 2-5pm Apr-Oct).

The town of **Langnau** is known for its ornamental crockery and has several demonstration potteries *(Schautöpferei)*, as does nearby **Trubschachen**, reached by train or bus. Ask the tourist office.

From Burgdorf to Wynigen, there's an interesting three-hour Planetenweg **hiking** path. Afterwards, you can catch the train back to **Burgdorf**, whose main attraction is a **Franz Gertsch museum** (☎ 034 421 40 20; Platanenstrasse 3; adult/child Sfr10/5; ☻ 11am-7pm Tue-Fri, 10am-5pm Sat & Sun) showcasing the works of Switzerland's foremost photorealist painter.

Sleeping

SYHA hostel (☎ 034 402 45 26; www.youthhostel.ch/lang nau; Mooseggstrasse 32, Langnau; dm Sfr25; ☺ reception 7-9am & 5-8pm) Langnau also has a hostel, in a quaint, farmhouse-style chalet. The huge overhanging roof is charming, but accommodation is quite basic. The hostel is a 10-minute walk from the station. It's closed early February and from late September to mid-October.

Hotel Hirschen (☎ 034 402 15 17; www.hotel-hir schen.ch; Dorfstrasse 17, Langnau; s/d from Sfr105/170) This hotel is in a similar homey chalet, with country-style Swiss rooms and lots of ornamental Langnau crockery around the place.

Hotel Stadthaus (☎ 034 428 80 00; www.stadthaus .ch in German; Kirchbühl 2, Burgdorf; s/d Sfr230/290; ☒ P) Try this option for unadulterated luxury. The only five-star hotel for miles, this former city hall has every amenity as well as brilliant views.

Getting There & Away

Every hour there's a fast train (15 minutes) and a local train from Bern to Burgdorf. The fare in both cases is Sfr8.20. Langnau can be reached by direct train from Bern (Sfr12.80) or from Burgdorf (Sfr8.20).

SOLOTHURN

pop 15,130 / elevation 440m

Solothurn (Soleure in French) is a little town with a big cathedral; the imposing, 66m-tall façade of St Ursus' may take you by surprise as it looms up out of the pavement at one end of the dinky main street. Without it, this could almost be a French village – an impression that makes more sense when you learn of confirmed-Catholic Solothurn's long-standing links to France. But the presence of the cathedral standing majestically alongside its fountains, churches and city gates gives weight to Solothurn's claim to be the most beautiful baroque town in Switzerland.

Orientation & Information

The train station is south of the Aare River and there is an information office, money-exchange counters and bicycle rental (all open daily). North across the river lies the old town, less than a 10-minute walk. The core of the centre is Kronenplatz, dominated by the cathedral.

Tourist office (☎ 032 626 46 46; www.solothurn-city .ch; Hauptgasse 69; ☺ 8.30am-noon & 1.30-6pm Mon-Fri, 9am-noon Sat) Diagonally opposite the cathedral. Organises 1½-hour walking tours (Sfr5, 2.30pm Saturday May to September).

Sights & Activities

The main landmark is the monolithic 18th-century **Cathedral of St Ursus**. Externally, architect Gaetano Matteo Pisoni managed to restrain himself, with a classical Italianate style. Inside, the church erupts into a complete white-and-gilt trip of wedding-cake baroque.

Two minutes east of the cathedral is the **Baseltor**, the most attractive of the city gates. In the opposite direction, just a stone's throw west down Hauptgasse from St Ursus', you'll find the **Jesuit Church**. Its unprepossessing façade disguises an interior of baroque embellishments and stucco work. In fact, all the 'marble' in here is fake: it's just spruced-up wood and plaster.

A little further west lies the **Zeitglockenturm**, a fine 12th-century astronomical clock where the figures do a little turn on the hour and the clock hands are reversed so that the smaller one shows the minutes.

The nearby **Justice Fountain** (1561) might also produce a wry smile. It shows a blindfolded representation of Justice, holding aloft a sword, while the four most important contemporary figures in Europe sit at her feet. The Holy Roman Emperor, in red and white robes, is by Justice's right foot, then proceeding anticlockwise, you'll see the Pope, the Turkish Sultan and…the mayor of Solothurn!

MUSEUMS

The centrepiece of the **Kunstmuseum** (Museum of Fine Arts; ☎ 032 622 23 07; www.kunstmuseum-so.ch in German; Werkhofstrasse 30; admission by donation; ☺ 10am-noon & 2-5pm Tue-Fri, 10am-5pm Sat & Sun) is Ferdinand Hodler's famous portrait of William Tell. Before arriving in Switzerland, you might never have imagined the national hero as a red-haired, bearded goliath in a white hippy top and short pants, but you'll see this personification repeated many times. The Madonna of Solothurn (1522), by Holbein the Younger, is one of only a small number of other major works, but the museum does have interesting temporary exhibitions.

The **Altes Zeughaus** (Old Arsenal; ☎ 032 623 35 28; Zeughausplatz 1; adult/student & senior/family Sfr6/4/10; ⊙ 10am-noon & 2-5pm Tue-Sun May-Oct, 2-5pm Tue-Sun Nov-Apr) is a reminder that Solothurn was once a centre for mercenaries, many of whom fought for French kings. Among the canons and guns sit 400 suits of armour.

Sleeping & Eating

For a small town, Solothurn surprises with several funky hotels and restaurants.

SYHA hostel (☎ 032 623 17 06; www.youthhostel.ch /solothurn; Landhausquai 23; dm Sfr29-39; ⊙ reception 7.30-10am & 4.30-10.30pm; 💻 ✗) This hotel is one of the country's most modern – all stainless steel, glass and modern black chairs. Dorms are sometimes mixed gender, and the larger ones in the attic somewhat more basic. It's closed late November to mid-January.

Baseltor (☎ 032 622 34 22; www.baseltor.ch; Hauptgasse 79; s/d Sfr90/155; ✗) Above the popular restaurant (mains Sfr18 to Sfr36), you'll find a lovely hotel with a personal feel. There are nine simple but good-looking rooms (three in a separate annexe).

Hotel an der Aare (☎ 032 626 24 00; www.hotelaare .ch in German; Berntorstrasse 2; s/d from Sfr115/150; 💻 ✗ 🅿) The nursing quarters of the 18th-century Solothurn hospital (itself built in 14th-century style) have recently been converted into a stylish, modern hotel. Brightly coloured walls and furniture give warmth to the many stone and exposed-brick features, and the location right next to the Aare is lovely, especially for the bar and brasserie. However, beware as it's also not that far from the railway line.

Hotel Kreuz (☎ 032 622 20 20; www.kreuz-solothurn .ch in German; Kreuzgasse 4; s/d/tr without bathroom Sfr50/90/120) This nearby hotel has simple, low-lit but spacious rooms above a cheap organic restaurant (menus from Sfr15) run by a co-operative. Ring the bell for reception when the restaurant is shut. Deduct Sfr5 if staying more than one night.

Sol Heure (☎ 032 625 54 34; Ritterquai 10; mains Sfr17.50-20.50, daily menus Sfr15.50-17.50; ⊙ 11-12.30am Tue-Sun) When the sun is out, it seems half of Solothurn repairs to the outdoor riverside bar behind this trendy former warehouse. The food is casual, from red chicken curry to New Mexico burgers, but it's the buzzing atmosphere you come for anyway.

La Cantinetta Bindella (☎ 032 623 16 85; Ritterquai 3; mains Sfr15-40; ⊙ 10-12.30am Mon-Sat) Dine

AUTHOR'S CHOICE

Pittaria (Theatergasse 12; snacks Sfr7.50-13.50; ⊙ 10am-11pm Tue-Sat) We were first bowled over by this unusual kebab shop/deli a few years ago, and not just because of its mint tea and home-made mango chutney ladled onto its falafel in pita bread. All the food excels and the friendly, familiar atmosphere, where vintage photos of owner Sami Daher's family hang on sunny yellow walls, the bench seating is laid with Persian rugs and people chat to each other, means you don't want to leave. We weren't the only fans. In 2004 and 2005, Pittaria was named the best takeaway in Switzerland. An unusual accolade, to be sure, but it deserves the award.

on white tablecloths beneath the trees of this Italian restaurant's leafy private garden, just across the street from Sol Heure.

Getting There & Away

Solothurn has two trains an hour to Bern on the private RBS line (Sfr12.80, 40 minutes, railpasses valid). Regular trains also run to Basel (Sfr25, one to 1½ hours, change required) and Biel (Sfr10.40, 20 minutes). Boats also connect Solothurn to Biel (see p190). By road, the Weissenstein mountain impedes access directly north, but the N1/E25 motorway is nearby to the east of town, providing a fast route to Bern, Basel and Zürich. Take highway No 5 for Biel.

AROUND SOLOTHURN

The grand **Schloss Waldegg** (☎ 032 622 38 67; www.schloss-waldegg.ch; Feldbrunnen-St Niklaus; adult/student & senior/family Sfr6/4/10; ⊙ 2-5pm Tue-Thu & Sat, 10am-5pm Sun May-Oct, 10am-5pm Sun only Nov & Dec), a few kilometres north of town, was built in the 17th century and displays period furniture and paintings. Take bus No 4 from the station to the St Niklaus stop, then walk north past the church for a further 10 minutes. It's closed January and February.

The **Weissenstein** (1284m), north of Solothurn, is a mountain that's good for hiking, cross-country skiing or a scenic drive. A few kilometres northwest of Solothurn is **Lommiswil**, where a viewing platform (admission free) overlooks dinosaur footprints in the forest.

Zürich

ZÜRICH

Zürich is a city whose reputation precedes it – and does it a complete disservice, trashes its name, gives it a good kicking. A boring banking capital? *'Zu Reich'* (too rich), business-minded and uptight? The spotless Singapore of Europe? If Switzerland's largest metropolis once lived down to those dull descriptions, it certainly no longer does.

Contemporary Zürich might still be home to the world's fourth-biggest stock exchange and remain Switzerland's financial engine, but it's also (whisper it softly) surprisingly vibrant and trendy. Located on a picturesque river and lake whose water you can drink, easy to get around and a stranger to the hassled lifestyle that defines bigger cities, this affluent, fashion-conscious place enjoys the finest things in life.

Hundreds of new bars, restaurants and clubs have opened since the late 1990s and, since its Street Parade overtook London's Notting Hill Carnival, Zürich now hosts Europe's largest annual street party. Its former industrial quarter brims with nightlife venues catering to a youngish crowd, and this happening 'Züri-West' district has the same buzz as Berlin's Prenzlauerberg or Mitte. The infamous 'gnomes', as the British like to call Zürich's bankers, are still here, but sometimes they can astonish you by whizzing by on a Segway scooter.

Fortunately, the city's Protestant modesty saves it from ever becoming too *schmicki-micki* (chi-chi). With church steeples rising against a backdrop of hills and mountains, the medieval old town will also appeal to traditionalists.

HIGHLIGHTS

- Genuflecting before Marc Chagall's stained-glass windows in the **Fraumünster** (opposite)
- Admiring the Alberto Giacometti stick figures, Dada and other modern art in Zürich's **Kunsthaus** (p197)
- Sipping a hot *schoggi* (chocolate) and stock up on delicious souvenirs at **Café Schober** (p205)
- Heading to a **waterfront bar** (p198) in summer, either on Lake Zürich or the Limmat River
- Taking a train up **Uetliberg** (p208) for excellent hiking or panoramic views

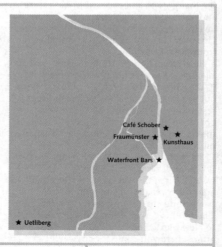

Café Schober ★
Fraumünster ★ ★ Kunsthaus
Waterfront Bars ★
★ Uetliberg

| ▪ POPULATION: 340,402 | ▪ AREA: 1729 SQ KM | ▪ LANGUAGE: GERMAN |

ORIENTATION

Zürich is on the northern bank of Zürichsee (Lake Zurich) with the Limmat River running further north still, splitting the medieval city centre in two. The narrow streets of the Niederdorf quarter on the river's eastern bank is crammed with noisy bars and restaurants; down the western bank runs the expensive Bahnhofstrasse and other shopping streets. The main Hauptbahnhof (train station) is at the northern end of Bahnfhofstrasse.

INFORMATION

Bookshops

Orell Füssli (Map p202; ☎ 0848 849 848; Bahnhofstrasse 70; ☉ 9am-8pm Mon-Fri, 9am-5pm Sat) Has an English-language section.

Travel Book Shop (Map p202; ☎ 044 252 38 83; Rindermarkt 20; ☉ 1-6pm Mon, 9am-6.30pm Tue-Fri, 9am-6pm Sat) English guidebooks and maps.

Discount Card

ZürichCard (per 24/72hr Sfr15/30) Available from the tourist office and the airport train station, this provides free public transport, free museums' admission and more.

Emergency

Police station (Map p202; ☎ 044 216 71 11; Bahnhofquai 3)

Internet Access

E-café.ch Urania (Map p202; ☎ 044 210 33 11; Uraniastrasse 3; per hr Sfr15; ☉ 7.30am-11pm Mon-Fri, 8.30am-11pm Sat, 10am-10pm Sun) Surf, type and print documents or connect your laptop here (Swiss-only power points, p313).

Quanta (Map p202; Limmatquai 94, im Niederdorf; per hr Sfr10, min charge Sfr5; ☉ 9am-midnight) Fairly noisy, but central.

Medical Services

Cantonal University Hospital (Map pp196-7; ☎ 044 255 11 11; Rämistrasse 100) For emergency medical and dental help, ring ☎ 044 261 61 00.

Bellevue Apotheke (Map p202; ☎ 044 252 56 00; Theaterstrasse 14) A 24-hour chemist.

Post

Hauptbahnhof post office (Map p202; ☉ 7.30am-6.30pm Mon-Fri, 7.30-11am Sat)

Sihlpost (Map pp196-7; ☎ 0848 84 84 42; Kasernenstrasse 95-97; ☉ 6.30am-10.30pm Mon-Fri, to 8pm Sat, 10am-10.30pm Sun)

---

01 BECOMES 044

The Zürich telephone prefix has changed from 01 to 044, but parallel dialling will operate until 31 March 2007. Before then, old Zürich numbers starting with 01 can still be dialled. From April 2007, however, try changing 01 to 044 – or search for a new number. The prefix 043 is also used in the region.

Tourist information

Zürich Tourism (Map p202; ☎ 044 215 40 00; www.zuerich.com; Hauptbahnhof; ☉ 8am-8.30pm Mon-Sat, 8.30am-6.30pm Sun May-Oct; 8.30am-7pm Mon-Sat, 9am-6.30pm Sun Nov-Apr) Offers excellent city walking tours and sells mountain day-trips.

SIGHTS

Churches

The 13th-century **Fraumünster** (Map p202; Münsterhof; ☉ 9am-6pm May-Sep, 10am-5pm Mar, Apr & Oct, 10am-4pm Nov-Feb) is renowned for its distinctive stained-glass windows, designed by the then elderly Russian–Jewish artist Marc Chagall in 1967.

The three main windows are, from left to right, the blue 'Jacob' window, with a ladder to heaven; the green 'Christ' window, featuring Mary, Joseph and the infant Jesus; and the yellow 'Zion' window depicting King David and Bathsheba being trumpeted into New Jerusalem. Additionally, the red-toned window on the left wall features various 'Prophets', while the 'Law' window opposite has Moses looking down on a disobedient people.

The window near the main exit of the church is by Augusto Giacometti.

More of Augusto Giacometti's work is on show across the river in the twin-towered **Grossmünster** (Map p202; ☉ 9am-6pm daily mid-Mar–Oct, 10am-5pm Nov–mid-Mar, tower closed Sun morning mid-Mar–Oct & all Sun Nov–mid-Mar). This landmark cathedral was founded by Charlemagne in the 9th century. But more importantly it's where preacher Huldrych Zwingli (1484–1531) began speaking out against the Catholic Church in the 16th century, and thus brought the Reformation and Protestantism's sober lifestyle to Zürich. Today, you can climb the **south tower** (admission Sfr2; ☉ 9.15am-5pm Mar-Oct).

From any position in the city, it's hard to overlook the 13th-century tower of **St Peterskirche** (Map p202; St Peter's Church; St Peterhofstatt). Its

ZÜRICH

ZÜRICH

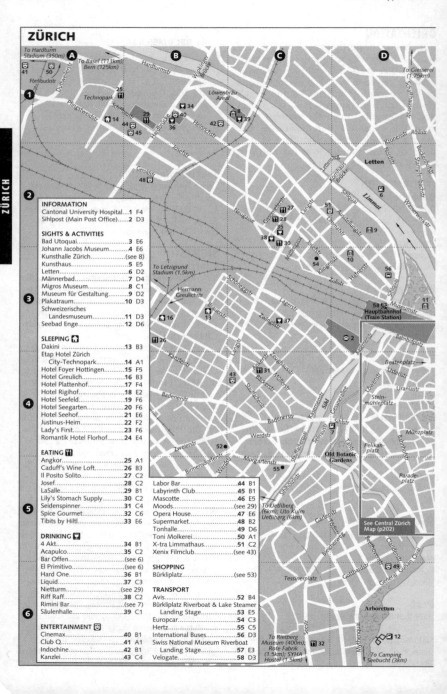

INFORMATION
Cantonal University Hospital...**1** F4
Sihlpost (Main Post Office).....**2** D3

SIGHTS & ACTIVITIES
Bad Utoquai.......................**3** E6
Johann Jacobs Museum........**4** E6
Kunsthalle Zürich................(see 8)
Kunsthaus...........................**5** E5
Letten................................**6** D2
Männerbad..........................**7** D4
Migros Museum...................**8** C1
Museum für Gestaltung........**9** D2
Plakatraum.........................**10** D3
Schweizerisches
    Landesmuseum...............**11** D3
Seebad Enge.......................**12** D6

SLEEPING
Dakini **13** B3
Etap Hotel Zürich
    City-Technopark..............**14** A1
Hotel Foyer Hottingen.........**15** F5
Hotel Greulich....................**16** B3
Hotel Plattenhof..................**17** F4
Hotel Rigihof......................**18** E2
Hotel Seefeld.....................**19** F6
Hotel Seegarten..................**20** F6
Hotel Seehof......................**21** E6
Justinus-Heim.....................**22** F2
Lady's First.........................**23** F6
Romantik Hotel Florhof........**24** E4

EATING
Angkor...............................**25** A1
Caduff's Wine Loft...............**26** B3
Il Posito Solito....................**27** C2
Josef..................................**28** C2
LaSalle...............................**29** B1
Lily's Stomach Supply...........**30** C2
Seidenspinner.....................**31** C4
Spice Gourmet....................**32** C6
Tibits by Hiltl......................**33** E6

DRINKING
4 Akt.................................**34** B1
Acapulco............................**35** C2
Bar Offen...........................(see 6)
El Primitivo.........................(see 6)
Hard One............................**36** B1
Liquid................................**37** C3
Nietturm............................(see 29)
Riff Raff.............................**38** C2
Rimini Bar..........................(see 7)
Säulenhalle........................**39** C1

ENTERTAINMENT
Cinemax.............................**40** B1
Club Q...............................**41** A1
Indochine...........................**42** B1
Kanzlei..............................**43** C4

Labor Bar...........................**44** B1
Labyrinth Club....................**45** B1
Mascotte............................**46** E5
Moods................................(see 29)
Opera House.......................**47** E6
Supermarket.......................**48** B2
Tonhalle.............................**49** D6
Toni Molkerei......................**50** A1
X-tra Limmathaus................**51** C2
Xenix Filmclub....................(see 43)

SHOPPING
Bürkliplatz.........................(see 53)

TRANSPORT
Avis...................................**52** B4
Bürkliplatz Riverboat & Lake Steamer
    Landing Stage.................**53** E5
Europcar............................**54** C3
Hertz.................................**55** C5
International Buses...............**56** D3
Swiss National Museum Riverboat
    Landing Stage.................**57** E3
Velogate............................**58** D3

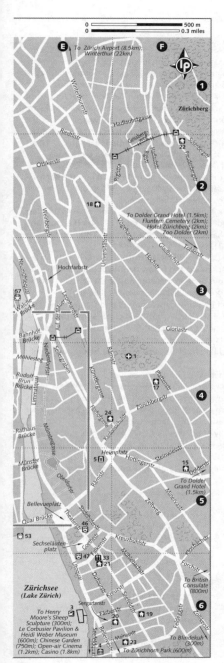

prominent clock face, 8.7m in diameter, is the largest in Europe.

Museums

Compact Zürich has 45 museums; get a comprehensive list from the tourist office.

KUNSTHAUS

After a major renovation in 2005, Zürich's **Museum of Fine Arts** (Map pp196-7; ☎ 044 253 84 84; www .kunsthaus.ch; Heimplatz 1; adult/student & senior Sfr12/7, free Sun; ◷ 10am-9pm Tue-Thu, 10am-5pm Fri-Sun) is looking better than ever, with its rich collection of Alberto Giacometti stick-figure sculptures, Monets, Van Goghs, Rodin sculptures and other 19th- and 20th-century art. Swiss artist Ferdinand Hodler is also represented.

LE CORBUSIER PAVILION

Many international visitors are mystified that Zürich doesn't make more of the stunning **Le Corbusier Pavilion and Heidi Weber museum** (Zürichhorn park; adult/concession Sfr12/8; ◷ 2-5pm Sat & Sun Jun-Sep). However, as a cash-strapped private museum its opening times are sadly limited. Looking like a Mondrian painting set in parkland, with differently coloured square panels, glass and steel, this was the last building designed by Le Corbusier (who died in 1965). Completed after his death, it long lay unused, but now contains many of his architectural plans, drawings, weavings, paintings, furniture and books – all collected by client, fan and friend Heidi Weber. The exterior alone is worth seeing.

MUSEUM FÜR GESTALTUNG

The exhibitions at Zürich's **Design Museum** (Map pp196-7; ☎ 043 446 67 67; www.museum-gestaltung .ch; Ausstellungstrasse 60; adult/concession Sfr7/4; ◷ 10am-8pm Tue-Thu, 10am-5pm Fri-Sun) are consistently impressive. The curators take such a broad interpretation of their brief that they have covered everything from Bollywood's love affair with Switzerland (see the boxed text The Hills are Alive with the Sound of Hindi, p155) to dendrites (tree-like structures found throughout nature). The **Plakatraum** (Poster Collection; Map pp196-7; Limmatstrasse 55-7; ◷ 1-5pm Tue-Sat) draws on a huge archive of vintage tourism, Dada and other posters.

SCHWEIZERISCHES LANDESMUSEUM

The big **Swiss National Museum** (Map pp196-7; ☎ 044 218 65 11; www.musee-suisse.ch; Museumstrasse 2;

ZÜRICH

WATERFRONT ZÜRICH

Zürich really comes into its own in its Mediterranean-like summer, when the green parks lining the lake are overrun with bathers, sunseekers, in-line skaters, footballers, lovers, picnickers, party animals, preeners and other hedonists. (Some police even patrol on rollerblades!) Between May and the middle of September, outdoor swimming areas are open around the lake and up the Limmat River.

Official swimming areas are usually rectangular wooden piers with a pavilion covering part of them and most offer massages, yoga, saunas and snacks. Admission is Sfr6, and swimming areas are open from 9am to 7pm in May and September and 9am to 8pm from June to August. One of the most central is **Seebad Enge** (Map pp196–7; Mythenquai 95), on the left shore near the laid-back Arboretum. On the opposite shore, adjacent to the Zürichhorn park, is **Bad Utoquai** (Map pp196–7; ☎ 044 251 61 51; Utoquai 49). Of course, there are plenty of free, unofficial places to take a dip, too.

Along the river, the 19th-century **Frauenbad** (Map p202; Stadthausquai) and its snack bar is only open to women during the day. Come nightfall, though, they let up to 150 men into the **Barfussbar** (Barefoot bar; Map p202; ☎ 044 261 75 68; www.barfussbar.ch; Stadthausquai; ⌚ from 8.30pm Wed-Sun) here. As the name implies, gents must leave their shoes at the entrance.

One favourite is **Letten** (Map pp196–7; Lettensteg), further north up the river, where Züri-West trendsetters swim, barbecue, skateboard, play volleyball, or just drink and chat on the grass and concrete. A former S-Bahn carriage from Berlin has been transformed into Bar Offen and there's the pavilion-style **El Primitivo** (Map pp196–7; ⌚ 11am-11pm).

Also highly recommended is the **Männerbad** (Map pp196–7; Schanzengraben), tucked away on the Venice-like Schanzengraben canal, behind the Hallenbad and below the Old Botanic Gardens. It's men-only by day, but women are welcome to join them in the evenings at the fantastic **Rimini Bar** (Map pp196–7; ☎ 044 211 9594; www.rimini.ch; ⌚ 7.30pm-midnight in good weather only).

Lake cruises (☎ 044 487 13 33; www.zsg.ch) run regularly between April and October and sporadically in winter, depending on the weather. They leave from Bürkliplatz (Map pp196–7). A small circular tour *(kleine Rundfahrt)*, takes 1½ hours (adult/child Sfr7.20/3.60, Swiss Pass and Eurail valid, Inter Rail 50% discount) and departs every 30 minutes from 9am to 7pm. A longer tour *(grosse Rundfahrt)* lasts four hours (adult/child Sfr22/11, passes valid as before) with eight daily departures from 9.30am to 5.30pm.

There are also other services to Rapperswil (see p208) or dinner cruises.

Riverboats (Limmatschiffe; ☎ 044 487 13 33; www.zsg.ch; Sfr3.60, day passes valid; ⌚ every 30 min Jun-Sep, reduced service in winter) run down the river and then do a small circle around the lake (55 minutes). Boats fill rapidly and your best chance of getting on board is at the Schweizerisches Landemuseum (Map pp196–7) or Zürichhorn Casino, rather than Bürkliplatz.

Boat hire is also possible on the lake, especially of pedalos and row boats. Prices start at Sfr16, plus Sfr50 to Sfr100 deposit, for 30 minutes. There's a rental site at Bürkliplatz (Map pp196–7), plus one near every official swimming area.

For a month from mid-July, there's an extremely popular waterside **open-air cinema** (☎ 0800 078 078; www.orangecinema.ch; Zürichhorn).

permanent collection adult/concession Sfr5/3, special exhibition prices vary; ⌚ 10am-5pm Tue-Sun) is a large cream cake of a museum that, however excellent, should be taken in small bites. The permanent collection includes a trail through Swiss history, plus there are usually enticing special exhibitions. A new annexe is under construction until 2008, but the museum should remain open throughout.

MUSEUM RIETBERG

An unexpectedly wonderful collection of African, Oriental and ancient American art is found in the **Museum Rietberg** (☎ 044 206 31 31; www.rietberg.ch; Gablerstrasse 15; permanent collection adult/concession Sfr6/3, special exhibitions Sfr5/3 extra; ⌚ 10am-5pm Tue-Sun, to 8pm Wed Apr-Sep; 10am-5pm Tue-Sun Oct-Mar). It's set in three villas in a leafy park.

MODERN ART MUSEUMS

Note that modern art exhibitions are frequently held in the airport, in its unused terminal.

Cabaret Voltaire (Map p202; ☎ 043 268 57 20; www.cabaretvoltaire.ch; Spiegelgasse 1; admission varies, free

COMPLETELY DADA

Antibourgeois, rebellious, nihilistic and deliberately nonsensical, the Dada art movement grew out of revulsion to WWI and the increasing mechanisation of modern life. Its proponents paved the way for nearly every form of contemporary art by using collage, extracting influences from indigenous art, applying abstract notions to writing, film and performance and taking manufactured objects and redefining them as art. Marcel Duchamp's somewhat damaged *Urinal* (a urinal as art piece) conveys the idea succinctly.

Dada artists worked in New York, Paris and Berlin, but the movement was born in Zürich. Hugo Ball, Tristan Tzara and Emmy Jenning's creation of the Cabaret Voltaire in February 1916 kicked off a series of raucous cabaret and performance art events at a room in a pub at Spiegelgasse 1, which has recently reopened (see opposite). The name Dada, according to the most generally accepted account, was chosen randomly by stabbing a knife through a French/German dictionary.

By 1923, the movement was to all intents and purposes dead, but its spirit lives on in the works of actual Dadaists like Georg Grosz, Hans Arp and Max Ernst and of those infected with its ideas such as Duchamp and photographer Man Ray. Dadaist works are in Zürich's Kunsthaus (p197) and the Poster Collection of the Museum für Gestaltung (p197).

to café/bar; 1-7pm Tue-Sun) is the birthplace of the iconoclastic Dada art movement (see the boxed text Completely Dada, above). It has been reopened as an exhibition space cum café/bar, dedicated to modern Swiss art and hosting Dada-related events.

Migros Museum (Map pp196-7; ☎ 044 277 20 50; www.migrosmuseum.ch; Limmatstrasse 270; adult/concession Sfr8/4, combined admission with Kunsthalle Sfr12/6; noon-6pm Tue-Fri, to 8pm Thu, 11am-5pm Sat & Sun) is one of two main museums in the converted Löwenbräu brewery, which also houses several galleries, a bookshop, a bar and a club.

JAMES JOYCE IN ZÜRICH

One of the greatest works of English literature, James Joyce's *Ulysses*, was written in Zürich and its author is buried here. Irish Joyce was just one disgruntled intellectual – Lenin and Trotsky were others – who took refuge in this neutral city during WWI, and he finished his epic during wartime exile here (1915–19). He returned shortly before dying in January 1941 and his carefully tended grave is found in Fluntern Cemetery; take tram No 6 to Zoo.

The **James Joyce Foundation** (Map p202; www.joycefoundation.ch; Augustinergasse 9; admission free; 10am-5pm Mon-Fri) hosts regular public readings in English from *Ulysses* (5.30pm to 7pm Tuesday) and *Finnegan's Wake* (4.30pm to 6pm and 7pm to 8.30pm Thursday).

Kunsthalle Zürich (Map pp196-7; ☎ 044 272 15 15; www.kunsthallezurich.ch; Limmatstrasse 270; adult/concession Sfr8/4, combined entry Sfr12/6; noon-6pm Tue-Fri, 11am-5pm Sat & Sun), like the Migros Museum, features changing exhibitions of contemporary art, particularly conceptual works.

OTHER MUSEUMS

Johann Jacobs Museum (Map pp196-7; ☎ 044 388 61 51; Seefeldquai 17; adult/concession Sfr5/3; 2-7pm Fri, 2-5pm Sat, 10am-5pm Sun) is as addictive as the coffee to which it is devoted. Temporary exhibitions range from the scientific effects of caffeine to displays of chinaware.

Beyer Museum (Map p202; ☎ 043 344 63 63; Bahnhofstrasse 31; adult/child Sfr5/free; 2-6pm Mon-Fri) is a small museum chronicling the rise of timekeeping, from striated medieval candles to modern watches.

Zoo

Zoo Dolder (www.zoo.ch; Zürichbergstrasse 221; adult/student Sfr16/8; 8am-6pm), up on the Zürichberg, has an expansive location, 1800 animals and a re-created rainforest. Take tram No 6 to Zoo station.

WALKING TOUR

Start at the Hauptbahnhof and head south along Bahnhofstrasse. This isn't the prettiest part of Zürich, but the many expensive shops will swiftly give you the measure of the place. The street, which follows the route of the former city walls, isn't exactly paved with gold, but it adds a certain thrill

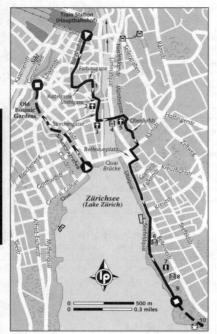

WALK FACTS

Start Hauptbahnhof
Finish Casino
Distance 5km
Duration 2 hours

to know that the bank vaults underfoot are full of that precious metal.

Turn left at Kuttelgasse and continue into Fortunagasse, before turning right into the **Lindenhof (1)**. This leafy raised terrace on the west bank of the river is where the Romans established their first customs post in 15 BC. Today it's a popular meeting spot, with views of terraced buildings lining the riverbank and the hills behind.

Now, head down the hill along Strehlgasse and Storchengasse, under the huge clock-face of **St Peter's (2**; p195). Take some time to look at the windows of the **Fraumünster (3**; p195), before crossing the bridge past the **Helmhaus (4**; www.helmhaus.org; Limmatquai 31; admission free; 🕑10am-6pm Tue-Sun, to 8pm Thu) contemporary art gallery. From

here, climb the stairs to the **Grossmünster (5**; p195).

To the north lies a narrow tangle of cobblestone medieval streets, most famously Niederdorfstasse. This is the main tourist drag and you're bound to wander through here at some point. For the moment, however, turn south and head along the slightly less congested and commercialised Oberdorfstrasse. Turn right at Rämistrasse, through Bellevue and begin the hugely enjoyable stroll along the eastern bank of the lake. Continue past the **Johann Jacobs Museum (6**; p199) and Henry Moore's **sheep sculpture (7)** until you come to **Le Corbusier Pavilion (8**; p197) and the **Chinese Garden (9)**. To save yourself the long trek back, continue to the **Casino (10)** and catch a city boat back up the river.

If you've still got energy to burn, a less well-known side of Zürich can be explored by wandering up the Schanzengraben canal and through the Old Botanic Gardens.

FESTIVALS & EVENTS

The following are just the most important; for a full list of events, see www.zuerich.com.

Sechseläuten During this Spring festival on the third Monday of April, guild members parade down the streets in historical costume and a fireworks-filled 'snowman' (the *Böögg*) is ignited to celebrate the end of winter.

Street Parade (☎ 044 215 40 00; www.street-parade .ch) This techno celebration in the middle of August is usually Europe's largest street party in any given year.

Knabenschiessen (www.knabenschiessen.ch in German) Huge shooting competition for 12- to 17-year olds in late September.

SLEEPING
Budget
HOSTELS

Note that Hotel Martahaus (opposite) and Hotel Foyer Hottingen (opposite) also have a few dorm beds each – for women only.

SYHA hostel (Map p202; ☎ 043 399 78 00; www.youth hostel.ch; Mütschellenstrasse 114, Wollishofen; dm Sfr38, s/d Sfr99/116; 🖳) Expensively overhauled in 2005, this huge hostel now features a swish reception/dining hall and sparkling modern bathrooms. Dorms remain quite small, though. Take tram No 7 to Morgental, or S-Bahn to Wollishofen.

City Backpacker (Hotel Biber; Map p202; ☎ 044 251 90 15; www.city-backpacker.ch; Niederdorfstrasse 5; dm Sfr31, sheets extra Sfr3, s/d Sfr66/92; 🕑 reception closed noon-3pm) Friendly and well equipped, if a trifle cramped. In summer, you can always overcome the claustrophobia by hanging out on the roof terrace.

B&B

Dakini (Map pp196-7; ☎ 044 291 42 20; www.dakini.ch; Brauerstrasse 87; s Sfr65-85, d Sfr90-135; 🖥) This relaxed B&B attracts a bohemian crowd of artists and performers, academics and trendy tourists who don't bat an eyelid at its location near the red-light district. Four double rooms and two singles are spread across a couple of apartments over two floors, sharing the kitchen and bathroom on each. Take tram No 8 to Bäckeranlange.

HOTELS

Justinusheim (Map pp196-7; ☎ 044 361 38 06; Freudenbergstrasse 146; s/d from Sfr40/80; s with bathroom Sfr70-80, d Sfr110-120) This student home usually has a few beds for travellers, and there are certainly plenty during university holidays. It's in a splendid, leafy location overlooking the city, yet only 10 minutes from its heart. Take tram No 10 to Seilbahn Rigiblick, then the funicular.

Etap Hotel Zürich City-Technopark (Map pp196-7; ☎ 044 276 20 00; www.etaphotel.com; Technoparkstrasse 2; s/d/tr Sfr82/92/102) Its capsule-sized bathrooms, industrial park location and garish décor render this completely charmless. However, you won't get clean, modern, in-room facilities and TV for less and it's very handy for clubbing in Züri-West. Take tram No 4 or 13 to Escher-Wyss-Platz.

CAMPING

Camping Seebucht (☎ 044 482 16 12; Seestrasse 559; adult/tent/car Sfr9.50/12/5; 🗓 1 May-30 Sep) Four kilometres from the city centre and on the western shore of the lake, this has good facilities. Take bus No 161 or 165 from Bürkliplatz.

Midrange

Hotel Martahaus (Map p202; ☎ 044 251 45 50; www.martahaus.ch; Zähringerstrasse 36; dm Sfr38, s/d Sfr85/100, with bathroom Sfr115/150) With 1970s black leather lounges in the very spacious breakfast room-cum-lounge and a roof terrace, this is a fun, friendly place to stay. Other features include a bar, laundry and gym. There's a lot of street noise, though, and the shared bathrooms are a bit of a squeeze.

Hotel Foyer Hottingen (Map pp196-7; ☎ 044 256 19 19; www.hotel-hottingen.ch; Hottingerstrasse 31; dm

---

HILLSIDE HIDEAWAYS

Two of Zürich's most memorable hotels overlook the city from the hills above.

Uto Kulm Uetliberg (☎ 044 457 66 66; www.utokulm.ch; Uetliberg; s Sfr150-300, d Sfr250-400, ste Sfr450-900) Luxurious Uto Kulm is perfect for a romantic retreat with its preponderance of spa baths and big beds. Take the S10 to Uetliberg (p208) and staff will collect you.

Hotel Zürichberg (☎ 044 268 35 35; www.zuerichberg.ch; Orellistrasse 21; s Sfr195-260, d Sfr270-340) This sleek hotel welcomes a mix of families and businesspeople. The original 19th-century pavilion has an oval-shaped modern annexe, clad in wood, where rooms are arranged around a circular interior ramp reminiscent of New York's Guggenheim museum. Take tram No 6 to Zoo.

Sfr38, s/d Sfr75/115; s with bathroom Sfr110-125, d Sfr155-165) Much the same deal as Hotel Martahaus, but with more muted décor, fewer facilities and a quieter location. The clientele is also slightly older and less funky.

Hotel Plattenhof (Map pp196-7; ☎ 044 251 19 10; www.plattenhof.ch; Plattenstrasse 26; new s/d Sfr235/305, old s/d Sfr165/205; 🅿 🔄) This youthful design hotel has low beds, in a vaguely Japanese style, plus mood lighting in its newest rooms. It's cool without being pretentious, and even the 'old' rooms are stylishly minimalist. Take tram No 6 to Platte.

Hotel Rössli (Map p202; ☎ 044 256 70 50; www.hotel-roessli.ch; Rössligasse 7; s Sfr180-200, d Sfr210-280, ste Sfr650-850) There's a calming, ascetic quality to this boutique hotel with its white walls and furnishings only occasionally disrupted by greys, mint greens or pale blues. It also has an elegant bar.

Hotel Seehof (Map pp196-7; ☎ 044 254 57 57; www.hotelseehof.ch; Seehofstrasse 11) A near-identical sister establishment of Hotel Rössli.

Lady's First (Map pp196-7; ☎ 044 380 80 10; www.ladysfirst.ch; Mainaustrasse 24; s Sfr195-230, d Sfr245-320; 🖥) Don't be fooled by the name; this renovated establishment now also welcomes men. Rooms provide a pleasant mixture of traditional parquet flooring and quality modern furnishings. The hotel spa and its accompanying roof terrace remain reserved for female guests only. Take tram No 4 to Feldeggstrasse.

ZÜRICH

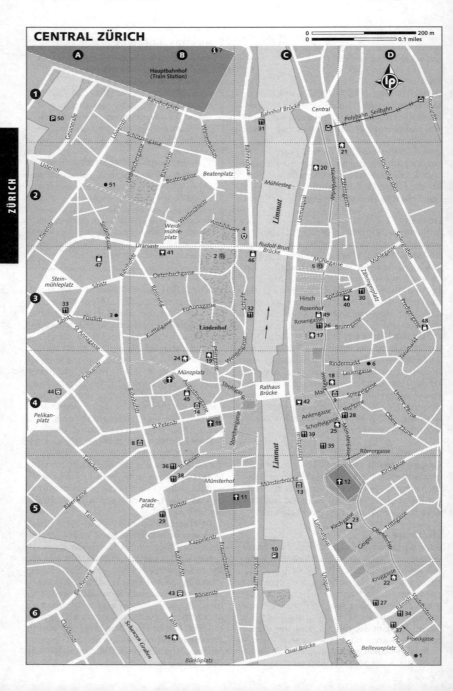

CENTRAL ZÜRICH

0   200 m
0   0.1 miles

Hotel Greulich (Map pp196–7; ☎ 043 243 42 43; www .greulich.ch; Hermann Greulich Strasse 56; s Sfr180-240, d Sfr255-320; ✗) It's hard to better *Condé Nast Traveller's* description of this super-sleek pad as 'bride-of-Bauhaus' functionalist. Behind the blue-grey outer walls, you find an ascetic inner courtyard with exposed concrete and evenly planted birch trees, and the minimalist, off-white rooms are laid out in facing bungalows along two sides of this. Chef David Martinez-Savany believes in genuine 'slow food' and serves much-lauded Spanish cuisine.

Hotel Seefeld (Map pp196–7; ☎ 044 387 41 41; www .hotel-seefeld.ch; Seefeldstrasse 63; s Sfr185-240, d Sfr290-360; 🖳 ✗ 🅿 🚆 🕭) The cool, modern design here is a trifle formulaic, but the range of facilities is excellent. Each floor is decorated in a different colour, so you can take your pick.

Hotel Seegarten (Map pp196–7; ☎ 044 388 37 37; www.hotel-seegarten.ch; Seegartenstrasse 14; s Sfr180-220,

d Sfr260-300) Rattan furniture and vintage tourist posters give this place a rustic Mediterranean atmosphere, which is reinforced by the proximity to the lake and the on-site Italian restaurant.

Hotel Kindli (Map p202; ☎ 043 888 76 76; www.kindli .ch; Pfalzgasse 1; s/d Sfr160/210, s with bathroom Sfr260-360, d Sfr360-420; ✗) This family-run hotel puts out the welcome mat for those who prefer cosy, traditional hotels, with its checked cushions and floral curtains. Tucked away in the old town on the west bank, in a 16th-century building, it's central but quiet.

Romantik Hotel Florhof (Map pp196–7; ☎ 044 250 26 26; www.florhof.ch; Florhofgasse 4; s Sfr220-290, d Sfr330-380) Another traditional hotel, this nestles in a lovely garden, a stone's throw from the Kunsthaus.

Also recommended:

Hotel Adler (Map p202; ☎ 044 266 96 96; www.hotel -adler.ch; Niederdorferstrasse 34; s/d from Sfr140/190; 🖳 ✗) Very pleasant, clean and comfortable, with tasteful trompe l'oeils of the Zürich skyline.

Hotel Limmatblick (Map p202; ☎ 044 254 60 00; www .limmatblick.ch; Limmatquai 136; s/d from Sfr190/200; 🖳 ✗) Small, stylish rooms dedicated to Dada artists. Central but noisy location.

Goldenes Schwert (Map p202; ☎ 044 250 70 80; www .gayhotel.ch; Marktgasse 14; s/d from Sfr130/165) Gay-friendly hotel with some elaborately themed rooms. The top floor gets the least noise from the downstairs disco.

Top End

Hotel Widder (Map p202; ☎ 044 224 25 26; www .widderhotel.ch; Rennweg 7; s/d from Sfr405/610) This

---

AUTHOR'S CHOICE

Hotel Otter (Map p202; ☎ 044 251 22 07; www .wueste.ch; Oberdorfstrasse 7; s Sfr100, d Sfr135-170) A true gem among Zürich hotels, this colourful place prides itself on being alternative. It certainly is that, with 17 rooms variously decorated with pink satin sheets and plastic beads, raised beds, wall murals, religious grottos and in one instance a hammock. A popular bar, the Wüste, is downstairs.

ZÜRICH

crisp and stylish hotel is a perfect example of the Swiss ability to combine modernity with traditional charm, with eight old townhouses given a Scandinavian-style makeover. Without the pompousness that permeates many similar establishments, the popular Widder Bar remains famous for its jazz and range of malt whiskeys.

Baur au Lac (Map p202; ☎ 044 220 50 20; www .bauraulac.ch; Talstrasse 1; s/d Sfr460/680; ✂ ▣ ✂ P) This is *the* most exclusive place in town (at least until the Dolder, following, reopens) – with sumptuous rooms, outstanding service, a spa and a private park.

Dolder Grand Hotel (☎ 044 269 30 00; www.dolder grand.ch; Kurhausstrasse 65) For many years, Europe's premier hotel, this 19th-century Zürichberg palace is getting a makeover from Sir Norman Foster, establishing it as one of the world's best on its reopening in spring 2007. See the website for prices when they become available.

EATING

Zürich's denizens have the choice of an astounding 2000 places to eat and party.

Budget

Tibits by Hiltl (Map pp196-7; ☎ 044 260 32 22; Seefeld-strasse 2; meals per 100g Sfr3.70; ✺ 6.30am-midnight daily, from 8am Sat & from 9am Sun) Tibits is where with-it, health-conscious Zürichers head for a light bite when meeting friends. There's a tasty vegetarian buffet, fresh fruit juices, coffees and cake.

Hiltl (Map p202; ☎ 044 227 70 00; Sihlstrasse 28; mains Sfr22-28; ✺ 10am-10.30pm) The original Hiltl was planning a renovation and temporary move to Paradeplatz, so call ahead.

Sternen Grill (Map p202; Bellevueplatz/Theatrestrasse 22; snacks from Sfr5-8; ✺ 11.30am-midnight) This is the city's most famous – and busiest – sausage stand; just follow the crowds streaming in for a tasty greasefest.

Eat And Meet/Schipfe 16 (Map p202; Schipfe 16; menus Sfr16-20; ✺ 10am-4pm Mon-Fri, drinks until 6pm) A pleasant dining room overlooking the Limmat River from the historic Schipfe area, this serves humble lunches, from Mediterranean to Indian to Swiss.

Café Zähringer (Map p202; Zähringerplatz 11; mains from Sfr18.50; ✺ 6pm-midnight Mon, 8am-midnight Tue-Sun) This very old-school alternative café serves up mostly organic, vegetarian food around communal tables.

For self-caterers there's a central **Coop supermarket** (Map p202; Bahnhofbrücke 1; ✺ 7am-8pm Mon-Fri, 7am-6pm Sat)

Midrange
SWISS

Traditional local cuisine is very rich, as epitomised by the city's signature dish of *Zürcher Geschnetzeltes*, or sliced veal in a creamy mushroom sauce.

Zeughauskeller (Map p202; ☎ 044 211 26 90; Bahn-hofstrasse 28a; most mains Sfr15-30; ✺ 11.30am-11pm) The menu at this huge, atmospheric beer hall offers 20 different kinds of sausages in eight languages, as well as numerous other Swiss specialities of a carnivorous and vegetarian variety.

Restaurant Kropf (Map p202; In Gassen 16; mains Sfr20-36; ✺ 11.30am-11.30pm Mon-Sat) Notable for its historic interior, with marble columns and ceiling murals, Kropf is more favoured by locals for its hearty Swiss staples and fine beers.

Adler's Swiss Chuchi (Map p202; ☎ 044 266 96 66; Rosengasse 10; most mains Sfr25-35; ✺ 11am-11pm) Adler's is a decent and simple, albeit touristy, option if you're looking for fondue or raclette.

Le Dezaley (Map p202; ☎ 044 251 61 29; Römergasse 7 & 9; small dishes from Sfr11, mains Sfr24-46; ✺ Mon-Sat) Tucked away in an alley below the Grossmünster, this is a little part of French Switzerland in Zürich and regarded as one of the places to try fondue.

INTERNATIONAL

Spice Gourmet (Map pp196-7; ☎ 044 201 05 66; Seestrasse 43; mains Sfr20-36; ✺ Mon-Sat) It's worth the short trip south of the centre to eat in the familiar surrounds of this 30-seat restaurant/shop, whose menu travels between India, Southeast Asia and South America.

Lily's Stomach Supply (Map pp196-7; ☎ 044 440 18 85; Langstrasse 197; most mains Sfr18-25; ✺ 11am-midnight Mon-Sat, 3pm-midnight Sun) This trendy noodle-bar's convenient location and casual, upbeat atmosphere is what's most appealing, although its food is generally quite respectable.

Il Posito Solito (Map pp196-7; ☎ 044 272 62 92; Gas-ometerstrasse 25; pizzas Sfr14-22, mains Sfr22-45; ✺ Mon-Sat) A meeting spot for the city's young trendsetters, this hectic, familiar Italian eatery reputedly serves Zürich's best pizzas. While not *entirely* convinced on that front,

ZÜRICH

AUTHOR'S CHOICE

Blindekuh (Blind Man's Bluff; ☎ 044 421 50 50; Mühlebachstrasse 148; lunch/evening mains from Sfr25/35; ⏱ 11.30am-2pm & 6-11pm Tue-Fri, 6-11pm Mon & Sat, bar 9-11pm daily) This eatery remains truly unusual, where you eat and drink in darkness. Run by people with impaired vision as a means of sharing their experience, this restaurant is booked out for months for dinner, but lunch (plus some last-minute evening) reservations are possible.

we'll always be tempted back by the pumpkin gnocchi and other homemade pasta.

Josef (Map pp196-7; ☎ 044 271 65 95; Gasometerstrasse 24; mains Sfr20-48; ⏱ Mon-Sat) A Züri-West stalwart, Josef frequently changes its décor and Swiss-Italian menu, but always has a good wine list and remains constantly popular with the in set.

Giesserei (☎ 044 205 10 10; Birchstrasse 108; mains Sfr24-38; ⏱ lunch & dinner Mon-Fri, dinner Sat, brunch & dinner Sun) This former factory in Oerlikon is a winner with its scuffed post-industrial atmosphere and pared-down menu (three starters, three mains and three desserts). Sufficient hip customers offset the suits from nearby PriceWaterhouseCoopers. Take tram No 11 to Regensbergbrücke.

Angkor (Map pp196-7; ☎ 043 205 28 88; Giessereistrasse 18; mains Sfr26-48) The Angkor's opulent Oriental interior and papyrus menu of authentically spicy Thai, Cambodian, Japanese and Chinese cuisine makes up for its concrete-wrapped Technopark location.

Top End

LaSalle (Map pp196-7; ☎ 044 258 70 71; Schiffbaustrasse 4; mains Sfr25-50; ⏱ 11am-midnight Mon-Tue, 11-1am Wed-Thu, 11-2am Fri, 6pm-2am Sat, 5pm-2am Sun) This modern Italian brasserie is a popular haunt for Zürich's beautiful people, where a huge glass cube bedecked with chandeliers and a long bar sits inside an even bigger converted warehouse (the so-called Schiffbauhaus).

Seidenspinner (Map pp196-7; ☎ 044 241 07 00; Ankerstrasse 120; most mains Sfr30-55; ⏱ 11am-midnight Tue-Sat) A favourite with the media and fashion crowd (it's attached to a leading fabric design shop), Silk-spinner boasts an extravagant interior, with huge flower arrangements and shards of mirrored glass covering the walls. Russian stroganoff and

borsch stand out on a mainly modern international menu.

Caduff's Wine Loft (Map pp196-7; ☎ 044 240 22 66; Kanzleistrasse 126; mains Sfr25-60, 4-course menu Sfr115; ⏱ Mon-Sat) A light-infused but deliberately understated interior draws your attention to the wine behind the long bar here. There are 2500 varieties, which the waiters will helpfully match with your Mediterranean/Swiss meal.

Zunfthaus zum Rüden (Map p202; ☎ 044 261 95 66; Limmatquai 42; mains Sfr45-70, menu Sfr140; ⏱ Mon-Fri) In the 14th century, Zürich's craftsmen formed themselves into 13 guilds, and this building belonged to the noble *Constaffel* society, whose ranks included the mayor for a time. In the stunning Gothic dining room, you can sample Swiss staples and seasonally changing international cuisine.

Kronenhalle (Map p202; ☎ 044 251 66 69; Rämistrasse 4; mains Sfr30-80; ⏱ noon-midnight) The city's top restaurant is a very upmarket, brasserie-style establishment, with white tablecloths and lots of dark wood. Impeccably mannered waiters move discreetly below Chagall, Miro, Matisse and Picasso originals.

DRINKING

For the main drinking options, see the boxed texts Waterfront Zürich, p198, and Zürich's Trendquartier, p206.

Wings (Map p202; ☎ 268 40 55; Limmatquai 54) When Swissair went bankrupt in 2001, some former employees set up this lounge bar using the airline's cutlery, crockery and even a few aeroplane seats. Given a few Hawaiian additions, it's Barry Manilow meets *Wallpaper** magazine.

Jules Verne Panorama Bar (Map p202; ☎ 043 888 66 66; Uraniastrasse 9; entry through Brasserie Lipp; ⏱ daily) Decked out like the basket of a hot-air balloon, this classic bar – welcoming all ages – boasts fantastic views.

Café Schober (Map p202; Napfgasse 4; ⏱ 8am-6.30pm Mon-Fri, to 5.30pm Sat, 10am-5.30pm Sun) A kitsch, fairy-tale grotto of a café, with huge bouquets of flowers tied with ribbons to ceiling arches, Schober serves a serious hot chocolate (made from real *schoggi* instead of cocoa powder) and shouldn't be missed.

Café Odeon (Map p202; Bellevueplatz) This onetime haunt of Lenin and the Dadaists is still a prime people-watching spot for gays and straights alike. Come for the Art Nouveau interior, but ignore the quite ordinary food.

ZÜRICH'S 'TRENDQUARTIER'

Zürich's former industrial area has, as in many cities, become its hippest neighbourhood, but the much-vaunted 'Züri-West' quarter (roughly west of the train station) actually straddles several districts.

Züri-West proper starts at Escher-Wyss Platz in the industrial surrounds of Kreis 5 (district 5). In the cluster of nightspots you'll find the relaxed **4 Akt** (Map pp196-7; ☎ 044 271 03 68; Heinrichstrasse 262) and the chic **Hard One** (Map pp196-7; ☎ 044 444 10 00; Heinrichstrasse 269). The latter is a glass cube of a lounge bar with great views, serving wine, whisky, champagne and cigars. At the back of the same building is the popular **Cinemax** (Map pp196-7; ☎ 044 273 22 22; Heinrichstrasse 269) multiplex.

Good views are also had from **Nietturm** (Map pp196-7; ☎ 044 258 70 71; Schiffbaustrasse 4; from 6pm Wed-Sun) in the nearby Schiffbauhaus. In this complex, which also hosts **La Salle** (see p205), you'll find the city's top jazz/funk club, **Moods** (Map pp196-7; ☎ 044 276 80 00; www.moods.ch; Schiffbaustrasse 6; ◷ from midnight Fri & Sat).

Clubs, bars, restaurants and hotels further west are also part of the industrial zone, but Züri-West is pretty loosely defined and also usually encompasses the (still slightly active) red-light district in Kreis 4 further east. Langstrasse is the main artery here, with popular bars clustered along its side streets. Neugasse, with retro **Acapulco** (Map pp196-7; ☎ 044 272 66 88; Neugasse 56; ◷ from 3pm) and cinema-cum-bistro bar **Riff Raff** (Map pp196-7; ☎ 044 444 22 05; Neugasse 57; ◷ from 8am Mon-Fri, from 10am Sat & Sun), is rich with possibilities, while a little further south is the fantastic **Liquid** (Map pp196-7; ☎ 044 291 12 91; Zwinglistrasse 12; ◷ from 5pm Tue-Fri, from 8pm Sat) with striped wallpaper and moulded plastic chairs.

Gasometerstrasse, parallel to Langstrasse, is also worth visiting for **Josef** (p205), **Il Posito Solito** (p204) and other bars and restaurants.

At the far northeast end of Langstrasse is the bar/lounge/restaurant/hotel/club complex **X-tra Limmathaus** (Map pp196-7; Limmatstrasse 118; ◷ Wed-Mon). This is mostly populated by teens and early 20s, although a broader public enjoys its Monday-night start to the week.

West along Limmatstrasse heading back towards Kreis 5, you'll find the new Löwenbräu Areal, a former brewery that now has contemporary art galleries, a bar and the sometimes uncomfortably mobbed **Säulenhalle** (Map pp196-7; ☎ 044 278 10 02; ◷ lounge bar from 5pm Tue-Sat, club from 11pm Thu-Sat).

Café Sprüngli (Map p202; ☎ 044 224 47 11; www .spruengli.ch; Bahnhofstrasse 21; ◷ 7am-6.30pm Mon-Fri, to 5.30pm Sat, 10am-5pm Sun) The mother of all chocolate shops. This roomy, buzzing main branch of the well-known chain also delivers chocolate worldwide.

ENTERTAINMENT

Züritipp is the city's events magazine, available around town and from the tourist office. Also look for the quarterly *Zürich Guide*. Tickets for events are available from the **Billettzentrale** (Map p202; ☎ 044 221 22 83; Bahnhofstrasse 9; ◷ 10am-6.30pm Mon-Fri, to 2pm Sat, closed Jul & Aug) or individual venues.

Nightclubs

Generally dress well and expect to pay Sfr15 to Sfr30 admission. See the boxed text Zürich's Trendquartier, above, for other tips.

Supermarket (Map pp196-7; ☎ 044 440 20 05; www .supermarket.li; Geroldstrasse 17; ◷ from 11pm Thu-Sat) Zürich's number one club is smaller than the name suggests, but boasts three cosy lounge bars around the dance floor, a covered back courtyard and an interesting roster of DJs playing house music. Watch out for 'Superyellow' nights in particular.

Mascotte (Map pp196-7; ☎ 044 260 15 80; www.mas cotte.ch; Theatrestrasse 17; ◷ Thu-Sun) The old variety hall 'Corso' is now a popular club with huge windows facing Sechseläutenplatz and the lake. It's renowned for Tuesday's Karaoke from Hell, where punters sing punk or metal songs accompanied by a live band.

Toni Molkerei (Map pp196-7; ☎ 044 273 23 60; Förrlibuckstrasse 109; ◷ from 10pm Wed-Sat) Based in a former dairy, this huge 20-something hangout is notable for the long rows of lounge chairs in its red-lit annexe, where vegetarian nibbles from Tibits/Hiltl are served.

Club Q (Map pp196-7; ☎ 044 444 40 50; www.club -q.ch; Förrlibückstrasse 151; ◷ from 11pm Thu-Sun) In a car park, this club is for those who take their dancing – to house, hip-hop and R&B – more seriously than seeing and being seen.

Labor Bar (Map pp196-7; ☎ 044 272 44 02; www
.laborbar.ch; Schiffbaustrasse 3; ☺ from 10pm Fri & Sat, from
9pm Sun) The set for local celebrity Kurt Ae-
schbacher's TV show, this is the epitome of
retro chic, with lots of Plexiglas and diffuse
coloured light. Always filled with beautiful
people, Friday is Celebreighties and Sunday
'for gays and friends'.

Indochine (Map pp196-7; ☎ 044 448 11 11; www.cl
ub-indochine.ch; Limmatstrasse 275; ☺ from 10pm Thu-Sat)
Models and rich kids mingle between the
dimly-lit fat Buddhas of this faux opium den.
It's Zürich's equivalent to London's China-
white or Paris's Buddha Bar.

Kaufleuten (Map p202; ☎ 044 225 33 22; www.kau
fleuten.com; Pelikanstrasse 18; ☺ from 11pm) An opulent Art Deco theatre with a stage, mezzanine floor and bars arranged around the
dance floor, Zürich's ritziest and most 'establishment' club plays house, hip-hop and
Latin rhythms to a slightly older crowd (ie
to, say, 45).

Cultural Centres

Rote Fabrik (for music ☎ 044 481 91 21, for theatre 044
482 42 12; www.rotefabrik.ch; Seestrasse 395; ☺ Tue-
Sun) This long-standing counter-cultural
institution has gone more mainstream in
recent years, but still stages rock concerts,
original-language films, theatre and dance
performances. There's also a bar and restaurant. Take bus No 161 or 165 from
Bürkliplatz.

Kanzlei (Map pp196-7; Kanzleistrasse 56; www.kan
zlei.ch) Kanzlei is similar to Rote Fabrik.

Xenix Filmclub (Map pp196-7; ☎ 044 242 04 11) A
cinema sitting alongside a bar and disco
(mostly funk, house, techno).

Gay & Lesbian Venues

Zürich has a lively gay scene, encompassing the previously mentioned Café Odeon
(p205). Other dedicated venues include the
bar **Barfüsser** (Map p202; Spitalgasse 14; ☺ daily)
and **Labyrinth Club** (Map pp196-7; Pfingstweidstrasse
70; ☺ Fri & Sat), the Zürich scene's top club.

Live Music

Tonhalle (Map pp196-7; ☎ 044 206 34 34; Claridenstrasse
7; tickets Sfr10-125) An opulent venue used by
Zürich's orchestra and chamber orchestra,
Tonhalle is patronised by the city's elite.

Opera House (Opernhaus; Map pp196-7; ☎ 044 268
66 66; Falkenstrasse 1) This also enjoys a worldwide reputation.

Sport

The local football team Grasshoppers plays
at **Hardturm Stadium** (Förrlibückstrasse). Catch tram
No 4 to Sportplatz Hardturm to get there.
However, **Letzigrund Stadium** (cnr Herden & Basler-
strasse) is being refurbished as the venue for
the Euro 2008 competition. Bus No 31 to
Letzipark will get you here.

SHOPPING

Neumarkt 17 (Map p202; Neumarkt 17) Selling cutting-edge furniture and homewares, this
store is just as famous for its own interior –
with ornamental wrought iron hanging over
a concrete 'chute' sitting above a reflective
water pool.

Fidelio (Map p202; Münzplatz 1) One of the city's
best clothes boutiques, Fidelio sells a wide
range of men's and women's wear, from
designer labels to street fashions.

Heimatwerk (Map p202; Rudolf Brun Brücke) Good-
quality, if touristy, souvenirs are found
here, including fondue pots, forks, toys and
classy handbags. Other branches are in the
train station and airport.

Jelmoli (Map p202; Seidengasse 1) The basement
food hall is the highlight of this legendary
department store.

The leading markets include the flea
markets at **Bürkliplatz** (Map pp196-7; ☺ 8am-4pm
Sat May-Oct) and **Rosenhof** (Map p202; ☺ 10am-9pm
Thu, 10am-4pm Sat Mar-Dec), but the tourist office
has details of more options.

GETTING THERE & AWAY
Air

Zürich airport (☎ 043 816 22 11; www.zurich-airport
.com) is a small international hub about 9km
north of the centre, with flights to most European capitals and to some in Africa, Asia
and North America.

Car & Motorcycle

The N3 approaches Zürich from the south
along the shore of Lake Zürich. The N1 is
the fastest route from Bern and Basel and
the main entry point from the west. The N1
also services routes to the north and east
of Zürich.

HIRE

Europcar (Map pp196-7; ☎ 044 271 56 56; Josefstrasse 53),
Hertz (Map pp196-7; ☎ 044 242 84 84; Morgartenstrasse 5)
and **Avis** (Map pp196-7; ☎ 044 296 87 87; Gartenhofstrasse
17) have airport branches. See p329 for rates.

ZÜRICH

Train

The busy Hauptbahnhof has direct trains to Stuttgart (Sfr95), Munich (Sfr90), Innsbruck (Sfr71) and Milan (Sfr75) and many other international destinations. There are also hourly departures to most major Swiss towns, such as Lucerne (Sfr22, 50 minutes), Bern (Sfr45, one hour) and Basel (Sfr30, 65 minutes).

GETTING AROUND
To/From the Airport

You're unlikely to need a taxi (around Sfr55). Up to eight trains an hour go to/from the Hauptbahnhof between around 6am and midnight, and the journey takes 12 minutes. (The so-called airport hotels, connected by road, take longer to reach!)

Bicycle

City bikes (www.zuerirollt.ch) may be borrowed or rented from various locations, including **Velogate** (Map pp196-7; ✪ 7.30am-9.30pm year-round), near platform 18 at the Hauptbahnhof; outside the department store **Globus** (Map p202; Usteristrasse; ✪ 7.30am-9.30pm May-Oct); and outside the **Opera House** (Map pp196-7; ✪ 7.30am-9.30pm May-Oct). A passport or identity card and Sfr20 must be left as a deposit. Rental is free if you bring the bike back after six hours for a pit-stop; otherwise it costs Sfr5 a day.

Boat

See the boxed text Waterfront Zürich, p198.

Car & Motorcycle

Parking is tricky and costly. The two most useful **car-parking garages** (www.parkhaeuser.ch; about Sfr32 a day) are opposite the main post office and on Uraniastrasse, next to the e-café. Otherwise street meters usually have a one-hour (Sfr2) or two-hour (Sfr5) maximum.

Public Transport

There's a unified system (www.zvv.ch) of buses, S-bahn suburban trains and, most importantly, trams. Services run from 5.30am to midnight, and tickets must be bought in advance. Every stop has a dispenser. Either type in the four-figure code for your destination or choose: a short single-trip *Kurzstrecke* ticket, valid for five stops (Sfr2.10; yellow button on dispenser); a single ticket for greater Zürich, valid for an hour (Sfr3.60; blue button); or a 24-hour city pass for the centre,

Zone 10 (Sfr7.20; green button). Tickets from dispensers don't need to be validated before travel; all others, such as the Zürichcard, must be stamped in the yellow 'Entwerfers' on the platforms. It's a Sfr80 fine if you're caught fare-evading.

A one-day pass for the whole canton costs Sfr30. Zürich's S-Bahn trains reach Baden, Schaffhausen, Stein am Rhein, Zug and Einsiedeln, but these are beyond the reach of the cantonal ticket.

Weekend night buses (around Sfr5, passes not valid) depart from Bellevue at 1am, 2am and 3am for suburban destinations.

Taxi

Taxis are expensive and usually unnecessary. It's not usual to hail them on the street; pick them up at the Hauptbahnhof or other ranks. Alternatively, call ☎ 044 444 44 44.

AROUND ZÜRICH

UETLIBERG
elevation 813m

One of the best half-day trips from Zürich starts off by taking the train (line S10) to Uetliberg at 813m (23 minutes, departures every 30 minutes). From here, you can take a panoramic two-hour **Planetenweg** (Planetary Path) running along the mountain ridge overlooking the lake to Felsenegg. En route you pass models of the planets in the solar system: all on a scale of one to 1000 million. At Felsenegg, a cable car descends every 10 minutes to Adliswil, from where frequent trains return to Zürich (line S4, 16 minutes). The day pass to buy is the Sfr14.40 Albis-Netzkarte, which gets you to Uetliberg and back, with unlimited travel downtown.

RAPPERSWIL
pop 7365 / elevation 405m

A pleasant excursion, especially for families, is to Rapperswil. It has a small, quaint old town and a well-known children's zoo. The **tourist office** (☎ 0848 811 500; www.zuerichsee.ch; Fischermarktplatz 1; ✪ 10am-5pm daily Apr-Oct, 1-5pm Nov-Mar) is by the lake, diagonally left (northwest) from the train station. In the same building, entered via the office, is a **Circus Museum** (adult/child Sfr4/2) detailing the history of Rapperswil's famous Knie family circus. (The circus itself is usually away on tour between March and November.)

Heading directly north of the train station, you come to the heart of the old town, with a 13th-century castle above it. Climb the hill for great views or to visit the small **Polish Museum** (☎ 055 210 18 62; www.museum-polskie.org; adult/child Sfr4/2; ☿ 1-5pm daily Apr-Oct, 1-5pm Sat & Sun Nov, Dec & Mar, closed Jan & Feb). The castle is also a popular wedding spot.

Knies Kinderzoo (☎ 055 220 67 60; www.knieskinder zoo.ch; Oberseestrasse; adult/child Sfr10/4.50; ☿ 9am-6pm mid-Mar–Oct) lies in the opposite direction, southeast of the station (signposted). Ponies, elephants and camels can be ridden, performing sea lions can be applauded and a whole host of creatures, from giraffes and apes to kangaroos and tortoises, can be admired and learnt about.

Staying overnight, **Jakob** (☎ 055 220 00 50; www.jakob-hotel.ch Hauptplatz 11; s/d/tr/f Sfr105/170/210/240; ☒) is the best midrange choice, with chic rooms in neutral tones. There's also a family-oriented **SYHA hostel** (☎ 055 210 99 27; www.youthhostel.ch; Hessenhofweg 10; dm/s/d Sfr28/50/78; ☿ closed Nov-Jan) near the lake in the suburb of Jona (catch the 'Südquartier' bus to Busskirch and then it's a 10-minute walk). Restaurants line Rapperswil's Fischmarktplatz, near the tourist office, and Hauptplatz, near Jakob.

Rapperswil can be reached by S5 or S7 from Zürich's main train station (one hour) or boat from Bürklipatz (two hours). The most cost-effective ticket for a day-trip is the 9-Uhr Tagespass (9 O'Clock Daypass; Sfr22), which is valid after 9am Monday to Friday and all day Saturday and Sunday; otherwise the fare is Sfr15 each way.

WINTERTHUR
pop 89,612 / elevation 447m

If ever there was a Swiss town to demonstrate the symbiosis between the financial services sector and art (ie millionaires' fondness for making tax-friendly investments in paintings and sculptures), leafy Winterthur is it. It gave its name to one of Europe's leading insurance companies, but is principally known for its amazing number of high-quality museums and galleries.

Information
Discount Card A museums pass costs Sfr16/25/28 for one/two/three days.

Post office (☎ 0848 888 888; Bahnhofplatz 8; ☿ 7.30am-7pm Mon-Fri, to 8pm Thu, 8am-5pm Sat)
Tourist office (☎ 052 267 67 00; www.winterthur -tourismus.ch; near platform 1, Hauptbahnhof; ☿ 8.30am-6.30pm Mon-Fri, 8.30am-4pm Sat)

Sights & Activities
Winterthur owes much of its eminence as an art mecca to collector Oskar Reinhart, a scion of a powerful banking and insurance family. His entire collection was bequeathed to the nation and entrusted to his hometown when he died in 1965. The **Sammlung Oskar Reinhart am Römerholz** (☎ 052 269 27 40; www.roemerholz.ch; Haldenstrasse 95; adult/student Sfr10/7; ☿ 10am-5pm Tue-Sun, to 8pm Wed) is particularly fascinating in the way it seeks to bridge the gap between traditional and modern art, juxtaposing the likes of Cézanne, Goya, Rembrandt and Rubens with Monet, Picasso, Renoir and Van Gogh. Take bus No 3 to Spital or get the Museums-Bus shuttle.

Reinhart's 500-strong collection of Swiss, German and Austrian artworks is on show at the **Museum Oskar Reinhart am Stadtgarten** (www .museumoskarreinhart.ch; Stadthausstrasse; adult/student Sfr8/6; ☿ 10am-5pm Tue-Sun), on the edges of the city park. A combined ticket for both museums is Sfr12/8).

Winterthur's outstanding **Fotomuseum** (Photo Museum; ☎ 052 234 10 34; Grüzenstrasse 44; admission varies; ☿ 11am-6pm Tue-Sun, to 8pm Wed) is another highlight among the city's total of 17, as is the **Kunstmuseum** (☎ 052 267 51 62; www.kwm.ch; adult/concession Sfr10/7; ☿ 10am-8pm Tue, 10am-5pm Wed-Sun), with its collection of 19th- and 20th-century art. See the tourist office for more details.

A Museums-Bus shuttle (Sfr5) leaves from the train station hourly between 9.45am and 4.45pm for the Sammlung Oskar Reinhart am Römerholz, Museum Oskar Reinhart am Stadtgarten and Kunstmuseum. On Sunday, the Fotomuseum is included in the circuit.

Just outside the city, there's an excellent exhibition at **Schloss Kyburg** (☎ 052 232 46 64; www.schlosskyburg.ch; adult/concession Sfr8/6; ☿ 10.30am-4.30pm Tue-Sun, to 5.30pm May-Oct, closed Dec & Jan). Mixing the ancient castle buildings with interactive technology, it's perfect for children. Take the S-bahn to Effretikon, then the bus to Kyburg. Ask the tourist office for the Kyburg leaflet, listing the times of the S-bahn train and bus connections. The journey takes 30 minutes each way.

ZÜRICH

ZÜRICH

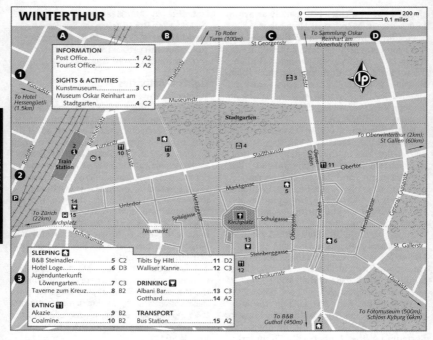

Sleeping

Most people will view Winterthur as a day trip from Zürich, but lower accommodation costs also make it a good base while visiting the larger city.

Jugendunterkunft Löwengarten (☎ 052 267 48 48; jugendunterkunft@win.ch; Wildbachstrasse 18; dm/s/d Sfr30/40/80, breakfast Sfr10 extra; ☒ reception 7-10.30am & 4-9.30pm, ☒ hostel closed Oct-Mar) Relatively quiet, fairly old hostel, with a kitchen and entertainment room upstairs, and a restaurant below.

Hotel Hessengüetli (☎ 052 224 32 32; www.hessen gueetli.ch; Oberfeldstrasse 10; s Sfr95-110, d Sfr140-150; P) Rooms here are modern and cheerful, if generic. In a quiet location a 10-minute bus ride from town, there's a Chinese restaurant attached. Take bus No 2 to Feldtal.

Taverne zum Kreuz (☎ 052 269 07 20; fax 052 260 07 39; Stadthausstrasse 10b/Im Stadtpark; s/d Sfr140/180) A charmingly lopsided half-timbered tavern from the 18th century, this has cosy rooms full of character.

Hotel Loge (☎ 052 268 12 00; www.hotelloge.ch; Graben 6; s/d Sfr160/200) Its strong business community means there are more expensive ho-

tels in Winterthur, but with its own bar, restaurant and even cinema, this designer place provides all the comfort and style you will ever need.

Also recommended:

B&B Guthof (☎ 052 233 52 43; www.bandb-guthof.ch; Guthof 3; s Sfr70-120, d Sfr110-160; ☒ P) Light, airy individually decorated rooms and a garden.

B&B Steinadler (☎ 052 212 53 25; www.steinadler.ch; Marktgasse 9, entrance via Obergasse; s/d 110/150; ☒) Pension under the roof of historic central building.

Eating

There's a cluster of bars and cheap restaurants along Neumarkt, offering a wide array of different ethnic cuisines.

Tibits by Hiltl (Oberer Graben 48; meals per 100g Sfr3.70; ☒ 6.30am-midnight daily, from 8am Sat & 9am Sun) The local branch of the Zürich buffet-style vegetarian café.

Coalmine (☎ 052 268 68 82; Turnerstrasse 1; most mains Sfr8-15; ☒ 8am-8pm Mon-Fri, 8am-6pm Sat) This cultural centre in the former coal cellar of the 'Folk Art' house is one of *the* places to be. As well as hosting gigs, author readings and art exhibitions, it has a bar and restaurant serving breakfast and lunch (and light eats at other times). Check out the floor-to-ceiling bookshelves.

Akazie (☎ 052 212 17 17; Stadthausstrasse 10; mains Sfr25-38, menus Sfr20-28; ⊙ 11am-midnight Mon-Sat) This restaurant serves nouvelle Mediterranean cuisine that come in old-fashioned portions.

Walliser Kanne (☎ 052 212 81 71; Steinberggasse 25; mains Sfr23-42; ⊙ lunch Mon, lunch & dinner Tue-Fri, dinner Sat) Try this rustic place for traditional Swiss specialities.

Drinking

Gotthard (☎ 052 212 09 05; Untertor) Winterthur's student population keeps the many bars humming all hours. Indeed, Gotthard literally keeps the taps flowing 24/7.

Albani Bar (☎ 052 212 69 96; Steinberggasse 16) The lounge lizard in you might also enjoy the dimly lit Albani, which has live music.

Roter Turm (23rd fl, Swisscom Tower, Theaterstrasse 17; ⊙ from 5pm Tue-Sat) You wouldn't want to spend all night in this fashionable but tiny space, but raise a glass to the view.

Getting There & Around

Four to five trains an hour run to Zürich airport (Sfr7.70, 15 minutes) and central Zürich (Sfr11.20). Many trains also go to Schaffhausen and Lake Constance (Bodensee). By road, the N1 (E60) motorway goes from Zürich, skirts Winterthur and continues to St Gallen and Austria. Main roads also lead to Constance (Konstanz) and Schaffhausen.

As local bus tickets to Oberwinterthur cost Sfr3.60, it's better to get a 24-hour pass for Sfr7.20 instead.

ZÜRICH

Central Switzerland

In its own way as gorgeous as the Bernese Oberland, Switzerland's geographical and political heartland has a more soothing beauty. The mountains hunching conspiratorially around Lake Lucerne at the core of the region are greener and less jagged, and a greater number of Alpine villages and larger towns make the place feel more lived-in and familiar.

The pact that kick-started the Swiss nation was signed here more than 700 years ago on the shores of Lake Uri, and Central Switzerland is the guardian of many Swiss founding tales and myths. Its far-east corner is William Tell country, where the legendary patriot is said to have shot an apple from his son's head and gone on the run. The nearby Rütli meadow is revered as the exact spot where Switzerland was signed into being in 1291; the village of Schwyz still proudly displays that original constitution.

Interesting stories attach themselves to many places, from the Christian miracle that made Einsiedeln a place of pilgrimage to the pagan superstitions surrounding several peaks. According to legend, the ghost of Pontius Pilate haunts Mt Pilatus, while mischievous elves inhabit the sides of Mt Rigi.

Taking a cable car up these panoramic mountains, and others like them such as Mt Titlis and the Stanserhorn, is one of the main pastimes here. Meanwhile, lake steamers bob from shore to shore, and there's plenty of scenic hiking and skiing to be enjoyed.

Of course, as the largest town, Lucerne itself remains pivotal to the experience. Built on water, with medieval bridges, old squares and a striking skyline, it's one of the country's main drawcards. Sometimes, when tour guides in medieval costume appear, it's even vaguely reminiscent of Venice. Fortunately, however, it never gets that choked or busy.

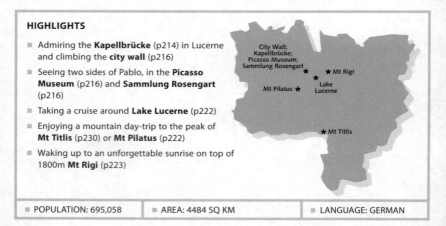

HIGHLIGHTS

- Admiring the **Kapellbrücke** (p214) in Lucerne and climbing the **city wall** (p216)
- Seeing two sides of Pablo, in the **Picasso Museum** (p216) and **Sammlung Rosengart** (p216)
- Taking a cruise around **Lake Lucerne** (p222)
- Enjoying a mountain day-trip to the peak of **Mt Titlis** (p230) or **Mt Pilatus** (p222)
- Waking up to an unforgettable sunrise on top of 1800m **Mt Rigi** (p223)

City Wall;
Kapellbrücke;
Picasso Museum;
Sammlung Rosengart ★

★ Mt Rigi

Mt Pilatus ★   Lake Lucerne

★ Mt Titlis

| POPULATION: 695,058 | AREA: 4484 SQ KM | LANGUAGE: GERMAN |

CENTRAL SWITZERLAND

Orientation & Information

The official tourist region of Central Switzerland (Zentralschweiz) has at its heart Lake Lucerne (the Vierwaldstättersee or Lake of the Four Forest Cantons), which is surrounded by the four cantons of Lucerne, Uri, Schwyz and Unterwalden (itself subdivided into the half-cantons of Nidwalden and Obwalden). Also included in this region is Switzerland's smallest rural canton of Zug, containing Lake Zug (Zugersee). In the north and west, Central Switzerland is fairly flat, but a southern tip reaches into the Alps as far as the St Gotthard Pass.

For information on the entire region, contact the tourist office in Lucerne (p214).

Getting There & Around

The nearest airport is Zürich, while road and rail connections are excellent in all directions. An interesting way to leave the region is on the William Tell Express (p331).

If you don't have a Swiss or Eurail Pass (both include lake journeys), you might want to consider purchasing the regional **Tell-Pass** (www.tell-pass.ch; per 7/15 days Sfr140/188; ⏲ Apr-Oct) for rail and boat travel. Sold by the Lucerne tourist office and at all boat stations, it provides travel for two/five days respectively, and half-price fares for the remainder.

The Vierwaldstättersee guest card, available whenever you're staying anywhere in this

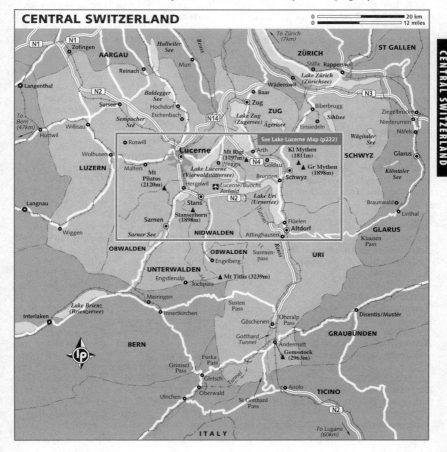

CENTRAL SWITZERLAND

region, is worth having; you should ask for it if your accommodation doesn't offer it. Benefits include various discounts on sporting facilities, 10% to 50% off certain cable cars, and reductions on museum admission in Lucerne and elsewhere.

LUCERNE

pop 57,817 / elevation 435m

Legend has it that an angel with a light showed Lucerne's first settlers where to build a chapel, and in good weather even an atheist might describe the city's location as heavensent. Lapped by a scenic lake, surrounded by mountains of myth – a picture of this once small fishing village and its wooden Kapellbrücke (Chapel Bridge) is enough to connote the very essence of Switzerland.

Between the 13th and 19th centuries, Lucerne (Luzern in German, or 'the city of lights') made its fortune as an essential stop on the trade route over the Alps. Then its charming medieval centre and its fabulous position began attracting tourists. It's never looked back.

Orientation

The city is on the western edge of its namesake lake, straddling the Reuss River. The medieval town centre is on the northern riverbank, within walking distance of the Hauptbahnhof (train station) on the southern side.

Information

BOOKSHOPS

Schweizerhof Buchhandlung (☎ 041 410 23 71; Schweizerhofquai 2; ☻ 1.30-6.30pm Mon, 8.30am-6.30pm Tue-Fri, 8am-4pm Sat)

DISCOUNT CARDS

Luzern Guide Stamped by your hotel, this entitles you to discounts on museum entry, some sporting facilities, car rental and lake cruises.

Museum Pass (per adult/child Sfr29/14.50) Free entry to all museums; valid for one month.

INTERNET ACCESS

Stadtbibliothek (Town Library; Löwenplatz 11; per hr Sfr4; ☻ 1.30-6pm Mon, 10am-6.30pm Tue-Fri, to 9pm Thu, 10am-4pm Sat)

Internetcafé (☎ 041 410 77 27; Löwengraben 31; per 15min Sfr4; ☻ 9am-9pm)

LAUNDRY

Jet Wash (☎ 041 240 01 51; Bruchstrasse 28; ☻ 8.30am-12.30pm & 2.30-6.30pm Mon-Thu, 8.30am-12.30pm Fri, 9am-2pm Sat)

MEDICAL SERVICES

Permanence Medical Center (☎ 041 211 14 44; Basement, Hauptbahnhof; ☻ 24hr)

MONEY

There are numerous ATMs all around the Hauptbahnhof.

Hauptbahnhof (☎ 041 227 36 46; ☻ 8.30am-6pm Mon-Fri, 9am-5pm Sat & Sun)

POST

Main post office (☎ 041 229 95 23; cnr Bahnhofstrasse & Bahnhofplatz; ☻ 7.30am-6.30pm Mon-Fri, 8am-4pm Sat) By the train station.

TOURIST INFORMATION

Luzern Tourism (enquiries ☎ 041 227 17 17, hotel reservations 041 227 17 27; www.luzern.org; Zentralstrasse 5; ☻ 8.30am-7.30pm Mon-Fri, 9am-7.30pm Sat & Sun mid-Jun–mid-Sep, to 6.30pm May & Oct, 8.30am-5.30pm Mon-Fri, 9am-1pm Sat & Sun Nov-Apr) Reached from either Zentralstrasse or from Platform 3 of the train station. Offers city walking tours.

Sights

MEDIEVAL BRIDGES

The **Kapellbrücke** (Chapel Bridge), crossing the Reuss River in the Old Town, is Lucerne's most potent symbol. It dates from the 14th century and the octagonal water tower remains original. However its sides and gabled roof are modern reconstructions, rebuilt after a disastrous fire in 1993.

The bridge is famous for the triangular, painted roof panels that line its ceiling, created by Heinrich Wägmann in 1614 and depicting important events from Swiss history and mythology. Fortunately, some 30 of these were also rescued from the blaze and have been replaced at either end of the bridge. Gaps between them have been retained as a constant reminder of the loss of others.

The **Spreuerbrücke** (Spreuer Bridge) further down the river is darker and smaller, but its 1408 structure and 17th-century paintings are all original. The roof panels' theme here is artist Caspar Meglinger's movie-storyboard-style sequence of paintings, *The Dance of Death*.

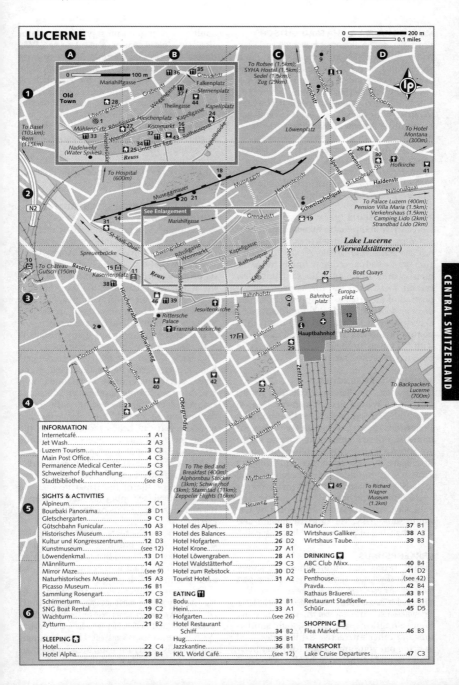

LUCERNE

CENTRAL SWITZERLAND

CENTRAL SWITZERLAND

MUSEGGMAUER & CHÂTEAU GUTSCH

From its medieval **Museggmauer** (city wall; admission free; 8am-7pm Apr-Oct), there are marvellous views over Lucerne's rooftops to the lake and mountains beyond. A walkway is open between the **Schirmerturm** (tower), where you enter, and the **Wachturm**, from where you have to retrace your steps. You can also ascend and descend the **Zytturm** or **Männliturm** (the latter not connected to the ramparts walkway).

At the time of writing, the hilltop **Château Gutsch** hotel was closed, its fate unknown. However, the Gütschbahn funicular (Sfr3 each way) continues to run up to the summit, where there are also breathtaking views.

PICASSO MUSEUM

Don't arrive at the **Picasso Museum** (041 410 35 33; Furrengasse 21; adult/student & senior Sfr8/6, combined with Sammlung Rosengart Sfr18/16; 10am-6pm Apr-Oct, 11am-5pm Nov-Mar) expecting to find many of the man's works. Although it does include a few ceramics and sketches, this is principally a portrait of the artist as an impish craftsman, lover and father. Nearly 200 photographs by David Douglas Duncan create a captivating picture of the last 17 years of Picasso's life with his family in their Cannes home. It's a uniquely revealing series.

SAMMLUNG ROSENGART

By contrast, the **Rosengart Collection** (041 220 16 60; www.rosengart.ch; Pilatusstrasse 10; adult/student Sfr15/9, combined with Picasso Museum Sfr18/16; 10am-6pm Apr-Oct, 11am-5pm Nov-Mar) *does* contain a significant amount of Picasso's own art. Showcasing the works retained by Angela Rosengart, a Swiss art dealer and friend of Picasso's, its ground floor is entirely devoted to the Spanish master. In the basement, there's a selection of sketches and small paintings by Paul Klee; upstairs you'll find works by Cezanne, Kandinsky, Miro and Modigliani, and a fine handful of pictures by Marc Chagall.

VERKEHRSHAUS

Planes, trains and automobiles are showcased in the huge, family-oriented **Transport Museum** (0848 852 020; www.verkehrshaus.org; Lidostrasse 5; adult/child/rail-pass holder/student Sfr24/10/12/22; 9am-6pm Apr-Oct, 10am-5pm Nov-Mar). They are found alongside space rockets, flight simulators and other interactive exhibits designed to bring out your inner child (or inner bully if you're one of the occasionally over-eager

adults). Switzerland's most popular museum also has a planetarium, a giant-screen **IMAX cinema** (www.imax.ch; adult/child Sfr16/12 extra, not covered by the Museum Pass; screenings hourly 11am-9pm) and the **Swiss Arena** – an eye-catching floor map of Switzerland and accompanying geographical puzzle. There's a collection of technology-related paintings, drawings and sculptures by Swiss artist Hans Erni. Finally, in good weather, a permanently moored hot-air balloon, the Hi-Flyer, will take you up 120m above the complex (call 041 370 20 20 after noon daily for details). Take bus No 6, 8 or 24 to get here.

KULTUR UND KONGRESSZENTRUM & KUNSTMUSEUM

A striking work of post-modern architecture in an otherwise largely historic city, Parisian architect Jean Nouvel's **KKL** (Arts & Congress Centre; www.kkl-luzern.ch; Europaplatz) really stands out with its prime waterfront location, neighbouring the main train station. But if you think it looks good, wait until you hear it. The acoustics of the main concert hall are as close to perfect as humankind has ever known – or at least that's the verdict of many musicians and conductors who have performed here. The trick is that the tall, narrow concert hall is partly built below the level of the lake's surface, is entirely surrounded by a reverberation chamber and has an adjustable suspended ceiling, all creating extra sound dampening. In the bubble of silence that has resulted, you can hear everything – to the point where audience members are even quite self-conscious about unwrapping sweets.

All the accolades showered upon the hall – it can be adjusted to any type of music – have raised the profile of the tripartite Lucerne Music Festival (see opposite). So increasingly it's one of the highlights on the global music calendar.

There are public **tours** (041 226 77 77; info@kkl-luzern.ch) of the building most Saturdays and Sundays at 11am, but they are only in German. Individual tours can, however, be arranged in English for groups.

Otherwise, you can enter the building to see the city's **Kunstmuseum** (Museum of Art; 041 226 78 00; www.kunstmuseumluzern.ch; Level K, KKL, Europaplatz; adult/child Sfr10/8, Sfr4 extra for special exhibits; 10am-5pm Tue-Sun, to 8pm Wed). The permanent collection is pretty uninspiring, but keep an eye out for temporary exhibitions.

VICTORIAN-ERA ATTRACTIONS

North of the old town, there's a cluster of 19th-century attractions for which Lucerne is famous but whose appeal is largely nostalgic. The renowned **Löwendenkmal** (Lion Monument; Denkmalstrasse) is dedicated to the Swiss soldiers who died in 1792 defending King Louis XVI and family during the French Revolution. Mark Twain once called this carved lion the 'saddest and most moving piece of rock in the world', but the sentiment might be lost on modern audiences.

Next door is the **Gletschergarten** (Glacier Garden; ☎ 041 410 43 40; www.glaciergarden.org; Denkmalstrasse 4; adult/student/child Sfr10/8/5; ☼ 9am-6pm Apr-Oct, 10am-5pm rest of year). This strip of rock bears the scars (including huge potholes) inflicted on it by the glacier that slid over it some 20 million years ago. The best thing about the garden, though, is its kitschy 1001-nights mirror maze. The **Alpineum** (☎ 041 410 40 64; www.alpineum.ch; Denkmalstrasse 11; adult/student Sfr5/4; ☼ 9am-12.30pm & 1.30-6pm Apr-Oct) opposite is a musty collection of Alpine relief maps and can be easily missed.

The renovated **Bourbaki Panorama** (☎ 041 412 30 30; www.bourbakipanorama.ch; Löwenplatz 11; adult/student & senior Sfr8/7; ☼ 9am-6pm) is a very professional depiction of the Franco-Prussian war of 1870–71, with a moving narrative (also in English) that brings to life the 1100-sq-metre circular painting of miserable-looking troops and civilians. All the same, it's hard to see the panorama appealing to those without a specific military interest.

OTHER MUSEUMS

Historisches Museum (History Museum; ☎ 041 228 54 24; www.hmluzern.ch; Pfistergasse 24; adult/child/student Sfr6/2.50/5; ☼ 10am-5pm Tue-Sun) is cleverly and carefully organised into a series of attention-grabbing themes, from lust and lasciviousness to government and tourism. Pick up a barcode-reading audio-guide, pick your topic and let yourself be guided through your chosen story in German or English.

The **Naturhistorisches Museum** (Museum of Natural History; ☎ 041 228 54 11; www.naturmuseum.ch Kasernenplatz 6; adult/child/student Sfr6/1.50/5; ☼ 10am-5pm Tue-Sun) offers an enticing entree into the natural world, especially for children, with lots of hands-on displays.

The **Richard Wagner Museum** (☎ 041 360 23 70; www.richard-wagner-museum.ch; Richard-Wagner-Weg 27; adult/student Sfr6/4; ☼ 10am-noon & 2-5pm Tue-Sun mid-Mar–Nov), housed in the composer's former residence in Tribschen, on the lake's southern shore, has a collection of historic musical instruments.

Activities

There's supervised swimming at the **Strandbad Lido** (☎ 041 370 38 06; adult/child Sfr6/3) near Camping Lido (see p219) or you can swim for free on the other bank of the lake by Seepark, off Alpenquai.

SNG (☎ 041 368 08 08; www.sng.ch), on the northern side of Seebrücke, rents out rowing boats, pedalos and small motor boats (from Sfr25/25/50 per hour, plus deposit) and offers cheap lake cruises (Sfr15).

If you can't choose between an ascent up Mts Rigi, Pilatus, Titlis or the Stanserhorn, you can cover them all quickly, as well as Lake Lucerne, on a **Zeppelin flight** (☎ 052 354 58 74, 052 354 58 88; www.skycruise.ch; flights from Sfr380; ☼ Wed-Sun May-Oct, subject to change). Blimps leave from Lucerne/Buochs airfield near Stans.

For snowshoe tours (from Sfr85) or adventure sports like tandem paragliding (for Sfr150), bungee jumping (Sfr160) and canyoning (from Sfr155), contact **Outventure** (☎ 041 611 14 41; www.outventure.ch; Stansstad).

Festivals & Events

Lucerne's six-day **Fasnacht** celebrations are more boisterous and fun than Basel's famous carnival. The party kicks off on 'Dirty Thursday' with the emergence of the character 'Fritschi' from a window in the town hall, when bands of musicians and revellers take to the streets. The carnival moves through increasingly raucous celebrations climaxing on Mardi Gras (Fat Tuesday), and is over on Ash Wednesday.

The musical **Lucerne Festival** (tickets ☎ 041 226 44 80, info 041 226 44 00; www.lucernefestival.ch) is divided into three separate seasons, Easter, summer and 'Piano' (in November). Concerts take place in the KKL (opposite).

Lucerne has several public holidays in addition to national ones: Corpus Christi (30 May), Assumption (15 August), St Leodegar's Day (2 October), All Saints' Day (1 November), Immaculate Conception (8 December), New Year's Eve and 2 January.

Walking Tour

Start by crossing the **Kapellbrücke** (**1**; p214) from the south to the north bank, admiring the illustrated roof panels in order as you go. Double back to the south bank along the modern, concrete Rathaussteg bridge, arriving in front of the **Jesuitenkirche (2)**, the oldest baroque church in Switzerland. Behind this lies the medieval **Franziskanerkirche (3)**, which has been frequently altered since its original construction in the 13th century. The nearby **Rittersche palace (4)** was built in 1577 for the city's mayor, but now houses the cantonal government.

Continue west along the south bank, past the **Nadelwehr (5)**, or water spikes, once used to regulate the river's water levels. Skirt left around the **Naturhistorisches Museum (6**; p217) and cross the **Spreuerbrücke (7**; p214).

You're now in Mühleplatz on the edge of the old city. Veer right into Weinmarkt, as you admire the painted façades on several of the historic buildings. Then exit into Hirschenplatz, where you'll see a building with a drawing of Goethe, boasting that the writer once lodged here in 1779. Follow Weggisgasse to the intersection with Mariahilfgasse and turn left up the hill.

At the top, follow the stairs up through the park to the **Musseggmauer (8)**. Climb the

Schirmerturm here and enjoy a walk to and fro along the city ramparts, before emerging in the same place.

Head left (northeast) out of the park and continue down Musseggstrasse, passing underneath an arch in the city wall and continuing on to Museumsplatz. Turn left until you come to the **Bourbaki Panorama (9**; p217) and Löwenplatz. Cross the square diagonally to have a quick look at Lucerne's famous **Löwendenkmal (10**; p217).

On the return leg, make a detour south to the **Hofkirche (11)**, on the site of Lucerne's first monastery. Even if you're not particularly interested in the part Romanesque, part Rennaissance church, there's a nice view from its broad stairs – and it's an ideal spot to gather your breath.

Finally, make your way back along Schweizerhofquai to Rathausquai and choose one of the restaurants or cafés facing the waterfront to enjoy a drink.

Sleeping
BUDGET
Hostels
Backpackers Lucerne (☎ 041 360 04 20; www.backpackerslucerne.ch; Alpenquai 42; dm Sfr28, d Sfr66; ☑ reception 7-10am & 4-11pm) Cheerfully decorated, with balconies overlooking the lake in a leafy spot, this friendly former students' residence makes a superlative backpackers' hostel. Facilities include kitchen and laundry. It's a 15-minute walk southeast of the train station.

WALK FACTS

Start Kapellbrücke
Finish Rathausquai
Distance 3.5km
Duration 1½ hours

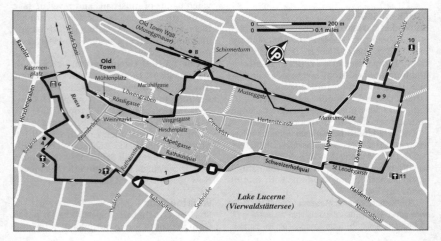

SYHA hostel (☎ 041 420 88 00; www.youthhostel.ch/luzern; Sedelstrasse 12; dm/d Sfr32.50/82; ⓦ check-in 2pm-midnight in summer, from 4pm in winter; 🖳 Ⓟ) Although modern, well-run and clean, this hostel's location north of the centre is not particularly convenient. It still gets busy in summer, though, when it's best to book. Get bus No 18 from the train station to Jugendherberge, bus No 19 to Rosenberg or bus No 1 to Schlossberg.

Pensions & Hotels
Tourist Hotel (☎ 041 410 24 74; www.touristhotel.ch; St-Karli-Quai 12; dm Sfr35-40, s/d Sfr70/100, with bathroom Sfr90/120; 🖳 ⊠) On the waterfront but away from the bustling tourist zone, this friendly budget hotel feels like an upmarket hostel, with spotless rooms in varying cheerful colour schemes. Some have balconies.

Bed and Breakfast (☎ 041 310 15 14; www.theBandB .ch; Taubenhausstrasse 34; s/d with shared bathroom Sfr80/120; ⊠ Ⓟ) On a good day, the atmosphere at this cosy, stylish residence feels like a bunch of friends – of varying ages – have got together for a calm, relaxing weekend. Rooms have white walls and parquet flooring, while there's a lovely old-fashioned bathroom with tub and pleasant garden. Take bus No 1 to Eichof.

Hotel Löwengraben (☎ 041 417 12 12; www.loewen graben.ch; Löwengraben 18; dm/s/d/ste Sfr30/120/165/165; ⊠) This revamped prison is a novelty, but fussier guests might find that the cheaper rooms all too accurately re-create the jail experience. With cell doors and barred windows, they consist of little more than a bed, bare floorboards and a prefabricated bathroom. They do for a short stay, however, while the suites are more congenial.

Also recommended:
Hotel Alpha (☎ 041 240 42 80; www.hotelalpha.ch; Zähringerstrasse 24; s/d Sfr75/110) Simple but clean lodgings, about a 10-minute walk from the centre.
Pension Villa Maria (☎ 041 370 21 19; villamaria@ bluewin.ch; Haldenstrasse 36; d with shared/private bathroom Sfr130/160; ⓦ closed Nov-Feb; Ⓟ) Friendly granny-chic pension near the Transport Museum. Most rooms share facilities.

Camping
Camping Lido (☎ 041 370 21 46; www.camping-international.ch; Lidostrasse 8; camp sites per adult/tent Sfr10/10, plus Sfr5 for electricity, cabin beds Sfr20; ⓦ 15 Mar–31 Oct) The well-equipped ground is on the lake's northern shore, east of town. It also has six-

bed wooden cabins (no breakfast, sleeping bag required). Get bus No 6, 8 or 24 or a boat to the Verkehrshaus.

MIDRANGE & TOP END
Most of the following hotels offer discounted rates during winter – sometimes up to one-third off.

Hotel zum Rebstock (☎ 041 410 35 81; www.here weare.ch; St-Leodegar-Strasse 3; s/d & tr Sfr160/260; Ⓟ) Spread over two houses – one still with medieval wooden beams and low ceilings – Rebstock's excellent rooms are tastefully decorated in a range of styles from urban to rustic and colonial to romantic. In three of them, funky tile decorations have been used to turn the bathrooms into works of art.

Hotel Hofgarten (☎ 041 410 88 88; www.hofgarten.ch; Stadthofstrasse 14; s/d/tr from Sfr195/295/335; 🖳 ⊠ Ⓟ) Rebstock's sister hotel also has striking, individually decorated rooms, but in a slightly more streamlined fashion. The Mies van der Rohe furniture in No 226 sets the tone.

Hotel des Alpes (☎ 041 410 58 25; www.desalpes -luzern.ch; Rathausquai 5; s/d from Sfr125/195) The best of the several hotels along this noisy strip, Hotel des Alpes' rooms are older in style, but the place is well-maintained and over-looks the river near the Kapellbrücke.

Hotel Waldstätterhof (☎ 041 227 12 71; www.hotel -waldstaetterhof.ch; Zentralstrasse 4; s Sfr150-170, d Sfr190-270; ⊠ Ⓟ) Surprisingly good for a hotel right opposite the train station, this temperance hotel has jauntily coloured modern rooms behind its faux Gothic, red-brick exterior.

Hotel des Balances (☎ 041 418 28 28; www.balances .ch; Weinmarkt 6; s Sfr200-350, d Sfr300-420; 🖳 Ⓟ) City tour guides frequently describe this four-star hotel's historic frescoed façade as the city's most beautiful, and the rooms inside are elegant, too. Be warned, however, that the Weinmarkt square can be noisy at night, so book rooms facing the river if possible.

Hotel Krone (☎ 041 419 44 00; www.krone-luzern .ch; Weinmarkt 12; s/d Sfr185/290) The central Krone combines an ornate historic façade with modern, pastel-coloured rooms through-out. Those facing the square are noisier.

Hotel Montana (☎ 041 419 00 00; www.hotel-mon tana.ch; Adligenswilerstrasse 22; s Sfr195-295, d Sfr320-440; 🖳 ⊠) This opulent Art Deco hotel perches on a hill overlooking the lake and is reached by its own funicular. Many of the generously sized bedrooms enjoy fantastic views, as do the breakfast room, terrace and the barrel-hall entrance.

Hotel (☎ 041 226 86 86; www.the-hotel.ch; Sempacherstrasse 14; ste from Sfr350-540; 🅿) Be a film star in your own bedtime in architect Jean Nouvel's low-lit design hotel, which features a scene from a different arthouse movie on the ceiling of each sleek matt-black suite.

Palace Luzern (☎ 041 416 16 16; www.palace-luzern .ch; Haldenstrasse 10; s Sfr390-560, d Sfr490-660) This huge luxury hotel on the waterfront is a favourite with the *Condé Nast* set for its *belle époque* style. Given its supposed pre-eminence, though, some finishes look a touch less than perfect. Some guests find it slightly overpriced.

Eating

Bodu (☎ 041 410 01 77; Kornmarkt 5; mains Sfr18-45) This French brasserie is a local institution, celebrated for its Parisian-café interior, Bordeaux wines and excellent river views. It specialises in Provençale cuisine, but also branches out into dishes from Piedmont and even the Antilles.

Hofgarten (☎ 041 41 0 01 77; Kornmarkt 5; soups & salads Sfr10, mains Sfr24-30, daily menus Sfr20) Enjoy the best vegetarian food in town in this restaurant's leafy garden. The specialities range from braised aubergine to Thai curry to vegetarian *Lozärner Chögalipaschtleti* (stuffed vol-au-vents), but the emphasis is always on fresh ingredients.

Jazzkantine (☎ 041 410 73 73; Grabenstrasse 8; snacks from Sfr6.50, mains Sfr19-25; 🕑 7-12.30am Mon-Sat, 4pm-12.30am Sun) With its stainless steel bar, sturdy wooden tables, chalkboard menus and wide selection of whiskies, this is a funky and rather smoky haunt, where you might have trouble catching a staff member's attention. Weeknight jazz workshops are followed by gigs on Saturday night.

KKL World Café (Europaplatz 1; sandwiches from Sfr8.50, mains Sfr16-19; 🕑 9am-midnight) This sleek-looking, casual bistro stocks muesli and sandwiches in its glass counters, but also offers a range of world dishes in woks at lunch and dinner.

Hotel Restaurant Schiff (☎ 041 418 52 52; Unter der Egg 8; mains Sfr20-45) Fish from Lake Lucerne, home-made Wurst and some of the city's most celebrated *Chögalipaschtleti* (vol-au-vents stuffed with meat and mushrooms – called *Kügelipastetli* in High German) are served at this old-fashioned but esteemed

AUTHOR'S CHOICE

Wirtshaus Taube (☎ 041 210 07 47; Burgerstrasse 3; mains Sfr18-40; 🕑 11am-midnight Mon-Sat) An excellent place to sample the local *Rüüdigi* cuisine, Taube has its own best-selling cookbook and a menu that goes well beyond Lucerne's trademark *Chögalipaschtleti* vol-au-vents. Lake fish, milk soup, rösti, calf's liver, homemade veal or pork sausages with onion sauce, venison and Alpine macaroni are just a few of the other dishes served in this updated but still cosy, former tavern.

restaurant. In summer, sit under the arcades facing the waterfront.

Wirtshaus Galliker (☎ 041 240 10 01; Schützenstrasse 1; mains Sfr20-50; 🕑 lunch & dinner Tue-Sat, closed Jul–mid-Aug) This very old fashioned restaurant is not without charm. The same family has owned it since 1856 and many groups of customers seem to be regulars, which bodes well for the traditional Lucerne cuisine.

Hug (☎ 041 410 10 92; Mühleplatz 6; lunch menus Sfr17-25; 🕑 7am-5pm Mon-Sat) This traditional café on the waterfront serves excellent breakfasts, delicious cakes and confectionery, plus cheap Swiss and Lucerne specialities. It's a successful local chain and has other outlets.

Heini (☎ 041 412 20 20; Am Falkenplatz) Heini has since mushroomed into a successful bakery/confectionery chain, but this was one of the original outlets and has an atmospheric 'grand café' as well as a takeaway shop.

Manor (cnr Theilingasse & Weggisgasse) This branch of the national supermarket restaurant chain is noteworthy for its panoramic roof terrace.

Drinking & Entertainment

Rathaus Bräuerei (☎ 041 410 52 57; Unter den Egg 2; 🕑 9am-midnight Wed-Sun, from 8am Tue & Sat) Sip home-brewed beer under the vaulted arches of this atmospheric tavern, or nab a pavement table and watch the river flow.

Penthouse (Astoria Hotel, Pilatusstrasse 29) This is a ritzy rooftop bar with plump sofas where, despite the great view, the clientele are busier discreetly checking each other out. On the ground floor in the same hotel, you'll find the door to the equally posh, but very popular Pravda nightclub (open Wednesday to Saturday) – a place where Ministry of Sound DJs have regular residencies.

ABC Club Mixx (☎ 041 240 88 77; www.abcmixx.ch; Pilatusplatz; ☺ daily) This plush mainstream club is unusually built inside a former cinema and retains some of the flock wallpaper in the entrance.

Loft (Haldenstrasse 21; ☺ Wed-Sun) With a steel-and-concrete minimalist design, this attracts a trendy, well-dressed, but unpretentious, young crowd and plays danceable house, Latin, hip-hop and urban sounds.

Schüür (☎ 041 368 10 30; www.schuur.ch; Tribschen-strasse 1; ☺ generally Wed-Sun) Laid-back DJ bar and club attracting a mixed crowd (late 20s, early 30s), although the mood depends on the programme of music. Turn left just after the railway bridge, then right.

Sedel (Emmenbrücke; ☺ always Fri & Sat, but sometimes also Mon & Thu) This formerly rundown, squat-like former prison was undergoing renovation at the time of writing, but should still maintain a fairly underground air with live industrial, experimental and punk music. It's near the SYHA hostel, behind Rotsee.

Restaurant Stadtkeller (☎ 041 410 47 33; Sternenplatz 3) Folkloric tourist trap.

Shopping

Fruit and vegetable stalls spring forth along the river quays every Tuesday and Saturday morning. There's also a **flea market** (Burgerstrasse/Reusssteg) each Saturday from May to October.

Getting There & Away

Hourly trains connect Lucerne to Interlaken (Sfr29, two hours, via the scenic Brünig Pass), Bern (Sfr34, 1¼ hours), Lugano (Sfr56, 2¾ hours) and Geneva (Sfr70, 3¼ hours, via Olten or Langnau). Zürich-bound trains are hourly (Sfr22, one hour).

The N2 (E9) motorway connecting Basel and Lugano passes by Lucerne, and the N14 provides the road link to Zürich.

BOAT

For information on boat transport, see p222. The departure points are the quays around Bahnhofplatz/Europaplatz.

Getting Around

Should you be going further than the largely pedestrianised Old Town, city buses leave from outside the Hauptbahnhof at Bahn-hofplatz. Tickets cost Sfr2 for a short journey, Sfr2.60 for one zone and Sfr3.80 for two. Ticket dispensers indicate the correct fare for each destination. The 24-hour pass (Sfr9.50) covers all zones, though with a stamped *Luzern* guide you can get a three-day bus ticket for Sfr14 and Swiss Pass holders travel free. There's an underground car park at the train station.

AROUND LUCERNE
Alphornbau Stocker

The Alphorn workshop **Stocker** (☎ 041 340 88 86; Industrie Schweighof, CH6010 Kriens-Luzern; admission free; ☺ 8am-noon & 2-6pm Mon-Fri, 9am-noon Sat) is south of Lucerne in Schweighof (take bus No 1 to Kriens, then bus No 16 to Oberkuoni-matt). Here you can learn all about how these huge, unwieldy Alpine instruments are made and have the chance not only to buy, but also to blow, your own horn.

Glasi Hergiswil

A visit to **Hergiswil Glassworks** (☎ 041 630 12 23; www.glasi.ch; Seestrasse 12; admission free; ☺ 9am-6pm Mon-Fri, 9am-4pm Sat; glass-blowing only until noon on Sat) is instructive and interesting, with the chance to see glass-blowing in action and buy souvenirs, after listening to an audiovisual history. The factory is between Lucerne and Alpnach-stad, and is an easy stopover on a round-trip up to Mt Pilatus (p222). Make sure your train stops at Hergiswil, however, as not all do.

LAKE LUCERNE

It's possible to feel the call of the mountains even while standing in downtown Lucerne. Majestic peaks hunch over the coastline of the adjacent Lake of the Four Forest Cantons, or Vierwaldstättersee – which twists and turns as much as the tongue does while saying that. (Little wonder English speakers use the shorthand Lake Lucerne.)

With Mt Pilatus, Mt Rigi and the Stanserhorn all having lookouts on their summits, you're really spoilt for choice. But, rest assured, any view across the shimmering expanse of water to the green hillsides, meadows and valleys beyond is never disappointing.

And apart from its many mountain lookout points, the lake also offers pleasant little tucked-away resorts, which can be reached by boat. The far eastern reach of Lake Lucerne – Lake Uri or Urnersee – has special significance for the Swiss, as it's home to the Rütli meadow where the country was supposedly born.

Getting Around

The **Lake Lucerne Navigation Company SGV** (☎ 041 367 67 67; www.lakelucerne.ch in German) operates boats (sometimes paddle-steamers) daily. This excludes the Lake Uri section of the lake, its most easterly finger, where services only go past Rütli in winter on Sundays and national holidays.

From Lucerne, destinations include Alpnachstad (one way/return Sfr19.20/20, 40 minutes each way), Weggis (Sfr13.80/21, 45 minutes), Vitznau (Sfr19.20/29, 55 minutes), Brunnen (Sfr28/42, 1¾ hours) and Flüelen (Sfr32/48, two hours). Longer trips are relatively much cheaper than short ones, and you can alight as often as you want. Swiss Pass and Eurail (on days selected for travel only) are valid on scheduled boat trips, while Inter Rail entitles you to half-price. Passes will get you discounts on selected mountain railways and cable cars. Ask about discounts for late afternoon or evening round trips during summer. There are also special dinner/dancing cruises on offer.

If driving, you'll find that roads run close to the shoreline most of the way around – excluding the stretch from Flüelen to Stansstad. Here, the N2 motorway ploughs a fairly straight line, sometimes underground and usually away from the water.

MT PILATUS

Looming over Lucerne from the southwest, **Mt Pilatus** (www.pilatus.com) is one of the region's most popular destinations. According to legend, this rugged 2120m peak was named after Pontius Pilate, whose corpse was thrown into a small lake on its summit and who has haunted its heights ever since. In reality, however, the moniker is more likely to derive from the Latin word *pileatus*, meaning covered in clouds – as the mountain frequently is.

The classic 'golden round-trip' takes bus No 1 to Kriens and the cable car, via Krienseregg and Fräkmüntegg, up to Mt Pilatus. From the summit, the world's steepest cog railway (at a maximum gradient of 48%) brings you down to Alpnachstad, from where a lake steamer heads back to Lucerne the same day.

The reverse route (Alpnachstad–Pilatus–Kriens–Lucerne) is much less crowded, however, and from November to May only the Kriens route is open, meaning you have to retrace your steps up the mountain and back during that time of year. Even this route is closed for the last two weeks of October, while the cable cars are serviced.

Total cost of the return trip is Sfr79.80 (Sfr40.80/43.20/52.30 with valid Swiss/Eurail/ Inter Rail passes). If you wish to walk part of the way, it is three hours down from the

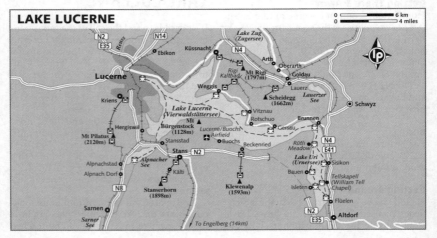

LAKE LUCERNE

summit to Alpnachstad, 3½ hours to Kriens and three hours down to Hergiswil boat station. The walk from Fräkmüntegg is easier.

It's more traditional, and arguably more worthwhile, to stay overnight at Mt Rigi (right), but there are two hotels found on Pilatus. The 19th-century **Pilatus Kulm** (☎ 041 670 12 55; hotels@pilatus.ch; s/d with shared bathroom Sfr80/125) and the modern **Hotel Bellevue** (s/d Sfr110/195) share the same reception in the circular building. There's also a self-service restaurant on this peak.

STANSERHORN

At 1898m, the **Stanserhorn** (www.stanserhorn.ch) is the second-tallest mountain on the lake. It also boasts the only revolving restaurant in the region, and offers 360-degree views looking back to Titlis.

The journey up is by 'old-timer' funicular from the village of Stans to Kälti, then a cable car. Both operate from mid-April to mid-November. The funicular's base station is a five-minute walk (signposted) from the Stans train station.

The return journey costs Sfr59 from Lucerne, or Sfr52 if you're staying in Stans. Alternatively, you can save more money by hiking up (4½ hours) or down (3½ hours) from the village. If you have a car you can save almost an hour by driving up to Kälti and parking there.

Stans is on the Lucerne–Engelberg railway (one way from Lucerne Sfr6.80). The **tourist office** (☎ 041 610 88 33; www.lakeluzern.ch; Bahnhofplatz 4; ◷ 9am-noon & 2-5pm) offers sightseeing trips in the village and helps out with accommodation. The expansive Dorfplatz, the hub of the charming town centre, is located behind the station, overlooked by an early baroque church and surrounded by pleasant streets to stroll. Here, too, is the well-regarded **Hotel Engel** (☎ 041 619 10 10; www.engelstans.ch; Dorfplatz 1; s/d/tr/f Sfr80/140/165/190), a striking mix of historic exterior and new designer rooms.

BECKENRIED

Beckenried, on the southern shore, is a bus ride from Stans. Just a few minutes' walk from the boat station is a cable car that makes the 10-minute ascent to **Klewenalp** (www.klewenalp.ch; one way/return Sfr19/30). This is a much-underrated skiing destination, especially for beginners, plus it offers many hiking and mountain biking trails heading into

the hills and valleys beyond. A map at the top outlines the options.

MT RIGI

Who would ever need TV when you have the astounding views from this 'Queen of the Mountains'? On a clear day, there's an impressive wall of mountain peaks to the south and east from 1797m-tall **Rigi** (www.rigi .ch) including Mt Titlis and the giants of the Jungfrau region. To the north and west, you overlook Arth-Goldau and the Zugersee, curving around until it almost joins Küssnacht and an arm of Lake Lucerne.

Most of all, sunrise is primetime viewing around here. Since the 19th century, tourists have been staying at the **Rigi Kulm Hotel** (☎ 041 855 03 03; rigikulm@bluewin.ch; dm Sfr32, s/d Sfr67/110, with bathroom Sfr105/186; ◷ closed mid-Nov-mid-Dec) and getting up before the crack of dawn to see the blazing sun light up the sky. (Today's hotel, a 20th-century re-creation of the original, is the only major establishment at the summit, and has two restaurants and a small snack kiosk).

After this, there's little left to do but to walk down this hikers' paradise of a mountain. For recommended routes, check www .rigi.ch. There are several easy walks (1½ to two hours) down from Rigi Kulm to Rigi Kaltbad (part-way down), with wonderful views. Or, ask at the tourist offices in **Lucerne** (☎ 041 227 17 17; Zentralstrasse 5) or **Weggis** (☎ 041 390 11 55) for information on the lengthy Rigi Lehnenweg route around the mountain.

Hiking up the mountain is another story. It's at least a 4½-hour trek from Weggis, but you could take the cable car from Küssnacht to Seeboldenalp (one way/return Sfr12/18) to shorten the journey. There are two paths from there, the shortest of which takes a little over two hours. The last section is quite steep, however. (While hiking on Rigi, watch out for the *Chlyni Lüüt*, tiny 'wild folk' with supernatural powers who in mythology once inhabited Rigi!)

For those of a less energetic bent, two rival rack railways carry passengers to the top. One runs from Arth-Goldau, the other from Vitznau. Either costs Sfr35/58 one way/return. The Arth-Goldau service closes for two weeks in late May, but Vitznau operates year-round.

The Vitznau track gives the further option of diverting at Rigi Kaltbad and taking

CENTRAL SWITZERLAND

the cable car to/from Weggis instead. The whole trip can be done from Lucerne for Sfr89 (Sfr29/29/44.50 with Swiss/Eurail/Inter Rail Pass).

Weggis
pop 3000 / elevation 440m

Sheltered from cold northerly winds by Mt Rigi, Weggis enjoys an unusually mild climate, sprouting a few palm trees and figs on the shores of the lake. Today, it's hard to believe this genteel resort was the birthplace of the rebellious 'Moderner Bund' art movement, the forerunner of Dada. Its small-town friendliness is extremely welcoming, but boats in and out of the resort are sparse in the evening and a few days' stopover generally suffices. A cable car runs from here up to Rigi Kaltbad (one way/return Sfr25/42).

The **tourist office** (☎ 041 390 11 55; www.weggis .ch; ☉ 8am-6pm Mon-Fri, 9am-2.30pm Sat & Sun in summer, 8am-5pm Mon-Fri in winter) is next to the boat station. Ask about bike rentals (per hour Sfr18).

Budget-Hotel Weggis (☎ 041 390 11 31; www.budget hotel.ch; Parkstrasse 29; s/d/tr Sfr47/76.50/86.50, with bathroom Sfr66.50/111.50/116.50; ☉ reception 3-9pm) keeps even pernickety customers happy, with its simple, if not especially atmospheric, rooms and high standards of cleanliness. This excellent cheap choice lies up the hill from the boat station.

SeeHotel Gotthard (☎ 041 390 21 14; www.gotthard -weggis.ch; s/d from Sfr135/210; ☉ closed mid-Oct–mid-Dec) is a pleasant midrange hotel with checked bedspreads and curtains and a handy location on the waterfront minutes from where boats dock.

Park Hotel Weggis (☎ 041 392 05 05; www.phw.ch; Herteinsteinstrasse 34; s/d from Sfr340/515; 🖳 ✖ 🅟) has two turreted buildings that house one of Switzerland's top five holiday hotels (it was good enough for the Brazilian national football team). It boasts elegant, understated designer rooms, outstanding service and restaurants, a well-equipped spa and even a private beach.

See-Café Weggis (☎ 041 390 17 38; Seestrasse 6; dishes Sfr13-25; ☉ 7am-11pm Jul & Aug, closed Thu Sep-Jun) is a popular local meeting place, serving down-to-earth meals, coffee and cake.

Grape (☎ 041 392 07 07; Seestrasse 60; pizza/pasta from Sfr14.50, mains from Sfr25; ☉ 10-12.30am) is a trendy Californian restaurant – part of the Park Hotel complex – serving wines from the Napa Valley alongside a range of delicious international cuisine. Asian and fusion dishes, Mexican classic and curries join wood-fired pizzas on the menu.

LAKE URI

With its many historical landmarks, the Lake Uri (Urnersee) section of Lake Lucerne is a popular outing for Swiss patriots. If you take the ferry from Brunnen towards Flüelen, the first sight you pass is a natural obelisk protruding from the water to a height of nearly 26m. Inscribed on it in gold lettering is a dedication to Friedrich Schiller, the author of the play *Wilhelm Tell*, which was so instrumental in creating the Tell legend.

Next stop is the **Rütli Meadow**. This is where the Oath of Eternal Alliance was supposedly signed by the three cantons of Uri, Schwyz and Nidwalden in 1291 and later where General Guisan gathered the Swiss army during WWII in a show of force against potential invaders. As such, this is hallowed ground to the Swiss and the focal point of national day celebrations on 1 August. On any ordinary day, there's always a flag flying proudly, and there's a small museum and a souvenir shop which doubles as a café.

Another port of call is the **Tellskapell** (William Tell Chapel). The walls are covered in murals depicting four episodes in the Tell legend, including the one that's supposed to have occurred on this spot, his escape from Gessler's boat (see the boxed text The William Tell Tale, opposite). There's a huge carillon that chimes behind the chapel.

After crossing into another founding canton, Uri, the boat finally pulls in at Flüelen. Flüelen is important because it's on the main road and rail route through the St Gotthard Pass, and historically it was a staging post for the mule trains making this crossing. Near the town is **Altdorf**, where William Tell is reputed to have performed his apple-shooting stunt. A statue of the man himself stands in the main square, and Schiller's play is sometimes performed in Altdorf's Tellspielhaus.

As well as making the round trip by boat (Sfr27) you can also circumnavigate Lake Uri on foot. You do that via the **Swiss Path** (www.weg-der-schweiz.ch) built to commemorate the 700th anniversary of the 1291 pact and running all the way from Rütli to Brunnen. The path is in 26 sections, each representing a different canton, from the founding three to Johnny-come-lately Jura (1979). The length of each section is determined by the canton's population and is marked off with a stone plaque. It would take stamina, and at least two days, to walk the whole 35km, but one or two sections between boat stops are manageable. The first and last stretches, from Rütli to Bauen and from Sisikon to Brunnen, are the hilliest. But Bauen to Flüelen (around 4½ hours) is almost flat and Flüelen to Sisikon (2½ hours) isn't too strenuous either.

BRUNNEN
pop 7000 / elevation 443m

Situated on the shore where Lake Lucerne and Lake Uri (Urnersee) meet at right angles, Brunnen enjoys mesmerising views south and west. As the local *Föhn* wind rushes down from the mountains, it creates the perfect conditions for sailing, windsurfing and paragliding.

Information
Tourist office (☎ 041 825 00 40; www.brunnen tourismus.ch; Bahnhofstrasse 15; ☼ 8.30am-6pm Mon-Fri, 9am-3pm Sat & Sun Jul & Aug; 8.30am-6pm Mon-Fri, 9am-1pm Sat Jun & Sep; 8.30am-noon & 1.30-5.30pm Mon-Fri Oct-May) Has information and Internet access. The office is less than five minutes from the train station (following the signs), which has money-exchange counters and bike rental available daily. Don't forget to ask about the guest card.

Activities
Most people will be suitably impressed by the wonderful views of Lakes Uri and Lucerne from the **Urmiberg** (cable car one way/return Sfr11/19). However, if you want to get even higher, contact **Touch and Go** (☎ 041 820 54 31; www.paragliding .ch; Parkstrasse 14) for tandem paragliding flights (from Sfr170).

Sleeping & Eating
Two camping grounds in west Brunnen are open in summer: **Camping Urmiberg** (☎ 041 820 33 27; camp sites per person/tent/car Sfr6.90/3.50/2.50) and **Camping Hopfreben** (☎ 041 820 18 73; camp sites per person/tent/car Sfr6.90/3.50/2.50).

THE WILLIAM TELL TALE

Really, the Swiss have a German playwright and an Italian musician to thank for their national hero. For without Friedrich Schiller's 1804 play *Wilhelm Tell* and Rossini's 1829 opera *Guillermo Tell*, the legend would not have so lodged in the global consciousness. After all, tales of sharp-shooting archers forced to knock objects off the heads of small boys had been doing the rounds in Norse mythology aeons earlier – pretty much ruling out the chance that any real William Tell existed. But when the Swiss began to chafe under the yoke of Austrian dominance during the 13th century, they made the story their own.

In their adaptation, the Austrian bailiff of Uri and Schwyz, Hermann Gessler, placed his hat on a pole in Altdorf town square. Everyone was required to bow to this symbol of Habsburg rule. However, William Tell from Bürglen neglected to do so and was stopped. Gessler knew of Tell's reputation with a crossbow and decreed he would forfeit his life and that of his son, unless he shot an apple off his son's head. To Gessler's disappointment, Tell succeeded. Yet Gessler noticed that Tell was hiding a second arrow, which Tell admitted was intended for Gessler, had Tell's son been harmed. Outraged, Gessler arrested Tell and took him on his boat, intending to imprison him for life in his fortress above Küssnacht.

As they crossed the lake, *Föhn* winds whipped up and threatened to capsize the boat. Tell, who was also a master helmsman, was untied to guide the boat to safety and took the chance to steer close to the shore. He leapt from the boat and onto a rock (at the site of the Tellskapell), at the same time pushing the boat back into the stormy waves. Realising his family would never be safe from Gessler, Tell raced to Küssnacht to ambush the tyrant. He hid by the Hohle Gasse, a sunken lane. As the bailiff and his entourage approached, Tell killed Gessler with a single arrow through the heart.

This version initially grew in Swiss legend through word of mouth, its first written incarnation appearing in the *Weisses Buch* (White Book) of Sarnen around 1470. But Schiller and Rossini put it on the world stage. Even today, Rossini's *William Tell Overture* remains instantly recognisable – even though that's more to do with another do-gooder outlaw, the Lone Ranger of classic TV fame.

CENTRAL SWITZERLAND

CENTRAL SWITZERLAND

Alpina (☎ 041 820 18 13; www.alpina-brunnen.ch; Gersauerstrasse 32; s Sfr90-120, d Sfr140-180, apt per week Sfr850; ☐ **P**) Though it lacks lake views, this family-run hotel is Brunnen's friendliest and most creative. Rooms have a cosy Swiss feel, which is offset by eye-catching arrangements of stones, plants and odd-shaped tree branches in the stairwell and public rooms. There's an Alpine garden in the grounds and homemade jam at breakfast. Book well ahead.

Hotel Alfa + Schmid (☎ 041 820 18 82; www.schmid alfa.ch; Axenstrasse 5-7; s Sfr60-90, d Sfr110-170) Spread across two buildings facing the lake, this hotel has a renowned restaurant and rooms to suit most tastes. Those in the Schmid building have been renovated, although the bedrooms still evince a traditional style, those in the Alfa are cosily modern. Budget rooms forego the best views.

Waldstätterhof (☎ 041 825 06 06; www.waldstaetter hof.ch; Waldstätterquai 6; s Sfr180-200, d Sfr270-320) Popular with honeymooners, including one-time English PM Winston Churchill, this grand hotel combines elegant rooms in neutral tones, lake views and a romantic atmosphere.

Weisses Rössli (☎ 041 820 10 22; fax 041 820 11 22; Bahnhofstrasse 8; s with shared/private bathroom Sfr45/80, d Sfr100/140) Recently rebuilt in its traditional 19th-century style after a devastating fire.

Mezcalito (☎ 041 820 08 08; Axenstrasse 9; mains from Sfr6-25; ☕ 11-1.30am, closed Sat & Sun in winter) This Mexican eatery is among the waterfront restaurants that are hard to miss.

Park Restaurant (☎ 041 825 47 26; Gersauerstrasse 8; mains Sfr12-24; ☕ 11am-5pm Sun-Wed, 11am-11pm Thu-Sun) Attached to the Aeskulap Klinik, this vegetarian and fish restaurant has a slightly worthy air about it, but you know the food is as healthy as it is tasty.

Dodo Bar & Café (Bahnhofstrasse 10) This place doubles as a very pleasant coffee house and a trendy bar.

Getting There & Away

By far the most pleasant way to get to Brunnen is to take a boat from Lucerne (Sfr28, 1¾ hours). The train (Sfr15.20, 45 minutes to one hour) is cheaper and quicker, although often a change in Arth-Goldau is necessary. There are also road connections from Lucerne, Zug and Fluelen.

SCHWYZ CANTON

Schwyz's claim to fame is that it gave Switzerland its name, and together with the communities of Uri and Nidwalden signed the Oath of Eternal Alliance of 1291. This birth certificate of the Swiss Confederation is still proudly displayed in Schwyz town.

SCHWYZ

pop 13,934 / elevation 517m

Schwyz seems an unassuming little village camped in farming land beneath the twin peaks of the Mythen mountains (1898m and 1811m). However, it is home to the most important document in Swiss history, is the birthplace of the original Swiss army knife and also provides the perfect jumping-off point for tours to the Hölloch Caves, Europe's largest underground caverns.

Orientation & Information

Schwyz train station is in the Seewen district, 2km from the centre. To reach the centre, take any bus outside the station marked Schwyz Post, and alight at Postplatz. The **tourist office** (☎ 041 810 19 91; www.wbs.ch; Bahnhofstrasse 4; ☕ 7.30am-noon & 1-6pm Mon-Fri, 8.30am-noon Sat) is by the bus station, with plenty of literature on the area.

Sights

The **Bundesbriefmuseum** (Museum of Federation; ☎ 041 819 20 64; www.sz.ch; Bahnhofstrasse 20; adult/student Sfr4/2.50; ☕ 9.30-11.30am & 1.30-5pm Mon-Fri, 9am-5pm Sat & Sun May-Oct; 9.30-11.30am & 1.30-5pm Mon-Fri, 1.30-5pm Sat & Sun Nov-Apr) is home to the 1291 charter of federation signed by Nidwalden, Schwyz and Uri, which is regarded as having launched modern Switzerland. It's accompanied by restatements in German (rather than the original Latin) after important military events, such as Morgarten in 1315, or as more cantons came aboard. There's some academic discussion in German and French about the authenticity of the 1291 document, as many historians question the accuracy of Switzerland's founding 'myths'.

An explanatory English booklet is available from the front desk.

In any case, the building's murals and other artworks, from Heinrich Danioth's *Fundamentum* on the façade to Walter Clénin's *Oath on the Rütli* in the main hall,

---

A WORTHY CROSS TO BEAR

Once you cross the border into Switzerland, you'll never have a second's doubt about which country you're visiting. The Swiss fly their national flag with a fervent patriotism, and the white cross on a red square flutters in thousands of private village gardens, as well as halfway up mountains and in the middle of waterfalls.

The flag is distinctive for being the world's only square flag, and locals might be attached to it simply because it looks so goddamn good. Its proportions are easy on the eye, and like all design classics, it's clear and simple.

However, if Switzerland's flag today is virtually a logo or brand image, it started life with a much more serious purpose; it was a means of identifying Swiss mercenaries on the battlefield. Two bits of white cloth were sewn onto the shirts of those from Central Switzerland fighting with Bernese troops during the 1339 Battle of Laupen, and this highly recognisable marker was gradually adopted for all Swiss soldiers.

General Henri Dufour, the victorious military leader in the Civil War, lobbied hard to finally persuade every canton to accept the red-and-white military flag as a federal emblem in 1840, but in the first decades of the new Swiss Confederation, debate raged about the emblem's proportions. Finally, in 1889 the federal parliament voted for the current incarnation. Five years later, the Geneva-based International Red Cross adopted the reverse image.

Today, the Swiss are happy to slather their national logo over a range of clothing, accessories and household items, from tacky to chic. And in 2005, a report announced that, despite the vast array of utterly astonishing scenery the country boasts, the best-selling postcard in Switzerland – outselling its nearest competitor by three to two – is the one of the national flag.

---

are more immediately appealing. Don't overlook Josef Rickenbacker's witty metal reliefs, *The Stations of the Swiss Cross*, in the portico – which you needn't pay to see.

The town's **Hauptplatz** (main square) is a pleasant place to sit while taking in the fountain and **Rathaus** (town hall), complete with 19th-century murals depicting the Battle of Morgarten and other historic events. On the other side of the square lies **St Martin's Church**.

The **Forum der Schweizer Geschichte** (Forum of Swiss History; ☎ 041 819 60 11; www.musee-suisse.ch, www.museenschwyz.ch; adult/student & senior Sfr8/6; ☷ 10am-5pm Tue-Sun) is well curated and has interesting displays, but is mostly of interest for its special exhibitions.

The **Ital Reding-Hofstatt** (☎ 041 811 45 05; www .irh.ch; Rickenbachstrasse 24; adult/student Sfr4/2.50; ☷ 2-5pm Tue-Fri, 10am-noon & 2-5pm Sat & Sun Apr-Nov) was once the home of a mercenary soldier, many of whom came from Schwyz and returned home with their booty. Now it's a museum revisiting its former master's lifestyle. Across the complex is House Bethlehem, a tiny proportioned ancient house dating back to 1287.

Off Hauptplatz and down Schmiedgasse, opposite the Mythencenter shopping complex, is **Victorinox** (☎ 041 818 12 11; www.victorinox .ch; Schmiedgasse 57, 6438 Ibach; ☷ 7.30am-noon &

1.15-4pm Mon-Fri, 8am-3pm Sat), the manufacturer of the original Swiss army knife. The company was founded in 1884 by Karl Elsener and, after a shaky start, hit pay dirt with its 'Officer's Knife'. You can't visit the factory here, but the shop has a vast array of knives, corkscrews and watches, where you can take pleasure in buying at the source.

Activities

The **Hölloch caves**, Europe's largest and the third biggest in the world, lie in Muotatal, some 35 minutes from Schwyz. More than 170km of tunnels carved out by underground streams have been mapped, while many remain unexplored. Book at **Trekking Team** (☎ 0848 808 007, 041 390 40 40; www.trekking.ch; short tours adult/child Sfr20/10, aperitif tours adult Sfr45, overnight tours from Sfr400), which even allows you to bivouac in the caves overnight. **Adventure Point** (☎ 079 247 74 72; www.adventurepoint .ch; Hirschen Hotel, Hinterdorfstrasse 14) also offers a range of activities.

Plenty of hikes begin from the nearby peak of **Stoos** (www.stoos.ch). Check the website or ask the tourist office for details.

Sleeping & Eating

Hirschen (☎ 041 811 12 76; www.hirschen-schwyz.ch; Hinterdorfstrasse 14; dm Sfr26; s/d Sfr48/80, with bathroom

Sfr58/100; ☾ reception 10am-noon & 4pm-midnight; 🖥 🗙) This is a cheerful backpacker's hostel on one side and a budget hotel on the other. A kitchen, laundry and young friendly atmosphere make up for the fairly basic dorms and bathrooms. To get here, follow the signs from Hauptplatz.

Wysses Rössli (☎ 041 811 19 22; roessli-schwyz.ch; Hauptplatz 3; s/d from Sfr130/200) Much of the accommodation in this four-star establishment has been renovated in a generic modern style, but it does retain several traditionally furnished and atmospheric older rooms.

Eating options are dotted in and around the main square, including the old-fashioned **Café Haug** (☎ 041 811 16 16; Postplatz 4; menus Sfr16.50-19; ☾ 7.30am-11pm Mon-Sat, to 6pm Sun), trendy **Kreuz & Quer** (☎ 041 810 01 01; Hauptplatz 7; snacks from Sfr8.50, mains Sfr22.50-38; ☾ 8.30am-midnight) and the historic **Ratskeller** (☎ 041 810 10 87; Strehlgasse 3; mains Sfr18-42; ☾ Mon-Sat) which specialises in Swiss and seasonal dishes.

Getting There & Away

Schwyz station is 30 minutes away from Zug (Sfr8.60) on the main north–south rail route (see p233 for more information); Lucerne is 40 minutes away (Sfr13.40). The Schwyz centre is only a few kilometres detour off the N4, which passes through Brunnen and Einsiedeln. (For details on transport to/from Einsiedeln, see opposite.)

EINSIEDELN

pop 12,747 / elevation 900m

Einsiedeln is to Switzerland what Lourdes is to France: its prime place of pilgrimage. And the ornate interior of Einsiedeln's huge church is so over-the-top, you might consider it worth seeing anyway. The story goes that in AD 964 the Bishop of Constance tried to consecrate the original monastery but was halted by a heavenly voice declaring 'Desist. God Himself has consecrated this building'. A papal order later recognised this as a genuine miracle.

Orientation & Information

Einsiedeln is south of Zürichsee (Lake Zürich) and by the western shore of the Sihlsee (Lake Sihl). The train station and the post office are together in the centre of town. In front of them is Dorfplatz square; head through this square and turn left into the main street, Hauptstrasse. The church is at the end of this street, overlooking Klosterplatz (a 10-minute walk). The **tourist office** (☎ 055 418 44 88; www.ein siedeln.ch in German; Hauptstrasse 85; ☾ 8.30am-5pm Mon-Fri, 9am-4pm Sat, 10am-1pm Sun) is near the church.

Sights & Activities

In Einsiedeln, all roads lead to the **Klosterkirche** (Abbey Church; www.kloster-einsiedeln.ch; Benzigerstrasse; ☾ 5.30am-8.30pm); you can follow the crowds flowing towards this baroque edifice, which was built between 1719 and 1735 by architect Caspar Moosbrugger. The holiest of holies is the **Black Madonna**, housed in a chapel by the entrance to the church. Most pilgrims' prayers are directed to this small statue, which has somehow survived three fires.

In front of the church is a large square where stalls sell kitsch religious souvenirs. Continuing the religious theme, there's a **Bethlehem diorama** (☎ 055 412 26 17; www.diorama .ch; Benzigerstrasse; adult/child Sfr4.50/2; ☾ 10am-5pm Apr-Nov) and, further down the same street, a **panorama painting of Calvary** (☎ 055 412 11 74), which is open the same hours as the diorama and costs the same.

On 14 September there's an annual torchlit procession to celebrate the **Festival of the Miraculous Dedication**.

The tourist office sells a variety of hiking maps (Sfr5 to Sfr12). The quickest and simplest walk begins by strolling through the monastery stables and continuing uphill along the path for 15 minutes to the **statue of St Benedikt** for an excellent view. Alternatively, a two-hour walk north of Einsiedeln and back will bring you to the narrow, wood-covered **Devil's Bridge** (Teufelsbrücke or Tüfelsbrugg), also built by abbey architect Caspar Moosbrugger. Ask the tourist office for details of this 'Etzel Wanderung'.

Sleeping

It's not really advisable to plan on staying in Einseideln, as material comfort seems to have taken a back seat to piety here.

Hotel Linde (☎ 055 418 48 48; www.linde-einsiedeln .ch; Klosterplatz; s/d from Sfr60/90, with bathroom Sfr110/160) This is the best bet in town with 17 nice, modern rooms, supplemented by some older budget rooms.

Hotel Rot Hut (☎ 055 412 22 41; fax 055 412 71 37; Hauptstrasse 80; s/d with shared bathroom Sfr65/100) If you get stuck, this might at least put a smile on your face with its kitschy 1970s décor.

Getting There & Away

Einsiedeln is in a rail cul-de-sac, so getting there usually involves changing at Biberbrugg. This is rarely a problem as arrivals/departures coincide. It is also within range of the canton of Zürich's S-Bahn trains. Zürich itself (Sfr16.20) is less than one hour away (via Wädenswil). There are trains to Lucerne (Sfr20.80, one hour), sometimes requiring a change at Goldau (70 minutes). From Einsiedeln to Schwyz, you can take the scenic 'back route' in summer: catch a postal bus to Oberiberg, then private bus (Swiss Pass not valid) from there.

By car, Einsiedeln is 5km off Hwy 8 between Schwyz and Rapperswil.

ENGELBERG

pop 3500 / elevation 1050m

Towering Mt Titlis has made Engelberg Central Switzerland's best-known ski resort, as well as a popular day trip from Lucerne. The relatively humble village sits in a quiet, idyllic valley that's lush and green in summer. However, the mountain is snow-capped all year and not only attracts summertime skiers and snowboarders, but also many Bollywood film crews and fans.

Orientation

The main street is Dorfstrasse (partially pedestrianised), where you'll find most of the town's shops and restaurants. Many of these close in November, but the influx of Indian tourists in May and June ensures more of the village now stays open at the other end of the winter and summer seasons.

Information

The half-canton of Obwalden, which includes Engelberg, has a religious holiday on 25 September.

Guest card Good for various discounts, including 10% off the Mt Titlis cable car.

Tourist office (☎ 041 639 77 77; www.engelberg.ch; Klosterstrasse 3; ⏰ 8am-6.30pm Mon-Sat, 2-6pm Sun in peak season, 8am-6.30pm Mon-Fri, 8am-5pm Sat rest of year) A five-minute walk from the train station, in the Tourist Center.

CENTRAL SWITZERLAND

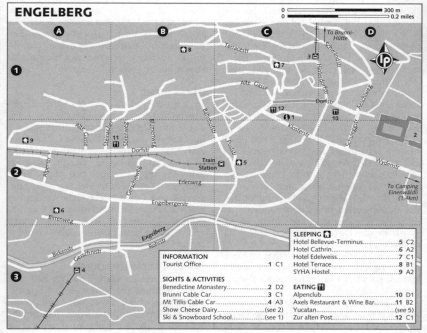

INFORMATION	
Tourist Office	1 C1

SIGHTS & ACTIVITIES	
Benedictine Monastery	2 D2
Brunni Cable Car	3 C1
Mt Titlis Cable Car	4 A3
Show Cheese Dairy	(see 2)
Ski & Snowboard School	(see 1)

SLEEPING 🛏	
Hotel Bellevue-Terminus	5 C2
Hotel Cathrin	6 A2
Hotel Edelweiss	7 C1
Hotel Terrace	8 B1
SYHA Hostel	9 A2

EATING 🍴	
Alpenclub	10 D1
Axels Restaurant & Wine Bar	11 B2
Yucatan	(see 5)
Zur alten Post	12 C1

Sights

ENGELBERG MONASTERY

Engelberg's **Benedictine Monastery** (☎ 041 639 61 19; tours around Sfr6; ☽ 45min tours 10am & 4pm daily, in English 10am Thu & Sat) is the only attraction in the village itself. The Engelberg valley was once ecclesiastically governed, independently of the Swiss Confederation, and the monastery was the seat of power. Now the resident monks teach instead of rule, but their home retains much of its former grandeur. Rebuilt after the last of several devastating fires in 1729, it contains rooms decorated with incredibly detailed wood inlays, and a baroque **monastery church** (admission free).

Inside the monastery, you'll also find a state-of-the-art **Show Cheese Dairy** (☎ 041 638 08 88; www.schaukaeserei-engelberg.ch; admission free; ☽ 9am-6.30pm Mon-Sat, 9am-5pm Sun) where you can watch the cheese-makers through a glass screen, enjoy their produce in the bistro or buy it in the shop.

Activities

MT TITLIS

Central Switzerland's tallest mountain, **Titlis** (www.titlis.ch), is known for being reached by the world's first revolving cable car. This was completed in 1992 and is still one of the few on the planet. However, that's the last leg of a breathtaking four-stage journey. First, you must ascend to Gerschnialp (1300m). Then, in the same small cable car, you glide over cow pastures and up to Trübsee (1800m). Transferring to a large gondola, you head for Stand (2450m). Finally, in Stand you board the Rotair (only the cabin inside revolves) for the passage over the dazzling Titlis Glacier.

The Titlis station (3020m) has all the usual array of restaurants and tourist attractions such as an ice cave. But on a good day, you want to head straight outside. To the 3239m summit, it's about a 45-minute hike (wear sturdy shoes). It doesn't look far but at this altitude you need to take it slowly. Otherwise, enjoy the snowboarding and skiing, either by participating or merely spectating. The **Ice Flyer chair lift** (adult/child Sfr10/6) will take you down to the glacier park where there are free 150m-long slides on rubber tyres. The nearby freestyle park has a half-pipe and good summer snowboarding.

The return trip to Titlis (30 to 45 minutes each way) costs Sfr79 from Engelberg, or Sfr95 from Lucerne. However, in good weather, you can walk some sections. Between Stand and Trübsee the Geologischer Wanderweg is open from July to September; it takes about two hours up and 1½ hours down. From Trübsee up to Jochpass (2207m) takes about 1½ hours (or there's a chair lift beyond the lake), and down to Engelberg takes around the same time. The tourist office's *Look Around* activity brochure sets out all the possibilities.

If you're hiking, destinations from Engelberg include Gerschnialp (one way/return Sfr6/9), Trübsee (Sfr18/26) or Stand (Sfr37/52). Reductions on all fares, including to Titlis, are 25% for Swiss Pass, and 20% for Eurail and Inter Rail. Ask about off-season reductions.

The cableway is open 8.30am to 5pm daily (last ascent/descent 3.40/4.50pm), but closes for maintenance for two weeks in early November.

BRUNNI

Brunni, on the opposite side of the valley, offers a series of untaxing, relaxing hikes. The cable car (one way/return in summer Sfr14/22) goes up to Ristis at 1600m. Here, there's a chairlift that takes you to the **Brunni Hütte** (☎ 041 637 37 32; www.berghuette.ch; adult/child Sfr52/35, breakfast Sfr10), a recently refurbished mountain hut that now has indoor plumbing. From here you can watch a magnificent sunset before spending the night.

OTHER HIKES

In summer, it's also possible to leave Engelberg on foot. The Surenenpass (2291m) is the scenic route to Attinghausen, from where a bus can take you to Altdorf and the southern end of Lake Uri. It takes around seven hours to get to Attinghausen; taking a cable car along the route can save two hours. From Jochpass a path goes to Meiringen via Engstlenalp and Tannalp. The highest point you reach is 2245m. From Meiringen it is easy to get to the Brienzersee. Acquire a decent map and check on snow conditions before trying any of these routes.

SKIING & SNOWBOARDING

Snowboarders populate Titlis, the half-pipe at Jochpass and the leisure park at Engstlenalp. Beginner skiers try around Brunni and near the lifts branching from Gerschnialp, while there are plenty of runs all around for more experienced skiers. A one-day pass costs Sfr52 (Sfr58 on weekends and holidays). Specific day passes cost Sfr18 for Gerschnialp and Sfr36 for Brunni.

Shops hire skiing and snowboarding equipment at fairly standard rates of about Sfr45 per day, which lower if you rent the equipment over a longer period.

There's a **Ski & Snowboard School** (☎ 041 639 54 54; www.skischule-engelberg.ch; Klosterstrasse 3) inside the tourist office. Engelberg hosts a ski-jump **World Cup** (☎ 041 639 77 33; www.weltcup-engelberg .ch) during December.

ADVENTURE SPORTS

Adrenaline sports are another Engelberg pastime. If you want to bungee jump from a cable car at the top of Mt Titlis, between May and October, you can. It's Sfr160 (Sfr150 on Friday) for the 130m dive. Contact **Outventure** (☎ 041 611 14 41; www.outventure.ch; Stansstad), which can also organise glacier-trekking, kayaking, rafting and canyoning.

Sleeping

Hotel Bellevue-Terminus (☎ 041 639 68 68; www.belle vue-engelberg.ch; Bahnhofplatz; s/d Sfr44/88, with bathroom Sfr100/170; ☻ year-round; ▯ Ⓟ) The very picture of faded grandeur, this Victorian-era hotel has lots of students and other youthful guests treading over its wonderfully creaky floorboards. Little wonder, since it offers great value and comfort for the price.

Hotel Edelweiss (☎ 041 639 78 78; www.edelweissen gelberg.ch; Terracestrasse 10; s/d from Sfr115/200) This grand old hotel has long been a family friendly establishment, with colourful paintings of clowns decorating its stairwell. All guests, though, will enjoy the views from its high-ceilinged dining room.

Hotel Terrace (☎ 041 639 66 66; www.terrace.ch; Terracestrasse 33; standard s/d from Sfr115/180, superior s/d from Sfr125/200; ☻ closed btwn seasons) The Terrace's dining room retains original Art Nouveau features, but its 180 rooms are somewhat newer and more ordinary, with overwhelmingly dusky pink hues. Still, the views are magnificent and you feel privileged catching the hotel's private funicular up the hill behind Engelberg. A favourite with Indian directors and film crews.

Hotel Cathrin (☎ 041 637 44 66; www.cathrin-engel berg.ch; Birrenweg 22; s/d from Sfr95/170; ☻ closed btwn seasons; ☒ Ⓟ) In a quiet location near the Mt Titlis cable car, this modern re-creation of a

chalet has sauna and fitness facilities, as well as a conservatory.

SYHA hostel (☎ 041 637 12 92; www.familienher berge.ch; Dorfstrasse 80; dm/d Sfr32.40/84.80; ☻ closed btwn seasons; ▯ Ⓟ) This hostel is 10 minutes back down the train line on the northern side of the tracks. It's clean, roomy and modern, but some of its dorms are impersonally large.

Camping Einenwäldli (☎ 041 637 19 49; www.eien waeldli.ch; camp sites per person/small tent/car Sfr8/8.50/2; ☻ year-round) This deluxe camping ground, attached to the Sporthotel Einenwäldli, has access to its restaurant and sauna facilities. The ski and shuttle buses will drop you less than a minute from the gate.

Eating & Drinking

Alpenclub (☎ 041 637 12 43; Dorfstrasse; mains Sfr18-48; ☻ 9am-late daily, closed Tue & Wed Jul & Aug) The atmosphere is wonderful in this low-ceilinged complex, with carved-back chairs and lampshades made from sepia-toned negatives of early mountaineering adventures. A longstanding local institution, it serves a mix of pizzas and Swiss food.

Axels Restaurant & Wine Bar (☎ 041 637 09 09; Dorfstrasse 50; mains Sfr40-50; ☻ 11.30am-2pm & 6pm-12.30am Wed-Sun) This chic minimalist restaurant wouldn't be out of place in Zürich or Geneva and indeed has garnered national attention with its Mediterranean-influenced cuisine. Head chef Axel Kirchner gently tweaks classic carpaccio, lasagne and risotto dishes, giving them a modern twist.

Zur Alten Post (☎ 041 637 25 24; Dorfstrasse; meals Sfr14.50-25; ☻ 8am-7pm) Nothing fancy, just a firm everyday favourite for coffee or a hearty lunch of rösti or Alpermagorinen (a form of macaroni cheese).

Mexican-style bar and restaurant **Yucatan** (Hotel Bellevue-Terminus) is the most popular après-ski place in town.

Getting There & Around

Engelberg is at the end of a train line, about an hour from Lucerne (Sfr15.60 one way). If coming on a day trip, check the Lucerne tourist office's special Mt Titlis excursion tickets.

Between early July and mid-October, a shuttle bus leaves the Engelberg train station roughly every half-hour for all the village's major hotels and attractions. It's free with a guest card or train ticket; Sfr1

CENTRAL SWITZERLAND

CENTRAL SWITZERLAND

without. In winter, there are free ski buses for getting to the slopes.

ZUG CANTON

ZUG

pop 22,917 / elevation 426m

To look at Zug, with its attractive medieval Old Town and placid lake, you might not immediately realise the enormous wealth beneath. With the lowest tax in Switzerland – about half the national average – this is the richest place in the country, but with typical Swiss modesty it doesn't boast about its riches. Undoubtedly, after an hour in town, you start to notice all the people in suits and a few more luxury cars than normal. However, like all good Swiss companies, Zugs go about their business quietly, leaving other visitors in peace to absorb the scenery.

Orientation

Zug hugs the northeastern shore of Zugersee. The train station is 1km north of the Old Town (Altstadt), and has bike rental and money-exchange counters. For the Old Town, follow the main train station exit into the roundabout at the head of Alpenstrasse (you'll see Confiserie Albert Meier to your left) and head south for another 700m.

Information

Tourist office (☎ 041 723 68 00; www.zug-tourismus .ch; Reisezentrum Zug, inside main train station; 9am-7pm Mon-Fri, 9am-4pm Sat, 9am-3pm Sun) Pick up a city map here.

Sights & Activities

It's hard not to be enchanted by Zug's medieval town centre. It starts at the town's emblem, the **Zytturm** (clock tower; Kolinplatz), whose distinctive tiled roof is in the blue and white cantonal colours. The heraldic shields below the 1557 clock face represent the first eight cantons to join the Confederation (Zug was the seventh in 1352). Walking through the clock's arch, you can veer off into the charming, pedestrian-only streets of Fischmarkt, Ober Altstadt and Unter Altstadt.

Uphill from the clock tower, opposite St Oswald's Church, is the **Museum in der Burg** (☎ 041 728 32 97; Kirchenstrasse; adult/child Sfr5/1, free Sun; 2-5pm Tue-Fri, 10am-noon & 2-5pm Sat & Sun). This is notable mainly for its 3D model of the town,

with commentary in German, French and English. Despite the narrative's stilted style, it's an excellent introduction to Zug – and its past tendency to partially sink into the lake.

On the waterfront, just north of the Old Town, is **Landsgemeindeplatz**. In this square there's an aviary of exotic birds, most strikingly a family of scarlet ibis (looking a bit homesick in colder weather).

The **Schönegg funicular** will take you up the Zugerberg (988m), where there are impressive views, or hiking trails for the more active. The Zug day pass (Sfr11.40) is the best deal, as it covers all bus rides and the funicular. Bus No 11 gets you to the lower funicular station.

City bikes (☎ 041 761 33 55; outside the Rathaus, Bundesplatz; 9am-9pm May-Oct) are loaned out for no cost (ID and monetary deposit required). On the waterfront, pedalos (per 30/60 minutes Sfr12/20) and other boats are for hire.

Sleeping

Camping Brüggli (☎ 041 741 84 22; Chamer Fussweg 36; camp sites per adult/tent/car Sfr7.80/7/4; Apr-Oct) On the shore of the lake, 2km west of the centre, this is a very attractive spot, with free swimming in the vicinity.

SYHA hostel (☎ 041 711 53 54; www.youthhostel.ch; Allmendstrasse 8; dm/d Sfr31/95; reception 7-10am & 5-10pm, hostel closed early Jan–early Mar;) Zug's hostel is clean and modern, and even has a communal kitchen. To walk here from the station, take the Dammstrasse/Grafenau exit, heading right in the direction of the Sportanlagen, then curving left and continuing past the hostel sign for about 10 minutes.

Hotel Guggital (☎ 041 711 28 21; www.hotel-gug gital.ch; Zugerbergstrasse 46; s Sfr115-160, d Sfr185-220;) This white building, with its distinctive three clover leafs, scenically overlooks the lake from a hill south of town. Although it principally caters to business travellers, it seems a perfect chill-out spot, as the priciest of its compact modern rooms have balconies. Bus No 11 will get you here from the Metalli exit from the train station.

Hotel Löwen am See (☎ 041 725 22 22; www .loewen-zug.ch; Landsgemeindeplatz; s/d from Sfr180/260;) The recently renovated rooms here are very civilised and several of them enjoy lake views. The hotel is also renowned for its downstairs Mediterranean restaurant, Domus, which is in a prime spot on the main square.

Ochsen Zug (☎ 041 729 32 32; www.ochsen-zug.ch; Am Kolinplatz; s/d/tw/ste Sfr175/210/255/320; ☒ Ⓟ) Although it dates from 1480 and once hosted Goethe, the Ochsen today is a business hotel and has been streamlined behind its quaint façade. Standard rooms are white and black with a few daubs of colour. Newer rooms use natural wood and fibres for an ecologically sound feel. The junior suite, No 503, has wonderful views of the Zytturm and the lake. Prices are about 10% to 20% cheaper on weekends.

Eating
The best restaurants congregate around Landsgemeindeplatz, and most have outdoor seating in summer. Fish from the lake is common; bream or *Zug Rotel* is a favourite.

Widder (☎ 041 711 03 16; Landsgemeindeplatz 12; mains Sfr16-38; ☺ 11am-midnight Mon-Sat, 11am-11pm Sun) Roof beams carved with Gothic words of wisdom give this tavern a traditional feel, but the menu is slightly unexpected. As well as Swiss and fish specialities, a page of South African dishes lists ostrich steak, biltong, Cape Town fish soup, Cape Malay curry and more.

Schiff (☎ 041 711 00 55; Graben 2; mains Sfr25-37; ☺ 11-12.30am summer, reduced hr winter) With a menu that seems equally split between fish and home-made pasta, this restaurant has a prime location on the main square, and the upstairs Panorama Bar to take advantage of the view.

Gasthaus Rathauskeller (☎ 041 711 00 58; Oberer Altstadt 1; meals in Bistro/Zunftstube from Sfr28/75; ☺ 11.30am-2.30pm & 3.30-10.30pm Tue-Sat) Both the ground-floor bistro and the elegant, traditional and pricey *haute cuisine* Zunftstube above are dotted with corporate customers, but somehow the service is so professional and the surrounds so pleasant that it just doesn't spoil the atmosphere.

Confiserie Albert Meier (☎ 041 711 10 49; www.die zugerkirschtorte.ch; Bahnhofplatz; ☺ 7am-6.30pm Mon-Fri, 8am-4pm Sat) A local speciality is *Zuger Kirschtorte*, a cherry cake made from pastry, biscuit, almond paste and butter cream, infused with strong cherry brandy. It's sold all over town, but this café claims to bake the best. And if it's not the best, at least it's the most convenient; you can get a sugar rush here minutes after leaving the train.

Getting There & Away
Zug is on the main north–south train route from Zürich (Sfr13.40) to Lugano, where trains from Zürich also branch off to Lucerne (Sfr16.40) and the Bernese Oberland.

By road, the north–south N4 (E31) runs from Zürich, sweeps around the western shore of Zugersee and joins the N2 (E35), which continues through the St Gotthard Pass and on to Lugano and Italy. Hwy 25 peels off the N4 north of Zug at Sihlbrugg, completes the corset around the eastern shore of the lake, then rejoins the N4 at Goldau.

Boats depart from Zug's Schiffsstation, north of Landsgemeindeplatz, travelling south to Arth in the summer and many other destinations around the lake. Swiss Pass holders get half-price travel.

GOTTHARD PASS

ANDERMATT
pop 1313 / elevation 1447m
At the southern end of the canton of Uri, Andermatt was once an important staging-post on the north–south St Gotthard route. Nowadays, the town is bypassed by the Gotthard Tunnel, but it remains a popular hiking and winter sports destination.

The train station is 400m north of the core of the village. The **tourist office** (☎ 041 887 14 54; www.andermatt.ch; ☺ 9am-noon & 2-5.30pm Mon-Sat Jul, Aug & Dec-Mar, 9am-noon & 2-5.30pm Mon-Fri rest of year), 200m to the left of the station, shares the same hut as the postal bus ticket office.

Sights & Activities
The **Gemsstock** peak (2963m) is a focal point for both hiking and skiing (intermediate and advanced). The journey to the top by cable car from Andermatt costs Sfr18/36 one way/return.

However, as Andermatt is a major army training centre, check beforehand that you're free to walk certain routes before heading up here. Ski passes cost Sfr53 per day for Gemsstock, Sfr42 for Nätschen/Gütsch and Sfr25 for Realp.

As Andermatt is situated near four major Alpine passes – Susten, Oberalp, St Gotthard and Furka – it's an excellent base for driving or bus tours. Check www.post bus.ch for the bus tours offered this year.

From Realp, along the flat valley, **steam trains** (www.furka-bergstrecke.ch) run to Furka from Friday to Sunday between mid-June and early October (daily from mid-July to late August). The **St Gotthard Museum** (☎ 091 869 15 25; adult/student & senior Sfr6/4; ☉ 9am-6pm Jun-Oct), on the St Gotthard Pass (2109m), is open only when the pass itself is. It chronicles the history of the pass and the Gotthard Tunnel (there's English text).

Sleeping

The tourist office can help find private rooms, but many places close in the low season.

Hotel Aurora (☎ 041 887 16 61; www.aurora-andermatt.ch; s/d Sfr90/150; Ⓟ) Despite its fairly unexciting modern exterior, this hotel on the far south side of the village is handy for the Gemsstock cable car, has good views and provides great value. It's popular with those doing motorcycle tours.

Hotel 3 Könige & Post (☎ 041 887 00 01; www.3koenige.ch Gotthardstrasse 69; s/d from Sfr95/190; Ⓟ) With nostalgic rooms in a traditional Swiss chalet near the centre of the village, this hotel – like most in Andermatt – has a sauna, but it also boasts a eucalyptus steam bath.

Kronen Hotel (☎ 041 887 00 88; www.kronenhotel .ch; Gotthardstrasse 64; s/d from Sfr95/180; Ⓟ) A friendly place with pleasant modern rooms. It's known for its Barrybar – named after the famous St Bernard dog – and has an excellent menu.

Getting There & Away

Andermatt is a stop on the Glacier Express from Zermatt to St Moritz. For north–south destinations, change at Göschenen, 15 minutes away. **Andermatt train station** (☎ 041 887 12 20) can supply details about the car-carrying trains over the Oberalp Pass (direction: Graubünden) and through the Furka Tunnel (the route to Valais). Postbuses stop by the train station. The Gotthard Tunnel (N2/E35) is one of the busiest north–south routes across the Alps. The 17km tunnel opened in 1980, and extends from Göschenen to close to Airolo in Ticino, bypassing Andermatt. Work is already underway building the new Gotthard Base Tunnel, designed for high-speed and freight trains. It should be completed in 2012.

Basel & Aargau

Welcome to Switzerland's most surprising 'culture vulture' region. Zürich and Geneva might be larger, but Basel can hold its own against them when it comes to high-quality galleries and museums. That's a good thing, too, for otherwise the flat, industrialised northwest of the country would have little to recommend it to visitors.

Long a patron of the arts, this densely populated area has a slew of major attractions for gallery lovers and architecture groupies. Basel's Beyeler Foundation boasts one of the most vital collections in Switzerland, there's an absorbing museum devoted to madcap sculptor Jean Tinguely, and showpieces by some of the world's best contemporary architects lie in nearby Weil am Rhein's impressive Vitra Design Museum.

Two of the most famous working architects on the planet, Jacques Herzog and Pierre de Meuron, hail from here. Yet, while international critics shower plaudits on their designs for London's Tate Modern, Beijing's 2008 Olympic Stadium and Munich's football arena, even they have some home-turf competition; local buildings by Ticino's Mario Botta and Italy's Renzo Piano often prove to be equally eye-catching.

Basel and Aargau cantons aren't just about cutting-edge postmodernity, however. The banks of the Rhine were settled more than 2000 years ago, and the best-preserved Roman remains in Switzerland are at Augusta Raurica. Basel's 11th-century cathedral and 16th-century town hall are landmarks, while sleepy Baden is like something from the 19th century.

The fact that the region borders France and Germany is often overplayed, creating the impression this is a more vibrant, cosmopolitan place than it is. Urbane, wealthy Basel is, at heart, a serious-minded business city. But, with its airport becoming more of an international hub, it could be on the verge of becoming not just more accessible but also less insular.

BASEL & AARGAU

HIGHLIGHTS

Vitra Design
★ Museum

★ Beyeler Foundation;
Jean Tinguely Museum;
Rhine River;
Tinguely Fountain

- Being wowed by the art and architecture of the superlative **Beyeler Foundation** (p237)
- Catching interior design exhibits across the German border in the **Vitra Design Museum** (p239)
- Admiring the sculptures of Jean Tinguely in the **Tinguely Fountain** (p239) and **Jean Tinguely Museum** (p237)
- Tracking down the works of internationally acclaimed local architects **Herzog & de Meuron** (p240)
- Jumping into the fast-moving Rhine River in summer or taking a **boat tour** (p243)

▪ POPULATION: 1 MILLION	▪ AREA: 1958 SQ KM	▪ LANGUAGE: GERMAN

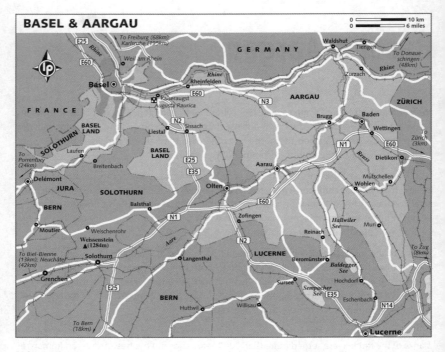

BASEL & AARGAU

Orientation

The region is well connected internationally via EuroAirport and has excellent rail and road links to France, Germany and the rest of Switzerland. For more details, see Getting There & Away, p243.

Information

Basel Tourism (opposite) will handle most queries for the entire region, but if you really want to get off the beaten path, ask **Aargau Tourism** (☎ 062 824 76 24; www.aargautourismus .ch in German) for extra tips.

BASEL

pop 166,290 / elevation 273m

Although it's famous for its Fasnacht and Vogel Gryff festivals in spring and winter, perhaps the best time to visit Basel is in summer. It is then when the city shucks off its notorious reserve to bask in, strangely for its northerly location, some of the hottest weather in Switzerland. As locals bob along in the fast-moving Rhine (Rhein)

River, cool off in the city's numerous fountains, whiz by on motor scooters, and dine and drink on overcrowded pavements, you could almost be in Italy, rather than on the dual border with France and Germany.

Of course, most visitors come for the city's many trade fairs and arrive during the more buttoned-down remainder of the year. For them, as well as other travellers during this period, the major distractions in Basel (Bâle in French, sometimes Basle in English) are a couple of the country's best art collections and some compelling modern buildings.

Orientation

The Old Town and most sights are on the south bank in Grossbasel (Greater Basel). On the north bank is Kleinbasel (Little Basel). Historically, the 'Klein' tag was a term derogatory of the working-class locality. The relief bust of *Lälle Keenig*, or 'Tongue King' (at the crossroads at the southern end of the Mittlere Brücke), sticking his tongue out at the northern section, just about sums up the old attitude.

Grossbasel has the SBB Bahnhof, the train station for travel within Switzerland. Tram No 1 and 8 leave from here for the Old Town centre. In Kleinbasel is the Badischer Bahnhof (BBF), for trains to Germany.

Information
BOOKSHOPS
Bider & Tanner (☎ 061 206 99 99; Aeschenvorstadt 2; ☽ 9am-6.30pm Mon-Fri, to 8pm Thu, 9am-5pm Sat) English books, reference books on German and Schwyzertütsch, travel guides and maps.

DISCOUNT CARD
BaselCard (Sfr20/27/35 for 24/48/72hr) Offers entry to 26 museums (permanent collections only) and Basel Zoo (www .zoobasel.ch in German), plus guided tours and ferry rides.

INTERNET ACCESS
Net-Bar (☎ 061 271 13 50; www.net-bar.ch; Steinenvorstadt 53; per hr Sfr11.50; ☽ 9.30am-midnight Mon-Thu, to 1am Fri, 11.30-1am Sat, 2-11pm Sun)

MEDICAL SERVICES
Cantonal Hospital (☎ 061 265 25 25; Petersgraben 2)

POST
Main post office (☎ 061 266 16 16; Rudengasse 1; ☽ 7.30am-6.30pm Mon-Fri, to 8pm Thu, 8am-5pm Sat)
Post office (☎ 061 278 54 35; Post Passage 9; SBB Train station; ☽ 7.30am-9pm Mon-Fri, 8am-5pm Sat, 3-8pm Sun)

TOURIST INFORMATION
Main tourist office (☎ 061 268 68 68; www.basel tourismus.ch; Stadtcasino, Barfüsserplatz; ☽ 8.30am-6pm Mon-Fri, 10am-5pm Sat, 10am-4pm Sun) At this address until 2007; afterwards check website for new office location. Organises English-language city tours (Sfr15; ☽ daily May-Oct, rest of the year Sat).
Tourist office (☎ 061 268 68 68; Train Station; ☽ 8.30am-6.30pm Mon-Fri, 9am-2pm Sat & Sun)

Sights
MUSEUMS & GALLERIES
For more on the city's 35 varied museums and galleries (including the very central and obvious History Museum) grab the relevant tourist office booklet.

Fondation Beyeler
Of all the private Swiss collections made public, former art dealers Hildy and Ernst Beyeler's is the most astounding. In the **Beyeler Foundation** (☎ 061 645 97 00; www.beyeler.com; Baselstrasse 101; adult/senior/student/child Sfr21/18/12/10,

reduced entry Sfr12/10/6/4; ☽ 10am-6pm, to 8pm Wed), sculptures by Miró and Max Ernst are juxtaposed against similar tribal figures, while 19th- and 20th-century works from the likes of Picasso and Rothko hang on the walls of leading Italian architect Renzo Piano's light-filled, open-plan building. To get here catch the No 6 tram to Riehen.

Museum Jean Tinguely
Built by leading Ticino architect Mario Botta, the **Museum Jean Tinguely** (☎ 061 681 93 20; www .tinguely.ch; Paul Sacher Anlage 1; adult/student & senior Sfr10/7; ☽ 11am-7pm Tue-Sun) resonates with playful mischievousness. Unfortunately, you're not allowed to touch most of Tinguely's 'kinetic' sculptures, which would rattle, shake or twirl if you did, but with springs, feathers and wheels radiating at every angle they look appealingly like the work of a mad scientist. Catch bus No 31 or 36 to get here.

Schaulager
The latest hometown construction by celebrity architectural duo Herzog & de Meuron evinces a kind of 'stone-age minimalism', with the sharply cornered and otherwise white gallery partly rendered in earth dug out from around the foundations. There's an asymmetrical gatehouse to the **Schaulager** (☎ 061 335 32 32; www.schaulager.org; Ruchfeldstrasse 19, Münchenstein; adult/concession Sfr14/12; ☽ noon-6pm Tue-Fri, to 7pm Thu, 10am-5pm Sat & Sun May-Sep) and a huge video screen on the front façade giving you a foretaste of the rolling temporary exhibitions in the angled, generously sized interior. Open to the public in summer only, the gallery welcomes artists, museum workers and teachers throughout the year. Catch the No 11 tram here.

Museum of Fine Arts
The **Kunstmuseum** (☎ 061 206 62 62; www.kunst museumbasel.ch; St Albangraben 16; adult/student Sfr10/5, incl Museum of Contemporary Art, free 1st Sun each month; ☽ 10am-5pm Tue-Sun) concentrates on two periods: from 1400 to 1600, and from 1800 to the present day. The medieval collection includes the world's largest number of Holbein works. The smaller contemporary collection features Picassos and Rodins, and spills over into the **Museum of Contemporary Art** (Museum für Gegenwartskunst; ☎ 061 206 62 62; www.kunstmuseumbasel.ch; St Alban-Rheinweg 60; adult/student Sfr10/5, incl Museum of Fine Arts, free 1st Sun each month; ☽ 11am-5pm Tue-Sun).

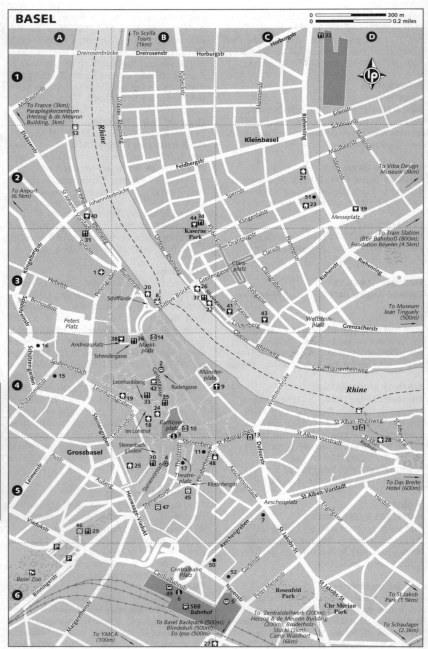

Vitra Design Museum

Always fancied seeing the amazingly organic Bilbao Guggenheim Museum in Spain and find yourself in Basel? Then, pop across the German border to the **Vitra Design Museum** (☎ +49 7621 702 32 00; www.design-museum.de; Charles Eames Strasse 1, Weil am Rhein; adult/student €6.50/5, Basel-Card valid; ☾ 11am-6pm Tue-Sun) for a small taste of the same. Not only is the main museum building by the Guggenheim's creator, Frank Gehry; the surrounding factory complex of famous furniture manufacturer Vitra, comprises buildings by other cutting-edge architects such as Tadao Ando, Zaha Hadid and Alvaro Siza. Exhibitions cover all aspects of interior design. The museum is a 30-minute bus ride from Claraplatz; catch bus No 55 to the Vitra stop.

Activities

The tourist office's *Experiencing Basel...* pamphlet lists five walks across town, all starting from Marktplatz (Market Square). There you'll find the vivid red **Rathaus** (town hall), built in the 16th century and since restored. One walk takes you to the fabulous 11th-century **cathedral** (Münster), a mix of Gothic exteriors and Romanesque interiors. The tomb of the famous Renaissance humanist Erasmus of Rotterdam (1466–1536), who lived and died in the city, lies in the cathedral's northern aisle. Another takes you west through the former artisans' district to the 600-year-old **Spalentor** city gate, a remnant of the former city wall.

Another walk passes the **Tinguely Fountain** (Theaterplatz), which will seem familiar to anyone who's seen the famous Stravinsky fountain outside Paris's Pompidou Centre. In Paris, however, Swiss sculptor Jean Tinguely's madcap machinery is accompanied by the plump day-glo figures of his wife and collaborator Niki de Saint Phalle. This Basel fountain is all his own doing (see also the Tinguely Museum p237).

Between mid-April and mid-October **Basler Personenschiffahrt** (☎ 061 639 95 00; www .bpg.ch in German) operates city/harbour **boat cruises** (Sfr14; departing 12.15pm Tue-Sat) and trips to Rheinfelden (one way/return Sfr38/50, departing 1.10pm Tue-Sat, 8.25am & 10.40am Sun & public holidays). All cruises depart from Schifflände, near the Mittlere Brücke. Various evening entertainment cruises are also offered.

Swimming in the Rhine River is a very popular summer pastime, too.

Festivals & Events

Basel makes much of its huge **Fasnacht** spring carnival, even though many people prefer Lucerne's exuberant celebrations. The festival kicks off at 4am exactly on the Monday after Ash Wednesday with the **Morgestraich**. The streetlights are suddenly extinguished and the procession starts to wend its way through the central district. Participants

INFORMATION	
Cantonal Hospital	1 A3
Main Post Office	2 B4
Main Tourist Office	3 B4
Net-Bar	4 B5
Post Office	5 C6
Tourist Office	6 B6

SIGHTS & ACTIVITIES	
Bank for International Settlements Building	7 C5
Basler Personenschiffahrt Boat Cruises	8 B3
Cathedral (Münster)	9 C4
History Museum	10 B4
Kunsthalle	11 B5
Museum of Contemporary Arts (Museum für Gegenwartskunst)	12 D4
Museum of Fine Arts (Kunstmuseum)	13 C4
Rathaus (Town Hall)	14 B4
Schützenmattstrasse 11 (Herzog & de Meuron Building)	15 A4
Spalentor City Gate	16 A4
Tinguely Fountain	17 B5

SLEEPING 🏠	
Au Violon	18 B4
Der Teufelhof	19 B4
Drei Könige am Rhein	20 B3
easyHotel	21 C2
Hotel Krafft	22 B3
Hotel Locanda	23 C2
Hotel Stadthof	24 B4
Hotel Steinenschanze	25 B5
Merian am Rhein	26 B3
SYHA Basel City Hostel	27 B6
SYHA Hostel	28 D5

EATING 🍴	
Acqua Osteria	29 A5
Balthazar	30 B5
Café de L'imprimerie	31 A3
Erlkönig	32 D1
Gleich	33 B4
Parterre	34 B2
Susu's	35 B4
Weinstube Gifthüttli	36 B4
Zum Schmale Wurf	37 B3

DRINKING 🍷 🍸	
Bar der Roten Engel	38 B4

Bar Rouge	39 D2
Cargo-Bar	40 A2
Fischerstube	41 C3
Fumare/Non Fumare	42 B4
Hirscheneck	43 C3
Kaserne	44 B2

ENTERTAINMENT 🎭	
Atlantis	45 B5
Die Kuppel	46 A5
Mad Max	47 B5
nt/Areal	(see 32)
Stadtcasino	(see 3)

SHOPPING 🛍	
Bider & Tanner (Bookshop)	48 B5

TRANSPORT	
Airport Bus Departures	49 B6
Avis	50 B6
CityRent	51 C2
Hertz	52 C6
Schifflände Main Boat Landing Stage	53 A2

BASEL & AARGAU

EXPLORING ARCHITECTURAL BASEL

Basel likes to boast that it has buildings by seven winners of architecture's prestigious Pritzker Prize, unprecedented for a city this small. Four of those winners – Frank Gehry, Alvaro Siza, Tadao Ando and Zaha Hadid – are actually found just across the German border from Basel at the **Vitra Design Museum** (p239). However, some works by Herzog & de Meuron are slightly more central. The Basel-based duo is internationally renowned for designing London's Tate Modern art gallery, the Olympic Stadium for Beijing 2008 and the Münich football arena. In Basel, as well as the **Schaulager** (p237) & **St Jakob Park** (p243) you'll find their wonderful lace-iron façade at **Schützenmattstrasse 11** and the matt-black **Zentralstellwerk** at Münchensteinerstrasse 115 – the latter is surely the only railway goods depot to be an architectural icon! Another interesting detour is to the duo's **Paraplegikerzentrum** (rehabilitation centre) near the French border. Take tram No 3 to Burgfelden Grenze, walk a little further north and follow the signs to the right.

Italian architect Renzo Piano is responsible for the remarkable **Beyeler Foundation** (p237) and British-Iraqi Zaha Hadid is due to build over the Stadtcasino at Barfüsserplatz in upcoming years.

He hasn't won the Pritzker, but Ticino architect Mario Botta is also worth checking out; see his **Tinguely Museum** (p237) and the grey-striped offices of the **Bank for International Settlements** at Aeschenplatz 1 (incidentally, the bank most seriously implicated in the 1990s Holocaust scandal, p30).

For more, including works by seventh Pritzker winner Richard Meier, grab a copy of the tourist office's free *Architektur in Basel/Architecture in Basel* pamphlet.

---

wear elaborate costumes and masks, and there's a little bit of carousing in the streets. The main parades are on the Monday and Wednesday afternoons, with Tuesday afternoon reserved for the children's parade.

It's also worth visiting Liestal (Sfr4.80, 30 minutes by train from Basel) on the Sunday evening before Morgestraich for the **Chienbäse**, a dramatic fire parade.

The city's other big festival is the **Vogel Gryff** at the end of January, which symbolically chases away winter from Kleinbasel. The three key figures – the griffin (*Vogel Gryff*), the savage (*Wilder Mann*) and the lion (*Leu*) – dance to the beat of drums on a raft on the Rhine, facing the town. Later they dance in the streets of Kleinbasel.

Trade fairs have long played an important part in the city's calendar. Leading events include the **MUBA** (www.muba.ch in German) Swiss industries fair every spring, the **Herbstmesse** (Autumn Fair) in October, the **Baselworld: The Watch and Jewellery Show** (www.baselworld.ch) in March and **ART Basel** (www.artbasel.ch), the contemporary art fair in June.

The **Swiss Indoors** (www.davidoffswissindoors.ch) tennis championship, held every October, is Switzerland's biggest annual sporting event.

Sleeping

You must book ahead if coming for a convention or trade fair, when prices also rise.

There are no trade fairs in July or August, but annoyingly some Basel hotels also close then. When you check in, remember to ask for your **mobility ticket**, which entitles you to free use of public transport.

BUDGET

For a wide range of B&Bs, visit the website www.bbbasel.ch.

Hostels

Basel Backpack (☎ 061 333 00 37; www.baselbackpack .ch; Dornacherstrasse 192; dm Sfr31, s/d/f Sfr80/96/144, breakfast Sfr7 extra; 🖳 🗙) Expensively converted from a factory, this friendly independent hostel has cheerful, colour-coded eight-bed dorms and more sedate doubles and family rooms.

SYHA hostel (☎ 061 278 97 39; www.youthhostel.ch /basel; St Alban Kirchrain; dm Sfr31-41, s/d from Sfr80/82; 🕑 reception 7-10am & 2-10pm; 🖳 🅿) This is the older of the two official hostels in town, less conveniently but more attractively located in a quiet, leafy spot. Take the No 3 tram to St Alban Tor.

Also recommended:

YMCA (☎ 061 361 73 09; www.ymcahostelbasel.ch; Gempenstrasse 64; dm Sfr21-32, breakfast Sfr7, d Sfr104-124; 🕑 reception 6.30-11am & 3.30-11pm; 🖳) New, well-equipped & family-oriented hostel.

SYHA Basel City hostel (☎ 061 365 99 60; www.youth hostel.ch/basel.city; Pfeffingerstasse 8; s/d Sfr75/90, with bathroom Sfr80/118; 🕑 reception 7-10am & 5-10pm, hostel

BASEL & AARGAU

closed Nov & Dec; 🖳) Convenient new hostel, just across from the train station, with singles and twins/doubles only.

Hotels

easyHotel (www.easyhotel.com; Riehenring 109; r from Sfr30; ⊠) What's plastic and orange and cheap all over? Yep, after the no-frills airline easyJet, here's the second instalment in Stelios Haji-Ioannou's hotel empire. Rooms are functional, clean, modern and, if not especially aesthetically appealing, slightly better than in the London outlet. Variable pricing sees costs rise at busy times (up to Sfr130 when we looked, but could go above that). Book well ahead, and if possible get a room with air-conditioning so you won't have to open a window onto the noisy street.

Hotel Stadthof (☎ 061 261 87 11; www.stadthof.ch; Gerbergasse 84; s/d Sfr80/120) You'll need to book ahead at this cheap, spartan, but nonetheless very decent central hotel. Breakfast is not included.

Camping

Camp Waldhort (☎ 061 711 64 29; www.camping-waldhort.ch in German; Heideweg 16, Reinach; adult/child/tent Sfr8/4.50/11; ☙ Mar-Oct) Six kilometres south of the SBB train station is this camping option. Catch the No 11 tram to Landhof.

MIDRANGE

Au Violon (☎ 061 269 87 11; www.au-violon.com; Im Lohnhof 4; s Srf100-110, d Sfr150-190) The doors are one of the few hints that quaint, atmospheric Au Violon was once a prison. Its understated rooms are decently sized (most comprise two former cells) and decorated in relaxing neutral tones. The hotel overlooks the city from its quiet, leafy hilltop location and has a well-respected restaurant.

Hotel Krafft (☎ 061 690 91 30; www.hotelkrafft.ch; Rheingasse 12; s/d Sfr145/230, with river view Sfr180/290, ste with river view Sfr380) The renovated Krafft will appeal to design-savvy urbanites. Sculptural modern chandeliers have been added to its creaky-floored dining room overlooking the Rhine, and minimalist tea bars (all stainless steel, grey and Japanese teapots) now adorn each landing of the spiral stairs. Rooms have a tasteful 1950s retro feel and classic furniture from the likes of Charles and Ray Eames. The riverbank is a popular night-time spot, however, so in summer this won't suit light sleepers.

Der Teufelhof (☎ 061 261 10 10; www.teufelhof.com; Leonhardsgraben 47; Galeriehotel s/d from Sfr180/255, r in Kunsthotel Sfr290-450; ⊠ P) The more expensive Kunsthotel comprises eight modern rooms (and one suite) each decorated by a different artist, with features like musical-score murals and all sorts of dreamlike optical illusions (although the rooms were due to be revamped in summer 2006). The larger Galeriehotel annex is more about stylish everyday design. Sleek public areas and an excellent restaurant cap off a thoroughly elegant package.

Hotel Locanda (☎ 061 699 20 20; www.hotel-locanda .ch; Drahtzugstrasse 61; s/d from Sfr110/170; ☙ closed Jul) Away from the three leading midrange hotels already mentioned, you're looking at secondary options, dictated by price or availability. This is a humble but clean hotel featuring white walls, yellow duvets and new bathrooms.

Hotel Steinenschanze (☎ 061 272 53 53; www .steinenschanze.ch; Steinengraben 69; s Sfr120-210, d Sfr180-260) The rooms here are slightly more old-fashioned than the sparkling lobby might suggest, but they are extremely well maintained and comfortable.

Das Breite Hotel (☎ 061 315 65 65; www.dasbreite hotel.ch; Zürcherstrasse 149; s/d from Sfr130/170) This forward-thinking modern hotel, opened in late 2005, employs adults with disabilities – which generally means the service to guests is extra attentive and friendly.

Merian am Rhein (☎ 061 690 91 30; Rheingasse 12; s/d from Sfr91/158, s/d with bathroom from Sfr139/182; 🖳 ⊠ P) This decent four-star establishment boasts well-appointed modern rooms, lots of business facilities and a respected restaurant. The location, while central, can be a trifle noisy on summer evenings.

TOP END

Drei Könige am Rhein (☎ 061 260 50 50; www.drei -koenige-basel.ch; Blumenrain 8) Due to be reopened in 2006 after a major refurbishment, the indisputably top address in town is set to be even better. Guests throughout its history have included Princess (later Queen) Victoria, Napoleon, Voltaire and Dickens.

Eating

Basel also has a branch of the eat-in-the-dark restaurant **Blindekuh** (☎ 061 336 33 00; www .blindekuh.ch in German; Dornacherstrasse 192). See p205.

Café de L'imprimerie (☎ 061 262 36 06; St Johanns Vorstadt 19; 2-course menus Sfr14.50-16.50; ☙ lunch &

dinner Mon-Fri, dinner Sat) This converted print shop makes an unpretentious bistro, with chalky walls and heavy wooden tables. Filling meals at affordable prices mean it's a fond local haunt.

Zum Schmale Wurf (☎ 061 683 33 25; Rheingasse 10; dishes Sfr10-30, midday menus Sfr16.50 & Sfr18.50; 🕑 lunch & dinner Mon-Fri, dinner Sat & Sun) Delicious smells and an air of intergenerational bonhomie waft over this Italian antipasto, pasta and *carne* heaven on the river. Lunchtime menus also occasionally branch out into global cuisine, with *merguez* sausages or jambalaya.

Susu's (☎ 061 261 67 80; Gerbergasse 73; soups from Sfr8.50, mains Sfr25-45) Acqua Osteria (see boxed text right) is trendier, but this place is just as likable for its versatility. Downstairs is good for everyday coffee or a casual lunch of spicy corn soup, while the stylish bar/restaurant upstairs is suitable for everything from a romantic tete â tete to a company get-together. The seasonally changing menu innovatively mixes Asian and Mediterranean influences, but usually finishes with *Schoggiträume* (chocolate dreams) – four shades of delicious chocolate mousse served in a line of shot glasses.

Erlkönig (☎ 061 683 33 22; NT/Areal, Erlenstrasse; mains Sfr28-36; 🕑 dinner Wed-Sun) It's a bit of a schlep to reach Erlkönig, but you know you're off the tourist trail. Located in the nt/Areal (opposite) it's a very cool merger of squat bar/restaurant and formal dining room, serving Basler and modern international cuisine. Take tram No 1 or 14 to Musicaltheater or the No 33 bus to Mattenstrasse.

Parterre (☎ 061 695 89 98; Klybeckstrasse 1b; mains Sfr24-32; 🕑 dinner Mon-Sat, snacks & light meals served 8am-midnight Mon-Fri, 10am-midnight Sat) Unusual dishes such as pork chop marinated in beer with apricot chutney, or green curry in tortilla shells over fried sweet potato, *mostly* come off in this slightly alternative place overlooking the Kaserne park. There's an array of newspapers and magazines, some English, to read over coffee and cake.

Weinstube Gifthüttli (☎ 061 261 16 56; Schneidergasse 11; mains Sfr18-48; 🕑 lunch & dinner Mon-Sat) It's received wisdom that this is the best place to sample local cuisine, although – if you're like us – you might find that, despite the ornate interior and impressive menu of various cordon bleus, it's slightly a victim of its own success.

AUTHOR'S CHOICE

Acqua Osteria (☎ 061 271 63 00; Binningerstrasse 14; dishes Sfr12-36; 🕑 lunch & dinner Mon-Fri, dinner Sat) For a special experience, head to these converted waterworks beside a quiet stream and the club Kuppel. The atmosphere is a mix of glam and industrial, with brown leather banquettes, candles and chandeliers – one over the open kitchen made from cooking utensils – inside bare concrete walls and floors. The food is Tuscan and the fact the ever-changing chalkboard menu is written in Italian might be more pretentious if this weren't multilingual Switzerland. Staff will explain all, but do book if you want a table. Basel's beautiful people drink in the attached lounge bar.

Gleich (☎ 061 261 48 83; Leonhardsberg 1; buffets from Sfr17.50; 🕑 10.30am-9.30pm Mon-Fri) This vegetarian restaurant is quiet and rather ascetic, but it's not bad for a healthy bite.

Eo Ipso (☎ 061 333 14 90; Dornacherstrasse 192; most mains Sfr38; 🕑 9am-1am Tue-Fri, 5pm-2am Sat, bar only 5pm-midnight Mon) Lip-smackingly fresh produce underpins a menu ranging from Italian to American to Japanese at this trendy bistro.

Also recommended.

Balthazar (☎ 061 281 81 51; Steinenbachgässlein 34; lunch specials Sfr25-35, other mains Sfr25-50; 🕑 lunch & dinner Mon-Fri, dinner Sat) Popular, upmarket Mediterranean restaurant, with fine wines and delicately flavoured dishes.

Bruderholz-Stucki (☎ 061 361 82 22; Bruderholzallee 42; lunch menus & à la carte evening mains from Sfr75; 🕑 lunch & dinner Tue-Sat) Gault Millau–rated *haute cuisine* in the suburbs.

Drinking

Both Steinenvorstadt and Barfüsserplatz teem with teens and 20-somethings on the weekends.

Bar Rouge (☎ 061 361 30 31; Messeplatz 10; 🕑 from 5pm Mon-Sat, from 8pm Sun) This plush red bar with panoramic views from the 31st floor of the *Messeturm* (or convention tower) is the city's most memorable. Hipsters, and a few suits early on weekday evenings, come to appreciate the regular DJs and films. It closes for parts of July and August, so ring ahead then.

fumare/non fumare (☎ 061 263 36 63; Gerbergasse 30; 🕑 8-1am Mon-Fri, 9am-2pm Sat, 10am-midnight Sun) Overlooking Marktplatz, this Italian feeling café/bar is a great spot to watch the world go by. And when you've finished doing that, you can retire to the buzzy atmosphere of the Mitte bar behind.

Cargo-Bar (☎ 061 321 00 72; St Johanns Rheinweg 46) A nice half-way house between cool and alternative, located in a tucked-away spot on the river. There are lots of art installations, live gigs, video shows and DJs.

Fischerstube (☎ 061 692 66 35; Rheingasse 45; ⏰ 9.30am-midnight Mon-Fri, to 2am Sat, 5pm-midnight Sun) An atmospheric, smoky beer hall, with long tables, Fischerstube is famous for its Ueli-bier. It also serves Wurst and a three-course 'Bier Menu' (Sfr42), where every course features the amber liquid, even the soup and the dessert.

For even more casual outings, try the studenty **Bar der Roten Engel** (☎ 061 261 20 08; Andreasplatz 15), the alternative **Kaserne** (Klybeckstrasse 1b) or the downright grungy **Hirscheneck** (☎ 061 692 73 33; Lindenberg 23).

Entertainment
LIVE MUSIC
The **Basel Symphony Orchestra** (www.sinfonieorchesterbasel.ch) and **Basel Chamber Orchestra** (www.kammerorchesterbasel.ch) both play at the Stadtcasino; ask the tourist office for details.

NIGHTCLUBS
Die Kuppel (☎ 061 270 99 39; www.kuppel.ch in German; Binningerstrasse 14; ⏰ from 9pm Tue & 10pm Thu-Sat) This is an atmospheric wooden dome, with a dance floor and cocktail bar, located in a secluded park. Salsa, soul, house and '70s/'80s are regularly on the bill.

nt/Areal (☎ 061 683 33 22; www.areal.org in German; Erlenstrasse 21; ⏰ from 7pm Wed-Sun) A meeting point for young Baslers in the former goods yard of the German railways. In summer, outdoor projectors play light shows, while customers tuck into food and drinks inside Erlkönig (see Eating, p241). From the Areal sign at the intersection of Mattenstrasse and Erlenstrasse, head 300m straight ahead. Either catch tram No 1 or 14 to Musicaltheater or the bus No 33 to Mattenstrasse.

Atlantis (☎ 061 228 96 96; www.atlan-tis.ch in German; Klosterbergstrasse 13; ⏰ from 6pm Tue-Fri) Bar/club Atlantis remains popular with smartly dressed punters, but it's not as unforgettably unique as the preceding two venues.

Mad Max (☎ 061 281 61 14; www.mad-max.ch; Steinentorstrasse 35; ⏰ from 10.30pm Fri & Sat) Huge club playing everything from rock to trance and house, and enforcing a strange door policy – nobody under 28 (or 26 for women) is allowed in.

SPORT
FC Basel, the leaders of the Swiss football league, play at St Jakob Park, some 2km east of the main train station. The stadium, by Herzog & de Meuron, is the prototype of their mega-famous Munich creation. Its translucent skin looks best when lit up, which only happens during games, every week or so. Take tram No 14 to get there.

Getting There & Away
AIR
EuroAirport (☎ 061 325 31 11; www.euroairport.com) serves Basel (as well as Mulhouse, France and Freiburg, Germany). Located 5km north in France, it has several routes to London on Swiss International Air Lines and low-cost carrier easyJet, with direct flights to many continental cities, including Alicante, Amsterdam, Barcelona, Brussels, Frankfurt, Hamburg, Madrid, Naples, Paris and Rome.

BOAT
An enjoyable, if slow, way to travel to/from Basel is via boat along the Rhine. The landing stage is between Johanniterbrücke and Dreirosenbrücke.

Viking River Cruises (☎ 1-818-227 1234; www.vikingrivers.com; 21820 Burbank Blvd, Woodland Hills, California) runs an eight-day trip from Amsterdam starting from around UK£1565. **Travel Renaissance** (☎ 0870 850 1690; The Bothy, Albury Park, Albury, Surrey GU5 9BU) is the company's representative in the UK, or you can call it in Germany (☎ 0800 258 46 65) or Switzerland (☎ 0800 84 54 64).

Also try **Scylla Tours** (☎ 061 638 81 81; www.scylla-tours.com; Uferstrasse 90).

CAR & MOTORCYCLE
The E25/E60 motorway heads down from Strasbourg and passes by EuroAirport, and the E35/A5 hugs the German side of the Rhine.

Rental
Try **Hertz** (☎ 061 205 92 22; Nauenstrasse 33) and **Avis** (☎ 061 206 95 45; Aeschengraben 31) in the Hilton Hotel. They also have branches near the SBB station and the airport. A Smart Car from **City-Rent** (☎ 061 685 70 01; www.cityrent.ch; Hotel Alexander,

BASEL & AARGAU

ACID HOUSE

Home to the giant Roche and Novartis companies, the Basel region is the epicentre of Switzerland's multi-billion franc pharmaceutical industry. However, it's not just prescription drugs that have seen the light of day here. In 1943, a chemist at the company Sandoz searching for a migraine cure accidentally absorbed an experimental compound through the skin of his fingertips and, oops, took the world's first 'acid trip'.

The chemist was Albert Hofmann and the drug was lysergic acid diethylamide, or LSD, which provoked a series of mind-bending, psychedelic hallucinations. Hofmann liked this experience so much, he tried the drug again, and he wasn't even deterred by his first bad trip, in which he thought a demon had invaded him and his neighbour was a witch.

Later, LSD was taken up by writers and artists, such as Aldous Huxley, who saw it as a creative force. Its mind-bending properties also made it a favourite with the 'far out' flower-power generation of the 1960s. From 1953, the CIA conducted extensive tests on LSD as a truth drug, ultimately deciding that – doh! – the testimony of people on acid was entirely unreliable. Tests on whether the drug had any clinical value were curtailed when it was outlawed in 1966.

But whatever LSD's destructive potential, it certainly didn't do Herr Hofmann much harm. He was still alive as various fans in Basel and abroad celebrated his 100th birthday in 2006.

Riehenring 83; per hr/day/week Sfr7/55/370 plus mileage) is a great way to zip around town.

TRAIN

Basel has two main train stations: the Swiss/French train station (SBB Bahnhof) in the city's south and the German train station (Badischer Bahnhof or BBF) on the northern bank.

Services within Switzerland leave from the SBB Bahnhof; there are two fast trains an hour to Geneva (Sfr67, 2¾ hours) and Zürich (Sfr30, one hour). Trains to France also leave from this station, although from the special SNCF section within it. There are services to Paris (Sfr51, six daily, five hours), Brussels (Sfr110, three daily, seven hours) and Strasbourg (Sfr19, 17 daily, 1½ hours).

Fast intercity services into Germany stop at both stations, but if you want to get to a smaller town in southern Germany, you will need to board at the Badischer Bahnhof (BBF). Two to three trains an hour run to Freiburg (€10 to €18, 30 minutes). Main destinations via BBF are Frankfurt (€60, plus German rail supplement for fast trains, 2¾ to 3¾ hours depending on service) and Berlin (€110, seven to 9½ hours).

Getting Around

Buses run every 20 to 30 minutes from 5am to around 11.30pm between the airport and the train station (Sfr2.80, 15 minutes). The trip by **taxi** (☎ 061 691 77 88, 061 271 22 22) costs around Sfr35.

Once you've booked into a hotel, your mobility ticket covers all public transport (including back to the airport). If you're not staying in town, tickets for buses and trams cost Sfr1.80/2.60/8 for up to four stops/the central zone/day pass.

There are several parking garages between the SBB station and the pedestrian zone. Expect to pay at least Sfr1.50 an hour. Small ferries cross the Rhine at various points (Sfr1.20, day passes not valid).

The SBB train station has **bike rental** (☺ 7am-9pm).

AROUND BASEL
Augusta Raurica

By the Rhine, these **Roman ruins** (admission free; ☺ 10am-5pm Mar-Oct, to 4.30pm Nov-Feb) are Switzerland's largest. They're the last remnants of a colony founded in 43 BC that had grown to 20,000 citizens by the 2nd century. Today, restored features include an open-air theatre and several temples. There's also a **Römermuseum** (Roman Museum; ☎ 061 816 22 22; admission Sfr5, BaselCard valid; ☺ 1-5pm Mon, 10am-5pm Tue-Sun, closed noon-1.30pm Nov-Feb), which features an authentic Roman house among its exhibits.

The train trip from Basel to Kaiseraugst takes 15 minutes (Sfr5.20 each way); it's then a 10-minute walk to the site. In summer, taking the boat is another option (single/return Sfr28/47; see p239).

The Basel tourist office (p237) also runs **guided tours** (adult/child Sfr15/7; ☺ 3pm Sun May-Oct).

AARGAU CANTON

BADEN

pop 16,193 / elevation 388m

Baden is an old-school spa; people have been coming here since Roman times, either for its mineral baths' curative properties or to escape the stresses of the world. And although it's not the health resort featured in Thomas Mann's classic novel *The Magic Mountain* – that was Davos – parts of this sleepy, nostalgic town still feel as if they're straight from those pages.

Orientation & Information

From the train station, you head either south for the Altstadt (Old Town) or north to the spa centre, which are a total 20 minutes' walk apart.

Post office (☎ 056 200 24 01; Bahnhofstrasse 31; ☻ 7.30am-6.30pm Mon-Fri, 8am-4pm Sat)

Tourist office (☎ 056 200 83 83; www.baden.ch; Bahnhofplatz 1; ☻ noon-7pm Mon, 9.30am-7pm Tue-Fri, 9.30am-4pm Sat)

Sights & Activities

There are 19 mineral-rich **sulphur springs** in Baden, believed to be helpful in treating rheumatism, respiratory, cardiovascular and even some neurological disorders. The tourist office can point you in the direction of treatments.

Pools in all the major hotels are open to everyone; entry ranges between Sfr5 and Sfr16, but whirlpool baths, saunas, solariums and special treatments cost more. The only pool large enough for swimming is the **Thermalbad** (☎ 056 203 91 12; www.thermalbaden.ch in German; adult/child Sfr16/10, plus Sfr5 for a dressing cabin; ☻ 7.30am-9pm Mon-Fri, 7.30am-8pm Sat & Sun) in the Hotel Verenahof.

The Old Town centre includes a **covered bridge** (Holzbrücke) and step-gabled houses.

If you're feeling keen, you can climb the hundreds of stairs near the **city tower** (Stadtturm) for a bird's-eye view from the ruined castle on the hill. West of the spas is **Stiftung Langmatt** (☎ 056 222 58 42; www.langmatt.ch; Römerstrasse 30; adult/student Sfr10/5; ☻ 2-5pm Tue-Fri, 11am-5pm Sat & Sun Apr-Oct), a stately home full of French Impressionist art.

Sleeping & Eating

SYHA hostel (☎ 056 221 67 36; www.youthhostel.ch /baden; Kanalstrasse 7; dm Sfr29-35, s/d Sfr78/88; ☻ closed mid-Dec–Feb; check-in 5-10pm; ✂ P) One of Switzerland's best-looking hostels, this has grey slate floors, earth-red walls and top-quality materials throughout. It's as quiet as the rest of the town, though. Walk from the train station to the Old Town, cross the Limmat River at Hochbrücke, and take the first right into Kanalstrasse to find it.

Atrium-Hotel Blume (☎ 056 222 55 69; www.blume -baden.ch; Kurplatz 4; s/d from Sfr85/150, with bathroom from Sfr135/240) An atmospheric old place featuring a wonderful inner courtyard with a fountain and plants; it also has a small thermal pool.

La Trattoria (☎ 056 222 64 64; Theaterplatz 2; mains Sfr13-30, midday menus Sfr12-20; ☻ lunch & dinner) This deservedly popular pizzeria also does seasonally changing specialities and Swiss staples such as *Ghackets mit Hörnli* and *Älpler Makkaroni*.

Roter Turm (☎ 056 222 85 25; Rathausgasse 5; mains from Sfr25-40; ☻ 9am-midnight Mon-Sat, meals served at lunch & dinner) This is a fairly upmarket dining room, with modern European, mainly Italian, cuisine alongside traditional dishes such as cordon bleu calf.

Getting There & Away

Baden is 17 minutes away from Zürich by train (Sfr9.80). It is also within Zürich's S-Bahn network (lines S6 and S12, 30 minutes). By road, follow the N1/E60 motorway to Zürich.

BASEL & AARGAU

Northeastern Switzerland

This is Switzerland's forgotten hinterland – at least, if such a well-explored country can be said to have one. While most tourists arrive in search of show-stopping natural scenery, this neat little corner tends more towards picture-book pretty. It offers more cultural delights, like the perfectly preserved medieval town of Stein am Rhein, the ostentatious bay windows of Schaffhausen or the magnificently ornate library of St Gallen's cathedral. Appenzell's contribution to this mix is a long line in rural tradition and a fine line in stinky cheeses.

On the northern border where Switzerland segues into Germany, the two can seem indistinguishable. The relatively flat landscape attracts cyclists from all directions, while castles line both the German and Swiss shores of Lake Constance and the Rhine River. Even as you head further south, a series of rolling hills, carefully tended pastures and manicured apple orchards continue to make this feel like one of Switzerland's physically tamest regions.

But Mother Nature didn't entirely leave here without true spectacle. Outside Schaffhausen, brave souls stand on a rock in the middle of the Rhine Falls – Europe's largest waterfall – as 600 cubic metres of water per second pound by. The stretch of the Rhine between Schaffhausen and Lake Constance is among the river's most beautiful cruises, and the snaggle-tooth shapes of the Churfirsten Mountains invite comparison with the Matterhorn.

Perhaps the car-free resort of Braunwald sums up the region's symbolic position within the country. Braunwald doesn't enjoy the same in-your-face views as resorts in the Bernese Oberland. But it's amazing in its own right and as undiscovered as Switzerland gets.

HIGHLIGHTS

- Marvelling at the perfectly preserved medieval town centre of **Stein am Rhein** (p250)
- Standing in the middle of the **Rheinfall** (p250), Europe's largest waterfall
- Letting every Swiss stereotype come to life in mouth-watering **Appenzell** (p255)
- Hitting the books in **St Gallen's Stiftsbibliothek** (p252), a superb rococo masterpiece
- Discovering car-free **Braunwald** (p260) in one of the country's least-visited regions

Rheinfall ★ Stein am Rhein ★

St Gallen ★
Appenzell ★

Braunwald ★

■ POPULATION: 865,855　　■ AREA: 4418 SQ KM　　■ LANGUAGE: GERMAN

NORTHEASTERN SWITZERLAND

Orientation & Information

The tourist region of Ostschweiz (Eastern Switzerland) unites several easterly Swiss cantons with Liechtenstein (p305). Information can be found on the pages of Switzerland Tourism (www.myswitzerland.com) or the official website of Ostschweiz Tourismus (www.ostschweiz-i.ch in German). Otherwise, enquire at the St Gallen tourist office (p252).

Getting There & Around

This area lies between Zürich and Friedrichshafen (Germany) airports and can be conveniently reached from either by public or private transport. Road and rail link Zürich with Schaffhausen, Stein am Rhein,

St Gallen and even Linthal, for Braunwald. Alternatively, a ferry will bring you across the lake from Friedrichshafen to Romanshorn, which also has good car and train links.

Several areas, such as the Bodensee region around Lake Constance and Appenzellerland, offer regional passes. For details, see the individual sections.

SCHAFFHAUSEN CANTON

Cyclists love touring this relatively flat region of the country, and accommodation (particularly cheaper accommodation) books up swiftly on weekends. However, excellent

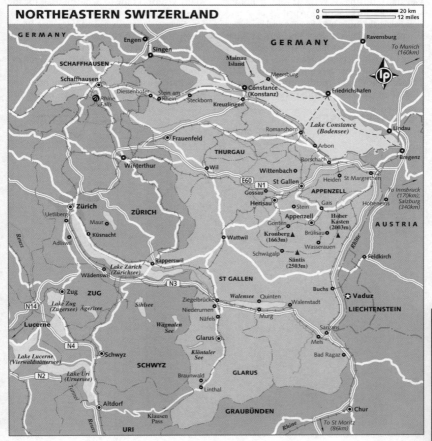

NORTHEASTERN SWITZERLAND

transport and manageable distances make it an easy day trip from Zürich (p194), too.

SCHAFFHAUSEN

pop 33,450 / elevation 404m

Schaffhausen is the kind of quaint medieval town one typically finds in Germany and, sitting on the northern shore of the Rhine not far from the border, it nearly is. Ornate frescoes and 'oriel' (bay) windows adorn the pastel-coloured houses lining the stone pavements of its pedestrian-only Old Town. Amidst this, on a vine-covered hill, stands the city's signature fortress, the circular Munot.

Despite this highly visible landmark, allied pilots really did 'mistake' Schaffhausen for Germany during WWII, dropping bombs on the outskirts – on 1 April 1944 – and making it the only bit of Swiss soil to take a direct hit during the war. This and another bombing of the city post–April Fools' Day were officially declared accidents. However, rumour has it they were a warning to Schaffhausen's powerful munitions industry to stop illicit dealings with the Nazi regime.

Orientation

The train station, served by Swiss and German trains, lies parallel to one of the main streets, Vorstadt. Cross the road and head straight ahead about 150m to find yourself in the thick of things.

Information

Main post office (☎ 052 630 03 40; Bahnhofstrasse 34; ☼ 7am-6.30pm Mon-Fri, 8am-5pm Sat) Opposite the train station.

Tourist office (☎ 052 632 40 20; www.schaffhausen -tourismus.ch; Herrenacker 15; ☼ 9.30am-6pm Mon-Fri, 9.30am-4pm Sat, plus 9.30am-3.30pm Sun Jul & Aug) Has one free Internet terminal.

Sights & Activities

Many visitors come to Schaffhausen for the nearby Rheinfall (Rhine Falls; see p250). However, it's worth spending a few hours seeing the Old Town, too. The tourist office offers **walking tours** (adult/child Sfr12/6; ☼ 2pm Tue, Thu & Sat May-Oct), with wine-tasting tours another possibility.

Schaffhausen is often nicknamed the *Erkerstadt* in German because of its 170

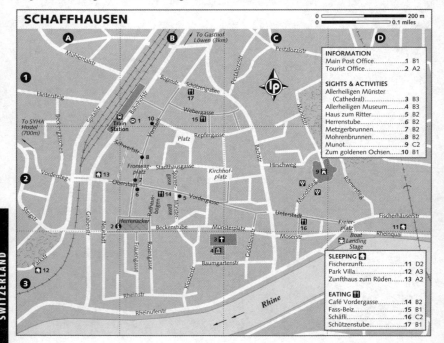

SCHAFFHAUSEN

0 ———————— 200 m
0 ———————— 0.1 miles

To Gasthof Löwen (3km)

To SYHA Hostel (700m)

Erkers, or oriel bay windows, which citizens built as a display of their wealth. One of the most noteworthy windows belongs to the 17th-century **Zum goldenen Ochsen** (Vorstadt 17). Further south, past the 16th-century Mohrenbrunnen (Moor fountain) is the old market place, Fronwagplatz, which is dominated by the Metzgerbrunnen (Butcher's fountain with a William Tell-type figure) and a large clock tower.

As you face the clock, you'll see the late baroque **Herrenstube** (Fronwagplatz 3), built in 1748 and once the drinking hole of Schaffhausen nobles. To your left, a street away, lies the town's most famous building, **Haus zum Ritter** (Vordergasse 65), built in 1492. Its detailed renaissance-style fresco is a copy, and if you're keen you can see parts of the 16th-century originals in the **Allerheiligen Museum** (☎ 052 633 07 77; www.allerheiligen.ch; Klosterplatz; admission free; ☾ 11am-5pm Tue-Sun). However, overall, this museum is rather unfocused and you'd be better off devoting time to the attached **Allerheiligen Münster** (All Saints' Cathedral; ☾ 10am-noon & 2-5pm Tue-Sun) instead.

East of Haus zum Ritter, Vordergasse eventually becomes Unterstadt, where you'll find the stairs to the 16th-century **Munot** (admission free; ☾ 8am-8pm May-Sep, 9am-5pm Oct-Apr). The circular shape of Schaffhausen's fortress is highly unusual and it was built by forced labour following the Reformation. Inside its dimly lit interior, a relatively slippery circular ramp leads up to a large roof terrace, where you can grab a drink while enjoying the views over Schaffhausen's rooftops. Alternatively, the wooden door to the right as you enter the Munot leads to stairs that run through the vines of the surrounding hill.

The 45km boat trip from Schaffhausen to Konstanz is considered one of the Rhine's more beautiful stretches, lined as it is with castles, quaint villages and lush countryside. **Boat trips** (☎ 052 634 08 88; www.urh.ch or www.river ticket.ch; Freier Platz; one way/return Sfr21/30; ☾ 4 times daily May-Sep, four times Sat & Sun Apr) head to/from Konstanz via the island of Reichenau and Stein am Rhein. The journey takes 3¾ hours heading downstream to Schaffhausen and 4¾ hours going the other way.

Sleeping

SYHA hostel (☎ 052 625 88 00; www.youthhostel.ch /schaffhausen; Randenstrasse 65; dm Sfr25.50; ☾ reception closed 9am-5pm, hostel closed Nov-Feb; ☐ P) This old pile of a mansion has clean, modern bathrooms, although the 10-bed mixed dorms are a bit musty. Set in leafy grounds, it's 15 minutes by foot west of the train station, or take bus No 6 to Hallenbad.

Gasthof Löwen (☎ 052 643 22 08; fax 052 643 22 88; Im Höfli 2; s/d with shared bathroom from Sfr65/110) Decent pension about 3km north of the centre. Take Bus No 5.

Park Villa (☎ 052 635 60 60; www.parkvilla.ch; Parkstrasse 18; s/d from Sfr80/130, with bathroom from Sfr170/180; P) The eclectic furniture in this faintly Gothic house resembles a private antique collection, with a various array of four-poster beds, Persian carpets, chandeliers, patterned wallpaper, fake Ming vases and so on, in individually decorated rooms. South of the station on the western side of the tracks, the hotel faces a pleasant park, and has quirky sculptures in its own garden.

Zunfthaus zum Rüden (☎ 052 632 36 36; www.rue den.ch; Oberstadt 20; s/d Sfr150/180; ☐) Refurbished guildhall with character, despite being mainly a business hotel.

Fischerzunft (☎ 052 632 05 05; www.fischerzunft.ch; Bahnhofstrasse 46; s/d from Sfr142/215) One of Switzerland's most opulent hotels, this has a subtle Oriental theme, with printed silks in the bedrooms and subtle Asian flavours in its sinfully expensive restaurant (menus up to Sfr265!).

Eating

Café Vordergasse (☎ 052 625 42 49; Vordergasse 79; snacks & light meals Sfr5-16; ☾ Mon-Sat) This deservedly popular Art Nouveau–style tearoom has an international flavour, with a range of sandwiches, salads, quiches and even hummus in pita bread. Mango lassis, Indian and African teas and even unusual juices like lychee are on the menu, too.

Fass-Beiz (☎ 052 625 46 10; Webergasse 13; meals Sfr7.50-25; ☾ Mon-Sat) This tucked-away alternative bar-café enjoys a laid-back atmosphere and serves sandwiches and tasty sit-down dishes, with an excellent vegetarian selection. There are music gigs and theatre performances in the cellar below.

Schäfli (☎ 052 625 11 47; Understadt 21; menus Sfr15-22; ☾ Tue-Sat) This solidly unpretentious place near the stairs to the Munot serves a range of classic Swiss dishes from cheese dumplings to *Geschnetzeltes* veal.

Schützenstube (☎ 052 625 42 49; Schützengraben 27; mains Sfr18-38; ☾ Mon-Fri) The ornate historic exterior might lead you to suspect a tourist trap, but this comfy tavern usually contains plenty of locals. The emphasis is on fresh seasonal ingredients, with the chef sometimes emerging from the kitchen to check diners are happy with their meals.

Getting There & Away

There are hourly trains to/from Zürich (Sfr17.60, 40 minutes). Local trains head half hourly to Stein am Rhein, Kreuzlingen, Romanshorn and either Rorschach or St Gallen. After 7pm, these services terminate at Romanshorn.

Schaffhausen also has excellent road connections radiating out in all directions.

RHEINFALL

The roar of water, the tang of salt spray and the chatter of hordes of day-trippers announce the presence of Europe's largest waterfalls. The **Rhine Falls** (www.rhinefalls.com) might not give Niagara much competition in terms of height (23m), width (150m) or even flow of water (600 cu metres per second in summer), but it's certainly a stunning sight when you arrive to see people standing on the tall rock in the middle, with the Swiss flag patriotically flying above.

Two castles overlook the falls. The smaller **Schlössli Worth** is on the north bank facing the falling water and is surrounded by touristy restaurants, shops, an information centre and small ferry wharves. The more imposing **Schloss Laufen** on the southern bank overlooks the falls at closer quarters, as they rush over the cliffs.

They are several ways to reach the falls, which governs where you arrive. If you catch bus No 1 or 6 from Schaffhausen train station to Neuhausen Zentrum (Sfr2.20), you'll follow the yellow footprints on the pavement until you come to a point where you can go right towards Schlössli Worth or left across the combined train/footbridge to Schloss Laufen.

If you come by local train from Schaffhausen or Winterthur to Schloss Laufen am Rheinfall (April to October only), you'll need to climb the hill to the castle. And if travelling by car, you'll pull up in the car park behind it.

Most views of the falls are free, but perhaps unsurprisingly, you pay for the best. To get close up to the rushing waters on the south side of the falls, you pay Sfr1 at the Schloss Laufen souvenir shop (open daily) to descend the staircase to the Känzeli viewing platform.

During summer, **ferries** (☎ 052 672 48 11; www.maendli.ch) flit in and out of the water at the bottom of the falls. Some merely cross from Schlössli Worth to Schloss Laufen (adult/child Sfr2.50/1.50), but the most unusual excursion is the 'Felsenfahrt Panorama Sicht' journey (adult/child Sfr6.50/3.50) to the tall rock in the middle of the falls, where you can climb to the top and watch the water rush all around you.

On the Swiss National Day, 1 August, there are spectacular fireworks over the falls.

If you're interested in the sound of the waterfall lulling you to sleep at night, there's an **SYHA hostel** (☎ 052 659 61 52; www.youthhostel.ch; dm Sfr25.50; ☽ reception closed 9am-5pm, hostel closed mid-Oct–mid-Mar) inside Schloss Laufen.

STEIN AM RHEIN

pop 3000 / elevation 407m

Stein am Rhein is a village straight out of Hans Christian Anderson fairytales: its immaculate appearance is something you'd only really expect in a children's picture book. The effect is most overwhelming in its cobblestone Rathausplatz, where dinky half-timbered houses decorated with ornate frescoes sit shoulder to shoulder in a united front against modernity.

This is frequently regarded as Switzerland's most beautiful town square, but the waterfront and a few side streets are also well worth exploring – which over one million tourists a year do. If you wish to avoid the worst crush, come on a weekday and stay until after 5pm.

Orientation & Information

The train station is on the southern side of the Rhine, while the Old Town lies on the northern bank. To make the short walk from the station (which has bicycle rental and lockers), head straight along Bahnhofstrasse. Turn right, then left and cross the bridge. Veering left, you'll enter the pedestrianised Rathausplatz.

The tiny **tourist office** (☎ 052 742 20 90; www.steinamrein.ch; Oberstadt 3; ☽ 9.30am-noon & 1.30-5pm Mon-Fri) is found to the east (right) of this square. Hotels can help with information when the office is closed. If arriving by ship, simply head inland, and you'll soon arrive at Unterstadt, with Rathausplatz to your right.

Sights & Activities

The **Rathaus** (town hall) stands at the eastern end of **Rathausplatz**, around which the 16th-century houses are named according to the pictures with which they are adorned. So, for example, there is *Hirschen* (Stag), *Roter Ochsen* (Red Ox), *Sonne* (Sun) and *Weisse Adler* (White Eagle).

The point of Stein am Rhein is really to just wander around soaking up the atmosphere – while ducking the costumed tour guides and pony-trap rides. However, one four-storey house has been converted into the surprisingly diverting **Museum Lindwurm** (☎ 052 741 25 12; Understadt 18; adult/student Sfr5/3; ✆ 10am-5pm Wed-Mon Mar-Oct), which evokes the bourgeois lifestyle of the mid-19th century. The living rooms, servants' quarters and kitchen replicate the conditions enjoyed by the family who once lived here, while there are stables, too.

Around the town, there are several gate towers built in the 14th century, including one at the end of Unterstadt.

Sleeping & Eating

SYHA hostel (☎ 0527411255; www.youthhostel.ch/stein amrhein; Hemishoferstrasse 87; dm Sfr24.50; ✆ reception closed 9am-5.30pm, hostel closed Nov-Feb) Hemishoferstrasse is the continuation of Understadt to the west, and about 1.5km from the centre of town you'll find Stein am Rhein's pleasant hostel, some two minutes from the beach.

Mühlethal Gasthaus (☎ 052 741 27 25; Öhningerstrasse; s/d Sfr75/100) This place, 200m east of the tourist office, is good value with compact rooms.

Rheingerbe (☎ 052 741 29 91; www.rheingerbe.ch; Rathausplatz 2; s/d Sfr85/150) The compact rooms here are old-fashioned, but that seems entirely fitting in Stein am Rhein. You need to book to get a river-view room.

Rheinfels (☎ 741 21 44; www.rheinfels.ch; Rathausplatz 2; s/d Sfr135/190) Up the creaky staircase, past the suit of armour (or straight up the lift instead), this atmospheric hotel has generously sized rooms, decorated in an older style with lots of pink and brown, but many with river views.

Grenzstein (☎ 052 741 51 44; camp sites per adult/ tent Sfr7/7; ✆ year-round) This smallish camping

site is 2km from Stein village, beside the Rhine. Good facilities onsite include washing machines, camp shop and restaurant.

Eating, like sightseeing, is very much a question of wandering around and seeing what takes your fancy.

Sonne (☎ 052 741 21 28; Rathausplatz 13; mains Sfr30-50; ✆ Thu-Mon) It's the oldest restaurant in town (the building is a cracked and crumbly 1463 slice of architecture). Fish dishes are delicate of texture, though rich in taste. There are also seasonal specialities.

Both hotels Rheingerbe (mains Sfr18 to Sfr28) and Rheinfels (mains Sfr35 to Sfr40) have highly rated fish restaurants.

Burg Hohenklingen (✆ Tue-Sun Mar-Dec) Up the hill above the town, Burg Hohenklingen provides a commanding view and a commendable restaurant.

Getting There & Away

Travel by train to Zürich costs Sfr23. Stein am Rhein is also on the hourly train route that links Schaffhausen (Sfr7.20) to the west with Rorschach (Sfr19) or St Gallen (Sfr23) to the east.

A boat trip along this stretch of the Rhine is pleasant if you have time (see p249), although you see many of the same sights during the quicker train or car journey. The latter follows Hwy 13, along the southern bank of the river.

ST GALLEN CANTON

ST GALLEN

pop 69,900 / elevation 670m

St Gallen's history as the 'writing room of Europe' is still evident in its principal attraction today. The ornate rococo library of its huge Catholic abbey remains its central focus. However, you don't have to be a complete bookworm to enjoy the place.

Its Old Town forms an attractive core, perfect for wandering, and with street names hung in large writing across their entrance, it's hard to get lost. Meanwhile, St Gallen's new outdoor 'City Lounge' provides a very modern counterpoint.

Orientation

The pedestrian-only Old Town, containing most major sights, is five to 10 minutes east of the train station.

Information

Main post office (☎ 071 499 73 04; Bahnhofplatz 5; ☺ 7am-7.30pm Mon-Fri, to 8pm Thu, 7am-4pm Sat, 3-6pm Sun)

Tourist office (☎ 071 227 37 37; www.st.gallen-boden see.ch; Bahnhofplatz 1a; ☺ 9am-noon & 1-6pm Mon-Fri, 9am-noon Sat)

Sights

STIFTSBIBLIOTHEK & CATHEDRAL

St Gallen's 16th-century **Abbey Library** (www .stiftsbibliothek.ch; adult/student & senior/child Sfr7/5/ free; ☺ 10am-5pm Mon-Sat, to 4pm Sun Apr-Oct; 10am-noon & 1.30-5pm Mon-Sat, to 4pm Sun Dec-Mar) is one of the world's oldest libraries and the finest example of rococo architecture in Switzerland. Filled with priceless books

and manuscripts painstakingly handwritten by monks during the Middle Ages, it's a dimly-lit confection of ceiling frescoes, stucco, cherubs and parquetry. Only 30,000 of the total 150,000 volumes are in the library at any one time, and only a handful in display cases, arranged into special exhibitions by theme.

Above you, carved wooden balustrades prop up a mezzanine floor of yet more books. If there's a tour guide in the library at the time (and you usually don't have to wait long for one) you might be lucky enough to see the monks' filing system, cleverly hidden in the wall panels.

Perhaps not surprisingly, the numerous school groups who tour the library are most

ST GALLEN

0 _____ 200 m
0 _____ 0.1 miles

INFORMATION	
Main Post Office	1 A3
Tourist Office	2 B3

SIGHTS & ACTIVITIES	
Abbey Library	3 C3
Cathedral	4 C3
Stadtlounge	5 B4
Textilmuseum	6 B3

SLEEPING 🛏	
Einstein Hotel	7 C4
Hotel Dom	8 C3
Hotel Metropol	9 B3
Hotel Vadian	10 C3

EATING 🍴	
Bäumli	11 C3
Metzgerei Gemperli	12 C3
Migros Supermarket & Restaurant	13 B4
Seeger	14 B2
Wirtschaft zur Alten Post	15 C3
Zum Goldenen Schäfli	16 C2

TRANSPORT	
Appenzeller Bahnen	17 A4
City Bus Stands	18 A3
Postbus Departures	19 A3
Trogenerbahn Stop	20 A4

To Winterthur (60km); Zürich (85km)

To David 38 (200m); Appenzell (15km)

To SYHA Hostel (500m)

NORTHEASTERN SWITZERLAND

THE LEGEND OF ST GALLEN

St Gallen all began with a bush, a bear and an Irish monk who should have watched where he was going. Or at least, so the legend goes. In AD 612, itinerant Gallus fell into a briar, but considered the stumble a calling from God rather than sheer coincidence. After a fortuitous encounter with a bear, in which he persuaded it to bring him a log, take some bread in return and leave him in peace, he used the log to begin building a hermitage. The result eventually became St Gallen's cathedral – allegedly.

enthralled by the 2700-year-old mummified corpse in the far corner.

The twin-towered **cathedral** (9am-6pm Mon, Thu & Fri, to 5pm Tue, 10am-5pm Wed, 9am-3.30pm Sat, noon-7pm Sun, but closed during services) is only slightly less ornate than its library, with dark-green ceiling frescoes and stucco embellishments. The remainder of the wall in the northeast corner of the Abbey complex is used to separate the Catholic and Protestant areas of town.

STADTLOUNGE

Historic St Gallen has recently given over part of its Bleicheli quarter to a stunningly modern art installation by Pipilotti Rist and Carlos Martinez. A rubberised red tennis-court coating has been spread over the ground between Gartenstrasse, Schreinerstrasse and Vadianstrasse, and this 'carpet' also covers a range of outdoor furniture like chairs, sofas, and tables, as well as a car.

This Stadtlounge project is intended as an 'outdoor living room' where people are encouraged to linger and chat. Huge bubbles hang over the street as lamps to add to the feeling of warmth.

BAY WINDOWS

St Gallen boasts a fine selection of elaborate 'oriel' bay windows, especially around Gallusplatz, Spisergasse, Schmiedgasse and Kugelgasse. **Walking tours** (adult/child Sf15/10; 2pm Mon, Wed, Thu, Fri & Sat May-Oct, plus 2pm Sun Jul & Aug) leave from outside the tourist office.

TEXTILMUSEUM

St Gallen has long been an important hub of the Swiss textile industry, and the **Textil-museum** (071 222 17 44; www.textilmuseum.ch; adult/student Sfr5/2; 10am-noon & 2-5pm Tue-Sat, 10am-5pm Sun, plus 10am-5pm 1st Wed of every month) is its most interesting. It traces the history of cloth-making in the town, but isn't all linen and old lace. Every season, there's also a selection of the latest fabrics waiting to be snapped up by haute-couture houses in Italy.

Sleeping

St Gallen is a business town, and frequent exhibitions and conferences can make beds scarce and prices high. Busy times are usually April and October.

SYHA Hostel (071 245 47 77; www.youthhostel.ch /st.gallen; Jüchstrasse 25; dm Sfr27, s/d/q per person Sfr46.50/36/31, r per person Sfr34; reception closed 9.30am-5pm, hostel closed mid-Dec–Mar) Signposts mark the 15-minute walk from the Old Town to this modern, quality hostel. However, it's easier to take the orange Trogenerbahn from outside the train station to 'Schülerhaus' (Sfr2.60) and walk a few minutes up the hill until you see the hostel on the left.

Hotel Vadian (071 223 60 80; fax 071 222 47 48; Gallusstrasse 36; s/d from Sfr75/120, with bathroom Sfr105/165) This 'alcohol-free' hotel offers good value with sparse modern rooms given a bit of personal character with the occasional decorative feature.

Hotel Dom (071 227 71 71; www.hoteldom.ch; Webergasse 22; s/d Sfr90/110, with bathroom Sfr130/190; P) The friendly service is the selling point at this clean, comfortable and extremely convenient three-star establishment. The staff are all people with minor disabilities, who put a lot of loving care into their work – including the art which decorates the place.

Hotel Metropol (071 228 32 32; www.hotel-metropol.ch; Bahnhofplatz 3; s/d from Sfr155/225; P) Rooms here are new and very stylish with lots of matt lacquer, white linen, broad-striped curtains and original art. There are blackout blinds to keep out the light from the train-station surrounds, and an excellent restaurant.

Einstein Hotel (071 227 55 55; www.einstein.ch; Berneggstrasse 2; standard s/d from Sfr200/250, superior from Sfr275/300; P) Even demanding rich Russians seem mollified by the levels of service and luxury at St Gallen's premier hotel. One wing contains the slightly older standard rooms. The superior rooms are brighter, airier, more hi-tech and spacious.

> **AUTHOR'S CHOICE**
>
> **Zum Goldenen Schäfli** (☎ 071 223 27 27; Metzgergasse 5; mains Sfr20-45; ✆ closed Sun in summer) This delightfully cosy 1st-floor restaurant has a distinctly sloping floor and eye-catching, sloping apéritif glasses to match. The glasses, silverware and flowers crowd the white tablecloths and a tiled medieval oven sits in the corner. The house speciality is tripe in white-wine sauce and meat dishes are numerous, but Schäfli also has half-a-dozen vegetarian choices, including home-made pasta.

Eating

FIRST-FLOOR RESTAURANTS

St Gallen is noted for its '1st Stock Beizli', which are traditional taverns situated on the first floor of half-timbered houses.

Bäumli (☎ 071 222 11 74; Schmiedgasse 18; mains Sfr20-45; ✆ Wed-Sun Aug-Jun) This cheap and homey option showcases all the typical first-floor specialities, from bratwurst with fried onions to lamb cutlets, Wiener Schnitzel, Cordon Bleus, *Geschnetzeltes* veal and *Mostbröggli* (smoked beef jerky).

Wirtschaft Zur Alten Post (☎ 071 222 66 01; Gallusstrasse 4; mains Sfr30-42; ✆ Tue-Sat) Things are a little ritzier at this upmarket *beizl*, where Swiss dishes are complemented with the likes of lamb on chilli risotto or mussels in lemongrass broth.

OTHER CUISINE

Seeger (☎ 071 222 97 90; Oberer Graben 2; mains Sfr9-27) This relaxed café attracts a broad mix of customers, with a few suits and ladies who lunch found among 20-somethings. Brunch is also served on weekends.

David 38 (☎ 071 223 28 38; Davidstrasse 38; mains Sfr20-42; ✆ Mon-Sat) This trendy upmarket bistro is a hit with the business set, with its range of fish and modern international cuisine.

Inexpensive restaurants are strung out along Marktplatz. St Gallen is also known for its Olma bratwurst, served plain in a *bürli*, or bun. Sausage stands are ubiquitous, but the best outlet is at **Metzgerei Gemperli** (cnr Schmiedgasse & Webergasse; sausages from Sfr6.50). For another budget option and self-catering, check out Migros Supermarket and Restaurant.

Getting There & Away

It's a short train or bus ride to/from Romanshorn (Sfr10.40). There are also regular trains to Bregenz in Austria (Sfr18), Chur (Sfr35) and Zürich (Sfr30, 70 minutes via Winterthur).

By car, the main link is the N1 motorway, which runs from Zürich and Winterthur to the Austrian border. It passes close to the centre of town, just slightly to the north.

Getting Around

Single journeys on the bus cost Sfr2.60, while it's Sfr8 for a day pass or Sfr32 for one week. Individual bus tickets are not valid on the Trogenerbahn, where the fare depends upon distance, but the general day passes *are* valid (as far as Rank station).

APPENZELLERLAND

The Appenzellers are the butt of many a cruel joke by their fellow Swiss. Just as Tasmanians are to Australians and Newfoundlanders are to Canadians, these are the nation's country bumpkins, reputedly slow on the uptake. Or as it would be delightfully described in Schwyzertütsch, they *hätte ä langi Laitig* (have a very long cable). It takes a while after you tug for them to get the message.

The roots of this backward reputation are fairly easy to divine. Innerhoden, one of the two semi-cantons that make up Appenzellerland (the other is Ausserrhoden), unusually still holds a yearly open-air parliament, and it didn't permit women to vote until 1991, to take just one example. Even then, the Supreme Court had to intervene.

In a general sense, however, many foreign visitors find the Appenzellers' devotion to rural tradition immensely charming and just what they expected from Switzerland. Maybe some things are best left unchanged. Appenzellerland has beautiful villages, mostly untouched by modern times. Life moves along at an enviably relaxed pace – the contented locals may know more than they are credited with.

Information

People who stay three days or longer in the region are eligible for the free Appenzeller Ferienkarte, which offers transport, sporting and museum discounts. Ask at the Appenzell tourist office (see below).

APPENZELL

pop 5530 / elevation 785m

Appenzell is a feast both for the eyes and the stomach. Behind the highly decorative façades of its traditional Swiss buildings lie numerous cafés, *confiseries* (confectionery shops), cheese shops, delicatessens, butchers and restaurants all offering local specialities. (Inevitably, given Appenzell's popularity with guided bus tours, there are plenty of shops selling tacky trinkets, too.)

This pastel-coloured Innerhoden village is suitable for lunch and a wander on a Sunday afternoon, or you could come for longer and explore the surrounding hills. Whichever you choose, remember to come hungry and with enough space in your luggage for chocolate, cheese and alcoholic souvenirs.

Orientation & Information

The train station (with money-exchange facilities and bike rental) is 400m from the centre of town. Take the exit marked 'Ortszentrum' and continue north roughly straight ahead (veering slightly left around the lilac house) until you come to Hauptgasse. The Landsgemeindeplatz is to your left (west); to your right (east), 100m along or so, is the **tourist office** (☎ 071 788 96 41; www .appenzell.ch; Hauptgasse 4; ☺ 9am-noon & 1.30-6pm Mon-Fri, 10am-noon & 2-5pm Sat & Sun Apr-Oct, 9am-noon & 2-5pm Mon-Fri, 2-5pm Sat & Sun Nov-Mar).

Sights & Activities

Appenzell's main focus is the **Landsgemeindeplatz**. This is not just the square where the open-air parliament takes place the last Sunday of every April, with locals wearing traditional dress and voting (in the case of the men, by raising a short dagger). It's one of the most picturesque spots in town all year round, with several elaborately painted hotels and restaurants around its edges.

The buildings along Hauptgasse are also worth admiring. The village **church** along here has gold and silver figures flanking a baroque altar. Nearby, beside the tourist office, is the **Appenzell Museum** (adult/student Sfr6/4; ☺ closed Mon in winter), which will fill you in on traditional customs and lifestyle – although you'll learn more at the museum in Stein (p256).

On the other side of the train station from the town is the **Museum Liner** (☎ 071 788 18 00; www.museumliner.ch; Unterrainstrasse 5; adult/ concession Sfr9/6; ☺ 10am-noon & 2-5pm Tue-Fri, 11am-5pm Sat & Sun Apr-Oct; 2-5pm Tue-Fri, 11am-5pm Sat & Sun Nov-Mar). This is Appenzell's contemporary art gallery, but the building is more interesting than the collection within.

There are numerous hikes in the region – so many in fact that it's simplest to ask for recommendations at the tourist office or pick up one of its brochures. Many hiking trails are lined with mountain restaurants, where you can restock on calories. One unusual trail is the **Barefoot Path** from Appenzell to Gonten, where you really don't need shoes. In Gonten there is also a **natural moor bath** (see the boxed text Spas & Thermal Springs, p47).

Sleeping

Gasthaus Traube (☎ 071 787 14 07; www.hotel -traube.ch; s Sfr85-110, d Sfr150-180; ☺ Mar-Jan) The most charming place in town isn't even the most expensive, but it does have just seven rooms. These are small, but feature wooden beds and new bathrooms with

---

SAY CHEESE

Appenzell is best known for its **strong-smelling cheeses** (www.appenzeller.ch). They make excellent fondues when mixed with fresh herbs and alcohol, and restaurants also dish them up in the form of *Käseschnitte* (cheese on toast), *Chäshöornli* (irregularly formed cheese dumplings with fried onions) or *Chääsmageroone* (macaroni cheese).

An Appenzell *Chäsflade* is a savoury cheese tart with coriander, and a *Chäshappech* is a pancake made with cheese, flour, milk, beer and eggs, and fried in oil. With raclette also popular, vegans might want to drown their sorrows in *Saurem Most* (local cider) or *Alpenbitter*, a herbal alcoholic drink a la Jägermeister that's another Appenzell speciality.

Local menus also feature lots of rösti, pork cutlets, veal, calf's liver and rabbit, but change regularly to accommodate seasonal specialities (ie venison and pumpkin in autumn). Appenzell produces a wide range of its own confectionery.

sliding frosted-glass doors. The modernist, tan-leather chairs are memorable, as is the staff's friendliness. This guesthouse is just off Landsgemeindeplatz, behind Hotel Säntis.

Hotel Appenzell (☎ 071 788 15 15; www.hotel -appenzell.ch; Landsgemeindeplatz; s/d Sfr125/210, with discounts for longer stays; ✗) Rooms in this attractive traditional building are generously sized, with wooden beds and slightly older bathrooms. The yellow decoration on the lower floor is much brighter and uplifting than the dusky pink on the upper.

Hotel Adler (☎ 071 787 13 89; www.adlerhotel.ch; Adlerplatz 5; 'Appenzeller' r Sfr180-200, ste Sfr240-260; ✗ Ⓟ) Overall, this place could do with some renovation, but it's worth staying in one of the 10 traditionally decorated 'Appenzeller' rooms. They feature painted wardrobes and some have tiled ovens as decoration; No 34 is particularly attractive. The hotel is near the eastern end of Hauptgasse, further still than the tourist office, on the other side of the street.

Hotel Säntis (☎ 071 788 11 11; www.saentis-appen zell.ch; Landsgemeindeplatz; s Sfr120-180, d Sfr180-300; ▢ ✗ Ⓟ) Appenzell's luxury option has one of the most striking façades on Landsgemeindeplatz and a romantic atmosphere throughout. Large rooms all have modern bathrooms; some come with four-poster beds.

A decent cheap option is **Gasthaus Hof** (☎ 071 787 22 10; www.gasthaus-hof.ch; Engelgasse 4; s/d/tr/q Sfr90/130/180/220), just off Landsgemeindeplatz. Four kilometres away in Kau, **Gasthaus Eischen** (☎ 071 787 50 30; www.eischen.ch; ☽ Mar-Jan) has an attached camping site.

Eating

Most places charge roughly Sfr12 for *Käseschnitte* (cheese on toast) and snacks, or Sfr20 to Sfr40 for main courses. Many of the best restaurants are in the hotels.

Hotel Appenzell (☎ 071 788 15 15; Landsgemeindeplatz) In many people's opinion this is the best place to try for its wide-ranging seasonal menu that includes vegetarian dishes. The restaurant, through the hotel's mouthwatering *Conditorei*, has a non-smoking section.

Gasthaus Traube (☎ 071 787 14 07; ☽ Tue-Sun) The restaurant on the first floor has the atmosphere of a traditional 'Stube' or tavern. It's a good place to try fondue or calf's liver. It is off Landsgemeindeplatz.

Gasthaus Hof (☎ 071 787 22 10; Engelgasse 4) Very smoky, very old-school restaurant with plenty of local bonhomie. Menus are attractively displayed and explained in several languages at the door.

Hotel Freudenberg (☎ 071 787 12 40; Riedstrasse 57; ☽ Tue-Mon Dec-Oct) Ten minutes' walk up the hill from the train station, in the opposite direction from the town, this family-run restaurant has a terrace with panoramic views of Appenzell and around.

Hotel Säntis (☎ 071 788 11 11; Landsgemeindeplatz) Säntis has several restaurants including a ground floor restaurant and terrace, serving all the usual Appenzell specialities, including fondue. Upstairs is more formal.

Getting There & Away

The narrow-gauge Appenzell train leaves from the front and to the right of the main St Gallen station (Swiss Pass and Eurail valid; Inter Rail half-price). To Appenzell (Sfr10.40) it takes 50 minutes. There are two routes so you can go back a different way. Departures from St Gallen are approximately every half-hour, via Gais or Herisau.

STEIN

En route to/from Appenzell, it's worth dropping into Stein for its **Volkskunde Museum** (Folklore Museum; www.appenzeller-museum-stein .ch; adult/student/child Sfr7/6/3.50; ☽ 1.30-5pm Mon, 10am-noon & 1.30-5pm Tue-Sat, 10am-6pm Sun Apr-Oct, 10am-5pm Sun only Nov-Mar). This gives a comprehensive and interesting rundown on traditional life in the region.

Should you not yet have had your fill of cheese, there's also the **Appenzeller Schaukäserie** (Appenzell Showcase Cheese Dairy; ☎ 071 368 50 70; www.showcheese.ch; admission free; ☽ 9am-7pm May-Oct, to 6pm Nov-Apr). It runs through the manufacturing process, explaining how cheeses like the famous Räss get their sweaty-socks smell (a coating of herbs and brine, apparently). Try to get here between 9am and 2pm, after which there's nothing much to see. The restaurant offers cheese-based dishes and cheese tastings. On Sunday, from 9am to 11am, there's an all-you-can-eat breakfast buffet (Sfr22.50).

Hourly buses go from the Appenzell train station to Stein (15 minutes, Sfr9.80, Swiss Pass valid) and drop you right opposite the cheese dairy.

NORTHEASTERN SWITZERLAND

SÄNTIS

Small in Swiss terms, Säntis (2503m) is the highest local peak, and offers a marvellous panorama encompassing Bodensee, Zürichsee, the Alps and the Vorarlberg Mountains. To get there, take the train from Appenzell to Urnäsch and transfer to the bus (approximately hourly) to Schwägalp (total fare Sfr16). From Schwägalp, the cable car, **Säntisbahn** (☎ 071 365 65 65; www.saentis bahn.ch; one way/return Sfr24/34; ☉ 7.30am-6.30pm summer, 8.30am-5pm rest of year) ascends to the summit every 30 minutes.

From Säntis, you can walk along the ridge to the neighbouring peak of Ebenalp (1640m) in about 3½ hours. At Wildkirchli on Ebenalp there are prehistoric caves showing traces of Stone Age habitation. The descent to Seealpsee on foot takes 1½ hours. Alternatively, a **cable car** (☎ 071 799 12 12; www.ebenalp.ch; one way/return Sfr18/25 in summer, Sfr25/33 in winter) runs between the summit and Wasserauen approximately every 30 minutes. Wasserauen and Appenzell are connected by rail (Sfr3.80).

LAKE CONSTANCE

Before package holidays began carrying large numbers of locals and their beach towels abroad in the 1970s and '80s, Lake Constance (Bodensee) was the German Mediterranean. Lionised in poetry and song – just like the River Rhine that flows into it – it's still a hugely popular destination with neighbouring Germans, Austrians and Swiss. The 'Swabian Sea', as it's nicknamed, is a great place to wind down for a few days and enjoy the water. Although even Swiss people admit that the towns on the northern German shore are more attractive, cyclists do like to tour through the very pleasant green countryside between the less-developed Swiss resorts, stopping briefly en route.

Orientation

Lake Constance is shared by Switzerland with its more affordable neighbourhoods Germany (country code ☎ 49) and Austria (country code ☎ 43).

Konstanz is the largest town on the lake and sits on the end of the peninsula between the two western arms, the Überlinger

See and the Unter See. Konstanz proper is in Germany, although the adjoining town of Kreuzlingen is Swiss and they are both really part of the same conurbation. Romanshorn, Arbon and Rorschach are also on the Swiss side. Other noteworthy tourist centres include Bregenz in Austria.

Information

DISCOUNT CARDS

The Bodensee Erlebniskarte (Sfr82/105/149 for 3/7/14 days) is sold from March to October and entitles the holder to free unlimited ferry travel and entrance to many museums, including the Zeppelin Museum in Friedrichshafen, a return journey up the Säntisbahn (left), walking tours in St Gallen and more.

MONEY

Almost without fail, shops, restaurants and other businesses in the region accept neighbouring currencies.

Getting There & Away

Ryanair (www.ryanair.com) flies from London Stansted to **Friedrichshafen Airport** (www.fly -away.de) in Germany. Friedrichshafen is connected by (car) ferry to Romanshorn on the Swiss side of the lake, with connections onwards to other towns in the region, as well as to St Gallen and Zürich.

There are good rail connections from Zürich to Konstanz. From Germany, they come south from Munich to Konstanz. Trains from Austria come via Bregenz and enter Switzerland at St Margrethen.

An enjoyable way to enter the region is to take a cruise along the Rhine from Schaffhausen to Konstanz (p249).

Access to the lake by road is good on all sides. From Zürich, the N1 (E60) motorway runs east, via Winterthur and St Gallen, to the Austrian border near Rorschach. The N7 branches off just after Winterthur and leads to Kreuzlingen.

Getting Around

Ferries (Switzerland ☎ 071 466 78 88; www.sbsag.ch; Austria ☎ 05574 428 68; www.bodenseeschifffahrt.at; Germany ☎ 07531 28 13 89; www.bsb-online.com) travel across, along or around the lake from early March to late October, with the more frequent services starting in late May. These boats are dubbed the *Weissen Flotte* or

NORTHEASTERN SWITZERLAND

white fleet. A Swiss Pass is valid only on the Swiss side of the lake.

Trains tend to be the easiest way to get around on the Swiss side, buses on the German bank.

The B31 road hugs the northern shore of the lake, but it can get busy. Likewise on the southern shore, where Hwy 13 shadows the train line around the lake, linking all the Swiss resorts mentioned in this section.

A 270km bike track encircles the lake and is well signposted. Train stations in the region mostly rent out bikes (p327).

KONSTANZ

☎ 07531 / pop 79,000

Konstanz (Constance) is the bustling, cosmopolitan hub of the Bodensee; one in seven inhabitants – affectionately known as *Seehas* (sea hares) – is a student at the university.

The **tourist office** (☎ 133 030; www.konstanz.de /tourismus; Bahnhofplatz 13; ⊙ 9am-6.30pm Mon-Fri, 9am-4pm Sat, 10am-1pm Sun Apr-Oct, 9.30am-12.30pm & 2-6pm Mon-Fri Nov-Mar) is a few minutes' walk north (right) of the main train-station exit. There's a 24-hour hotel board in front, and another information counter near the ferry landing.

Konstanz's moment of glory came in 1414–18, when the Council of Konstanz convened here to elect a single pope and tried, unsuccessfully, to heal the schism in the Catholic church. That council convened inside the enormous **Münster** (cathedral), which showcases various architectural styles from 1052 to 1856. The Gothic spire can be climbed for truly vertiginous views.

Stretching north from the cathedral to the Rhine is the old quarter of **Niederburg**, with lots of tight winding alleys.

There are several **museums** in town, but Konstanz's most astonishing attraction is a little out of the centre, reached by ferry or via bus 4 from the main train station. It's **Insel Mainau** (☎ 303 0; www.mainau.de; adult/child €11/3.40, Apr-Nov €6/3; ⊙ 7am-8pm Mar-Oct, 9am-6pm Nov-Apr), an island landscaped with 45 hectares of splendid gardens, including a tropical garden, an Italian garden, a butterfly enclosure and a palm house (closed winter). There's also a baroque church and various arboretums. It can get crowded in summer, when it's best to come late or early. It's possible to take bikes onto the island. To rent one, try **Pro Velo** (☎ 293 29; Konzilstrasse 3).

Sleeping

DJH hostel (☎ 322 60; fax 311 63; Zur Allmannshöhe 18; dm junior/senior €22/28; ⊙ Mar-Oct) Although it's located in a converted water tower, this hostel's rooms are fairly bland and institutional. Catch bus No 4 from the station to Jugendherberge or you can take bus No 1 to Allmansdorf-Post.

Barbarossa (☎ 128 990; www.barbarossa-hotel .com; Obermarkt 8-12; s €40-65, d €90-110) With its three categories of rooms, this labyrinthine hotel caters for most budgets and tastes, but is very popular in summer so you should book. The cheaper rooms are modern and simple; the costlier ones are more traditional and atmospheric.

Campingplatz Bodensee (☎ 322 60; fax 07531 311 63; Zur Allmannshöhe 18; ⊙ Mar-Oct) This modern camp site, only built in 1995, is in the neighbourhood of the car-ferry port. It hires out surfboards and canoes. Take bus No 4 to get there.

KREUZLINGEN

pop 16,770 / elevation 404m

Kreuzlingen is little more than an appendage to Konstanz and not as attractive as the larger town. There's a good **SYHA hostel** (☎ 071 688 26 63; www.youthhostel.ch/kreuzlingen; Promenadenstrasse 7; dm Sfr28.50; ⊙ Mar-Nov), but otherwise the most sensible thing to do is to change trains at Kreuzlingen station and head straight to Konstanz (Sfr2.80, three minutes); there is no passport control. Should you need more details, try the **tourist information counter** (☎ 071 672 38 40; www.kreuz lingen-tourismus.ch; TCS Travel Agency, Hauptstrasse 39; ⊙ 8.30am-noon & 1.45-6pm Mon-Fri, 8.30am-noon Sat). Direct trains run every 30 minutes between Kreuzlingen and Schaffhausen (one hour).

FRIEDRICHSHAFEN

☎ 07541 / pop 57,500

Friedrichshafen, in Germany, will forever be associated with the Zeppelin, the early cigar-shaped craft of the skies. The first of Graf (Duke) Zeppelin's airships made its inaugural flight over Lake Constance in 1900 and several years ago these rigid-framed 'blimps' were resurrected here as a tourist attraction. **Deutsche Zeppelin Reederei** (☎ 0700 9377 2001; www.zeppelinflug.de; 30min/1hr from €250/335; ⊙ Apr-Nov) offers sightseeing flights over Lake Constance or Friedrichshafen. There's also the **Zeppelin Museum**

(☎ 380 10; www.zeppelin-museum.de; Seestrasse 22; adult/senior/student & child €7.50/6.50/3; ☺ 9am-5pm Jul-Sep, 9am-5pm Tue-Sun May, Jun & Oct, 10am-5pm Nov-Apr), with a small re-creation of the crafts' train-like sleeping cabins and smoking room. The audio guide makes it much more exciting.

The **tourist office** (☎ 300 10, for 24hr hotel booking ☎ 194 12; www.friedrichshafen.ws; Bahnhofplatz 2; ☺ 9am-6pm Mon-Fri, 9am-1pm Sat May-Sep, 9am-noon & 2-5pm Mon-Fri Apr & Oct, 9am-noon & 2-4pm Mon-Fri Nov-Mar) is just outside the Friedrichshafen Stadt train station and can book everything from Zeppelin flights to accommodation.

To get to Friedrichshafen's busy **DJH Hostel** (☎ 724 04; Lindauer Strasse 3; dm junior/senior 19/21.70), take bus No 7587 from the Friedrichshafen Stadt train station. **Gasthof Rebstock** (☎ 216 94; www.gasthof-rebstock-fn.de; Werastrasse 35; s/d €50/70; P) is a pleasant, family-run pension with simple but fresh and tidy rooms, a short walk southeast of the same train station. Reception is closed Fridays, so ring ahead.

There are two trains an hour (€1.50, 15 minutes) from the **airport** (www.fly-away.de) to Friedrichshafen Stadt and Friedrichshafen Hafen, where you'll find the Zeppelin Museum and ferries. A **car ferry** (☎ 923 8389; www.bsb-online.com; adult/child/family €6.20/3/30, car €14, Swiss francs accepted) runs between Friedrichshafen and Romanshorn hourly from at least 8.30am to 5.30pm, with extra early and late services most days. The landing stage and passport control in Romanshorn are next to the train station. From Friedrichshafen, you can also take a ferry to anywhere on the lake.

ROMANSHORN & ARBON
pop 8950 & 13,110 / elevation 398m
Despite its one prominent church spire, Romanshorn is of minimal sightseeing interest – little more than a staging point as you go to/from Friedrichshafen on the ferry. If you do decide to stay, the **tourist office** (☎ 071 463 32 32; www.romanshorn.ch; ☺ 10am-noon & 2-6.30pm Mon-Fri, 10am-noon Sat Apr-Sep; 10am-noon & 2-5pm Mon-Fri, 10am-noon Sat Oct-Mar) is in the train station.

The medieval village of Arbon is prettier, either for a day trip spent wandering and admiring its half-timbered houses and ancient chapels, or for a day or two's quiet relaxation and water sports. It's on the train

line between Zürich and Rorschach, and there are direct connections to Romanshorn and Schaffhausen.

Leaving the train station, walk 10 minutes north (left) up Bahnhofstrasse, until you come to a lakeside intersection with Hafenstrasse heading right and Hauptstrasse left. Continue another five minutes to the left until you come to Schmiedgasse on your right and the **tourist office** (☎ 071 440 13 80; Schmiedgasse 40). You're now in the historic town centre, with its 16th-century castle and accompanying **historical museum** (admission Sfr3; ☺ 2-5pm May-Sep, Sun only Apr & Oct).

There's a good range of places to stay from the cheerful **Hotel Rotes Kreuz** (☎ 071 446 19 18; www.hotelroteskreuz.ch; Hafenstrasse 3; s/d Sfr70/140) and comfortable **Hotel Park** (☎ 071 446 11 19; www.hotelpark.ch; Parkstrasse 7; s/d Sfr85/150) to the more upmarket **Gasthof Frohsinn** (☎ 071 447 84 84; www.frohsinn-arbon.ch; Romanshornerstrasse 15; s Sfr105-120, d Sfr160-175) and **Gasthaus Römerhof** (☎ 071 447 30 30; www.gasthausroemerhof.ch; Hauptstrasse; s/d from Sfr120/180). Both of these last two have good restaurants, and Frohsinn also has a microbrewery.

RORSCHACH
pop 8640 / elevation 398m
Nothing to do with the psychiatric ink-blot tests with which it shares its name, the quiet resort of Rorschach sits on the waterfront below a wooded hill. Although something of a faded beauty these days, the town does have some fine 16th- to 18th-century houses with oriel windows.

There are three train stations, which can be confusing. If coming from St Gallen, alight at Rorschach Stadt station (Sfr6) and walk 500m east through the centre to Rorschach Hafen station (which is on the line from Romanshorn, Arbon, Kreuzlingen and Schaffhausen). Here, you will find the **tourist office** (☎ 071 841 70 34; www.tourist-rorschach.ch; Hauptstrasse 63; ☺ 9.30-11.45am & 2-5.30pm Tue-Fri, 2-5.30pm Mon Apr-Oct, plus 9.30am-noon Sat Jun-Sep, 2-5.30pm Mon-Fri Nov-Mar) and the cogwheel train which leaves to the **health resort** of Heiden.

The Rorschach Hafen station is also handily located on Haupstrasse. Walk left (east) from the station to see some fine oriel windows, particularly at Nos 33, 31 and the town hall, No 29. Walk right from the train station to find the main hotels,

NORTHEASTERN SWITZERLAND

AUTHOR'S CHOICE

Schloss Wartegg (☎ 071 858 62 62; http://wartegg.ch; Rorschacherberg; s/d/f Sfr120/185/205; 🖥 P) Want to spoil yourselves while exploring the Lake Constance and nearby Appenzellerland regions? If you have a car, book into this magnificent schloss on the hillside above Rorschach, a 10-minute drive away. This 16th-century former royal Austrian castle, set in leafy grounds on the hill above Rorschach, was converted to a sleek modern hotel in 1999, with an emphasis on wood and other natural materials, offset with lots of white and a few muted tones. There's a playroom and special facilities for children as well as a turquoise-coloured spa tub – 'Switzerland's most beautiful bath' – and an excellent restaurant.

including the individualistic **Hotel Rössli** (☎ 071 844 68 68; www.hotel-roessli.ch; Hauptstrasse 88; s/d from Sfr105/135) and **Hotel Mozart** (☎ 071 844 47 47; www.mozart-rorschach.ch; Hafenzentrum; s/d from Sfr105/150; P), which is outwardly all tacky reflective gold, but inside features a mix of pleasant modern and traditional rooms.

Behind the Rorschach Hafen station there's also the **Automobil, Motorrad und Automaten Museum** (adult/child Sfr8/5; 🕙 1.30-6pm Mon-Sat, 10am-6pm Sun Mar-Jun & Sep-Nov, 10am-6pm daily Jul & Aug; 1-6pm Dec-Feb), with ancient cars and motorcycles.

About the only time you need to alight at the main Rorschach station is if you're staying at the lakeside **SYHA Hostel** (☎ 071 844 97 12; www.jugendherberge-rorschach.ch; Hauptstrasse 92; dm Sfr25.50).

BREGENZ
☎ 5574 / pop 27,500

With its face to the waters of the lake and its disproportionate number of expensive clothes stores, Bregenz feels more like a posh seaside village than the provincial Austrian capital it is. The town is busiest during the spectacular annual **Bregenz Festival** (☎ 407-6; www.bregenzerfestspiele.com; 🕙 Aug), when opera, rock and classical music are performed on a vast waterborne stage on the edge of the lake. At other times, there are spectacular views and **hiking** atop the nearby Pfänder mountain (1064m). A **cable car** (☎ 42 16 00; www.pfaenderbahn.at; adult/senior

return €9.80/8.80; 🕙 9am-7pm, closed 2 weeks in Nov) carries you up and back.

There's a hotel board with free phone by the train station, while the **tourist office** (☎ 495 90; www.bregenz.at; Bahnhofstrasse 14; 🕙 9am-noon Mon-Sat & 1-5pm Mon-Fri, 9am-7pm Mon-Sat during the Bregenz Festival) is on the edge of the town centre.

The HI **Jugendgästehaus Bregenz** (☎ 428 67; www.jgh.at; Mehrerauerstrasse 5; dm summer/winter from €19/17, s/d available in winter for extra €7) is near the skateboard park visible from the train station. Rooms are modern and comfortable, most with five or six beds and private bathrooms.

Pension Gunz (☎ /fax 436 57; Anton Schneider Strasse 38; d from €54, s/d with bathroom from €31/56; reception 🕙 Wed-Mon) is a humble, but comfy enough abode, with an attached restaurant.

GLARNERLAND & AROUND

At the bottom of eastern Switzerland, connected to the centre of the country only by the narrow Klausenpass, this little pocket gets relatively little attention. That doesn't mean it's undeserving, however, just that you have more of it to yourself. Besides the car-free resort of Braunwald and the dramatic Churfirsten mountains, Glarnerland offers breathtaking hiking, low-key skiing and snowboarding, and plenty of climbing and adrenaline sports. For more information, contact **Glarner Tourismus** (☎ 055 610 21 25; tourismus@glarusnet.ch).

BRAUNWALD
elevation 1256m

Car-free Braunwald basks in sunshine on the side of a steep hill, gazing at the snow-capped Tödi mountain (3614m) and the pastures in the valley below. It's not *quite* as breathtaking as Mürren (p165) or Wengen (p156) in the Bernese Oberland, but it feels like more of a discovery, and the air really does feel clean up here.

The resort is reached via the Braunwaldbahn (one way/return Sfr7.20/14.40, Swiss Pass holders free, seven minutes travelling continuously), which climbs the hill from the Linthal Braunwaldbahn station in the valley.

Braunwald Tourism (☎ 055 653 65 65; www
.braunwald.ch; ☺ 8.30-11.45am & 2.15-5.30pm Mon-Fri,
plus Sat Jul-Nov) is on the top floor of the funicular station (go around the back), next
to the **post office** (☎ 055 643 16 05; ☺ 8.30-11.45am
& 3-5.30pm Mon-Fri, 8.30-10am Sat).

To the left of the station, **Hotel Alpenblick**
(☎ 055 643 15 14; www.alpenblick-braunwald.ch; per 30
min Sf7; ☺ 24hr) runs an Internet café and offers public wireless LAN.

Braunwald is a hiker's paradise, and you'll
find pamphlets at the funicular station outlining several hiking routes, including to the
Oberblegisee, a well-known local lake. Mountain climbing is also a popular pastime, as are
skiing and snowboarding. The tourist office
or your hotel can help with more details.

When entering or leaving the region,
think about doing so over the vertiginous
Klausen Pass (right for details), which is an
attraction in its own right.

Sleeping & Eating

Call ahead if you want help in carting your
luggage up the steep mountainside.

Hostel Adrenalin (☎ 079 347 29 05; www.adrenalin
.gl; r Sfr35, bedding & towels each Sfr5, breakfast Sfr8,
surcharge for short stays) Less than two minutes
from the funicular station, this hostel is
the hub of the young snowboarding and
adventure-sports community in winter,
with video games and lots of parties. However, it can be quiet in summer. A converted
budget hotel, it consists of 50% singles and
doubles, and 50% dorms. Most feature lots
of orange.

Alexander's Tödiblick (☎ 055 653 63 63; www
.holidayswitzerland.com; s Sfr75-130, d Sfr150-260, s/d
with shared bathrooms from Sfr60/120) You instantly
feel at ease in this rustic chalet hotel. The
rooms are traditionally Swiss, with old-
fashioned but spotless bathrooms and balconies, the owners are charming and the
restaurant – worth visiting even if you're
not staying – serves good home-cooking,
with fresh-made pasta, local specialities,
vegetarian options and herbal teas (mains
Sfr20 to Sfr35).

Märchenhotel Bellevue (☎ 055 653 71 71; www
.maerchenhotel.ch; r per person Sfr185, child under 6yr free,
various discounts and weekly packages available) Is this
the best family hotel in the world? A converted grand Victorian hotel, it combines
elegant modern rooms and saunas and bars
for parents with all manner of playthings
for children. So while youngsters enjoy the
theatrical props, computer games, climbing
wall and the fibreglass cow that you 'milk'
in the breakfast room, adults can relax in
the top-floor, glass-walled spa, with its
amazing views. The name means fairytale
(the owner tells one every evening) and it
really is.

Getting There & Away

The Glarner Sprinter train (www.glarner
sprinter.ch) runs hourly between Linthal
Braunwaldbahn and Ziegelbrücke (40 minutes) every day, from where there are handy
connections to Zürich (Sfr27, 1½ hours
from Linthal Braunwaldbahn). It's a one-
hour drive to/from Zürich along the A3.

From June to October, postbuses travel
daily (usually around 3pm) from Linthal
main train station (two minutes down the
line from Linthal Braunwaldbahn) to Altdorf (Sfr34, 2¼ hours) via the spectacular Klausen Pass. For the latest schedules,
check www.postbus.ch. Alternatively, ask
Braunwald Tourism or at the Linthal
Braunwaldbahn station.

WALENSEE

This lake is guarded by the Churfirsten
Mountains to the north. Wedged between
the steep rocks and rippling water is **Quinten**,
a tiny hamlet with just a couple of guest-
houses. There's no road – you have to walk
from Walenstadt (one hour), the nearest
train station, or take a boat. Boats go year-
round from Murg on the southern shore,
though other boat tours of the lake are in the
summer only. Contact **Schiffsbetrieb Walensee**
(☎ 081 738 12 08) for details. The main train
route from Zürich to Sargans passes along
the southern shore of the lake.

Graubünden

Switzerland, we are told (and often can't help feeling), is so utterly tidy, so irritatingly perfect that it feels like you shouldn't touch anything for fear you'll spoil the postcard. Graubünden (Grisons, Grigioni, Grishun), many Swiss from other cantons will tell you in admiring tones, is so, well, wild.

The roads are mostly narrow, winding and often pockmarked. In the countless valleys that slice up the rugged landscape are scattered villages that retain a rough-diamond rural edge largely lost in the picture-perfect hamlets of the rest of the country. Or should that be rough-emerald? Great carpets of deep-green felt seem to have been draped over the valleys and lower hills of this, the country's biggest canton. From the little explored western valleys to the picturesque Engadine, much untamed beauty and bucolic village charm awaits discovery.

Beyond the ancient capital, Chur, the canton is a little short on high culture but boasts more than 11,000km of walking trails, 1500km of downhill ski slopes and more than 600 lakes. Graubünden is also home to the country's only (and Europe's oldest) national park, the Swiss National Park (Parc Naziunal Svizzer).

But Graubünden is wild in another way. If many country villages still get by on small-scale farming, others have been propelled to wealth by the dazzling winter-sports industry. Indeed, half the population is involved in tourism. Who hasn't heard of the ultra-chic ski resorts of St Moritz, Davos and Klosters? And don't forget the thermal baths. Several are scattered across the canton, led by those of Vals and Scuol.

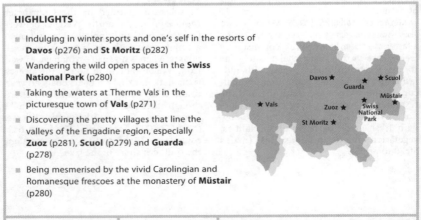

HIGHLIGHTS

- Indulging in winter sports and one's self in the resorts of **Davos** (p276) and **St Moritz** (p282)

- Wandering the wild open spaces in the **Swiss National Park** (p280)

- Taking the waters at Therme Vals in the picturesque town of **Vals** (p271)

- Discovering the pretty villages that line the valleys of the Engadine region, especially **Zuoz** (p281), **Scuol** (p279) and **Guarda** (p278)

- Being mesmerised by the vivid Carolingian and Romanesque frescoes at the monastery of **Müstair** (p280)

■ POPULATION: 186,100   ■ AREA: 7105 SQ KM   ■ LANGUAGE: GERMAN, ROMANSCH & ITALIAN

GRAUBÜNDEN

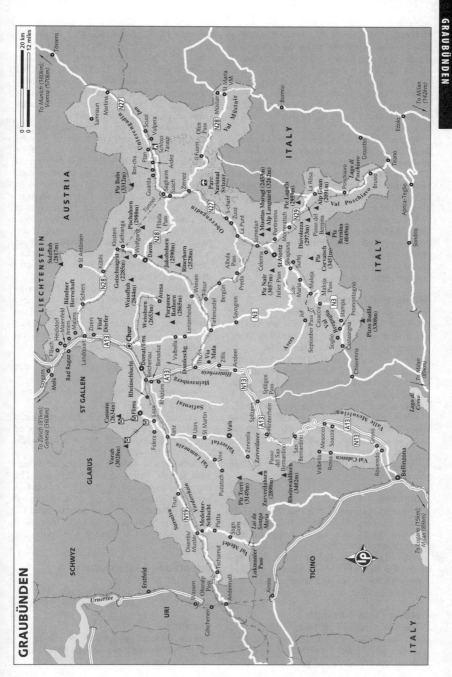

History

The canton's openness to all-comers today is a far cry from its inward-looking and diffident past. Down through the centuries, the people of this rugged area lived largely in isolated, rural pockets, mistrustful of outsiders and, aided by the near impregnable mountain terrain, able to resist most would-be conquerors.

In medieval times the region was known as Rhaetia, and was loosely bound by an association of three leagues (Drei Bünde). The modern name for the canton derives from the *Grauer Bund,* or Grey League. Graubünden joined the Swiss Confederation in 1803.

However, much more important was the year 1864, when a local hotel owner in St Moritz invited summer guests to stay over for the winter – for free. In this way, winter tourism in Graubünden, and later all Switzerland, was launched.

Orientation & Information

Two major rivers traverse the rugged terrain: the Rhine (with two main source rivers in the canton) and the Inn. The Alps stretch out across most of the region, which explains why the canton is so sparsely populated – around 26 inhabitants per square kilometre. The September Pass, Julier Pass and Maloja Pass have been key transit routes across the Alps since Roman times.

Chur, the capital, houses the cantonal tourist office, **Graubünden Ferien** (☎ 081 254 24 24; www.graubuenden.ch & www.rhein.ch; Alexanderstrasse 24; ☺ 8am-5pm Mon-Fri), located in the building marked 'Publicitas', 200m east of the train station.

Language

In the north (around Chur and Davos) German is spoken, in the south Italian and in between (St Moritz, Lower Engadine and parts of the Vorderrhein Valley in the west) mostly Romansch. German speakers account for 65% of the Graubünden population, with those speaking Romansch around 15% and around 20% Italian.

Getting There & Around

Three main passes lead from northern and western Graubünden into the southeast Engadine region: Julier (open year-round), Albula (summer only) and Flüela (year-round, but may close in bad weather). These approximately correspond to three exit points into Italy: Maloja, Bernina and Fuorn/Ofen (all open year-round). The Oberalp Pass, the route west to Andermatt, is closed in winter but, as at Albula, there is the option of taking the car-carrying train instead. Carry snow chains or use winter tyres in winter.

Graubünden offers a regional transport pass (Sfr120/150) valid for seven or 14 days from May to October. You get two/four days respectively of unlimited free travel on all Rhätische Bahn (RhB) trains (which serve the canton), the SBB line between Chur and Bad Ragaz, the RhB bus between Tirano and Lugano and postal buses within the canton. For the remaining days of validity you pay half price. Throughout the pass's validity you will pay half price on most cable cars and funiculars, the Furka–Oberalp line between Disentis/Mustér and Brig, and Davos city buses.

A winter version issued from 1 November to 30 April (Sfr90) gives two days' free travel and three days' half-price travel on RhB trains in a seven-day period. It also gives you five days' half-price travel on postal and Engadine buses.

CHUR

pop 31,900 / elevation 585m

Chur (pronounced 'ch' as in a Scottish loch) is Switzerland's oldest continually inhabited city. The old centre still retains a few medieval reminders and is a pleasant concentrate of history and culture in a region otherwise largely bereft of urban interest. The city was almost destroyed by fire in 1464. A wave of German-speaking artisans arrived to rebuild and, in the process, managed inadvertently to suppress the local lingo. So it was *abunansvair* Romansch and *Guten Tag* to German.

Orientation & Information

INTERNET ACCESS

Street Café (☎ 081 253 7 14; Grabenstrasse 47; per 20min Sfr5; ☺ 9am-midnight Sun-Thu, 9am-2am Fri & Sat)

LAUNDRY

Malteser's Wäsch-Egga (Grabenstrasse; wash/dry Sfr7/4; ☺ 9am-midnight Mon-Sat, noon-midnight Sun) Self-service laundry.

MONEY

You can change money at the **train station** (🕑 7am-8pm). A handy central bank with ATMs is the UBS branch on Poststrasse.

POST

Post office (Postplatz, 🕑 7.30am-6.30pm Mon-Fri, 8am-noon Sat) Just outside the Old Town.

TOURIST INFORMATION

Tourist office (☎ 081 252 18 18; www.churtourismus .ch; Grabenstrasse 5; 🕑 1.30-6pm Mon, 8.30am-noon & 1.30-6pm Tue-Fri, 9am-noon Sat) Has a town map that carries potted explanations of every conceivable sight.

Sights & Activities

Apart from three surviving medieval towers and the late Romanesque-Gothic cathedral, the bulk of the old city dates to the 16th century. A stroll reveals brightly painted façades along the mostly pedestrian-only streets. Aside from what is mentioned below, the city is home to a series of second-tier museums, whose subjects range from wine to sewing machines!

The **Obertor**, just in from the Plessur river, marks the main medieval entrance into the old town. Along with the stout, stone **Maltesertor** (once the medieval powder and munitions tower), on the corner of Grabenstrasse and Engadinstrasse, and the **Sennhofturmn** (nowadays part of the city's prison), it is all that remains of the city's defensive walls. Just inside Obertor, a produce market is held on Saturday mornings.

The **Kathedrale** (cathedral; ☎ 081 258 60 00; www.bistum-chur.ch in German; Hof; 🕑 7.30am-6pm) was established in 1150 on the site of earlier churches, dating back as far as the 5th century AD. The modern exterior, added centuries later, is nothing to write home about but inside are some notable treasures. Of the church's seven altars, the High Altar is the most important. Built by Jakob Russ from 1486 to 1492, it contains a splendid triptych. The striking stained-glass windows over the west entrance to the church were done in the late 19th century. Although it is possible to enter a side aisle, the bulk of the church is off limits while restoration work continues, at least until late 2006.

Some of the religious art and reliquaries once housed in the cathedral crypt are now on show in the **Rätisches Museum** (☎ 081 257 28 89; www.rm.gr.ch in German; Hofstrasse 1; adult/ senior & student/child under 16yr Sfr6/4/free; 🕑 10am-noon & 2-5pm Tue-Sun). Over three floors and in the loft spreads a permanent exhibition that encapsulates much of what is known of the canton's history. Displays include a few Roman artefacts, coins, weapons and armour, household items from down the centuries and a section on Alpine rural tools and gizmos.

The nearby 1491 **St Martinskirche** (Martinsplatz; 🕑 for services) contains three stained-glass windows by Augusto Giacometti.

To get a better idea of the artistic legacy of Augusto (1877–1947), his cousin Giovanni (1868–1933) and Giovanni's son Alberto (1901–66), head for the **Bündner Kunstmuseum** (Museum of Fine Arts; ☎ 081 257 28 68; www.buendner-kunstmuseum.ch; Postplatz; adult/senior & student/child under 16yr Sfr10/5/free; 🕑 10am-noon & 2-5pm Tue-Sun, to 8pm Thu). The Giacometti clan, and Alberto in particular (all born in the Val Bregaglia in southern Graubünden), are the only local artists to have made an impression worldwide and their works occupy much of the top floor of this art museum (housed in a delightful 19th-century mansion) dedicated to Graubünden artists. A room on the ground floor is given over to works by Chur-born Angelika Kaufmann (1741–1807), and in the basement are works by a host of contemporary artists, including Lenz Klotz and HR Giger.

Had enough of enclosed spaces? Take the cable car up to **Brambrüesch** (☎ 081 250 55 90; www.brambruesch.ch in German; Kasernenstrasse 15; return fare adult/child Sfr22/11; 🕑 8.30am-5pm mid-Jun–late Oct) for a hike in the heights (1600m). In winter it is in action again, in combination with a couple of ski lifts, to allow locals a little practice before heading off for more serious ski action elsewhere in the canton.

Sleeping

Hotel Zunfthaus Räblüta (☎ 081 252 13 57; www .rebleuten.ch in German; Pfisterplatz 1; s/d with shower Sfr80/140) It oozes 500 years of history, but never fear; this classic has been redecorated once or twice since it was built! The 12 rooms are fresh and inviting. Especially romantic (but don't bump your head) are those in the loft.

Hotel Franziskaner (☎ 081 252 12 61; fax 081 252 12 79; Kupfergasse 18; s/d Sfr65/110, d with bathroom up to Sfr160) This hotel in the Old Town is neatly positioned over a pretty but somewhat

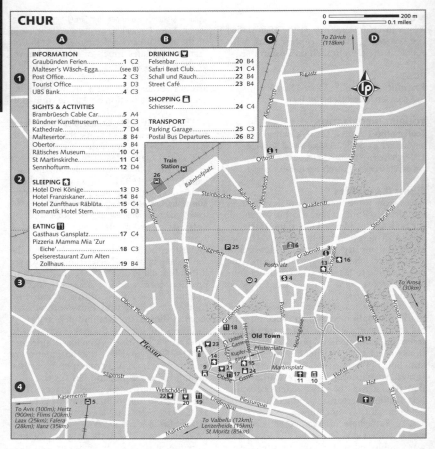

CHUR

0 ————— 200 m
0 ————— 0.1 miles

INFORMATION
Graubünden Ferien...............1 C2
Malteser's Wäsch-Egga.........(see 8)
Post Office.........................2 C3
Tourist Office.....................3 D3
UBS Bank..........................4 C3

SIGHTS & ACTIVITIES
Brambrüesch Cable Car..........5 A4
Bündner Kunstmuseum..........6 C3
Kathedrale.........................7 D4
Maltesertor.......................8 B4
Obertor.............................9 B4
Rätisches Museum................10 C4
St Martinskirche..................11 C4
Sennhofturm......................12 D4

SLEEPING
Hotel Drei Könige................13 D3
Hotel Franziskaner...............14 B4
Hotel Zunfthaus Räblüta........15 C4
Romantik Hotel Stern...........16 D3

EATING
Gasthaus Gansplatz..............17 C4
Pizzeria Mamma Mia 'Zur
  Eiche'............................18 C3
Speiserestaurant Zum Alten
  Zollhaus.........................19 B4

DRINKING
Felsenbar..........................20 B4
Safari Beat Club..................21 C4
Schall und Rauch.................22 B4
Street Café........................23 B4

SHOPPING
Schiesser..........................24 C4

TRANSPORT
Parking Garage...................25 C3
Postal Bus Departures...........26 B2

---

boisterous square (on Friday and Saturday nights) inside Obertor. The rooms are bright, comfortable and clean, with pine furniture.

Hotel Drei Könige (☎ 081 252 17 58; www.drei koenige.ch in German; Reichsgasse 18; s/d Sfr120/160; (P)) Room décor varies from the timber-lined to plain bright white. The hotel has been greeting guests since the 18th century. The bar/café has a laid-back charm, occasionally with live jazz nights.

Romantik Hotel Stern (☎ 081 252 57 57; www .stern-chur.ch in German; Reichsgasse 11; s/d Sfr145/290; (P)) Although it's been in the business for several centuries, this attractive hotel on the edge of the Old Town has a fresh, crisp feel. Rooms are generally light and decked

out with warm timber furniture. The hotel restaurant is also worth a visit.

Eating

Speiserestaurant Zum Alten Zollhaus (☎ 081 252 33 98; Malixerstrasse 1; meals Sfr60-70; ⏰ 11.30am-midnight) Welcome to what is easily the most atmospheric of Chur's old-time eateries. Black- and white-clad waitresses bustle beneath centuries-old timber beams serving up local and Swiss German dishes. In autumn there's an extensive hunters' menu, with all sorts of freshly hunted game.

Gasthaus Gansplatz (☎ 081 252 14 57; Obere Gasse 34; meals Sfr60-70; ⏰ 9am-midnight Tue-Sat, 11am-5pm Sun) Lacking the smoky, centuries-old atmosphere of the Zollhaus, this spot is nevertheless good for local cuisine, including such oddities as *capuns* and *bizochel* (see p51).

Pizzeria Mamma Mia 'Zur Eiche' (☎ 081 252 22 20; Grabenstrasse 39; pizza & pasta Sfr13-22; ☺ daily) To set you in the mood, a statue with dribbling fountain greets you inside the entrance. Pizzas and pasta are the order of the day, but you can have a perch fillet (*Eglifilet*) and a brief range of meat dishes. When it's warm, make sure to eat in the garden terrace.

Drinking

A restless student population has led to high-density bar activity in the Old Town. Until midnight Sunday to Thursday, the scene is on Untere Gasse, basically a row of bars. On the weekend, here and elsewhere in town, it gets a little sillier with generalised 2am closing. Down on Welschdörfli they don't have to wait for the weekends. However, with a few notable exceptions, it is dominated by girly-bars.

Street Café (☎ 081 253 79 14 14; Grabenstrasse 47; ☺ 9am-midnight Sun-Thu, 9-2am Fri & Sat) This is one of the trendier hang-outs for the earlier part of the evening. There's foosball and computer games. It's best to sit outside if weather permits.

Safari Beat Club (www.safari-beatclub.ch in German; Kupfergasse 11; ☺ 8pm-midnight Wed-Thu & Sun, 8pm-2am Fri & Sat) Wander into what seems a half-derelict arcade and look (to your left) for the pitiless armoured door – yank it and you're in. The club, whose innards are quite visible from the street and is littered with flora gamely suggestive of safari territory, sometimes pumps out music beyond 2am on the weekend.

Schall und Rauch (www.schallundrau.ch in German; Welschdörfli; ☺ 5pm-2am Wed-Sat, 3pm-2am Sun) 'Sound & Smoke' attracts all sorts. Lounge lizard music, such as Gotan Project, wafts across the red and orange stage-lit bar. At one end is a mezzanine, at the other a flat-screen TV with a loop fireplace sequence to give you a warm feeling even without imbibing.

Felsenbar (www.felsenbar.ch; Welschdörfli 1; ☺ 8pm-2am Tue-Thu, 8pm-4am Fri & Sat) The all-black décor and inevitably sociable set around the horseshoe bar give this spot a busy, underground feel. Throw in some dance music as the night wears on and the atmosphere becomes pleasantly rowdier.

Shopping

Schiesser (☎ 081 252 35 73; Obere Gasse 22) So impressed by local meat and sausage specialities that you'd like to take some home? Head for Schiesser, where there is wind-dried *Bündnerfleisch, Rohschinken* (cured ham) and all sorts of *salsiz* (sausage) to salivate over.

Getting There & Away

There are rail connections to Klosters and Davos (Sfr30, 1½ hours), and fast trains to Sargans, for Liechtenstein (Sfr9.80, 22 to 25 minutes), and Zürich (Sfr36, 1¼ to 1½ hours). Postal buses leave from the terminus above the train station. The A13 motorway runs north from Chur to Zürich and Lake Constance.

Getting Around

Bahnhofplatz is the hub for all local buses, which cost Sfr2.20 per journey (valid for changes for 30 minutes). At around 8pm the routes combine and services become less frequent.

The old centre is mostly pedestrian-only. For parking, look for signs to several parking garages on the edge of the old quarter (eg on Gäuggelistrasse).

CAR RENTAL

If you plan to hire a car, try **Avis** (☎ 081 252 39 73; Kasernenstrasse 37), in the Claus Carrosserie car body shop; or **Hertz** (☎ 081 252 32 22; Triststrasse 15).

AROUND CHUR

Chur is within easy access of a number of ski areas.

LENZERHEIDE & VALBELLA
elevation 1470m & 1540m

These linked resorts, on either side of Heidsee, bombard you with their beauty. There's a woodland wonderland, as well as plenty of soaring peaks. Skiing on the 155km of slopes is mainly geared towards beginners and intermediates. A one-day ski pass costs Sfr55 for adults, Sfr50 for seniors, Sfr37 for youths and students, or Sfr18 for children to 12 years old.

The **Parpaner Rothorn** (2865m) is the highest point reached by cable car. Several walking trails wend their way from the summit. In summer, you can lose yourself along 170km of marked hiking trails.

The **Lenzerheide tourist office** (☎ 081 385 11 20; www.lenzerheide.ch; Voa Principala; ◷ 8.30am-6pm Mon-Fri, 8.30am-noon Sat) is on the main road.

Sleeping & Eating

There are 23 hotels in Lenzerheide and Valbella, and more in nearby towns. You could also opt for longer stays in holiday apartments and chalets.

Hotel Pöstli (☎ 081 384 11 60; www.stall-lenzerheide .ch in German; Hauptstrasse 37; s/d Sfr84/158) A pleasant option in central Lenzerheide. Rooms are full of timber and the downstairs restaurant dishes up local cuisine and national favourites like fondue and raclette. If you want early nights it might not be for you, as they sometimes crank up the après-ski music.

Hotel Guardaval (☎ 081 385 85 85; www.guardaval .ch in German; meals Sfr100; ◷ closed May) In Sporz, about 3km southwest of Lenzerheide, this hotel offers high cuisine, with meat and fish options, in a charming setting. Try for a table on the open timber gallery.

Getting There & Away

Either resort is easily reached by an hourly bus from Chur (Sfr9.80, 40 minutes). They're on the route from Chur to St Moritz spanning the Julier Pass.

AROSA

pop 2270 / elevation 1800m
Once a near inaccessible rural settlement and then, from the late 19th century, a sanatorium for the unhealthy wealthy, Arosa is today a mid-level ski and hiking resort. Plans are in the air to build a linking lift with the Lenzerheide and Valbella ski stations. Although only 30km southeast of Chur, getting there is nothing short of spectacular. The road climbs about 1100m from Chur in a series of curves so challenging that Arosa is one of the few sizeable settlements in the country not reached by postal buses. The scenic train ride from Chur makes an excellent alternative. Some hotels and restaurants close for lack of interest in the off season.

Orientation & Information

Arosa has two parts: Ausserarosa (Outer Arosa) is the main resort, grouped around

the shores of Obersee (Upper Lake) at the train terminus; and Innerarosa is the older section of the original village. The train station has money-exchange counters, luggage storage and bike rental.

From Oberseeplatz, go along Poststrasse, heading uphill in the direction of Innerarosa. Within five minutes you'll reach the **tourist office** (☎ 081 378 70 20; www.arosa.ch; Poststrasse; ◷ 8am-noon & 1.30-6pm Mon-Fri, 9am-1pm Sat plus 2-4pm Sat mid-Jun–mid-Aug, 9am-noon Sun May-Nov, 9am-6pm Mon-Fri, 9am-5pm Sat, 4-5.30pm Sun Dec-Apr).

The post office is at Oberseeplatz.

In summer, grab the Arosa Card (Sfr8) which gives unlimited access to the two ski lifts in operation, local buses, pedalos and rowing boats available on the Obersee. If you stay overnight you get the card for free from your hotel.

Activities

Arosa has 100km of **skiing**, suitable for mixed abilities, based on three main mountains. Beginners have a good choice of runs. Contact the **ski school** (☎ 081 378 75 00 50; www .sssa.ch; Seeblickstrasse; ◷ 8.30am-5.30pm Mon-Sat) for lessons. The highest skiing point is the Weisshorn at 2653m. Ski passes cost Sfr55 for one day and Sfr276 for one week (there are senior/youth reductions). In addition to downhill and cross-country skiing, Arosa features several ice-skating rinks (natural and artificial), curling and tobogganing (from Tschuggen down to the village).

Arosa has 200km of maintained **hiking** trails, with good options even in winter. The walk up to Weisshorn from the village takes about 3½ hours and the panorama is extensive. From the **Hörnli** top station (2513m) via the Hörnli Express cable car you can embark on several circuits or even walk west to Lenzerheide (p267), a hike of around three hours. A 1½ walk will get you to Weisshorn.

Sleeping

Praval (☎ 081 377 11 40; www.praval.ch in German; Innere Poststrasse, Innerarosa; s/d Sfr120/240) A pleasing mountain chalet-style house, the Praval offers comfortable rooms; the best easily are those south-facing doubles with balconies and wide views over a deep valley. It's just off the road and fairly close to the Hörnli Express ski lift.

Sonnenhalde (☎ 081 378 44 44; www.sonnenhalde -arosa.ch in German; Innerarosa; s/d Sfr82/248; Ⓟ) A three-storey, dark timber house, it's located just by the Brüggli bus stop. The single rooms are small and have shared bathroom facilities. The doubles are rather more generous, with timber beds and carpet. Best of all are the family suites with four beds, private bathroom and balcony.

Hotel Alpensonne (☎ 081 377 15 47; www.hotelalpensonne.ch in German; Innere Poststrasse, Innerarosa; s/d Sfr178/376; P Sfr12) Also close to the Brüggli bus stop, this place offers tempting south-facing doubles with balconies and breathtaking views. The cosiest are those on the top loft floor, with sloping timber ceilings. They also have a steam bath and sauna on the premises.

Eating

Restaurant Grishuna (☎ 081 377 17 01; Poststrasse, Innerarosa; meals Sfr35-50; ♥ Wed-Mon, closed mid-Sep–Oct) This corner spot near the Brüggli bus stop may first catch your eye because of the enormous cowbells hanging in the window. But they whip up a storm in the kitchen. Swiss German dishes prevail, but a handful of pasta options are thrown in and a series of *Kinderteller* (at Sfr11) for kids.

Alpenblick (☎ 081 377 14 28; meals Sfr40-50; ♥ daily) Sitting right below the Hörnli Express cable car, this country-style chalet makes good on the Alp views from the terrace and serves up solid meat dishes, fondue and a killer homemade *Apfelstrudel*.

Orelli (☎ 081 377 12 08; Poststrasse; salad buffet per plate Sfr14, veg dishes Sfr16-22; ♥ Thu-Tue) Known for its all-too-healthy salad bar and alcohol-free policy, Orelli's also serves up a limited range of vegetarian dishes and carnivorous options with organic products. Rooms with shower and TV are also available for up to Sfr175 per person half-board.

Getting There & Away

The only way to get to Arosa is from Chur; take the hourly narrow-gauge train that leaves from in front of the train station (Sfr13.40, one hour). It's a winding, scenic journey chugging past mountains, pine trees, streams and bridges. The train crosses the oldest steel and concrete rail bridge ever built. At 62m high over a ravine, it is a dizzying engineering feat completed in 1914.

Buses in the resort are free if you have the Arosa Card or ski pass. Drivers should note a traffic ban from midnight to 6am.

FLIMS, LAAX & FALERA

They say that if the snow ain't falling anywhere else, you'll surely find some around Flims, Laax and Falera. These three towns, 20km west of Chur, form a single ski area known as the Weisses Arena (White Arena), with 220km of slopes catering for all levels. Laax in particular is known as a Mecca for snowboarders, who spice the local nightlife up too. The resort is barely two hours by train and bus (less by car) from Zürich airport.

Orientation & Information

The three towns that make up the backbone of the ski resort are strung northeast to southwest over 15km. Flims is the biggest, divided into the larger, residential Flims Dorf to the north, and the leafier Flims Waldhaus, 1km away. The ski lifts lie between the two. Laax is also divided into two. The sleepy old town, Lag Grond, with its pretty houses and peaceful lake, lies to the south; and Laax Murschetg, where the lifts are located, is 1km to the north. The third of the towns, Falera, is the smallest and quietest. There are **tourist offices** in all three, the main one in **Flims Dorf** (☎ 081 920 92 00; www.alpenarena.ch; Via Nova; ♥ 8am-6pm Mon-Fri, 8am-4pm Sat May-Oct; 8am-5pm Mon-Sat Nov-Apr). Another useful website is www.laax.com.

Sights
FALERA
Those in search of a touch of history will be drawn to the Romanesque **St Remigiuskirche** in Falera, set on a grassy hill that has been a site of worship since prehistoric times (as attested by the line-up of modest menhirs leading up to it). Inside the shingle-roofed church, the left wall is completely covered by a mid-17th-century fresco depicting the Last Supper. From the cemetery you can see deep into the Vorderrhein valley.

LAG DA CAUMA
Known in German as Caumasee, this turquoise lake is about a 15-minute hike or a five-minute stroll and then ride by lift, south of Flims Waldhaus in the midst of thick woods. It is a pretty location and great for a cool summer swim. You can hire a rowboat and eat at a restaurant terrace overlooking the lake.

Activities

SKIING & SNOWBOARDING

The ski slopes range as high as 3000m and are mostly intermediate or easy, although there are some 45km of more challenging runs. A one-day ski pass includes ski buses and costs Sfr62 (plus Sfr5 for the KeyCard that you use to access the lifts). There are 60km of cross-country skiing trails. Laax was the first Swiss resort to allow snowboarders to use the lifts back in 1985, and remains a Mecca for the snow surfers, with two huge half-pipes (one said to be the biggest in the world) and a freestyle park huddled around the unfortunately named Crap Sogn Gion peak. The season starts in late October on the glacier and, depending on snowfalls, in mid-December elsewhere.

HIKING

In summer, the hiking network covers 250km. At the Cassons summit there is a circular walking route, the *Naturlehrpfad*, that yields a flush of flora and fauna.

RIVER RAFTING

The raging Rhine (Rhein in German) has two main sources, both in Graubünden: the Vorderrhein (which rises just south of the Oberalp Pass in the far west of the canton) and the Hinterrhein (which itself has several sources in the south of the canton). Try river-rafting on the 17km turbulent stretch of the Vorderrhein between Ilanz and Reichenau, taking you through the **Rheinschlucht** (Rhine gorge), somewhat optimistically dubbed 'Switzerland's Grand Canyon', but impressive enough nevertheless. In summer, **Swissraft** (☎ 081 911 52 50; www.swissraft.ch) offers half-/full-day rafting for Sfr109/160. The meeting spot is Ilanz train station. You can get the same dramatic views of the gorge on westward-bound trains, but without the thrills and spills.

Sleeping

There is just one hotel in Falera, more than a dozen options in Laax and 30 hotels in Flims. The area is teeming with holiday houses and apartments that sleep up to eight people. Book through www.alpenarena.ch.

Riders Palace (☎ 081 927 97 00; www.riderspalace.ch; Laax Murschetg; dm Sfr30-60; d per person up to Sfr200; 🖳) It may look like some awful 1970s housing estate, but this place, a magnet for partying snowboarders, is a curious slice of designer cool for the snow party animal (hotel motto: sleeping is for dreamers). You can go for basic but comfortable bunk-bed accommodation or stylish rooms (with baths by Philippe Starck). The pricing system is a trifle complicated and can include your ski pass. The so-called Multimedia rooms are doubles/triples with Playstation, video recorder, DVD player and Dolby surround sound. The whole place is wi-fi enabled and located 200m from the Laax lifts.

Hotel Grischuna (☎ 081 911 11 39; www.hotel-grischuna.ch in German; Promenade, Flims Waldhaus; s/d Sfr100/200) On the road linking Flims Dorf with Flims Waldhaus and a short walk from the ski lifts, this is a simple family affair with a rustic restaurant (meals Sfr35 to Sfr55; open Tuesday to Sunday). It serves a three-course daily menu for Sfr28 as well as regional specialities à la carte.

Hotel Cresta (☎ 081 911 35 35; www.cresta.ch; Via Passadi, Flims Waldhaus; s/d Sfr145/290) Modern digs tucked away in the wooded back lanes of Waldhaus, this place is a water-baby's dream, with saunas, steam baths, Jacuzzis, pool, solarium and massage options. Oh, and they have rather nice rooms too.

Eating

Restaurant Pöstli Laax (☎ 081 921 44 66; www.poestlilaax.ch in German; Via Principala 54; lunch Sfr25-35, dinner mains Sfr35-40; 🏵 Tue-Sun) An endearing building in the old part of Laax, this spot (aside from seven charming rooms) offers local cooking presented with care. Choose between the warm dining area, with heavy wooden beams, the vaulted cellar or the covered winter garden.

Restaurant Barga (☎ 081 928 28 28; www.adula.ch; Via Les Sorts Sut 3, Flims Waldhaus; tasting menus Sfr75-110; 🏵 mid-Dec–Apr, mid-May–mid-Nov) Housed in the Hotel Adula, this classy French gastropalace is the place to come for a fireside romantic meal. Opting for one of the set tasting menus takes the complication out of choosing from a long list of local and French-oriented dishes.

Drinking

Bars are generally shut from mid-April to June and late September to mid-November.

Riders Palace (☎ 081 927 97 00; www.riderspalace.ch; Laax Murschetg; 🏵 4pm-4am) Its lobby bar opens for the après-ski scene and continues until well into the night, and occasionally with live acts.

Crap Bar (☎ 081 927 99 45; Laax-Murschetg lifts; ⏰ 4pm-2am) A hit with skiers and snowboarders coming off the pistes in Laax. Made out of 24 tonnes of granite, it is right by the Laax Murschetg lifts and makes a great place to end the day and/or start the evening.

Getting There & Away

Postal buses run to Flims and the other villages in the White Arena area hourly from Chur (Sfr12.40 to Flims Dorf, 30 minutes). A local free shuttle bus connects the three villages.

WEST OF CHUR

The mainly Romansch-speaking Surselva area west of Chur stretches out along the lonely N19 highway that snakes its way west towards Uri canton and, not far beyond, to the great southern Alpine canton of Valais. Beyond the ski fun of Flims, Laax and Falera (p269), the pickings are slim along this road, although a few points along the Vorderrhein river are worth a stop. More impelling are a couple of wild valleys extending south of the road, which itself trails out in Alpine wilderness as it rises to the wind-chilled **Oberalp Pass** (2044m) that separates Graubünden from Uri. About 4km south of the pass, near the tiny Lai da Tuma lake, lies hidden the source of the Vorderrhein river.

ILANZ

A bustling town with a pleasant enough old centre, Ilanz is for most visitors largely a transport hub. The main N19 road ribbons westward, passing through various towns in the predominantly German-speaking Obersaxen area before reaching the Romansch monastery village of Disentis/Mustér (p272) Ilanz is also the departure point for exploration of two pretty southern valleys.

VALSERTAL & VAL LUMNEZIA

Initially following the course of the Glogn (or Glenner) stream south, the Valsertal (Vals Valley) drive is delightful, passing a handful of hamlets, such as Uors and St Martin, before arriving at the star attraction, **Vals** (1252m). After St Martin, the valley tightens and deepens. A dense web of forest folds its canopy over the narrow, snaking road. About 2km short of the village, you emerge into one of those typically Graubünden Alpine plains, green and liberally scattered with houses and summer shepherds' huts.

Vals, home to the Valser mineral water, stretches 2km along its glittering stream. The secret of this place and its soothing waters is well and truly out since Basil-born architect Peter Zumthor created Therme Vals, the unique thermal bath installation that opened in 1996 on the site of the old baths.

Sights

Therme Vals (☎ 081 926 80 80; www.therme-vals .ch; Vals; admission Sfr30, most treatments Sfr55-255; ⏰ 11am-8pm Tue-Sun, 11am-9pm Mon mid-Jun–mid-Apr) is a must. Using 60,000 stone sheets of local quartzite, Zumthor created the most magical setting for baths in a country that has no shortage of fine thermal bathing installations.

Aside from the main heated indoor and outdoor pools, which are a treat in themselves, you will discover in this grey-stone labyrinth all sorts of watery nooks and crannies, cleverly lit and full of cavernous atmosphere. Try the deep heat Feuerbad (42°C), the perfumed Blütenbad or the hideaway Grottenbad. Have a hum in the latter and enjoy the otherworldly acoustics! Sweat out all those impurities in the Dampfstein (steam rooms with rising temperatures).

Less well known than the baths is an exhilarating 8km trip south to the impossibly turquoise lake of **Zervreilasee**. The drive takes you up through a claustrophobic 2km tunnel that would be more at home in a coalmine. Access is generally only possible from June to October. From above the lake, various hiking options present themselves. There is some modest downhill skiing in the heights above Vals.

Running parallel to the Valsertal from Ilanz, and then gradually branching away to the southwest, is the **Val Lumnezia**, as generously broad and sunlit green (in summer) as the Valsertal is deep and narrow. The road runs high along the west flank of the valley. Where it dips out of sight of the valley you arrive in **Vrin**, a cheerful huddle of rural houses gathered around a brightly frescoed church. The asphalt peters out 8km further on in Puzatsch.

Sleeping

Apart from holiday houses for rent, Vals offers eight hotel options.

Gasthaus Edelweiss (☎ 081 935 11 33; edelweiss vals@bluewin.ch; Dorfsplatz; r per person Sfr59) Located right on the village square this place has timber-lined rooms and bathrooms on each floor. It has its own good restaurant serving up local dishes such as *capuns* and variations on *späzli*. The hotel can get you Sfr5 off entry to the baths.

Hotel Therme (☎ 081 926 80 80; www.therme-vals .ch; s/d Sfr245/410) In this frightful 1960s colossus, Peter Zumthor has redesigned the rooms. In some cases, the hotel's annexes have not been given the Zumthor makeover, and are consequently cheaper and, frankly, ugly. Use of the bath facilities is included in the price.

Hotel Pensiun Pez Terri (☎ 081 931 12 55; s/d Sfr60/120) Located in Vrin, on the road through the middle of the village, this is a cheerful and rustic old place. Rooms are all loaded with timber and soft beds. Chomp on the hearty local cooking downstairs.

Getting There & Away

Postal buses run more or less hourly to Vrin (Sfr12.40, 47 minutes) and Vals (Sfr11.40, one hour) from Ilanz (itself reached by regular train from Chur, Sfr14.20). The Vals bus goes on to Zervreila from June to October, taking an extra 25 minutes.

DISENTIS/MUSTÉR & VAL MEDEL

An average sort of village by the picturesque standards of the canton, Disentis or Mustér ('monastery' in Romansch), boasts a far-from-average Benedictine monastery

---

AUTHOR'S CHOICE

Hotel Alpsu (☎ 081 947 51 17; www.hotelalpsu .ch in German; s/d Sfr72/136; **P**) On the main street smack in the middle of Disentis, this place is a gem. With lots of woodwork, rooms are cosily appointed and each quite unique. In one you find a grand four-poster, in another exposed wood beams and an open plan situation with bubble bath opposite the bed. Just as good is the restaurant (meals Sfr50 to Sfr60; open daily). The friendly staff do fine renditions of *capuns* and *bizochel*.

MAGIC MUSHROOMS

There was a time when there were customs stations on the passes that lead from Graubünden to Ticino. They are long gone but, come autumn, cantonal police are again stationed on some passes, in particular the Lukmanier Pass, on the lookout for 'bandits' sneaking out kilos of luscious mushrooms. No, it's not drug-trafficking. The magic of these mushrooms is the flavour they bring to a risotto. The people of Ticino and their Italian cousins can't get enough of them and they pour across the cantonal border to fill up their picnic baskets with the autumn crop. There's just one hitch. The legal limit is 2kg per person per day. And the police take a dim view of cheats. On one early September weekend in 2005, 30 people were fined for excessive picking – one mushroomer was caught with 70kg of the tasty tubers!

---

with baubly baroque church attached. As early as the 8th century a modest monastery stood on this site. The present immense complex dates to the early 18th century. To the immediate left of the entrance into the church is a door that leads you down a corridor to the **Klostermuseum** (admission free; 2-5pm Tue, Thu & Sat Jun-Oct, 2-5pm Wed Christmas-Easter), filled with memorabilia on the history of the monastery. Then head left upstairs to the **Marienkirche**, a chapel with Romanesque origins which is filled with *ex-voto* images from people far and wide in need of (or giving thanks for) some miraculous intervention from the Virgin Mary.

You can follow the road south of Disentis down the **Val Medel** valley, which starts in dramatic style with the **Medelser-Schlucht** (Medel Gorge). You pass through several villages, of which **Platta** is noteworthy for its shingle-roof Romanesque church. About 20km on, by the **Lai da Sontga Maria** lake and surrounded by 3000m peaks, the road hits the **Lukmanier Pass** (Passo di Lucomagno, 1914m) and crosses into Ticino canton.

Disentis/Mustér is where Matterhorn-Gotthard trains from Brig via Andermatt (Sfr16.80, 50 minutes) in Valais terminate and local RhB trains heading to Chur (Sfr26, 1¼ hours) start. They leave in both directions every hour. Five buses a day rumble over the Lukmanier Pass, four of them heading on to Biasca in Ticino.

SOUTH OF CHUR

The main route south of Chur passes castle ruins and the town of Zillis (whose church is a treasure trove of Romanesque art), and heads on into the remote Italian-speaking Mesolcina valley on the way to Ticino.

VIA MALA & AVERS VALLEY

The A13 motorway and railway south of Chur at first head west to Reichenau before swinging south along the Hinterrhein river between the Domleschg mountain range to the east and the Heinzenberg to the west. A string of villages and ruined robber-knight castles dot the way to **Thusis**, a busy town whose main interest lies in the fabulous views from the **Obertagstein** castle ruin about an hour's walk from the centre. Trains from Chur en route for St Moritz call in here, before swinging east to make for the ski resort via Tiefencastel.

South of Thusis, take the N13 rather than the motorway to get an idea of how the Via Mala (Bad Way), through a deep gorge, must once have been as scary a route as chroniclers down the centuries suggest. It opens out just before the town of **Zillis**, known for its **St Martinskirche** (adult/child Sfr4/2; ☼ 10am-6pm Apr-Oct). This modest church is of interest for its wooden Romanesque ceiling, which is divided into 153 extraordinarily vivid painted panels depicting the life of Christ until, oddly, his crowning with thorns, followed by scenes of the life of St Martin.

To really get out into the wild, head south another 8km past **Andeer** (known for its modest thermal baths and home to five hotels and a camping ground) for the junction with the road into the remote **Avers valley** (four hotels in hamlets along the way). This lonely trail snakes 24km south, at first amid thick forests and then in a bare Alpine valley, through tiny hamlets to reach **Juf** (2126m), a disappointing huddle of houses claiming to be the highest permanently populated village in Europe.

Postal buses run between Thusis and Bellinzona in Ticino (Sfr38, two to 2½ hours) stopping at Zillis, Andeer, Splügen and towns along the Valle Mesolcina. Buses from Andeer run to Juf (Sfr15.20, 55 minutes).

SPLÜGEN & VALLE MESOLCINA

From the Avers turn-off, the main roads branch west into an area known as the Rheinwald (Rhine Forest), whose main town is **Splügen**. The Via Mala Ferien website (www.splugen.ch in German) covers Splügen and around, the Avers area, Andeer and Zillis. Splügen is an intriguing place for its mix of dark timber Walser (people from the Upper Valais) farm houses and bright-white mansions of trading families made wealthy by 19th-century commerce with Italy over the nearby Splügen and San Bernardino mountain passes. Apart from the riverside camping ground you could stay at **Hotel Pratigiana** (☎ 081 664 14 76; Hauptstrasse 1; s/d Sfr80/160; Ⓟ), a stout white building in the centre and one of five hotel options.

The road south of Splügen leads 9km to the like-named pass into Italy, while the main roads continue west 8km before swinging south to the Passo del San Bernardino (you can take the tunnel when the pass is closed) that drops into the **Valle Mesolcina**, the most Italian part of Graubünden. The main towns of Mesocco (look out for the hilltop castle ruins nearby, which are visible from the highway), Soazza and Roveredo are not overly interesting, although the latter has some lively eateries and bars.

Just north of Roveredo, the wild and barely visited **Val Calanca** opens up to the north, with a 19km road that terminates in the hamlet of **Rossa**, from where a dirt track continues another 5km north past **Valbella** into the wilderness. Several wild and woolly hiking trails roll out in the heights above the narrow valley. From Roveredo, it is about 10km to Bellinzona (p288), the capital of Ticino canton.

See Via Mala & Avers Valley (left) for transport information. In addition, buses run every 1½ hours or so up the Val Calanca to Rossa from Bellinzona (Sfr16.20, 1½ hours) via Roveredo (change at Grono, on the intersection with the Val Calanca road).

NORTH OF CHUR

A quick trip north will bring you to the region's premier wine region, the Bündner Herrschaft, and the kitsch delights of Heidiland. You can also take the waters at nearby Bad Ragaz.

BÜNDNER HERRSCHAFT

The A13 motorway blasts northward from Chur and through the wine-growing region known as the **Fünf Dörfer** (Five Villages), of which **Zizers** is perhaps the prettiest. The road runs into the industrial town and transport crossroads of **Landquart**, in which you won't want to waste time stopping.

Instead follow the narrow country lane out of Landquart for Malans, which takes you into territory known as the Bündner Herrschaft. This is the canton's premier wine region, dominated by the Blauburgunder (aka Pinot Noir) grape variety that makes for some memorable reds. This is also, rather sickeningly, Heidiland.

Malans & Jenins

Through vineyards and woods you arrive in **Malans**, dominated by the private castle of the Salis dynasty, a name in local wine and historic rivals to the Planta clan, whose townhouses line the village square. The **Weisskreuz** (☎ 081 322 81 61; Rathausgasse 148; meal Sfr60-100; ☯ daily) is a renowned local eatery in an atmospheric 17th-century building with terrace. A few kilometres north is **Jenins**, a less noble looking village worth a stop for a glass or two of the local tipple and perhaps a snooze in **Gasthaus Zur Traube** (☎ 081 302 18 26; Unterdorf 1; s/d Sfr47/94; restaurant & bar ☯ 11.45am-midnight Mon-Wed, 4pm-midnight Fri, 10am-midnight Sat & Sun).

You can get trains from Chur to Malans (Sfr6.60, 21 to 34 minutes), some requiring a change in Landquart. To push on to Jenins (from Sfr9.20, 33 minutes from Chur) you have to get a connecting postal bus from Landquart, Malans or Maienfeld.

Maienfeld & Heididorf

The most impressive of these wine towns is **Maienfeld**, another 2km through magical woods and vineyards. Dominated by a colourfully frescoed **Rathaus** (town hall) and haughty church, it is worth hanging out for the local cuisine. Head for **Schloss Brandis** (☎ 081 302 24 23; meals Sfr50-80; ☯ 11am-midnight Mon-Tue, 10am-midnight Wed-Sun), a mighty medieval tower (in the square off a street called Vorderwinkel) that houses one of the canton's best restaurants. The full menu, dripping with meaty suggestions, is available from midday to 2pm and 6pm to 10pm, and a limited menu the rest of the time.

A series of set menus are around Sfr40 to Sfr50, excluding wine. If you feel like a little wine-tasting, try the personable **Vinothek von Salis** (☎ 081 302 50 57; Kruseckgasse 3; ☯ 2-6pm Mon-Fri, 9.30am-4pm Sat), where you can try if you want to buy. If your German is up to it, Frau Möhr will tell you everything you need to know about the local tipples.

Each year the four Bündner Herrschaft towns (Maienfeld, Malans, Jenins and Fläsch) take turns to celebrate the **Städlifest**, a lively wine harvest celebration with much drinking, eating and merrymaking in the otherwise normally dead quiet streets, held on the last weekend of September.

OK, we have held out, but Maienfeld is where to start your Heidiland experience. Johanna Spyri (1827–1901) had the idea of basing the story in the countryside around Maienfeld, and the locals had the worse idea of identifying one local village as Heidi's. It is now called, oh dear, **Heididorf**, a 25-minute walk from Maienfeld (signposted) across pretty country. In peak periods you might be able to get the Heidi Express bus, which will pass by the rather awful Heidihof Hotel. Apart from the **Heidihaus** (☎ 081 330 19 12; www.heidi-swiss.ch; adult/child 6-16yr/child under 6yr Sfr5/2/free; ☯ 9am-5pm Mar-Nov), where of course she never lived because she never existed, you could visit the Heidishop and buy some Heidi colouring-in books, Heidi videos or just plain Heidikitsch. Then you could follow the Heidiweg (Heidipath) into the surrounding hills (Heidialp). When you're done, you might be in need of some Heidiwein for your Heidiheadache…or perhaps just hit the N13 road and Heiditail it out of here north into Liechtenstein.

Maienfeld is on the Chur–Bad Ragaz train line.

Bad Ragaz

pop 5041 / elevation 502m

The perfect cure for a case of Heidiness could be the baths of Bad Ragaz, a couple of kilometres west of Maienfeld. **Tamina Therme** (☎ 081 303 27 41; www.resortragaz.ch; baths only adult/child under 12yr Sfr17/12; ☯ 7.30am-9pm) is a couple of kilometres south of the town centre (local buses run hourly from the train station). In the bath business since 1840, Bad Ragaz has attracted the likes of Douglas Fairbanks and Mary Pickford. Children under three may not enter. Bad Ragaz is on the Chur–Zürich train line. Trains from Chur via Maienfeld run hourly (Sfr7.80, 15 to 20 minutes).

KLOSTERS & DAVOS

Following the N28 road east away from Landquart you enter the broad plains valley of the Prättigau, which stretches east to the understatedly chic ski resort of Klosters. Several valley roads spike off the highway before Klosters, and the one leading to **St Antönien** is the most attractive. There are no specific sights, just high Alpine country dotted by villages and Walser houses, the typical burned wood constructions raised by this rural folk since migrating here from the eastern Valais from the 13th century on.

KLOSTERS

pop 3800 / elevation 1194m
Britain's Royals love this ski resort because of its old-fashioned charm and lack of a brash and flash nightlife. The slopes don't get much more sophisticated.

Orientation & Information
Klosters is split into two sections. Klosters Platz is the more important, grouped around the train station. Right of the station is the **tourist office** (☎ 081 410 20 20; www.klosters.ch; Alte Bahnhofstrasse 6; ☼ 8.30am-6pm Mon-Fri, 8.30am-4pm Sat). The post office is opposite the station.

Two kilometres to the left of the station is the smaller enclave of Klosters Dorf, with several hotels, a tourist office and the Madrisa cable car. Klosters buses are free with a Guest Card (which also gives discounts on local sport activities and other items) or ski pass.

Activities
There are 315km of **ski runs** in the Davos/ Klosters region, which is covered by the general Regionalpass (adult/youth/child Sfr61/41/21 a day). One-day passes for specific areas are marginally cheaper.

Above Klosters at 2300m is the Gotschnagrat, accessible from the cable car by the train station. It gives access to the gulp-inducing Gotschnawang. Not only is the word hard to say, but the ski run is one of the most difficult there is. On the other side of the valley, the Madrisa region has runs favouring beginners and intermediates, as well as a kids' day care centre **Kinderhort Madrisa**

(1st hr Sfr10, each hr after Sfr5; ☼ 9.30am-4pm). The Klosters' runs are linked to the Weissfluh area in Davos (p276). For more information on skiing in the resorts, check out www.davosklosters.ch. Hiking and mountain biking are options in summer.

Sleeping
The tourist office supplies lists of private rooms (from Sfr20 per person) and numerous holiday apartments.

Soldanella (☎ 081 422 13 16; www.youthhostel .ch/klosters; Talstrasse 73; dm incl breakfast winter/summer Sfr42/28.50; ☼ reception closed 10am-5pm, hostel closed btwn seasons) Soldanella, the SYHA hostel set in two mountain chalet-style buildings, is a 12-minute, mostly uphill trek from the station. Half of the straightforward rooms are singles and doubles and there's no curfew.

Rustico (☎ 081 410 22 88; www.rusticohotel.com; Landstrasse 194; s/d Sfr77/92; 🖳 🅿) The 10 double rooms here are spacious, with parquet floors and comfy beds. The ones in the loft, with timber ceilings, are the cosiest. The hotel, near the Gotschnabahn ski lift in Klosters Platz, has a sauna.

Hotel Alpina (☎ 081 410 24 24; www.alpina-klosters .ch; Bahnhofplatz; s/d Sfr285/450; ☼ late Nov–mid-Apr & mid-Jun–mid-Oct; 🖳 🅿) Opposite the station, this hotel has luxurious rooms. Prices are highest in the guesthouse section, but you will appreciate the Jacuzzis. Some may also like the Feng Shui layout, parquet floors and non-smoking status of some rooms. Use of the swimming pool, sauna and fitness room is included.

Eating
Hotel Alpina (☎ 081 410 24 24; www.alpina-klosters .ch; Bahnhofplatz; meals Sfr62; ☼ daily) This hotel's restaurant is considered one of the best in eastern Switzerland (along with the nearby Walserhof) and serves a mouth-watering array of international dishes.

Salzi's Sonne (☎ 081 422 13 49; Landstrasse 155; meat mains Sfr35-40; ☼ Wed-Sun) Along the road towards Dorf from Platz, Salzi's Sonne serves a broad selection of dishes, including pasta, fondue (Sfr28 per person) and richly flavoured regional dishes. One of the house specialities is beef stroganoff.

Gasthaus Bargis (☎ 081 422 55 77; Kantonsstrasse 8; meals Sfr35-50; ☼ Wed-Sun) A typical timber fronted house for the region, this is a good spot for simple local fare on the road into

GRAUBÜNDEN

Klosters Dorf. When the sun is shining, eat on the terrace, with its views across Klosters and the countryside.

Getting There & Away

See Davos (p278), as Klosters is on the same train route between Landquart and Filisur. Klosters and Davos are linked by free buses for those with Guest Cards or ski passes.

DAVOS

pop 10,900 / elevation 1560m

Nine kilometres on from Klosters, Davos is the brasher of the two resorts and frankly not that attractive. Once a famous health resort, it has recently got a name for itself as the annual meeting point for the crème de la crème of world capitalism, the World Economic Forum (WEF to those in the know).

Global chat fests aside, the serious business here is skiing. Those bold of body and swift of ski brave some savage slopes, including the legendary Parsenn-Weissfluh area, where runs descend up to 2000m.

Orientation & Information

Davos is a 4km-long strip beside the train line and the Landwasser river. It comprises two contiguous areas, each with a train station: Davos Platz and the older Davos Dorf. The **main tourist office** (☎ 081 415 21 21; www .davos.ch; Promenade 67; ☼ 8.30am-6.30pm Mon-Fri, 9am-5.30pm Sat, 10am-noon & 3-5.30pm Sun) is in Platz. Hours are reduced in low season (spring and autumn). Another tourist office, opposite the Dorf train station, is closed on Sundays. The **post office** (Bahnhofstrasse 3; ☼ 7.45am-6.30pm Mon-Fri, 8.30am-noon Sat) is in Davos Platz.

The Visitor's Card allows free travel on local buses and trains, as does the general ski pass (and the Swiss Pass). There's a self-service laundry, **Waschsalon** (☎ 081 416 32 70; Promenade 102; ☼ 8am-6.30pm Mon-Fri). **Expert RoRo** (☎ 081 420 11 11; Promenade 123; per 20/60min Sfr5/12) has Internet access.

Sights

Davos is mostly an outdoor experience. But if you want some time away from fresh air, there are compact museums with limited opening hours in and around town – such as the ski-obsessed **Wintersportmuseum** (☎ 081 413 24 84; www.wintersportmuseum.ch in German; Promenadestrasse 43; adult/child Sfr5/3; ☼ 4.30-6.30pm Tue, Thu & Sat Dec-Mar & Jul-Oct).

Kirchner Museum (☎ 081 413 22 02; Ernst-Ludwig-Kirchner-Platz; adult/senior & student/child Sfr10/8/5; ☼ 10am-6pm Tue-Sun Christmas-Easter & 15 Jul–end Sep, 2-6pm Tue-Sun rest of year) displays the world's largest collection of works by the German expressionist painter (1880–1938). Kirchner, afflicted by pulmonary problems and later a weakness in the hands that made painting difficult, first came to Davos for treatment in 1917. He later returned and, as the Nazis rose to power in his home country, remained and painted some extraordinary scenes of the area around Davos. When the Nazis classified Kirchner as a 'degenerate artist' and emptied German galleries of his works, he was overcome with despair and took his own life in 1938.

Activities

The Weissfluh ski area goes as high as 2844m, from where you can **ski** to Küblis, more than 2000m lower and 12km away. Alternatively, you can take the demanding run to Wolfgang (1629m) or the scenic slopes to Klosters. Across the valley, Brämabüel and Jakobshorn (the latter beloved of snowboarders) offer equally good skiing, and the nearby areas of Pischa and Rinerhorn are within easy reach of Davos. See p275 for ski pass prices.

There are several ski and snowboard schools, including the **Schweizer Schneesportschule** (☎ 081 416 24 54; www.ssd.ch; Promenade 157). Some 75km of cross-country trails open from December to April.

The mountains of Davos and Klosters together provide 450km of marked **hiking** paths and 600km of **mountain bike** tracks. Other possible activities, depending on the season, include swimming, para-gliding, hang gliding, wind-surfing and sailing on **Davoser See** (Davos Lake), ice-skating, tobogganing and more. At the **Sportzentrum** (☎ 081 415 36 00; Talstrasse 41) you can get into handball, volleyball and more – it is free for overnight guests.

Festivals & Events

Davos hosts an **International Music Festival** from late July to mid-August, featuring a variety of classical works and young performers. It is preceded by a week-long jazz festival. In December there's a Nordic skiing World Cup event.

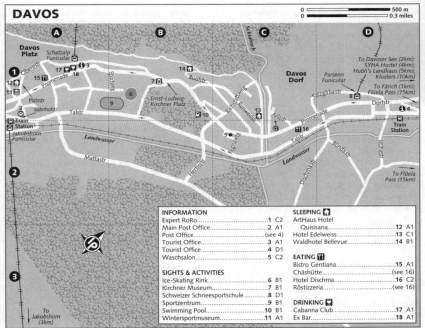

DAVOS

INFORMATION
Expert RoRo.....................................**1** C2
Main Post Office..............................**2** A1
Post Office..................................(see **4**)
Tourist Office..................................**3** A1
Tourist Office..................................**4** D1
Waschsalon.....................................**5** C2

SIGHTS & ACTIVITIES
Ice-Skating Rink.............................**6** B1
Kirchner Museum.............................**7** B1
Schweizer Schneesportschule.........**8** D1
Sportzentrum..................................**9** B1
Swimming Pool.............................**10** B1
Wintersportmuseum.....................**11** A1

SLEEPING
ArtHaus Hotel
  Quisisana...................................**12** A1
Hotel Edelweiss.............................**13** C1
Waldhotel Bellevue.......................**14** B1

EATING
Bistro Gentiana.............................**15** A1
Chäshütte....................................(see **16**)
Hotel Dischma.............................**16** C2
Röstizzeria..................................(see **16**)

DRINKING
Cabanna Club...............................**17** A1
Ex Bar..**18** A1

Sleeping

Hubli's Landhaus (☎ 081 417 10 10; www.hublis.ch in German; Kantonsstrasse, Davos Laret; s/d Sfr157/244; 🖵 🅿) Between Davos Dorf and Klosters, this is a gorgeous country inn with appealing, light rooms decked out in dark timber furniture. There are cheaper rooms without a private toilet. There's a sauna and just nearby is a peaceful mountain lake. The Davos bus stops virtually out the front. What's more, they have a fine restaurant (meals Sfr45 to Sfr60; open Tuesday to Sunday) with a Michelin star. What about *gebratene Lachsschnitzel an Balsamicsauce* (roasted salmon fillets in balsamic vinegar sauce)?

Hotel Edelweiss (☎ 081 416 10 33; www.edelweiss -davos.ch; Rossweidstrasse 9; s/d Sfr115/190; 🅿) The hotel is a friendly, middle-sized place where finding a room should be no problem. The better rooms in this one-time sanatorium have generous, south-facing balconies. There are also some spacious family rooms for up to four. The water is solar heated.

ArtHaus Hotel Quisisana (☎ 081 413 51 04; www .arthaushotel.ch; Platzstrasse 5; s/d Sfr149/258) Two themes dominate the rooms: light, timber furnishings and art on the walls. The sun-filled rooms are otherwise quite different in shape and décor from one another. The owner, Diego do Clavadetscher, is an artist and the entire interior of this bright-red building is liberally sprinkled with his works and nice designer touches.

Waldhotel Bellevue (☎ 081 415 37 47; www.waldho tel-bellevue.ch; Buolstrasse 3; s/d Sfr265/450; 🚠 🅿) One of the nicest things about this one-time sanatorium (which became the Magic Mountain in Thomas Mann's eponymous 1924 novel) is pampering yourself in the Wellness centre, with various baths, saunas, steam baths and more. Rooms are comfortable, if a little on the standard side, although the bathrooms are stylishly designed. From your balcony there are nice views of the mountains.

Eating

Bistro Gentiana (☎ 081 413 56 49; Promenade 53; meals Sfr35-55; 🕐 Thu-Tue summer, daily winter, closed May) This bistro specialises in snail dishes (*Schnecken*) and meat and cheese fondues. A dish of six juicy snails oven-cooked in mushroom heads costs Sfr29.50.

GRAUBÜNDEN

Hotel Dischma (☎ 081 410 12 50; Promenade 128) brings several eating choices together under one roof. For a reasonable pizza or rösti try the **Röstizzeria** (meals Sfr25-35; ☒ Dec-Apr, dinner only Jun-Oct). The downstairs **Chäshütte** (meals Sfr35-40; ☒ dinner only Dec-Apr), or cheese hut, specialises in bubbling fondue.

Drinking

Ex Bar (☎ 081 413 56 45; Promenade 63; ☒ 6pm-3am daily Dec-Apr) There's Europop on the jukebox, free salty popcorn at the bar, a chandelier on the ceiling and a huge stuffed toy reindeer hanging over the door. It frequently stays open later than the official closing time.

Cabanna Club (☎ 081 415 42 01; Promenade 63; ☒ 8pm-3am Dec-Apr) Located in Hotel Europe, this is a busy disco in winter, but if you've had enough of jiving, there are always the pool tables. Closing time seems equally flexible here.

Getting There & Away

For trains to Chur (Sfr26, 1½ hours) or Zürich (Sfr49, two hours 25 minutes), you will change at Landquart. For St Moritz (Sfr27, 1½ hours), take the train at Davos Platz and change at Filisur. For the hourly service to Scuol (Sfr27, 1¼ hours) in the Unterengadin, take the train from Davos Dorf and change at Klosters.

THE ENGADINE

The almost 3000km long Inn river (En in Romansch) has its source in the Graubünden Alps around the Maloja Pass and gives its name to its long valley, the Engadine (Engadin in German, Engiadina in Romansch).

The valley is carved into two sections: the Oberengadin (Upper Engadine) from Maloja to Zernez; and the Unterengadin (Lower Engadine), stretching from Zernez to Martina, by the Austrian border.

The Oberengadin is dominated by the glitz and glamour of chichi skiing in St Moritz and neighbouring resorts, while the Unterengadin, actually comprising two valleys and home to the country's only national park, is characterised by its pretty villages with sgraffito decorated houses and stunning countryside. It is one of the best places to hear Romansch spoken, although the lingua franca is German.

Chalandamarz, a spring and youth festival, is celebrated in the Engadine on 1 March. The **Schlitteda**, an ancient custom involving a procession of colourful horse-drawn sleds, can be seen in St Moritz, Pontresina and Silvaplana in January.

UNTERENGADIN

Known to the Romansch-speaking locals as the Bassa Engiadina (Lower Engadine), this thickly wooded eastern end of Switzerland juts like a wolf's snout into neighbouring Austria and Italy. From Davos, the N28 highway climbs up to the barren Flüela Pass (2383m) in a series of loops before dropping over the other side, opening up majestic vistas of crags and valleys, with silver slivers of mountain streams and patches of brown Alpine grass.

The road descends to **Susch**, close to the exit point of Sagliains for the car train that passes along the Vereina Tunnel from Selfranga (just outside Klosters), the only way to make the trip when snow falls close to the pass. The trains run every 30 to 60 minutes during the day and cost Sfr27 to Sfr40 per car, depending on the season.

From Susch you can head 6km south to Zernez and then east into the Swiss National Park and Val Müstair, or further southwest to the Oberengadin.

Or you can follow the Inn on its gradual eastern progress to Austria.

From Guarda to Scuol
pop 170 / elevation 1653m

Six kilometres east of Susch, a side road bends up north of the N28 to **Guarda**. The cobblestone streets of this impossibly pretty village are lined by quaintly squat houses draped in light-hearted sgraffito decoration. It lies above the valley floor on a winding route that leaves the main road and offers sweeping views. Guarda is 30 minutes' walk from its valley-floor train station by the steep footpath, or you can take the postal bus (Sfr2.60), which runs every two hours in the daytime. It makes for a peaceful overnight stop and a good place to go hiking. A trail leads 8km north to a spot in the foothills of the Piz Buin peak (3312m). So now you know where the name of the sun screen comes from!

Plenty of pretty lodgings are available in the traditional houses of Guarda. At the top (eastern) end is the **Hotel Piz Buin** (☎ 081 861 30

00; www.pizbuin.ch; s Sfr105, d Sfr140-220). Its singles are a little pokey, though comfortable, and there is a range of doubles. The house is full of rustic clutter, while the rooms are lean and clean, the best of them clad in stone pine (Arvenholz).

A couple of wooded kilometres east is the hamlet of **Bos-cha**, but by car you can't get any further. To continue on the high road you first have to return to the low road and follow the signs up to **Ardez**, a small village set in striking country and with a ruined medieval tower just on its flank. Another 8km brings you to **Ftan** (with several accommodation options), from where the narrow road slithers down to the main attraction of the valley, Scuol.

Scuol

pop 2160 / elevation 1250m

Attracted by one of the best thermal bathing complexes in the country (second only to Vals, see p271), visitors to Scuol are pleasantly surprised by the ingenious beauty of the sgraffito decoration of the town's houses, many of them centuries old and gaily restored in the past few decades.

ORIENTATION & INFORMATION

The train station is more than 1km west of the village centre. The **tourist office** (☎ 081 861 22 22; Stradun; ☻ 8am-6.30pm Mon-Fri, 9am-6pm Sat, 10am-noon & 2-5pm Sun) is in the centre of town, above the Old Town that is gathered down around the river.

SIGHTS & ACTIVITIES

Lower Scuol (the Old Town) has quaint Engadine dwellings and cobblestone squares. There's a **museum** (☎ 081 861 22 22; Dorfplatz; adult/child Sfr5/2) devoted to the Unterengadin, open limited hours in summer and winter. The mighty **Schloss Tarasp** (☎ 081 864 93 68; admission Sfr5, tour adult/child Sfr7.20/3.20; guided visits 2.30pm Jun–mid-Jul, 11am, 2.30pm, 3.30pm & 4.30pm mid-Jul–Aug, 2.30pm & 3.30pm Sep–mid-Oct) castle, a 6km drive to the south and out of view of the town, was built in AD 1040 and controlled by the Austrians until 1803.

Engadin Bad Scuol (☎ 081 861 20 00; Via dals Bogns; adult/child 6-16yr/child under 6yr/child under 1yr Sfr25/18/5/free) presents various options. The standard bathing entry gives 2½ hours in a series of pools with all sorts of gadgets that turn on and off, from a whirlpool that drags you around the outside pool to various massaging jets and waterfalls. You can also use the sauna. The big attraction is the 2¼ hour Roman-Irish bath, which combines a series of different baths, massages and relaxation, all done naked. You must book this in advance (people aged 16 and over).

There is **skiing** above Scuol up to 2800m, with a total of 80km of runs – the longest is 12km. A one-day pass costs Sfr50/40/25 for adults/youths and seniors/children. **Engadin Adventure** (☎ 081 861 14 19; www.engadin-adventure .ch) offers a choice of **white-water rafting** trips from Sfr95.

SLEEPING & EATING

Three attractive hotels are bundled together in the Old Town of Scuol. Plenty more line Stradun, the main street of the modern town.

Hotel Traube (☎ 081 861 07 00; www.traube.ch; Stradun; meals Sfr30-40; ☻ noon-10.30pm Mon & Thu-Sun, 6-10.30pm Tue-Wed) This is a simple eatery (with rooms upstairs), on the main road at the junction with Via de l'Ospidal. Staff offer local and more general Swiss dishes.

GETTING THERE & AWAY

The train from St Moritz (Sfr25, 1½ hours), with a change at Samedan, terminates at Scuol-Tarasp station. There are direct trains from Klosters (Sfr24, 45 minutes). From Scuol, the train to Guarda (Sfr6.60) takes 12 minutes. Postal buses from the station

---

AUTHOR'S CHOICE

Hotel Engiadina (☎ 081 864 14 21; www .engiadina-scuol.ch; d Sfr178-380) This boutique charmer is the pick of the Old Town crop. You can opt for a simple double with shower and loo or go for a fully renovated stone pine room. Some are white-washed and vaulted, in the style of the old Engadine houses; others have warm timber ceilings. Bathrooms are modern and stylish. Best of all is the award-winning restaurant (tasting menu Sfr78; open Tuesday to Saturday), where you can try a mix of local and international cuisine in candle-lit surroundings. The *Ftaner Lammrücken mit Tomatenkruste auf Ratatouille und Olivengnocchi* (a juicy lamb cut in a tomato crust with ratatouille and olive gnocchi) is delicious.

operate year-round to Tarasp (Sfr4.60, 26 minutes), Samnaun and Austria (as far as Landeck).

Samnaun

pop 819 / elevation 1377m

The drive east along the Inn to the Austrian border is beautiful if otherwise eventless. You could choose to make a detour that takes you briefly into Austria and then back into a remote corner of Switzerland to the incongruous duty-free town of Samnaun. In winter there is a little skiing but for the floods of local Swiss and Austrians who pour in, it's the tax-free goods (from petrol and cigarettes to watches and clothes) that attracts the traffic.

Müstair

pop 830 / elevation 1375m

It seems extraordinary that one of Europe's great early Christian treasures should be tucked away in such a remote corner of central Europe. But when Charlemagne supposedly founded a monastery and a church here in the 9th century, this was a strategically placed spot below one of the mountain passes (Ofen Pass) that separate northern Europe from Italy and the heart of Christendom.

Just before the Italian border at the end of Val Müstair, you could reach Müstair from Samnaun by dropping down through a brief stretch of Austrian territory and a slice of Italy. Or approach from Zernez through the national park (see below).

For information on lodgings along the Val Müstair, check with the village **tourist office** (☎ 081 858 50 00; www.muestair.ch).

The Carolingian (9th century) and Romanesque (12th century) frescoes that plaster the interior of the church of the **Kloster St Johann** (St John's Monastery; ☎ 081 851 62 28; admission free; ☒ 9am-noon & 1.30-5pm), known in Romansch as the Baselgia San Jon, are remarkable for their lively colour. Beneath the Carolingian representations of Christ in glory in the apses, are Romanesque stories that concentrate on the grisly ends of John the Baptist, St Peter (crucified), St Paul (decapitation) and St Steven (stoned to death). Above it all reign images of Christ seated in heavenly majesty. Next door, the **museum** (adult/child Sfr12/6) takes you through part of the monastery complex, with bits and pieces of Carolingian art and other objects.

Postal buses run along the valley between Zernez and Müstair (70 minutes).

Swiss National Park (Parc Naziunal Svizzer)

The road west from Müstair stretches 34km over the Ofen Pass (Pass dal Fuorn, 2149m) and through the thick woods of Switzerland's only national park and on to **Zernez**, which is home to the **Chasa dal Parc Naziunal**

A LITTLE ANIMAL MAGIC

If you'd like a break from people and their playthings, the Swiss National Park provides an ideal spot far from the madding crowd. It's a place to enjoy the vast, untrammelled countryside.

The park was established in 1914, the first such park to be created in Europe. At 172 sq km, it is smaller than most American and Canadian national parks, but the command of conservation is more rigorously adhered to. The key principle is to keep things natural. This even means holding down the number of paths to a minimum, to lessen the impact of human curiosity.

Such care has led to a flourishing of flora and fauna. You can also view a number of animals that are not usually seen – ibex, marmot, chamois and deer roam through the park at will.

A three-hour walk from S-chanf to Trupchun is especially popular in October when you can get close to large deer. The Naturlehrpfad circuit near Il Fuorn gives an opportunity to see bearded vultures, released into the wild since 1991.

In summer 2005, one of the descendants of the handful of Slovenian brown bears released into the wild in northern Italy since the 1990s caused a storm by wandering over the border into the Val Müstair near the Ofen Pass (Pass dal Fuorn). He came to join the small number of wolves that have again been roaming the east of the canton since 2002. The appearance of the bear attracted floods of animal spotters, but the hullabaloo was short-lived, as the bear wandered back into Italy. In September he was back and upsetting locals by killing a dozen or more sheep to keep hunger at bay.

Svizzer (National Park House; ☎ 081 856 13 78; www.nationalpark.ch; ❤ 8.30am-6pm daily, to 10pm Tue Jun–Oct). It is on the main road just as it leaves the east end of town and is open the same months as the park. It provides hiking details with locations to see particular animals.

There's no charge to enter the park and parking is free. Walkers can enter by trails from Zernez, S-chanf and Scuol. Deviating from the paths is not permitted. Regulations prohibit camping, littering, lighting fires, cycling, picking flowers, bringing dogs into the park or disturbing the animals in any way. Fines of up to Sfr500 may be imposed for violations.

SLEEPING & EATING

There are several hotel and restaurant options in Zernez and a couple in the park itself.

Chamanna Cluozza (☎ 081 856 12 35; cluozza@hotmail.com; dm Sfr27, d per person Sfr37, half-board per person Sfr68; ❤ late Jun–Oct) With 70 beds mostly in typical Alpine hut dorms, this timber-fronted but basic sleeping option is great for walkers who want to wake up in the middle of it all. It's about a three-hour hike from Zernez.

Hotel Bär & Post (☎ 081 851 55 00; www.baer-post.ch; s/d Sfr90/160) In business since 1905, this is one of the best options in town and on the main road. The best rooms are particularly spacious, the local stone pine predominates and there's also a sauna on the premises. The restaurant, decked out in typical timber style for the region, is a good place to sample local cooking (mains up to Sfr40; open daily).

Il Fuorn (☎ 081 856 12 26; www.ilfuorn.ch; dm Sfr19, s/d from Sfr75/140, half-board extra Sfr30; ❤ Jun–Oct) In the middle of the national park by the main road, it is a handy hulk of a place with surprisingly pleasant rooms. Unless you want to opt for the very basic dorm with huddled together mattresses. Trout is big on the *stübli* menu.

GETTING THERE & AWAY

Trains run regularly from Zernez to St Moritz (Sfr16.80, 50 minutes), stopping at S-chanf, Zuoz and Celerina. For the latter and St Moritz, change at Samedan.

OBERENGADIN

As much as the Unterengadin is loaded with rural charm, the Oberengadin is charged with skiing adrenaline. St Moritz, possibly the most chichi resort of the lot in Switzerland, is joined by a string of other skiing resorts along the Oberengadin valley and nearby Pontresina. A regional ski pass thus covers 350km of downhill runs.

Zuoz

pop 1224 / elevation 1750m

Zuoz, a small town 13km southwest of Zernez, is fully in the Engadine tradition, with colourful sgraffito decorated houses and windows in the church chancel designed by Augusto Giacometti. Skiing from here is limited but the town is one of the prettiest in the Oberengadin.

You'll find several hotels, private rooms and restaurants. **Hotel Belvair** (☎ 081 854 20 23; www.hotel-belvair.ch; s/d Sfr165/310; ❤ Jun–mid-Oct, Dec–Apr) is a somewhat sprawling affair at the entrance to town from the main road, vaguely rose-coloured and with spacious rooms. Better still, the hotel has a Wellness centre with whirlpool, sauna and small gym.

Occupying one side of the central square is **Hotel Crusch Alva** (☎ 081 854 13 19; www.hotelcruschalva.ch; r up to Sfr115 per person; ❤ Jun–Oct, Dec–Apr). The 13 rooms in this beautifully maintained 500-year-old Engadine house are full of timber-flavoured rustic charm. On the 1st floor the little *stüva* (parlour) is like a 19th-century drawing room and is where to sit down to a meal of fondue, meat or fish (set meals from Sfr25; open Thursday to Tuesday).

Celerina

This resort (Schlarigna in Romansch) by the Inn River is about a 45-minute walk northeast of St Moritz and shares the same ski slopes. Known for its Olympic **bob run** (☎ 081 830 02 00; www.olympia-bobrun.ch), the 1.6km-long bobsleigh run is the world's oldest and the only one made from natural ice. It starts by St Moritzer. One 130km/h 'taxi-ride' trip costs Sfr210. The **cresta run** (☎ 081 833 46 09; www.cresta-run.com) was created by British tourists in 1885. Over 1km, it starts near the Schiefer Turm in St Moritz. A set of five rides costs Sfr450 (and Sfr44 a ride thereafter).

The **tourist office** (☎ 081 830 00 11; www.celerina.ch; cnr Via Maistra & Via da la Staziun; ❤ 8.30am-noon & 2-6.30pm Mon-Fri, plus 10am-noon & 3-5pm Sat in season) is in the village centre.

There are several hotels and restaurants in and around Celerina, although it is not

GRAUBÜNDEN

the most attractive location and a little on the quiet side.

Hotel Cresta Run (☎ 081 833 09 19; www.hotel-cresta-run.ch; Via Maistra; d Sfr80; Ⓟ) is on a minor road directly linking Celerina and St Moritz, about 500m south of Celerina's town centre. It's a simple family hotel with its own restaurant and pizzeria set right by the finish of the Crest bob run.

Celerina is easily reached from St Moritz by train (Sfr2.80, three minutes) or by local bus.

ST MORITZ

pop 5010 / elevation 1856m

St Moritz (San Murezzan in Romansch) is where the wealthy come to enjoy their riches. With its smugly perfect lake and aloof mountains, the town also looks a million dollars. Those still waiting to make their first billion usually stay around the lake in St Moritz Bad.

Visitors can enjoy a huge variety of winter and summer sports. There is diverse downhill, plus cross-country skiing. Health treatments are also part of the package.

After all, those wealthy boys and girls want to be around as long as possible to keep spending all that lovely lolly.

Orientation & Information

St Moritz exudes health and wealth from the slopes overlooking the lake that shares its name (St Moritzer See in German, Lej da San Murezzan in Romansch). Uphill from the lakeside train station on Via Serlas is the post office and five minutes further on is the **tourist office** (☎ 081 837 33 33; www.stmoritz.ch; Via Maistra 12; ☯ 9am-6.30pm Mon-Fri, 9am-6pm Sat, 4-6pm Sun Dec-Easter & mid-Jun–mid-Sep, 9am-noon & 2-6pm Mon-Fri, 9am-noon Sat rest of the year). St Moritz Bad is about 2km southwest of the main town, St Moritz Dorf. Local buses run between the two, as do postal buses. Not much stays open during November, May and early June.

Sights

The **Engadiner Museum** (☎ 081 833 43 33; Via dal Bagn 39; adult/child Sfr5/2.50; ☯ 10am-noon & 2-5pm Mon-Fri, 10am-noon Sun Dec-Apr & Jun-Oct) gives a good introduction to the style of dwellings and simple interiors you may encounter if

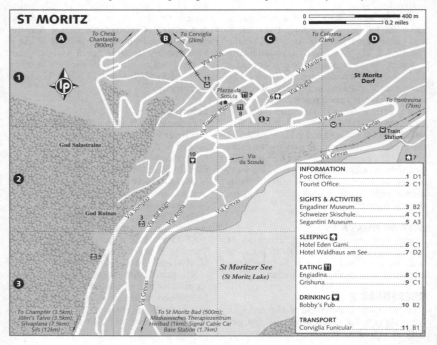

ST MORITZ

Scale	
0	400 m
0	0.2 miles

To Chesa Chantarella (900m)
To Corviglia (2km)
To Celerina (2km)
St Moritz Dorf
To Pontresina (7km)
Via Tinus
Via Maistra
Via Veglia
Via Serlas
Via Serlas
Via Grevas
Plazza da Scuola
Train Station
God Salastrains
Via Tavrler Plazza
Via da Scuola
God Ruinas
Via Somplaz
Via dal Bagn
Via Arona
Via Grevas
Via Grevas
St Moritzer See
(St Moritz Lake)
Via Grevas

To Champfèr (3.5km); Jöhri's Talvo (3.5km); Silvaplana (7.5km); Sils (12km)
To St Moritz Bad (500m); Medizinisches Therapiezentrum Heilbad (1km); Signal Cable Car Base Station (1.7km)

INFORMATION
Post Office......................................1 D1
Tourist Office..................................2 C1

SIGHTS & ACTIVITIES
Engadiner Museum...........................3 B2
Schweizer Skischule.........................4 C1
Segantini Museum............................5 A3

SLEEPING 🏠
Hotel Eden Garni.............................6 C1
Hotel Waldhaus am See....................7 D2

EATING 🍴
Engiadina.......................................8 C1
Grishuna..9 C1

DRINKING 🍷
Bobby's Pub....................................10 B2

TRANSPORT
Corviglia Funicular...........................11 B1

you explore the Engadine Valley. Traditional stoves and archaeological finds complete the collection.

The **Segantini Museum** (☎ 081 833 44 54; www.segantini-museum.ch; Via Somplaz 30; adult/student/child Sfr10/7/3; ☽ 10am-noon & 2-6pm Tue-Sun Dec-Apr & mid-May–mid-Oct) is devoted to local 19th-century artist Giovanni Segantini (1858–99), who specialised in majestic mountain scenes.

Activities

SKIING

The **downhill skiing** area adjacent to St Moritz centres on Corviglia (2486m), accessible by funicular from Dorf. From Bad a cable car goes to Signal (shorter queues), giving access to the slopes of Piz Nair. A ski pass for both areas costs up to Sfr61 (child/youth 13 to 17 Sfr30/55) for one day. If you ski on Piz Corvatsch, above nearby Silvaplana, you can ski back down to Bad via the demanding Hahnensee run. The first Swiss ski school was founded in St Moritz in 1929. Today skiing or snowboarding tuition (Sfr70 per day) can still be had at one of several ski schools, such as the **Schweizer Skischule** (☎ 081 830 01 01; www.skischool.ch; Plazza da Scuola 16; ☽ 9am-7pm Mon-Sat).

You can get a general ski pass to cover all the slopes including Silvaplana, Sils, Celerina, Zuoz, Pontresina and Diavolezza. One day costs Sfr70/47/24 in high season for adults/youths aged 13 to 17/children, although you couldn't possibly touch more than a fraction of the area in one day. Seven days costs Sfr376/252/128.

The region also boasts 160km of cross-country trails. The famous **Engadine Ski Marathon** takes place on the second Sunday in March. It starts at Maloja, crosses over the frozen lakes at Sils and Silvaplana, passes by the southeast side of St Moritzer See and finishes between Zuoz and S-chanf, a distance of some 42km.

Visit the website www.skiengadin.ch for more information about skiing facilities and services.

HIKING & OTHER ACTIVITIES

There are 120km of marked hiking paths. Many are open in winter. The tourist office has a map giving suggestions (in English) for walking throughout Oberengadin. Above St Moritz soars Piz Nair (3057m), and the summit provides a marvellous perspective of Alpine peaks and the lakes and valley below.

You can play golf, fish, paraglide and indulge in many other sports. Enjoy the experience of a 'treatment' in the **Medizinisches Therapiezentrum Heilbad** (☎ 081 833 30 62; www.heilbad-stmoritz.ch; Plazza Paracelsus 2; admission to mineral water baths Sfr35; ☽ 8am-noon & 2-7pm Mon-Fri, 8am-noon Sat).

Sleeping

Chesa Chantarella (☎ 081 833 33 55; www.chesa-chantarella.ch; Via Salastrains; s/d Sfr95/190; ☽ Jun-Sep & Dec-Apr; P) High up over the town, this is a charming, knock-about sort of place that also happens to house one of the town's better value eateries for local cooking and fondue.

Hotel Eden Garni (☎ 081 830 81 00; www.edenstmoritz.ch; Via Veglia; s/d Sfr138/284; ▯ P) Smack in the heart of St Moritz Dorf, this is a reasonable midrange option with an attractive central atrium. The views from the fairly standard top-floor rooms are great.

Hotel Waldhaus am See (☎ 081 836 60 00; www.waldhaus-am-se.ch; s/d Sfr170/320; ▯ P) Brilliantly located in grounds overlooking the lake and a short walk from the train station, this place has pleasant rooms, many with enticing views over the lake and mountains. It has its own sizzling restaurant too, with grilled meat specialties.

Eating

Engiadina (☎ 081 833 32 65; Plazza da Scuola 2; ☽ Mon-Sat) This comfortable, cosy place is famous for fondue, and that's the best thing to eat here (from Sfr32 per person – Sfr38.50 with champagne!). It's open year round.

Jöhri's Talvo (☎ 081 833 44 55; Via Gunels 15; ☽ Tue-Sun) This place, beyond Bad in nearby Champfér, is the best valley restaurant, serving up fish and local dishes in rustic surroundings.

Grishuna (☎ 081 837 04 04; Via Maistra 17; mains Sfr25-40; ☽ daily Jun–mid-Oct & Dec-Apr) Housed on the first floor of the not-too-promising looking Hotel Monopol, this place is appreciated by local residents as much as visitors for its elegantly presented local dishes.

Drinking

Around 20 bars and clubs have dancing and/or music. While you bop to the beat your wallet might also be waltzing itself wafer-thin, because nights out in St Moritz can be nasty on the banknotes.

GRAUBÜNDEN

Bobby's Pub (☎ 081 834 42 83; Via dal Bagn 50a; ☺ 10-1am) This vaguely pub-type place, with undulating bar and a wide selection of beers, attracts young snowboarding types in season, and just about everyone in town out of season, being one of the few places open year round.

Getting There & Away

The **Glacier Express** (www.glacierexpress.ch) links St Moritz to Zermatt (Sfr129, plus Sfr9 reservation fee) via the 2033m Oberalp Pass. The majestic route takes 7½ hours to cover the 290km and crosses 291 bridges. In summer you pay Sfr15 or Sfr30 reservation fee, depending on the train.

Regular trains, as many as one every 30 minutes, run from Zürich to St Moritz (Sfr67, three hours 20 minutes) with one change (at Landquart or Chur) along the way. Those via Landquart pass through Klosters, Zernez, Zuoz and Samedan. Via Chur they take a different route via Reichenau, Thusis, Tiefencastel and Celerina.

Postal buses run every 30 to 60 minutes from St Moritz southwest to Maloja (Sfr9.80, 35 minutes) with stops at Silvaplana (Sfr3.80, 14 minutes) and Sils (Sfr6.60, 21 minutes). For Pontresina and beyond, see Bernina Pass Rd (right).

SILVAPLANA, SILS-MARIA & MALOJA

Sitting between two lakes 7.5km southwest of St Moritz, **Silvaplana** (Silvaplauna in Romansch) is a centre for water sports, especially windsurfing. Across the causeway is **Surlej**, providing access to ski slopes and marvellous views from Piz Corvatsch (3451m).

Another 4km brings you to **Sils-Maria** (Segl in Romansch). It has two parts: Baselgia by the lake and Maria at the foot of the mountains, where most amenities are located. A cable car ascends to Furtschellas (2312m), where there is a network of hiking trails and ski slopes.

Sils might be a quiet lakeside country village now, but the rumble of existential philosophy once reverberated around these mountains, courtesy of fiery Friedrich Nietzsche. The German giant of the inner mind spent his summers in Sils from 1881 to 1888, writing essential texts concerning the travails of modern man, including *Also Sprach Zarathustra (Thus Spake Zarathustra)*. The **Nietzsche Haus** (☎ 081 826 53 69; www

.nietzschehaus.ch; adult/student & senior/child under 12yr Sfr6/3/free; ☺ 3-6pm Tue-Sun mid-Jun–mid-Oct & late Dec–mid-Apr) has many photos of and letters penned by the man with the mighty moustache, as well as other memorabilia.

In Sils you could stay at one of several places. About the cheapest is **Pensiun Schulze** (☎ 081 826 52 13; s/d Sfr85/160), on the main street in Sils above the Gran Café. It offers simple rooms, the better with their own shower. In another class altogether is nearby **Hotel Pensiun Privata** (☎ 081 832 62 00; www.pensiunprivata.ch; s/d Sfr190/340), where rooms have timber lined walls and ceilings, views over the woods, broad beds and antique-style furniture. It also has a fine restaurant.

For sheer luxury try the century-old **Hotel Waldhaus** (☎ 081 838 51 00; www.waldhaus-sils.ch; s/d with half board up to Sfr395/800; ☺ mid-Jun–Oct & mid-Dec–mid-Apr; ☒ P). This palace of 150 rooms, set on a rise amid the woods, is a jump back into the past. Along with modern installations (pool, sauna, Turkish baths, tennis courts) the owners have been careful to maintain the old charm of the grand public areas (and hire a three-man orchestra to perfume the evening air with light classics). Rooms vary enormously in type, size and décor.

The road from Sils follows the north shore of its lake to the one-street village of **Maloja** and, shortly after, the **Maloja Pass** that separates the Engadine from the Val Bregaglia. The artist Giovanni Segantini lived in the village from 1894. His **studio** (Atelier; adult/child Sfr3/1.50; ☺ 3-5pm Wed & Sun mid-Jun–mid-Oct & Jan–mid-Apr) can be visited. Paintings are also on display in the **Belvedere Tower** (admission free; ☺ 9am-5pm daily Jun–mid-Oct & Jan-Apr). There are several places to stay and eat here.

All these towns are on the postal bus route from St Moritz.

BERNINA PASS ROAD

The road runs from Celerina southeast to Tirano in Italy, linking Val Bernina and Val Poschiavo by way of the Bernina Pass at 2323m. There is some great hiking in the bare, brooding mountains – shown in more detail in various hiking maps available from the tourist office in Pontresina.

As many as 10 trains run via Pontresina (Sfr4.50, 11 minutes) direct to Tirano (Sfr27, 2½ hours) in northern Italy.

PONTRESINA & AROUND
pop 1880 / elevation 1800m

Pontresina, at the mouth of the Val Bernina, makes a nice alternative base to St Moritz. Check out the pentagonal Moorish tower and the Santa Maria chapel, with frescoes dating from the 13th and 15th centuries.

From the train station, west of the village, cross the two rivers, Rosegg and Bernina, for the centre and the **tourist office** (☎ 081 838 83 00; www.pontresina.ch; Rondo Bldg, Via Maistra; ☺ 9.30am-noon & 2-6pm Mon-Sat, 3-6pm Sun mid-Dec–Apr, 9.30am-noon & 2-6pm Mon-Fri, 9.30am-noon Sat May–mid-Dec).

There's not much skiing from Pontresina's own mountain, Alp Languard (3262m), but use the resort as a base to explore slopes further down the valley, at **Piz Lagalb** (2959m) and **Diavolezza** (2973m). Combined ski passes for the two cost Sfr50/38/19 per adult/student/child (or get the Engadin regional skiing pass mentioned in the St Moritz section, p283). In summer, it's worth getting the cable cars to either for views. A walking trail leads down from Diavolezza to Morteratsch.

Sleeping

Pension Valtellina (☎ 081 842 64 06; Via Maistra; s/d with hall shower Sfr60/112) This old-style Engadine house between the tourist office and post office has 14 quaint, old-style rooms.

Hotel Albris (☎ 081 838 80 40; www.albris.ch; Via Maistra; s/d Sfr145/260; ☐ P) This is a popular three-star place near the post office with spacious, well-appointed rooms featuring timber ceilings, quality pine furniture and modern bathrooms. Downstairs they have a fine restaurant (meals Sfr60 to Sfr70; open daily) and a wellness centre.

VAL POSCHIAVO

Once over the **Bernina Pass** (2328m), you drop into the sunny Italian-speaking Val Poschiavo. A good lookout point is Alp Grüm (2091m), reached on foot (two hours) from the Ospizio Bernina eatery at the pass. Fourteen kilometres south of the pass lies **Poschiavo**, 15km short of the border with Italy. Hang out at a café on the pretty central square, Plazza da Cumün. **Hotel Albrici** (☎ 081 844 01 73; www.hotelalbrici.ch; Plazza da Cumün; s/d Sfr90/140) is an historic lodging whose spacious rooms have polished timber floors, antique furniture and buckets of charm. The restaurant serves up local meals and pizza, or banquets in the 17th-century Sala delle Sibille.

You could pop down from St Moritz one day for a change of speed. Just past the glittering **Lago di Poschiavo**, the town of **Brusio** is known for its distinctive circular train viaduct. Another 5km and you reach **Tirano**, just over the Italian border.

VAL BREGAGLIA

From the Maloja Pass (1815m), the road spirals down into the Val Bregaglia (Bergell in German) valley, cutting a course southwest into Italy. The road then splits, with one arm leading north and back into Switzerland via the Splügen Pass, and the other going south to Lago di Como and on to Milan. The postal bus from St Moritz to Lugano branches off from the Milan road to circle the western shore of the lake.

As you proceed down the valley, the villages betray an increasing Italian influence. **Stampa** was the home of the artist Alberto Giacometti (1901–66), and is the location of the valley's **tourist office** (☎ 081 822 15 55; www.bregaglia.ch; ☺ 9-11.30am & 3-5.30pm Mon-Fri, 9-11.30am Sat).

Soglio (1050m), a hamlet near the Italian border, faces the smooth-sided Pizzo Badile (3308m) peak on a south-facing ledge, reached from the valley floor by a narrow road. The village, a warren of lanes and stone houses, lies at the end of a steep, thickly wooded trail away from the main road and is the starting point for **hiking** trails, most notably the historic Panorama Hochweg. It takes around four hours to reach Casaccia, 11km distant and down in the valley. There are several modest accommodation options along with the gleaming white four-storey **Palazzo Salis** (☎ 081 822 12 08; www.palazzosalis.ch; d per person Sfr80-135; ☺ early Mar-late Nov). About 50m up from the post office is this truly regal resting place, with portraits on the walls, suits of armour and ornate furniture. Built in 1630 and in the hotel business since the beginning of the 20th century, it has rooms with stucco or wooden ceilings, antique furniture (some of it four centuries old) and bottles of charm. It also has a restaurant (mains Sfr20-35).

Buses from St Moritz to Castasegna travel along Val Bregaglia. Alight at the post office at Promontogno and take the bus to Soglio from there (Sfr3 each way, six to 10 departures per day, 12 minutes).

Ticino

The summer air is rich and hot. The peacock-proud posers propel their scooters in and out of traffic. Italian weather. Italian style. And that's not to mention the Italian ice cream, Italian pizza, Italian architecture, Italian language. But this isn't Rome, Florence or Naples. It's the Switzerland that Heidi never mentioned.

Ticino (Tessin in German and French) is a strange mix. Classic, dark-haired Latin lookers rub shoulders with equally style-conscious blue-eyed blondes. There is a certain vibrant snappiness in the air of towns like Lugano. But this is Switzerland, after all, and the temperament is tamer than further south. A lusty love for Italian comfort food and full-bodied wines is balanced by a healthy respect for rules and regulations. And in the scattered valley hamlets the Italian spoken has a halting lilt that marks its distance from the honeyed heat of southern Italian conversation. The very manner of the people is demonstrative of how the canton manages a blend of Swiss cool and Italian passion.

The region offers a little of everything. A touch of the shimmering lake life can be had in Lugano and Locarno. Their mirror-like lakes, dotted by colourful villages with mansions and palm trees, are framed by grand, verdant mountains. To the north, the region's capital, Bellinzona is a quieter but stunning medieval fortress town. Those in search of rural quiet have come to the right place. Various valleys spread across the length of the northern half of the canton, blessed by homely hamlets, Romanesque chapels and endless hiking options past lakes and roaring mountain streams.

HIGHLIGHTS

- Taking an aristocratic amble around Bellinzona's three **castles** (p289)
- Losing yourself in the high valleys, especially **Val Bavona** (p303), of the Valle Maggia
- Drinking in the lake views from Lugano's **Monte Brè** (p296) and **Monte San Salvatore** (p296)
- Feasting on the cream of the silver screen at Locarno's **Festival Internazionale di Film** (p300) in August
- Catching the spectacular **Centovalli Railway** (p302) to Domodossola in Italy

★ Val Bavona

★ Valle Maggia

Centovalli ★
Railway

★ Festival
Internazionale
di Film

★ Bellinzona

Monte Brè
★

★ Monte San
Salvatore

| ■ POPULATION: 314,600 | ■ AREA: 2812.5 SQ KM | ■ LANGUAGE: ITALIAN |

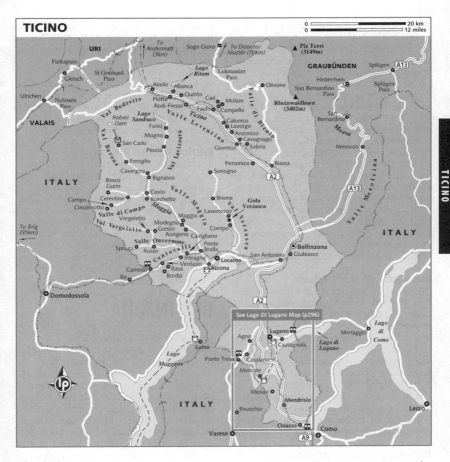

TICINO

TICINO

History

Ticino, long a poor, rural buffer area between the Swiss German cantons north of the Alps and Italy to the south, was absorbed by the Swiss in the late 15th century after centuries of changing hands between the lords of Como and the dukes of Milan. In earlier days it had been a loosely controlled Lombard fiefdom and, before that, a Roman frontier stronghold.

When the founding cantons of the Swiss confederation, Uri, Scwhyz and Unterwalden, had secured their independence of Habsburg Austrian control, they decided to move to protect the soft Alpine underbelly to the south. This they managed to do with surprising alacrity, defeating a su-

perior Milanese force at Giornico in the Valle Levantina in 1478 and taking fortified Bellinzona in 1503.

Napoleon came to upset the Swiss apple cart in 1798 and ended Swiss German domination of Ticino. For a while it became an independent republic, then in 1803 it entered the new Swiss Confederation concocted by Napoleon as a free and equal canton.

Only since WWII has it been able to emerge from its struggling rural slumber, and nowadays the region thrives as a services (mostly banking) centre and tourist attraction, especially for Swiss Germans looking for a little Italian style without leaving home. The establishment of a university at Lugano in 1996 was a significant step, as the Italian-speaking population had long been caught between two hard options: study elsewhere in Switzerland in another language, or overcome bureaucratic hell to gain admission to Italian universities.

The region has its problems. With such a small percentage of the Swiss population, it counts for little in big national decisions. Wages are lower than in most of the rest of Switzerland. Ticinesi are attracted by big brother Italy, but often suffer a sense of indifference, when not inferiority (not aided by the parading Gucci brigade that pops up from Milan on weekends), next to their southern cousins. Staunchly (but independently) Swiss, they don't readily identify with many political choices made north of the Alps, although recently Ticino has swung to the right on subjects like immigration and the debate on how far to become involved with the EU (answer: as little as possible).

Orientation & Information

Ticino is the country's fourth-largest canton, bordering with Graubünden to the north and east, a small stretch of the Valais to the west, and with Italy to west, south and southeast. The climate is mild on the lakes and a little more extreme in the rural valleys. Average afternoon temperatures for Lugano are around 28°C in July and August, 17°C in April and September and 7°C in December and January. Locarno gets more than 2300 hours of sunshine per year.

In addition to the normal Swiss national holidays, the following public holidays are taken in Ticino:

Epiphany (Epifania or La Befana) 6 January
St Joseph's Day (Festa di San Giuseppe) 19 March
Labour Day (Festa del Lavoro) 1 May
Corpus Christi variable date
Sts Peter and Paul Day (Festa di SS Pietro e Paolo) 29 June
Feast of the Assumption (Assunzione or Ferragosto) 15 August
All Saints' Day (Ognissanti) 1 November
Feast of the Immaculate Conception (Immaculata Concezione) 8 December

The regional tourist office is the **Ente Ticinese per il Turismo** (☎ 091 825 70 56; www.ticino.tourism .ch; Villa Turrita, Via Lugano 12, Bellinzona; ☺ 8am-noon & 2-6pm Mon-Fri).

Pick up a copy of the *Ticino Camping* brochure, which details the canton's 40 camping

grounds. Ask about the 30-odd mountain huts run by the **Federazione Alpinistica Ticinese** (FAT; www.capanneti.ch) along the canton's hiking trails.

Wine is a big part of the Ticino experience. Pick up the *Le Strade del Vino* mapguide. It details wineries around the canton, their opening hours and products. To learn more about the Ticino love affair with Merlot, have a look at www.ticinowine.ch.

Getting There & Around

The Lugano Region Pass gives free travel on Lago di Lugano, and on regional public transport in and around Lugano (including the funiculars up Monte Brè and San Salvatore). It also gives free or reduced rides on the cable cars and rack and pinion railways in the area, as well as half-price transport to and around Locarno and on Lago Maggiore. The price is Sfr72/96 for three/seven days. It is available for 2nd class only and issued from around Easter to October.

BELLINZONA

pop 16,890 / elevation 230m
Strategically placed at the conversion point of several valleys leading down from the Alps, Bellinzona is visually unique. Inhabited since Neolithic times, it is dominated by three grey-stone, fairy-tale medieval castles that have attracted everyone from Swiss invaders to painters like William Turner. Turner may have liked the place, but Bellinzona has a surprisingly low tourist profile, in spite of its castles together forming one of only six Unesco World Heritage sites in Switzerland.

The rocky central hill upon which rises the main castle, Castelgrande, was a Roman frontier post and Lombard defensive tower, and was later developed as a heavily fortified town controlled by Milan. The three castles and valley walls could not stop the Swiss German confederate troops from overwhelming the city in 1503, thus deciding Ticino's fate for the following three centuries.

Information

Bisi (☎ 091 825 21 31; Via Magoria 10; Internet access per hr Sfr5; ☺ 2-7pm Mon-Fri)
Post office (Viale Stazione 18) To get here, walk left of the train station for five minutes.

Tourist office (☎ 091 825 21 31; www.bellinzona turismo.ch; Piazza Nosetto; ☺ 10am-6pm) In the restored Renaissance Palazzo Civico (town hall).

Sights & Activities

A stroll around the cobblestone pedestrian-only old core of town is a treat. Keep an eye out for fresco-adorned churches and close-knit townhouses. South of Piazza dell'Independenza, the medieval huddle gives way to elegant, if ageing, villas.

CASTLES

Without doubt, the city's three imposing castles are the main draw. To visit all three, get a general ticket (adult/concession Sfr8/4), which is valid indefinitely.

Castelgrande (☎ 091 825 81 45; Monte San Michele; admission to grounds free; ☺ 9am-midnight), dating from the 6th century, is the biggest fortification and is in the town centre. You can walk (head up Scalinata San Michele from Piazza Collegiata) or take the lift, buried deep in the rocky hill, from Piazza del Sole. The castle's **Museo Archeologico** (Archaeological Museum; adult/concession Sfr4/2; ☺ 10am-6pm) has a modest collection of finds from the hill dating to prehistoric times. More engaging is the display of 15th-century decorations taken from the ceiling of a former noble house in central Bellinzona. The pictures range from weird animals (late medieval ideas on what a camel looked like were curious) to a humorous series on the 'world

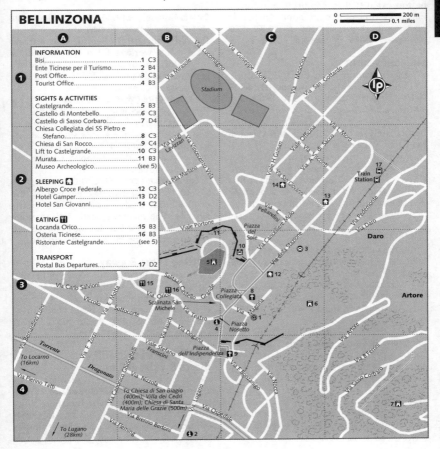

BELLINZONA

INFORMATION	
Bisi..**1** C3	
Ente Ticinese per il Turismo.............**2** B4	
Post Office....................................**3** C3	
Tourist Office.................................**4** B3	
SIGHTS & ACTIVITIES	
Castelgrande.................................**5** B3	
Castello di Montebello.....................**6** C3	
Castello di Sasso Corbaro................**7** D4	
Chiesa Collegiata dei SS Pietro e	
Stefano....................................**8** C3	
Chiesa di San Rocco........................**9** C4	
Lift to Castelgrande........................**10** C3	
Murata..**11** B3	
Museo Archeologico....................(see 5)	
SLEEPING 🛏	
Albergo Croce Federale...................**12** C3	
Hotel Gamper................................**13** D2	
Hotel San Giovanni.........................**14** C2	
EATING 🍴	
Locanda Orico...............................**15** B3	
Osteria Ticinese.............................**16** B3	
Ristorante Castelgrande.................(see 5)	
TRANSPORT	
Postal Bus Departures.....................**17** D2	

0 ————— 200 m
0 ————— 0.1 miles

Stadium

Train Station

Piazza del Sole

Daro

Artore

Scalinata San Michele

Piazza Collegiata

Piazza Nosetto

Piazza dell'Indipendenza

To Locarno (16km)

Torrente

Dragonato

To Pierino Tatti

To Lugano (28km)

To Chiesa di San Biagio (400m); Villa dei Cedri (400m); Chiesa di Santa Maria delle Grazie (500m)

TICINO

upside down'. Examples of the latter include an ox driving a man-pulled plough and a sex-crazed woman chasing a chaste man (!). The uncomfortable black seats you sit on for the 12-minute audiovisual on the castle's history were designed by Mario Botta and cost around Sfr1000 a pop!

After wandering the grounds and the museum, head west along the **Murata** (Walls; admission free; 9am-7pm Apr-Sep, 10am-5pm Oct-Mar).

Castello di Montebello (☎ 091 825 13 42; Salita ai Castelli; admission to castle free, museum adult/concession Sfr4/2; 10am-8pm) is slightly above the town and has a smaller museum that continues the study of medieval Bellinzona. From here it's a 3.5km climb uphill to **Castello di Sasso Corbaro**. At this point you should be too exhausted to explore the grounds, but lucky you – there are none. The castle hosts temporary **exhibitions** (☎ 091 825 59 06; adult/concession Sfr4/2; 10am-8pm).

CHURCHES & ART
Wandering south from the train station, you will first see the **Chiesa Collegiata dei SS Pietro e Stefano** (Piazza della Collegiata; 8am-1pm & 4-6pm), a Renaissance church with baroque touches and rich in frescoes inside. More immediately eye-catching is the **Chiesa di San Rocco** (Piazza dell'Indipendenza; 7-11am & 2-5pm), with its huge fresco of St Christopher and a smaller one of the Virgin Mary and Christ. Similarly decorated is the 14th-century **Chiesa di San Biagio** (Piazza San Biagio; 7am-noon & 2-5pm), the difference being that these frescoes are not 20th-century restorations. It stands 500m south of Piazza dell'Indipendenza.

Off the same square is the elegant **Villa dei Cedri**, set in lush **gardens** (admission free; 8am-8pm Apr-Sep, 9am-5pm Oct-Mar) and home to the city's **art collection** (adult/concession Sfr8/5; 2-6pm Tue-Fri, 11am-6pm Sat, Sun & holidays), mostly local and northern Italian works of the 19th and 20th centuries.

West over the railway line stands the **Chiesa di Santa Maria delle Grazie** (Via Convento; closed for restoration), a 15th-century church with an extraordinary fresco (much damaged by fire in 1997) of Christ's Crucifixion.

Sleeping
None of the functional hotels will win charm awards. Most are strung out along Via della Stazione.

Albergo Croce Federale (☎ 091 825 16 67; fax 091 826 25 50; Viale della Stazione 12; s/d Sfr100/150) The only place just inside the old town (part of the city wall stands menacingly behind it), this is a pleasant stop. Rooms are straightforward but light, and the restaurant downstairs is cheerful.

Hotel San Giovanni (☎ 091 825 19 19; www.hotel zimmer.ch; Via San Giovanni 7; s/d Sfr50/90, d with shower Sfr120) The single main quality of this place is the low price of the cluttered rooms (with shared bathroom).

Hotel Gamper (☎ 091 825 37 92; hotel-gamper@ bluemail.ch; Viale Stazione 29; s/d Sfr110/140) The top-floor box-like rooms offer good views. Rooms are functional and clean.

Eating
Osteria Ticinese (☎ 091 825 16 73; Via Orico 3; pasta Sfr11-15, mains Sfr13-16; daily) On the edge of the old centre, this cheerful spot attracts local office workers for a simple midday meal. Portions of standard Italian fare are generous, and you'll probably be fine with just pasta or a main.

Locanda Orico (☎ 091 825 15 18; Via Orico 13; pasta Sfr30-40, mains Sfr45-50; Tue-Sat) Behind the lace curtains in this low-slung temple to good food you come across such creations as *gnocchi di patate al timo annegati in un puree di zucca* (thyme gnocchi bathed in pumpkin puree).

Castelgrande (☎ 091 826 23 53; Castelgrande; mains Sfr35-60; Tue-Sun) It's not often you get the chance to eat inside a Unesco World Heritage site. The medieval castle setting alone is enough to bewitch. Elegantly presented Italian and Ticino cuisine will help too.

Getting There & Away
Bellinzona is on the train route connecting Locarno (Sfr7.80, 30 minutes) and Lugano (Sfr11.40, 30 minutes). It is also on the Zurich–Milan route. Postal buses head northeast to Chur (Sfr47). Postal buses depart from beside the train station.

NORTH OF BELLINZONA
Biasca & Valle di Blenio
Biasca is, with the vague exception of its 13th-century **Chiesa di SS Pietro e Paolo**, of little interest but an important transport junction. If you pass through, head for the series of *grotti* on Via ai Grotti, a series of simple, traditional eateries huddled around simple

stone huts backing into the rocky mountain wall. **Grotto Greina** (☎ 091 862 15 27; Via ai Grotti 36; mains Sfr18-30; ☺ 10-1am Tue-Sun Apr-Oct) is a good example, serving up lashings of grilled meats with polenta. Trains run twice an hour from Bellinzona (Sfr7.20, 12 minutes).

Directly north of Biasca, the Valle di Blenio splits off the main route and heads for the Lukmanier Pass (Passo di Lucomagno). It is a barren-looking valley, laced with potential hiking options and modest skiing near the pass.

The main town along the way is **Olivone**, where you will find a **tourist office** (☎ 091 872 14 87; www.blenioturismo.ch). Staff can help with hiking tips in the surrounding mountains, among the least explored in the country. **Albergo Olivone e Posta** (☎ 091 872 13 66; fax 091 872 16 87; Via Lucomagno; s/d Sfr85/140) is the most enticing hotel, a sturdy establishment at the northern entrance to town. It has a decent restaurant (closed Sunday).

From Bellinzona get the train to Biasca (Sfr20.60, one hour) and change to the postal bus.

Valle Leventina

From Biasca, the motorway powers northwest to Airolo and on to the St Gotthard Pass into central Switzerland. Taking this road you'd never know that high above it is strung a series of hamlets offering superlative views, great walking (the Strada Alta, partly asphalted, runs about 45km from Biasca to Airolo) and the occasional fine feed.

About 7km northwest of Biasca, head for Personico for its **Grotto Val d'Ambra** (☎ 091 864 18 29; mains Sfr16-28; ☺ Thu-Tue Apr-Oct), 500m outside the village. More than a century old, this is one of the most traditional of Ticino's *grotti*. The main restaurant building has a cosy dining area full of timber furniture. Outside, on balmy summer days, up to 100 people gather around the rough granite tables scattered about the dozen or so shaded *grotti* (the original stone buildings once used as houses and storage).

About 4km further, **Giornico** (site of a major defeat of the Milanese by Swiss Confederate forces in 1478) boasts two Romanesque bridges, the finest example of a Romanesque church in Ticino (**Chiesa di San Nicolao**, on the south bank of the Ticino river), a picturesque old centre and a couple of decent places to stay and eat. For the latter, follow

the signs to **Grotto Rodai** (☎ 091 864 21 48; mains Sfr16-30; ☺ Tue-Sun Apr–mid-Oct), a typical *grotto* (simple stone structure, usually built into the side of a hill or mountainside).

If driving, you can head up to the Strada Alta, high up on the north flank of the Ticino river valley, at several locations. From Lavorgo, 4km northwest of Giornico, a road winds up to the hamlets of **Anzonico**, **Cavagnago** and **Sobrio**. About 7km further on, another road leads from Faido to high points like **Campello**, **Molare** and **Carí**. At Molare you'll find a handy eatery on summer weekends, the **Locanda Chià d'Au** (☺ Fri dinner only & Sat & Sun Apr-Oct), behind the church.

At **Rodi-Fiesso**, the broad valley floor narrows to a claustrophobic gorge. Just outside the eastern entry to town, a Swiss customs and control point has guarded the way to the St Gotthard Pass since the 16th century. Today the restored **Dazio Grande** (☎ 091 874 60 66; Via San Gottardo; s/d Sfr85/125) has modern rooms, a small museum on the post's history and a restaurant (set menu Sfr38, open Tuesday to Sunday).

About 7km northwest of Rodi-Fiesso, you reach the sleepy valley town of Piotta. On the north side of the motorway here, Europe's steepest **funicular** (adult/child/senior one way Sfr13/6/11) heads up above the Strada Alta to **Lago Ritom**, a high dam from where walkers can head into the mountains. There's a restaurant with a few rooms (per person Sfr55, open April to October) behind the dam.

Airolo is a surprisingly big settlement at the head of the Valle Leventina, but not of great interest. If you want to cross the Alps into central Switzerland, this is the easiest route to follow. The Passo di San Gottardo (St Gotthard Pass) lies 7km north of Airolo. You can opt for the 17km tunnel or, when snow doesn't close it, the mountain road. The hourly train to Airolo from Bellinzona (Sfr20.80, 52 minutes) continues as far as Zürich and passes through the valley towns. From these you can connect by occasional postal bus to the hamlets of the Strada Alta.

You can sleep deep below the pass, underground! **La Claustra** (☎ 091 880 50 55; www.laclaustra.ch; San Gottardo; s/d Sfr180/280; ☺ May-Oct) is a combination of Wellness hotel, restaurant, library, wine cellar (the 2003 Gransegreto Merlot is delicious) and seminar centre, all at 2050m above sea level buried deep in the rock beneath the St Gotthard Pass in what was once one of the most impregnable of Swiss army bunkers, the San Carlo artillery base. Clearly, none of the 17 rooms, all individually laid out and decorated, come with views. Water comes from underground sources. Take a postal bus from Airolo to the pass. Booking ahead is essential.

West of Airolo, the quiet **Val Bedretto** climbs, slowly at first and then in sweeping curves through the bald Alpine terrain to reach another mountain crossing, the Nufenen Pass in the eastern Valais (see p140). The area is beloved of hikers in search of tranquillity.

LUGANO

pop 48,120 / elevation 270m

Ticino's lush lake isn't its only liquid asset. The largest city in the canton is also the country's third most important banking centre.

Visitors can only wonder how so many locals can work in stuffy banks when they could be wandering the spaghetti maze of steep cobblestone streets that untangle themselves at the edge of the lake. And how can they resist the water sports and hill-walking opportunities available to them?

Orientation

Lugano is on the shores of Lago di Lugano. The train station stands above and to the west of the Old Town. Take the stairs or the funicular (Sfr1.10, open 5.20am to 11.50pm) down to the centre, a patchwork of interlocking *piazze*. The most important one, Piazza della Riforma, is presided over by the 1844 neoclassical Municipio (town hall).

Paradiso, a southern suburb, is the departure point for the funicular to Monte San Salvatore (vaguely reminiscent of Rio's). The other mountain looming over the town, Monte Brè, is to the east. The airport is 3km west of the train station.

Information

INTERNET ACCESS

Manor department store (Servizio Clienti area, 3rd fl, Salita Chiattone 10; per 30min Sfr5; ☼ 8.15am-6.30pm Mon-Fri, to 9pm Thu, 8.15am-6pm Sat)

MEDICAL SERVICES

Doctor/dentist ☎ 111
Ospedale Civico (☎ 091 805 61 11; Via Tesserete 46) Hospital north of the city centre.

POST

Post office (Via Della Posta 7; ☼ 7.30am-6.15pm Mon-Fri, 8am-4pm Sat) In centre of Old Town.

TOURIST INFORMATION

Tourist office (☎ 091 913 32 32; www.lugano-tourism .ch; Municipio Bldg, Riva Giocondo Albertolli; ☼ 9am-7pm Mon-Fri, 9am-5pm Sat, 10am-5pm Sun & holidays Apr-Oct, 9am-noon & 2-5pm Mon-Fri Nov-Mar)

Sights

OLD TOWN & CHURCHES

Wander through the mostly porticoed lanes woven around the busy main square, Piazza della Riforma (which is even more lively when the Tuesday and Friday morning markets are held). Via Nassa is the main shopping street and indicates there is no shortage of liquid cash in this town.

The simple Romanesque **Chiesa di Santa Maria degli Angioli** (St Mary of the Angels; Piazza Luini; ☼ 8am-5pm), against which a now crumbling former hotel was built, contains two frescoes by Bernardino Luini dating from 1529. Covering the entire wall that divides the church in two is a grand didactic illustration of the Crucifixion. The closer you look, the more scenes of Christ's Passion are revealed, along with others of him being taken down from the cross and his resurrection. The power and vivacity of the colours are astounding. Less alive is Luini's depiction of the Last Supper on the left wall. Much of the remainder of the church, in particular the apse, is also gaily frescoed.

Below the train station, the **Cattedrale di San Lorenzo** (St Lawrence Cathedral; ☼ 8am-5pm) contains some fine frescoes and ornately decorated statues.

MUSEUMS & GALLERIES

The **Museo Cantonale d'Arte** (Cantonal Art Museum; ☎ 091 910 47 80; www.museo-cantonale-arte.ch; Via Canova 10; adult/student Sfr7/5, special exhibitions Sfr10/7; ☼ 2-5pm Tue, 10am-5pm Wed-Sun) celebrates the work of modern artists from the region. There's more creativity from the cutting edge at the **Museo d'Arte Moderna** (Modern Art Museum; ☎ 058 866 69 09; www.mdam.ch; Riva Antonio Caccia 5; adult/11-14yr/15-18yr/student & senior Sfr11/3/5/8; ☼ 9am-7pm Tue-Sun). Housed in Villa Malpensata, it is one of the city's main art spaces.

Another is **Galleria Gottardo** (☎ 091 808 19 88; Via San Franscini 12; admission free; ☼ 2-5pm Tue, 11am-5pm Wed-Sat), the private foundation of the Banca

TICINO

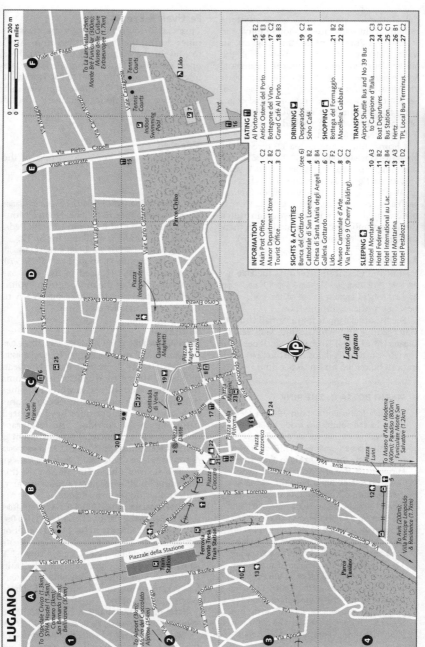

LUGANO

INFORMATION
Main Post Office.	.1 C2
Manor Department Store.	.2 B2
Tourist Office.	.3 C3

SIGHTS & ACTIVITIES
Banca del Gottardo.	(see 6)
Cattedrale di San Lorenzo.	.4 B2
Chiesa di Santa Maria degli Angeli.	.5 B4
Galleria Gottardo.	.6 C1
Lido.	.7 F2
Museo Cantonale d'Arte.	.8 C2
Via Pretorio 9 (Cherry Building).	.9 C2

SLEEPING
Hostel Montarina.	.10 A3
Hotel Federale.	.11 B2
Hotel International au Lac.	.12 B4
Hotel Montarina.	.13 A3
Hotel Pestalozzi.	.14 D2

EATING
Al Portone.	.15 E2
Antica Osteria del Porto.	.16 E3
Bottegone del Vino.	.17 C2
Grand Café Al Porto.	.18 B3

DRINKING
Desperados.	.19 C2
Soho Café.	.20 B1

SHOPPING
Bottega del Formaggio.	.21 B2
Macelleria Gabbani.	.22 B2

TRANSPORT
Airport Shuttle Bus and No 39 Bus to Campione d'Italia.	.23 C3
Boat Departures.	.24 C1
Bus Station.	.25 C1
Hertz.	.26 B1
TPL Local Bus Terminus.	.27 C2

del Gottardo, which puts on exhibitions ranging from sculpture to photography.

About 1.7km from central Lugano, in Villa Heleneum at Via Cortivo 24, is the **Museo delle Culture Extraeuropee** (Museum of Non-European Cultures; ☎ 058 866 69 09; www.lugano .ch/cultura; adult/student Sfr5/3; ◷ 10am-5pm Wed-Sun Easter–early Nov). The brew of tribal relics from far-off countries includes a collection of masks and statues soaked in sexuality. Take bus No 1 to get there.

Chomp into some cocoa culture at the **Museo del Cioccolato Alprose** (☎ 091 611 88 56; www .alprose.ch; Via Rompada 36, Casalano; adult/child Sfr4/1; ◷ 9am-6pm Mon-Fri, 9am-5pm Sat & Sun). This is a great place to take the children or anyone with a sweet tooth. As well as getting a choc-olate-coated history lesson, you can watch the sugary substance being made. Get there by the Ferrovia Ponte Tresa train (Sfr6).

Activities

East of the Cassarate stream is the **Lido** (per day Sfr6; ◷ 9.30am-6pm May-Jun & Sep, 9.30am-7.30pm Jul-Aug, reduced opening hr rest of the year), with beaches and a swimming pool.

See the official guide for information about water-skiing and windsurfing. **Club Nautico-Lugano** (☎ 091 649 61 39) charges Sfr10 per hour for windsurfing. Pedalos near the boat land-ing can be rented for Sfr16 per hour.

MARIO BOTTA IN THE PINK

Lugano's Mario Botta (born 1943 in Men-drisio to the south) has made an interna-tional name for himself as a leading light in contemporary architecture. Best known for his work abroad (like San Francisco's Museum of Modern Art and the Kyobo Tower in Seoul), Botta has also left an in-delible mark on and around Lugano. The grand 12-storey Casino in Campione d'Italia is one example. Botta seems to have a thing about right angles and the colour pink. In the centre of town, his landmarks include the **Banca del Gottardo** (Via San Franscini 12), a series of interconnected monoliths; the pink brick office block at **Via Pretorio 9** (known to locals as the Cherry Building because of the cherry tree planted on the roof); and the roof of the TPL local bus terminal on Corso Pestalozzi. At night it is illuminated…in a light pink.

Festivals & Events

This classy town takes in some classical tunes during the **Lugano Festival** from April to May in the Palazzo dei Congressi. Free open-air music festivals include **Estival Jazz** in early July and the **Blues to Bop Festival** at the end of August. The lake explodes in a display of pyrotechnical wizardry around midnight on 1 August, Switzerland's **Na-tional Day**.

Sleeping

Many hotels close for at least part of the winter.

BUDGET

Hostel Montarina (☎ 091 966 72 72; www.montarina .ch; Via Montarina 1; dm Sfr25) The Hostel Mon-tarina has rooms with four to 16 bunk beds. A buffet breakfast is available for Sfr12.

SYHA hostel (☎ 091 966 27 28; www.luganoyouth hostel.ch; Via Cantonale 13, Savosa; dm/s/d Sfr25/55/80; ◷ mid-Mar–Oct; ⏻) Housed in the Villa Sa-vosa, this is one of the more enticing youth hostels in the country. Take bus No 5 to Crocifisso. Breakfast costs Sfr8.

MIDRANGE

Hotel Pestalozzi (☎ 091 921 46 46; www.attuale.com /pestalozzi.html; Piazza Independenza 9; s/d with bath-room Sfr98/174; ⏼) A renovated Art Nouveau building, this is a good central deal. Rooms have a fresh feel, with crisp white and blues dominating the decoration. Some rooms have air-con. Cheaper ones have a shared bathroom in the corridor. The restaurant downstairs is a no-alcohol establishment.

Hotel Montarina (☎ 091 966 72 72; www.monta rina.ch; Via Montarina 1; s/d Sfr80/120; ◷ mid-Mar–Oct; ⏻ Ⓟ) Behind the train station is this charming hotel, whose best rooms are airy, with timber floors and antiques.

Hotel Federale (☎ 091 910 08 08; www.hotel-feder ale.ch; Via Regazzoni 8; s Sfr160, d Sfr190-260; ◷ Feb-Dec; Ⓟ ▱) If you can afford the grand top floor doubles with lake views, this place beats many multi-stellar places hands down. A short luggage-laden stumble from the train station, it is in a quiet spot with immacu-lately kept rooms and friendly staff. There is wi-fi in the lobby.

Hotel International au Lac (☎ 091 922 75 41; www.hotel-international.ch; Via Nassa 88; s/d Sfr185/298; ◷ Apr-Oct; Ⓟ ⏼ ⏻) From the balconies of the front rooms you will look straight out over Lago di Lugano the lake. These are the best, but other cheaper rooms are scattered about the hotel. Rooms are comfortable, with a smattering of antique furniture. Out the back is a pool within the walled garden.

TOP END

Villa Principe Leopoldo & Residence (☎ 091 985 88 55; www.leopoldohotel.com; Via Montalbano 5; s/d up to Sfr680/794; P ✕ ☒ ☐ ☒) This red-tiled residence set in sculptured gardens was built in 1926 for Prince Leopold von Hohenzollern, of the exiled German royal family. It oozes a regal, nostalgic atmosphere. The entrance looks away from the lake, but the gardens and many splendid rooms do not.

Eating

For pizza or overpriced pasta, any of the places around Piazza della Riforma are pleasant and lively enough.

Grand Café Al Porto (☎ 091 910 51 30; Via Pessina 3; ☽ 8am-6.30pm Mon-Sat) This café, which began life way back in 1803, has several fine rooms for dining too. Be sure to take a look at the frescoed Cenacolo Fiorentino, once a monastery dining hall, upstairs. It's used for private functions.

L'Antica Osteria del Porto (☎ 091 971 42 00; Via Foce 9; mains Sfr25-35; ☽ Wed-Mon) Set back from Lugano's sailing club, this is the place for savouring local fish and Ticinese dishes like brasato di manzo al Merlot con polenta gratinata e legume (grilled beef with polenta and vegetables). The terrace overlooking the Cassarate stream is pleasant, and you also have lake views.

Al Portone (☎ 091 923 55 11; Viale Cassarate 3; mains Sfr30-50; ☽ Tue-Sat) For an upmarket meal, this place remains a sure bet for demanding gourmands. It has a lunchtime set menu (Sfr58) and a tasting feast menu at night (Sfr120). How about guance di vitello confits al Merlot Redegonda e funghi (confit of veal cheeks in Ticino Merlot and mushrooms)?

San Bernardo (☎ 091 941 01 00; Tèra d'Súra; meals Sfr60-80; ☽ lunch & dinner Tue-Sat, lunch Sun) Head out of town for the warren of medieval alleys in Comano, where you'll discover this gourmet getaway. Opt for the summer pergola or muted designer dining room. The menu changes frequently and the emphasis is on slight twists to old recipes. The quadrotti di zucca (squares of pumpkin-filled

AUTHOR'S CHOICE

Bottegone del Vino (☎ 091 922 76 89; Via Magatti 3; mains Sfr30-45; ☽ Mon-Sat) Favoured by the local banking brigade at lunchtime, this is a great place to taste fine local wines over a well-prepared meal. The manzo marinato su letto di spinaci (marinated slices of uncooked beef on a bed of spinach) is perfect with a Merlot. The décor has a classic timelessness, with elegant timber furniture and cream table linen. Knowledgeable waiters fuss around the tables and are only too happy to suggest the perfect Ticino tipple to go with your food.

pasta with a sweetish chestnut sauce) melt in the mouth. Take a taxi.

Drinking

Soho Café (☎ 091 922 60 80; Corso Pestalozzi 3; ☽ 10-1am Mon-Fri, 4pm-1am Sat) So that's where they are! All those good-looking Lugano townies crowd in to this long, orange-lit bar for cocktails. Generally chilled DJ music is turned up enough to create a buzz but not so much you can't hear yourself talk.

La Lanchetta (☎ 091 971 55 51; Via Castagnola 16; ☽ 10am-midnight Sun-Thu, 10-1am Fri & Sat) Sitting on the lake opposite the Hotel Cassarate Lago, this hip, dimly lit bar is perfect for pre-dinner drinks. Furniture and dress sense is black, although there is a little tongue-shaped snug that glows white.

Desperados (☎ 091 921 11 97; Via al Forte 4; ☽ 10pm-5am) This late-night disco bar is hot, cramped and sweaty – in other words the perfect nightclub. The entrance is on a tiny square off Vicolo Orfanotrofio.

Shopping

Macelleria Gabbani (☎ 091 911 30 80; www.gabbani .ch; Via Pessina 12) You'll find it hard to miss the giant sausages hanging out the front of this irresistible delicatessen. The same people operate a tempting cheese shop, the **Bottega del Formaggio**, across the road.

Getting There & Away

AIR

From **Agno airport** (☎ 091 612 11 11; www.lugano -airport.ch), **Darwin Airline** (www.darwinairline.com) flies to London (City) via Bern, Rome (Fiumicino), Geneva and Olbia (in Sardinia).

TICINO

Flybaboo (www.flybaboo.com) flies to Geneva and **Swiss** (www.swiss.com) to Zürich.

BUS

Lugano is on the same road and rail route as Bellinzona. To St Moritz, one postal bus runs direct via Italy at least Friday to Sunday (daily late June to mid-October and late December to early January). The cost is Sfr67 (plus Sfr15 if you are using Swiss travel passes for a reduction) and it takes four hours. Reserve at the bus station, the train station information office or on ☎ 091 807 85 20. All postal buses leave from the main bus depot at Via Serafino Balestra, but you can pick up the St Moritz and some other buses outside the train station 15 minutes later.

TRAIN & BOAT

For further train and boat information, see p290 and right.

CAR & MOTORCYCLE

You can hire cars at **Hertz** (☎ 091 923 46 75; Via San Gottardo 13) and **Avis** (☎ 091 913 41 51; Via Clemente Maraini 14).

Getting Around

A shuttle bus runs to the airport from Piazza Manzoni (one way/return Sfr10/18) and the train station (Sfr8/15). Get timetables from the tourist office. A **taxi** (☎ 091 971 21 21, 091 971 91 91) to the airport costs around Sfr20.

Bus No 1 runs from Castagnola in the east through the centre to Paradiso, while bus No 2 runs from central Lugano to Paradiso via the train station. A single trip costs Sfr1.20 to Sfr2 (ticket dispensers indicate the appropriate rate) or it's Sfr5 for a one-day pass. The main local bus terminus in central Lugano is on Corso Pestalozzi.

AROUND LUGANO

The tourist office has picked out some of the best lakeside walks and written guides on them. If you'd rather float than use your feet, relaxing in a boat can be a blast.

For a bird's eye view of Lugano and the lake, head for the hills. The **funicular** (☎ 091 971 31 71; www.montebre.ch; one way/return Sfr14/20) from Cassarate (walk or take Bus No 1 from central Lugano) scales Monte Brè (925m). From Cassarate a first funicular takes you to Suvigliana (free up, Sfr1.60 down) to

connect with the main funicular. Or take bus No 12 from the main post office to Brè village and walk about 15 minutes.

From Paradiso, the **funicular** (☎ 091 985 28 28; www.montesansalvatore.ch; one way/return Sfr17/24) to Monte San Salvatore operates from mid-March to mid-November. Aside from the views, the walk down to Paradiso or Melide is an hour well spent. Children aged five to 16 pay half and those under five travel for free.

LAGO DI LUGANO

Much can be seen in one day if you don't fancy a longer excursion. Boats are operated by the **Società Navigazione del Lago di Lugano** (☎ 091 971 52 23; www.lakelugano.ch). Examples of return fares from Lugano are Gandria (Sfr19.80), Melide (Sfr30.40 with entry to Swissminiatur included) and Morcote (Sfr28.90). If you want to visit several places, buy a pass: one/three days cost Sfr34/51 and one week costs Sfr62. There are reduced fares for children.

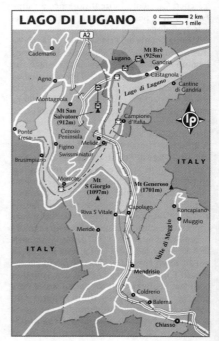

The departure point from Lugano is by Piazza della Riforma. Boats sail year-round, but the service is more frequent from late March to late October. During this time some boats go as far as Ponte Tresa, so you could go one way by boat and return to Lugano on the Ponte Tresa train. The Swiss Pass is valid and the Half-Fare Card gets reductions.

Trains run to Melide (Sfr3.20, six minutes). For Morcote (Sfr7.80, 30 minutes), get the bus from the Paradiso train station.

GANDRIA

Gandria is an attractive, compact village almost dipping into the water. A popular trip is to take the boat from Lugano and walk back along the shore to Castagnola (around 40 minutes), where you can visit Villa Heleneum and/or Villa Favorita, or simply continue back to Lugano by foot or bus No 1.

Across the lake from Gandria is the **Museo delle Dogane Svizzere** (Swiss Customs Museum; ☎ 091 923 98 43; admission free; ☼ 1.30-5.30pm late Mar–early Oct), at Cantine di Gandria, and accessible by boat. It tells the history of customs (and more interestingly smuggling) in this border area. On display are confiscated smugglers' boats that once operated on the lake.

CAMPIONE D'ITALIA

It's hard to tell, but this really is a part of Italy surrounded by Switzerland. There are no border formalities (but take your passport anyway); many cars in the village have Swiss number plates and they use Swiss telephones and Swiss francs.

Euros (and any other hard currency), however, are equally welcome as there are none of the Swiss restrictions on gambling in Campione d'Italia. The 12-storey **casino** (☎ 091 640 11 11; www.casinocampione.it; admission free; ☼ noon-5am), converted by Lugano's favourite architect, Mario Botta, into Europe's biggest in 2005, does a brisk business. Smart dress is required. From noon to midnight you can take the No 39 bus from Lugano's Piazza Manzoni (one way/return Sfr7.40/12.80) to Campione d'Italia. The last return bus leaves at 12.40am, and then there's one at 6.39am.

MONTE GENEROSO

The fine panorama provided by this summit (1701m) includes lakes, Alps and the Apennines on a clear day. It can be reached by boat (except in winter), train (Sfr5.40) or car to Capolago, then the rack and pinion **train** (☎ 091 630 51 11; www.montegeneroso.ch; adult/ under 5/6-12yr/senior & student return Sfr38/free/19/29; ☼ up to 10 a day Apr-Oct & early Dec–early Jan).

CERESIO PENINSULA

South of Lugano, this peninsula is created by the looping shoreline of Lake Lugano. Walking trails dissect the interior and small villages dot the lakeside. The postal bus from Lugano to Morcote goes via either Melide or Figino, and departs approximately hourly. Year-round boats also connect Morcote and Melide to Lugano.

Montagnola

The German novelist Hermann Hesse (1877–1962) chose to live in this small town in 1919 after the horrors of WWI had separated him from his family. As the years wore on and crisis followed crisis in Germany, topped by the rise of the Nazis, he saw little reason to return home. He wrote some of his greatest works here, at first in an apartment in Casa Camuzzi. Nearby, in Torre Camuzzi, is the **Museo Hermann Hesse** (☎ 091 993 37 70; www.hessemontagnola .ch; Torre Camuzzi; adult/child Sfr6/5; ☼ 10am-12.30pm & 2-6.30pm Tue-Sun Mar-Oct, 10am-12.30pm & 2-6.30pm Sat & Sun Nov-Feb). Personal objects, some of the thousands of watercolours he painted in Ticino, books and other odds and ends help re-create something of Hesse's life. From Lugano, get the Ferrovia Ponte Tresa train to Sorengo and change for a postal bus (Sfr3.20, 37 minutes).

Melide

Melide is a bulge of shore from which the A2 motorway slices across the lake. The main attraction is **Swissminiatur** (☎ 091 640 10 60; www.swissminiatur.ch; adult/child Sfr13/7; ☼ 9am-6pm mid-Mar–end Oct), where you'll find 1:25 scale models of more than 120 national attractions. It's the quick and easy way to see Switzerland in a day.

Morcote

With its narrow cobbled lanes and endless nooks and crannies, this peaceful former fishing village (population 710) clusters at the foot of Monte Abostora. Narrow stairways lead to **Chiesa di Santa Maria del Sasso**, a 15-minute climb. Views are excellent, and the church has frescoes (16th century) and carved faces on the organ. From there continue another 15 minutes upstairs to **Vico di Morcote**, a pleasant high altitude hamlet. About 5km further is Carona, worth a visit for the **Parco Botanico San Grato** (admission free). Apart from a stroll, you can see displays of **falconry** (adult/child/student Sfr14/10/12; 11am & 3pm Mon-Sat, 11am, 3pm & 5pm Sun & holidays).

Parco Scherrer (091 996 21 25; adult/child /student & senior Sfr7/1/5; 10am-5pm mid-Mar–Oct, to 6pm Jul & Aug), 400m left (west) from the boat stop, offers a bustling range of architectural styles, including copies of famous buildings and generic types (eg Temple of Nefertiti, Siamese teahouse). It's all set in subtropical parkland.

There are several lakeside sleeping options. **Albergo della Posta** (091 996 11 27; www.hotelmor cote.com; Piazza Grande; s/d Sfr135/190) has charming little rooms (10 in all), most with views across the lake. It has its own restaurant.

The walk along the shore to Melide takes around 50 minutes.

MENDRISIO & AROUND
pop 6640 / elevation 354m

South of Lago di Lugano is the Mendrisiotto and Lower Ceresio. It is a fine area for walking tours around the rolling valleys and unspoilt villages. Mendrisio is the district capital and has a useful **tourist office** (091 646 57 61; www.mendrisiotourism.ch). It has several interesting old churches and buildings, and is worth a visit for the **Maundy Thursday Procession** or the **Wine Harvest** in September.

For a good value bite, seek **Trattoria Romano Nuovo** (091 646 11 89; Via Andreoni 20; set lunch Sfr12, mains Sfr12-25; Mon-Sat), a family-run spot with abundant Ticino dishes and, better still, offerings from the owners' native Emilia in Italy (such as tortellini and tagliatelle).

Postal buses run from Lugano (Sfr6.60).

Exiting southeast from Mendrisio, a side road leads about 15km uphill and north along the **Valle di Muggio**, known for its cheese. This pretty drive ends abruptly in the hamlet of **Roncapiano**. Hiking enthusiasts

---

WHAT'S COOKING IN TICINO?

If eating and drinking is your idea of a great time, Ticino is a must-visit. It's not just about standard pizza and pasta either. Some of your most satisfying eating experiences in Ticino will happen in *grotti*, rustic, out-of-the-way eateries, where in the warmer months you can sit outside at granite tables for wholesome local fare. Some are mentioned in this chapter, but fan(atic)s might want to track down the tri-lingual *Guida a Grotti e Osterie*, available in bookshops in Lugano and Locarno.

What rösti is to the Swiss Germans, polenta is to the people of Ticino. This maize-based staple alone is stodgy, but coupled with other ingredients becomes another ballgame. You might find it with *brasato* (braised beef) or *capretto in umido alla Mesolcinese*, a tangy kid meat stew with a touch of cinnamon and cooked in red wine. Polenta is good served with any game meat *(cacciagione)* in autumn.

Cazzöla is a meat dish with a savoury selection teaming up on one plate, served with cabbage and potatoes. More delicate dishes include *cicitt* (small sausages) and *mazza casalinga* (a selection of delicatessen cuts).

Plenty of enticing dishes from Italy have found their way over the border. Indeed, many restaurants in Ticino are run by Italians. Risotto (rice-based) dishes are common. A good version is with *funghi* (mushrooms), especially in autumn during the mushroom-picking season.

Down on lakes Lugano and Maggiore expect to find fish on the menus, especially *persico* (perch), *coregone* (whitefish) and *salmerino* (a cross between salmon and trout, only smaller).

Various cheeses are produced in Ticino. *Robiola* is a soft cow's milk cheese that comes in small discs. A cool, fresh alternative is *robiolino*, tubes of cow's milk cheese. Goat's cheese can also be found, along with various types of *formaggella*, a harder, crusty cheese.

Portions tend to be generous in Ticino, so the Italian habit of eating a *primo* (first course, generally of pasta) followed by a *secondo* (main) is by no means obligatory. Prices often make such gluttony onerous on the bank account anyway. Another common option is to have *mezza porzione* (half serving) of a first course and then a full serve of a second course.

For some broader tips on Swiss food and wine, see p51.

could start a climb of 2½ hours to **Monte Generoso** from here.

MERIDE
pop 330 / elevation 583m

The **Museo dei Fossili** (Fossil Museum; ☎ 091 646 37 80; www.montesangiorgio.ch; admission free; ☼ 8am-6pm) in Meride, to the northwest of Mendrisio town, displays vestiges of the first creatures to inhabit the region – reptiles and fish dating back more than 200 million years. It may sound a little dry but the finds are important enough to warrant Unesco recognition of the area around Monte San Giorgio (where they were uncovered) as a World Heritage site in 2003. Near the town is a circular **nature trail.** You can reach Meride from Lugano by postal bus (Sfr10.40).

LOCARNO

pop 14,320 / elevation 205m

With its palm trees and much vaunted 2300 hours of sunshine a year, Locarno has attracted northern tourists to its warm, Mediterranean-style setting since the late 19th century. The lowest town in Switzerland, it seemed like a soothing spot to host the 1925 peace conference intended to bring stability to Europe after WWI. Long before, the Romans had appreciated its strategic position on the lake and Maggia river for trade.

Orientation & Information

Five minutes' walk west of the train station is the town's core, Piazza Grande. The **tourist office** (☎ 091 791 00 91; www.maggiore.ch; Largo Zorzi 1; ☼ 9am-6pm Mon-Fri, 10am-6pm Sat & holidays, 10am-1.30pm & 2.30-5pm Sun mid-Mar–Oct, 9.30am-noon & 1.30-5pm Mon-Fri, 10am-noon & 1.30-5pm Sat Nov–mid-Mar) is nearby. Ask about the Lago Maggiore Guest Card and its discounts.

Piazza Grande is home to the post office, a shopping arcade and cafés with outside tables. North and west of the piazza is the old part of town *(città vecchia)*.

Sights
SANTUARIO DELLA MADONNA DEL SASSO

Overlooking the town, this sanctuary was built after the Virgin Mary supposedly appeared in a vision to a monk, Bartolomeo d'Ivrea, in 1480. There's a small **museum**

(☎ 091 743 62 65; Via del Santuario 2; adult/student & child Sfr2.50/1.50; ☼ 2-5pm), a **church** (☼ 8am-6.45pm) and several rather rough, near life-size statue groups (including one of the Last Supper) in niches on the stairway. The best-known painting in the church is *La Fuga in Egitto* (Flight to Egypt), painted in 1522 by Bramantino.

Contrasting in style are the naive votive paintings by the church entrance, where the Madonna and Child appear as ghostly apparitions in life-and-death situations.

A funicular runs every 15 minutes from the town centre (Sfr4.50 up, Sfr6.60 return) past the sanctuary to Orisella, but the 20-minute walk up is not all that demanding (take Via al Sasso off Via Cappuccini) in spite of being a chapel lined path known as the Via Crucis.

OLD TOWN

Plod the Italianate piazzas and arcades, and admire the Lombard houses. There are some interesting churches. Built in the 17th century, the **Chiesa Nuova** (New Church; Via Cittadella) has an almost sickeningly ornate baroque ceiling. Outside, left of the entrance, stands a giant statue of St Christopher with disproportionately tiny feet. The 16th-century **Chiesa di San Francesco** (Piazza San Francesco) has frescoes by Baldassare Orelli, while the **Chiesa di Sant'Antonio** is best known for its altar to the *Cristo Morto* (Dead Christ).

Castello Visconteo (Piazza Castello; adult/student Sfr7/5; ☼ 10am-noon & 2-5pm Tue-Sun), dating from the 15th century and named after the Visconti clan that long ruled Milan, today houses a museum with Roman and Bronze Age exhibits. Locarno is believed to have been a glass-manufacturing town in Roman times, which accounts for the strong showing of glass artefacts in the museum. This labyrinth of a castle, whose nucleus was raised around the 10th century, also hosts a small display (in Italian) on the Locarno Treaty.

Activities

From the Orisella funicular stop, a cable car goes to **Cardada**, and then a chair lift soars to **Cimetta** (www.cardada.ch in Italian and German; return adult/6-16yr Sfr33/11; ☼ 8am-8pm Mon-Sat Jun-Sep, 9am-6pm Mon-Thu, 8am-8pm Fri & Sat Oct-May) at 1672m. From either stop there are fine views and walking trails. Paragliding is possible up here, as is winter skiing.

TICINO

Locarno's climate is perfect for lolling about the lake. **Giardini Jean Arp** (Jean Arp Gardens) is a lakeside park off Lungolago Motta, with sculptures by the surrealist artist scattered among the palm trees. It is free to swim in various convenient spots around the lake.

Festivals & Events

Locarno has hosted the two-week **Festival Internazionale di Film** (International Film Festival; ☎ 091 756 21 21; www.pardo.ch; Via Luini 3, CH-6600 Locarno), which has been held in August, since 1948. Cinemas are used during the day but at night, films are screened in the open air on a giant screen set up in the Piazza Grande.

Sleeping

Vecchia Locarno (☎ 091 751 65 02; www.hotel-vecchia-locarno.ch; Via della Motta 10; s/d Sfr50/95) Rooms are gathered around a sunny internal courtyard, evoking a Mediterranean mood, and some have views over the old town centre and hills. The digs are simple enough, but comfortable (heaters are provided in the colder months). Bathrooms are in the corridor.

Albergo Ristorante Citadella (☎ 091 751 58 85; www.cittadella.ch; Via Cittadella 18; s/d Sfr100/170) Aside from its well-known restaurant, this spot has a handful of pretty little rooms, individually decorated.

Grand Hotel Locarno (☎ 091 743 02 82; www.grand-hotel-locarno.ch; Via Sempione 17; s/d Sfr160/340; 🚫 🖳 🅿) Grand in name and looks, this

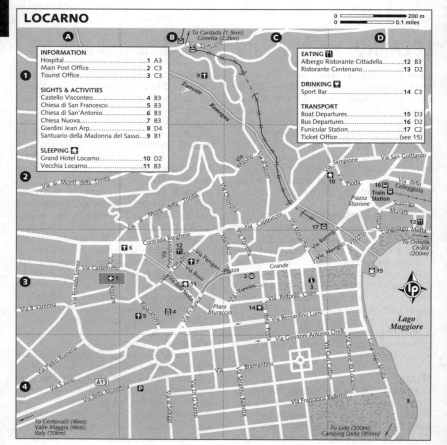

LOCARNO

INFORMATION	
Hospital	1 A3
Main Post Office	2 C3
Tourist Office	3 C3

SIGHTS & ACTIVITIES	
Castello Visconteo	4 B3
Chiesa di San Francesco	5 B3
Chiesa di San'Antonio	6 B3
Chiesa Nuova	7 B3
Giardini Jean Arp	8 D4
Santuario della Madonna del Sasso	9 B1

SLEEPING	
Grand Hotel Locarno	10 D2
Vecchia Locarno	11 B3

EATING	
Albergo Ristorante Cittadella	12 B3
Ristorante Centenario	13 D2

DRINKING	
Sport Bar	14 C3

TRANSPORT	
Boat Departures	15 D3
Bus Departures	16 D2
Funicular Station	17 C2
Ticket Office	(see 15)

To Cardada (1.5km);
Cimetta (2.2km)

To Osteria Chiara (200m)

Lago Maggiore

To Centovalli (4km);
Valle Maggia (4km);
Italy (10km)

To Lido (300m);
Camping Delta (850m)

AUTHOR'S CHOICE

Osteria Chiara (☎ 091 743 32 96; Vicolo della Chiara 1; pasta & mains Sfr15-30; ☺ Tue-Sat) Tucked away on a cobbled lane, this has all the cosy feel of a *grotto*. Sit at granite tables beneath the pergola or at timber tables by the fireplace for chunky dishes of *malfatti con zucca al timo* (big gnocchi-style pasta with pumpkin and thyme). From the lake follow the signs up Vicolo dei Nessi.

---

is an old-style relic of *belle époque* proportions standing in its own grounds. Rooms are a trifle faded but the best of them exude the luxury of bygone years in this historic building. Most of the 1925 Locarno peace talk delegations lodged here.

Camping Delta (☎ 091 751 60 81; www.campingdelta .com; camp sites Sfr37-47, plus per adult/child/senior & student Sfr18/6/16; ☺ Mar-Oct) Although pricey, this camping ground has great facilities and is brilliantly located between the shores of Lago Maggiore and the Maggia river.

Eating

Albergo Ristorante Cittadella (☎ 091 751 58 85; Via Cittadella 18; mains Sfr30-50; ☺ Tue-Sun) This is the place to go if you enjoy fine fish – the upstairs section does not serve anything else. Downstairs the menu is not quite so focused on the aquatic and includes pizza for Sfr12 to Sfr19.50.

Ristorante Centenario (☎ 091 743 82 22; Lungolago Motta 17; set meals Sfr58-130, mains Sfr40-55; ☺ Tue-Sat) Although some think Locarno's temple to French *haute cuisine* is a trifle stuffy, this lakeside gem is a guarantee of fine dining. Making no concessions to anyone, even the menu is in French. Tuck into some *carré d'agneau rôti au romarin* (roast lamb cooked in rosemary).

Drinking

Sport Bar (Via della Posta 4; ☺ 8-1am Mon-Fri, 10-1am Sat, 2pm-1am Sun) A fairly run-of-the-mill place by day, this rough and tumble bar with the red walled dance space out the back and beer garden on the side is an extremely popular hangout with Locarno's young and restless.

Getting There & Away

Trains run every one to two hours from Brig (Sfr50, 2½ hours), passing through Italy (bring your passport). Change trains at Domodossola.

Postal buses to the surrounding valleys leave from outside the train station, and boats (see below) from near Piazza Grande. There is cheap parking (per day SFr3) along Via della Morettina.

AROUND LOCARNO
Lago Maggiore

Only the northeast corner of Lago Maggiore is in Switzerland; the rest slices into Italy's Lombardy region. **Navigazione Lago Maggiore** (NLM; ☎ 091 751 61 40; www.navigazione laghi.it) operates boats across the entire lake. Limited day passes cost Sfr13.40, but the Sfr23 version is valid for the entire Swiss basin. There are various options for visiting the Italian side of the lake.

Ascona

Ascona is Locarno's smaller twin (population 5060) across the Maggia river delta.

SIGHTS & ACTIVITIES

The late 19th century saw the arrival of 'back to nature' utopians and anarchists from northern Europe in Ascona. Their aspirations and eccentricities are the subject of the **Museo Casa Anatta** (☎ 091 791 01 81; www.mon teverita.org; Via Collina 78; adult/student & senior Sfr6/4; ☺ 3-7pm Tue-Sun Jul & Aug, 2.30-6pm Tue-Sun Apr-Jun & Sep-Oct) on Monte Verità (take the small bus to Buxi from the post office; Sfr1).

The **Museo Comunale d'Arte Moderna** (☎ 091 759 81 40; Via Borgo 34; adult/concession Sfr7/5; ☺ 10am-noon & 3-6pm Tue-Sat, 4-6pm Sun), in Palazzo Pancaldi, includes paintings by artists connected with the town, among them Paul Klee, Ben Nicholson, Alexej Jawlensky and Hans Arp.

The **Collegio Papio** (Via Cappelle), now a high school, boasts a fine Lombard courtyard and includes the 15th-century **Chiesa Santa Maria della Misericordia**, with medieval frescoes.

For 55 years Ascona has hosted **Settimane Musicali**, an international classical music festival lasting from the end of August to mid-October.

SLEEPING & EATING

Ascona is bursting with hotels and eateries, especially along the lakefront.

Ristorante Antica Posta (☎ 091 791 04 26; www .ti-gastro.ch/anticaposta; Via Borgo; s/d Sfr100/200) Aside from having a pleasant restaurant gathered around an internal courtyard, this place offers 10 simple rooms in the heart of town.

Ristorante della Carrà (☎ 091 791 44 52; Via Carràdei Nasi; mains Sfr25-45; ☯ daily) Hidden inside off the street is this cosy courtyard with pergola, along with the inside dining area. Consider the *costata fiorentina alla griglia* (Sfr44), a grilled slab of prime beef. Fish is also available.

Castello del Sole (☎ 091 791 02 02; www.castellodelsole.com; Via Muraccio 142; s/d up to Sfr410/780; P ⌘ ⌾) One of the most enticing upper range hotels in Ticino is set in magnificent gardens; this is *the* place to pamper yourself.

GETTING THERE & AWAY

Bus No 31 from Locarno's train station and Piazza Grande stops at Ascona's post office with departures every 15 minutes (Sfr2.80). Boat services on Lago Maggiore stop at Ascona.

WESTERN VALLEYS

The valleys ranging to the north and west of Locarno team with grey stone villages, gushing mountain streams, cosy retreats, traditional *grotti* and there are some endless walking opportunities.

CENTOVALLI

The 'hundred valleys' is the westward valley route to Domodossola in Italy, known on the Italian side as Val Vigezzo.

As you head west of the busy traffic junction of Ponte Brolla (with several fine eateries), 4km west of Locarno, the road winds out in a string of tight curves, often with surprisingly heavy traffic, high on the north flank of the Melezzo stream, which is largely held in check by a dam.

The quiet towns with their stone houses and heavy slate roofs, mostly high above the road and railway line on either side of the valley, make tranquil bases for mountain hikes. Among the best stops are **Verdasio**, **Rasa** and **Bordei**. Rasa is only accessible by cable car from Verdasio. **Ristorante al Pentolino** (☎ 091 780 81 00; d Sfr120; restaurant ☯ Wed-Sun), in the heart of Verdasio, offers nicely renovated rooms. You can enjoy hearty cooking at any time of the day (11am to 10.30pm, Sfr30 to Sfr35) at the granite tables beneath the pergola.

At **Re**, on the Italian side, there is a procession of pilgrims on 30 April each year, a tradition that originated when a painting of the Madonna was reported to have started bleeding when struck by a ball in 1480. More startling than the legend is the bulbous basilica built in the name of the Madonna del Sangue (Madonna of the Blood) in 1922–50.

A picturesque train along the valley, trundling across numerous precarious-looking viaducts, leaves from Locarno for Domodossola (Sfr30 return, two hours each way). There are up to 11 departures a day. Take your passport.

VALLE ONSERNONE

Once known for its granite mines, this is one of the least visited of Ticino's valleys. About 10km west of Locarno along the Centovalli route, take a right at Cavigliano and swing northwest into barely inhabited territory. Clusters of stone houses form attractive hamlets along the way.

Shortly after Russo, a west branch road leads to **Spruga** (a popular starting point for walks with Swiss German visitors). The main road curves further north into the **Val Vergeletto**, whose main town bears the same name. It is a quiet, old place, except for the roar of the mountain stream past its houses and church. About 2km further west is the delightful **Locanda Zott** (☎ 091 797 10 98; r per person half-board Sfr66), with its child-friendly atmosphere, busy downstairs restaurant and renovated rooms upstairs, some with their own shower. The road peters out 6km west and the territory is great for hiking.

Make the excursion to nearby **Gresso**, perched high above Vergeletto at 999m. The views are great from this unadorned, close-knit hamlet where you may find a lone *osteria* open for lunch.

Up to five daily buses run from Locarno to Spruga. Change at Russo for Vergeletto and Gresso.

VALLE MAGGIA

This mostly broad, sunny valley follows the river of the same name from Ponte Brolla, passing small villages, until at Cevio (the valley's main town) it splits, the first of several divisions into smaller valleys. The valley's **tourist office** (☎ 091 753 28 85; www.vallemaggia.ch) is in Maggia.

Among the earlier villages, **Modegno** and **Aurigeno** are worth a stop and look around. The former is a quiet conglomeration of grey stone houses, while the latter is known for its colourful frescoes. **Maggia** itself is handy for stocking up at the supermarket but otherwise without great charm.

Cevio, 12km northwest, holds more interest. Admire the colourful façade of the 16th-century **Pretorio**, covered in the family coats-of-arms of many of the town's rulers, mostly in the 17th century. About 1km away, the core of the old town is graced with 16th-century mansions. A short walk away (signposted) are *grotti*, cellars carved out of great blocks of granite that tumbled onto the town here in a landslide. There is a handful of hotels and eateries here.

Take the road for Bosco Gurin and after 1km, a side road to **Boschetto** that leads over a stream (note the riverside *grotti* of **Rovana**). This mostly abandoned hamlet is a starting point for local walks and has a haunting quality.

The road to Bosco Gurin slices up in seemingly endless hairpin bends to **Cerentino**, where the road forks. You have a couple of eating options here. The right fork leads 5.5km to **Bosco Gurin**, a minor ski centre (with a couple of hotels) and pleasantly sun-kissed high pasture village of slate-roofed, white-washed houses. It is the only town in Ticino where the majority language is German, a heritage of Valais immigrants. The other fork from Cerentino leads up the 8km-long **Valle di Campo** along a winding forest road to another broad, sunny, upland valley. The prettiest of its towns is **Campo**, with its scattered houses and Romanesque belltower. The valley is closed off (great views) by **Cimalmotto**, where you can stay and eat in the rustic **Pensione Alpina** (☎ 091 754 11 91; www .pensionealpina.ch; r per person Sfr45; ✆ Apr–Oct).

Back in Cevio, the Valle Maggia road continues 3km to Bignasco, where you turn west for the **Val Bavona**, the prettiest of them all. A smooth road follows a mountain stream on its course through narrow meadows cradled between steep rocky walls. Its series of tightly huddled stone and slate-roofed hamlets is protected by a local foundation, but only inhabited from April to October. The valley sees no direct sunlight from November to February. For all that, its hamlets are irresistible. **Foroglio**

is dominated by a powerful waterfall (a 10-minute walk away) and home to **Ristorante La Froda** (☎ 091 754 11 81; meals Sfr45; ✆ daily Apr–Oct). Sit at one of five timber tables by a crackling fire for heaped serves of melt-in-the-mouth *stinco di maiale* (pork shank), served with the best polenta you are likely to taste. Wash down with a glass of Merlot. On summer days, lunch on the terrace in view of the waterfall.

At the end of the valley, just after San Carlo, a **cable car** (adult/child return Sfr20/10; ✆ mid-Jun–mid-Oct) rides up to the **Robiei dam** and nearby lakes, great for a day's hiking. A bus runs four times a day from Bignasco to San Carlo, from April to October.

From Bignasco it is 17km to **Fusio**, another pretty town surrounded by woods at the head of the **Val Lavizzara**. Stop in **Mogno** on the way to see the extraordinary 1996 cylindrical church designed by Mario Botta. The grey (Maggia granite) and white (marble from Peccia) interior doorway has a strangely neo-Romanesque air. From Fusio the road leads to the dam holding back the emerald **Lago Sambuco**, from where you can hike on to other artificial lakes as well as north over the mountains into Valle Leventina. In Fusio, the **Antica Osteria Dazio** (☎ 091 755 11 62; www.hats.ch; s/d Sfr170/220; ✆ Mar–Nov; ℗) is a beautifully renovated place to sleep, with loads of timber and Alpine charm. It has a restaurant, too.

Regular buses run from Locarno to Cevio and Bignasco, from where you make less regular connections into the side valleys.

VAL VERZASCA

About 4km northeast of Locarno, this rugged 26km valley snakes north past the impressive Vogorno dam, which is fed by the gushing Verzasca (green waters), a delightful river whose white stones lend the transparent mountain water a scintillating emerald hue.

Just beyond the Vogorno lake, look to the left and you will see the picture-postcard hamlet of **Corripo** seemingly pasted on to the thickly wooded mountain flank. To reach it you cross the **Gola Verzasca**, a delightful little gorge. Up in Corripo you can eat (and possibly from 2006, sleep) at the basic **Osteria Corripo** (☎ 091 745 18 71; pasta Sfr12; ✆ Wed-Mon Apr-Oct).

About 5km upstream, **Lavertezzo** is known for its narrow, double-humped, Romanesque bridge (rebuilt from scratch after the 1951

TICINO

floods destroyed it) and natural pools in the icy stream. Be careful, as storms upstream can turn the river into a raging torrent in no time. Stay at riverside **Osteria Vittoria** (☎ 091 746 15 81; s/d Sfr100/149), a bustling family lodge with its own restaurant and garden. Most rooms have balconies with views over the Verzasca.

Another 12km takes you to **Sonogno**, a once abandoned hamlet at the head of the valley that has been resuscitated largely due to tourism.

Postal buses operate to Sonogno from Locarno only every two hours (Sfr17, 70 minutes).

Liechtenstein

If Liechtenstein didn't exist, someone would have invented it. A tiny mountain principality governed by an iron-willed monarch in the heart of 21st-century Europe, it certainly has novelty value.

Only 25km long by 6km wide – just larger than Manhattan – Liechtenstein doesn't have an international airport, and access from Switzerland is by local bus. However, the country proves to be a rich banking state and the world's largest exporter of false teeth.

Liechtensteiners sing different German lyrics to the tune of God Save the Queen in their national anthem, but they sure hope the Lord preserves theirs. For while head of state Prince Hans Adam II and his son, Prince Alois, have constitutional powers unprecedented in Europe, the royal presence helps give this theme-park micro-nation its tourist appeal.

Most come to Liechtenstein just to say they've been, and tour buses regularly disgorge day-trippers in search of souvenir passport stamps. But, if you're going to make the effort to come this way, it's pointless not to venture further, however briefly. With friendly locals and magnificent views, the place comes into its own away from soulless modern Vaduz.

In fact, the more you read about Fürstentum Liechtenstein (FL) the easier it is to see it as the model for Ruritania – the mythical kingdom conjured up in fiction as diverse as *The Prisoner of Zenda* and Evelyn Waugh's *Vile Bodies*.

Someone would have invented it? Oh, they did.

LIECHTENSTEIN

HIGHLIGHTS

- Getting a souvenir passport stamp and sending a postcard
- Climbing the short trail up to **Schloss Vaduz** (p308) for wonderful views
- Journeying uphill to **Triesenberg** (p310) to learn about the Walser community
- Taking the family to **Malbun** (p310) for undemanding hiking and skiing
- Indulging in some extreme hiking along the legendary **Fürstensteig trail** (p310)

★ Fürstensteig Trail

Schloss ★ Vaduz

★ Triesenberg

★ Malbun

■ POPULATION: 34,294 | ■ AREA: 160 SQ KM | ■ LANGUAGE: GERMAN

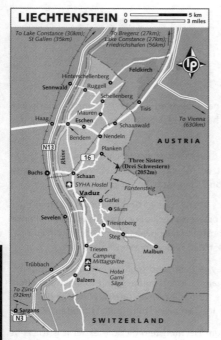

History

The country's history started when an Austrian prince, Johann Adam Von Liechtenstein, purchased the counties of Schellenberg (1699) and Vaduz (1712) from impoverished German nobles. Soon afterwards, the territory acquired his name and became a principality under the Holy Roman Empire. It gained independence in 1866, and in 1923 formed a customs union with Switzerland.

Even then, none of the ruling Liechtensteins had bothered to leave their Viennese palace to see the country. It wasn't until 1938 that Prince Franz Josef II became the first monarch to live in the principality, when he and his much-loved wife, Gina, began dramatically transforming a poor rural nation into today's rich banking state. Their son, Prince Hans Adam II, ascended the throne on the prince's death in 1989.

The country's use of the Swiss franc encourages people to see it as a mere extension of its neighbour, but Liechtenstein has very different foreign policies, having joined the UN and the European Economic Area (EEA) relatively early, in 1990 and 1995 respectively. Known as a tax haven, the principality banned customers from banking money anonymously in 2000, after allegations of money laundering. However, it remains under pressure to introduce more reforms.

In 2003, Hans Adam demanded sweeping powers to dismiss the elected government, appoint judges and reject proposed laws. Opponents warned of dictatorship, but the prince threatened to stomp off back to Austria if he didn't get his way, and the population – possibly worried about what an empty Schloss Vaduz would do to tourism – backed him in a referendum. The following year, Hans Adam handed the day-to-day running of the country to his son Alois, although he remains head of state.

IT'S LIECHTENSTEIN TRIVIA TIME!

- Liechtenstein is the only country in the world named after the people who purchased it.
- In its last military engagement in 1866, none of its 80 soldiers was killed. In fact, 81 returned, including a new Italian 'friend'. The army was disbanded soon afterwards.
- Low business taxes means 75,000 companies are registered here – twice the number of people.
- Worth UK£3.3 billion, the royal family is richer than any other in Europe, including the English monarchy.
- The surname of national football coach Ralf Loose is pronounced 'loser', which kind of suits his struggling team.
- Until 2005, Liechtenstein's cows were fed hemp – related to cannabis – to keep them chilled and producing 'better' milk. The practice was only stopped after worries about the active drug THC reaching the human food chain.

Orientation

Liechtenstein is slightly larger than Manhattan but feels much smaller, because two-thirds is mountainous. A thin plain – the basin of the River Rhine separating Liechtenstein from Switzerland – runs down the country's western edge. The main north–south thoroughfare follows this.

The plain is wider and lower in the north, which is called the Unterland (lowland), while the south is described as the Oberland (highland).

Entering the country from Buchs, you first reach Schaan, which virtually merges into Vaduz and then Triesen further south. Further south still is Balzers. Entering from Sargans you do the journey in reverse.

From Triesen, you can take the steep, winding road west up to Triesenberg and Malbun (1600m).

North of Schaan are quiet villages like Planken and Schellenberg.

Information

Tourist information abroad is distributed by Switzerland Tourism (www.myswitzerland.com). Prices here are comparable to those in Switzerland. Shops usually open 8am to noon and 1.30pm to 6.30pm Monday to Friday, and 8am to 4pm Saturday, although souvenir shops also open on high-season Sundays. Banks open the same weekday hours, except they shut around 4.30pm. The country now runs its own postal and phone systems, but continues to use Swiss currency.

Devoutly Catholic, Liechtenstein takes off all the main religious feast days, plus Labour Day (1 May) and National Day (August 15), totalling a healthy 22 public holidays annually.

The official language is German, though most speak an Alemannic dialect. The Austrian 'Grüss Gott' is as common as the Swiss 'Grüezi'. English is widely spoken.

Getting There & Away

The nearest airports are Friedrichshafen (Germany) and Zürich, with train connections to the Swiss border towns of Buchs (via Romanshorn) and Sargans. From each of these towns there are usually three buses to Vaduz (Sfr2.40/3.60 from Buchs/Sargans, Swiss Pass valid). Buses run every 30 minutes from the Austrian border town of Feldkirch;

> **THE INSIDE READ**
>
> While Liechtenstein sounds quite wacky, in reality it has the reassuring familiarity of a small village where everyone knows everyone else's business. Liechtensteiners are warm-hearted folk who know what's important in life, as you soon realise reading Charlie Connelly's amusing *Stamping Grounds: Liechtenstein's Quest for the World Cup*. We don't mean it as a back-handed compliment when we say that football fan Connelly has managed to write possibly the longest and most engrossing book about Liechtenstein there's ever been.

you sometimes have to change at Schaan to reach Vaduz.

A few local Buchs–Feldkirch trains stop at Schaan (bus tickets are valid).

By road, route 16 from Switzerland passes through Liechtenstein via Schaan and ends at Feldkirch. The N13 follows the Rhine along the border; minor roads cross into Liechtenstein at each motorway exit.

Getting Around

Buses traverse the country. Single fares are Sfr2.40/3.60 for two/three zones, while a weekly bus pass costs Sfr10/5 per adult/child. The latter is available from post offices and tourist offices. Swiss travel passes are valid on all main routes. Timetables are posted at stops. Check when the last bus leaves, as some services finish early.

For bicycle hire, try the Swiss train stations in Buchs or Sargans, or **Sigi's Velo Shop** (☎ 384 27 50; www.sigis-veloshop.li; Balzers; per day from Sfr30).

For a taxi, try calling ☎ 233 35 35 or ☎ 232 18 66.

VADUZ

pop 5005 / elevation 455m

Poor Vaduz. It's all that most visitors to Liechtenstein see, and it feels like its soul has been sold to cater to the whims of its banks and the hordes of whirlwind tourists who alight for 17 minutes on guided bus tours. Souvenir shops, tax-free luxury-goods stores and cube-shaped concrete buildings dominate the antiseptic small pedestrian centre beneath the steep castle hill.

But don't be disheartened. Traces of the quaint village that existed just 50 years ago

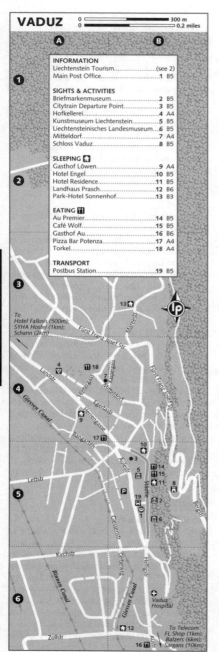

VADUZ

0 _____ 300 m
0 _____ 0.2 miles

INFORMATION
Liechtenstein Tourism.....................(see 2)
Main Post Office................................**1** B5

SIGHTS & ACTIVITIES
Briefmarkenmuseum.........................**2** B5
Citytrain Departure Point...................**3** B5
Hofkellerei..**4** A4
Kunstmuseum Liechtenstein..............**5** B5
Liechtensteinisches Landesmuseum...**6** B5
Mitteldorf..**7** A4
Schloss Vaduz...................................**8** B5

SLEEPING
Gasthof Löwen..................................**9** A4
Hotel Engel......................................**10** B5
Hotel Residence...............................**11** B5
Landhaus Prasch..............................**12** B6
Park-Hotel Sonnenhof......................**13** B3

EATING
Au Premier......................................**14** B5
Café Wolf...**15** B5
Gasthof Au.......................................**16** B6
Pizza Bar Potenza............................**17** A4
Torkel..**18** A4

TRANSPORT
Postbus Station................................**19** B5

To
Hotel Falknis (500m);
SYHA Hostel (1km);
Schaan (2km)

To Telecom
FL Shop (1km);
Balzers (6km);
Sargans (10km)

still exist, and there are a couple of good museums. Plus, there is the rest of the country to see…

Orientation

Two streets, Städtle and Äulestrasse, diverge and then rejoin, enclosing the centre of town. Everything of practical importance is near this small area, including the bus station and open-air car parking. Städtle is pedestrian only.

Information

Liechtenstein Tourism (☎ 239 63 00; www.touris mus.li; Briefmarkenmuseum, Städtle 37; ⏱ 9am-noon & 1.30-5pm daily May-Oct, 9am-noon & 1.30-5pm Mon-Fri Nov-Apr) Offers souvenir passport stamps for Sfr2, plus all usual assistance.
Main post office (Äulestrasse 38; ⏱ 7.45am-6pm Mon-Fri, 8-11am Sat)
Telecom FL Shop (☎ 237 74 00; Austrasse 77; ⏱ 9am-noon & 1.30-6.30pm Mon-Fri, 9am-1pm Sat) Free Internet access.

Sights & Activities

Schloss Vaduz (Vaduz Castle) looms over the capital from the hill above and although it's closed to the public, it's worth making the climb for the magnificent vistas. Take the path beside Hotel Engel and follow the signs; there's also a network of walking trails along the ridge. For a peek inside the castle grounds, arrive on 15 August, Liechtenstein's National Day, when there are magnificent fireworks and the prince invites all 34,294 Liechtensteiners over to his place for a glass of wine or beer.

In the centre, the well-designed **Liechtensteinisches Landesmuseum** (National Museum; ☎ 239 68 20; www.landesmuseum.li; Städtle 43; adult/concession Sfr8/5; ⏱ 10am-5pm Tue-Sun, to 8pm Wed) provides a surprisingly interesting romp through the principality's history, from medieval witchtrials and burnings to the manufacture of false teeth.

The mainstay of the **Kunstmuseum Liechtenstein** (☎ 235 030 00; www.kunstmuseum.li; Städtle 32; adult/concession Sfr8/5; ⏱ 10am-5pm Tue-Sun, to 8pm Thu) is temporary exhibitions of contemporary art, not the prince's collection of old masters, which was relocated to the Liechtenstein Museum in Vienna. There are some 20th-century classics on the ground floor.

The **Briefmarkenmuseum** (Postage Stamp Museum; ☎ 236 61 05; Städtle 37; admission free; ⏱ 10am-noon & 1.30-5pm), above the tourist office, is only mildly diverting. Liechtenstein once made a packet producing souvenir stamps for enthusiasts, but that market has been hit by the rise of email. Here you'll find all national stamps issued since 1912, and the post office has an adjoining **philatelic section** (8.30am-noon & 1.30-4.30pm Mon-Fri) for collectors.

To see how Vaduz once looked, head northeast from the pedestrian zone to **Mitteldorf**. This and the surrounding streets form a charming quarter of traditional houses and verdant gardens. Nearby lies the prince's wine cellar, the **Hofkellerei** (232 10 18; www.hofkellerei.li; Feldstrasse 4). It is possible to sample the wines here only in a large group and if you have booked.

Every afternoon from May to October at 4.30pm, a touristy **Citytrain** (777 34 90; www .citytrain.li; adult/child Sfr9/5) makes a 35-minute circuit of Vaduz.

Sleeping

Vaduz is the most convenient base, but other towns are more charming for longer stays, so ask the tourist office.

Hotel Engel (236 17 17; www.hotelengel.li; Städtle 13; s/d from Sfr110/165; ☐ ☒ ℗) Renovated Hotel Engel has modern but soulless rooms. There's an Asian restaurant (Thai and Chinese) wafting tempting aromas through the hallways, but the bonus for laptop-owners is free Internet in all the rooms.

Gasthof Löwen (232 00 66; www.hotel-loewen .li; Herrengasse 35; s Sfr210-255, d Sfr265-335; ℗) Historic and creakily elegant, this 600-year old guesthouse has eight spacious rooms with antique furniture and modern bathrooms. There's a cosy bar, fine-dining restaurant and a rear outdoor terrace overlooking grapevines and with views up at the castle.

Hotel Residence (239 20 20; www.residence .li; Städtle 23; s/d from Sfr195/260; ☒ ℗) Vaduz's newest hotel is a modern designer number with lots of seagrass and muted colour schemes.

Park-Hotel Sonnenhof (239 02 02; www.sonnen hof.li; Mareestrasse 29; s Sfr250-320, d Sfr300-490, s/d from Sfr360/460; ☒ closed Christmas/New Year; ☐ ℗ ☎) The staff's pride in this small luxury establishment is palpable. The rooms keep FIFA executives and business tycoons more than happy, while the hillside views, solarium, ornate restaurant, cobbled courtyards, tin-

AUTHOR'S CHOICE

Torkel (232 44 10; Hintergasse 9; dishes Sfr40-60; ☒ lunch & dinner Mon-Fri, dinner Sat) Just above the prince's vineyards sits His Majesty's ivy-clad restaurant, where Hans Adam II likes to take business colleagues. The garden terrace enjoys a wonderful perspective of the castle above, while the ancient, wood-lined interior is cosy in winter. Food mixes classic with modern and has a couple of unusual veggie options (eg Quorn steak with white-truffle jus).

kling fountains and manicured gardens all create a privileged atmosphere. Check out the sci-fi robot lawnmower, too!

Also available:

Landhaus Prasch (232 46 63; www.news.li/touri /prasch; Zollstrasse 16; s/d from Sfr100/120; ☒ Apr-Oct; ☎) Quaint place with a sauna and whirlpool.

Hotel Falknis (232 63 77; Landstrasse 92; s/d with shared bathroom Sfr55/110; ℗) Basic rooms some 15 minutes on foot north of the centre – or take the bus.

Eating

Pizza Bar Potenza (Herrengasse 9; Sfr12-20; ☒ 11am-7pm Mon-Sat) Delicious aromas waft from this deservedly popular deli-cum-pizzeria. There's not much seating, but most customers seem happy to stand at the benches, or take away.

Café Wolf (Städtle 29; mains Sfr16-36) This relaxed café and restaurant have pavement tables in summer and a menu that mixes Swiss and international cuisine.

Gasthof Au (232 11 17; Austrasse 2; mains Sfr15-32; ☒ Wed-Sun) Based on Charlie Connelly's humorous descriptions (see the boxed text The Inside Read, p307), we might not recommend staying at 'Griselda's', but the garden restaurant is known for its good local food.

Au Premier (232 22 22; Hotel Real, Städtle 21; menus Sfr95 & Sfr135) Hotel Real's historic rooms could do with freshening up, but its gourmet restaurant holds its own, with classic French and seasonal specialities artfully arranged on large white plates with the hotel crest. There are 20,000 bottles of wine in the cellar.

AROUND VADUZ
Sights

Away from the capital, one's impression of Liechtenstein swiftly improves, thanks to magnificent Alpine scenery.

LIECHTENSTEIN

LIECHTENSTEIN

Triesenberg (bus No 10 from Vaduz) is perched on a terrace above the Rhine Valley and has a **Heimatmuseum** (☎ 262 19 26; www .triesenberg.li; adult/concession Sfr2/1; 1.30-5.30pm Tue-Fri, 1.30-5pm Sat Sep-May; plus 2-5pm Sun Jun-Aug), which tells the intriguing story of the Walsers. This German-speaking 'tribe' from Valais emigrated across Europe in the 13th century and settled in many places, including Liechtenstein, where they still speak their own dialect.

Hinterschellenberg (bus No 50, 51 or 52 from Schaan Post) has a **monument** commemorating the night in 1945 when a band of 500 Russian soldiers crossed the border to escape slavery in the German army. There's a **restaurant** (☺ Fri-Tue) and you can usually walk across the Austrian border, and back, unimpeded.

In **Balzers** (bus No 1 from Vaduz) is the 13th-century **Burg Gutenberg**. Until recently, this castle belonged to a Liechtenstein woman and her Mexican film-producer husband who gave it an over-the-top interior. Now sold back to the state, it's only open for concerts, but cuts a striking figure on the horizon and boasts nice strolls in the vicinity.

Hiking

There are 400km of hiking trails. The tourist office produces a booklet *Wanderungen für Familien und Geniesser* (Hikes for families and connoisseurs) and sells the *Liechtenstein Hiking Map* (Sfr15.50).

The country's most famous trail is the **Fürstensteig**, a rite of passage for nearly every Liechtensteiner. You must be fit and not suffer from vertigo, as in places the path is narrow, reinforced with rope handholds and/or falls away to a sheer drop. The hike, which takes up to four hours, begins at the **Berggasthaus Gaflei** (bus No 30 from Triesenberg). Travel light and wear good shoes.

A steep two-hour climb from **Planken** (bus No 20 from Schaan Post) brings you to the panoramic **Gafadurahütte** (☎ 262 89 27; www.alpenverein.li). From here, over the **Three Sisters** mountain, you can meet up with the Fürstensteig.

Sleeping

Hotel Garni Säga (☎ 392 43 77; www.saega.li; Alte Landstrasse 17; s/d Sfr95/160; 🖳 🅿) This modern family-run pension, next door to the camp site, has very pleasant, sunny rooms.

SYHA Hostel (☎ 232 50 22; www.youthhostel.ch /schaan; Untere Rütigasse 6; dm Sfr30.50, d Sfr82; ☺ mid-Mar–Oct, reception closed 10am-5pm) Renovated a few years ago, this hostel caters particularly to cyclists and families. Halfway between Schaan and Vaduz, it's within easy walking distance of either.

Camping Mittagspitze (☎ 392 36 77, 392 23 11; adult/child/car Sfr8.50/4.50/4, tent Sfr5-8, dm adult/child Sfr22/13; 🛒) This well-equipped camp site in a leafy spot is excellent for families, with a playground and pool as well as a restaurant, TV lounge and kiosk. It's south of Triesen.

MALBUN

pop 35 / elevation 1600m

At the end of the road from Vaduz, the 1600m-high resort of Malbun feels – in the nicest possible sense – like the edge of the earth. Craning your neck to glimpse the surrounding peaks, you reflect that this natural bowl high in the mountains could be perfect for holing up with a broken heart or living out an apocalypse.

It's not really as remote as it seems, and in high season Malbun does get mobbed. However, generally it's perfect for unwinding, especially with the family. The skiing is inexpensive, if not too extensive, while the hiking is relaxing and beautiful.

Between seasons, though, be warned that Malbun becomes a deserted cul-de-sac. As one local puts it, 'You can run naked down the main street in November and no-one will see you'. (Not an invitation to try…)

Information

Bancomat ATM by the lower bus stop, accepting all major cards.

Tourist office (☎ 263 65 77; www.malbun.li; ☺ 9am-noon & 1.30-5pm Mon-Sat Jun-Oct & mid-Dec–mid-Apr) On the main street, not far from Hotel Walserhof.

Activities

As you pass the nursery slopes on the way into Malbun, you realise this is a resort aimed at beginners, with a few intermediate and cross-country runs thrown in. Indeed, older British royals like Princes Charles learnt to ski here, before shifting their allegiance to Klosters.

There's still a ski, and now a snowboard, school. A general ski pass (including the Sareis chairlift) for a day/week costs Sfr37/169 for adults and Sfr25/110 for children. One

day's equipment rental from **Malbun Sport**
(☎ 263 37 55; malbun_sport@adon.li; ☯ 8am-6pm
Mon-Fri, plus Sat & Sun in high season) costs Sfr50 including skis, shoes and poles.

Some hiking trails, including to **Sassfürkle**,
stay open during the winter. During the
summer, other treks include the **Furstin-Gina
Path**, with views over Austria, Switzerland
and Liechtenstein. This walk starts at the
top of the Sareis chairlift (Sfr7.50/12 single/
return in summer) and returns to Malbun.

Sleeping & Eating

Alpenhotel Malbun (☎ 263 11 81; www.alpenhotel
.li; s/d from Sfr55/110, with bathroom Sfr65/130; [P] [☎])
Rooms in the sienna-coloured main chalet
are as cute as pie, with doors painted in
traditional farmhouse patterns, and polished golden wood. They're tiny, though,
and the shared facilities quite basic. En suite
rooms in the nearby annexe are larger and
comfier but straight from the 1970s. Pop
into the main building's restaurant to enjoy
the kitschy Alpine décor, warm atmosphere
and decent food.

Hotel Gorfion-Malbun (☎ 264 18 83; www.s-ho
tels.com; s Sfr100-210, d & f Sfr160-380; [🖵] [✕] [P] [☎])

Malbun's most spacious and upmarket
hotel is spread across two chalet-style buildings. Undergoing progressive renovation,
it has a sleek modern lobby and pool, but
a traditional lounge. It caters brilliantly for
children and if you fancy one of its all-
in packages, the huge buffets are full of
healthy, tasty food.

For supplies, visit **Schädler** (☎ 263 40 55;
☯ 8am-6pm in high season, 8am-12.30pm & 1.30-6pm
rest of year). There's also a mountain restaurant atop the Sareis chairlift.

Getting There & Around

Bus 10 travels hourly from Vaduz to Malbun between 7.20am and 6.20pm every day
(Sfr3.60, Swiss Pass valid), returning between 8.20am and 7.20pm.

AROUND MALBUN

Two kilometres before Malbun is the Väluna
Valley, the main **cross-country skiing** area. The
trail, illuminated in winter, starts at Steg.
Nearby is the simple but charming **Berggasthaus Sücka** (☎ 263 25 79; www.suecka-erlebnis.li;
dm Sfr34, d Sfr100; [P]), which also has a restaurant open from Tuesday to Sunday.

LIECHTENSTEIN

Directory

CONTENTS

ACCOMMODATION

Switzerland offers every type of accommodation you've heard of, and some you might not – such as 'sleeping in straw' (see opposite). Local tourist offices always have listings and will book hotels and pensions for you for little or no commission.

This guidebook runs the gamut from budget to midrange and top-end accommodation. The budget category includes camping, dormitories, farm stays, hostels and simple hotels and pensions, which frequently offer rooms without private bathroom facilities. These all generally cost less than Sfr150 for a double, although this might differ slightly, depending on whether you're staying in a city or the countryside.

Midrange accommodation – with all the comforts of private bathroom, TV, telephone and more – rises to approximately Sfr350 for a double, again depending on where you're staying. Above this price you will certainly be enjoying time-honoured Swiss luxury.

Rates in main cities stay constant throughout the year (apart for Christmas). But in small towns and resorts, there are low, middle and high seasons. Some have two high seasons: one in summer and one in winter. Changeover dates differ from place to place, so check in advance. In budget hotels the seasonal differences are less marked.

Unless otherwise noted, hotel prices in this guide always include breakfast.

B&Bs/Private Rooms

More than 350 B&Bs throughout Switzerland can be found at www.bnb.ch. Private houses in rural areas also frequently offer inexpensive 'room(s) vacant' (*Zimmer frei, chambres libres* or *camere libere* in German/French/English).

Camping

There are about 450 camp sites in the country, classified from one to five stars depending on their amenities and convenience of location. They are often scenically situated in an out-of-the-way place by a river or lake, so having your own transport is useful. Charges per night are from around Sfr8 per person plus Sfr6 to Sfr12 for a tent, and from an additional Sfr4 for a car. Telephone ahead, as in the high season camps might be full, and at the start or end of the season camps may close if demand is low or the weather poor.

BOOK ACCOMMODATION ONLINE

For more accommodation reviews and recommendations by Lonely Planet authors, check out the online booking service at www.lonelyplanet.com. You'll find the true, insider lowdown on the best places to stay. Reviews are thorough and independent. Best of all, you can book online.

PRACTICALITIES

■ Major newspapers include the *Neue Zürcher Zeitung* (www.nzz.ch in German) and *Tages Anzeiger* (www.tagesanzeiger.ch in German) in Zürich, *Le Temps* (www.letemps.ch in French) and *La Tribune de Genève* (www.tdg.ch in French) in Geneva and the Lugano-based *Corriere del Ticino* (www.cdt.ch in Italian). More populist papers include the free tabloid *20 Minuten* (www.20min.ch in German) and the right-wing *Blick* (www.blick.ch in German). *Facts* (www.facts.ch in German) is a glossy news monthly, while *Cream* (www.cream-magazine.ch) is an English magazine published every two months.

■ Public broadcast media are largely broken down along linguistic lines. German-language SF-DRS operates three TV and five radio stations. The French and Italian TV operators are TSR and RTSI respectively, with RSR and RSI being their radio equivalents. RR is a Romansch radio station.

■ Swissinfo (www.swissinfo.org) is a national news website available in several languages, including English. World Radio Geneva (FM 88.4) is an English-language station broadcasting music and news throughout the Lake Geneva region. Check online for BBC World Service frequencies (www.bbc.co.uk/worldservice/schedules).

■ The PAL system (not compatible with the North American and Japanese NTSC system) is used for videos. DVDs are the universal standard.

■ Electrical supply is 220V, 50Hz. Swiss sockets are recessed, hexagonally shaped and incompatible with most plugs from abroad (including 'universal' adapters). Fortunately, you will also usually find at least one standard, three-pin continental socket in every building.

■ Metric measurements are used. Like other continental Europeans, the Swiss indicate decimals with commas and thousands with full points.

For details on camping in Switzerland contact the **Schweizerischer Camping und Caravanning Verband** (Swiss Camping & Caravanning Federation, SCCV; ☎ 061 302 26 26; www.sccv.ch) and **Verband Schweizer Campings** (Swiss Camping Association; ☎ 033 823 35 23; www.swisscamps.ch; Seestrasse 119, CH-3800 Interlaken). Another useful Internet site is www.camping.ch.

The **Touring Club der Schweiz** (Swiss Touring Club, TCS; ☎ 022 417 27 27; www.tcs.ch in German, French & Italian; Chemin de Blandonnet, Case postale 820, CH-1214, Vernier/Geneva) also publishes a comprehensive guide to Swiss camp sites.

Free camping *(Wildes Camping)* is not strictly allowed and should be discreet, but it is perfectly viable in the wide-open mountain spaces, and is fairly common in places like Ticino. If the police come across you, they may not do anything (especially if you've been responsible with your rubbish) or they may move you on. A fine is theoretically possible.

Dormitories & Alpine Huts

Dormitory accommodation (*Touristenlager* or *Massenlager* in German, *dortoir* in French) has been well established for years

in ski and other resorts. Take care in studying accommodation lists, as dormitories may only take groups. Mattresses are often crammed side by side in massive bunks in these places; however, there are usually no curfews and the doors aren't usually locked during the day. Some camp sites offer simple dorm beds too.

Student dorms in university towns may also be offered during holidays.

There's been a move in recent years to upgrade the accommodation in Alpine huts – including indoor plumbing – although most remain quite basic. There are some 150 huts, all maintained by the **Schweizer Alpenclub** (Swiss Alpine Club; ☎ 031 370 1818; www.sac-cas.ch in German & French). They're rarely full and you'll probably be offered a place on the floor rather than being turned away. If there's no warden, payment depends on an honesty system, and there will be a book for signing in. Prices are comparable to those of youth hostels.

Farm Stays

When their cows are out to pasture in summer, Swiss farmers often charge travellers a small fee to sleep in their empty barns. At Sfr20, plus a few sundries (usually Sfr1 to Sfr2 for showers, breakfast etc), 'sleeping in straw' is not only cheap, but also a great experience. Many straw pallets come with blankets – though it's advisable to ask ahead.

A booklet listing participating farms is available from **Aventure sur la paille/Abenteuer im Stroh** (☎ 024 445 16 31; www.aventure-sur-la-paille .ch, www.abenteuer-stroh.ch).

Some farms take paying guests in their farmhouses, too.

Hostels

The word for youth hostel is *Jugendher-berge* in German, *auberge de jeunesse* in French and *alloggio per giovanni* in Italian. The national hostel organisation is the **Schweizer Jugendherbergen** (Swiss Youth Hostel Association, SYHA; ☎ 044 360 14 14; www.youth hostel.ch), which is affiliated with Hostelling International (HI) and runs 61 hostels. These range from older, institutional affairs to some very modern establishments bordering on designer accommodation. If you're not an IYHA member (over/under 18 Sfr33/22), you'll pay a Sfr6 'guest fee'. Six guest fees add up to a full international membership card. Bed prices mostly range from Sfr30 to Sfr35, although a few start at Sfr25.

Hostels do get full; telephone reservations are not accepted but bookings can be made via the website. During busy times a three-day maximum stay may apply.

As well as official youth hostels, there are many backpacker hostels in Switzerland. These tend to be more flexible in their regulations, reception times and opening hours, and are generally free of school groups. Membership is not required, but more than 20 of these hostels are loosely affiliated under **Swiss Backpackers** (☎ 033 823 46 46; www.swissbackpackers.ch).

Look out also for **Naturfreundehaus** (Friends of Nature; www.nfhouse.org) hostels.

Hotels & Pensions

Despite the great reputation of Swiss hotels, the standard at the lower end of the market is pretty variable. The cheapest rooms are those without private toilet and shower, although they often have a sink (*lavabo*). For these, prices start at around Sfr40/70 (single/double) in a small town, or Sfr80/100 in

cities and top resorts. Count on at least Sfr10 to Sfr20 more per person for a room with shower. In low-budget accommodation, the private shower may be merely a shower cubicle rather than a proper en suite bathroom.

If you're staying in mostly one- or two-star hotels, **Swiss Budget Hotels** (☎ 0848 805 508; www.rooms.ch) produces a national booklet of good-quality cheaper hotels and has regular special offers.

A *Frühstückspension* or *Hotel-Garni* serves only breakfast, and does not offer half or full board. Small pensions with a restaurant often have a 'rest day', when check-in may not be possible, unless by prior arrangement (so telephone ahead).

If you move into the realm of the three- or four-star pension or hotel, you are assured of decent comfort. There'll be a room telephone, TV and maybe even a mini-bar.

However, it's in five-star establishments that Swiss excellence comes into its own. The places are palatial and the service is impeccable. Luxury establishments like Zürich's Baur au Lac and Gstaad's Palace hotel are world renowned.

Self-Catering Apartments

Self-catering accommodation is available in holiday chalets, apartments and bungalows. These are often booked out well in advance – for peak times, reserve six to 12 months ahead. In low season, you can sometimes get apartments on demand. A minimum stay of one week (Saturday to Saturday) is common. Local tourist offices will send lists if requested. **REKA** (Schweizer Reisekasse; ☎ 031 329 66 33; www.reka.ch) has special deals in the low season. **Interhome** (Zürich ☎ 01 497 22 22; www.inter home.ch; USA ☎ 305-940 2299; Australia ☎ 02-9453 2744; UK ☎ 020-8891 1294) has offices in several countries and gives one-third off bookings made in the week preceding the rental period.

BUSINESS HOURS

Most shops are open from 8am to 6.30pm Monday to Friday, sometimes with a one-to two-hour break for lunch at noon in smaller towns. In larger cities, there's often a late shopping day until 9pm, typically on Thursday or Friday. Closing times on Saturday are usually 4pm or 5pm. In some places souvenir shops can open on Sunday, although it is unusual for other shops to be open on that day – exceptions are Zürich's Shop Ville and supermarkets at some train stations.

Offices are typically open from about 8am to noon and 2pm to 5pm Monday to Friday. Banks are open from 8.30am to 4.30pm Monday to Friday, with late opening usually one day a week.

CHILDREN

Orderly and clean, Switzerland is perfect for family travel and promotes itself as such. **Swiss Railways** (www.rail.ch) offers a Family Card (see p327), while **Switzerland Tourism** (www.myswitzerland.com) lists hotels that provide special family facilities (eg supervised play rooms). Click on 'Family Vacations' in the menu for details.

Places that might interest kids include: the Swiss Games Museum (p87) in Vevey; the frogs in Estavayer's Regional Museum (p103); the mirror maze in Lucerne's Glacier Garden; the Knie children's zoo in Rapperswil; Teddyland on Schynige Platte in the Jungfrau Region; the Freilichtmuseum Ballenburg near Brienz. There's also the Crans Montana children's festival in February.

Individual chapters contain more tips for families. For general advice, see Lonely Planet's *Travel with Children*.

CLIMATE CHARTS

You'll need to be prepared for a range of temperatures, as the mountains create a variety of local and regional microclimates. That said, most of the country has a central European climate, with daytime temperatures around 18° to 28°C in summer and -2° to 7°C in winter. The coldest area is the Jura, in particular the Brevine Valley. By contrast, Ticino in the south has a hot Mediterranean climate.

Summer tends to bring a lot of sun, but also the most rain, and there were terrible floods in 1999 and 2005. Look out for the Föhn, a hot, dry wind that sweeps down into the valleys and can be oppressively uncomfortable (though some find its warming effect refreshing). It can strike at any time of the year, but especially in spring and autumn.

For more information about when to visit Switzerland, see p18.

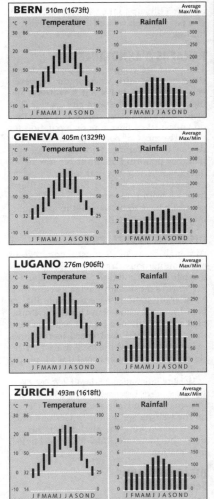

CUSTOMS

Visitors are subject to duty-free limits. Visitors from Europe may import 200 cigarettes, 50 cigars or 250g of pipe tobacco. Visitors from non-European countries may import twice as much. The allowance for alcoholic beverages is the same for everyone: 1L for beverages containing more than 15% alcohol by volume, and 2L for beverages containing less than 15%. Alcohol and tobacco may only be brought in by people aged 17 or over. Gifts up to the value of Sfr100 may also be imported, as well as food provisions for one day.

DANGERS & ANNOYANCES

The Swiss are relatively rule-oriented, and street crime is fairly uncommon. However, you should still always watch your belongings; pickpockets thrive in city crowds. The Swiss police aren't very visible, but when they do appear, they have a poor reputation for their treatment of people of non-European descent or appearance, with some suggesting that they perform random street searches of questionable necessity and so on.

Several cities, such as Zürich and Bern, have a heroin problem, but these days you generally have to be way off the main thoroughfares to notice it.

DISABLED TRAVELLERS

Although many of its most scenic regions are mountainous, travellers with physical disabilities will still find Switzerland one of the world's most easily navigable countries. Most train stations have a mobile lift for boarding trains, and many hotels have disabled access (although budget pensions tend not to have lifts). **Switzerland Tourism** (www.myswitzerland.com) and the local tourist offices should be able to offer travel tips for people with physical disabilities.

Mobility International Schweiz (☎ 062 206 88 35; www.mis-ch.ch; Froburgstrasse 4, CH-4600 Olten) has information and a travel agency. Details on the website are mainly in German only, but it is working on an English translation, and there are links to some English information.

DISCOUNT CARDS
Senior Cards

Senior citizens are not entitled to discounts on Swiss railways, but they do get many discounts on museum admission, ski passes and some cable cars. Numerous hotels also offer low-season discounts. **Switzerland Tourism** (www.myswitzerland.com) can send you a list of these hotels.

Proof of age is needed for museum and transport discounts. The discounts often start for those as young as 62, although sometimes a higher limit is observed. The abbreviation for senior citizens is AHV in German and AVS in French.

Student & Youth Cards

An International Student Identity Card (ISIC) can get the card-holder discounts on admission prices, air and international train tickets and even some ski passes. If you're under 26 but not a student, you can apply for the IYTC (International Youth Travel Card). This is not so useful, but may get you some price reductions in lieu of an ISIC. Both cards should be issued by student unions and by youth-oriented travel agencies in your home country.

The travel agencies **STA Travel** (www.statravel .ch) and **Globetrotter** (www.globetrotter.ch in German) can issue ISIC cards (Sfr20).

Visitors' Cards

In many resorts and a few cities there's a visitors' card, sometimes called a guest card (Gästekarte), which provides various useful benefits such as reduced prices for museums, swimming pools or cable cars. Cards are issued by your accommodation (even hostels and camp sites), though if you're in a holiday apartment you'll need to get one from the tourist office. They're well worth having, so if your hotel doesn't supply one automatically, ask if such a scheme exists.

Swiss Museum Pass

Regular or long-term visitors to Switzerland might want to consider buying a **Swiss Museum Pass** (www.museumpass.ch; adult/concession/family Sfr111/99/202) which offers entry to the permanent collection (only) of 400 museums. See the website for details.

EMBASSIES & CONSULATES
Swiss Embassies

For a comprehensive list of Swiss embassies abroad, go to www.eda.admin.ch. The following is a selection of countries that have Swiss embassies:

Australia (☎ 2-6162 8400; www.eda.admin.ch/aus tralia; 7 Melbourne Ave, Forrest, Canberra, ACT 2603)

Canada (☎ 613-235 1837; www.eda.admin.ch/canada; 5 Marlborough Ave, Ottawa, Ontario K1N 8E6)

Ireland (☎ 01-218 6382; www.eda.admin.ch/dublin; 6 Ailesbury Rd, Ballsbridge, Dublin 4)

New Zealand (☎ 04-472 1593; vertretung@wel.rep .admin.ch; 22 Panama St, Wellington)

South Africa (☎ 012-452 06 60; www.eda.admin .ch/pretoria; 225 Veale St, Parc Nouveau, New Muckleneuk 0181, Pretoria)

UK (☎ 020-7616 6000; www.eda.admin.ch/london;
16-18 Montague Pl, London W1H 2BQ)
USA (☎ 202-745 7900; www.eda.admin.ch/washington;
2900 Cathedral Ave NW, Washington DC 20008-3499)

Embassies & Consulates in Switzerland

All embassies are found in Bern. Consulates
can be found in several other cities, particularly in Zürich and Geneva. Australia and
New Zealand have no embassy in Switzerland, but each has a consulate in Geneva.
Most of Bern's embassies are located southeast of the Kirchenfeldbrücke. For a comprehensive list, go to www.eda.admin.ch.

Australia (☎ 022 799 91 00; www.australia.ch; Chemin
des Fins 2, Grand-Saconnex, Geneva)
Austria (Map p180; ☎ 031 356 52 52; bern-ob@bmaa
.gv.at; Kirchenfeldstrasse 77-79, Bern)
Canada Bern (Map p180; ☎ 031 357 32 00; www.canada
-ambassade.ch; Kirchenfeldstrasse 88); Geneva (Map p62;
☎ 022 919 92 00; 5 Ave de l'Ariana)
France Bern (☎ 031 359 21 11; www.ambafrance-ch.org
in German & French; Schosshaldenstrasse 46); Geneva
(☎ 022 319 00 00; www.consulfrance-geneve.org in
French; 11 Rue J Imbert Galloix)
Germany Bern (☎ 031-359 41 11; www.bern.diplo.de in
German & French; Willadingweg 83); Basel (☎ 061 693 33
03; Schwarzwaldallee 200)
Ireland (Map p180; ☎ 031-352 14 42; Kirchenfeld-
strasse 68, Bern)
Italy (Map p180; ☎ 031 350 07 77; Elfenstrasse 14, Bern)
South Africa (Map p180; ☎ 031 350 13 13; www.south
africa.ch; Alpenstrasse 29, Bern)
Netherlands (Map p180; ☎ 031 350 87 00; www.nl
embassy.ch; Kollerweg 11, Bern)
New Zealand (Map p62; ☎ 022 929 03 50; Chemin des
Fins 2, Grand-Saconnex, Geneva)
UK Bern (Map p180; ☎ 031 359 77 00; www.britain-in
-switzerland.ch; Thunstrasse 50); Geneva (Map p62; ☎ 022
918 24 00; Rue de Vermont 37-39); Zürich (☎ 01 383 65
60; Hegibachstrasse 47)
USA Bern (☎ 031 357 70 11; http://bern.usembassy.gov;
Jubiläumsstrasse 93); Geneva (☎ 022 840 51 60; Rue
Versonnex 7); Zürich (☎ 01 422 25 66; Dufourstrasse 101)

FESTIVALS & EVENTS

Numerous events take place at a local level
throughout the year, so check with tourist offices, especially for markets (Märit)
and traditional fairs (Chilbi). Following is
a brief selection of the main events; more
information and additional special events
are mentioned in the destination sections
of this guidebook and at www.switzerland
.com. For details on the Alpine Games

(Unspunnenfest), held every 10 years, see
p149.
January Costumed sleigh rides in the Engadine and the
Lauberhorn ski race at Wengen. International Hot Air
Balloon Week is held in Château d'Oex and the Vogel Gryff
festival is in Basel.
February Carnival time (Fasnacht) in many towns,
particularly in Catholic cantons, with parades, costumes
and musicians. Basel's Fasnacht is best known, but it's also
lively in Lucerne and Fribourg.
March Engadine Skiing Marathon, Graubünden. Cow fight-
ing (yes, the cows fight each other!) starts at the end of the
month in lower Valais and continues for most of the summer.
April Meeting of the Landsgemeinde in Appenzell.
May Celebrations for May Day, especially in St Gallen and
in Vaud.
June The annual performance of William Tell starts in
Interlaken, and continues until early September. There are
open-air music festivals in Ticino (late June to August).
July Montreux Jazz Festival, Nyon Rock Festival.
August National Day (1 August) celebrations and fireworks,
and Swiss wrestling in the Emmental. The middle of the
month sees Zürich's Street Parade, the start of the Geneva
Festival and the International Festival of Music in Lucerne.
September Teens test their shooting ability (Knaben-
schiessen) in Zürich, and a religious festival in Einsiedeln.
October Vintage festivals in wine-growing regions such
as Morges, Neuchâtel and Lugano.
November Open-air festivals on the fourth Monday in
November including the onion market (Zibelmärit) in Bern.
December St Nicholas Day celebrations on 6 December
and the Escalade festival in Geneva.

FOOD

Swiss food has an Italian, French or German flavour, depending on which part of the
country you're in. (Your tastebuds will thank
you most if it's an Italian region.) Although
fondue and rösti are available, so too is a
wide range of international cuisine.

This guide includes options for all tastes
and budgets. At budget restaurants, you
can expect to fill up for less than Sfr25 per
person. Midrange establishment events will
set you back between Sfr25 and Sfr75 each,
while bills in fine-dining restaurants can
easily rise to Sfr200 per person (or more).

See p51 for more on eating and drinking
in Switzerland.

GAY & LESBIAN TRAVELLERS

Attitudes to homosexuality are progressive.
Gay marriage is recognised (although gay
couples are not permitted to adopt children
or have fertility treatment) and the age of

consent for gay sex is the same as for heterosexuals, at 16 years.

All major cities have gay and lesbian bars. The **Cruiser magazine** (☎ 044 388 41 54; www.cruiser.ch in German; Sfr6.50) has extensive listings of organisations, places and events. Other useful websites include: www.gay.ch (in German) www.pinkcross.ch (in German and French) and www.lesbian.ch (in German). Pride marches are held in Geneva (early July) and Zürich (mid-July).

HOLIDAYS

National holidays in Switzerland are:
New Year's Day 1 January
Easter March/April; Good Friday, Easter Sunday and Monday
Ascension Day 40th day after Easter
Whit Sunday & Monday 7th week after Easter
National Day 1 August
Christmas Day 25 December
St Stephen's Day 26 December

Some cantons observe their own special holidays and religious days, eg 2 January, 1 May (Labour Day), Corpus Christi, 15 August (Assumption) and 1 November (All Saints' Day). Ticino and Lucerne are the luckiest cantons, enjoying an extra eight/seven public holidays respectively. The third Sunday in September is a federal fast day, and some cantons (eg Vaud and Neuchâtel) take the following Monday as a holiday.

INSURANCE

Since free health treatment in Switzerland is very limited, it's all the more important to have the correct travel insurance. In addition, if you're trekking in the mountains, you might want to check whether your policy covers helicopter rescue and emergency repatriation. When skiing or snowboarding, you can buy 'winter sports' cover, available from most insurance companies at a premium. A few winter-sports policies can also be extended, at a cost, to adventure sports, such as canyoning, rafting and skydiving.

Worldwide cover to travellers from over 44 countries is available online at www.lonelyplanet.com/travel_services.

For more on health insurance, see p334.

INTERNET ACCESS

Using Swiss Internet cafés and terminals can be quite frustrating. Not only are they expensive (on average Sfr10 to Sfr16 per hour), but many public computers are deliberately equipped with only web browser software. That frequently means that if you want to do anything mildly technical – like reading an email attachment – the set-up won't allow it. It's a good idea to warn your family and friends of this.

Some of the larger public libraries have cheaper terminals and some hotel rooms have easy-to-use modem plugs. Nearly all Swisscom phone boxes now have an electronic phonebook, which allows you to send short emails worldwide for just Sfr1.50 each.

LEGAL MATTERS

Swiss police have wide-ranging powers of detention allowing them to hold a person without charges or a trial, so be extra careful to stay on the right side of the law. If approached by them, you will be required to show your passport, so carry it at all times.

There are some minor legal variations between the 26 cantons. In Zürich, for example, women are not allowed to use or carry pepper spray (*Pfefferspray*) to deter attackers, whereas in neighbouring Aargau, they are. Similarly, busking (playing music in the streets) may be allowed in some places and not in others. If in doubt, ask.

Drugs

Moves to decriminalise cannabis in Switzerland were abandoned in October 2003, but you will still notice a fair bit of dope around. In the cities, police tend not to do much about it, but if they do decide to enforce the law you face a fine of up to Sfr400. Possession of over about 30g of cannabis, or any amount of a harder drug, may mean being looked upon as a dealer, and you'll possibly be liable for a larger fine, jail or deportation.

MAPS

Hallwag, Kümmerly + Frey (☎ 031 850 31 31; www.swisstravelcenter.ch; Grubenstrasse 109, CH-3322 Schönbühl) has a vast range of road atlases, city maps and hiking maps, which can be bought online. Swiss Hiking Federation maps and maps produced by the Bundesamt for Topographie (sometimes down to 1:15,000 scale) are also found in most travel bookshops. The *Swiss Travel System* brochure, free from Switzerland Tourism and major train stations, has a clear A3 map of bus and train routes. For more detail, buy the Swiss Federal Railway rail map from a Swiss train station.

In Swiss cities and towns, the local tourist information office will have free maps and brochures.

MONEY

Swiss francs are divided into 100 centimes (*Rappen* in German-speaking Switzerland). There are notes for 10, 20, 50, 100, 500 and 1000 francs, and coins for five, 10, 20 and 50 centimes, as well as for one, two and five francs.

See p19 for information about costs in Switzerland.

ATMs

Automated teller machines (ATMs) – called Bancomats in banks and Postomats in post offices – are common, and are accessible 24 hours a day. They can be used with most international bank or credit cards to withdraw Swiss francs, and they have English instructions. Your bank or credit-card company will usually charge a 1% to 2.5% fee, and there may also be a small charge at the ATM end.

Cash

Many businesses throughout Switzerland, including most hotels, some restaurants and souvenir shops, will accept payment in euros. However, any change will be given in Swiss francs, at the rate of exchange calculated on the day.

Credit Cards

The use of credit cards is less widespread than in the UK or USA and not all shops, hotels or restaurants will accept them. When they do, EuroCard/MasterCard and Visa are the most popular.

International Transfers

Western Union (☎ 0800 007 107) has a receiving agent in most towns. Charges, paid by the sender, are on a sliding scale, depending on the amount sent.

Moneychangers

You can change money at banks, as well as at airports and nearly every train station daily until late into the evening. Whereas banks tend to charge about 5% commis-

sion, some money-exchange bureaus don't charge commission at all. Exchange rates are *slightly* better for travellers cheques than for cash, but there's not much difference.

For bank opening hours and exchange rates, see the inside front cover of this guidebook.

Tipping

Tipping is not normally necessary, as hotels, restaurants, bars and even some taxis are legally required to include a 15% service charge in bills. However, if you've been very happy with a meal or service you could round up the bill (locals often do); hotel and railway porters will expect a franc or two per bag. Bargaining is virtually nonexistent, though you could certainly try asking for a discount on your hotel room in the low season.

Travellers Cheques

All major travellers cheques are accepted, especially American Express, Visa or Thomas Cook. You can call **American Express** (☎ 0800 550 100) on its toll-free number if you lose your Amex travellers cheques.

POST

Post office opening times vary, but they're usually open from at least 8am to noon and 2pm to 5pm Monday to Friday, and from 8.30am to noon on Saturday. The larger post offices stay open during lunchtime and also have an emergency counter (*Dringlichschalter*) outside normal operating hours (eg lunchtime, evening, Saturday afternoon, Sunday evening), but transactions are subject to a Sfr1 to Sfr2 surcharge. Many post offices have an ATM.

Postal Rates

Within Switzerland, deliveries are either by A-Post (delivered next working day) or B-Post (taking three working days). Standard letters (up to 100g) and postcards sent A-Post cost Sfr1. Sending them by B-Post costs Sfr0.85.

For international deliveries, the main categories of post are priority/prioritaire and economy/economique. Priority deliveries to Europe take two to four days, and to elsewhere roughly seven days. Economy service to Europe takes four to eight days and, to other destinations, seven to 12 days. Rates for priority/economy letters under 20g to Europe are Sfr1.30/1.20. Equivalent rates to countries outside Europe are Sfr1.80/1.40. Prices for posting items to countries bordering the Mediterranean are the same as those for Europe.

Paketpost rates are cheaper for heavier items than for Briefpost (letter post). An 'Urgent' service is also available for same-day or next-day international deliveries; for prices and other details contact **Swiss Post** (☎ 0848 454 545; www.post.ch).

SHOPPING

You can't miss the cowbells and cuckoo clocks, sold by numerous souvenir shops. The upmarket Heimat/Heimatwerk shops also stock textiles, ceramics, quality fondue sets, toys and trendy handbags.

However, Switzerland is a land of brands and it's also worth keeping some room in your suitcase for the following:

Bags and satchels Switzerland is home to Freitag (www.freitag.ch), the manufacturer of trendy, courier-style satchels made from recycled plastic.

Colouring pencils The world's first water-soluble brand of pencil was Switzerland's Caran d'Ache (www.caran dache.ch). A boxful still makes a delightful present for the little sister, artist or architect back home.

Footwear Bally (www.bally.ch) is known abroad, but the stay-at-home national chain Navyboot (www.navyboot.ch) also does some great high-stepping boots and shoes.

Swiss army knives The leading and original brand is Victorinox (www.victorinox.ch), although Wenger (www.wenger-knife.ch) also does a decent range. Knives can cost anything from Sfr7.50 to Sfr200 or more, depending on functionality.

Watches If you can't stretch to a TAG Heuer, Rolex, Cartier or Patek Philippe, then a Swatch (www.swatch.ch) will let you tell the time in style without first having to consult your bank manager.

Water bottles Sigg (www.sigg.ch) is a world leader in this field; one of its brightly coloured, aluminium-coated flasks has even been immortalised in New York's Museum of Modern Art.

Taxes & Refunds

VAT (MWST in German, TVA in French) is levied on goods and services at a rate of 7.6%, except on hotel bills, when it's only 3.6%. Nonresidents can claim the tax back on purchases over Sfr400. (This doesn't apply to services or hotel/restaurant bills.) Before making a purchase, ensure that the shop has the required paperwork for you

to make a claim. Refunds are given at main border crossings and at Geneva and Zürich airports, or you can claim later by post.

SOLO TRAVELLERS

Solo travellers should experience no particular problems and will be perfectly safe. You'll meet people staying in hostels, of course; however, the Swiss are also pretty chatty and friendly, and will often strike up impromptu conversations.

TELEPHONE

The main telephone provider is **Swisscom** (☎ 0800 800 114; www.swisscom.com), which evolved from the former state-run monopoly. The minimum charge in its numerous phone boxes is 60c, which then increases by 10c increments. Coin-operated call boxes also take euros, but it's more common for public phones to take only phone 'taxcards', which come in values of Sfr5, Sfr10 and Sfr20, and can be purchased from post offices and other outlets, newsagencies, shops etc. Many telephones take credit cards.

To find a phone number in Switzerland, check the telephone book or dial ☎ 111 (minimum charge Sfr1.60, Sfr0.25 for the first minute and national tariffs thereafter). Alternatively, the residential **white pages** (www.weisseseiten.ch) and the business **yellow pages** (www.gelbeseiten.ch) have listings in German, French, Italian and English.

There's no surcharge for calling the international operator (☎ 1141), although you are not able do this from public telephone boxes. Operator-connected international calls can be made collect via ☎ 0800 265 532.

Since 2005, Swiss private customers have been able to buy fixed-line phones with SMS (text message) capability.

Phone Codes

The country code for Switzerland is ☎ 41. When telephoning Switzerland from abroad you drop the initial zero from the number, hence to call a number in Bern you dial ☎ 41 31 (preceded by the overseas access code of the country you're dialling from).

The international access code from Switzerland is ☎ 00. To call Britain (country code ☎ 44), you would start dialling with ☎ 00 44.

Telephone numbers with the code 0800 are toll-free, and those with 0848 are

WARNING: DIAL ALL NUMBERS

Regional codes do not exist in Switzerland. Although the numbers for a particular city or town share the same three-digit prefix (for example Bern 031, Geneva 022), numbers always must be dialled in full, even when calling from next door – literally.

charged at the local rate. Numbers beginning with 156 or 157 are always charged at the premium rate. Numbers with the code 079 are mobile phone numbers.

Tariffs & International Phonecards

There are only two national tariffs to fixed line phones: Sfr0.08 per minute for daytime calls Monday to Friday, anywhere in Switzerland, and Sfr0.04 per minute after 5pm, before 8am and on weekends. When calling Swisscom mobiles, the equivalent rates are Sfr0.41/0.31, and for other mobiles it's Sfr0.55/0.45.

The normal/cheap tariff for international dialling to fixed-line phones is Sfr0.12/0.10 per minute for a range of countries including Australia, Britain, Canada, New Zealand and the USA, and Sfr0.25/0.20 to countries including Ireland, Japan and the Netherlands. For further details see www.swisscom-fixnet.ch. Of course, many hotels add a premium to these rates.

You can usually save money on the normal international tariff by buying prepaid cards – Swisscom sells them to the value of Sfr10, Sfr20, Sfr50 and Sfr100. Or look for prepaid cards from rival operators. For example, the **Mobile Zone** (www.mobilezone.ch in German, French & Italian) chain of shops has Sfr20 or Sfr50 Discount Call cards, which can be used via local mobile phones, private phones and phone boxes. Check the website for the nearest branch.

Mobile Phones

Most phones on European GSM networks will work in Switzerland perfectly, though you should check with your provider about costs. Alternatively, prepay local SIM cards are available from the three network operators – **Orange** (www.orange.ch), **Sunrise** (www.sunrise.ch) and **Swisscom Mobile** (www.swisscom-mobile.ch).

It's easy to buy these via the nationwide **Mobile Zone** (www.mobilezone.ch in German, French &

Italian) chain of shops. Check the website for the nearest branch. Prices start at about Sfr40 to Sfr50 for a card with Sfr20 of talk-time.

All prepay cards must be officially registered, so take your passport when you go to buy.

TIME

Swiss time is GMT/UTC plus one hour. If it's noon in Bern it's 11am in London, 6am in New York and Toronto, 3am in San Francisco, 9pm in Sydney and 11pm in Auckland. Daylight-saving time comes into effect at midnight on the last Saturday in March, when the clocks are moved forward one hour; they go back again on the last Saturday in October. The Swiss use the 24-hour clock when writing times.

Note that in German *halb* is used to indicate the half-hour before the hour, hence *halb acht* means 7.30, not 8.30.

TOILETS

Public toilets are usually pretty clean. Urinals are often free, and many cubicles are too, but some of the latter may have a charge of between Sfr0.20 and Sfr0.50. The spotless Mr Clean range of facilities in most train stations is more expensive, costing Sfr2. Toilet cubicles in supermarket and department-store restaurants are generally free; they're for customers only, but who will know?

TOURIST INFORMATION

Switzerland Tourism abroad and local tourist offices in Switzerland are helpful and have plenty of literature in English. They usually also have information for travellers with special requirements.

Regional Tourist Offices

Generally, these tend not to accept personal callers, but will answer written queries. For a list, see Switzerland Tourism's website (www.myswitzerland.com).

Local Tourist Offices

For detailed resort information, you are always better off contacting the local tourist office. Information is free (maps nearly always are too) and somebody will invariably speak English. Local tourist offices are widespread and will often book hotel rooms, tours and excursions for you. In German-speaking Switzerland the offices are called

DIRECTORY

Verkehrsbüro, or *Kurverein* in some resorts. In French they are called *office du tourisme* and in Italian, *ufficio turistico*.

Tourist Offices Abroad

The headquarters of **Switzerland Tourism** (☎ 044 288 11 11; www.myswitzerland.com; PO Box 695, CH-8027, Zürich) will provide written information, but accepts no personal visits. Swiss tourist offices abroad include the following:

France (☎ 00800 100 200 30; info@myswitzerland .com; Porte de la Suisse, 11 bis, rue Scribe, F-75009 Paris) Closed to the public; only provides information by phone, email or post.

Japan (☎ 03-5401 5426; info@switzerland.com; Toranomon Daini Waiko Bldg 3F, 5-2-6, Toranomon, Minato-ku Tokyo 105-0001)

UK (☎ 020 7420 4900, 00800 100 200 30; info.uk@ switzerland.com; 30 Bedford St, London WC2E 9ED)

USA (☎ 1877 794 8037; info.usa@switzerland.com; Swiss Center, 608 Fifth Ave, New York, NY 10020)

Switzerland Tourism has no Australian office, but you can get information from its website, from Zürich HQ (info@switzerland .com), from the embassy in **Canberra** (☎ 02-6162 8400; www.eda.admin.ch/australia; 7 Melbourne Ave, Forrest, Canberra, ACT 2603) or any major Australian travel agent.

There are several other offices in Europe and around the world, all listed on the website under 'Contact'.

VISAS

Visas are not required if you hold a passport for the UK, Ireland, the USA, Canada, Australia, New Zealand or South Africa, whether visiting as a tourist or on business. Citizens of the EU, Norwegians and Icelanders may also enter Switzerland without a visa. A maximum three-month stay applies, although passports are rarely stamped. Citizens of several African, Asian and Arab countries, plus Eastern European and Balkan states, require visas. See www .foreigners.ch for details, and check with the local embassy or a reputable travel agency before travelling.

In Switzerland, carry your passport at all times and guard it carefully. Swiss citizens

are required always to carry personal identification, so you will also need to be able to identify yourself at any time.

WOMEN TRAVELLERS

Minor sexual harassment (catcalls and the like) is much less common than in some neighbouring countries, such as Italy and France, but, in our experience at least, it's a teensy bit more common than in others, like Germany and Austria. Common sense is the best guide to dealing with potentially dangerous situations such as hitching or walking alone at night.

WORK
Work Permits

Citizens of the EU, plus Norwegians and Icelanders, may work in Switzerland for up to 90 days a year without a permit. However, these workers still have to register with the Swiss cantonal authorities before arrival.

Other foreigners and EU citizens on longer assignments will need a permit. For details visit www.foreigners.ch. If you get caught working illegally you can be fined and deported.

These rules can change at any time, so do some research beforehand.

Types of Work

Language skills are particularly crucial for work in service industries. Generally, the ski resorts are the most likely places to find a position. *Working in Ski Resorts – Europe* (paperback) by Victoria Pybus provides detailed information. Within Switzerland, check through ads for hotel and restaurant positions in the weekly newspaper *hotel + tourismus revue* (Sfr4.30), which is mostly in German. A useful web resource for service-industry jobs is www.gastronet.ch.

In October, work is available in vineyards in Vaud and Valais. Conditions are usually better than in other countries.

WWOOF (Worldwide Opportunities on Organic Farms; www.dataway.ch/~reini/wwoof; Postfach 59, CH-8124, Maur) finds people volunteer work on small organic farms throughout Switzerland.

Transport

GETTING THERE & AWAY

When visiting Switzerland from outside Europe, it's worth investigating whether it's cheaper to fly to a European 'gateway' city and travel on from there. London and Frankfurt are the most obvious candidates.

Flights, tours and rail tickets can be booked online at wfthww.lonelyplanet.com /travel_services.

ENTERING THE COUNTRY

Formalities are kept to a minimum when entering Switzerland by air, rail or road, although passports will be checked.

Passport

Ensure your passport is valid until well after you plan to end your trip – six months is a safe minimum. Swiss citizens are required to always carry personal identification, so carry your passport at all times and guard it carefully. Citizens of many European countries don't need a passport to travel to Switzerland; a national identity card may suffice. Check with your travel agent or the Swiss embassy before departure.

> **THINGS CHANGE**
>
> The information in this chapter is particularly vulnerable to change. Check directly with the airline or a travel agent to make sure you understand how a fare (and ticket you may buy) works and be aware of the security requirements for international travel. The details given in this chapter should be regarded as pointers and not a substitute for your own careful, up-to-date research.

AIR

Airlines

More than 100 scheduled airlines fly to/ from Switzerland, the most important of which are listed below. Lufthansa part-owns Swiss International Air Lines and their two timetables have been integrated.

Air France (☎ 022 827 87 87; www.airfrance.com)
American Airlines (☎ 044 654 52 56; www.aa.com)
British Airways (www.ba.com); Zürich (☎ 0848 845 845); Geneva (☎ 0848 801 010)
Continental Airlines (☎ 0800 776 464; www .continental.com)
Darwin Airline (☎ 0800 177 177; www.darwinairline .com)
Lufthansa Airlines (☎ 0845 773 7747; www.lufthansa .com)
Qantas Airways (☎ 0845 774 7767; www.qantas.com)
Swiss International Air Lines (☎ 0848 852 000; www.swiss.com)
South African Airways (☎ 0870 747 1111; www .flysaa.com)
United Airlines (☎ 0845 844 4777; www.ual.com)

Low-Cost Airlines

This market changes often, so keep an eye out for new entrants and be aware that current players might abandon certain routes.

Air Berlin (☎ 0848 737 800; www.airberlin.com)
easyJet (☎ 0848 888 222; www.easyjet.com)
flybe (☎ + 44 0 1392 268 500; www.flybe.com)
Germanwings (www.germanwings.com)
Helvetic (☎ 043 557 90 99; www.helvetic.com)
SkyEurope (☎ 043 557 90 99; www.skyeurope.com)

Airports

The two main Swiss airports are **Zürich Airport** (☎ 043 816 22 11; www.zurich-airport.com), **Geneva**

International Airport (☎ 022 717 71 11; www.gva .ch), and increasingly **EuroAirport** (☎ 061 325 31 11; www.euroairport.com), serving Basel (as well as Mulhouse, France and Freiburg, Germany).

Bern-Belp (☎ 031 960 21 21; www.flughafenbern .ch) and **Lugano Airport** (www.lugano-airport.ch) are secondary airports, but growing.

For more details, see the relevant destination chapters. Bear in mind that **Friedrichshafen** (www.fly-away.de) in Germany and **Aeroportidi Milano Linate & Malpensa** (www.sea -aeroportimilano.it) in Italy are airports close to the Swiss border.

Tickets

Two agents, **Flight Centre** (www.flightcentre.com) and **STA Travel** (www.statravel.com), operate in many of the regions discussed here.

Check for cheap fares in major newspapers and try the following online booking sites (or their local versions):

■ www.cheapflights.com
■ www.ebookers.com
■ www.expedia.com
■ www.lastminute.com
■ www.opodo.com
■ www.travelocity.com

Africa

South Africa is the best place on the continent to buy tickets to Switzerland. **Swiss International Air Lines** (☎ 0860 040 506; www.swiss .com) has direct flights daily from Johannesburg to Zürich (from 4500 rand in low season).

Asia

With tourism from India the fastest growing sector of the Swiss tourism market, **Swiss International Air Lines** (Delhi ☎ 91-011 2341; 5th fl, World Trade Tower, Barakhamba Lane; Mumbai ☎ 022-2287 01 22; 1st fl, Hoechst House, 193 Nariman Point) has plenty of offices in the country. It operates nonstop flights to Zürich from Mumbai, with connecting flights to/from Geneva.

Expect to pay about 38,000 rupees in the low season, or try **STIC Travels** (☎ 11-233 57 468; www.stictravel.com) for cheaper tickets.

Direct flights also go to Zürich from Bangkok, Hong Kong, Singapore and Tokyo.

Australia & New Zealand

The Sydney-based **Swiss Travel Centre** (☎ 02 9250 9320; www.swisstravel.com.au) has specially negotiated airfares to Switzerland.

FLY-RAIL BAGGAGE SERVICE

Passengers on all flights into Geneva and Zürich airports are able to send their luggage directly on to any one of 116 Swiss train stations, without having to wait for their bags at the airport. Similarly, upon departure they can check their luggage at any of these train stations up to 24 hours before their flight and pick it up at their destination point. The charge is Sfr20/ US$15 per item of luggage. Bulky items such as bicycles and surfboards are excluded. For details, email reservation@stc .ch. Alternatively, visit www.rail.ch or www .myswitzerland.com to find sales points in your country. Similar luggage forwarding is possible within the country (see p333).

Swiss International Air Lines (☎ 1300-724 666, 02-8251 3950; c/o Walshes World Agencies, Level 3, 117 York St, Sydney 2000) has linked services with Air New Zealand, British Airways, Qantas and Singapore Airlines. Expect to pay up to AUD$3200 or NZ$2700 in the low season.

Thai Airways (☎ 02-9844 0999; www.thaiairways .com.au; 75-79 Pitt St, Sydney 2001) has the most convenient services, flying from Sydney to Bangkok with timed connections to Geneva.

Canada

Travel CUTS (☎ 1-866-246 9762; www.travelcuts.com) is Canada's national student travel agency.

Swiss International Air Lines (☎ 1 877 359 7947; www.swiss.com) has direct flights daily from Montreal to Zürich (from C$600 return in the low season) and other code-share services via New York.

Continental Europe

The number of low-cost flights has mushroomed in recent years. If you book very early – and are lucky – you might find flights for as little as €22 each way (plus taxes).

Air Berlin (☎ www.airberlin.com) flies to Zürich from dozens of destinations in Germany, Italy, Spain and Portugal. Beware that you need to book very early with this particular low-cost carrier to get the best deal.

easyJet (www.easyjet.com; France ☎ 08-25 08 25 08; Netherlands ☎ 023-568 4880; Spain ☎ 90-229 9992) has flights to Geneva and Basel from about two dozen destinations. See the website for details.

Germanwings (www.germanwings.com) operates from Cologne-Bonn, Germany to Zürich.

Helvetic (www.helvetic.com) flies to Zürich from Italy, Portugal, Spain, the Czech Republic and Hungary.

SkyEurope (www.skyeurope.com) flies from Basel and Zürich to Austria (Vienna) and Slovakia (Bratislava and Kosice).

Aside from **STA Travel** (www.statravel.com), agencies in major European cities include the following:

NBBS Reiswinkels (☎ 0900 10 20 300; www.nbbs.nl in Dutch; Linnaeusstraat 28, Amsterdam)

Passaggi (☎ 00800 191 020 04; www.passaggi.it in Italian; Galleria Stazione Termini, 00 185 Rome)

Voyages Wasteels (☎ 0825 887 070; www.wasteels.fr in French; 11 rue Dupuytren, 756006 Paris)

UK

London is a major centre for discounted air tickets. Including taxes, you should be able to find a scheduled return flight for between UK£120 and UK£200.

The two main scheduled carriers are **British Airways** (☎ 0845-773 3377; www.ba.com) and **Swiss International Air Lines** (☎ 0845-601 0956; www.swiss.com), which both have services leaving from Heathrow and London City airports.

Ticino carrier **Darwin Airline** (☎ +41 (0) 800 177 177 international toll free; www.darwin-airline.com) flies from London City Airport (to Bern and Lugano only).

Several low-cost carriers travel between the UK and Switzerland, including **easyJet** (☎ 0870-600 0000; www.easyjet.com) and **Helvetic** (☎ 020 7026 3464; www.helvetic.com). Note that if you travel **Air Berlin** (☎ 0870 738 8880; www.air berlin.com) or **Germanwings** (☎ 0870 252 1250; www.germanwings.com) your flight will be routed via Germany.

During the winter skiing season only, **Bmibaby** (☎ 0870 264 2229; www.bmibaby.com) flies to Geneva from Birmingham, Cardiff, Manchester and Nottingham to Geneva.

Budget travel agencies include **Trailfinders** (☎ 0845 058 5858; www.trailfinders.com) and **Bridge the World** (☎ 0870 444 7474; www.bridgetheworld.com).

USA

In the USA, try consolidators (budget travel agencies), such as **Air Brokers** (☎ 1-888-883 3273; www.airbrokers.com), **Airline Consolidator** (☎ 1-888-468 5385; www.airlineconsolidator.com) and **Airtech** (☎ 212-219 7000; www.airtech.com).

Scheduled fares start at approximately US$450 for return flights to Switzerland. **American Airlines** (☎ 1 800 433 7300; www.aa.com) and **Swiss International Air Lines** (☎ 1 877 359 7947; www.swiss.com) code-share on several nonstop flights per day to Zürich from New York (both JFK and Newark), Boston, Chicago, Los Angeles, Miami and Washington, as well as direct flights to Geneva. **Continental Airlines** (☎ 1-800-231 0856; www.continental.com) also has nonstop flights from Newark, while **Delta** (☎ 1-800-221 1212; www.delta.com) flies nonstop from Atlanta.

LAND
Bus

Eurolines (www.eurolines.com), via local operator **Alsa+Eggman** (☎ 0900 573 747 per min Sfr1.50, Geneva ☎ 022 716 91 10, Zürich ☎ 043 366 64 30; www.alsa-eggmann.ch), operates services on about 35

ROAD TOLLS

There's a one-off charge of Sfr40 to use Swiss motorways and semi-motorways, identified by green signs. The charge is payable at the border (in cash, including euros) or from Swiss tourist offices abroad (see p322). The sticker *(vignette)* you receive upon paying the tax can also be bought at post offices and petrol stations. It must be displayed on the windscreen and is valid for a calendar year, with one month's leeway. If you're caught without it, you'll be fined Sfr100. A separate *vignette* is required for trailers and caravans. Motorcyclists are also charged the Sfr40. For more details, see www.vignette.ch.

Generally, it's easy enough to avoid motorways and hence not bother with the *vignette*. However, note that a *vignette* is also necessary to use either the Gotthard Tunnel (between Ticino and Uri) or the San Bernardino Tunnel (between Ticino and Graubünden).

On the Swiss–Italian border you'll need to pay an additional toll if using the Grand St Bernard Tunnel between Aosta, Italy, and Wallis (toll for cars/motorcycles one way from Italy Sfr38.40 /20.40, from Switzerland Sfr29/17).

routes to/from Austria, Croatia, Hungary, Germany, Montenegro, Poland, Portugal, Romania, Serbia, Slovakia and Spain.

See p331 for further bus services.

Car & Motorcycle

There are fast, well-maintained motorways (freeways) to Switzerland through all surrounding countries. The German motorways (Autobahnen) have no tolls, whereas the Austrian, Czech, French (autoroute) and Italian (autostrada) and Slovak motorways do.

The Alps present a natural barrier to entering Switzerland, so main roads generally head through tunnels (see the boxed text Road Tolls, p325 for information about the costs involved). Smaller roads are scenically more interesting, but special care is needed when negotiating mountain passes. Some, like the N5 (E21) route from Champagnole (in France) to Geneva, aren't recommended if you have no previous experience driving in the mountains. See p328 for more on getting around using this mode of transport.

PAPERWORK & PREPARATIONS

An EU driving licence is acceptable throughout Europe for up to a year. Third-party motor insurance is a minimum requirement: get proof of this in the form of a Green Card, issued by your insurers. Also ask for a 'European Accident Statement' form. Taking out a European breakdown assistance policy is a good investment.

A warning triangle, to be displayed in the event of a breakdown, is compulsory almost everywhere in Europe, including Switzerland. Recommended accessories include a first-aid kit (compulsory in Austria, Slovenia, Croatia and Greece), a spare bulb kit and a fire extinguisher. In the UK, contact the **RAC** (☎ 0906-470 1740, per min 60p; www .rac.co.uk) or the **AA** (☎ 0870-550 0600; www.theaa .com) for travel information.

For more on Swiss motoring regulations, see p74.

Train

Taking the train is more expensive and time-consuming than flying within Europe. However, some travellers enjoy the experience, and it can seem somehow appropriate to arrive in environmentally friendly Switzerland via a relatively green mode of transport. Contact www.raileurope.co.uk, www.raileurope .com or your local European rail operator.

From the UK, the quickest train route is via **Eurostar** (www.eurostar.com) to Paris and then onwards by French TGV (train à grande vitesse). A fare to Geneva generally costs between UK£150 and UK£200 for adults between 26 and 59 years, with slight discounts for those under 26 or over 60. Allow approximately nine hours for this trip, or 10 to Zürich.

There are several trains a day from Paris to Geneva and Lausanne, taking 3½ to four hours. The trip from Paris to Bern takes 4½ hours by TGV.

Zürich is the country's busiest international terminus. Four daily trains (four hours) connect with München. Two daytime trains (nine hours) and one night train leave for Vienna, from where there are extensive onward connections to/from cities in eastern Europe.

Most connections from Germany pass through Zürich or Basel. Nearly all connections from Italy pass through Milan before branching off to Zürich, Lucerne, Bern or Lausanne.

SEA & RIVER

Switzerland can be reached by steamer from several lakes, although it's a slightly more unusual option. From Germany, you come via Lake Constance (p257); from Italy via Lago Maggiore (p301); and from France along Lake Geneva (p85).

It's also possible to cruise down the Rhine River to Basel (p243).

GETTING AROUND

Despite a headline-grabbing three-hour power outage in 2005, and disruptions after that year's terrible flooding, Switzerland's fully integrated public transport system is one of the most efficient in the world. The Swiss think nothing of coordinating schedules with only a few minutes' leeway between arrivals and departures. Missing a connection through a late arrival is rare.

Travel within the country is expensive, however, and visitors who are planning to use public transport on inter-city routes

SWISS TRAVEL PASSES

The following national travel passes generally offer betters savings than Eurail or Inter Rail passes (see p333) on extensive travel within Switzerland. Most can be purchased before arrival in Switzerland from **Switzerland Tourism** (☎ 044 288 11 11; www.myswitzerland.com; PO Box 695, CH-8027, Zürich) or on arrival from major transport centres such as the main train stations in Zürich or Geneva. The Half-Fare Card, however, is rarely available abroad. For more details, go to www.rail.ch and search for 'travel passes'.

Swiss Pass

The Swiss Pass entitles the holder to unlimited travel on almost every train, boat and bus service in the country, and on trams and buses in 35 towns. Reductions of 25% apply on funiculars, cable cars and private railways such as Jungfrau Railways. The following prices are for 2nd-class passes; 1st class is 50% higher. If you are under 26, you are entitled to a Swiss Youth Pass, which is 25% cheaper in each instance.

- four days (Sfr245)
- eight days (Sfr350)
- 15 days (Sfr425)
- 22 days (Sfr490)
- one month (Sfr545)

Swiss Flexi Pass

This pass allows you to nominate a certain number of days (anywhere from three to eight) during a month in which you can enjoy unlimited travel.

- three days (Sfr230)
- eight days (Sfr420)

Half-Fare Card

Almost every Swiss person owns one of these. As the name suggests, you pay only half-fare on trains with this card, plus you get some discounts on local-network buses and trams. If you plan to use many cable cars, the Half-Fare Card might be a better option than the Swiss Pass, as the reduction is greater (50% as against 25%), and the cheapest version pays for itself after only three or four mountain trips.

- One month (Sfr99)
- One year (Sfr150; photo necessary)

Family Card

A free Family Card is also available, offering free travel (on trains, buses and boats – even on some cable cars) for children aged between six and 16 accompanied by at least one of their parents. Children within that age bracket and travelling with an adult who is not a relative get 50% off.

Regional Passes

Network passes valid only within a particular region are available in several parts of the country. Such passes are available from train stations in the region and more details can be found in individual destination chapters.

---

are strongly advised to consider one of the passes listed in the boxed text Swiss Travel Passes, above.

Timetables often refer to *Werktags* (work days), which means Monday to Saturday, unless there is the qualification '*ausser Samstag*' (except Saturday).

AIR

Internal flights are of little interest to most visitors, owing to Switzerland's compact size and excellent rail transport. However, **Swiss International Air Lines** (www.swiss.com) does serve all major hubs, such as EuroAirport, Geneva and Zürich airports. Return fares start from about Sfr250.

Some mountain resorts have helicopter operators offering flights around the Alps. There are also scenic Zeppelin airship rides over Lakes Lucerne (p217) and Constance (p258).

BICYCLE

For information on the experience of biking around Switzerland and national cycle routes, see p43.

Hire

Rent A Bike (www.rent-a-bike.ch in German & French) hires out bikes at around 100 train stations. Prices start at Sfr23 for a half day, and Sfr31 for a full day, and there are discounts for

Swiss travel pass–holders. Counters are open daily, usually from the crack of dawn until some time in the evening. If you inform staff beforehand, you can return your bike to any other station with a rental counter, but it costs Sfr6 more. There's a huge demand for these rental bikes during summer, so try to reserve your bike at least a day or two ahead.

Many **SYHA Hostels** (www.youthhostel.ch) also now rent out bikes, even to nonguests. Prices are Sfr10 for a half day and Sfr15 for a full day, although you will have to leave a Sfr100 deposit. Booking is also necessary.

There is free bike rental in Bern (p184), Geneva (p66), Zug (p232) and Zürich (p208).

Transport

One bike per passenger can be taken on slower trains, and sometimes even on Inter-City (IC) or EuroCity (EC) trains, when there is enough room in the luggage carriage (Sfr15, or Sfr10 with valid Swiss travel pass). Between 31 March and 31 October, you must book (SFr5) to take your bike on ICN (inter-city tilting) trains.

Trains that do not permit accompanied bikes are marked with a crossed-out pictogram in the timetable. Sending your bike unaccompanied costs Sfr16 to Sfr32, depending on its size.

BOAT

All the larger lakes are serviced by steamers operated by Swiss Federal Railways (SBB/CFF/FFS), or allied private companies for which national travel passes are valid. Lakes covered include Geneva, Constance, Lucerne, Lugano, Neuchâtel, Biel, Murten, Thun, Brienz and Zug, but not Lago Maggiore. Railpasses are not valid for cruises offered by smaller boat companies. The **Swiss Boat Pass** (Sfr35; valid for 1 year) gives you a 50% discount on travel on the country's 14 largest lakes.

BUS

Yellow 'postal buses' (Postbus in German, Car Postal in French, Auto Postale in Italian) supplement the rail network, following postal routes and linking towns to the more inaccessible mountain regions. They are extremely regular, and departures tie in with train arrivals. Bus stations are invariably next to train stations. Travel is one class only.

For a flat fee of Sfr12, your luggage can be sent on ahead to a post office and picked up later – especially useful for hikers relying on the postal bus network.

For those schlepping home late from a club or rushing to make a red-eye flight, there are several **Nightbuses** (☎ 0900 100 201; http://mct.sbb.ch/mct/nightbird in German & French) on weekends.

Bus Passes

All Swiss national travel passes (see the boxed text Swiss Travel Passes, p327) are valid on postal buses; however, a few tourist-oriented Alpine routes levy a surcharge (usually around Sfr15, but sometimes Sfr25). Details are given in the relevant chapters.

Costs

Postal bus fares are comparable to train fares (see p332). All-day scenic journeys, for example, can cost between Sfr35 to Sfr85.

Reservations

Tickets are usually purchased from the driver, though on some scenic routes over the Alps (eg, the Lugano–St Moritz run) advance reservations are necessary. See www.postbus.ch for details.

CAR & MOTORCYCLE

If you're deciding whether to travel by car or motorcycle, you should consider the effect your exhaust emissions will have on the Alpine environment. You might also find it frustrating to have to concentrate on the road while magnificent scenery unfolds all around. Public transport is excellent in city centres, where parking can make cars an inconvenience.

Automobile Associations

The **Swiss Touring Club** (Touring Club der Schweiz, TCS; ☎ 022 417 27 27; www.tcs.ch in German, French & Italian; Chemin de Blandonnet, Case postale 820, CH-1214, Vernier/Geneva) and **Swiss Automobile Club** (Automobil-Club der Schweiz, ACS; ☎ 031 328 31 11; www.acs.ch; Wasserwerkgasse 39, CH-3000, Bern 13) are internationally affiliated and can provide details on driving in Switzerland.

The larger TCS operates the national 24-hour **emergency breakdown service** (☎ 140). The service is free for members of the Swiss motoring clubs or their affiliates;

anybody else has to pay (charges are Sfr80 to Sfr320).

Bring Your Own Vehicle
For information on bringing your own transport into Switzerland, see p326.

Driving Licence
EU and US licences are accepted in Switzerland for up to one year. Otherwise, you should obtain an International Driving Permit (IDP).

Fuel
Unleaded (*bleifrei, sans plomb, senza plombo*) petrol is standard, found at green pumps, but diesel is also widely available (black pumps). At the time of writing, unleaded fuel cost Sfr1.58 per litre, diesel Sfr1.68. For the latest prices, go to www.theaa.com and search for 'fuel'.

Hire
Car rental is expensive, especially if hiring from a multinational firm. It's cheaper to book ahead from your own country, but you're still looking at Sfr350 to Sfr500 per week. The minimum rental age is usually 25, but falls to 20 with some local firms, and you will always need a credit card. It is possible to drive Swiss hire-cars into most EU countries, including the 10 member states that joined in 2004. However, you cannot take them to Greece. Other off-limits countries include Albania, Bosnia, Bulgaria, Serbia, Turkey and Ukraine.

National (local rate) and international reservation numbers and web addresses include the following:

Avis (☎ 0848 811 818; www.avis.ch)
Europcar (☎ 0848 808 099; www.europcar.ch)
Hertz (☎ 0848 811 010; www.hertz.ch)
Holiday Autos (www.holidayautos.com) Australia (☎ 1300 554 432); Switzerland (☎ 056 675 75 85); UK (☎ 0870 400 0099); USA (☎ 1-800 422 7737)
Sixt (☎ 0848 884 444)
Thrifty (Australia ☎ 1300 367 227; www.thrifty.com .au; New Zealand ☎ 09-309 0111; www.thrifty.co.nz; UK ☎ 01494 751 600; www.thrifty.co.uk).

Insurance
See p326.

TRANSPORT

ROAD DISTANCES (KM)

	Basel	Bellinzona	Bern	Biel-Bienne	Brig	Chur	Fribourg	Geneva	Interlaken	Lausanne	Lugano	Lucerne	Neuchâtel	St Gallen	St Moritz	Schaffhausen	Sion
Bellinzona	241																
Bern	97	253															
Biel-Bienne	93	247	41														
Brig	190	161	91	129													
Chur	228	115	242	237	174												
Fribourg	132	285	34	71	179	274											
Geneva	267	420	171	209	214	409	138										
Interlaken	153	195	57	92	73	209	92	230									
Lausanne	203	359	107	146	151	346	72	62	167								
Lugano	267	28	279	273	187	141	331	446	221	383							
Lucerne	103	140	115	107	149	140	147	280	71	218	166						
Neuchâtel	141	294	46	31	141	283	43	123	104	73	320	156					
St Gallen	191	217	204	197	288	102	236	371	225	307	243	138	244				
St Moritz	313	150	327	321	241	85	359	494	294	430	176	225	368	178			
Schaffhausen	161	246	115	167	259	182	205	340	228	276	272	108	214	80	266		
Sion	252	214	160	195	53	399	128	161	86	98	240	271	166	356	294	329	
Zürich	113	195	125	119	208	118	157	292	177	229	221	57	166	81	203	51	281

TRANSPORT

Road Conditions

Swiss roads are well built, well signposted and well maintained, but you should stay in low gear on steep stretches and carry snow chains in winter.

Most major Alpine passes are negotiable year-round, depending on the current weather. However, you will often have to use a tunnel instead at the Great St Bernard, St Gotthard and San Bernardino passes. Passes that are open only from June to October are Albula, Furka, Grimsel, Klausen, Oberalp, Susten and Umbrail. Other passes are Lukmanier (open May to November), Nufenen and (June to September), Splügen (May to October).

Phone ☎ 163 for up-to-the-hour traffic conditions (recorded information in French, German, Italian and English).

You can take your car on trains through the following tunnels and passes, among others:

Lötschberg Tunnel (☎ 0900 55 33 33 premium rate; www.bls.ch; hMar-Oct) From Kandersteg to Goppenstein or Iselle.

Furka Pass (☎ 027 927 77 71; www.mgbahn.ch; Y year-round) From Oberwald to Realp.

Flüela Pass (☎ 081 288 37 37; www.rhb.ch; Y year-round)

Road Rules

A handbook on Swiss traffic regulations (in English) is available from cantonal registration offices and at some customs posts. The minimum driving age for cars and motorcycles is 18, and for mopeds it's 14.

The Swiss drive on the right-hand side of the road. If in doubt, always give priority to traffic approaching from the right. On mountain roads, the ascending vehicle has priority, unless a postal bus is involved, as it always has right of way. Postal bus drivers let rip a multitone bugle when approaching blind corners. In towns, allow trams plenty of respect, and stop behind a halted tram to give way to disembarking passengers.

The speed limit is 50km/h in towns (though certain stretches may be as low as 30km/h), 80km/h on main roads outside towns, 100km/h on single-carriage motorways and 120km/h on dual-carriage motorways. Car occupants must wear a seat belt at all times where fitted, and vehicles must carry a breakdown-warning triangle, which must be readily accessible (ie not in the boot).

Dipped headlights must be turned on in all tunnels, and are recommended for motorcyclists during the day. Headlights must be used in rain or poor visibility. Both motorcyclists and their passengers must wear crash helmets.

Switzerland is tough on drink-driving. The blood alcohol content (BAC) limit is 0.05%, and if caught exceeding this limit you may face a heavy fine, a driving ban or even imprisonment. If you're involved in a car accident, the police must be called if anyone receives more than superficial injuries.

Proof of ownership of a private vehicle should always be carried. Within Switzerland, you can drive a vehicle registered abroad for up to 12 months, but its plates should be clearly visible.

Road Signs

Almost all road signs use internationally recognised conventions. Signs you may not have seen before are: a crisscrossed white tyre on a blue circular background, which means snow chains are compulsory; and a yellow bugle on a square blue background, which indicates a mountain postal road where you must obey instructions given by postal bus drivers.

Urban Parking

Street parking in the centre (assuming traffic isn't banned, as it often is) is controlled by parking meters during working hours (8am to 7pm Monday to Saturday). Parking costs around Sfr1 to Sfr1.50 per hour, with maximum time limits from 30 minutes to two hours. Central streets outside these metered areas are usually marked as blue zones, allowing a 1½-hour stay during working hours, or as (increasingly rare) red zones, with a 15-hour maximum. In either of the latter two cases, you need to display a parking disc in your window indicating the time you first parked. Discs are available for free from tourist offices, car-rental companies and police stations.

LOCAL TRANSPORT
Public Transport

All local city transport is linked via the same ticketing system, so you can change lines on one ticket. Usually you must buy tickets before boarding, from ticket dispensers at

SCENIC JOURNEYS

Trains, buses and boats are more than the means of getting from A to B in Switzerland. On some routes with stunning views, the journey really is the destination. Switzerland boasts the following routes among its classic sightseeing journeys. Bear in mind that you can choose just one leg of the trip, and that scheduled services ply the same routes for standard fares. In addition to these journeys, almost any train in the Jungfrau region (p151) will also provide beautiful scenery.

Panorama Trains

The following have panoramic coaches with extended-height windows:

The **Glacier Express** (Brig ☎ 027 927 71 24 or 027 927 77 77, Chur ☎ 081 288 61 00; www.glacierexpress .ch; 2nd/1st class Sfr129/215, seat reservations supplements Sfr9-17; ⏱ 7½hr, daily) runs between Zermatt and St Moritz, Chur or Davos. It's a spectacular journey over the Alps, past the lakes of central Switzerland and on to the rolling countryside of Graubünden. The Brig–Zermatt Alpine leg makes for pretty powerful viewing, as does the area between Disentis/Mustér and Brig. See p23.

The **Golden Pass Route** (☎ 033 828 32 32; www.goldenpass.ch, www.mob.ch; one way 2nd/1st class Sfr67/111; ⏱ 5hr, 4 trips daily) travels between Lucerne to Montreux, from the wonderful landscape of central Switzerland over the Brünig Pass to Gstaad and then down to the waters and vineyards of the Lake Geneva area. The journey is in three legs, and you must change trains twice. The Lucerne–Interlaken leg (2nd/1st class Sfr30/60, two hours) is best around the Brünig Pass, while the Montreux–Zweisimmen section (Sfr29/58; two hours) really comes to life from Montreux to Château d'Oex, especially on the climb/descent from Lake Geneva. The Interlaken–Zweisimmen section (Sfr24/48) takes an hour. Regular trains, without panoramic windows, work the whole route hourly.

The **Bernina Express** (☎ 081 288 63 26; www.rhb.ch; one way 2nd/1st class Sfr74/110, Swiss pass free, reservations obligatory in summer Sfr7; ⏱ 2½hr, daily) cuts 145km through Engadine from Chur to Ticino. The train travels through viaducts and switchback tunnels, past glaciers, streams and Alpine flowers and up through the 2253m Bernina Pass without a rack and pinion system. Between May and October, you can opt to continue onwards from Ticino to Lugano by bus.

Other scenic rail routes include the following:

Chocolate train (www.mob.ch) Touristy return trip in a Pullman car from Montreux to the chocolate factory at Broc.

Mont Blanc/St Bernard Expresses (www.tmrsa.ch) From Martigny to Chamonix, France, or over the St Bernard Pass.

Voralpen Express (www.voralpen-express.ch) Lake Constance to Lake Lucerne, through St Gallen, Rapperswil and Romanshorn.

Rail/Boat

Several journeys combine panorama trains with lake steamers.

The **William Tell Express** (Lucerne ☎ 041 367 67 67, Locarno ☎ 027 922 81 51; www.lakelucerne.ch; 2nd/1st class Sfr73/111, Swiss Pass free, obligatory reservation Sfr47; ⏱ May-Oct) starts with a wonderful three-hour cruise across Lake Lucerne to Flüelen, from where a train wends its way through ravines and past mountains to Locarno.

The **Rhône Express** (www.rhoneexpress.ch; 2nd/1st class Sfr105/162, Swiss Pass free, obligatory reservation Sfr45) combines a 1st-class boat ride on a historic steamer across Lake Geneva from Geneva to Montreux, followed by a scheduled service to Visp, and a change to a panoramic train at Visp to the Matterhorn and Zermatt.

Postal Bus

The **Palm Express** (St Moritz ☎ 081 837 67 64, Lugano ☎ 091 807 85 20; www.palmexpress.ch; tickets Sfr62, Swiss Pass free, obligatory reservation Sfr10) travels between Lugano and St Moritz, skirting the Mediterranean-style Lakes Lugano and Como (in Italy) before rising into the mountains via the Maloja Pass into Engadine.

For details on four passes tours, see p174. Another half a dozen scenic Alpine routes can be found at www.postbus.ch.

TRANSPORT

stops. Very occasionally you can also buy from machines on board.

In some Swiss towns, single tickets may give a time limit (eg one hour) for travel within a particular zone, and you can only break the journey within that time. Multi-strip tickets may be available at a discount (validate them in the on-board machine at the outset of the journey), or one-day passes are even better value.

Inspectors regularly check for people travelling without tickets. Those found without a ticket pay an on-the-spot fine of up to Sfr80.

Taxi

Taxis are rarely necessary, but you can usually find them outside train stations or telephone for them (see individual chapters for details). They are always metered, and prices are high.

MOUNTAIN TRANSPORT

The Swiss have many words to describe mountain transport. They are: funicular (*Standseilbahn* in German, *funiculaire* in French), a cable car (*Luftseilbahn, téléphérique, funivia*), a gondola (*Gondelbahn, télécabine, telecabinoia*) and also a cable chair/chair lift (*Sesselbahn, télésiège, seggiovia*). All are subject to regular safety inspections.

TOURS

Numerous day trips can be booked through local tourist offices. The country is so compact that excursions to major national attractions are offered from most towns. A trip to Jungfraujoch, for example, is available from Zürich, Geneva, Bern, Lucerne and Interlaken.

Most of these tours represent reasonable value. They are good if you are pressed for time and sometimes cheaper than organising it yourself.

TRAIN

The Swiss rail network combines state-run and private operations. The **Swiss Federal Railway** (www.rail.ch, www.sbb.ch/en) is abbreviated to SBB in German, CFF in French and FFS in Italian. All major train stations are connected to each other by hourly departures, which are normally between 6am and midnight.

Long-distance trains usually have a dining car. Smoking is banned on all trains and train stations.

Classes

Most travellers will find spick-and-span 2nd-class compartments perfectly acceptable for their needs. However, these carriages are sometimes fairly full, especially when the army is on the move, and occasionally you'll have to stand.

The 1st-class carriages are even more comfortable and spacious. Fewer passengers use 1st class, which also offers power points for laptops to let you work onboard.

Exactly where 1st- and 2nd-class sections will draw up alongside the platform (see opposite) is usually announced over the loudspeaker, or shown on a bulletin board. A few private lines may not have 1st-class compartments.

Costs

Ordinary fares are relatively expensive, at about Sfr30 per 100km. A national travel pass (see the boxed text Swiss Travel Passes, p327) will undoubtedly save you money. Return fares are only cheaper than two singles for longer trips. Special deals are sometimes available in the low season.

All fares quoted in this guide are for 2nd-class travel unless stated otherwise; 1st-class fares average 50% to 65% higher.

Information

All stations, large and small, can provide advice in English, and free timetable booklets are invariably available. There's a Switzerland-wide number for **train information** (☎ 0900 300 300); calls are charged at Sfr1.19 per minute.

ROUND-TRIP TICKETS

If you have a specific itinerary and are certain you won't be changing your route, a *Rundfahrt* (*billet circulaire* in French) ticket is worth investigating as a sometimes cheaper alternative to a Swiss travel pass. Such tickets allow you to journey in a circular loop and, because they are valid for a month, it's possible to break your journey for several days at various cities and towns along the way.

MAJOR SWISS RAIL ROUTES

Train schedules are revised every December, so double-check all fares and frequencies quoted here.

Luggage

Train stations invariably offer luggage storage, either at a special counter (usually Sfr8 per piece) or in 24-hour lockers (Sfr3 to Sfr4 for a small locker, Sfr4 to Sfr6 for a large one).

Nearly every station allows ticket-holders to send their luggage ahead – yes, even after 9/11 – where you can dispatch your bag before 9am and collect it at your destination station after 6pm. This is especially useful if you're visiting several different locations in a day before your overnight stop. This 'fast baggage' service is Sfr20 per item (up to 25kg) and your luggage will be screened.

Platforms

Station announcements, in German, French, English and frequently Italian, state on which track (*Gleis* in German, *voie* in French, *binario* in Italian) a particular train is due. Station platforms are quite long and are divided into sections, A to D. Pay special attention to announcements, as sometimes small rural trains wait at the furthest end of the platform.

Reservations & Tickets

Seat reservations are advisable for longer journeys in the high season and usually cost an extra Sfr5.

Some smaller, rural rail routes, marked with a yellow eye pictogram, have a 'self-control' ticketing system. On these routes, be sure to buy a ticket before boarding, or you'll risk a fine. Ticket inspectors do appear quite frequently.

Single train tickets for journeys over 80km are valid for two days. It is possible to break the journey on the same ticket – but tell the conductor before your ticket is punched.

Return tickets over 160km are valid for a month and similarly allow you to break your journey.

Train Passes

European railpasses (www.raileurope.co.uk, www.raileurope.com), including Eurail and Inter Rail passes, are valid on Swiss national railways. However, you cannot use them on postal buses, city transport, cable cars or private train lines (eg the Zermatt route and the Jungfraubahn routes at the heart of the Bernese Oberland). So, while they're practical if you're covering several countries in one journey, they're less useful than Swiss travel passes (p327) for exploring the really scenic regions of Switzerland.

Health

CONTENTS

Travel health depends on your pre-departure preparations, your daily health care while travelling and how well you handle any medical problem that does develop. In Switzerland, you face no unusual threats to your health.

BEFORE YOU GO

Make sure you're healthy before you start travelling. If you require a particular medication take an adequate supply, as it may not be available locally. Take part of the packaging showing the generic name rather than the brand, which will make getting replacements easier. It's a good idea to have a legible prescription or letter from your doctor to show that you legally use the medication, to avoid any problems.

INSURANCE

Make sure that you have adequate health insurance (see p318). There is no free state health service in Switzerland (Swiss citizens and residents are all obliged to take out some form of private health insurance) and all treatment must generally be paid for. The EU and Switzerland have a reciprocal agreement on basic health-care provisions.

Although there is a public system in Switzerland, it is not really free as all residents in Switzerland have to pay for health insurance.

EU members are covered to an extent, but should take out private travel/health cover. Treatment in a public ward of a public hospital is covered by the European Health Insurance Card (EHIC, which replaced the old E111 form in 2005), the card European citizens use to obtain reciprocal health care in other EU member states. There is a nonrefundable excess charge for every 30-day period in hospital. EU citizens with the EHIC pay half of the full cost of ambulances (road and air). Go to any doctor registered with the Swiss health system. Dental care, except emergency accident treatment, is not covered at all. You will generally have to pay up front and claim a refund from **Gemeinsame Einrichtung KVG** (☎ +41 32 625 48 20; Gibelinstrasse 25, Postfach CH-4503 Solothurn).

RECOMMENDED VACCINATIONS

No immunisations are required to enter Switzerland, but generally it's a good idea to make sure your tetanus, diphtheria and polio vaccinations are up to date before travelling. You may also like to consider immunisation against tick-borne encephalitis if you are going to be in rural areas. Check with your doctor and leave plenty of time for shots – ideally six weeks before travel. The US-based **Centers for Disease Control & Prevention** (www.cdc.gov) also has information.

Although there is no risk of yellow fever in Switzerland, if you are arriving from a yellow fever-infected area (ie most of sub-Saharan Africa and parts of South America) you'll need proof of yellow fever vaccination before you will be allowed to enter the country.

INTERNET RESOURCES

EU citizens should see the website of their national health system for travel advice and what the European Health Insurance Card (EHIC) entitles them to in Switzerland. In the case of the UK, check the NHS website (www.dh.gov.uk).

FURTHER READING

Lonely Planet's *Travel with Children* includes helpful advice on travel health for younger children. There are also excellent travel-health sites on the Internet. From the Lonely Planet home page there are links at www .lonelyplanet.com/weblinks/wlheal.htm to the World Health Organization and the US Centers for Disease Control & Prevention.

IN TRANSIT

DEEP VEIN THROMBOSIS (DVT)

Blood clots may form in the legs during plane flights, chiefly because of prolonged immobility (the longer the flight, the greater the risk). The chief symptom of DVT is swelling or pain of the foot, ankle or calf, usually but not always on just one side. When a blood clot travels to the lungs, it may cause chest pain and breathing difficulties. Travellers with any of these symptoms should immediately seek medical attention. To prevent the development of DVT on long flights you should walk about the cabin, contract the leg muscles while sitting, drink plenty of fluids and avoid alcohol and tobacco.

JET LAG & MOTION SICKNESS

To avoid jet lag try drinking plenty of nonalcoholic fluids and eating light meals. Upon arrival, get exposure to natural sunlight and readjust your schedule (for meals, sleep etc) as soon as possible.

IN SWITZERLAND

Self-diagnosis and treatment can be risky, so you should always seek medical help. An embassy, consulate or five-star hotel can usually recommend a local doctor or clinic. The quality of health care in Switzerland is generally very high, whether in public or private hospitals. See opposite for more information.

INFECTIOUS DISEASES

HIV & AIDS

Infection with the human immunodeficiency virus (HIV) may lead to acquired immune deficiency syndrome (AIDS), which is a fatal disease. Any exposure to blood, blood products or body fluids may put the individual at risk. The disease is often transmitted through sexual contact or dirty needles – vaccinations, acupuncture, tattooing and body piercing can be potentially as dangerous as intravenous drug use. HIV/AIDS can also be spread through infected blood transfusions; blood used for transfusions in European hospitals is screened for HIV and should be safe.

TRAVELLER'S DIARRHOEA

Simple things like a change of water, food or climate can all cause a mild bout of diarrhoea, but a few rushed toilet trips with no other symptoms is not indicative of a major problem.

Dehydration is the main danger with any diarrhoea, particularly in children or the elderly as dehydration can occur quite quickly. Under all circumstances *fluid replacement* (at least equal to the volume being lost) is the most important thing to remember. Weak black tea with a little sugar, soda water, or soft drinks allowed to go flat and diluted 50% with clean water, are all good. Stick to a bland diet as you recover.

Swiss restaurants generally have very high standards of hygiene, and food poisoning is rare – although, naturally, always possible. Some of the country's dairy products have very high levels of fat, however.

ENVIRONMENTAL HAZARDS

Altitude Sickness

This disorder can occur above 3000m, but very few treks or ski runs in the Austrian, French, Italian or Swiss Alps reach heights of 3000m or more – Mont Blanc is one exception – so altitude sickness is unlikely. Headache, vomiting, dizziness, extreme faintness, and difficulty in breathing and sleeping are all signs to heed. Treat mild symptoms with rest and simple painkillers. If mild symptoms persist or get worse, descend to a lower altitude and seek medical advice.

Bites & Stings

RABIES

Switzerland is one of the few European countries to be have been declared free of rabies.

SNAKES

Switzerland is home to several types of snakes, a couple of which can deliver a nasty, although not fatal, bite. They are more prevalent in the mountains. To minimise

HEALTH

your chances of being bitten always wear boots, socks and long trousers when walking through undergrowth where snakes may be present. Don't put your hands into holes and crevices, and be careful when collecting firewood.

If bitten by a snake that could be venomous, immediately wrap the bitten limb tightly, as you would for a sprained ankle, and then attach a splint to immobilise it. Keep the victim still and seek medical help. Tourniquets and sucking out the poison are now comprehensively discredited.

TICKS

These small creatures can be found throughout Switzerland up to an altitude of 1200m, and typically live in underbrush at the forest edge or beside walking tracks. A tiny proportion carry viral encephalitis, which may become serious if not detected early (see below).

You should always check all over your body if you have been walking through a potentially tick-infested area, as ticks can cause skin infections and other more serious diseases. If a tick is found attached, press down around the tick's head with tweezers, grab the head and gently pull upwards. Avoid pulling the rear of the body as this may squeeze the tick's gut contents through the attached mouth-parts into the skin, increasing the risk of infection and disease. Smearing chemicals on the tick will not make it let go and is not recommended.

Lyme Disease

This is an infection transmitted by ticks that may be acquired in Europe. The illness usually begins with a spreading rash at the site of the tick bite and is accompanied by fever, headache, extreme fatigue, aching joints and muscles, and mild neck stiffness. If untreated, these symptoms usually resolve over several weeks, but over subsequent weeks or months, disorders of the nervous system, heart and joints may develop. Treatment works best early in the illness. Medical help should be sought.

Tick-Borne Encephalitis

This disease is a cerebral inflammation carried by a virus. Tick-borne encephalitis can occur in most forest and rural areas of Switzerland. If you have been bitten, even having removed the tick, you should keep an eye out for symptoms, including blotches around the bite, which is sometimes pale in the middle. Headache, stiffness and other flu-like symptoms, as well as extreme tiredness, appearing a week or two after the bite, can progress to more serious problems. Medical help must be sought. A vaccination is available and is the best protection.

Hypothermia

The weather in Europe's mountains can be extremely changeable at any time of the year. Skiers and hikers should always be prepared for very cold and wet weather.

Hypothermia will occur when the body loses heat faster than it can produce it and the core temperature of the body falls. It is surprisingly easy to progress from very cold to dangerously cold due to a combination of wind, wet clothing, fatigue and hunger, even if the air temperature is above freezing. It is best to dress in layers; silk, wool and some of the new artificial fibres are all good insulating materials. A hat is important, as a lot of heat is lost through the head. A strong, waterproof outer layer (and a 'space' blanket for emergencies) is essential. Carry basic supplies, including food containing simple sugars to generate heat quickly and fluid to drink.

Symptoms of hypothermia are exhaustion, numb skin (particularly toes and fingers), shivering, slurred speech, irrational or violent behaviour, lethargy, stumbling, dizzy spells, muscle cramps and violent bursts of energy. Irrationality may take the form of sufferers claiming they are warm and trying to take off their clothes.

To treat mild hypothermia, first get the person out of the wind and/or rain, remove their clothing if it's wet and replace it with dry, warm clothing. Give them hot liquids – not alcohol – and high-kilojoule, easily digestible food. Do not rub victims; instead, allow them to slowly warm themselves. This should be enough to treat the early stages of hypothermia. The early recognition and treatment of mild hypothermia is the only way to prevent severe hypothermia, which is a critical condition.

Sunburn

You can get sunburnt surprisingly quickly, even through cloud, and particularly at high altitude. Use a sunscreen, a hat and a barrier cream for your nose and lips. Calamine lotion or a commercial after-sun preparation are good for mild sunburn. Protect your eyes with good-quality sunglasses, particularly if you will be near water, sand or snow.

Water

Not only can you rely on tap water in Switzerland, but the water from most of the country's tens of thousands of fountains is also drinkable. Occasionally you will come across a tap or fountain labelled *Kein Trinkwasser* or *eau non potable,* and that means it's *not* drinking quality.

If you will be drinking water from rivers, lakes or streams – even crystal-clear Alpine streams – you should take steps to purify it. The simplest way of purifying water is to boil it thoroughly. Vigorous boiling should be satisfactory; however, at high altitude water boils at a lower temperature, so germs are less likely to be killed. Boil it for longer in these environments. Consider purchasing a water filter for a long trip. Alternatively, iodine is effective in purifying water and is available in tablet form. Follow the directions carefully and remember that too much iodine can be harmful.

HEALTH

Language

CONTENTS

In the corner of Europe where the German, French and Italian language areas meet, Switzerland (Schweiz, Suisse, Svizzera) has three official federal languages: German (spoken by about 64% of the population), French (19%) and Italian (8%). A fourth language, Rhaeto-Romanic, or Romansch, is spoken by less than 1% of the population, mainly in the canton of Graubünden. Derived from Latin, Romansch is a linguistic relic that, along with Friulian and Ladin across the border in Italy, has survived in the isolation of the mountain valleys. Since 1996,

---

TALK OF THE TOWN

Occasionally, it's hard to remember there's a language divide in Switzerland, when the person at the next table flits from German to French and a widespread form of thanks, *merci vielmals* mixes the two. Undoubtedly, the much-vaunted Röstigraben (Rösti ditch) still divides French- and German-speaking parts of the country, both in language and culture, but visitors will more often be charmed by the country's linguistic ambidextrousness. By the time you leave Switzerland you might well be in thrall of the way many Swiss Germans say *Salut* as if it were 'Sally' or bid you farewell with *Adieu* rather than *Tschüss*. You might relish the drawn-out, sing-song vowels of the interchangable Swiss German greetings *Grueza* or *Gruezi wohl*. However, don't worry if you don't even begin to understand anything more complicated in Schwyzertütsch, not even many French or Italian Swiss do.

Romansch has enjoyed status as a semi-official federal language, together with guarantees for its preservation and promotion.

Being Understood in English

Regardless of how the list of official languages reads, day-to-day language use is somewhat different. In order of predominance, the country's spoken languages are: German, English, French and Italian. Surprising as it is, English is increasingly the *lingua franca* in Swiss companies spanning several of the country's language regions. Children in Zürich and seven other German-speaking cantons are, controversially, starting to learn English in school before they're even taught French.

Most Swiss, particularly those working in service industries (tourist office staff, telephone operators, hotel and office receptionists, restaurant staff and shopkeepers), already speak excellent English. In German Switzerland, you'll also meet many fluent English speakers in other walks of life, especially in the cities. To a progressively lesser extent, the same is true in French,

LANGUAGE AREAS

- Romansch
- German
- French
- Italian

Italian and Romansch-speaking Switzerland. You'll rarely get stuck, but that's no excuse not to have a go in the local lingo.

FRENCH

SWISS FRENCH

Neuchâtel is where the purest form of French is spoken, yet you won't find much difference from standard French, wherever you go. Of course there are some local expressions and regional accents. A female waitress is a *sommelière*, not a *serveuse*, and a postal box is a *case postale*, not a *bôite postale*. Although the normal French numbers are understood, some locals use *septante* for 70, *huitante* for 80, and *nonante* for 90. Swiss Romande is a term used to refer to French-speaking Switzerland.

PRONUNCIATION

Most letters in the French alphabet are pronounced more or less the same as their English counterparts; a few that may cause confusion are listed below. The combinations *un* and *on* in the pronunciation guides are nasal sounds – the 'n' is not pronounced; *zh* is pronounced as the 's' in 'measure.'

c	before **e** and **i**, as the 's' in 'sit' before **a**, **o** and **u** it's pronounced as English 'k'
ç	always the 's' in 'sit'
h	always silent
j	as the 's' in 'leisure'
r	from the back of the throat while constricting the muscles to restrict the flow of air
n, m	where a syllable ends in a single **n** or **m**, these letters are not pronounced, but the preceding vowel is given a nasal pronunciation
s	often not pronounced in plurals or at the end of words

GENDER

All nouns in French are either masculine or feminine and adjectives reflect the gender of the noun they modify. The feminine form of many nouns and adjectives is indicated by a silent **e** added to the masculine form, as in *ami* and *amie* (the masculine and feminine for 'friend'). In the following phrases both masculine and feminine forms have been indicated where necessary. The masculine form comes first and is separated from the feminine by a slash. The gender of a noun is often indicated by a preceding article: 'the/a/some,' *le/un/du* (m), *la/une/ de la* (f).

ACCOMMODATION

I'm looking for a ...
Je cherche ...	zher shersh ...
guesthouse	
une pension (de famille)	ewn pon·syon (der fa·mee·yer)
hotel	
un hôtel	un o·tel
youth hostel	
une auberge de jeunesse	ewn o·berzh der zher·nes

What is the address?
Quelle est l'adresse?
kel e la·dres
Could you write the address, please?
Est-ce que vous pourriez écrire l'adresse, s'il vous plaît?
e·sker voo poo·ryay e·kreer la·dres seel voo play
Do you have any rooms available?
Est-ce que vous avez des chambres libres?
e·sker voo·za·vay day shom·brer lee·brer
May I see it?
Est-ce que je peux voir la chambre?
es·ker zher per vwa la shom·brer
Where is the bathroom?
Où est la salle de bains? oo e la sal der bun

I'd like (a) ...
Je voudrais ...	zher voo·dray ...
single room	
une chambre à un lit	ewn shom·brer a un lee
double-bed room	
une chambre avec un grand lit	ewn shom·brer a·vek un gron lee
twin room (with two beds)	
une chambre avec des lits jumeaux	ewn shom·brer a·vek day lee zhew·mo

How much is it ...? *Quel est le prix ...?* kel e ler pree ...
per night	*par nuit*	par nwee
per person	*par personne*	par per·son

CONVERSATION & ESSENTIALS

You'll find that any attempt to communicate in French will be very much appreciated. Even if the only sentence you can muster is *Pardon, madame/monsieur/mademoiselle, parlez-vous anglais?* (Excuse me, Madam/Sir/Miss, do you speak English?), you're sure to be more warmly received than if you blindly address a stranger in English.

An important distinction is made in French between *tu* and *vous*, which both mean 'you'; *tu* is only used when addressing people you know well, children or animals. If you're addressing an adult who isn't a personal friend, *vous* should be used unless the person invites you to use *tu*.

Hello.	*Bonjour.*	bon-zhoor
Goodbye.	*Au revoir.*	o-rer-vwa
Yes.	*Oui.*	wee
No.	*Non.*	no
Please.	*S'il vous plaît.*	seel voo play
Thank you.	*Merci.*	mair-see
You're welcome.	*Je vous en prie.*	zher voo-zon pree
	De rien. (inf)	der ree-en
Excuse me.	*Excusez-moi.*	ek-skew-zay-mwa
Sorry. (forgive me)	*Pardon.*	par-don

What's your name?
Comment vous appelez-vous?
ko-mon voo-za-pay-lay voo
My name is ...
Je m'appelle ...
zher ma-pel ...
Do you speak English?
Parlez-vous anglais?
par-lay-voo ong-lay
I don't understand.
Je ne comprends pas.
zher ner kom-pron pa
Could you write it down, please?
Est-ce que vous pourriez l'écrire, s'il vous plaît?
es-ker voo poo-ryay le-kreer seel voo play

NUMBERS

0	*zero*	ze-ro
1	*un*	un
2	*deux*	der
3	*trois*	twa
4	*quatre*	ka-trer
5	*cinq*	sungk
6	*six*	sees
7	*sept*	set

EMERGENCIES

Help!
Au secours!   o skoor
There's been an accident!
Il y a eu un accident!   eel ya ew un ak-see-don
I'm lost.
Je me suis égaré/e. (m/f)   zhe me swee-zay-ga-ray
Leave me alone!
Fichez-moi la paix!   fee-shay-mwa la pay

Call ... !	*Appelez ... !*	a-play ...
a doctor	*un médecin*	un med-sun
the police	*la police*	la po-lees

8	*huit*	weet
9	*neuf*	nerf
10	*dix*	dees
11	*onze*	onz
12	*douze*	dooz
13	*treize*	trez
14	*quatorze*	ka-torz
15	*quinze*	kunz
16	*seize*	sez
17	*dix-sept*	dee-set
18	*dix-huit*	dee-zweet
19	*dix-neuf*	deez-nerf
20	*vingt*	vung
21	*vingt et un*	vung tay un
22	*vingt-deux*	vung-der
30	*trente*	tront
40	*quarante*	ka-ront
50	*cinquante*	sung-kont
60	*soixante*	swa-sont
70	*soixante-dix*	swa-son-dees
80	*quatre-vingts*	ka-trer-vung
90	*quatre-vingt-dix*	ka-trer-vung-dees
100	*cent*	son
1000	*mille*	meel

SHOPPING & SERVICES

I'd like to buy ...
Je voudrais acheter ...   zher voo-dray zash-tay ...
How much is it?
C'est combien?   say kom-byun

Can I pay by ...?
Est-ce que je peux payer avec ...?
es-ker zher per pay-yay a-vek ...

credit card	*ma carte de crédit*	ma kart der kre-dee
travellers cheques	*des chèques de voyage*	day shek der vwa-yazh

LANGUAGE

I'm looking for ...	Je cherche ...	zhe shersh ...
a bank	une banque	ewn bonk
the ... embassy	l'ambassade de ...	lam·ba·sahd der ...
the hospital	l'hôpital	lo·pee·tal
the market	le marché	ler mar·shay
the police	la police	la po·lees
the post office	le bureau de poste	ler bew·ro der post
a public phone	une cabine téléphonique	ewn ka·been te·le·fo·neek
a public toilet	les toilettes	lay twa·let
the tourist office	l'office de tourisme	lo·fees der too·rees·mer

SIGNS	
Entrée	Entrance
Sortie	Exit
Renseignements	Information
Ouvert	Open
Fermé	Closed
Interdit	Prohibited
Toilettes/WC	Toilets
Hommes	Men
Femmes	Women

TIME & DATES

What time is it?
Quelle heure est-il? kel er e til

It's (8) o'clock.
Il est (huit) heures. il e (weet) er

It's half past ...
Il est ... heures et demie. il e ... er e der·mee

in the morning
du matin dew ma·tun

in the afternoon
de l'après-midi der la·pray·mee·dee

in the evening
du soir dew swar

Monday	lundi	lun·dee
Tuesday	mardi	mar·dee
Wednesday	mercredi	mair·krer·dee
Thursday	jeudi	zher·dee
Friday	vendredi	von·drer·dee
Saturday	samedi	sam·dee
Sunday	dimanche	dee·monsh

January	janvier	zhon·vyay
February	février	fev·ryay
March	mars	mars
April	avril	a·vreel
May	mai	may
June	juin	zhwun
July	juillet	zhwee·yay
August	août	oot
September	septembre	sep·tom·brer
October	octobre	ok·to·brer
November	novembre	no·vom·brer
December	décembre	day·som·brer

TRANSPORT

What time does ... leave/arrive?	À quelle heure part/arrive ...?	a kel er par/a·reev ...
bus	le bus	ler bews
train	le train	ler trun

I'd like a ... ticket.
Je voudrais un billet ... zher voo·dray un bee·yay ...

one-way		
simple		sum·pler
return		
aller-retour		a·lay rer·toor
1st class		
de première classe		der prem·yair klas
2nd class		
de deuxième classe		der der·zyem klas

the first	le premier (m)	ler prer·myay
	la première (f)	la prer·myair
the last	le dernier (m)	ler dair·nyay
	la dernière (f)	la dair·nyair
train station	la gare	la gar

Directions

I want to go to ...
Je voudrais aller à ... zher voo·dray a·lay a ...

Where is ...?
Où est ...? oo e ...

Go straight ahead.
Continuez tout droit. kon·teen·way too drwa

Turn left.
Tournez à gauche. toor·nay a gosh

Turn right.
Tournez à droite. toor·nay a drwat

near (to)/far (from)
près (de)/loin (de) pray (der)/lwun (der)

Can you show me (on the map)?
Pouvez-vous m'indiquer (sur la carte)? poo·vay·voo mun·dee·kay (sewr la kart)

GERMAN

SWISS GERMAN

Though German-speaking Swiss have little trouble with standard High German, they use Swiss German, or Schwyzertütsch, in private conversation and in most unofficial situations. Contrary to the worldwide trend

LANGUAGE

of erosion of dialects, its usage is actually increasing. Swiss German covers a wide variety of melodic dialects that can differ quite markedly from High German, often more closely resembling the German of hundreds of years ago than the modern version. It's as different to High German as Dutch is. Swiss German is an oral language, rarely written down, and indeed there is no standard written form – they can't even agree on how to spell 'Schwyzertütsch')! While newspapers and books almost invariably use High German and it's also used in news broadcasts, schools and the parliament, people are more comfortable with their own Swiss German, and may even attempt a completely different language when speaking to foreigners rather than resort to High German.

Germans themselves often have trouble understanding Schwyzertütsch. To English speakers' ears High German sounds like it's full of rasping 'ch' sounds, but even Germans will joke that *Schwyzertütsch ist keine Sprache, sondern eine Halsentzündung* (Swiss German isn't really a language, it's a throat infection).

To make matters even more complicated, regional dialects are strongly differentiated for such a small country, thanks to the isolating effect of mountain ranges (and the lack of a written 'standard').

With no written form and so many dialects, it's impossible to provide a proper vocabulary for Swiss German. The commonly used greeting is *Grüezi* (Hello) and 'tram' is *Tram*, not *Strassenbahn*. Versions of French words are often used: 'thank you' is not *danke* but *merci* (though pronounced as 'mur-see' rather than the correct French, 'mair-see'); 'bicycle' is *vélo*, not *Fahrrad*; 'ice cream' is *glace*, not *Sahneneis*. In pronunciation, double vowel sounds are common – 'good' sounds more like 'gu-et' than the High German *gut*. Visitors will probably also note the frequent use of the suffix *-li* to indicate the diminutive, or as a term of endearment.

For more information, read *Dialect and High German in German-Speaking Switzerland*, published by Pro Helvetia, the Arts Council of Switzerland. For a more indepth guide to High German, get a copy of Lonely Planet's *German Phrasebook*.

PRONUNCIATION
Vowels

German	Pronunciation Guide
*h*at	**a** (eg the 'u' in 'run')
*h*abe	**ah** (eg 'father')
*m*ein	**ai** (eg 'aisle')
*B*är	**air** (eg 'hair', with no 'r' sound)
*B*oot	**aw** (eg 'saw')
*l*eben	**ay** (eg 'say')
*B*ett/*M*änner	**e** (eg 'bed')
*fl*iegen	**ee** (eg 'thief')
*sch*ön	**er** (eg 'her', with no 'r' sound)
*m*it	**i** (eg 'bit')
*K*offer	**o** (eg 'pot')
*L*eute/*H*äuser	**oy** (eg 'toy')
*Sch*uhe	**oo** (eg 'moon')
*H*aus	**ow** (eg 'how')
*z*üruck	**ü** ('ee' said with rounded lips)
*u*nter	**u** (eg 'put')

Consonants

The only two tricky consonant sounds in German are **ch** and **r**. All other consonants are pronounced much the same as their English counterparts (except **sch**, which is always as the 'sh' in 'shoe'). The **ch** sound is generally like the 'ch' in *Bach* or Scottish *loch* – like a hiss from the back of the throat. When **ch** occurs after the vowels **e** and **i** it's more like a 'sh' sound, produced with the tongue more forward in the mouth. In this book we've simplified things by using the one symbol **kh** for both sounds. The **r** sound is different from English, and it isn't rolled like in Italian or Spanish. It's pronounced at the back of the throat, almost like saying a 'g' sound, but with some friction – it's a bit like gargling.

Word Stress

As a general rule, word stress in German msotly falls on the first syllable. In the pronunciation guides in the following words and phrases, the stressed syllable is shown in italics.

ACCOMMODATION
Where's a ...?

Wo ist ...?	vaw ist ...
guesthouse	
eine Pension	*ai*-ne pahng-*zyawn*
hotel	
ein Hotel	ain ho-*tel*
inn	
ein Gasthof	ain *gast*-hawf

youth hostel
eine Jugendherberge *ai*·ne yoo·gent·her·ber·ge

What's the address?
Wie ist die Adresse? vee ist dee a·*dre*·se

May I see it?
Kann ich es sehen? kan ikh es *zay*·en

Do you have a ... room?
Haben Sie ein ...? *hah*·ben zee ain ...

single
Einzelzimmer *ain*·tsel·tsi·mer

double
Doppelzimmer mit do·pel·tsi·mer mit
einem Doppelbett *ai*·nem do·pel·bet

twin
Doppelzimmer mit zwei do·pel·tsi·mer mit tsvai
Einzelbetten *ain*·tsel·be·ten

How much is it per ...?
Wie viel kostet es pro ...? vee feel *kos*·tet es praw ...

night
Nacht nakht

person
Person per·*zawn*

CONVERSATION & ESSENTIALS

You should be aware that German uses polite and informal forms for 'you' (*Sie* and *Du* respectively). When addressing people you don't know well you should always use the polite form (though younger people will be less inclined to expect it). In this language guide we use the polite form unless indicated by 'inf' (for 'informal') in brackets.

If you need to ask for assistance from a stranger, remember to always introduce your request with a simple *Enschuldigung* (Excuse me, ...).

Good ... *Guten ...* *goo*·ten ...
morning *Morgen* *mor*·gen
afternoon *Tag* tahk
evening *Abend* *ah*·bent

Hello.
Guten Tag. *goo*·ten tahk

Goodbye.
Auf Wiedersehen. owf *vee*·der·zay·en

Yes.
Ja. yah

No.
Nein. nain

Please.
Bitte. *bi*·te

Thank you (very much).
Danke./Vielen Dank. dang·ke/*fee*·len dangk

You're welcome.
Bitte (sehr). *bi*·te (zair)

Excuse me, ... (before asking for help or directions)
Entschuldigung. ent·*shul*·di·gung

Sorry.
Entschuldigung. ent·*shul*·di·gung

What's your name?
Wie ist Ihr Name? (pol) vee ist eer *nah*·me
Wie heisst du? (inf) vee haist doo

My name is ...
Mein Name ist .../ main *nah*·me ist .../
Ich heisse ... ikh *hai*·se ...

Do you speak English?
Sprechen Sie Englisch? shpre·khen zee *eng*·lish

I (don't) understand.
Ich verstehe (nicht). ikh fer·*shtay*·e (nikht)

Could you please write it down?
Könnten Sie das bitte kern·ten zee das *bi*·te
aufschreiben? owf·shrai·ben

EMERGENCIES

Help!
Hilfe! *hil*·fe

I'm sick.
Ich bin krank. ikh bin krangk

Call a doctor!
Rufen Sie einen Arzt! roo·fen zee *ai*·nen artst

Call the police!
Rufen Sie die Polizei! roo·fen zee dee po·li·*tsai*

I'm lost.
Ich habe mich verirrt. ikh *hah*·be mikh fer·*irt*

Go away!
Gehen Sie weg! *gay*·en zee vek

NUMBERS

1	*ains*	aints
2	*zwei*	tsvai
3	*drei*	drai
4	*vier*	feer
5	*fünf*	fünf
6	*sechs*	zeks
7	*sieben*	*zee*·ben
8	*acht*	akht
9	*neun*	noyn
10	*zehn*	tsayn
11	*elf*	elf
12	*zwölf*	zverlf
13	*dreizehn*	*drai*·tsayn
14	*vierzehn*	*feer*·tsayn

LANGUAGE

15	fünfzehn	fünf·tsayn
16	sechzehn	zeks·tsayn
17	siebzehn	zeep·tsayn
18	achtzehn	akh·tsayn
19	neunzehn	noyn·tsayn
20	zwanzig	tsvan·tsikh
21	einundzwanzig	ain·unt·tsvan·tsikh
30	dreizig	drai·tsikh
31	einunddreizig	ain·und·drai·tsikh
40	vierzig	feer·tsikh
50	fünfzig	fünf·tsikh
60	sechzig	zekh·tsikh
70	siebzig	zeep·tsikh
80	achtzig	akh·tsikh
90	neunzig	noyn·tsikh
100	hundert	hun·dert
1000	tausend	tow·sent
2000	zwei tausend	tsvai tow·sent

SIGNS

Polizei	Police
Eingang	Entrance
Ausgang	Exit
Offen	Open
Geschlossen	Closed
Kein Zutritt	No Entry
Rauchen Verboten	No Smoking
Verboten	Prohibited
Toiletten (WC)	Toilets
Herren	Men
Damen	Women

SHOPPING & SERVICES

I'm looking for ...
Ich suche ... ikh zoo·khe ...
How much (is this)?
Wie viel (kostet das)? vee feel (kos·tet das)

Do you accept ...?
Nehmen Sie ...? nay·men zee ...
  credit cards
  Kreditkarten kre·deet·kar·ten
  travellers cheques
  Reiseschecks rai·ze·sheks

a bank	eine Bank	ai·ne bangk
a chemist	die Apotheke	dee a·po·tay·ke
the ... embassy	die ... Botschaft	dee ... bot·shaft
the hospital	das Krankenhaus	das krang·ken·hows
the market	der Markt	dair markt
the police	die Polizei	dee po·li·tsai
the post office	das Postamt	das post·amt
a public phone	ein öffentliches Telefon	ain er·fent·li·khes te·le·fawn
a public toilet	eine öffentliche Toilette	ain er·fent·li·khe te·le·fawn

What time does it open/close?
Wann macht er/sie/es auf/zu? (m/f/n)
van makht air/zee/es owf/tsoo

TIME & DATES

What time is it?
Wie spät ist es? vee shpayt ist es
It's (one) o'clock.
Es ist (ein) Uhr. es ist (ain) oor

Twenty past one.
Zwanzig nach eins. tsvan·tsikh nahkh ains
am
  morgens/vormittags mor·gens/fawr·mi·tahks
pm
  nachmittags/abends nahkh·mi·tahks/ah·bents

Monday	Montag	mawn·tahk
Tuesday	Dienstag	deens·tahk
Wednesday	Mittwoch	mit·vokh
Thursday	Donnerstag	do·ners·tahk
Friday	Freitag	frai·tahk
Saturday	Samstag	zams·tahk
Sunday	Sonntag	zon·tahk

January	Januar	yan·u·ahr
February	Februar	fay·bru·ahr
March	März	merts
April	April	a·pril
May	Mai	mai
June	Juni	yoo·ni
July	Juli	yoo·li
August	August	ow·gust
September	September	zep·tem·ber
October	Oktober	ok·taw·ber
November	November	no·vem·ber
December	Dezember	de·tsem·ber

TRANSPORT

What time does the ... leave?
Wann fährt ... ab?
van fairt ... ap

bus	der Bus	dair bus
train	der Zug	dair tsook

What time's the ... bus?
Wann fährt der ... Bus?
van fairt dair ... bus

first	erste	ers·te
last	letzte	lets·te
next	nächste	naykhs·te

LANGUAGE

A ... ticket to ...
Einen ... nach ...   *ai·*nen ... nahkh ...
   one-way
   einfache Fahrkarte   ain·fa·khe *fahr·*kar·te
   return
   Rückfahrkarte   rük·fahr·kar·te
   1st-class
   Fahrkarte erster Klasse   *fahr·*kar·te *ers·*ter *kla·*se
   2nd-class
   Fahrkarte zweiter Klasse   *fahr·*kar·te *tsvai·*ter *kla·*se

Directions
Where's (a bank)?
   Wo ist (eine Bank).?
   vaw ist (*ai·*ne bangk)
Can you show me (on the map)?
   Können Sie es mir (auf der Karte) zeigen?
   *ker·*nen zee es meer (owf dair *kar·*te) *tsai·*gen

Turn ...	*Biegen Sie ... ab.*	*bee·*gen zee ... ap
left/right	*links/rechts*	lingks/rekhts

straight ahead	*geradeaus*	ge·rah·de·*ows*
near	*nahe*	*nah·*e
far away	*weit weg*	vait vek

ITALIAN

SWISS ITALIAN
There are some differences between the
Ticinese dialect and standard Italian, but
they aren't very significant. You may come
across some people saying *bun di* instead of
buon giorno (good morning/day) or *buona
noc* (pronounced 'nockh') instead of *buona
notte* (goodnight).

PRONUNCIATION
Vowels
Vowels are generally more clipped than in
English:

a	as in 'art', eg *caro* (dear); sometimes short, eg *amico/a* (friend)
e	short, as in 'let', eg *mettere* (to put); long, as in 'there', eg *mela* (apple)
i	short, as in 'it', eg *inizio* (start); long, as in 'marine', eg *vino* (wine)
o	short, as in 'dot', eg *donna* (woman); long, as in 'port', eg *ora* (hour)
u	as the 'oo' in 'book', eg *puro* (pure)

Consonants
c	as the 'k' in 'kit' before **a**, **o** and **u**; as the 'ch' in 'choose' before **e** and **i**
ch	as the 'k' in 'kit'
g	as the 'g' in 'get' before **a**, **o**, **u** and **h**; as the 'j' in 'jet' before **e** and **i**
gli	as the 'lli' in 'million'
gn	as the 'ny' in 'canyon'
h	always silent
r	a rolled 'rr' sound
sc	as the 'sh' in 'sheep' before **e** and **i**; as 'sk' before **a**, **o**, **u** and **h**
z	as the 'ts' in 'lights'; at the beginning of a word, it's most commonly as the 'ds' in 'suds'

A double consonant is pronounced as a
longer, more forceful sound than a single
consonant.

Word Stress
Stress is indicated in our pronunciation
guide by italics. Word stress generally falls
on the second-last syllable, as in spa·*ghet*·ti,
but when a word has an accent, the stress
falls on that syllable, as in cit·*tà* (city).

ACCOMMODATION
I'm looking for a ...	*Cerco ...*	*cher·*ko ...
guesthouse	*una pensione*	*oo·*na pen·*syo·*ne
hotel	*un albergo*	oon al·*ber·*go
youth hostel	*un ostello per la gioventù*	oon os·*te·*lo per la jo·ven·*too*

What is the address?
   Qual'è l'indirizzo?   kwa·*le* leen·dee·*ree·*tso
Could you write the address, please?
   Può scrivere l'indirizzo, per favore?   pwo *skree·*ve·re leen·dee·*ree·*tso per fa·*vo·*re
Do you have any rooms available?
   Avete camere libere?   a·*ve·*te *ka·*me·re *lee·*be·re
May I see it?
   Posso vederla?   *po·*so ve·*der·*la

I'd like a ... room.		
Vorrei una camera ...		vo·*ray* oo·na *ka·*me·ra ...
single		
singola		*seen·*go·la
double		
matrimoniale		ma·tree·mo·*nya·*le
twin-bed		
doppia		*do·*pya

How much is it ...?	*Quanto costa ...?*	*kwan·*to *ko·*sta ...
per night	*per la notte*	per la *no·*te
per person	*per persona*	per per·*so·*na

CONVERSATION & ESSENTIALS

Hello.	*Buongiorno.*	bwon-*jor*-no
	Ciao. (inf)	chow
Goodbye.	*Arrivederci.*	a-ree-ve-*der*-chee
	Ciao. (inf)	chow
Good evening.	*Buonasera.*	bwo-na-*se*-a
(from early afternoon onwards)		
Good night.	*Buonanotte.*	bwo-na-*no*-te
Yes.	*Sì.*	see
No.	*No.*	no
Please.	*Per favore/*	per fa-*vo*-re
	Per piacere.	per pya-*chay*-re
Thank you.	*Grazie.*	*gra*-tsye
That's fine/	*Prego.*	*pre*-go
You're welcome.		
Excuse me.	*Mi scusi.*	mee *skoo*-zee
Sorry (forgive	*Mi scusi/*	mee *skoo*-zee/
me).	*Mi perdoni.*	mee per-*do*-nee

What's your name?
Come si chiama?   ko-me see *kya*-ma
My name is ...
Mi chiamo ...   mee *kya*-mo ...
Do you speak English?
Parla inglese?   *par*-la een-*gle*-ze
I don't understand.
Non capisco.   non ka-*pee*-sko
Please write it down.
Può scriverlo, per   pwo *skree*-ver-lo per
favore?   fa-*vo*-re

EMERGENCIES

Help!
Aiuto!   a-*yoo*-to
I'm ill.
Mi sento male.   mee *sen*-to *ma*-le
I'm lost.
Mi sono perso/a.   mee *so*-no *per*-so/a
Go away!
Lasciami in pace!   la-sha-mi een *pa*-che
Vai via! (inf)   va-ee *vee*-a

Call ...!	*Chiami ...!*	kee-*ya*-mee ...
a doctor	*un dottore/*	oon do-*to*-re/
	un medico	oon *me*-dee-ko
the police	*la polizia*	la po-lee-*tsee*-ya

NUMBERS

0	*zero*	*dze*-ro
1	*uno*	*oo*-no
2	*due*	*doo*-e
3	*tre*	tre
4	*quattro*	*kwa*-tro
5	*cinque*	*cheen*-kwe
6	*sei*	say
7	*sette*	*se*-te
8	*otto*	*o*-to
9	*nove*	*no*-ve
10	*dieci*	*dye*-chee
11	*undici*	*oon*-dee-chee
12	*dodici*	do-*dee*-chee
13	*tredici*	tre-*dee*-chee
14	*quattordici*	kwa-*tor*-dee-chee
15	*quindici*	*kween*-dee-chee
16	*sedici*	*se*-dee-chee
17	*diciassette*	dee-cha-*se*-te
18	*diciotto*	dee-*cho*-to
19	*diciannove*	dee-cha-*no*-ve
20	*venti*	*ven*-tee
21	*ventuno*	ven-*too*-no
22	*ventidue*	ven-tee-*doo*-e
30	*trenta*	*tren*-ta
40	*quaranta*	kwa-*ran*-ta
50	*cinquanta*	cheen-*kwan*-ta
60	*sessanta*	se-*san*-ta
70	*settanta*	se-*tan*-ta
80	*ottanta*	o-*tan*-ta
90	*novanta*	no-*van*-ta
100	*cento*	*chen*-to
1000	*mille*	*mee*-le

SHOPPING & SERVICES

I'd like to buy ...
Vorrei comprare ...   vo-*ray* kom-*pra*-re ...
How much is it?
Quanto costa?   *kwan*-to *ko*-sta
Do you accept credit cards?
Accettate carte   a-che-*ta*-te *kar*-te
di credito?   dee *kre*-dee-to

I want to change ...
Voglio cambiare ...   vo-lyo kam-*bya*-re ...
  money
  del denaro   del de-*na*-ro
  travellers cheques
  assegni dee viaggio   a-*se*-nyee dee vee-*a*-jo

I'm looking for ...	*Cerco ...*	*cher*-ko ...
a bank	*un banco*	oon *ban*-ko
the ... embassy	*l'ambasciata*	lam-ba-*sha*-ta
	di ...	dee ...
the market	*il mercato*	eel mer-*ka*-to
the post office	*la posta*	la *po*-sta
a public toilet	*un gabinetto*	oon ga-bee-*ne*-to
the tourist	*l'ufficio*	loo-*fee*-cho
office	*di turismo*	dee too-*reez*-mo

LANGUAGE

TIME & DATES
What time is it?
Che ore sono?		ke *o*·re *so*·no

It's (8 o'clock).
Sono (le otto).		*so*·no (le *o*·to)

in the morning
| *di mattina* | | dee ma·*tee*·na |

in the afternoon
| *di pomeriggio* | | dee po·me·*ree*·jo |

in the evening
| *di sera* | | dee *se*·ra |

Monday	*lunedì*	loo·ne·*dee*
Tuesday	*martedì*	mar·te·*dee*
Wednesday	*mercoledì*	mer·ko·le·*dee*
Thursday	*giovedì*	jo·ve·*dee*
Friday	*venerdì*	ve·ner·*dee*
Saturday	*sabato*	*sa*·ba·to
Sunday	*domenica*	do·*me*·nee·ka

January	*gennaio*	je·*na*·yo
February	*febbraio*	fe·*bra*·yo
March	*marzo*	*mar*·tso
April	*aprile*	a·*pree*·le
May	*maggio*	*ma*·jo
June	*giugno*	*joo*·nyo
July	*luglio*	*loo*·lyo
August	*agosto*	a·*gos*·to
September	*settembre*	se·*tem*·bre
October	*ottobre*	o·*to*·bre
November	*novembre*	no·*vem*·bre
December	*dicembre*	dee·*chem*·bre

TRANSPORT
What time does the ... leave/arrive?
A che ora parte/arriva ...?		a ke *o*·ra par·te/a·*ree*·va ...

(city) bus		
l'autobus		*low*·to·boos
(intercity) bus		
il pullman		eel *pool*·man
train		
il treno		eel *tre*·no

I'd like a ... ticket.
Vorrei un biglietto ...		vo·*ray* oon bee·*lye*·to ...
one-way		
di solo andata		dee *so*·lo an·*da*·ta
return		
di andata e ritorno		dee an·*da*·ta e ree·*toor*·no
1st class		
di prima classe		dee *pree*·ma *kla*·se
2nd class		
di seconda classe		dee se·*kon*·da *kla*·se

SIGNS	
Ingresso/Entrata	Entrance
Uscita	Exit
Informazione	Information
Aperto	Open
Chiuso	Closed
Proibito/Vietato	Prohibited
Polizia/Carabinieri	Police
Gabinetti/Bagni	Toilets
Uomini	Men
Donne	Women

the first	*il primo*	eel *pree*·mo
the last	*l'ultimo*	*lool*·tee·mo
train station	*stazione*	sta·*tsyo*·ne

Directions
Where is ...?
Dov'è ...?		do·*ve* ...

Go straight ahead.
| *Si va sempre diritto.* | | see va *sem*·pre dee·*ree*·to |
| *Vai sempre diritto.* (inf) | | *va*·ee *sem*·pre dee·*ree*·to |

Turn left.
| *Giri a sinistra.* | | *jee*·ree a see·*nee*·stra |

Turn right.
| *Giri a destra.* | | *jee*·ree a *de*·stra |

Can you show me (on the map)?
| *Può mostrarmelo* | | pwo mos·*trar*·me·lo |
| *(sulla pianta)?* | | (soo·la *pyan*·ta) |

ROMANSCH

Romansch dialects tend to be restricted to their own particular mountain valley. Usage is gradually being undermined by the steady encroachment of German, and linguists fear that the language may eventually disappear altogether. There are so many dialects that not all the Romansch words listed here will be understood. The main street in villages is usually called Via Maistra.

A FEW WORDS & PHRASES
Please.	*Anzi.*
Thank you.	*Grazia.*
Hello.	*Allegra.*
Good morning.	*Bun di.*
Good evening.	*Buna saira.*
Good night.	*Buna notg.*
Goodbye.	*Adieu/Abunansvair.*
tourist office	*societad da traffic*
room	*la chombra*
bed	*il letg*

closed	*serrà*	**Wednesday**	*Marculdi*
left	*sanester*	**Thursday**	*la Gievgia*
right	*dretg*	**Friday**	*Venderdi*
woman	*la dunna*	**Saturday**	*Sanda*
man	*l'um*	**Sunday**	*Dumengia*
cross-country skiing	*il passlung*		
food	*mangiar*	**1**	*in*
bread	*il paun*	**2**	*dus*
cheese	*il chaschiel*	**3**	*trais*
fish	*il pesch*	**4**	*quatter*
ham	*il schambun*	**5**	*tschinch*
milk	*il latg*	**6**	*ses*
wine	*il vin*	**7**	*set*
		8	*och*
Monday	*Lündeschdi*	**9**	*nouv*
Tuesday	*il Mardi*	**10**	*diesch*

LANGUAGE

Alternative Place Names

ABBREVIATIONS

(E) = English
(F) = French
(G) = German
(I) = Italian
(R) = Romansch

Basel (E, G) – Basle (E), Bâle (F), Basilea (I)
Bern (E, G) – Berne (E, F), Berna (I)
Bernese Mittelland (E) – Berner Mittelland (G), Le Plateau Bernois (F)
Bernese Oberland (E) – Berner Oberland (G)
Biel (G) – Bienne (F)
Bodensee (G) – Lake Constance (E)
Brienzersee (G) – Lake Brienz (E)
Brig (E, G) – Brigue (F)

Chur (E, G) – Coire (F)

Fribourg (E, F) – Freiburg (G), Friburgo (I)

Geneva (E) – Genève (F), Genf (G), Ginevra (I)
Graubünden (E, G) – Grisons (F), Grigioni (I), Grishun (R)

Lake Geneva (E) – Lac Léman or Lac du Genève (F), Genfer See (G)
Lake Geneva Region (E) –Région du Léman (F), Genferseegebiet (G)
Lago Maggiore (I) – Lake Maggiore (E)
Leuk (E,G) – Loeche (F)
Leukerbad (E,G) – Loeche-les-Bains (F)
Lower Valais (E) – Unterwallis (G), Bas Valais (F)
Lucerne (E, F) – Luzern (G), Lucerna (I)

Matterhorn (E, G) – Cervino (I)
Mont Blanc (F) – Monte Bianco (I)

Neuchâtel (E, F) – Neuenburg (G)

Rhine River (E) – Rhein (G), Rhin (F)

St Gallen (E, G) – St Gall (F), San Gallo (I)
St Moritz (E, G) – Saint Moritz (F), San Murezzan (R)
St Peter's Island (E) – St Peterinsel (G), Île de St Pierre (F)
Sarine River (E) – Saane (G), Sarine (F)
Schaffhausen (E, G) – Schaffhouse (F), Sciafusa (I)
Sierre (E, F) – Siders (G)
Sion (E, F) – Sitten (G)
Solothurn (E, G) – Soleure (F), Soletta (I)
Switzerland (E) – Suisse (F), Schweiz (G), Svizzerra (I), Svizzra (R)

Thunersee (G) – Lake Thun (E), Lac de Thoune (F)
Ticino (E, I) – Tessin (G, F)

Upper Valais (E) – Oberwallis (G), Haut Valais (F)

Valais (E, F) – Wallis (G)
Vaud (E, F) – Waadt (G)
Vierwaldstättersee (G) – Lake Lucerne (E)
Visp (E,G) – Viège (F)

Winterthur (E, G) – Winterthour (F)

Zug (E, G) – Zoug (F)
Zugersee (G) – Lake Zug (E), Lac de Zoug (F)
Zürich (G) – Zurich (E, F), Zurigo (I)

Behind the Scenes

THIS BOOK

This 5th edition of Switzerland was written and researched by Damien Simonis, Sarah Johnstone and Nicola Williams. Damien and Sarah also wrote and researched the 4th edition, with some contributions from Lorne Jackson. The first three editions were written and researched by Mark Honan. This guidebook was commissioned in Lonely Planet's London office, and produced by the following:

Commissioning Editor Judith Bamber
Coordinating Editor Justin Flynn
Coordinating Cartographer Corey Hutchison
Coordinating Layout Designer Yvonne Bischofberger
Managing Cartographer Mark Griffiths
Assisting Editors Lauren Rollheiser, Brooke Clark, Susie Ashworth, Helen Koehne, Trent Holden
Assisting Cartographers Marion Byass, Helen Rowley, Natasha Velleley, Emma McNicol
Assisting Layout Designers Jacqui Saunders, Wibowo Rusli
Cover Designer Pepi Bluck
Indexer Kristin Odijk
Project Manager Glenn van der Knijff
Language Content Coordinator Quentin Frayne

Thanks to Tashi Wheeler, Meagan Williams, Fabrice Rocher, Melanie Dankel, Jacqueline McLeod, Indra Kilfoyle, Evan Jones, Celia Wood, Sally Darmody, Adriana Mammarella

THANKS
DAMIEN SIMONIS

Thanks in general go to the staff of the tourist offices around Vaud, Valais, Graubünden and Ticino, whose reams of knowledge and general information smoothed the way.

A big *merci* to Georges-Alain and Delphine Claret for their priceless tips on the Lower Valais. Likewise to Anne Gaudard, who had some useful information (and much more that I could not have possibly included in the scope of this book) on customs in the Upper Valais.

In Ticino, I owe a big *grazie* to Monica Bonetti in Lugano, who rolled out the welcome mat, pumped me with local tips and took me briefly into the orbit of friends (thanks for the fun dinner to Rolf, Umberto and company).

I would also like to thank fellow writers Sarah Johnstone and Nicola Williams for living up to their reputations as frighteningly efficient and diligent operators! Their contributions to this modest tome have been invaluable.

Big thank-yous go to my brother Des, for keeping things under control on the home front in the UK during long absences and especially to Janique, for her support and help in collecting info when I couldn't be in Switzerland. She also joined me for a wonderful voyage of discovery in the deepest, darkest valleys of Graubünden and various nooks and crannies of Valais.

SARAH JOHNSTONE

Thanks are due to many people, particularly Davide Caenaro, Jennifer Davies, Colin Tivendale, and Peter in Zürich, Hansine Johnston on Zürich from Geneva, Katrin Dürennberger and Rudolf Suter in Basel, Sandra Schär and Muriel Freudiger in Bern, Astrid Nahköstin, Marco Hermann and colleagues

---

THE LONELY PLANET STORY

The story begins with a classic travel adventure: Tony and Maureen Wheeler's 1972 journey across Europe and Asia to Australia. There was no useful information about the overland trail then, so Tony and Maureen published the first Lonely Planet guidebook to meet a growing need.

From a kitchen table, Lonely Planet has grown to become the largest independent travel publisher in the world, with offices in Melbourne (Australia), Oakland (USA) and London (UK). Today Lonely Planet guidebooks cover the globe. There is an ever-growing list of books and information in a variety of media. Some things haven't changed. The main aim is still to make it possible for adventurous travellers to get out there – to explore and better understand the world.

At Lonely Planet we believe travellers can make a positive contribution to the countries they visit – if they respect their host communities and spend their money wisely. Every year 5% of company profit is donated to charities around the world.

in St Gallen, Martina Michel-Hoch and Sheila in Liechtenstein. Chris and Ursula were an invaluable help in proving that Interlaken does have some decent places to eat – who would have thunk it? Thanks also to fellow authors Damien and Nicola; we didn't speak much, but when we did it was a pleasure to work with you. Finally, cheers to Charlie Connelly, whose book on Liechtenstein stopped me from cracking too many easy jokes about that tiny, but vertiginous, country. It's even left me thinking that, one day, I might hike the scary Fürstensteig.

NICOLA WILLIAMS

Brief my three chapters might be, but I do have several friends in Geneva to thank, not least Matthias' foodie colleagues from the World Economic Forum in Cologny who revealed their tip-top dining spots in the city: Marie-Laure Burgener, Carla Boeckman and Stephanie Nassenstein. Elsewhere thanks to Lyon-based journalist and former Geneva resident Joanna Kelly for yet more eating tips; to the Maison du Gruyère in that deliciously cheesy corner of Switzerland; and last but far from least, to my darling Matthias for dragging me here.

OUR READERS

Many thanks to the travellers who used the last edition and wrote to us with helpful hints, useful advice and interesting anecdotes:

Jan Achten, Ben Andrew, Dominik Bach, Mehdi Bazargan, Ant Biring, Jullian Blight, Damon Burn, Charlotte Cibeira, Christine Cooper, Antonio Crego, Christoph Doenni, Heather Ebbott, Stian Eriksen, Rolf Ernst, Yuet Yee Foo, Andrew Forrest, Michael Fust, Ainsley Gallagher, Corinna Giezendanner, Lucas Giradet, Elli Goeke, Ronalie Green, Stephanie Guilbert, Stefanie Hug, Russell Huntington, Brendon Hyde, Jo Johnston, Raphael Keller, Richard Kennett, Dave Kiely, Mary Ellen Kitler, Jeff Knox, Christoph Landolt, Sonia Läuchli, Karen Lee, Matjaz Leu, Gabor Lovei, Marilyn Magnus, Dudley McFadden, J McLintock, Jim Meyer, Vera

SEND US YOUR FEEDBACK

We love to hear from travellers – your comments keep us on our toes and help make our books better. Our well-travelled team reads every word on what you loved or loathed about this book. Although we cannot reply individually to postal submissions, we always guarantee that your feedback goes straight to the appropriate authors, in time for the next edition. Each person who sends us information is thanked in the next edition – and the most useful submissions are rewarded with a free book.

To send us your updates – and find out about Lonely Planet events, newsletters and travel news – visit our award-winning website: **www.lonelyplanet.com/feedback**.

Note: We may edit, reproduce and incorporate your comments in Lonely Planet products such as guidebooks, websites and digital products, so let us know if you don't want your comments reproduced or your name acknowledged. For a copy of our privacy policy visit www.lonelyplanet.com/privacy.

Näf, Janet Neilson, Manfred Neumann, Ott Nik, Keith O'Brien, Dave Olson, Paul Ozorak, Pattaraplurk Pattarachote, Geoffrey Peake, Matthäus Pfatschbacher, Camille Poshoglian, Cesar Prieto, Sanjay Sabnis, Jean-Frederic Salazar, Jutta Schaller, Daniela Scharfetter-Lauterjung, Alan Schneider, Sujit Sen, Daniel Sparing, Robert Stagg, Lola Suttie, Chaiya Thepsangpraw, Boyd & Fay Thompson, Susi Türler, Lode Vermeersch, Ian Waters, Anna White, Norman Williams, Jack Wilson, Michael Winward, Michael & Judy Wray, Chia-Nan Yen, Annabella Yim, Sepp Zahner, Mohamad Hafiz Zolkipli.

ACKNOWLEDGMENTS

Many thanks to the following for the use of their content:

Globe on back cover ©Mountain High Maps 1993 Digital Wisdom, Inc.

Index

INDEX

INDEX

000 Map pages
000 Photograph pages

INDEX